Educational Leadership

A Problem-Based Approach

THIRD EDITION

William G. Cunningham

Old Dominion University

Paula A. Cordeiro

University of San Diego

Boston • New York • San Francisco
Mexico City • Montreal • Toronto • London • Madrid • Munich • Paris
Hong Kong • Singapore • Tokyo • Cape Town • Sydney

Senior Editor: *Arnis K. Burvikovs*
Series Editorial Assistant: *Kelly Hopkins*
Marketing Manager: *Tara Kelly*
Production Editor: *Janet Domingo*
Editorial Production Service: *Walsh & Associates, Inc.*
Composition Buyer: *Andrew Turso*
Manufacturing Buyer: *Andrew Turso*
Electronic Composition: *Omegatype Typography, Inc.*
Cover Administrator: *Kristina Mose-Libon*

For related titles and support material, visit our online catalog at www.ablongman.com.

Between the time website information is gathered and then published, it is not unusual for some sites to have closed. Also, the transcription of URLs can result in typographical errors. The publisher would appreciate notification where these errors occur so they may be corrected in subsequent editions.

Library of Congress Cataloging-in-Publication Data

Cunningham, William G.
    Educational leadership : a problem-based approach / William G. Cunningham, Paula A. Cordeiro.—3rd ed.
        p. cm.
    Includes bibliographical references and indexes.
    ISBN 0-205-46634-6
    1. School management and organization—Study and teaching (Higher)—United States.   2. Problem-based learning—United States.   3. School administrators—Training of—United States.   I. Cordeiro, Paula A.   II. Title.

LB1738.5.C86 2006
71.2—dc23

2005045820

Printed in the United States of America

10 9 8 7 6 5 4 3   09 08 07 06

Contents

Preface   xv

1 *Administrative Theory, Values Clarification, and Leadership Responsibility*   *1*

- **Flem Snopes High School: A New Administrative Team**   **1**

Educational Leadership   *3*

Human Capital and the Accumulated Knowledge Base   *7*

Administrative Process and Knowledge   *8*
Philosophical Frames and Epistemological Influences   9
Paradigms and the Scientific-Rational Approach   11
Political, Critical, and Constructivist Frames of Reference   12
Critical-Contextual, Gender, and Race   13
Postmodernism, Poststructuralism   15
- **Grounding Moral Educational Leadership in the Intrinsically Moral Enterprise of Learning,** *by Robert J. Starratt*   **18**

Ethical Models   *19*
The Ethic of Caring   19
The Ethic of Justice   19
The Ethic of Critique   20

Foundations of Ethical Behavior: Standards for Good Practice   *20*
Codes of Ethics   21

Administrative Platforms   *21*

The Knowledge Base in Educational Administration   *25*
- **The Knowledge Base in Educational Administration: A Postmodernist Perspective,** *by Robert Donmoyer, The University of San Diego*   **27**

Conclusion   *28*

Portfolio Artifacts   *29*

Terms   29

Suggested Readings   29

2 *Context and Perspective for Educational Leaders*   *30*

- **Nanuck Middle School: Understanding the Context**   **30**

Contextual Knowledge   *31*

Broad, Complex Context   *32*

Federal Turning-Points   *33*
  Education Origins   34
  Land Grant   34
  Relief   38
  National Defense   38
  Equal Educational Opportunity   39
  World Class Economic Competitiveness
  and Support—1980 to Present   41

Establishing National Goals   *43*
- **Thoughts for Leaders of Educational Institutions in Transition,**
  *by Luvern L. Cunningham, Novice G. Fawcett Professor of Educational
  Administration (Emeritus), The Ohio State University*   **44**

The 1990s and Beyond   *46*
  No Child Left Behind   47

New Technological Demands   *49*

State Roles and Responses   *50*

Equity and Social Justice   *54*

Challenges in the Twenty-First Century   *55*

Conclusion   *57*

Portfolio Artifacts   *59*

Terms   *59*

Suggested Readings   *59*

3 *School Reform*   *60*

- **Scrivner Middle School: Reform at Scrivner**   **60**
- **Leading Innovative Schools,** *by Stephanie Pace Marshall, Ph.D.,
  Mathematics and Science Academy, Aurora, Illinois*   **61**

The Context for School Reform   *63*

Finding New Directions   64

Common Themes in a Changing World   66

Innovative Programs   *67*

Other Innovative Models and Their Benefits   75

• **A Framework for School Improvement,** *by Carl Glickman, Lew Allen, and James Weiss, The University of Georgia*   **76**

Harnessing Technology   *77*

Technology Opens New Opportunities   80

Administrative Applications   80

• **Wilson Elementary School District: Five Steps to a Successful Technology Program,** *by Jane M. Juliano, Ph.D., Principal, Wilson Charter High School, Phoenix, Arizona*   **82**

The Leadership Challenge   *84*

Conclusion   *88*

Portfolio Artifacts   *89*

Terms   *90*

Suggested Readings   *90*

4   *Diversity and Community Relations*   *91*

• **Oakes High School: Cultures Clash in Fairhaven**   **91**

Diversity in Schools   *93*

Socioeconomic Status and Social Class   93

U.S. Population Demographics   93

Cultural Identity   94

Cultural Transitions   97

Sexual Identity   99

Prejudice and Discrimination   *100*

Discrimination in Schools   *101*

Competing Perspectives: Theories, Models, and Approaches to Race, Class, and Gender   *102*

Cultural Deficiency Approach   103

Cultural Difference Approach   104

Human Relations Approach   104

Single-Group Studies Approach   105

Multicultural Education Approach   106

Social Justice Education Approach   106

Segregation, Desegregation, and Integration   **109**
Magnet Schools   109
Language Diversity in U.S. Schools: Program Options   110
• **Promoting Linguistically Diverse Learners' Academic Success,**
by Viviana Alexandrowicz, University of San Diego   **111**

English Language Learners in U.S. Public Schools   **113**
English Only, English Plus, and Programs
for Nonstandard English Speakers   113
• **Developing Programs of School, Family, and Community
Partnerships: Administrators Make a Difference,** *by Joyce L. Epstein,
Director, Center on School, Family, and Community Partnerships,
Johns Hopkins University*   **114**

Connecting Schools and Community Organizations   **116**

Conclusion   **118**

Portfolio Artifacts   **118**

Terms   **118**

Suggested Readings   **119**

5 *School District Organizational Structure
and Leadership*   **120**

• **Alta Vista School: Data Disaggregation**   **120**

The Local Role   **122**

The Local School Division   **122**

The School Board   **124**

The School Division Superintendent   **127**

Central Office Operations   **130**
• **Local School Structures and Arrangements,**
by Marilyn Tallerico, Syracuse University   **133**

The School Administrator   **135**
Changing Roles   136
Critical Incidents   138

Politics of the Principalship   **140**
Principal: Instructional Leader or School Manager?   141

School Safety Audit   **143**
• **Putting "Cs" into the Village,** *by Paul C. Houston, Ed.D.,
Executive Director, American Association of School Administrators*   **144**

Parental Involvement   **145**

Assistant Principal (AP)   *147*

Conclusion   *148*

Portfolio Artifacts   *150*

Terms   *150*

Suggested Readings   *150*

Appendix 5.A: The Joint AASA–NSBA Superintendent Guidelines   *151*

6   Leadership Theory and Practice   153

• **Atlas Shrug High School: Failing Health**   153

Assessing Leadership Characteristics   *155*

Paradigms of Leadership: A Growing Knowledge Base   *156*

Leadership Instrument Analyses   *157*
McGregor's Theories X and Y   158
NREL Behavior Matrix   160
Early Studies   162
The Ohio State Studies   163
The New Managerial Grid   165
Situational and Contingency Leadership   167
University of Michigan Studies   176

Recent Works on Leadership   *178*
Search for Excellence   178
The 7 Habits of Highly Effective People and Alignment   179
The Learning Organization   181
The New Science of Leadership   182
Total Quality Management (TQM)   183
School-Based Management (SBM)   185
Cultural Leadership   185
Transformational Leadership   187

Leadership Traits or Skills   *189*

Conclusion   *190*

Portfolio Artifacts   *191*

Terms   *191*

Suggested Readings   *192*

Appendix 6.A: Directions for Scoring Box 6.1: The X–Y Scale   *192*

Appendix 6.B: Directions for Interpreting Box 6.4:
The Behavior Matrix   *193*

Appendix 6.C: Directions for Scoring Box 6.5:
Leadership Behavior Survey   196

Appendix 6.D: Directions for Scoring Box 6.6:
Measuring Preferred Management Styles   197

Appendix 6.E: Twenty-One Combined Domains
of Effective School Leadership   199

7   *Successful School Leadership   201*

• **Packer Middle School: An Interview for a Principalship**   201

Leadership Matters   201

Adult Learning   204

Effective School Leadership Practices   205
   • **Leadership and the Change Process,**
     by Michael Fullan, University of Toronto   **208**

Structures That Provide Opportunities for Teacher Collaboration   209
   Study Groups   209
   Instructional Walk-Throughs   210
   Teacher Conferences   211
   School Visitations   211
   District and/or School Instructional Conferences   211
   • **Principals as Instructional Leaders: Modeling and Supporting Teaching**
     and Learning, *by Paul V. Bredeson, University of Wisconsin–Madison*   **212**

Supporting the Change Process   214

The Teacher Selection Process   214

Conclusion   215

Endnote   216

Terms   216

Suggested Readings   216

8   *Program Development, Delivery, and Assessment   217*

• **Linton Elementary School: Program Improvement**   217

Conceptions of Academic Achievement   218
   Theories of Intelligence   218
   Types of Knowledge   219
   Learning Transfer   221

Constructivism: A New Conception of Learning   222
Building a Culture of Learning   223

Teaching and Learning Approaches   **224**
Apprenticeship Learning   225
Cooperative Learning   225
Problem-Based Learning   226

Curriculum Design and Educational Programming   **227**
Functions of Curriculum   227
• **Principal as Curriculum Leader,** *by Allan A. Glatthorn,
University of East Carolina*   **228**
The Standards Movement   229

Curricular and Instructional Change   **230**
Developing Curriculum and Programs   231
Designing and Managing the Curriculum   232
• **Seeing the Curriculum Whole: The Function of a Real
Educational Leader,** *by Laurel N. Tanner, Temple University*   **233**

Program Improvement and Evaluation   **235**

Utilizing Time   **236**
Year-Round Education   236
Block Scheduling   237
Looping   238
Time on Task   239

Assessing Student Progress   **239**
Portfolios   240
• **Assessing Student Performance,** *by Grant Wiggins, President and Director
for the Center on Learning Assessment and School Structure (C.L.A.S.S.)*   **240**
Reporting Student Progress   242
Presenting Student Outcomes to the Community   243

Conclusion   **245**

Portfolio Artifacts   **246**

Terms   **246**

Suggested Readings   **247**

9 *Pupil Personnel Services*   **248**

• **Edgar Allen Poe Middle School: Special Education**   **248**
Pupil Personnel–Student Service Team   **249**
Counseling, Guidance, Psychological Services   **251**

Special Education and Remedial Instruction   252

Inclusion   255

• **Leadership for Special Services,**
    by *Judy Mantle, University of San Diego*   **257**

School Health Services   258

Child Accounting and School Safety   259

School Security   260

Student Discipline   261

Pupil Appraisal, Testing, and Diagnostics   265

Extracurricular Activities   266

Conclusion   270

Portfolio Artifacts   271

Terms   271

Suggested Readings   272

10   *Human Resource Management*   273

• **Lincoln Elementary School: Staffing Problems**   **273**

Taking Care of the Staff   276

Job Analysis, Classification, and Staff Planning   277

Job Analysis   280

Job Classification   281

Staff Planning   282

Recruitment   283

Selection   285

Alternative Selection Approaches   287

Performance Appraisal and Evaluation   289

Planning the Evaluation   290

Collecting Information   291

Using Information   292

Staff Development   294

Employee Assistance and Wellness Programs   298

• **Human Resource Administration in the Third Millennium,**
    by *Ronald Rebore, St. Louis University*   **299**

Organizational Development   300

Wage and Salary Considerations   301

Benefits   303

Collective Bargaining   304

Employee Records and Reports   305

Employee Litigation   305

Conclusion   306

Portfolio Artifacts   306

Terms   307

Suggested Readings   307

11 *Laws and Policies   308*

• **Benton I.S.D: Not Following School Board Policy   308**

Legal Responsibility   309
Learning about Schools and Legal Issues   309

The U.S. Legal System   309
Federal Role in Education   309
Federal Courts   310
• **Understanding Court Decisions,** *by Perry A. Zirkel and
Kathleen A. Sullivan, Lehigh University*   **312**
The State's Legal Role in Education   314
State Legislatures, Administrative Agencies,
and Local Boards of Control   315
School Districts and Litigation   316

Legal Issues and Schools   317
Due Process   318
Freedom of Speech and Expression   319
Discipline and Students with Disabilities   319
The Confidentiality of Student Records   321
• **Student Rights,** *by Charles J. Russo, University of Dayton*   **321**
Torts   322

Monitoring Compliance with Policies and Procedures   323
• **Legal and Ethical Dimensions of Educational Leadership,**
by Martha McCarthy, Indiana University   **324**

Conclusion   327

Portfolio Artifacts   328

Terms   328

Suggested Readings   328

Court Cases   329

12 *Resource Allocation and Management*   *330*

- **Oceanview School District: Identifying Funding Sources for Meadows High**   330

Financing Schools   *330*
Taxes   331

Federal Involvement in Financing Schools   *332*

State Involvement in Financing Schools   *332*

Local Involvement in Financing Schools   *335*

Vouchers   *336*

Nontraditional Revenue Sources   *336*
School Foundations   337

Revenue Sources for Independent Schools   *338*
- **Obtaining Funding for Educational Programs,** *by Harvey B. Polansky, Ph.D., Superintendent of Schools, Southington, Connecticut*   **338**

Grant Writing   *339*

Budgeting, Accounting, and Facility Management   *340*
The Budgeting Process   340

Types of Budgeting   *343*
Line-Item Budgeting   343
Planning, Programming, Budgeting System (PPBS)   344
Zero-Based Budgeting   344
Incremental Budgeting   345
Trends in Budgeting and Management   346

Activity Funds   *347*

Fiscal Accounting   *348*

The Audit   *349*
- **Acquiring, Allocating, and Accounting for Resources,** *by Richard A. King, University of Northern Colorado*   **349**

Managing School Supplies and Equipment   *351*

Maintaining School Buildings and Grounds   *351*

Conclusion   *351*

Portfolio Artifacts   *352*

Terms   *353*

Suggested Readings   *353*

13 *Problem-Based Learning Projects*   354

Problem-Based Learning   354
- **Problem-Based Learning in Educational Leadership,** *by Ed Bridges, Stanford University, and Philip Hallinger, Vanderbilt University*   **356**

Facilitating Groups   358
- **Understanding Group Process,** *by Cheryl Getz, University of San Diego*   **359**
- **Project 1: Safe Havens: Developing School-Based Health Clinics,** *by Ellen Smith Sloan, Southern Connecticut State University*   **362**
- **Project 2: A Jalapeño in a Candy Jar: Addressing Cultural Diversity,** *by Paula A. Cordeiro, University of San Diego*   **368**
- **Project 3: Atoms and Bits: A Technology Project,** *by Barbara S. Campbell, Wolcott Public School, Connecticut*   **373**
- **Project 4: Data Management and Analysis (DMA) and Decision Making at Madison High School,** *by William G. Cunningham, Old Dominion University*   **380**
- **Project 5: Marveling at the Results: Power, Roles, Relationships, and School Reform,** *by William G. Cunningham, Old Dominion University*   **384**

References and Bibliography   **392**

Name Index   **420**

Subject Index   **428**

Preface

Educational Leadership: A Problem-Based Approach provides a comprehensive discussion of the field of educational administration. The book describes how successful and effective schools and administrators operate in an increasingly challenging, fast-paced, demanding, and perhaps revolutionary environment. Readers are offered an integrated view of the knowledge base, research, and practice of administration within a context of multiple perspectives and a wide range of thinking.

Each chapter builds a strong foundation on which to sustain an educational career. The book uses the most widely recognized research and best administrative practices to focus attention on the very latest challenges facing our discipline. Readers are encouraged to be introspective and reflective as they apply the collective wisdom within the field to the current issues in the context of today's education. Through hundreds of vignettes, problem-based challenges, concrete examples, original expert essays, assessment instruments, collected artifacts, and reflective writings, the book focuses the reader's attention on the successful application of the expansive knowledge contained within. This book will be invaluable for anyone who wishes to take on greater leadership responsibility in education.

The book's format allows the reader to choose among areas of concentration and those of review. Some chapters are important to a reader because of his or her present professional status, whereas others may be simply informative. Although the topics flow logically from one chapter to the next, selected chapters and even portions of chapters can be studied separately, or in a different sequence depending on the needs of the reader or instructor.

Earlier chapters can be skipped without losing touch with the essence of later chapters, or vice versa, although we recommend that you scan them to obtain a sense of their content. Each topic is introduced and placed in a practical perspective as part of an integral system of leadership that is developed throughout a person's professional life. This text provides a comprehensive reference of key information useful in improving educational practice.

Each chapter follows the same basic format and begins with a vignette that reflects the life of a school administrator. Questions and comments are located throughout each chapter to make overall theory-practice connections, to encourage readers to enrich their understanding of problems in practice, and to suggest how leadership might be applied in a variety of settings. Illustrations, expert opinions, quotes, Internet addresses, and examples are often used to highlight key points, trends, and issues.

Each chapter concludes with suggested activities through which readers can begin to build their educational leadership platforms. Artifacts can be collected to demonstrate a reader's ability to connect knowledge to his or her responsibilities. The portfolio artifacts and reflective writings can be collected for each chapter to create a cumulative portfolio documenting the reader's growth and understanding of administrative practice.

A number of nationally noted scholars and practitioners from a variety of fields have provided original, expert reflections on critical topics within each chapter. These contributions provide insights into many key areas of educational administration from those who have been involved in the most promising activities within the field. The objective of providing these important insights is to model and encourage readers in the development of well-thought-out and supported analysis of key issues. They also allow the reader to relate his or her reflective thinking to that of noted experts in the field. Each contribution encourages the reader to think through, discuss, and debate key issues surrounding educational administration.

The first chapter explores and develops philosophical frames, values, ethics, and practices in educational administration. The next three chapters examine context, sociocultural issues, major reform initiatives, cultural diversity, and community relations. Chapters 5 to 7 focus on school district organization and successful leadership. Readers are asked to assess their own leadership styles using the instruments provided. Attention then shifts to operational responsibilities and legal regulatory issues in Chapters 8 through 12. The book explores major leadership responsibilities related to curriculum, instruction, and program development; pupil personnel; human resource management; legal and compliance issues; and finance and stewardship. A brief overview of problem-based learning (PBL), two expert inquiries, and five PBL projects comprise the final chapter.

The five PBL projects can be used in a variety of ways. One approach is to schedule a project before reading the text. The text can serve as a resource when readers select only chapters that are necessary to address issues adequately and appropriately. Another way to incorporate the projects is for readers to complete a project approximately midway through the book. This approach permits readers to become comfortable with the content, begin the development of an administrative platform, and possibly begin developing a portfolio. Alternatively, a PBL project could be used as a culminating activity. No solutions are provided. The PBL projects are designed to stimulate inquiry, to create deep reflection, to work on group dynamics and to challenge perspectives regarding key issues, values, and needs.

The authors appreciate the wise counsel of their editor, Arnis E. Burvikovs. Much of the content of this book is drawn from the life work of researchers, scholars, and practitioners who have dedicated their professional lives to an improved understanding of education and administration. We appreciate their dedication and critically important insights. We are also indebted to reviewers for previous editions who provided invaluable feedback, insights, and resources: Bruce Barnett, University of Northern Colorado; Martin Burlingame, Oklahoma State University; Tom Glass, University of Memphis; Maria-Luisa Gonzalez, New Mexico State University; Larry W. Hughes, University of Houston; Richard A. King, University of

Northern Colorado; Otis Lovette, University of Louisiana at Monroe; Rosita L. Mercano, Northern Illinois University; and Ulrich C. Reitzug, University of North Carolina, Greensboro. Special thanks go to each of the experts, who contributed original pieces reflecting on the contents of the chapters and who have made such significant contributions to our field. Particular thanks go to Dawn Hall and Sheila Jones, whose proofreading and typing helped to make this book a reality.

Many friends and colleagues who teach and practice educational administration provided counsel, inspiration, and direction as they have given of their time and interest. Last, but certainly not least, are the thousands of educational leadership students who first breathe such exciting life into this subject and then into our schools. We wish them Godspeed on their noble journeys. To them all, we offer appreciation and great thanks.

We would like to thank the reviewers of this edition for their time and input: John C. Daresh, University of Texas–El Paso; Lynn H. Doyle, Old Dominion University; and Mark D. Myers, Indiana University–Purdue University Fort Wayne.

We would also like to thank our parents, Jerry and Margaret Cunningham and Manuel Cordeiro; sister, Gail Penn; spouse, Sandra L. Cunningham; children Kerri and her husband Chuck Joyner and Michael and his wife Dottie; and grandchildren, Cierra, Merrick, Keenan, Shealyn, Braidyn and Alayna for their continuing encouragement and support and the happiness and love we enjoy. Many, many thanks to David J. O'Brien for his careful editing of the first drafts. His insights and support are deeply appreciated.

We hope you find this book worthy of the greatness of the people who have had such profound influences on our lives. Part of each is in this work.

William G. Cunningham
Paula A. Cordeiro

Interstate School Leaders Licensure Consortium

Standards Covered in This Text

Standard 1 A school administrator is an educational leader who promotes the success of all students by facilitating the development, articulation, implementation, and stewardship of a vision of learning that is shared and supported by the school community.

Chapters
2, 3, 4, 7, 8, 9, 13

Standard 2 A school administrator is an educational leader who promotes the success of all students by advocating, nurturing, and sustaining a school culture and an instructional program conducive to student learning and staff professional development.

Chapters
1, 3, 5, 6, 7, 8, 9, 10, 13

Standard 3 A school administrator is an educational leader who promotes the success of all students by ensuring management of the organization, operations, and resources for a safe, efficient, and effective learning environment.

Chapters
5, 6, 10, 11, 12, 13

Standard 4 A school administrator is an educational leader who promotes the success of all students by collaborating with families and community members, responding to diverse community interests and needs, and mobilizing resources.

Chapters
2, 4, 9, 11, 12, 13

Standard 5 A school administrator is an educational leader who promotes the success of all students by acting with integrity, with fairness, and in an ethical manner.

Chapters
1, 4, 11, 13

Standard 6 A school administrator is an educational leader who promotes the success of all students by understanding, responding to, and influencing the larger political, social, economic, legal, and cultural context.

Chapters
2, 3, 5, 11, 13

1

Administrative Theory, Values Clarification, and Leadership Responsibility

A New Administrative Team

Superintendent Vivian Armstid of the Flem Snopes school district wants to develop a leadership team at the high school that would support the upcoming school renewal effort. Thus, Flem Snopes school district is in the process of selecting a high school principal and two assistant principals to lead major reform efforts that would occur over the next three to five years at Flem Snopes High School. Superintendent Armstid, in stressing the importance of this selection decision, stated, "It is essential that we select the candidates who we believe are best able to take on the challenging roles of principal and assistant principal during our important renewal effort at the high school. We have narrowed the field down to seven candidates, all of whom are well prepared to assume this important challenge. The major differences among these candidates can be found in their values, beliefs, philosophies, and knowledge bases about leadership, which ultimately will shape the way that renewal will be approached in this school. Some of these differences seem mutually exclusive of one another and your responsibility will be to rank order these candidates based on their be-

lief system, style, and paradigm of leadership. The highest ranked individual will be considered for the principal position and the second- and third-ranked for the two assistant principal positions."

As part of the interview, each of the seven candidates for administrative positions were asked to briefly state his or her administrative platform related to the enormously complex job of administration. The contrasting belief systems of the seven candidates are as follows:

• Mr. Wayne stated: "The leader must be the role model for his teachers. He is strong and courageous, willing to take risks, and try new things, with a desire to excel. Charisma is very important. You view the principalship as a character you play who models the expectations you have for your staff. You must be a person of action, engaged in great deeds, eliminating negative forces at every turn, and inspiring your employees. You show them you're willing to work as hard as you want them to work. Leaders must be people of action modeling excellence at every possible opportunity."

• Ms. Taylor viewed leadership slightly differently, explaining: "You must carefully lay out standards, divide the work that must be done, and identify those who have the expertise to be productive and efficient. Success depends on getting the small day-to-day operations functioning well. If you can't get the bills paid and have people arrive on time, return phone calls, and have schedules that work, you won't go very far. Effective management and effective leadership are somewhat the same. Both require that people know what is expected of them and have the organization and resources needed to get the job done."

• Mr. Newton offered a different perspective: "Leadership is first and foremost about making effective decisions. If the leader makes good decisions, everything else will fall into place. The leader must ensure that the organization objectively evaluates what is known and makes his or her decision on the basis of research, facts, and rationality. Relationships between decisions and the aims to be achieved must be carefully established and evaluated. Standards are used to define the expectations related to the level of performance deemed acceptable. When people know the leader will ensure that decisions are logical and objective and based on the latest knowledge and research, they will support him or her because they are the best possible decisions given the circumstances. Leaders must know about key subjects like development, curriculum, and finance and study them in depth. Leadership is using the right information for making decisions. Such leaders have a strong knowledge base, are aware of the latest research, and have a clear focus on the goals. Leaders are persuasive and convince others that the goals are worth achieving. Once that has occurred, the work will be achieved in an effective and efficient manner."

• Ms. Maynard held different views related to leadership: "It is the formal structure, communication networks, the relationships of people, and organizational climate that are important in leadership efforts. The employee's strongest motivation is for survival, status, power, and recognition, and leaders help those within the organization to obtain such motivators. Leaders create productive relationships within the organization and sometimes outside. It is the patterns and operating procedures of the organization that shape the people who work within it. Leaders must understand and be able to work through the inner structures to accomplish results. It's who you call, when to be nice, when to bite the bullet and decide. Good relationships and collaboration certainly help. Who you are and the power you have are important, but people's behaviors are shaped by policies, procedures, job descriptions, organizational hierarchy, and other such structural components. They must believe the mission will benefit all members of the group and will be compatible with formal organizational beliefs. Leadership depends on running a tight organizational ship."

• Mr. Browne believed: "Leaders do not deal with matters that are scientific or even orderly but those that are philosophical and ethical. Leadership is being fair and honest and having a sense of what is right and what is wrong. That means that issues like human rights, justice, loyalty, trust, integrity, respect, duty, and other such virtues are important. A person's moral responsibility and duty are very important. The job of the leader is consciousness-raising and ensuring good moral behavior on the part of all employees and a sense of collective responsibility. Leadership requires critical reflection and analysis of the human condition and all human action to determine what is important, right, and helpful. Employees should be responsible, inquisitive, probing, reflective, and critical in their thinking. Leaders are fair, honest, moral, and consistent and thus earn and grant respect. Leaders increase sensitivity to moral issues that arise and develop moral, ethical, and legal responses."

• Ms. Gilligan suggested: "Leadership is caring for and being sensitive to the needs of others and understanding responsibilities and relationships. It should emphasize feelings, compassion, generosity, assisting, nurturing, and caring for others. We all bear a responsibility for the ethical perfection of others. You have to be willing to listen to people and set aside your agenda; just because it's good for you does not mean it's good for others. Decisions are good when they help others in their personal and professional lives. Leaders must be ethical, sincere, and encouraging. Leadership's primary purpose is developing the best in staff so they will benefit children."

• Mr. Wheatly stated: "Organizations are fluid, with no final destination possible and therefore no certainty—no possibility of a true or accurate account. As a result, leadership becomes the management of discourse that is influenced by multiple interpretations, multiple realities, changing views, and different perspectives, even about leadership for school reform. Uncertainty, instability, differences, disagreements, or volatility often throws organizations into chaos; under proper conditions, however, this chaos is a catalyst for renewal and enhancement. Leadership can come from just about anyone, and conflict and dissension are not necessarily a bad thing. Individual differences can often be used as a learning tool. The leader must provide those proper conditions and comfort levels to allow such knowledge and instability to do its work. Order does not come from avoiding differences; people must be free to interact with the turbulent changing environment in order to respond and regenerate. This means a willingness to listen to people and set aside your own personal agenda. Listening is the fuel for reflecting and reframing situations. Leadership organizes complexity, provides information, remains fluid, and encourages constant improvement."

These candidates will carry out their work, make decisions, and set the mood of the school on the basis of their administrative platforms. Thus, deciding which of these individuals and related platforms will best serve the high school is a very important decision. This information helps in determining how these candidates (1) will structure a positive, productive environment for school renewal, (2) will manage conflict, and (3) will motivate people. After reflecting on the platforms, you are asked to develop your reasoning and ranking based on how well you believe these candidates will lead the renewal, work at the tasks, interact with others, make decisions, motivate people, and ultimately achieve success. You will want to consider the characteristics that you like and dislike about the styles in order to select the ones you believe to be most appropriate. You might also consider how styles complement or assist and where there might be conflicts among the styles when these individuals would be closely associated or working together. Most important, you are to select the best administrative team to provide leadership for Flem Snopes High School.

✻ **Why is Superintendent Armstid stressing the importance of "values, beliefs, philosophies, and knowledge bases" in selecting an administrative team for Flem Snopes High School?**

Educational Leadership

The first fifteen years of the twenty-first century provides one of the great opportunities to obtain educational administration positions. According to the U.S. Department of Labor, over 50 percent of the nations 93,200 principals will retire over the next thirteen years. This has created a shortage of qualified applicants that was confirmed by Educational Research Services (1998; 2000). The 1998 report stated that "There is a shortage of qualified candidates for principal vacancies in the United States. About half of the surveyed districts reported that there was a shortage of qualified candidates for the principal positions they had attempted to fill.

This shortage has occurred among all types of schools (rural, urban, and suburban) and among all levels of vacancies (elementary, junior high/middle, and high school). However, these interviewees did not indicate that they were dissatisfied with the people they hired, only that they perceived there to be a shortage of qualified candidates" (p. 9).

The number of qualified candidates willing to assume positions of school leadership is growing smaller (Young, Petersen, & Short, 2002). According to NASSP, half of all surveyed districts, including 45 percent of those classified as suburban, reported shortages of qualified candidates for principalships at all levels—elementary (45 percent), middle (55 percent), and high school (55 percent). As a result, school districts across the country are studying ways to increase the number of candidates for administrative positions at almost all levels, including the superintendency.

School districts are identifying future leaders who can think thoroughly and quickly about complex issues, collaborate with diverse groups, show good judgment, stay on the cutting-edge of school improvement, and lead needed school reforms. These leaders will be risk-takers and coalition-builders who can obtain broad support.

In all states, educational leaders will have to meet established educational administrative licensure requirements. Over forty states now require a master's degree with some administrative courses for an administrative and supervision license. These state requirements were developed to ensure the quality of the preparation of our future practicing school leaders. They exist to protect the health, safety, and welfare of the public and to ensure knowledge and skills important for competent practice. In addition, many states and local districts now offer leadership academies to complement the training received in universities and to provide inservice development for practicing administrators.

A growing number of states, particularly southern states, have established cut scores on various forms of assessment as a prerequisite to receiving licensure. A licensure test is designed to determine if individuals possess occupation-relevant knowledge and skills at the time of entry into their profession. The belief is that school administrators should be held accountable to the same high standards as teachers. The ISLLC standards (see Box 1.1) guide and shape the six-hour Educational Testing Service (ETS) School Leadership Licensure Assessment and the scoring of the exercises.

Practitioner-oriented professional associations also provide input on the identification, preparation, and practice of educational leaders. They have local, state, and national meetings, academies, and conferences for the purpose of providing professional development while shaping the latest thinking in educational leadership. They publish newsletters, journals, and books that help administrative students and practitioners to keep current in their field. They have a long-standing commitment to the improvement of education and have championed the cause for innovation and experimentation.

Those preparing to be administrators as well as practicing administrators will want to associate with a professional association that best meets their needs. Some of the older and well-known professional associations are the following:

Professional Association	Example of a Major Practitioner Audience
Council of Chief State School Officers (CCSSO)	State superintendents
National School Board Association (NASB)	School board members
American Association of School Administrators (AASA)	Superintendents
Association for Supervision and Curriculum Development (ASCD)	Central office personnel and supervisors
National Association of Secondary School Principals (NASSP)	High school principals
Middle School Principal Association (MSPA)	Middle school principals
National Association of Elementary School Principals (NAESP)	Elementary school principals
National Education Association (NEA)	Teachers
American Federation of Teachers (AFT)	Teachers

BOX 1.1 • ISLLC Standards for School Leaders

Standard 1   – VISION

A school administrator is an educational leader who promotes the success of all students by facilitating the development, articulation, implementation, and stewardship of a vision of learning that is shared and supported by the school community.

Standard 2 – CULTURE/INSTRUCTION

A school administrator is an educational leader who promotes the success of all students by advocating, nurturing, and sustaining a school culture and an instructional program conducive to student learning and staff professional growth.

Standard 3 – MANAGEMENT

A school administrator is an educational leader who promotes the success of all students by ensuring management of the organization, operations, and resources for a safe, efficient, and effective learning environment.

Standard 4 – COMMUNITY

A school administrator is an educational leader who promotes the success of all students by collaborating with families and community members, responding to diverse community interests and needs, and mobilizing resources.

Standard 5 – ETHICS

A school administrator is an educational leader who promotes the success of all students by acting with integrity, with fairness, and in an ethical manner.

Standard 6

A school administrator is an educational leader who promotes the success of all students by understanding, responding to, and influencing the larger political, social, economic, legal, and cultural context.

The Interstate School Leaders Licensure Consortium (ISLLC) Standards were developed by the Council of Chief State School Officers (CCSSO) and member states. Copies may be downloaded from the Council's website at www.ccsso.org.

Council of Chief State School Officers. (1996). *Interstate School Leaders Licensure Consortium (ISLLC) standards for school leaders*. Washington, DC: Author.

One example of the profound influence that professional associations might have on the preparation of future school administrators can be found in the work of the CCSSO. The CCSSO, in conjunction with the National Policy Board for Educational Administration (NPBEA)—a joint board representing a number of educational professional associations—created the Interstate School Leaders Licensure Consortium (ISLLC) to develop standards for the preparation and assessment of school leaders. These six standards were adopted by a majority of the states and influenced state administrative licensure requirements, the design of the ETS Administrative Assessment, and the development of educational administrative programs across the United States. (For more information see www.npbea.org.)

Schools; school divisions; state departments of, and the federal office of, education; professional associations; and universities form a rich network of organizations focused on the improvement of the teaching/learning process and education, by enhancing organizational and individual effectiveness. Administrators benefit from a knowledge base, skills, ethical principles, and contextual understanding that provide the intellectual grounding needed for effective leadership. They build on a core of knowledge and skills in which theory and practice are integrated to improve performance.

Effective administrators are prepared to respond to the larger political, social, economic, legal, and cultural context of schools. Administrators are expected to apply a variety of policies, laws, regulations, and procedures in creative ways. They are expected to operate and maintain safe and clean buildings, equipment, and grounds while keeping attention focused on instruction.

When you assume the role of an educational administrator, you will influence the direction of schooling so that each student leaves school having the capacity to engage in self-governance and self-development and to access the economic benefits of our society.

Thomas Jefferson noted that schooling is necessary for democracy to survive. Administrators are expected to be a catalyst in that process by which multiple voices, conflicting values, and diverse expectations are molded into a vision for education. The vision must meet the tests of justice, fairness, and equity. Thus, schooling is a profoundly human enterprise, an institution that nourishes liberty and democracy and provides access to economic benefits. It is also a technological one integrating the latest in technological advances into the curriculum and instructional process.

Communicating, facilitating, team building, coaching, managing conflict, involving others in decision making, and acting politically are a few of the major skills to be developed in the context of technological advancement, assessment and accountability, diversity, new knowledge, limited resources, and many other contextual elements. Effective administration requires cooperation among departments, government agencies, staff members, professional groups, political office holders, school board members, media, universities, publishers, and many others.

It is not easy to conceptualize what educational administrators need to know and to be able to do. Although there is no sense of total agreement, conceptually there is widely accepted agreement that there are some foundational factors central to the practice of educational administration. Certainly the mission includes commitment to effective operation and continuous improvement of our schools, but it is far more than that. The desirable aspects of effective leadership are influenced by beliefs related to caring, pedagogy, moral stewardship, renewal, accountability, passion, charisma, civility, economic utility, reform, democratic character, and competence. According to Leithwood and Duke (1999), the elaboration of educational administrative knowledge "is illustrated in efforts to deepen understanding of those sources of leadership legitimation as well as to extend knowledge of the practices associated with each different approach to leadership. The outcome of this process, although not synthesized well to date, are conceptions of leadership in school that are increasingly complex (a good thing), multidimensional, ecologically valid, defensible, and user-friendly" (p. 65). The need is to provide a comprehensive account of educational leadership without oversimplifying its complex, dynamic, interactive nature.

Human Capital and the Accumulated Knowledge Base

There exists a diverse variety of perspectives and alternative (sometimes conflictive) views as to how one might better understand educational administration. These views tend to rise and fall in importance in relation to the social and political events of the times. However, Willower and Forsyth (1999) find that there are a number of unifying elements in the scholarship in educational administration which provide a variety of frameworks for addressing educational problems. They state "regardless of how infrequently or imperfectly knowledge and values currently are employed to guide practice, it is genuinely possible for their use to be more widely internalized by reflective individuals and institutionalized in educational organizations" (p. 15). The decision as to what will best serve the practitioner will most likely come down to its utility when it is being employed and the benefits of its results.

Certainly, educational administration practice is a blending of knowledge, practice, politics, ethics, traditions, and new visions. No one perspective or approach will provide a complete and universal explanation for practitioners; however, great benefit is derived by having an understanding of these diverse perspectives. The challenge then becomes in finding ways to integrate the different perspectives, values, and approaches so as to improve the outcomes of education and the functioning of educational organizations (Donmoyer, 1999a).

Some experts (Coleman, 1990; Strober, 1990) suggest that human capital within the organization is this accumulated knowledge along with the skills that influence the capacity to be successful and productive. Social capital focuses on resources that can be utilized to promote productive activity, resources such as one's knowledge and skill base that can be developed by educational leaders and shared with others. This shared knowledge and belief system shapes interactions among organizational members and helps to sustain productive social relationships. The knowledge and skill base connects the organization to previously developed understanding. Administrators are the keepers of the conventional practice and wisdom of the time, wisdom composed of the professional knowledge, norms, and values that transcend the work site and even the times during which the individual works (Smylie & Hart, 1999).

Administrative Process and Knowledge

When we consider management, we typically place greater emphasis on organizational policies and procedures, whereas leadership focuses on the dynamics and direction of the organization. However, Leithwood and Duke (1999) suggest, "The distinction between management and leadership contributes little or nothing to an understanding of leadership conceived as a set of relationships" (p. 67). Given that concern, the two terms are often used in the literature, and therefore, an understanding of how the terms are used can be important.

Leadership has to do with guiding improvement and infusing an organization with meaning and purpose, whereas *management* is involved with stewardship and accountability for all types of resources. Management also focuses on implementing routines in an organization and ensuring its smooth operation. Joel Barker (1992) states, "You manage within a paradigm, you lead between paradigms" (p. 164). The line between these two concepts remains fuzzy for some, and the terms are occasionally used synonymously.

The study of administration is grounded in science and philosophy, in theories and ethics. According to Barnett (1991), many with an interest in educational administration believe it is very important for administrators to understand and develop belief systems and philosophies for their practice. Thus a person's epistemology—the way a person thinks and determines reality and the way that person approaches work—is critically important. Bolman and Deal (1993) conclude:

> Wise and effective leadership is more important than ever, but it requires a complex array of lenses to distinguish traps and deadends from promising opportunities. Multiframe thinking reduces administrators' stress and enhances their effectiveness. (p. 31)

The premise is that good theory provides useful knowledge to guide effective practice. The administrator's skills and abilities are improved by both theory and practice. As John Dewey suggested long ago, there is nothing as practical as a good theory. Theories provide the conceptual tools to focus the work of the administrator: They are guides to action. They provide a reasonable base for tactics and strategies that might improve the educational administrator's success. William Greenfield (1995) states, "More complete knowledge of these two realms (the nature and centrality of leadership in schools and the demand environment [context] to which it responds) will provide a basis for more powerful theories about school administration, more informed preparation curricula, and more concrete guidance regarding the specific intentions, strategies, behaviors, and process associated with effective leadership in schools" (p. 80).

✳ **How might you begin to rank order the different thinking regarding the role of the principal?**

Philosophical Frames and Epistemological Influences

Paradigms can provide a general overview of the development of prominent conceptualizations and transformations of ideas about administration. Paradigms identify the main components in such a way that they embody how something operates.

Table 1.1 presents Heck and Hallinger's (1999, p. 142) conceptualization of philosophical frames and epistemological influences on research in educational administration. They state:

> During the past decade, the fields of education and management have both been in the midst of paradigm shifts. These shifts have led to the reconsideration of the theoretical conceptualizations as well as research methods. (p. 142)

Table 1.1 illustrates the identifiable research strands (alternative ways of knowing and understanding educational administration). Studies are presented in the table according to their multiple perspectives of knowledge, philosophical foundations, research orientation, leadership model, and method. Donmoyer (1999b), in reviewing Heck and Hallinger's work, suggests that

> Heck and Hallinger ground their framework in three conceptions of knowledge—positivist, interpretive, and critical-contextual—which are reasonable facsimiles of Guba and Lincoln's (1994) positivist/postpositivist, naturalistic/constructivist, and critical theory paradigms. (p. 621)

The approach used to understand and classify the thinking that influences theory and knowledge development in educational administration is highly debated. There is much turbulence in regard to types of epistemology, research orientation, and knowledge bases when it comes to educational administration. Such turbulence portrays "the rifts and currents alive in our field today." Before studying the field, it is important to gain an understanding of the many perspectives that influence the knowledge base in existence today.

For example, the dominate paradigm of science has been eclipsed in the postmodern age. The claim that administration is a closed "scientific" system faces severe challenges (Callahan, 1962; Greenfield, 1988; Willower, 1979). Griffiths (1979) criticizes science and the "cult of efficiency" for failing to provide ethical guidance and to theorize gender issues and for being unable to support political analysis or to adjudicate conflicts of interest. He suggests that educational administration as a field is in intellectual turmoil. Feminist criticisms of Carol Gilligan (1982) and Charol Shakeshaft (1986) demonstrate the neglect of gender issues in administrative theory and research. Concern is expressed by James Banks (1993) that educational administrative research might also be racially biased.

Most criticism of logical empiricism and science has come about because of difficulties with empirical adequacy as a criterion of theory choice (Evers & Lakomski, 1996; Greenfield, 1993; Hodgkinson, 1991). Useful patterns to explain organization and educational administration "draw on more criteria than just empirical adequacy—such as consistency, simplicity, comprehensiveness, utility of explanation, learnability and fecundity" (Evers & Lakomski, 1996, p. 386).

TABLE 1.1 *Framework of Approaches for Studying School Leadership*

Knowledge	Positivist		Interpretive		Critical-Contextual			
Lens	*Structural-Functional (Rational)*		*Political-Constructivist*	*Conflict*	*Critical Constructivist*	*Feminist*	*Gender Culture*	*(No Lens) Postmodern*
Research Orientation	Nature of Work	Administrator Effects	Sense-Making in Schools		Sense-Making about Social Constructions (Whose interests are served?)			Post-Structural Pragmatic
Example Studies	Peterson (1978) Kmetz & Willower (1981) Martin & Willower (1982) Chung & Miskel (1989)	Scott & Teddie (1887) Eberts & Stone (1988) Hallinger et al. (1989) Bamburg & Andrews (1990) Synder & Ebmeier (1992) Brewer (1993) Hannaway & Talbert (1993) Bass & Avolio (1989) Leithwood (1994) Silins (1994)	Gronn (1984a) Ball (1987) Greenfield (1991) Blase (1993)	Varenne (1978, 1983) Wolcott (1973) Leithwood & Stager (1989) Ogawa (1991) Duke & Iwanicki (1992) Hart (1994) Murphy & Beck (1995) Anderson & Shirley (1995) Cooper & Heck (1995) Begley (1996) Walker et al. (1996) Lum (1997)	Lomotey (1989, 1993) Anderson (1991) Keith (1996)	Reagan (1990) Chase (1992) Oritz (1992)	Dillard (1995) Benham (1997) Benham & Cooper (1998)	Blount (1993) Bloom & Munro (1995) Gronn & Ribbins (1996) Robinson (1996)
Leadership	None	Instructional Transformational	Micropolitics	Symbolic, Metaphorical Values-oriented Social Cognition	Moral-Educative (Social Responsibility)			Nontraditional Interim Informal
Method	Descriptive	Quantitative Modeling	Ethnography, Case Study, Historical		Critical Ethnography			Biography, Narrative

Source: R. Heck & P. Hallinger (1999). "Next generation methods for the study of leadership and school improvement," in *Handbook of research on educational administration* by J. Murphy and K. Seashore Louis, 1999, San Francisco: Jossey-Bass. Copyright © 1999 by Jossey-Bass. This material is used by permission of John Wiley & Sons, Inc.

Wayne Hoy (1994) describes the turmoil produced by the debate over the appropriate theories and methodologies for knowing about educational organization and administration as the "great paradigm wars." Logical empiricism, traditional science, behaviorism, critical theory, subjectivism, feminism, and postmodernism all provide alternative and often conflicting perspectives within administrative theory.

✱ **Why is there debate on what paradigm of administration is most appropriate?**

Paradigms and the Scientific-Rational Approach

Paradigms come from the traditional sciences; they are frameworks of thought that rest on a belief system and some scientific data and facts. Paradigms are the way we understand and explain our world. They are our way of perceiving, thinking, valuing, and achieving based on our particular explanations of complex behavior. Barker (1992) states, "A paradigm is a set of rules and regulations (written or unwritten) that does two things: (1) it establishes or defines boundaries; and (2) it tells you how to behave inside the boundaries in order to be successful" (p. 32). We see the world through our paradigms. "What may be perfectly visible, perfectly obvious to persons with one paradigm may be quite literally invisible to persons with a different paradigm" (p. 86).

In its simplest form, a paradigm is the set of rules by which something operates. When an organization's paradigm changes, the way it operates changes as well. This shift usually results in confusion, turbulence, and chaos as the changes dramatically upset the existing theoretical explanation and status quo. The changing of the rules, theory, or paradigms is the earliest sign of a significant change in our understanding of the world.

Scientists see unfounded explanations as ideologies. Under the influence of ideologies, decisions are based on personal interpretation and not on rational inquiry and analysis and scientific methods. Usually politics, not science, is used to mediate discordant ideologies, disparate value systems, and conflicting points of view. Scientists do not hold ideology in high regard because it is often based on speculation or a body of unproven doctrine. They often do not accept ideologies as truth because the concepts rest on "self-evident" or "unexamined" truths (English, 1993, p. 49). English suggests that paradigms in the social sciences are highly likely to emerge from ideologies rather than scientific theories because they cannot be tested against objective realities. Scientists suggest that paradigms based on ideology are much less challengeable and thus less provable than those that are based on theory (Barker, 1992). Basing decision on thought processes other than science can result in an organization's continual floundering, as it is buffeted by constantly shifting and unproved ideologies.

✱ **Which of the principal candidates seem to take the more scientific approaches? On what basis did you draw this conclusion?**

Political, Critical, and Constructivist Frames of Reference

Thomas Greenfield (1978, 1979, 1980, 1985, 1988) forcefully attacked many assumptions embedded in the scientific-rationality movement. He believed that ends cannot be separated from means, facts from underlying values, or rational thinking and action from preferences, passions, and ideologies. Each type of thinking and acting is subjective rationality—justifiable from the thinker's perspective. Greenfield recognized, as important, the truly irrational outbursts that influence our everyday lives and the course of history—that drive humans to do what they do. Inquiry must proceed from a variety of perspectives, and not solely the sciences. Greenfield suggested that educational administration can benefit from philosophy, history, law, political theory, sociology, and anthropology as well.

Investigation that adequately grasps administrational and organizational complexity must identify motives, emotions, attitudes, abilities, intentions, preferences, values, beliefs, relationships, and many other factors that complicate administrative practice. Understanding organizational structures, functions, and roles requires critical examination of ideology, power, force, authority, legitimization, and conflict.

William Greenfield (1995) suggested that the school is unlike other institutions because of its highly educated, autonomous, and practically permanent teacher workforce; the moral character of the school as an institution; and a milieu characterized by continuous and unpredictable threats to its stability. Schools are what Evers and Lakomski (1996) describe as a human invention or naturalistic system. Critical theorists believe that leadership should focus attention on collective intentions, the means of their achievement, and the conditions for individual empowerment. Forms of coercion are found on the disempowerment end of the continuum while methods of facilitation are on the empowerment end.

Administrators must have an awareness of competing value orientations if they hope to survive. Heslep (1997) suggests that

> being committed to the principles of moral value, moral rights, and moral duty as the fundamental standards for their judgments, those engaged in educational leadership must not approve ends and means that are inconsistent with these principles. . . . What they necessitate is that in forming judgments those engaged in educational leadership appreciate the knowledge, freedom, purposefulness, deliberativeness, and so on of all affected moral agents, respect the rights of such agents to these matters, and be cognizant of the duties of all concerned to foster freedom and knowledge in leadership of that kind. (pp. 77–78)

The net effect of these types of critiques was to call into question the legitimacy and appropriateness of a single knowledge base, based on the scientific-rationality approach and the professional status of such a knowledge base (Donmoyer, 1999a). Critical theorists challenge certain entrenched meanings, motives, or values. Such challenges open up possibilities for new types of responses and free us from the rigidity of science. The result can be an educative and transformational process in which organizational aspects such as vision, goals, practices, rewards, structures, policies, and controls might be altered. However, those in power often must be motivated to consent to such changes. This usually requires relinquishing traditional concepts and practices that are well established, defined, and defended (Robinson, 1994).

Because revolution is impractical and destructive, change will require the supportive involvement of those who control and benefit from the present conditions. Some critical theorists question whether a morality base can work for both the oppressed and the oppressor simultaneously. Certainly mutual acknowledgment of common interests can sustain a transformation, but what occurs when such acknowledgments do not exist? Participants either sacrifice debate and conflict in the interest of collaboration, or they exercise power in a way that jeopardizes collaboration (Bridges, 1986). Regardless of such power struggles over renewed and reformed practices, critical theorists argue that administrators are not neutral, rational, scientific bureaucrats. They operate from a value base that affects their views, decisions, and actions (Scribner, Aleman, & Maxcy, 2003).

Critical-Contextual, Gender, and Race

Feminist theorists begin with a desire to offer a reconceptualization of administration based strongly on the beliefs and values of women. The present administrative knowledge base developed under a white male perspective. This knowledge base is universal only to the extent that women and people of color respond like white males do. Carol Gilligan (1982) challenges the dominant ethic of justice and proposes an ethic of care and conceptualizes moral maturity as caring for and sensitivity to the needs of others. She writes:

> As we have listened for centuries to the voices of men and the theories of development that their experience informs, so we have come more recently to notice not only the silence of women but that the different voice of women lies in the truth of an ethic of care, the tie between relationship and responsibility, and the origins of aggression in the failure of connection. The failure to see the different reality of women's lives and to hear the differences in their voices stems in part from the assumption that there is a single mode of social experience and interpretation. . . .
>
> While an ethic of justice proceeds from the premise of equality—that everyone should be treated the same—an ethic of care rests on the premise of nonviolence—that no one should be hurt. (1993, pp. 173–174)

Feminist critique (Noddings, 1992) stresses the importance of all people and an ethics of relationship and care. The emphasis is "on living together, on creating, on maintaining, and enhancing positive relations" (p. 21). Feminist theories encourage administrators to challenge the conflicts between self-interest and the desire to "act on behalf of others." Noddings suggests that administrative decisions are related to how we are situated, who we are, and to whom we are related. Feminist critique stresses the importance of engaging in public, moral deliberation and making and revising decisions according to the results of such debate and not solely on technical, rational, scientific, and political expertise. The emphasis is on responsibility and relationships as much as on rights and rules.

Charol Shakeshaft (1995) focuses on differences in the way male and female administrators perceive situations. Her work is based on the belief that gender and race differences influence behavior and perspective. For example, male administrators are less likely to promote women into positions of close working proximity because they feel uncomfortable in a close working relationship and are concerned with image problems among colleagues, subordinates, and family members. Women seem to value community and relationship building more than men do. Men typically receive more feedback, and more types of feedback, than women do. Furthermore, women often receive positive feedback even when their performance is less than ideal, depriving them of an equal opportunity to improve their performance. Males fear the prospect of women's tears and often hold back negative comments. The work environment of women is also one that has elements of sexual fear and threats that can be perceived as unsafe. Shakeshaft concludes:

> The point of examining these differences is not to say one approach is right and one is wrong (the way theory and practice up to now have done), but rather to help us understand that males and females may be coming from very different places, and that unless we understand these differences, we aren't likely to work well together. . . .
>
> The traditional literature of educational administration not only leaves women without a clear understanding of issues important to them, but also deprives men of understanding how their cultural identity as males interacts with women's cultural identity as females and the effects this interaction has on organizational dynamics. (pp. 153–154)

Starratt (1991) suggests that educational administrators need to draw on both care (understanding, sensitivity, nurturing) and justice (rationality, rights, laws) to create ethical schools.

Recent concern has been expressed (Banks, 1995; 1993) that administrative epistemologies used in research and practice might be racially biased. Banks suggests that "all knowledge reflects the values and interests of its creators" (1993, p. 4). With our dominant frames of reference for educational administration, views from other races or cultures can be relegated to the margins in terms of legitimacy. Schewick and Young (1997) state:

> as we teach and promote epistemologies like positivism to post-modernism, we are at least implicitly teaching and promoting the social history of the dominant race at the exclusion of people of color, scholars of color and the possibility for research based on other race/culture epistemologies. We can, however, use our opposition to racism to consider the question of whether our dominant epistemologies are racially biased and, if they are, to begin to change the situation. (p. 11)

The bottom line is that a person's perception of truth and scientific inquiry can be blurred by his or her system of beliefs, assumptions, values, contexts, words, and, ultimately, decisions. These marginalized people become invisible because people in the dominant group refuse to see them.

Foster (1986) suggests that in the objective world of fact, conclusions are based on empirical evidence; in the moral world of rightness, they are based on sanctioned discourse and debates about values such as truth, justice, and equality. Foster approaches administration and leadership as praxis—a practical action aimed at clarifying and resolving social conditions:

> Praxis must be thought of as practical action, informed by theory, that attempts to change various conditions. In one respect, then, change involves a raising of consciousness about possibilities by penetrating the dominating ideas or total ideologies and analyzing the possible forms of life. This orientation, while political and cultural, is also critical, because it suggests that we attempt to cut through the "natural" taken-for-granted status quo to explore new arrangements. (p. 167)

For Foster, leadership requires critical reflection and analysis by all in a process of empowerment and transformation.

Administrators must reflect on and consider the moral consequences of their actions. Their decisions affect the interest and welfare of a large, diverse group of people. Administrative decisions must be grounded in deliberate reflection and consideration of moral issues and the consequences of actions based on those decisions and not solely on scientific inquiry. The well-being of the child serving as the fundamental value, "persons along the axis of oppression (whether teachers, administrators, students, or staff) must endure first-hand the discriminatory polices and practices engaged in by majority group members unaware of the influence of their actions on others" (W. D. Greenfield, 1993, p. 269).

Postmodernism, Poststructuralism

Postmodernists suggest that no foundations exist for knowledge and therefore no successful way to represent reality exists. "Postmodernists argue that all forms of knowing have equal legitimacy, all expressions are acceptable forms of voice, and there are no hierarchies of wisdom" (Glickman, 1998, p. 40). "Those who write from a postmodern perspective tend to question the value of rationality, to reject grand theory, to favor local knowledge over systemic understanding, to eschew large-scale studies, and to view the world as an indeterminate place beyond coherent description" (Constas, 1998, p. 27).

For the practitioner who confronts the day-to-day operation of the school, utility can be the only criterion under the pressure of today's environment. Cornel West (1992, p. 65) suggests, "new cultural politics of difference . . . align themselves with demoralized, demobilized, depoliticized, and disorganized people in order to empower and enable social action."

Postmodernism addresses the importance of creativity, imagination, and vision. In a rapidly changing environment, organizations must articulate realistic, credible, attractive futures. Progress is the "realization of a vision" that is used to guide successful improvement. It begins as a statement of dreams that develop from inspiration and creative insights. Such thinking is more imagery than words, more perception than conception. It is the presentation of scenarios and visions that express dreams and are tempered with an understanding of what is possible—a belief in what should and can be. In discussing these frames of references, Evers and Lakomski (1996, p. 140) state:

> Really massive gains over experience come from manipulating theory formulations so that they apply to matters beyond experience, enabling us to think hypothetically and act accordingly. The imagination so augmented can explore policy and decision option spaces that have not been lived through, perhaps not with precision, owing

to the friability of current administrative theory and its context dependence, but with a modest prospect of beating chance. (p. 140)

Bolman and Deal (1995) suggest that leaders have lost touch with some of these precious gifts, with what gives our lives passion and purpose. As they suggest it is "about the search for something bigger. . . . Seek new sources of vigor, meaning, and hope to enrich your life and leave a better legacy for those who come after you" (pp. 11–12). These sources animate, inspire, and transform as they operate on the emotional and spiritual resources and on its values, commitment, and aspirations. They provide a deep, noble sense of purpose and inspiration.

Other recent lines of inquiry focus on studying the culture of organizations and the leader's role in developing and modifying that culture. Most argue that the cultural focus is closely akin to the subjectivist and critical theory view in its underlying assumptions regarding the importance of the shared values, beliefs, and ideology.

A minority express concern that such cultural approaches are simply an expansion of the behaviorist and structuralist control models espoused by the scientific, rationalist community. They attempt to influence thought as well as action, to make a shift toward ideological control. Foster (1986) worries that it is the leader's conception of organizational culture that is promoted. The existing culture, however, might protect the status quo and thus need to be changed to stimulate the imaginative process.

Even the critics of postmodernism recognize that it too has something to offer to our understanding of epistemology and knowledge development. Constas (1998) states:

> we are meant to believe that postmodernism can rescue us from the dominant and oppressive conditions created by modernist/scientific discourse. There is, however, reason to believe that postmodernism (deconstruct, interrogate, genderize) itself contains a measure of veiled censorship that regulates the discourse of educational inquiry. . . . We need to consider the idea that the postmodern version of educational inquiry is just another variety of discourse in education and should not be granted special privileges . . . because I believe that an overreliance on any one disciplinary perspective is necessarily confining, it is worth exploring the way educational research may be situated, explained and enlivened. (pp. 30–31)

The debate continues between subjectivity and objectivity, values and facts, and empiricism and philosophy. The most reasoned position seems to suggest that all these perspectives offer the possibility for improved understanding of educational administration. As growth in all forms of knowledge occurs, it supports an improvement in our reasoning and decision making, and ultimately in our administrative ability. A balanced perspective (Willower, 1996) suggests that science, ethics, and practice should not be sharply separated but should be allowed to inform each other. We should not cut ourselves off from any of the knowledge sources that can inform wise choices. Science, ethics, philosophy, and creativity should not be sharply separated and placed in mutually exclusive warring camps.

Paradigms need not be mutually exclusive; considered in concert, they all contribute to theory development and practice. Prestine (1995) states:

These and other issues caution us that in the debate over the establishment of a knowledge base, it would seem to be wise to err on the side of inclusion rather than exclusion, divergence rather than convergence. If educational administration is to remain a vibrant and dynamic field, one that pushes on the edge of the envelope, as it were, we must not be confined by rigid prespecification of boundaries or meticulous categorization of knowledge. (pp. 281–282)

According to Marshall and Anderson (1995), theories, when used heuristically, are lenses or windows that provide a particular view of social phenomena, opening up vistas not to be seen from other windows/theories. In this way, new theoretical perspectives can make visible those aspects of traditional educational phenomena made invisible by previous theoretical frames. New theories can also illuminate previously ignored phenomena, opening up new areas for critical examination (p. 169).

Not all are equally useful in all situations, but each may have something to offer in different facets of educational administration. Informed administrators can value multiple ways of viewing situations from differing epistemologies and take actions beyond those offered by any single perspective (Capper, 1991). Bjork, Lindle, and Van Meter (1999) expand on this theme, stressing the importance of administrators not only acquiring knowledge but also being able to apply it to improve schooling. They suggest that knowledge, in the field of educational administration, demands relevance and usefulness.

There is now widespread recognition of the need to blend approaches, such as description-evaluation, fact-value, quantitative-qualitative, in enquiries as to the nature of educational administration, each being influenced by the context in which it will be applied. Chapman, Sackney, and Aspin (1999), in characterizing the present state of the revolution in the field, suggest that:

> Until the late 1960s, structural-functionalism and statistical paradigms shaped the research agenda. The shift from quantitative to qualitative approaches in the study of educational administration represents a change in basic philosophy. In part, the shift from structural functionalism and statistical inferences to interpretive paradigms (such as phenomenology, culturalism, social interactionism) has resulted in the popularity of qualitative methods. The result has been the usage of various labels: ethnography, participant observation, fieldwork, qualitative methods, case studies, and naturalistic inquiry; these approaches are all attempts to understand educational processes *in situ*.
>
> Intersections of gender, race, and class now serve as important analytical categories in fields of study. These intersections, made viable through the interdisciplinary fields such as women's studies, embody strong political and social concerns, moving theory and research away from previous and now discredited intellectualist conceptions of an "ivory-tower" separation between theory and practice, directly into the world of practice. (p. 93)

Understanding and expanding the knowledge base carries with it the expectation that the knowledge base will be applied to administration in such a way that it improves practice.

✳ **Characterize each of the following individuals' approaches or paradigms, and comment on their strengths and weaknesses: (a) Mr. Wayne, (b) Ms. Taylor, (c) Mr. Newton, (d) Ms. Maynard, (e) Mr. Browne, (f) Ms. Gilligan, (g) Mr. Wheatley.**

Grounding Moral Educational Leadership in the Intrinsically Moral Enterprise of Learning

ROBERT J. STARRATT • *Boston College*

The moral demands of educational leadership go well beyond considerations of specific acts of moral choice (when to tell or withhold the truth about what one knows about a student; whether to compromise with pressure groups who want to impose a point of view in certain areas of the curriculum or lose one's job over the issue; whether to retain a mediocre teacher with political connections, and so on). The much more essential work of moral educational leadership is to create a schoolwide learning environment that promotes the moral integrity of learning as the pursuit of the truth about oneself and one's world, however complex and difficult that task may be.

Schooling implicates learners in the enterprise of appropriating the way by which their society interprets and understands itself and the world. These knowledges help or hinder learners to identify who they are (as citizens, as workers, as gendered and racial beings, or simply as human beings), what they are worth, what they are responsible for, how they exist in nature and society, and how they might conduct themselves in their personal and public lives. Since these knowledges are received or presented as heuristic as well as an expressive cultural production of that society (McCarthy, 1997), schools ought to assist the learner in exploring how these knowledges were generated and on what assumptions that generation rests.

Learning involves an encounter with an aspect of reality, albeit an interpreted and culturally grounded reality. The learner cannot intentionally deny its existence or arbitrarily make it into its opposite without disfiguring the integrity of that reality and violating the intrinsic moral obligation to acknowledge on its own terms the reality one encounters. Learning requires a coming to terms with what a person is learning, whether it is a scientific fact such as "ice floats on water," a historical assertion that "Lincoln freed the slaves," or a depiction of a moneylender like Shylock in *The Merchant of Venice.* That learning conveys a multitude of meanings, some of which should be honored (slavery is immoral), some of which should be questioned (since most of the mass of an iceberg is below water, how can it be said to float on water? Where does money come from and how is it accumulated?), and some of which should be repudiated or denounced (Hitler's assertion of the superiority of the Aryan race).

The obligation to come to terms with what one knows, to explore its use and its misuse, to avoid its distortion or manipulation is both a moral and an intellectual obligation (if for scholars, why not for younger learners as well?). Learning is a moral search as well as an intellectual search for truth—truth about ourselves, about our community, about our history, about our cultural and physical world. The truth, of course, will never be final or complete; rather, it will be tentative, incomplete, fallible, partial, and generative. But the truth will ultimately involve human beings with choices about themselves and about the kinds of communities they want to create.

This is what schools are supposed to be about. Hence, those who would lead schools toward this approach to teaching and learning are inescapably involved in a moral enterprise. This understanding of moral educational leadership implies a different conversation between educational leaders and other teachers and parents about curriculum, about assessment of student performances, and about teacher assessment. It also implies a different kind of academic preparation of administrators, one in which the moral dimensions of their own learning are continuously explored and the ongoing creation and reconstruction of their own self-identity is pursued.

Ethical Models

Figure 1.1 depicts Starratt's model (1994) of the three ethics: caring, justice, and critique. Each of these overlapping ethics raises different questions that school leaders need to consider.

The Ethic of Caring

The notion of an ethic of caring has been promoted by Carol Gilligan (1982) and Nel Noddings. According to Noddings (1992), "Caring is a way of being in relation, not a set of specific behaviors" (p. 17). Caring includes modeling, dialogue, practice, and confirmation. Modeling for educators means demonstrating to students that we care, rather than simply saying it. Dialogue must be in the sense that Paolo Freire (1973) espouses, open-ended and sincere. This dialogue allows teachers to show they care by listening to their students fully. Noddings's fourth component of caring—confirmation—involves affirming and encouraging the best in others. Noddings believes that "when we confirm someone, we spot a better self and encourage its development" (p. 25).

The Ethic of Justice

Justice involves equity and fairness in relation to individual and community choice. How a school is governed is a crucial part of the ethic of justice. The ethic of justice demands that administrators serve as advocates for students, including

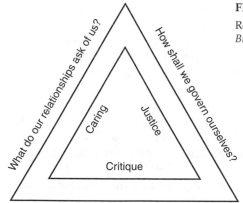

FIGURE 1.1   *The Multidimensional Ethic*

Reprinted with permission from Falmer Press from *Building an Ethical School* by R. J. Starratt.

advocating for optimal learning conditions. Justice addresses issues of educational equity, opportunity of resources, emotional and physical security, and health and social environment.

Justice involves individuals acting impartially and a community that governs its actions fairly. As Starratt maintains, "To promote a just social order in the school, the school community must carry out an ongoing critique of those structural features of the school that work against human beings" (p. 194). One habit of the heart that schools must embrace is the habit of questioning and self-criticism. If the questions raised come from the ethics of caring and justice, they are closely related to the ethic of critique.

The Ethic of Critique

The ethic of critique is based on critical theory. According to Foster (1986), critical theory "questions the framework of the way we organize our lives or the way our lives are organized for us" (p. 72). Foster argues that the school administrator must be a critical theoretician. Through dialogue, she or he must ask and help others to ask questions that challenge the status quo. The ethic of critique promotes questions such as: Who benefits from this? Who holds power? Whose voice has not been heard? Who is privileged?

The ethic of critique facilitates conversation and dialogue between people in organizations. It is crucial to the ethic of critique that conflict be addressed with civility.

✳   **How might the values and beliefs of the administrators you selected influence their decision making and conflict resolution?**

Foundations of Ethical Behavior: Standards for Good Practice

Greenfield (1990), Noddings (1992), Starratt (1996), Beck (1994), and others writing on the topic of ethics have identified standards of good practice that can serve school administrators as a foundation for ethical behavior. Standards of good practice include being conscious (aware and informed), encouraging dialogue, modeling, and being reflective.

In recent years researchers have described various approaches educational administrators can use to help develop skills to function as ethical school leaders (Craig, 1999; Duke & Grogan, 1997; Mertz, 1997; Shapiro & Stefkovich, 1997). These skills and approaches include:

- Examining situations from a variety of perspectives, including feminism, postmodernism, liberation theology, and critical theory
- Writing personal essays, or educational platforms, describing ethical principles or values that students subscribe to
- Examining dilemmas from consequentialist and nonconsequentialist points of view

- Utilizing data from values instruments such as the Personal Values Inventory and the Hall-Tonna Inventory that supply information on several areas of human growth
- Comparing and contrasting ethical codes of conduct from a variety of organizations
- Learning and using group dynamics training
- Reading ethical dilemmas rooted in particular contextual variables since "leadership does not exist apart from context" (Duke & Grogan, 1997, p. 145)

Craig (1994) believes that "virtue can be developed through arduous practice" and that "treating others justly and respectfully over a long period of time may result in a virtuous person" (p. 134).

Codes of Ethics

According to Shapiro and Stefkovich (1997), a legal perspective focuses on the interpretation of state and federal codes of ethics. These codes are rule bound. Box 1.2 on page 22 depicts the Statement of Ethics of the National Association of Secondary School Principals (NASSP). Similar standards exist for many professional associations.

These ten standards can be viewed as a beginning step for a school administrator when developing a personal educational platform that includes the principles he or she advocates. As Covey notes (1989), "Principles are not practices. A practice is a specific activity or action. A practice that works in one circumstance will not necessarily work in another. . . . Principles are guidelines of human conduct that are proven to have enduring permanent value" (p. 35). This NASSP code of ethics contains some principles that educational administrators might want to include when developing a personal platform.

Administrative Platforms

The earlier sections describe the many frames of reference, conceptual understandings, ways of knowing, and ethical beliefs relevant to the enormously complex job of administering an organization. They include a set of contrasting beliefs, opinions, values, and attitudes that can provide a foundation for practice. Senge and colleagues (2000) state: "Reflection and inquiry are not practiced much: People everywhere are impeded from working together effectively by the conflicting views of the world. But the discovery of oneself, the ability to see something in your own behavior that was invisible to you before, and appreciation of what's productive and what's painful in your attitudes—awareness of these capabilities seems pretty intrinsic to the human condition. . . . There is something integral in the core idea that manifests at all different levels and can be seen from all different angles" (pp. 560–561). It is thus important that administrators and those whom they influence have a clear understanding of the foundational principles, conceptualizations, philosophy, and narratives on which they base their judgments.

BOX 1.2 • *Statement of Ethics for School Administrators*

Issue

An educational administrator's professional behavior must conform to an ethical code. The code must be idealistic and at the same time practical so that it can apply reasonably to all educational administrators. The administrator acknowledges that the schools belong to the public they serve for the purpose of providing educational opportunities to all. However, the administrator assumes responsibility for providing professional leadership in the school and community. This responsibility requires the administrator to maintain standards of exemplary professional conduct. It must be recognized that the administrator's actions will be viewed and appraised by the community, professional associates, and students. To these ends, the administrator subscribes to the following statement of standards.

The educational administrator

1. Makes the well-being of students the fundamental value of all decision making and actions.
2. Fulfills professional responsibilities with honesty and integrity.

3. Supports the principle of due process and protects the civil and human rights of all individuals.
4. Obeys local, state, and national laws.
5. Implements the governing board of education's policies and administrative rules and regulations.
6. Pursues appropriate measures to correct those laws, policies, and regulations that are not consistent with sound educational goals.
7. Avoids using positions for personal gain through political, social, religious, economic, or other influences.
8. Accepts academic degrees or professional certification only from duly accredited institutions.
9. Maintains the standards and seeks to improve the effectiveness of the profession through research and continuing professional development.
10. Honors all contracts until fulfillment, release, or dissolution mutually agreed upon by all parties.

Approved by the NASSP Board of Directors; November 1973; Revised July 2001.

This statement was originally developed by a task force representing the National Association of Secondary School Principals, National Association of Elementary School Principals, American Association of School Administrators, Association of School Business Officials, American Association of School Personnel Administrators, and the National Council of Administrative Women in Education.

Empathy, intuition, honesty, optimism, self-esteem, self-confidence, determination, and self-awareness are essential to good leadership. In addition to administrative knowledge and skills, beliefs, opinions, values, and attitudes provide the foundation for the actions of leaders. They are seen by the school community as the educational values and beliefs of the leader and often become the mood of the school. These relatively intangible qualities of the principalship spur leaders, their staff, and the entire school to superior performance. Leadership often requires making strong and positive personal connections with a number of people in which you come in contact.

Leaders will need to build up the necessary human capital to get the most out of their people. People need to connect emotionally as well as intellectually in order to succeed. Good leaders do not communicate with people because they need something, but to enjoy the shared experience of working toward exciting outcomes. They have a genuine interest in the staff and their optimal performance. Leaders provide the support and encouragement often needed for individual outstanding performance but also as part of a larger organizational purpose.

There is some wisdom in establishing the right level of passion and emotion when communicating with others. Too much or too little can easily turn others off to what you are saying. Simple things like eye contact can be very important as well as effective listening and oral communication skills. Sensing where to focus attention is certainly another one of those intangible hard-to-describe skills. These are all embodied in the platform upon which one stands.

Everyone harbors some biases and faults that can skew their thinking and decision making. Certainly it is important to be aware of biases and bad traits so that they can be monitored and their impact controlled. Most of us have some small cracks in our character that have the ability to greatly damage what otherwise might have been a great success. There have been very high-profile examples in government, business, investing, athletics, but administrators in all professions have these needs to control some of their passions.

This is a very delicate line to walk, however, because one who never lets his or her guard down or opens up to others and is very controlled tends to turn off others, as well as organizational creativity, and causes the breakdown of trust. This trait can create a work culture that lacks honesty because the tough and challenging questions never get asked. The risk of losing goodwill dominates all that is done. This closed culture never gets beneath the surface of tough realities and the heart to take heat and grief. Sergiovanni and Starratt (2001) refer to this personal philosophy as a *platform*. An individual's platform "is made up of those basic assumptions, beliefs, attitudes and values that are underpinnings of an educator's behavior" (2001, p. 84).

An educational leadership platform is a document that provides a description of one's values, beliefs, and philosophies about educational leadership. It is a self-reflective document providing a framework for administrative action. It helps administrators determine if their actions are aligned with their espoused beliefs. Barnett (1991) stresses the importance of platform development in helping administrators "to identify the moral dilemmas they will face as administrators and to articulate the standards of practice they will use in judging situations" (p. 135). The platform is a statement that systematically and accurately states the principles, ethics, and values that underlie a person's actions. It is crucial that administrators reflect on the basis of the choices they will ultimately make. Next come their ideas of how supervision and administration are related to these beliefs (Kottkamp, 1982).

Educators carry on their work, make decisions, and plan instruction on the basis of their platforms; thus, these platforms should be clearly articulated and espoused. This concept is based on the political model in which parties are expected to develop platforms to aid supporters and voters to make the clearest, best, most informed choices for themselves. Knowing the platform and being aware of any inconsistencies with practice or other platforms is immensely helpful. Argyris and Schön (1978) refer to these inconsistencies as differences between espoused theory and theory-in-use. Espoused theories detail philosophies, beliefs, values, assumptions, theories, and paradigms underlying behavior; theory-in-use represents the way people actually implement them. Argyris and Schön state:

> When someone is asked how he would behave under certain circumstances, the answer he usually gives is his espoused theory of action for the situation. This is the theory of action to which he gives allegiance and which, upon request, he communicates to others. However, the theory that actually governs his actions is his theory-in-use, which may or may not be compatible with his espoused theory; furthermore, the individual may or may not be aware of the incompatibility of the two theories. (p. 11)

Argyris and Schön (1978), Cunningham (1982), and Blake and McCanse (1991) suggest that the best first step in improving organizational functioning is for practitioners to discover and make explicit any differences between espoused theory and theory-in-use. An administrator needs to clearly state her or his espoused theory, that is, her or his administrative platform. The administrator then compares this platform to her or his behavior within the organization. When platform and behavior are incompatible, the administrator decides which to alter. It is best for all concerned when actual behavior is compatible with espoused values and theories. When it is not, trust breaks down and the organization becomes ineffective. Thus, the development of an educational and administrative platform is essential for all administrative action.

Individual platforms should be in general agreement with the philosophy, mission, goals, and direction of the school system. When they are not, administrators should endeavor to explain why such differences exist.

Platforms often include a statement of the person's philosophy of leadership, preferred leadership style, and the process by which he or she works with teachers, other school community members, and other foundational areas related to leadership practices. Ovando (2004) found platform development to be a powerful learning experience—self-awareness and value clarification. Platforms provided an opportunity for reflection while they serve "as a foundation for school leadership practice" (p. 37). The platform serves as a guide for school leadership performance as it is consulted as a point of reference. Sharing one's platform with peers is enlightening, enhances understanding, and is useful in bringing out areas of agreement and disagreement.

Sergiovanni and Starratt (1998) describe how to get started:

> Once we have written down the elements of our platform, we can with further reflection begin to group them in clusters and place them in some order of importance . . .
> [Some] will find the writing exercise too tedious and will seek out a colleague to discuss this whole question. The free flow of shared ideas frequently stimulates the process of clarification . . . Still others may go to a formal statement of goals that the school or system has in print to begin the process. (p. 244)

Sergiovanni and Starratt (1998) refer to this as a work in progress that should be periodically revisited and updated. Colleagues, students, and professors should challenge the leader to prove that his or her platform is more than espoused theory. The leader's theory in use must be observable in his or her actions.

They go on to suggest that regardless of how individual platforms are developed, administrators should compare them with those of other colleagues to provide themselves an opportunity to reflect on "areas of agreement or disagreement." Sometimes this comparison leads to modification and sometimes to acceptance of greater diversity in perspectives. It usually helps to build collegiality, understanding, alignment, and, when the platform is compatible with behavior, trust, integrity, cooperation, and continuous improvement, which creates organization effectiveness (Cunningham & Gresso, 1993). Chapter 6 provides a number of instruments that can be used for "guided reflection" related to values, beliefs, experiences, and, ultimately, practices.

✳ **Select one of the candidates from the vignette whose views are closest to your own and develop his or her administrative platform, paying particular attention to the value system it is based upon.**

The Knowledge Base in Educational Administration

There is considerable debate and little agreement regarding a specific knowledge base for educational administration (Hoy, 1994). Obviously, no "cookbook" tells practitioners what paradigms, values, methods, or models to use; what issues and operational areas to address; or how to apply specific skills in various different contexts. Administrative knowledge is a complex array of theories, ideologies, skills, ethical principles, paradigms, and practices that are applied to a diverse set of issues.

The synthesis of knowledge in educational administration can be conceptualized as comprising seven factors: functions, skills, ethics, structure, operational areas, context, and issues. Table 1.2 on page 26 presents a comprehensive model of the complexity of educational administration. Even though in practice factors cannot be separated, it is probably best to focus on and integrate one factor at a time. Each leads to some truth, but none by itself affords an adequate understanding. Together they provide a more complete understanding of educational administration.

Effective leaders understand all elements of educational administration and create a shared vision of school excellence that is translated into classroom practice. They raise teacher expectations for students, they support continued curricular and instructional improvement, and they reward and recognize all forms of excellence. Sergiovanni (2001) concludes:

> Schools must be run effectively and efficiently if they are to survive. Policies must be in place. Budgets must be set. Teachers must be assigned. Classes must be scheduled. Reports must be completed. Standardized tests must be given. Supplies must be purchased. The school must be kept clean. Students must be protected from violence. Classrooms must be orderly. These are essential tasks that guarantee the survival of the school as an organization. Yet, for the school to transform itself into an institution, a learning community must emerge. Institutionalization is the moral imperative. (p. 351)

✳ **What will be the principals' general responsibility in the Flem Snopes school renewal effort? What impact will the principal's philosophy, values, and platform have on the school?**

TABLE 1.2 *Key Factors in Effective Administration*

Administrative Functions*	Skills	Ethical Standards	Structure and Organization	Operational Areas	Context	Issues
• Plan	• Leadership	• Honesty	• President	• Finance	• Community	• Safe schools
• Organize	• Problem analysis	• Integrity	• U.S. Department of Education	• Curriculum and instruction	• Taxpayers	• Multiculturalism
• Actuate/direct	• Decision making	• Promise keeping	• Secretary of Education	• Human resource development	• Special-interest groups	• Inclusion
• Coordinate	• Implementing	• Loyalty/fidelity	• Governors	• Research and development	• Teachers/parents/kids	• Technology
• Control/evaluate	• Delegation	• Fairness	• State school boards	• Business and logistics	• Chamber of commerce	• Synchronous and asynchronous learning
	• Supervising and motivating	• Concern for others	• State superintendents	• Physical plant	• College professors/researchers	• Standardized testing (high-stakes testing)
	• Interpersonal sensitivity	• Respect for others	• State departments of education	• Pupil personnel	• Media/TV	• Assessment
	• Oral communication	• Law-abiding/civic duty	• Local school boards		• City council	• Vouchers
	• Written communication	• Pursuit of excellence	• Superintendents		• Religious organizations	• Charter schools
	• Research measurement evaluation	• Personal accountability	• Central Administrators		• Private business	• School choice
	• Legal, policy, and political applications		• Principals		• Professional associations	• Constructivist curriculum
	• Public relations		• Teachers		• Textbook manufacturers	• Global education
	• Technology		• PTA		• Industry	• Environmentalism
	• Social				• Government	• Alternative certification
					• International groups	• Best practices
					• Technologists	• Comprehensive school reform
						• Preschool education
						• Childhood obesity
						• Differentiated instruction

*Henri Fayole (1949).

The Knowledge Base in Educational Administration:
A Postmodernist Perspective

ROBERT DONMOYER • *The University of San Diego*

The search for a scientific knowledge base for the educational administration field has taken various forms during the past 100 years. Initially, scholars in the emerging field took their cue from efficiency experts in business. For instance, Elwood P. Cubberly, who often has been called the father of the educational administration field, wrote in 1909: "Our schools are, in a sense, factories in which the raw products (children) are to be shaped and fashioned into the products to meet the various demands of life" (p. 383). Cubberly, like many other twentieth-century scholars (e.g., Thorndike, 1910; Good, Biddle, and Brophy, 1975), assumed that educational researchers could, through experimentation, create a knowledge base that would lead to standardizing the teaching and learning process. This belief turned out to be wrong.

Later, educational administration scholars, motivated at least in part by the failure of Cubberly and his contemporaries to produce a definitive knowledge base that could be used to "choreograph" educational practice, focused their work on creating social science theory. They assumed that the theories scholars generated (not the findings of particular studies, per se) could direct educational practice. The lack of success of this so-called theory movement can be seen in PRIMIS, a computerized set of documents developed by the University Council of Educational Administration (Hoy, 1994) that ostensibly organizes the knowledge base for the field. Rather than providing a coherent and relatively consistent vision of educational administration practice, the document base presents a plethora of different—and at times conflicting—theoretical perspectives. These perspectives can be useful to school administrators as they think about what actions to take and which policies to implement; a theoretical knowledge base containing many different, often conflicting theories, however, does not provide the sort of direction to administrators and policymakers that theory movement advocates envisioned. (For a more detailed discussion of the issue, see Donmoyer, 1999a.)

As is often the case, there are echoes of the past in the present. It is a virtual certainty that current efforts to develop a definitive knowledge base for the field will be no more successful than efforts in the past have been because of two problems that have not—and will not—go away.

One of these is the idiosyncrasy problem. Anthropologists allude to this problem when they note that normally there is as much variation within a culture or group as there is between cultures and groups. Observant teachers certainly understand what anthropologists are talking about. They know (either from experience or from reading research), for example, that fourth-grade African American males tend to respond positively to certain strategies and negatively to others; however, they also know that not all African American fourth graders fit the general pattern. Skilled teachers understand that they must always see children as unique individuals rather than merely as types; by contrast, researchers intent on producing a general knowledge base for the field can only speak in terms of general categories. Consequently, the knowledge researchers produce, though not useless, cannot be translated into formulas or recipes that policymakers and administrators can mandate for schools and classrooms with certainty about the results. Indeed, the problem of idiosyncrasy suggests that deviation from a "scientifically validated" standardized program will be required for certain students to succeed.

The second problem, which can be labeled *the problem of values*, can best be explained by using an example: Assume that a team of researchers has been hired to determine whether a kindergarten program created from the developmental theories of Piaget produces more learning than a kindergarten program that is rooted in Skinnerian behaviorism. Before the team can begin to study the programs and their effects, the team must answer a question that, ultimately, is a value question: How should learning be defined in the study? If the researcher values the way Piaget conceptualizes learning, he or she almost certainly will select a definition—and outcome measures consistent with the definition—that reflects Piaget's view of learning. The same can be said of a researcher who prefers Skinner's way of thinking. Whatever definition is selected will have a significant impact on which program is judged more successful; the definition—and the values implicit in it—will determine what data count and, in fact, what data get counted. That is why educational research in the past—and any educational research that will be done in the future—will suggest differing, and possibly even contradictory, courses of action.

So, do the two problems discussed above mean that educational administration cannot develop a knowledge base? And, since a knowledge base is generally thought to be a prerequisite for classifying a field as a profession, does that mean that educational administrators cannot be considered professionals? Not necessarily.

There is at least one very prestigious profession, the profession of law, in which what counts most is not a knowledge of facts and theories but, rather, a knowledge of how to think and reason. To be sure, lawyers do understand legal principles and know about particular legal cases. This knowledge is secondary, however, to knowledge about how to employ legal principles and case knowledge in the process of legal reasoning about a particular case. It would seem that reasoning that applies general principles to particular contexts (and also enriches the general principles with each application to a particular case) may be as important in the educational administration field as it is in the field of law. Consequently, although the knowledge base question in educational administration has not generally been conceptualized in this way in the past, the legal reasoning analogy appears to be fertile territory to explore in future efforts to legitimate educational administration as a profession.

Conclusion

Our frames of reference, our paradigms, and our mental models are invisible elements that influence the way we think and our ability to envision the future. We can operate "without thinking" if we never reflect upon frames of reference or develop platforms which make our belief systems explicit. New frames can accentuate previously unnoticed possibilities; new relationships, previously unseen, can become viable. For these reasons administrators should continually revisit and reflect on their platforms.

Significant improvements can start with the system that is already in place, but it always can be radically improved (Rhodes, 1997). Our practice is held captive by our theory, our knowledge base, and our experiences. We must ensure that the ideas, positions, and theories that enjoy privileged positions of unquestioned supremacy and thus are viewed as the "truth" are themselves questioned when new ways of seeing things evolve. The challenge is in how we pursue knowledge and how knowledge is expanded.

Knowledge grows within those who discipline themselves to think about what is known and still needs to be known. In this way, we learn from one another and we develop new insights. We are called to learn from those who have come before us and from our contemporaries so that we can be prepared to leave our imprints on our organizations and professions. This is the real stuff of leadership. A cross-fertilization of ideas occurs and new research, knowledge, values, and best practices can be synthesized into a schoolwide plan. The ultimate assessment of all educational leaders remains whether they "promote the success of all students." That is the lasting core value that guides administrative and organizational action.

✳ **Which candidates did you select for the principal and two assistant principals of Flem Snopes High School, and what was your rationale for selecting these candidates?**

Portfolio Artifacts

- Write a one-page statement of your philosophy of education.
- Write a one-page statement of your philosophy of leadership.
- Define the values or ethics that guide your behavior as an educational leader.
- Develop a comprehensive administrative platform.
- Analyze the values and philosophical frame of reference existing at a school and relate it to teacher morale and/or student performance.
- Examine past agendas of school board meetings or attend a school board meeting and relate the work of the school board to your philosophy and values.

- Describe how your leadership behavior models personal and professional ethics, integrity, justice, and fairness.
- Reflect upon your philosophy, ethics, and administrative platform, recognizing their impact and influence on the performance of others.
- Engage in professional and personal development.
- Attend a conference or a superintendent's administrative meeting and report back on the content and what you learned.
- Read an administrative job description and relate it to an administrative frame of reference.
- Examine an administrative evaluation system and relate it to your administrative platform.

Terms

Administrative platforms	Frames of reference	Management
Epistemology	Human capital	Paradigms
Ethics	ISLLC Standards	Postmodernism
ETS SLLA	Knowledge base	Qualitative research
Feminist critique	Leadership	School renewal

Suggested Readings

Beckner, W. (2004). *Ethics of educational leaders.* Boston: Allyn and Bacon.

Begley, P. (Ed.). (1999). *Values and educational leadership.* Albany: State University of New York Press.

Bell, D. (2002). *Ethical ambition.* New York: Bloomsbury.

Donmoyer, R., Scheurich, J., & Imber, M. (1995). *The knowledge base in education administration.* Albany: State University of New York Press.

Fullan, M. (2003). *The moral imperative of school leadership.* Thousand Oaks, CA: Corwin.

Gardiner, M., Enomoto, E., & Grogan, M. (2000). *Coloring outside the lines.* Albany: State University of New York Press.

Glickman, C. (2003). *Holding sacred ground: Essays on leadership, courage, and endurance in our schools.* San Francisco, CA: Jossey-Bass.

Murphy, J., & Louis, K. (1999). *Handbook of research in educational administration.* San Francisco: Jossey-Bass.

Shapiro, J., & Stefkovich, J. (2001). *Ethical leadership and decision making in education.* Mahwah, NJ: Lawrence Erlbaum Associates.

Starratt, R. (2004). *Ethical leadership.* San Francisco, CA: Jossey-Bass.

Tschanneh-Moran, M. (2004). *Trust matters: Leadership for successful schools.* San Francisco, CA: Jossey-Bass.

Context and Perspective for Educational Leaders

NANUCK MIDDLE SCHOOL
Understanding the Context

You are the new principal of Nanuck Middle School. The principal whom you replaced is quite bitter in the fact that he was not appreciated for maintaining a fine school while confusion, conflict, and criticism, abounded. He stated, "They did not understand the many problems I faced from hiring teachers to maintaining accountability." The teachers seem to be fed up with the lack of respect they receive and concerned about the inability to envision the kind of school the community and state were demanding. Since the salaries of members of the community had significantly outpaced those of educators, in a professional association survey they ranked "salary" as their number one concern. Safety and discipline were also high on their list. Family life within the community had deteriorated and tension within the school was on the increase.

In discussing the principal position with you, Superintendent Melville said, "The previous principal was unable to read the federal, state, and local demands and school board and district expectations for the school and thus generated resistance, divisiveness, and mistrust, which ultimately ended in ideological battlegrounds and no school improvement." You are concerned that the curriculum, instruction, and support services have not stayed up with current demands.

The federal government is placing a strong emphasis on an education preparing students to be successful in most sectors of the U.S. economy. The theme of this movement is creating a high school diploma that counts. The proposal now being debated within the state is the creation of Opportunity Grants (vouchers) for students to allow them to select the school they want to attend if the school they are attending receives low marks. They are encouraged to attend schools that will enhance their skills in the workforce and prepare them for success in college or in the workplace.

If a school does not meet high academic standards regarding the "must have" competencies, the students are encouraged to use their Opportunity Grants to go to better schools. The creation of this competition in public education is believed, by policymakers, to improve public education.

Another major theme for school reform that is gaining support and enthusiasm is small schools with less bureaucracy and more personal environments. A number of schools in your district have applied for and received grants from foundations over the past few years to develop these small, personalized charter schools that use best practices. In addition, there are also a number of excellent small private schools within the district. Both small charter and private schools have achieved success on the state standardized tests and are fully accredited. Other schools within the district have not been doing as well and a number of schools have performance levels that are not considered acceptable. Nanuck Middle School is considered a low performing school.

There is much controversy regarding these new initiatives. A number of parents within your school attendance zone see the recent focus on standards and tests as creating a factory approach to education. There is also a strong movement within the state to suggest that much of this reform is to discredit public schools and provide a new emphasis for privatization. They use the concept of school choice and the creation of Opportunity Grants as examples of how this transition might take place. You have been drawn into the middle of this debate in that your district has a grant from the state to test the concept of Opportunity Grants. The 2004–2006 Washington, DC, plan was considered a model program for implementing this grant. The theme is that we can no longer "keep children in schools in need of improvement."

Nanuck Middle School has received accreditation but needs improvement. You are considered a "challenged school" that is not meeting its challenges. You have the highest number of students eligible for free/reduced price lunches in the district. Your school is not meeting full accreditation, the staff has been somewhat humiliated, and morale is very low. Parents have now been granted a green light to abandon Nanuck Middle School and 160 (approximately 13 percent) students have opted to use their Opportunity Grants to transfer to other public and private schools next year. The parents of those leaving sometimes mention their concern about public school ideology and finding schools that are more relevant to their belief systems. With drops in enrollment at Nanuck and a few other schools, the loss of students within the public schools, the overcrowding of students in high-performing and charter schools, and everyone involved feeling great pressure and tension, the superintendent and board have become very concerned.

You have been instructed to reflect upon the new experimental Opportunity Grant program and to make suggestions on what should be done next. You are to focus on potential allies to make the public schools better able to serve all children, to work on any campaign needed to improve the present situation, to shift resources, and to take the best next steps for the school and district given its present context.

✱   **How will you begin to gain control of Nanuck Middle School given the present context?**

Contextual Knowledge

Most experts today recognize and accept the importance of context to the practice of educational administration. They might not agree on how best to characterize context, but few question its importance. Duke (1998) states: "As people interact, they are guided by their perception of context. These perceptions, by shaping speech and action, help to generate context, even as context influences interactions" (p. 172). He later reinforces this point: "One clear message from the preceding review of recent scholarship is that leadership is situated. It cannot be understood, in other words, apart from context. The context of leadership, however, may be characterized in various ways" (p. 182). Leaders today cannot be successful without having a broad understanding of the social, political, and economic dynamics that influence and are shaped by American education. Administrators must at least be aware of the ideologies, political pressures, and shifting economic and social conditions, if they are to provide effective educational leadership.

The sheer number of groups offering ideas on how to improve education has drastically increased as have the number of competing reform agendas. Efforts to improve education have been described as waves of reform with each washing over an education system that is having a hard time gaining its balance. Because of general disappointment regarding most of these reform efforts, there is now a call for shifting the responsibility for reform. Not only might schooling change but so might the roles, responsibilities, and procedures of the educational leaders.

To a great extent, the quality of American education depends on the effectiveness of school leaders to be able to respond to diverse groups and pressures as they continuously work to improve schools (Edmonds, 1979; Lezotte, 1988). The call is for leaders with political savvy, a moral compass, who understand the social, economic, and human demands, the governmental and community agendas, as well as the professional expectations and responsibilities of the work. Schools are part of a much larger global system, linked to society through both formal and informal structures of governance and influence that shape almost all educational decisions. (For more information see: www.ed.gov/.)

✳ **How will the existing contextual factors shape what you will do as the principal of Nanuck Middle School? What contextual factors will have the most significant impact in the near future?**

Broad, Complex Context

Schooling is a federal interest, a state responsibility, and a local operation. The United States has fifty systems of public education that are being strongly influenced by world, national, state, and local pressures and expectations (see Chapter 5 for greater detail). James W. Guthrie and Rodney J. Reed (1991) capture the complexity of the system:

> The United States maintains an educational system which is probably more diverse, disparate, decentralized, and dynamic than any other in the world. This system depends only slightly upon national government to make education policy or to provide financial support for educational institutions. Instead, governmental authority for American education is distributed primarily among the fifty states, which in turn, delegate administrative responsibility to thousands of local school districts. The consequence is fifty systems of public tax-supported lower and higher education in which most policy is made by fifty sets of state officials, governors, legislators, judges, state boards of education, and their counterparts in thousands of local communities. As if this were not sufficiently complex, there exists a parallel system of private or nonpublic institutions, generally outside of government, for both higher and lower education. (p. 22)

Add to this the significant number of interest groups—the *Encyclopedia of Associations* lists 1,221 national and international education associations—and you begin to understand the diversity of thinking local school leaders must be prepared to contend with, even before they face students and their parents.

Citizens across the nation are becoming increasingly interested in what is taught, read, viewed, and discussed in our public schools. A policy network newsletter of the National School Boards Association states:

> Parents, students, school board members, and administrators all have an obvious interest regarding what goes on in our schools, but so do people with no local affiliation or direct connections to the district. People representing the political spectrum of ideas and beliefs, people worried about social mores and the future of a sometimes less than admirable society look to the public schools as a mechanism to foster change or to stifle it. (Morris, 1992, p. 1)

People use pressure, legislation, mandates, and other forms of political action to make decisions conform to their interests. The educational leader is responsible for ensuring that the final decisions are representative of the whole and are in the best interests of the children.

Educational leaders are caught among conflicting desires of elected and governmental officials, diverse communities, teachers and staff, boards of education, interest groups, students and families, educational experts, and others, all of whom have their own agendas. The related pressures seem to be increasing along with the ever-growing number of social problems and issues that find their ways into the schools. As educators become enmeshed in the web of issues being debated by various constituencies, they can find themselves at the center of the controversies, particularly if they do not understand the history and objectives of the groups with which they are dealing.

Razik and Swanson (1995) suggest:

> For better or for worse, this is, indeed a dynamic and exciting period in human history. Because of the fluidity of the situation, it is a period of unparalleled opportunity and potential danger. To capitalize on the opportunities and to minimize the dangers demands extraordinarily wise leadership in all sectors and in all enterprises including education. . . .
>
> The context of educational leadership today is different from any other time in history. It is essential that contemporary issues and processes be understood if leadership is to result in relevant action. (pp. 70–71)

The challenge of leaders is to identify the "turning-points" and be prepared to exert necessary leadership.

✳ **With which individuals or groups should you as principal at Nanuck Middle School meet on a regular basis?**

Federal Turning-Points

The involvement of the federal government in education has shifted directions during the past 250 years and is sometimes categorized by eras of influence. This is not a precise categorization since once an era begins, some of the impact from that period continues to influence education during later eras. What follows is one way of looking at the historical involvement of the federal government in U.S. education.

Education Origins

Education was not mentioned in the U.S. Constitution. As a result of the Tenth Amendment, ratified in 1791, it became a responsibility of each state. As states adopted constitutions, they consolidated powers over education that had been exercised by local communities. The states established minimum standards and guidelines, leaving a large amount of the power for operating the school systems to local communities. The American school system was built on a concept of universal opportunity for education to all of its citizens. Thousands of acts and laws passed in each of the states placed schools in the public domain, granting compulsory taxing power, setting schools up as quasi-municipal corporations, establishing legal rights, setting up standards, providing for governance, and so forth.

Names like Horace Mann, Henry Barnard, William H. McGuffey, Johann Herbart, and later John Dewey were powerful forces in shaping American education. The American people began to look to public education to meet the challenges of a rapidly changing civilization. School enrollments increased by geometric proportions, and public education became one of the great enterprises in the nation. At the same time, social and economic concerns in a changing world were making new demands on schooling.

Because the constitution is silent about support for public education, the federal government must use implied powers for which it does have responsibility to support involvement in education. These implied powers come from the general welfare clause, parts of the First Amendment, and both the due process and equal protection clauses of the Fourteenth Amendment. To date, five major federal responsibilities have been used to justify federal involvement in education: (1) land grant, (2) public relief and welfare, (3) national defense, (4) equal opportunity, and (5) economic competitiveness and school safety as shown in Table 2.1. This table is not inclusive but provides a sampling of legislation related to education. In addition, a number of pieces of legislation, although not directed specifically at education, certainly have a significant impact—such as the Fair Labor Standards Act and the Equal Employment Opportunity Act.

Land Grant

As early as 1785, with the orderly distribution of public land through surveying and setting land aside for specific purposes, land-grant schools came into being. The Ohio Statehood Enabling Act was the first of the enabling acts that provided land grants for public schools in newly created states. Each of these enabling acts, by which territories became states, required provisions for a system of public education. Later, in 1862, the Morrill Act provided lands for the establishment of colleges and universities. In 1867, the U.S. Office of Education was created under the Department of the Interior for the purpose of collecting "statistics and facts as shall

TABLE 2.1 *Federal Involvement in Education*

Law		Purpose
Land Grant, Agriculture, and Vocation		
Land Ordinance	1785	Provided for orderly distribution of public land by surveying the land
Northwest Ordinance	1787	Encouraged use of public monies for the maintenance of public schools in the newly created townships
Ohio Statehood Enabling	1802	First of the enabling acts, which provided land grants for public schools in newly created states
Smith–Lever Act	1914	Created Agricultural Extension Service to "aid in diffusing . . . useful and practical information on subjects pertaining to agriculture and home economics"
Smith–Hughes Act	1917	Provided matching funds to help states develop high school vocational programs
Relief		
"New Deal" Activity	1930s	Encouraged education as part of the Public Works Administration, Civilian Conservation Corps, National Youth Administration, Works Progress Administration, and others
Lanham Act	1941	Provided funds to construct and operate schools where federal activity created burdens on local governments; expanded in 1980 by Impact Laws 815 and 874, which provided money for school construction and district operating costs, respectively
National School Lunch Program	1946	Provided funds for school lunch programs in public and nonpublic school; expanded in 1954 to include a school milk program
National Defense		
School Construction Act	1957	Provided $325 million/year for four years for financing school construction
National Defense Education Act	1958	Provided graduate fellowships in education—particularly in the sciences, mathematics, and foreign languages; extended in 1964 (supported student loans, local-state-national partnership, encouraged curriculum reform)
Peace Corps Act	1961	Established a program to supply teachers and technicians for underdeveloped nations for two-year time periods
Manpower Development and Training Act	1962	Established up-to-date training programs for youth whose lack of education prevented them from obtaining employment
Equal Educational Opportunity		
Vocational Education Act	1963	Extended 1950 impact laws and NDEA and provided funds for construction of vocational schools and development of expanded vocational education offerings

(continued)

TABLE 2.1 *Continued*

Law		Purpose
Economic Opportunity Act	1964	Provided the legislative weapon for the War on Poverty; intended to improve the lot of the disadvantaged through educational and community projects: Head Start, Job Corps, Neighborhood Youth Corps, VISTA, and other work-experience and community programs
Civil Rights Act	1964	Intended to discourage racial discrimination throughout society with particular emphasis on hastening desegregation in the nation's schools
Elementary and Secondary Education Act	1965	Provided large sums of money for a broad range of educational concerns. Improved state department of education, compensatory education, and innovative programs
Education Professions Development Act	1967	Amended the 1965 Higher Education Act to improve the preservice and inservice training of educational personnel
Bilingual Education Act	1968	Provided funds for instruction of children with limited English proficiency
Emergency School Aid Act	1972	Provided federal support for voluntary desegregation of local schools
Rehabilitation Act	1973	Provided for accommodation of the disabled student with the service necessary to provide high-quality education
Family Educational Rights and Privacy Act	1974	Established a student's right to privacy
Education for All Handicapped Children Act (PL 94-142)	1976	Forbade exclusion of or discrimination against persons solely because of their handicapping condition (Provided some funds for children in poverty)

World Class Economic Competitiveness and Safety

Law		Purpose
Education Consolidation Improvement Act	1981	Provided for block grants that state and local education agencies could use for certain broadly defined educational programs
National Assessment of Educational Progress	1983	Created a national testing program for the assessment of educational results
Education for Economic Security Act	1985	Provided for education and development to maintain economic position regarding high-technology
Tax Reform Act	1986	Lowered the taxes on high-income earners and raised the taxes on middle- to upper-middle wage earners
American with Disabilities Act	1990	Protected the rights of individuals with disabilities through high standards, accommodations, and employment practices and services
Job Training Partnership	1991	Designed program to help at-risk youth be successful in schools and jobs
Civil Rights Act	1991	Extended punitive damages and jury trial to those who have been discriminated against

TABLE 2.1 *Continued*

Law		Purpose
Family and Medical Leave Act	1993	Allowed employees to take twelve weeks a year of unpaid leave for circumstances such as childbirth, adoption, illness of family member
Goals 2000: Educate America Act	1994	Established eight national goals for public education (two new goals concerning teacher education and parental participation); provided funds for standards-based reforms
The Violent Crime Control and Law Enforcement Act	1994	Attacked youth crime, including tough enforcement provisions and crime prevention programs oriented toward youth
Improving American Schools Act	1994	(Reauthorization of the ESEA Act) Strongly encouraged state and LEA's involvement in education, especially in setting high standards; moved ESEA toward school-based reform; promoted innovative programs
Safe and Drug-Free Schools and Communities Act	1994	(Reauthorization of title IV) Supported school and community efforts in the war against drugs
Telecommunications Act	1996	Mandated FCC to make telecommunications services affordable for all schools and libraries
Amendments to the Individuals with Disabilities Education Act	1997	Attempted to overcome barriers that have prevented children with disabilities from being educated effectively
Education Flexibility Partnership Act	1999	Provided for greater flexibility in applying certain federal education regulations
Alternative Routes to Teacher Certification Act	2001	Provided for the establishment of a commission to review and make recommendations to Congress and the states on alternative and nontraditional routes to teacher certification
No Child Left Behind Act	2002	Developed school accountability for results, provided freedom to states and communities, encouraged proven educational methods, and provided more choices for parents
Teacher Preparation Act	2002	Allowed educators to take reasonable steps to maintain discipline without fear of litigation
Education Sciences Reform Act	2002	Overhauled the office of Educational Research and Improvement (OERI); eliminated OERI and replaced it with a new Academy of Education Science that could oversee educational research, statistics gathering, program evaluation, and dissemination of information
Teacher Recruitment and Retention Act	2003	Provided for loan forgiveness for math, science, and special education teachers and for those in the poorest of poor and some rural schools
Washington D.C. School Choice Act	2003	Provided additional educational choices to District of Columbia schools through "opportunity scholarships" for children to attend better schools

show the condition and progress of education in the several states and territories. . . ." Henry Barnard was instrumental in the creation of this office and served as the first U.S. Commissioner of Education.

Relief

The country was entering into the Great Depression of the 1930s and initially relief acts were more to help the youth of the country who could not find jobs than they were to improve education. This legislation began with the development of vocational programs through the Smith–Hughes Act in 1917, but the heart of this legislation was in the New Deal activity in the 1930s, intended to train youth and place them in meaningful employment. The Impact Aid laws were enacted to help school systems that had a large amount of nontaxable federal property within the school district. The results of these laws include the familiar school lunch and school milk programs.

National Defense

In 1939, the U.S. Office of Education was transferred to the Federal Security Agency. The first act passed under the national security and defense emphasis was the National Science Foundation Act in 1950. This act provided funds for study and research in scientific fields and was administered by the National Science Board composed of twenty-four members and a director. The Hoover task force, Commission on Government Organization, created in 1955, concluded that the U.S. Office of Education had "meager influence and no control." In addition, of the 3 billion federal dollars being spent on education at the time, only 1 percent went through the U.S. Office of Education. The rest went through a number of blue-ribbon boards and commissions and over twenty other federal agencies. The commission recommended a number of changes in the executive branch of government. In 1953 the Department of Health, Education, and Welfare was created, placing greater responsibility for the administration and control of educational matters within this office. The 1954 cooperative research program was enacted under the leadership of U.S. Commissioner Samuel Brownell.

The Soviet Union's launching of Sputnik in October 1957 opened the floodgates of seething criticism of the American educational system. It was a rude awakening to Americans who had been taught that most Soviets did not have access to electricity or running water; unfairly or not, the schools were blamed for the Soviets' technical success over America. From all sides came demands for changes in the way Americans were schooled. National security and defense were increasingly used as a justification for greater federal involvement in education. The result was the passage of the largest federal legislation to date as the National Defense Education Act (NDEA) of 1958. This act was to address changes in curriculum, methods, and requirements, including higher standards, more training in science and mathematics, better provision for bright students, and harder study for all students. The act was particularly designed to strengthen science, mathematics, and foreign languages. This legislation introduced the era of excellence with its emphasis on enrichment, ability grouping, gifted education, and accelerated and enrichment programs. It also established more local-state-national partnerships to improve American education. This was the first piece of legislation aimed specifically at improving instruction in academic or nonvocational subjects and in broadening the involvement of those influencing curriculum and instruction.

Equal Educational Opportunity

Before the 1950s, inner-city poor urban communities, particularly African American communities, saw education as their only hope for improved quality of life. The education system had shown some signs of meeting their needs through the approaches that grew out of progressive child-centered education. Progressive educators argued that teachers had the responsibility of making education relevant to the needs and background of the child. John Dewey was identified as the leader of this movement. Dewey believed that society should be interpreted to children through their daily living in the classroom, in a framework that is genuine and meaningful to them as students. It was during this time that education began to become accessible to all, enabling students to progress at their own speed. The reforms that grew out of the NDEA act and related thinking reversed the progressive child-centered focus and reverted to a subject-centered focus on basics, achieving excellence, with major focus on math, science, and foreign language skills. The curriculum was expanded to include much more learning within each grade level. Those who could not keep up often failed and later dropped out of school.

At the same time, U.S. Supreme Court and legislative activity were placing greater attention on equal opportunity without discrimination. Although we have reserved the discussion of the influence of the courts to Chapter 11, there have been a few cases that have had such a profound impact on U.S. education that they must be included in any discussion of the context. Certainly the *Brown v. Board of Education* in 1954 and the *Swann v. Charlotte-Mecklenburg Board of Education* in 1971 Supreme Court cases were such ground-breaking decisions. Both grew out of a long, protracted struggle for civil rights and the end of segregation. The two decades between these decisions marked an effort to counteract the racial discrimination—in housing, education, jobs, buses, restaurants, and other public places—that existed in the United States.

The *Brown v. Board of Education of Topeka* decision increased the number of African Americans and other minorities entering public schools. Some of the U.S. Supreme Court decisions at this time included the invalidation of school prayer, equality of voting rights and representation, a number of antidiscrimination decisions, and reaffirmation of the freedom of religion, speech, press, and association.

Amid the sense of volatility regarding fundamental civil liberties, especially within urban communities, legislators and others were providing a powerful political push to address growing concerns. Crime, especially among juveniles and young adults, had increased significantly. The signs of problems were easily seen in New York, Cleveland, and other cities in early 1964 through boycotts of city school systems. Redevelopment, education, and jobs were the major themes. A two-year period of rioting and looting began in the summer of 1964 in the Harlem and Bedford-Styvesant sections of New York. Other cities in which this tragic pattern was repeated were Rochester, Los Angeles (Watts), Springfield, Massachusetts; Chicago; Atlanta; San Francisco; Cleveland; Pittsburgh; Baltimore; St. Louis; Omaha; Milwaukee; Pompano Beach, Florida; Birmingham; and Tuscaloosa. Demonstrations and marches were also occurring throughout the nation.

The Kerner Commission on Civil Disorders was created in 1967 to investigate the riots. The report (U.S. Riot Commission, 1968) concluded that the typical rioter was an underemployed school dropout whose hopes were raised by earlier student-centered improvements, only to be later crushed by experiences with NDEA-supported school changes. These conditions created a climate that resulted in violence. The typical citizen within the community who tried to stop the riots—the counterrioter—was a high school graduate with a job. Education and income were the only factors that distinguished the counterrioters from the rioters. General practices of racism were also high on the Kerner list of causes. Overall, the assessment was that the push toward a curriculum that was discipline-oriented, as a return to intellectual rigor, had just the opposite effect and resulted in a reduction in the number of students taking intellectually rigorous courses.

This was the beginning of federal involvement in education for the purpose of encouraging equality of educational opportunity. The most significant piece of legislation under the equality movement is the Elementary and Secondary Education Act (ESEA) of 1965, a broad program of support to children from low-income families. The first six titles of this bill supported compensatory education, instructional materials, supplementary services, innovative programs, strengthening state departments, and libraries. Literature, such as Charles E. Silberman's *Crisis in the Classroom*, describing school as a "grim, joyless place" where spirit is repressed and the joy of learning and creating is lost, added support for student-centered innovations. The programs created under the ESEA legislation were now complemented by progress in Head Start programs, desegregation, student-centered education, and open classrooms.

In the 1970s, the busing of children to schools outside their neighborhoods to improve racial balances overshadowed all other education issues. The significant *Swann v. Charlotte-Mecklenburg Board of Education* decision established that there was "no basis for holding that the local school authorities may not be required to employ bus transportation as a tool of school desegregation. Desegregation plans cannot be limited to the walk-in school." This decision launched busing as a legal approach to achieving school desegregation when housing patterns blocked them from occurring naturally. This was another very turbulent period in American education. One of many examples of the backlash to racial busing occurred in the South Boston and Hyde Park sections of Boston, where police and National Guardsmen were required for approximately five weeks to establish order in the communities and schools. This experience was very similar to what was occurring in southern cities such as Birmingham, Alabama, and Little Rock, Arkansas.

Certainly an additional factor in forming national opinion was the increased interest in media, particularly television, to gain an understanding of what was occurring in America and the world. Television, for the first time, offered a glimpse into the difference between affluence and poverty, which later helped fuel the frustration and rage of those living in poverty. The vast resources of the media are able to solidify support, intentionally or unintentionally, for issues and reforms that they view as important and/or necessary.

The 1970s ended with a concern that a significant number of American youth did not perform satisfactorily on standardized tests of reading, writing, and arithmetic—the three Rs. The first major international comparison of achievement in mathematics revealed that U.S. student scores fell below those of Japan and Britain. At the same time, significant cutbacks were made in funding for public schools, the equalization of state educational funding formulas were challenged (*Rodriguez v. San Antonio Independent School District*), and the integration of American schools met with considerable success and optimism. A separate cabinet-level U.S. Department of Education came into existence on September 24, 1979. This new cabinet position was to fulfill a promise to the National Education Association (NEA) and to improve relations with U.S. teachers. There were a string of teacher strikes over issues such as salary increases, cost-of-living clauses, lesson-preparation time, class size, and extra-duty pay.

Perhaps most evident amidst the turmoil occurring in education since the 1950s was the minimum influence educational leaders were able to exert. They were constantly being whipsawed by political and judicial decisions and the social and economic conditions within their communities. They found themselves constantly reacting to political and community forums in which they were not partners. Educators had always seen themselves as apolitical, as experts and professionals in pedagogical matters. They began to realize that political issues outside education were having a profound impact on what was happening within education and that they had lost control of the agenda.

Responding to political demands, educators had built an integrated system of education, where a very high percentage of youth graduated from high school, meeting or exceeding minimum standards in schools that were barrier-free and open to all American youth regardless of race, gender, physical ability, or IQ.

World Class Economic Competitiveness and Support—1980 to Present

The 1980s began with teachers openly expressing dissatisfaction with their jobs— 41 percent responded to an NEA teacher poll that they would not become teachers if they had to do it over again. Educators argued that the tax revolt of the 1970s had reduced state and local funds to education, and federal cuts only contributed to the difficulties within local districts.

A blitz of national reports criticized U.S. education, including one by the U.S. Secretary of Education's appointed National Commission on Excellence in Education (1983). The report, titled *A Nation at Risk,* purposefully alarmist in tone, began:

> Our nation is at risk. Our once unchallenged preeminence in commerce, industry, science and technological innovation is being overtaken by competitors, throughout the world. The educational foundations of our society are presently being eroded by a rising tide of mediocrity that threatens our very future as a nation and a people. . . .

If an unfriendly foreign power had attempted to impose on America the mediocre educational performance that exists today, we might well have viewed it as an act of war.

American students compared unfavorably to foreign students and were weaker in inferential skills, science and math achievement had declined, and illiteracy was a huge national problem. The recommendations were to launch a core curriculum, raise academic standards, lengthen the school day and year, improve teacher quality, and attract capable teachers. National attention turned to the need for higher academic standards, tougher subjects, rigorous testing, and stiffer high school graduation requirements. Also important were high-level cognitive skills, critical thinking skills, active and authentic learning, technology application, logic and reasoning skills, functional and operational literacy, interpersonal skills, work ethic, multicultural respect, problem solving and reasoning, and analytical skills. Educators found that the collective American mood had swung once again—excellence was more important than equality of opportunity and equity. President Ronald Reagan was urging prayer in public schools, legislation for tuition tax credits, vouchers, choice in public and private schools, and a smaller federal role in education. Amid all the criticism of the schools there was a bright spot: 80 percent of the nation's school-age population now graduated from high school, far more than in most other countries.

Education had entered the political arena full swing, and regardless of causes, politicians felt compelled to make their mark on education. There is no sign that they will retreat from this position anytime in the near future.

The National Governors' Association 1986 report, *Time for Results,* states early on that, "Better schools mean better jobs." Governor Alexander's summary of the report (1986, p. 7) reaffirmed the governors' readiness to provide "the leadership needed to get results on the hard issues that confront the better school movement . . . (and) to lead the second wave of reform in American education policy." The governors shared the belief "that real excellence can't be imposed from a distance. Governors don't create excellent schools; communities—local school leaders, teachers, parents, and citizens—do." The states would work on recommendations, standards, assessment, and accountability.

At the same time, the Carnegie Forum on Education and the Economy (1986, p. 26) found that many teachers were "immensely frustrated—to the point of cynicism" by reform activities that they saw as bringing about very little change and showing a lack of respect for classroom teachers. They observed bureaucratic structures becoming more rigid, opportunities for exercising professional judgment decreasing, few or no real gains for students, and lack of professional respect for teachers. In a report titled *Results in Education: 1987,* the members of the National Governors' Association noted that "states will have to assume larger responsibilities for setting educational goals and defining outcome standards, while, at the same time, stimulating local inventiveness" (p. 3).

During this time, the country was developing a very wealthy class of people whose income was significantly higher than that of the middle class, creating the largest economic gap in U.S. history. In the United States, the wealthiest 1 percent of the population holds 36 percent of the country's wealth—a higher proportion than any other country in the world (Ginsberg, Lowi, & Weir, 1995). Sixty-four percent of the increase in earnings in the 1980s went to this top 1 percent. Over 50 percent of total U.S. income is now paid to the wealthiest 20 percent of the population. At the same time, the taxes on this extraordinarily wealthy group of Americans were being cut, placing the burden of government on the middle class. During the Ronald Reagan administration, the top personal tax bracket dropped from 70 percent to 28 percent and corporate taxes were cut in half. The Tax Reform Act of 1986 effected a 53 percent tax decrease for the wealthy and an 18 percent increase in federal taxes for middle- to upper-middle-class taxpayers (Barlett & Steele, 1994). The middle class carries an ever-increasing burden of fiscal responsibility for governmental activity.

Elshtain (1995) characterizes the thinking among some upper-socioeconomic groups in regard to the programs that were created to benefit the less fortunate. He states:

> Instead, they see a growing dependence on welfare, increased inner-city crime, an epidemic of out-of-wedlock births, and the like. They perceive, therefore, a pattern of redistribution through forms of assistance to people who do not seem to be as committed as they are to following the rules of the game by working hard and not expecting the government to shoulder their burdens. This, at least, is the widespread conviction, and it fuels popular anger and perplexity. As a result, programs geared to particular populations have lost . . . legitimacy. (pp. 3–4)

As a result, government began a period of scaling back services to its citizens, particularly middle- and lower-socioeconomic citizens, cutting taxes and increasing governmental efficiency.

✳ **Select contextual elements that are having and/or will have the most pronounced influence on Nanuck Middle School.**

Establishing National Goals

In 1989, school reform was developing from the most ideologically conservative political process of our times. In this setting, President George H. W. Bush and the nation's governors came together at the historic Educational Summit in Charlottesville, Virginia. All agreed that "the time has come, for the first time in the United States history, to establish clear national performance goals, goals that will make us internationally competitive." In 1991, the Educational Goals panel recommended national standards and related systems for student assessment. States and school districts are required to set standards for curriculum content and student performance to qualify for federal Chapter I funds.

The mood, as we entered the last decade of the century, was best summed up in a February 9, 1990, article, which appeared in *The Wall Street Journal*'s first education supplement.

Jobs are becoming more demanding, more complex. But our schools don't seem up to the task. They are producing students who lack the skills that business so desperately needs to compete in today's global economy and doing so, they are condemning students to a life devoid of meaningful employment.

Better corporate retraining may serve as a stopgap. But ultimately the burden of change rests with our schools. While debate rages about how change should come, almost everyone agrees that something has to be done. And quickly. (p. R1)

Thoughts for Leaders of Educational Institutions in Transition

LUVERN L. CUNNINGHAM • *Novice G. Fawcett Professor of Educational Administration (Emeritus), The Ohio State University*

This is a personal story invoking the privilege of experience and age.

Time, its inexorable movement traced across a half century. After one year as a teaching-principal in a small high school on the prairies of Nebraska, I was hired as a superintendent. The hiring took place on a Saturday night in the back room of a poolhall. I was 24. It was 1949. Nine years later, two superintendencies, one year as director of admissions at Midland Lutheran College, a master's degree at the University of Nebraska at Omaha, and a doctorate from the University of Oregon under my belt, I arrived at the University of Chicago. I was appointed assistant professor and assistant director of the Midwest Administration Center, probably the most prominent and respected center for research on problems and issues of school administration in the country. Later, in 1967, I became dean of the College of Education and Professor of Educational Administration at Ohio State University.

The late 1950s and 1960s were a period of intellectual ferment and excitement in school administration across the nation. The University Council for Educational Administration was created and thrived under the leadership of Jack Culberston. Its offices were at Ohio State. Students and faculty at Chicago had built up a full head of steam, generating fresh thinking about the theory and practice of school administration. It was a movement, and Chicago was in the thick of it. Research was underway. Important books, monographs, and articles were written. Regional, national, and international conferences

were convened on matters germane to educational administration. Students on completion were taking important positions in school systems and universities across the United States and Canada.

An inspiring transition to some, an enervating struggle to others, was underway in the 1950s. Concentration within the field of school administration from its humble beginnings to that point had been on technical matters. "Budgets, buildings, and buses" was a phrase often cited as a descriptor of the field. Textbooks of prominence focused on the nitty-gritty of running schools. Such topics as these were emphasized: courses of study, heating and lighting of buildings, selecting sites for schools and playgrounds, hiring and firing of employees, budgets, paying for schooling, legal questions, ordering books and supplies, organizing and reorganizing school districts and attendance areas, and preparing the school calendar. For the first forty years of the twentieth century, pencils, paper, blackboards, and chalk constituted technology; hectographs, mimeographs, typewriters, and A-V came later. Minimum credentials were required to be a principal or superintendent of schools.

In the 1950s, the center of gravity began to shift away from those items to such interests as leadership, political behavior, change process, decision making, policy development, policy analysis, administrative behavior, organizational behavior, attributes of leaders in educational administration, and administration as a social process. New theories and their advocates began to appear. The whole of the social sciences became the source of new ideas. Theories were drawn from economics, sociology, psychology, political science, even anthropology. Professional fields such as public administration, health administration, and business administration were explored for useful ways to think about administrative practice. Drawing from such disciplines and centers of practice is now commonplace, but it was not then.

The political, economic, and social context within which schooling was taking place was changing. The Russians launched and orbited Sputnik, the first artificial satellite, in 1957. Enrollments were growing, classrooms were needed, double sessions were widespread. There was a severe teacher shortage.

Collective bargaining entered the picture, and rumblings of dissatisfaction with school performance began to appear. A single book, *Why John Can't Read,* stirred people and aroused indignation across the country. The federal government stepped up its interest in education, prompted in some measure by Sputnik, leading to the national Defense Education Act and a spate of other federal programs aimed at improving academic achievement, reforming the curriculum, addressing problems of poverty, technology (language labs, for example), special education, and career.

Of singular significance in the 1950s was *Brown v. Board of Education,* the celebrated Topeka desegregation case of 1954, which changed public education profoundly in the United States. The decision launched the civil rights movement within public education. It, along with subsequent desegregation litigation, contributed to the 1967 Civil Rights Act and other public policy to follow. Nearly a half century later, its impact is still registering on the nation and its educational system. In some respects the struggle over issues of race and social class is only beginning. The dark cloud of poverty versus privilege, haves versus have-nots is more menacing than ever, burdening this generation as well as future generations of educational administrators.

In the new millennium, school administrators face continuing and emerging challenges. Finding money, spending it wisely, having standards and living up to them, intensifying the concentration on student learning, staying accountable, involving parents, leading and following in good balance are ongoing needs. Maintaining personal and professional focus; achieving comfort with chaos; making change your ally, not your enemy; locating the constructive place of technology in the scheme of things; carving out time for reflection; holding firm to values, traditions, and practices that sustain schools as democratic institutions; standing tall, more than ever before, for children, youth, and their families; facing squarely issues of race and social class; walking and sustaining the moral and ethical high ground: These are today's and tomorrow's imperatives.

External forces have always pounded educational institutions at all levels. Ironically, one of those forces, probably the most transforming, was the evolution of digital computing, centered initially at the University of Illinois and MIT. The "digitalization of civilization," a phrase borrowed from a recent issue of *Daedalus,* characterizes our current circumstances. It began in the 1940s, continuing through the decades at a blistering pace, outstripping the capacity of analysis to surmise its significance for the future. One person's reading of the tea leaves often seems as good as another's. The impact of digitalization at the change of centuries is so profound on all aspects of life and living that it seems unnecessary to belabor its presence except to say that administrators cannot relax in their struggle to tease out its meaning for their institutional stewardship.

My doctoral work at the University of Oregon in the middle 1950s was anchored heavily in the social sciences, especially political science and sociology. I moved from the intellectually familiar to the intellectually unknown. I found the stimulation exhilarating. These experiences have enhanced my thinking, research, writing, and administrative performance ever since. I urge administrators in the process of becoming to find a conceptual system that will guide them through a host of contextual and virtual realities and help them contain and understand the excitement of their experience. Otherwise, why make the trip?

The 1990s and Beyond

In 1991–1992, a total of thirty superintendents of urban school districts—Los Angeles, Atlanta, Boston, Cleveland, Columbus, Charlotte-Mecklenburg, Charleston, St. Louis, Kansas City, and Washington, DC, to name a few—lost their jobs. Carter and Cunningham (1997) suggest that the cost of turnover has weighed heavily on local school districts and the staff who are trying to hold them together. Paul Houston, executive director of the AASA, suggests:

> The current role is indeed a troubled one. The condition of children in this country has deteriorated, while the challenges facing them have escalated. And the critics are in full force. Superintendents find themselves defending the system they lead, demanding accountability so they can keep the doors open and morale up, while at the same time they must search for ways to transform the system to meet an uncertain future. . . . Much of the solution to this problem rests in the ability of school leaders to build conditions of support for schools from among those most interested in seeing schools succeed. (Carter & Cunningham, 1997, pp. ii–iv)

The 1990s were also a period of great concern regarding the large increase in juvenile violent crimes. More and more of our young were lost to crime and violence, prompting former President Bill Clinton to address the theme of reducing school violence and providing a safe learning environment. In a 1999 speech to the American Federation of Teachers, he stated:

> Our progress will come to nothing if our schools are not safe places, orderly places where teachers can teach, and children can learn. We also know that in too many American schools, there is lawlessness where there should be learning. There is chaos where there should be calm. There is disorder where there should be discipline. Make no mistake, this is a threat not to our classroom, but to America's public school system and, indeed, to the strength and vitality of our nation.

In March 1996, forty-nine corporate leaders; forty-one governors; and thirty educators, staff advisors, and policy experts (observers) attended the second national Education Summit. Louis V. Gerstner, CEO of IBM and cochair of the summit, stated, "Until we set standards and learn how to measure against them we can't assess the effectiveness of all the ideas that bounce off the walls of educational establishments." The attendees endorsed the idea of each state developing "internationally competitive academic standards" and rigorous new tests to measure whether students meet the standards.

The third national education summit occurred in the fall of 1999 when government and business leaders stressed the importance of standards and accountability. Texas had increased the number of students passing the state assessment test by 25 percent, although the accusations of fraudulent behavior in Houston Public schools that occurred almost seven years later clouded the accuracy of the reported test scores. By 2003, 48 states set standards for students and provided some sort of state-mandated testing in reading and math.

✳ **How might you and the staff begin to respond to the contextual demands being placed upon Nanuck Middle School?**

No Child Left Behind

The educational summits committed the nation to a process of measuring student progress on a set of broad educational goals. One of the more important pieces of legislation at the beginning of the twenty-first century is the No Child Left Behind Act of 2001 (NCLB), which was signed by the president on January 8, 2002. (www.ncslorg/programs/educ/nochild.htm) This is a reauthorization of the Elementary and Secondary Education Act of 1965. This act stresses the importance of accountability goals and that states, districts, and school administrators should strive to develop sets of goals that are complementary if not completely consistent with the national goals. Almost every state has adopted standards for the areas of reading/language arts and mathematics. Most states have also established student performance standards and state assessments (Nebraska and Iowa being two exceptions due to their state constitutions, which prohibit state assessment).

The NCLB law states that reading and math tests must be given each year to students in grades three through eight and to one grade in high school. The goal is to have all students proficient in both subjects by 2014. The appropriate tests must be in place by the 2005–2006 school year. By 2007–2008, states also must have standards in place in science that must be assessed at three different points during the students' progression through grades (www.nochildleftbehind.gov.links). This legislation encourages evidence-based schooling by looking at adequate yearly progress (AYP) on accountability goals for all students as well as breakdowns for the following subgroups:

- Economically disadvantaged
- Children with disabilities
- Children of different race and ethnicity
- Children with limited English proficiency

A minimum 95 percent participation rate for all schools is required. Each school system is responsible to collect and disaggregate data, determine AYP goals to ensure school accountability for students on achievement tests, identify schools needing improvement and corrective action, take corrective actions, provide supplemental educational services, and report results to the federal Department of Education. Schools that fail to achieve adequate progress might require corrective actions such as academic reviews, school improvement plans, adding new curriculum, increasing lengths of school year/day, appointing outside experts as advisors, restructuring of reconstituting school organization, replacing relevant staff and/or governance changes, and providing parental choice options. By 2013–2014, all schools must reach 100 percent proficiency.

There is also an expectation that there will be a highly qualified teacher in all classrooms. These are teachers demonstrating "subject knowledge," and "teaching skills" in reading, writing, mathematics and other basic subject areas that must be in place in every classroom by the end of the 2005–2006 school year. This requirement is also tied in with Title II of the Higher Education Act of 1998. The focus of grants in this area is on professional development in mathematics and science, reforming certification/licensing requirements, alternative routes (troops to teachers, career switchers, etc.) to certification, recruitment and retention initiatives, reforming tenure, teacher testing, and merit pay.

The NCLB act has been hotly debated in many arenas including political, academic, and research arenas and in local school systems and their communities. Criticism has included concerns regarding the narrowing of the instructional focus resulting in an impoverished definition of reading, writing, or mathematics; ignoring content domains not tested; questions regarding realistically obtainable goals for all children (Goldilock standards); stressing less desirable instructional practices to achieve goals; testing taking away from time for instruction; misalignment of instructional materials with tests; too much pressure on educators; treating all children the same; branding children, schools, and communities; to name but a few of the more prevalent themes. Some states have begun to seek federal waivers from some parts of the act.

Robert Linn (2003) believes that based on a straight-line projection of present rates of improvement it would take 57 years for grade 4 percentages of students to achieve the desired 100 percent level. Yet, school systems only have until 2014 to achieve this percentage. "Such a rapid acceleration would be nothing short of miraculous (p. 6)" according to Linn. He goes on to state: "The goals that NCLB sets for student achievement would be wonderful if they could be reached, but, unfortunately, they are quite unrealistic, so much so, that they are apt to do more to demoralize educators than to inspire them" (p. 10) Probably the greatest concern is the cost of this program to the states. The National Association of State Boards of Education estimated the cost of developing, scoring, and reporting results of reading and math tests at somewhere between $2.7 billion and a frightening $7 billion over the life of the new law. Science tests would cost extra. The Education Council reported a figure at between $300 and $400 million each year, which works out to be approximately $4 billion.

Rice and Malen (2003) studied school reconstitution and the consequences on the human costs associated with this reform. Reconstitution generally involves "removing a school's incumbent administrators and teachers (or large percentages of them) and replacing them with educators who, presumably, are more capable and committed" (Rice & Malen, 2003, p. 635). The results of their study casts doubts on the ability of reconstitution initiatives (like those in NCLB) to enhance human capital in low-performing schools. Reconstitution was found to result in a decline in qualifications of staff; increased costs; unreasonable demands on districts and states; lack of incentives for master teachers and administrators to go to reconstituted schools; lack of personnel, time, and support; increased costs, time, and energy to fill vacancies; staffing instability; weaker collegial structures, trust, and collaboration; blanket indictments and assaults; loss of efficacy and self-worth; and, alienation, all of which undermined the ability of the reform to achieve its major objectives (www.bc.edu/researchnbetpp).

Robert G. Marzano from the Mid-Continental Research and Learning (McREL) Institute and many others argue that standards and standardized testing holds the greatest hope for significantly improving student achievement. Over time, he believes that standards-based classroom tests can be at least as precise as external tests and that in the future they will balance each other and will lessen the need for a single high-stakes test.

The U.S. public still seemed quite supportive of high-stakes testing in 2004. They are concerned that students are not likely to become responsible and productive citizens without the acquisition of a standard set of skills (www.edexcellence .net/library/cizek.pdf).

New Technological Demands

The Congressional Office of Technology Assessment reported in 1995 that although the private sector demands workers with the skills needed to compete in the "information society," most schools lack key technologies. They also lack teachers who are properly trained to use the equipment that is readily available in other institutions. Educational leaders are now being asked to make technology a key part of the learning process. Between 1995 and 2000, the federal government granted over $8 billion to states to purchase technology equipment and related programs for schools.

The General Accounting Office reported that schools don't have facilities to make full use of computer, video, and other communications. More than half the schools lack modems and phone lines and were not linked to external networks; one-third complained of problems with electrical wiring; and less than 50 percent of the classrooms had access to voice mail. In 1999, there was a federal goal of connecting every school to the National Information Infrastructure (NII) and providing training for how to use this tremendous information communication library.

The International Society for Technology in Education (ISTE) released a set of computer proficiency standards titled the "National Technology Standards for Students" (NET-S). They also published a guidebook, *National Education Technology Standards for Students: Connecting Curriculum and Technology,* for school leaders, showing how to integrate the standards and technology throughout the curriculum (ISTE, 2000). The goal of school systems is to "produce technology-capable kids," meaning "kids who are able to use technology effectively by applying their technical skills."(For more information see: www.iste.org.)

In April 2001, the Collaborative for Technology Standards for School Administrators (TSSA) approved a set of technology standards that described what educational administrators should know about technology. For example, administrators must (a) demonstrate the ability to use technology to collect and analyze data and other information to improve decision making, vis-à-vis student academic achievement tests; (b) understand current technologies that can be integrated into all aspects of the teaching and learning process; (c) understand the elements and characteristics of long-range planning for the use of current and emerging technology; and (d) attain technology skills for instructional planning, budgeting, technical support, personnel, and safety.

The National Education Technology Standards for Administrators (NETS-A) states that administrators should "advocate, on the state and national levels, for policies, programs, and funding opportunities that support implementation of the district technology plan." This has become far more pressing because federal and state funding has resulted in educational technology rapidly spreading into K–12 schools across the nation (Nance, 2003). The recent issues now revolve around how students and staff should use this new educational technology. This has introduced issues related to legal matters, purchase/update of computer hardware and software, training needs, applications software, and programming for instruction and administration, as well as policy and procedural initiatives. Technology opens up access to massive amounts of current information and communication networks with people around the world as communication and computer technologies converge. (See Chapter 3.)

✳ **What additional issues will most likely develop over the next five years that you will need to consider in providing leadership at Nanuck Middle School? What factors will be important? Explain your answer.**

State Roles and Responses

Education is mentioned in every state constitution. The legislatures in every state other than Hawaii, a state school system, continue to follow the original pattern of local control of public education (see Chapter 5 for greater detail). State boards of education date back to 1784, and the first state superintendent of public instruction temporarily emerged in New York in 1812 and reemerged permanently in 1854. State superintendents have been successful in marshaling public opinion, lobbying state legislatures, providing professional leadership, establishing direction, and setting minimum standards. Although the state legislature is charged with the primary responsibility of maintaining a system of public education, the governor's desires are not lightly ignored. Governors influence education through their platform positions, educational appointments, and proposition and veto of bills. The state board of education is often appointed by the governor and determines policies and appoints the chief state school officer. The state department of education is responsible for implementing these policies. It originally collected data, then expanded into setting and maintaining minimum educational standards, inspecting and ensuring appropriate compliance, providing leadership through mandates and program development, and finally facilitating and supporting local efforts to improve education.

State education departments did not really come of age until after the passage of the Elementary and Secondary Education Act in 1965. Title V of this act provided money to significantly increase the number of state department officials as well as providing training, equipment, and encouragement for research and development efforts. Within three years after the passage of this act, many state departments of education doubled in size, with much of the support coming from federal funds.

The major areas of focus at the state level are academic standards, instructional programs, textbook selection, certification of personnel, facilities standards, financial support, data collection and distribution, testing, and regulation of non-public schools. Susan H. Fuhrman (1994) concluded:

> During the '70s and '80s, legislatures generated volumes of statutes related to education. In the 1970s, they revised school financing statutes to address wealth-related disparities among local districts; and they provided special programs, such as compensatory education, for the neediest students. In the early 1980s, they turned their attention to the performance of all students, increasing standards for high school graduation and mandating more testing to assess student progress . . . twenty-eight states enacted school finance reform measures between 1971 and 1981. By 1979–80, twenty-three states provided funds to local districts to support services for disadvantaged students; the same number offered financial assistance for instruction of limited English proficient students; and all fifty states had enacted special education programs that conformed to Public Law 94-142, although they varied in financing mechanisms. (pp. 30–31)

Educators at the local level question the staying power of state initiatives. The attitude sometimes seems to be "wake me up when this one's over!" In addition, state departments of education have been hampered in the 1990s by downsizing and having limited funds to support initiatives (John Murphy, 1993).

The major theme across America at the turn of the century was "get the scores up." Reform in 2001 was often a matter of conforming instruction to fit final tests. Students were exposed to sets of practice tests, drill and skill teaching and packaged programs, hustling through units and chapters to complete a year's worth of standards. This has created an era of "test-centered" curriculum. Critics expressed concern that this test-centered focus was on temporary acquisition of facts and skills rather than acquiring understanding and generating knowledge. Some argued the testing trivialized teachers' evaluations of students, grades, and other teacher responsibilities.

Tests are slowly becoming a major determiner of what the curriculum should and should not include, thus transferring control of the curriculum and teaching and learning to groups that control the exams. In expressing some concerns regarding the standards movement, and particularly the related sanctions, Linda Darling-Hammond and Beverly Falk (1997) state:

> Ultimately, raising standards for students so that they learn what they need to know requires raising standards for the system, so that it provides the kinds of teaching and school settings students need in order to learn. Grade retention as a solution to low achievement is merely a symbol of the failure of the system to teach successfully. Given the effects of retention, such a strategy for accountability foreshadows greater educational failure in the years ahead. Genuine accountability requires both higher standards and greater supports for student, teacher, and school learning. (p. 198)

Most state department initiatives are now dominated by standards and testing programs to provide records of the students' progress and in some cases to hold people accountable. (For more information see: www.mcrel.org.)

There is at least some evidence that state standardized testing is having a positive impact. Detert, Kopel, and Jenni (2000) state:

> Our data suggest that while educators may not agree with state-wide testing, the tests are serving as an impetus for continuous improvement efforts, including goal setting, baseline data, and benchmarks. Most sites with highly publicized state tests are using them successfully as a rallying point for improvement efforts and as a concrete reason to analyze and study their data and the processes relating to these tests. At least two of the sites in the sample reported that the data received from the state was useful and generated an excitement about understanding the causes of the scores and how to improve them. For example, a respondent at one site said: "We looked at holes in our [state test] scores and focused on those skills that needed attention." Another added: "We have in-house charts that show five year trends [of the state tests scores] by school and subject area." Furthermore, educators at this site have taken an additional step. Explained one respondent, "We have done a high school study of [the state test results]. When we found out [the reason for the results] the math department instituted a whole process for addressing this problem and improving these scores." (pp. 179–180)

A recent American Association of School Administrators poll found that 63 percent of the superintendent respondents do not believe that one test can accurately measure students' progress. The tests can provide useful feedback to improve instruction, but they should not be the only *benchmarks, competencies, performance standards,* or any other current term in the accountability movement.

Educators are challenging the fairness of sanctions and high-stakes tests, particularly when all students and teachers are held to the same standards, regardless of socioeconomic status or whether students can speak English. Also, knowing someone's position in a test distribution does not tell one what needs to be done to improve it. Another challenge is that tests are only a sample of what states need to know and may end up narrowing teacher focus. Dr. Rod Paige, the U.S. Secretary of Education in 2001, emphasizes:

> When you test, you give irrefutable and invaluable information on student progress to parents, teachers, administrators, community members and policymakers. By making the results visible, you give each of these stakeholders a powerful incentive for change where the results aren't good enough, and for recognition and growth were the results meet and exceed our standards.
>
> Without those results, all those who care deeply about the success of our schools and our students would persist in the hopeful but misguided belief that everyone and every school is making progress.
>
> We cannot be afraid to test and teach the children who need assistance the most, and we must not deprive them and their parents and teachers of the measure of their progress.

Efforts are now under way to find ways to allow schools to experiment and innovate beyond the "shackles of policy and tradition." By 1995, nearly half the states had authorized charter schools, and many were looking at various forms of school choice programs, school vouchers, year-round learning, and magnet schools.

By 2003, school choice had greatly expanded. Seventeen states have interdistrict open enrollment programs; thirty-seven states and the District of Columbia have passed charter school legislation; public voucher programs exist in three states; and numerous private voucher programs are operating mostly in urban areas. This new direction opens up the opportunity for businesspeople to operate schools for-profit and, if school vouchers are created, an opportunity that for-profit schools might replace public schools. Supporters argue that such approaches offer opportunities for improved student achievement. As a result, there is an increasing number of private organizations that provide support for education and who hope to both manage and operate schools. Arthur Levine (2000) suggests, "The private sector has two entrance points to the public school marketplace. They can directly enter by creating for-profit schools or managing exiting schools in the manner of Christopher Whittle's Edison Schools. Or one can enter the field by providing support services, learning materials as Sylvan does" (p. 8.) He believes the "companies that provide support and non-instructional services for elementary and secondary schools will be more lucrative than those that create or manage schools" (p. 9). The greatest concern expressed in for-profit schools is that the profit will take precedence over the children and that it will separate the diversity that exists in schools in this country by providing a different level of educational service, based largely on parents' wealth and what amount they can afford to pay for their children's education. There is also a concern that a fragmented educational system will be a threat to U.S. society, national unity, and democratic socialization creating a balkanization of U.S. society and growing segregationalism. (For more information see: www.ed.gov/programs/bastmp/sea.htm.)

The lower-socioeconomic communities have difficult times meeting the new standards. Studies completed on the National Assessment of Education Progress data showed variables such as number of parents living at home, parents' educational background, type of community, and poverty rate accounted for 89 percent of the differences in state test scores. Students in lower-socioeconomic communities have the most difficulty in meeting bottom-line expectations and sanctions without assistance. According to Fashola and Slavin (1998), the key reforms now needed are in curriculum and instruction, programs for at-risk students, and family support.

In 2002, New York Mayor Bloomberg reached an agreement with state legislative leaders that removed power from the local boards and gave him control over the schools. Another takeover occurred in Philadelphia in 2001, when the school board was disbanded and the state took control of the schools.

If the present conditions in education do not change, we can expect to see a further push toward increased privatization through charters, vouchers, public funding for private and parochial schools, and various forms of school takeovers. The case for vouchers received strong support in the Supreme Court's June 2003 decision in the Cleveland voucher case, *Zelman v. Simmon Harris*. By a 5–4 margin, the Supreme Court upheld a program in which school district voucher receipts were being used to attend religious schools on the grounds that it was a "true private choice" and thus not unconstitutional. The theme was that the programs were neutral in respect to religion and were a genuine expression of parent choice. In this way, the district/state may pay the tuition of students who wish to attend private schools, even religious schools. This ruling may not have a significant impact since 37 states have amendments that prohibit using public money to support religious schools; however, the voucher battle is expected to heat up in state legislatures. Washington, DC, has a voucher plan to start in fall 2004. Typically, referendums on vouchers and tuition tax credits have failed, especially when they take money away from public schools; however, the present political/legal climate is no longer clear on this issue.

French (1998) believes that privatization can be avoided if state education agencies "use their leverage and resources to marry rigor and diversity, equity and democracy, high expectations and multiple intelligences instead of uniformity, rigid standards, and narrow high-stakes tests. Our educational institutions need to act democratically" (p. 190). School choice, which many conservative higher- and some lower-socioeconomic groups argue will provide healthy competition in a free market economy, might create greater inequalities by acting as a sorting mechanism and class structure of schooling.

✳   **What role would your state most likely play in Nanuck's renewal efforts?**

Equity and Social Justice

Since the 1950s, there has been an increased concern as to whether U.S. education was fulfilling its goal of treating people equitably—equality of opportunity for all children. According to Linda Darling-Hammond (1997), annual educational spending in 1988 ranged from $1,000 per pupil to over $50,000 per pupil. Schools in the ninetieth percentile spent nearly ten times more than schools in the tenth percentile. Such conditions do not provide equitable treatment for economically disadvantaged students. In the past, this inequity has had a particularly harsh effect on African American, Latino, and Native American children. Darling-Hammond (1997, p. 273) suggests, "Perhaps the single greatest source of inequity in education is this disparity in the availability and distribution of well-qualified teachers" (www.leadershipforsocialjustic.org).

Equity or social justice can be discussed from a number of different perspectives—political, economic, opportunity, and results. The equity movement has resulted in the improvement of access of minority children, women, and the handicapped to various school programs and activities. The issues now have expanded to include financial equality. This issue is also receiving greater attention as a result of the achievement gaps and the extraordinary economic gaps among people. Pounder, Reitzug, and Young (2002, p. 270) talk about "inequitable outcomes" that are characterized by "patterned polarization" of school achievement and economic opportunity and welfare.

The focus on multicultural issues related to curriculum, instruction, textbooks, literature, and cultural studies also show an increasing interest in social justice. Pounder, Reitzug, and Young (2002) clearly illustrate the recent direction of the social justice discourse: "Literally millions of students, every year, are not served well by our schools. Schools across our nation in districts large and small with different resources and different student populations are failing to educate, failing to nurture, failing to develop, failing to protect, and failing to include all students . . . the students who are affected most are typically from marginalized groups (e.g., students of color, students with disabilities, low-income students, girls, and gay/ lesbian students)" (p. 271).

Social justice helps define part of the ethical, moral, and democratic dimension of the critical-contextual philosophical frame of reference. Such leaders will need to continuously stress the values of equity and excellence and ensure that it becomes part of the organizations vision. In discussing this type of leader, Schewich and Skrla (2003) found that such a leader "understands that it is our responsibility, even our sacred or spiritual responsibility—to create such schools. This leader understands that this responsibility is central to our country's long history of dedication to equity for all people—for working people, the poor, women, people of color, people with disabilities, for any people who have been excluded" (p. 100). This will not always be an easy position to take and leaders will want to be well connected to allies who can provide moral support. Most transformations will require strong, outstanding leaders and issues related to equity and social justice is no exception.

Grogan (2002) claims that the social justice leaders must continue to challenge the status quo, which favors one group over others. The primary goal is the improvement of "life chances" of children who have in the past been minimized by the system. Recently, the issues have been expanded to environmental pollution and domination over nature and oppressed groups. This focus is on understanding the relationships between ecological and cultural systems and not jeopardizing the environment for future generations (Furman & Gruenewald, 2004).

No country has taken the concerns of equality and social justice more seriously than the United States. This goal has necessitated "creating policies that favor children most at risk—policies that, by definition, are partial, biased and unequal." Given an unlevel playing field, only redistributive policies offer the possibilities of equalizing educational opportunities" (Cooper, Fusarelli, & Randall, 2004, p. 51).

A recent example of such legislature is the NCLB Act of 2002, which states that, "Assessment results and State progress objectives must be broken out by poverty, race, ethnicity, disability, and limited English proficiency to ensure that no group is left behind."

Challenges in the Twenty-First Century

According to a number of reports, many parents and communities are not attending to their children. Marian Wright Edelman, founder and president of the Children's Defense Fund, calls them "back seat" children. Two-parent income earners, single-parent homes, mobility, divorce, and very busy lifestyles have changed the experiences children have within the family. They are often confronted by social issues such as crime, neglect, poverty, abuse, disease, addiction, and violence. In *Beyond Rhetoric*, the National Commission on Children (1991) says of American children:

[A]mong all races and income groups, and in communities nationwide, many children are in jeopardy. They grow up in families whose lives are in turmoil. Their parents are too stressed and too drained to provide nurturing, structure and security that protect children and prepare them for adulthood. Some others are unsafe at home and in their neighborhoods. Many are poor, and some are homeless and hungry. (p. 5)

Dr. Edelman expressed her deep concern for the nation's "back seat" children in a report on the state of American children (Children's Defense Fund, 1991).

Nowhere is the paralysis of public and private conscience more evident than in the neglect and abandonment of millions of our shrinking pool of children, whose future will determine our nation's ability to compete and lead in a new era. (p. 7)

Some of the quality-of-life factors that are worsening include child abuse, the number of children in poverty, drug abuse, lack of health insurance coverage, out-of-pocket health costs, anger, selfishness, urban poverty, and crime. Other significant trends that affect education are national and global interdependence, increasing institutional change in both pace and complexity, the obsolescence of knowledge, terrorism, and a worsening ecology. The real buying power of American families is decreasing except among approximately 30 percent of the wealthiest Americans. Income and economic power are being concentrated in fewer and fewer hands. The world in which we live is shrinking, and we need a better understanding of other countries and cultures. Futurists suggest that the next two decades will produce more change than has occurred in the last century. The half-life of knowledge is approximately eight years—that is, half of what you learn will be obsolete in eight years. The world store of knowledge is growing at a geometrically increasing rate.

Minority, particularly Hispanic, populations will continue to increase faster than the overall population. The non-Hispanic white population will drop from 65 percent in 2003 to 56 percent by 2020. By 2025, nearly one in four school-aged children will be Hispanic. In June 2003, there were 291 million people in the United States, 8 million more than forecast. This increase was caused by immigration—primarily of Latinos, now the largest minority representing 38.8 million and growing by nearly 10 percent every two years. As more Americans marry across racial lines, however, such categories will perhaps be less meaningful.

Twenty-four percent of children in the United States live with one parent and 4 percent live with neither parents. Eighty-one percent of the youth report that they use alcohol by twelfth grade. Approximately 50 percent of twelfth graders reported moderate to heavy drinking. Thirty percent have ridden with a driver who had been drinking. Sixteen percent of all white children and 37 percent of all black and Hispanic children live in poverty. Non-English speaking students went from 2.8 to 5.0 percent in the past two decades. Eight percent have attempted suicide. Forty-five percent of high school students had reported sexual intercourse.

The number of older Americans—the graying population—is increasing within our society. Overall, the elderly are the fastest growing segment of the population. Today only one household in four has a school-age child. As fewer adults have contact with children in their daily lives, there will probably be less political support for children in the future. Labor-intensive work is being outsourced to other nations, forcing American labor to compete with low-income workers in Third World countries. (For more information see: www.lcweb.loc.gov.)

The estimated U.S. federal budget deficit, approaching $4 trillion somewhere over the next five years, may slow economic growth and further reduce federal support to cash strapped state and local education budgets. Students will need to be well equipped for work in a high-tech world. Most of the new generation can tolerate hardship on a national level as long as it does not affect their personal prosperity.

Support for public schools has been on the decline since the late 1980s, and criticism and frustration with government-provided services continues into the twenty-first century. As a result, more and more political figures, from city mayors to the U.S. president, have advocated reform for education. Five times more 20-year-olds would rather own a business than hold a key position in politics or government. These views are strengthened by the strong American belief in the superiority of capitalism and the free market system. Ultimately, the result has been insecurity, unrest, disunity, disaffection, alienation, and resistance that has resulted in "a crisis of confidence in government." Murphy (1999, pp. 414–415) states:

> The attraction of more market-oriented forms of school governance can be traced to some extent to internal processes of self-destruction in the educational system. Three patterns of self-destruction are most salient: (1) the perceived failure of public schooling to deliver a quality product; (2) the seeming inability of education to heal itself; and (3) a growing disconnect between the public and public education. The consequence is a significant reinforcement of the "common and widely reiterated observation of a declining confidence in public education . . . [and] the mounting criticisms of the established form and content of publicly-funded educational systems" (Mayberry, 1991, p. 1 [as cited in Murphy, 1999]).

✱ **What structure and process will best allow schools like Nanuck to be both proactive and responsive to contextual issues at the federal, state, and local levels?**

Conclusion

Federal and state involvement in U.S. education centers around the recurring themes of educational excellence and educational opportunity. Educational excellence seeks to set higher standards; strengthen the curriculum, particularly in math and the sciences; set higher requirements for course work and graduation; and develop more rigorous grading, testing, homework, and discipline. Educational opportunity prompts efforts to improve school attendance, provide needed services, ensure that all Americans achieve minimum standards, and provide for multiculturalism, inclusiveness, and diversity. Money can be spent for enrichment programs directed toward gifted students or for special education and inclusion programs for needy students, or for both. Seeing the current state of education as a dichotomy oversimplifies the diverse interests and initiatives that have been prominent in developing federal and state education policy. The demand is growing to offer more choices for kids with different learning styles and abilities. The bottom line is to create schools that are constantly improving themselves and meeting the ever-changing demands of society.

Local school leaders are often challenged by conflicting desires, expressed at the federal, state, and local levels as part of the "great national debate on education." Joel Spring (1998) found that

> Conservative interest groups such as the Christian coalition and Eagle Forum advocate reduction in federal regulations and control. On the other hand, some interest groups such as those representing the disadvantaged and the disabled feel protected by strong federal control. The new professionals at the state and local levels are concerned with any changes in regulations that threaten their interests. . . . Although state politicians welcome control over federal programs, they worry about reduced federal spending. (p. 107)

Tip O'Neill, a past, well-respected member of the U.S. House of Representatives, once said, "All local politics are local." While local control and grassroots democracy remain a cherished tradition, the political power of localities has eroded. Gerald Tirozzi (2003, p. 59) states: "The new focus of power has shifted to the nation's statehouses and witnessed a greater involvement at the federal level. This shift must be clearly understood by school leaders as they chart a course for their schools and districts. It is imperative that school administrators analyze and comprehend the significance of the educational "megatrends" of the past 35 years, all of which have been largely directed by the political process." He goes on to say: "Educational leaders can either allow the political process to continue to set the school reform agenda (p. 59)" or "they can be active and vocal participants in the discourse, informing and instructing the debate with their expertise and experience . . . Administering a school district or school in an environment that is politically motivated is not a spectator sport—it needs active participants. Let's take the field!" (p. 59).

There are still many seeds of optimism about the future given the challenges to be faced in education today. Cetron and Cetron (2004, p. 29) suggest the following: "Yet we are cautiously optimistic about the future of education. In any poll, U.S. voters—the people who must pay for our schools—consistently cite education as the highest priority . . . If technology brings new challenges for our schools, it also provides a means to make schools more effective.

Ten years from now, teachers and administrators may look back on this decade as one of the most trying periods that U.S. schools have ever experienced. But if educators implement the reforms that the future demands, they will also remember this period as the time when they learned to give all their students an education suited to the modern, high-tech world.

Despite the crush of competing agendas and distractions, educational leaders must help to bring everyone's attention and efforts to bear on important educational goals for the future. All who have a stake in successful schools must be involved in the efforts to improve them. Their challenge in the twenty-first century will be to spell out and develop successful schools.

✳ **How will you build the needed political support for Nanuck Middle School? How might you use the political model to improve conditions at Nanuck and to create a clear vision of school improvement?**

Portfolio Artifacts

- Reexamine and redefine a school's vision or mission. Identify and address any barriers to accomplishing the vision.
- Verify that a school's vision, program, and/or instructional practice operates consistently within the parameters of federal, state, and local laws, standards, policies, regulations, and statutory requirements.
- Share information with colleagues regarding new ideas and directions acquired from the state or federal department of education or professional meetings.
- Demonstrate an understanding and articulation of the context that is operating within your school district.

- Demonstrate an ability to use accountability systems to produce reports of local, state, and federal compliance.
- Influence and support public policy that will result in the improvement of schools and student learning.
- Work with a state or city legislature to write a bill and get it passed.
- Join and actively participate in a political party.
- Attend a Senate, House of Representatives, or city council, Chamber of Commerce, or civic organization meeting.

Terms

Adequate yearly progress (AYP)	Elementary and Secondary Education Act	School reconstitution
Accountability	Equal educational opportunity	Safe School Plan
"Back seat" children	Graying of America	School choice
Block grants	High-stakes testing	School effectiveness research
Brown decision	National Education Standards	*Swann v. Charlotte-Mecklenburg Board of Education*
Business partners	National goals	U.S. Department of Education
Charter school	National mosaic (not a melting pot)	Vested interests
Context	NCLB	Vision
Desegregation	Opportunity scholarships	Vouchers
Equity and social justice		

Suggested Readings

Campbell, R. E., Cunningham, L. L., Nystrand, R. O., & Uslan, M. D. (1980). *The organization and control of American schools.* Columbus, OH: Charles E. Merrill Publishing.

Cooper, B., Fusarelli, B., & Randall, E. (2004). *Better policies, better schools: Theories and applications.* Boston: Allyn and Bacon.

Duke, D. (2004). *The challenge of educational change.* Boston: Allyn and Bacon.

Fiore, D. (2004). *Introduction to educational administration: Standards, theories, and practice.* Larchmont, NY: Eye on Education.

Fowler, F. (2004). *Policy studies for educational leaders: An introduction.* Columbus, OH: Merrill/Prentice Hall.

Goodlad, J. I., & McMannon, T. J. (Eds.). (1997). *The public purpose of education and schooling.* San Francisco: Jossey-Bass.

Heck, R. (2004). *Studying educational and social policy.* Mahwah, NJ: Lawrence Erlbaum Associates.

Kohn, A. (2001). *School: The story of American public education.* Boston: Beacon Press.

Murphy, J., & Forsyth, P. B. (1999). *Educational administration: A decade of reform.* Thousand Oaks, CA: Corwin Press.

Sergiovanni, T. J., Burlingame, M., Coombs, F. S., & Thurston, P. W. (1999). *Educational governance and administration.* Boston: Allyn and Bacon.

Tyack, D. (2002). *The One Best System: A history of urban education.* Cambridge, MA: Harvard University Press.

Tyack, D. (2003). *Seeking common ground: public schools in diverse society.* Cambridge, MA: Harvard University Press.

3

School Reform

Reform at Scrivner

You are the principal at Scrivner Middle School. Your math, social studies, science, and English departments all seem to be ready to focus effort on improving student achievement in the areas of reading, writing, mathematics, and science. The school board and Superintendent Melville have asked that you select one of the standard models (see pages 68–74) for improving instruction, collecting information about the model, developing a proposal on why the model best fits Scrivner, and upon approval joining the network of nationwide educators involved in developing and implementing the model. It is quite important to the Board and Superintendent Melville that the model selected be compatible with the integration of technology into each of the core subject areas. The combined reform model and integrated technology plan will be used at a later time at Scrivner to develop a comprehensive school improvement plan. You are now doing some of the initial groundwork regarding possible content for the plan; the process for school improvement planning and the budget will be devised at a later date.

The school division does not have a policy regarding implementing curriculum and instructional reform to ensure consistent and quality decision making. A policy is needed regarding agreed-upon criteria for evaluating and approv-ing reforms for the school. In fact, a number of the teachers are familiar with national reform efforts underway by prominent individuals and groups nationwide that they believe could hold considerable promise for Scrivner Middle School. Each of the models will need to be evaluated in regard to its educational merit and the technology integration initiative in order to select the one that is most compatible with the school's need to realign its core curriculum. Some members of the community and a number of teachers who are loyal to the existing curriculum have already begun to express concern that you and some of the teachers are chasing after the latest fads and not supporting existing programs. The school student council made an appeal, however, that the principal and teachers come up with a plan to remedy "the shortcomings" at the school, so all students will be prepared to meet the challenges they will face as adults and to take on a meaningful role in society. To convince parents, teachers, and students, information will need to be available on successful CSR reform efforts that are underway in other school divisions. Final decisions regarding reform will be based on which CSR initiatives will be most compatible to the desires for Scrivner Middle School as well as on their potential impact on student achievement.

✳ **Develop some general guidelines regarding the content of curricular and instructional reforms and the criteria that will be used to evaluate the comprehensive school reform models.**

Leading Innovative Schools

STEPHANIE PACE MARSHALL, PH.D. • *Mathematics and Science Academy, Aurora, Illinois*

What does it take to lead an innovative school (and by that I mean a transformative and generative learning community) for the twenty-first century? What are the conditions that leaders-in-learning must create, to prepare students to be pioneers in an unknown land? Perhaps a bit of history is important. For three centuries, the dominant scientific worldview was the image of a static, repetitive, predictable, linear, and clockwork universe. This "Newtonian" worldview has influenced and defined almost every dimension of our own cultural and organization life, including our schools.

Consequently, as leaders we focused on predictive cause-and-effect models of human learning; we became preoccupied with things and efficiently managed our schools by reducing them to discrete observable and measurable parts. Deriving our insight from "Newtonian" science, we behaved as if we actually believed that by understanding the parts we would discern the behavior of the whole and that analysis would inevitably lead to synthesis.

By design, we constructed and operated our "Newtonian" schools as we understood our world, and this produced learning disabled institutions that have suppressed reflective thought, creativity, and the innate and inexhaustible capacity for lifelong learning.

The unexamined application of "Newtonian" laws to learning environments diminished our capacity for continuous growth and change because it diminished our capacity to grow the individual and collective intelligence, spirit, and hope of the whole system.

We designed a linear system built on predictive models of change and a belief that learning was incremental, when in fact human systems are not predictable; change is nonlinear and learning is dynamic and patterned. Human beings do not follow the logic of cause and effect. We crave connectedness and meaning, we seek lasting and deep relationships, we grow by sharing and not by keeping secrets, and we need to trust and be trusted to feel safe enough to dare.

As a result, leaders of innovative learning communities need to create learning and teaching environments that enable learners to direct their own learning toward greater rigor, coherence, and complexity; to increase their intellectual, social, and emotional engagement with others; and to foster collaborative and dynamic approaches to learning that enable learners to develop thoughtful and integrative ways of knowing.

We must create a learning culture that provides a forum for risk, novelty, experimentation, and challenge and that redirects and personalizes learning. We must create learning communities for learners of all ages that can give power, time, and voice to their inquiry and their creativity. Such a community is governed by the principles of learning, not school, and is:

- *Personalized, flexible, and coherent.* Questions that are significant to the human condition drive the curriculum, and knowledge is not separated in distinct and unconnected disciplines.
- *Internally and externally connected.* It is not bounded by physical, geographic, or temporal space (because learning happens everywhere, student learning must transcend classroom and school boundaries).
- *Rich in information and flexible and diverse learning experiences.* It has pathways for all learners (students are actively engaged in meaningful research and inquiry; they study "big and important concepts in the

context of interdisciplinary problems that matter and that are relevant to the real word; students are engaged in meaningful research and serious inquiry).

- *Intergenerational in the configuration of learning experiences.* Margaret Mead has said that the healthiest learning environment occurs when three generations are learning together.
- *Grounded in collaborative inquiry.* Students engage with adults and peers and draw on the experiences of the entire group; learners are honored as capable of creating and generating knowledge, not just acquiring information.
- *Focused on complex cognition, problem finding, and problem resolution.* Students are engaged in authentic and meaningful dialogue with members of the internal and external community; they are taught skills that enable them to deal with complexity and with ambiguity and paradox.

Creating these conditions for generative learning is the work of innovative leaders, and it is fundamental to the creation of an environment that enables exceptional learning for all students.

Parker Palmer (1998), in his simple, yet profound book *The Courage to Teach*, offers the following essential insight about leaders and leading within a learning setting:

> If we are to have communities of discourse about teaching and learning—communities that are intentional about the topics to be pursued and the ground rules to be practiced—we need leaders who can call people toward that vision.
>
> Good talk about good teaching is unlikely to happen if presidents and principals, deans and department chairs . . . do not expect it and invite it into being. . . . This kind of leadership . . . involves offering people excuses and permission to do things that they want to do but cannot initiate themselves. . . . (p. 156). Becoming a leader of that sort—one who opens, rather than occupies, space—requires [an] "inner journey" . . . beyond fear into authentic self-hood, a journey toward respecting otherness and understanding how committed and resourceful we all are.

As those inner qualities deepen the leader becomes better able to open spaces in which people feel invited to create communities of mutual support . . . leaders call us back to the heart of teaching and learning, to the work we share and to the shared passion behind that work. (p. 161)

Lee Bolman and Terry Deal (1995) in their book *Leading with Soul* confirm Palmer's assertion, "Leadership is a relation rooted in community . . . " (p. 56) [whose essence is] "not giving things or even providing visions, it is offering one's self and one's spirit" (p. 102).

As leaders we have been trying to fix the parts. We now realize we must first change the way we think and relate with one another. We must create a new way of seeing and being in the world and this will cause us to change what we do.

The seventeenth-century Newtonian worldview created a mechanistic and machine-based metaphor for leadership. Now we know much better. We must take our metaphor for leading, not from a machine but from the biologic of living systems in the natural world.

As leaders we must seek to gain insight from the paradoxes that continuously confront our systems. We must:

- Create comfort with ambiguity.
- Create opportunities to allow energy, information, and the human spirit to flow within and throughout the system by facilitating authentic dialogue about teaching and learning.
- Promote diversity of all kinds.
- Establish communal relationships of meaning by inviting the hearts and souls of people into the learning environment.
- Look for patterns and relationships and explicitly identify and name them in order to promote the organization's sense of self and integrity.
- Celebrate the power of community and the human spirit.
- Create common language to build common meaning.
- Create trusting response-able and love-able learning communities.

For leaders in innovative schools our role is not to control but to facilitate authentic learning by creating conversations that matter. Conversations of community that invite the entire organization into shaping its future and into answering questions:

1. What is possible now?
2. What do we want to be in the world?
3. How can the world be different because of us?

Until recently threats to organizational survival were largely external in nature and driven by precipitous events leaders could strategically defend against. Now our threats are mostly internal, and their dynamic and systematic complexity requires leaders who can think and act in integrated, systematic, and spiritful ways.

The vision of educational leadership for innovative schools has changed from knowing what to do in order to control and manage to knowing how to live in order to unleash the synergy of the system. This is both our greatest challenge and our greatest opportunity.

We need courageous leaders who can think and act in integrative, systematic, and soulful ways and who are not afraid to create transformational learning communities that learn their way into the future by inviting and engaging in development of the fullness of human capacity.

The Context for School Reform

The concerns of people are that the times have changed and yet education has not. Schools have greatly improved student access but remain basically the same when almost all other aspects of our lives have been revolutionized. The response to these concerns was rapid and dramatic. A flurry of legislative action established goals, standards, accountability, teacher qualification, and new structures. Universities completely restructured their teacher and principal preparation programs, and superintendents and school boards experimented with new approaches and structures within their school districts to be more responsive to needed changes.

We, as educators, have created structures, we better understand the process, and we have established significant new standards and measures of assessment; the most important journey, however, still lies ahead of us. Now that we have built the needed capacity to change we must begin to rethink all aspects of schooling, given new needs and expectations and new technologies. The call is to transform the classroom, curricula, instruction, staffing, and relationships to parents and community (Carter & Cunningham, 1997; Martin, 1993; Noddings, 1992).

In an analysis of reform efforts since the 1950s, Fullan (1993) concludes:

We have learned that neither centralization (federal, state, or district) nor decentralization (school) by itself works. We also see that reform strategies struggle between overcontrol and chaos. The realization that initiating multiple innovations is the problem has shifted our attention to more comprehensive perspectives but has failed to provide a solution. Evidently, change is more complex than we realized. (p. 122)

Rand Institute research found little evidence that schools have changed. Theodore Sizer's experiences suggest that change in schools is exceedingly difficult and incentives are weak. The Business Coalition for Educational Reform found that introducing new approaches in education is very difficult. The National Science Foundation maintains that schools have minimum technology, which typically services existing practices. In general, research suggests reforms have had minimal impact on the long-range functioning of classrooms and schools (Carter & Cunningham, 1997). Schlechty (1997) is concerned that "unfortunately, too many educators seem to lack the sense of urgency it will take to bring about the kinds of reforms that are needed if public education is to be a vital force in American life into the twenty-first century" (p. 17).

✳ **What will be needed for reform to be successful at Scrivner Middle School?**

Finding New Directions

The improvements that are now called for address "what and how" subjects are taught, as well as how progress is measured and evaluated. They get at the technical core of the teaching and learning process. Students' performance, experiences, preparation, and outcomes become the driving force for the new reforms.

Certainly no educational improvements will occur if an organization has not built in the capacity to change. To succeed the people in it must use a great deal of care to create a culture and approach that motivates and supports participants. According to Brown and Anfare (2003), the capacity to support continuous improvement requires the administrator's knowledge and skill in the following areas:

1. Understand the nature, needs, strengths, and limitations of staff members.
2. Understand the relevance of the reform in terms of need, practicality, and complexity.
3. Assess the readiness of staff to become involved.
4. Ensure that the necessary resources and support are available, including the time to accomplish the task.
5. Work collaboratively with a critical mass of diverse constituents (teachers, community members, parents, etc.).
6. Understand that change is difficult and will be met with resistance.
7. Acknowledge that teachers must "own" the intended reform.
8. Ensure that excessive authority is not imposed from above.
9. Provide the professional development and education necessary to properly implement the intended reform.
10. Remember that structural changes will not ensure fundamental changes in the purposes, priorities, and functioning of a school by themselves.
11. Acknowledge that reform is a developmental process (p. 30).

However, improvements will not occur unless educators are encouraged to think about the significant opportunities that exist for their schools. Without a strong vision of what great twenty-first century schools look like, it is highly unlikely that capacity-building efforts will have much impact on classrooms, schools, or students. Capacity and vision must proceed hand in hand if we are to achieve any level of success.

Much of the research on planning and innovation has focused on decision making and the implementation process (Allison, 1971; Cohen & March, 1974; Etizoni, 1986; Hughes & Achilles, 1971; Janis & Mann, 1977; Lindblom, 1980; March & Simon, 1968; Mintzberg, 1989). In relating this literature to education, Michael Fullan (1991) found a problem with thinking in terms of a single innovation as a means to improvement. He found such an outlook excessively limiting. Fullan states:

> Instead of tracing specific policies and innovations, we turn the problem on its head, and ask what does the array of innovative possibilities look like. . . . Changes that increase schools' and districts' capacity and performance for continuous improvement— is the generic solution needed.
>
> Taking on one innovation at a time is fire fighting and faddism. Institutional development of schools and districts increases coherence and capacity for sorting out and integrating the myriad of choices, acting on them, assessing progress, and redirecting energies. (p. 349)

Other authors see innovation as a series of choices that organizations and thus individuals are constantly confronting in order to decide what is better than the idea it supersedes (Hall & Hord, 1987; Rogers, 1995). Probably the most important factor related to the speed of adoption and its ultimate success is the relative advantage as perceived by those who influence the decision and its ultimate success.

Innovations typically begin with the recognition of a need or problem. This recognition can occur through the political process, the rise of social problems, or a sense of present difficulties and future needs. Everett Rogers (1995) states:

> Many, but not all, technical innovations come out of research. The purpose of research is to advance knowledge, practice and/or to solve practical problems. Rogers defines development as "the process of putting a new idea into a form that is expected to meet the needs of an audience of potential adopters. . . . This represents an arena in which researchers come together with change agents. How are innovations evaluated? One way is through clinical trials, scientific experiments that are designed to determine prospectively the effects of an innovation in terms of efficacy, safety and the like. (p. 160)

It takes the genius of creative ideas, a vision of the future, and a knowledge of where we need to be to spark individuals to improve schools. The capacity is essential, but so are the ideas. (For more information see: ericir.syr.edu.) Eventually, when innovations are successful and are an improvement on what currently exists, they are implemented by leaders who serve as the innovative catalysts in their disciplines.

Those participating in the improvement of schools will need to orient their common efforts toward a shared vision of improvement as they develop creative insights, invent new schools, and prepare all students for life in a knowledge society (Carter & Cunningham, 1997).

The creation of effective new schools ultimately depends on the ability of educators to visualize how improved schools look. Vision converts ideas, knowledge, experience, and futurist thinking into a reality that is clearly understood and achievable by practitioners. Vision provides the bridge between innovative ideas and purposeful, coordinated action. Therefore, it is critically important that educators be aware of the latest thinking, of what holds the greatest promise for improving education. The vision of an ideal school helps them to rework and reshape existing curriculum content, instructional methods, and delivery systems.

Educators must stop tinkering with the existing paradigms of education and rethink all aspects of schooling, given new needs and expectations and new technologies and to make the shift to a new paradigm (Sparks, 1997).

Common Themes in a Changing World

Professionals need some school-reform guidelines in order to know what to keep, what to throw away, and what to build anew. Recent studies suggest that it will be imperative for schools to emphasize lifelong learning, thinking, and problem solving.

This begins with preschool education, which some believe will provide lifetime dividends (Bracey, 2003). Research suggests that those who attend preschool have higher school completion rates, higher test scores, earn more money, have reduced crime rates, and fewer special education placements. There is still limited agreement on such outcomes, however, and on the effectiveness of preschool educational placements. As in many such programs, it is the cost-benefit analysis of the investment that is receiving attention.

They must also stress actively applying learning, moral reasoning, writing and speaking effectively, researching information, using new technologies, and listening to and understanding others. The traditional emphasis on acquiring knowledge and skills is giving way to a greater emphasis on learning how to think intelligently and the application of knowledge as needed within a specific context. The most recent guidelines are based on Bloom's (1956) higher order of learning: analysis, synthesis, and evaluation.

New schools are expected to provide many more learning options for students who have different learning styles and brain functioning. They must incorporate what we have learned from recent brain research, including that on infant and toddler development and learning (Gardner, 1993). Teachers need to help students develop understanding, inferential skills, and strategic knowledge and to advance their thinking skills. The most powerful models in instruction are interactive and generative—engaging and encouraging the learner to construct and produce knowledge in meaningful ways. Students teach others interactively and interact generatively with their teachers and peers (Education Commission of the States, 1991).

More than ever before, technology is at the forefront of a rapidly changing world. Information technology is driving change at an accelerated rate. Like their forebears, children must become pioneers as they move into a future of change and great adventure, where technology allows them to access information from anywhere in the world in a matter of seconds.

The American Association of School Administrators (1993) completed a study ranking critical elements in "preparing students for the twenty-first century." In part, the top-ranked items included:

1. *Academic content.* Use of math, logic, reasoning, and writing skills, functional/operational literacy; critical interpersonal skills; use of technology to assess or process information.

2. *Behaviors.* Exercise of honesty, integrity, the golden rule, respect for effort, the work ethic, discipline; respect for multiculturalism and diversity; appreciation for individual contributions, ability to work with team members.
3. *Essential skills.* Teaching of oral/written communication; critical thinking, problem solving, reasoning, analytical skills; responsibility for one's actions, discipline and ethics; ability to assess one's goals.
4. *Changes in schools.* Incorporation of "marketplace" technology in learning and as part of exit criteria; accommodation of new technology; promotion of active versus passive learning; provision of more time for professional development, particularly in technology; clarification of students' goals and standards; incorporation of more real-world projects; and increase in parental and community involvement in schools.

A child's education should be authentically grounded; subjects should be integrated (NCTAF, 1997). It is clear that we need citizens who can think strategically to create visions, learn in a constantly changing environment, build knowledge from a wide range of sources, understand systems in diverse contexts, and collaborate both locally and globally using technology.

The President's Committee of Advisors on Science and Technology's Report to the President (1997) stated that the private sector demands workers with the skills needed to compete in the "information society." There is a potential for radically different methods of teaching and learning using the range of technological possibilities—changing what is learned, how it is learned, how it is measured, and what the teacher does in the classroom. There is a clearly stated goal of connecting every school to the National Information Infrastructure (NII) and providing training on how to use this tremendous information communication library.

Technology will be a major supporting tool for all learning, and students will work on projects through distance learning with other students and professionals at diverse locations. The technology will be based on powerful learning paradigms that allow students and teachers to work on authentic and challenging problems, interact with real data in ways that allow student control, build knowledge within a learning community, and involve practicing professionals and community mentors. Virtual reality will be used to bring life to knowledge and classroom activities. The classroom will be a knowledge-building learning community.

The types of reforms required are major in scope, discontinuous with the past, and transformational. Box 3.1 summarizes some of these major new demands on education.

Innovative Programs

The new reforms must prove themselves in the classroom, and when successful they must be woven into the basic fabric of the school and school district (Cunningham & Gresso, 1993; Goety, Floden, & Oday, 1996; Murphy, 1991; Murphy & Hallinger, 1993; Elmore, Peterson, & McCarthy, 1996). (For more information see: www.temple.edu/iss/csr-info.htm.)

BOX 3.1 • *New Demands to Change Pedagogical Models*

From	To
Teacher–Curriculum-centered	Learner-centered
Acquisition of knowledge and skills	Intelligent thinking and knowledge application
Individual tasks	Collaborative work (speaking and listening skills)
Passive learning (listener)	Active learning (collaborator)
Printed media	Technological tools
Grade focus	Achievement focus
National perspective	Global perspective
Independent efforts	Combined efforts
Abstract learning (facts)	Authentic learning (relationships, inquiry, invention, understanding)
Rote learning (drill and practice)	Problem solving (communication, creativity, access, expression)
Paper-and-pencil tests (norm-referenced)	Demonstrations and performances (criterion-referenced)
Discipline-based	Integrative/interdisciplinary/ transdisciplinary approaches

One approach, called Comprehensive School Reform (CSR), seeks to improve student performance by addressing and aligning all aspects of the school's operations using the guiding philosophy, vision, and practices of a specific model. These models typically bring a clear blueprint for how the school should be operated in regard to standards, curriculum, and instructional practices. Interest in this approach grew in 1998 when Congress appropriated $150 million for the CSR Demonstration program presently called the CSR Program (CSRP) now under Title I of the NCLB Act. The CSRP encourages schools to adopt an established scientifically based, reform model.

According to Borman, Hewes, Overman, and Brown (2003), "Schools that implement CSR models for 5 years or more showed particularly strong effects, and the benefits were consistent across schools of varying poverty levels (p. 125)." These programs have now been implemented in thousands of schools serving millions of students and can be transported to schools throughout the United States. In many cases, the developer provides professional development, technical support, curricular materials, performance assessment, pedagogical practices, and so on to help educators successfully implement the philosophy and/or programs.

The U.S. Department of Education (2002) defines CSR on the basis of the following eleven components:

1. Employs proven methods for student learning, teaching, and school management that are founded on scientifically based research and effective practices and have been replicated successfully in schools.

2. Integrates instruction, assessment, classroom management, professional development, parental involvement, and school management.
3. Provides high-quality and continuous teacher and staff professional development and training.
4. Includes measurable goals for student academic achievement and establishes benchmarks for meeting those goals.
5. Is supported by teachers, principals, administrators, and other staff throughout the school.
6. Provides support for teachers, principals, administrators, and other school staff by creating shared leadership and a broad base of responsibility for reform efforts.
7. Provides for the meaningful involvement of parents and the local community in planning, implementing, and evaluating school improvement activities.
8. Uses high-quality external technical support and assistance from an entity that has experience and expertise in schoolwide reform and improvement, which may include an institution of higher education.
9. Includes a plan for the annual evaluation of the implementation of the school reforms and the student results achieved.
10. Identifies the available federal, state, local, and private financial and other resources that schools can use to coordinate services that support and sustain the school reform effort.
11. Meets one of the following requirements: Either the program has been found, through scientifically based research, to significantly improve the academic achievement of participating students, or strong evidence has shown that the program will significantly improve the academic achievement of participating children.

Borman and colleagues (2003) completed a meta-analysis of twenty-nine CSR models. Table 3.1 provides a presentation of their work related to number of sites, cost, and effectiveness categories. Some of the conclusions that they drew from their meta-analysis are the following:

- Effects of CSR appear greater than effects of other interventions.
- Methodological differences across studies tell more about the different effects than program components of CSR models.
- Models meeting the highest standard are the only CSR models to succeed across varying contexts and study designs and to be expected to improve test scores.
- The strong effect after the fifth year of implementation can be explained by cumulative impact or self-selection artifacts.

These researchers concluded:

> We challenge the developers and the educational research community to make a long-term commitment to research-proven educational reform and to establish a marketplace of scientifically based models capable of bringing comprehensive reform to the nation's schools (2003, p. 169–170).

TABLE 3.1 Listing of Programs Along with One of the Four Effectiveness Categories

Model	Number of Replication Sites	First-year cost Personnel	First-year cost Non-personnel	High Effectiveness Strongest Evidence	High Effectiveness Promising Evidence	Promising Evidence	Greatest Need for Additional Research
Accelerated Schools Projected	1,300	$13,543	$14,585			X	
America's Choice School Design	450	$104,181	$93,763			X	
Atlas Communities	105	$8,334	$93,763			X	
Audrey Cohen College	16	$78,135	$89,595				X
Center for Effective Schools	1,000	$52,175	$55,000				X
Child Development Program	165	$95,675	$65,000				X
Coalition of Essential Schools	1,000	$1	$250,000				X
Community for Learning	118	$78,135	$85,428				X
Community Learning Centers	15	$1	$61,700				X
Co-NECT Schools	198	$1	$612,582				X
Core Knowledge	1,020	$1	$58,341				X
Different Ways of Knowing	600	$1	$87,512				X
Direct Instruction	300	$52,090	$202,110	X			X
Edison Project	136	$13,023	$72,926				X
Expeditionary Learning Outward Bound	93	$1	$84,386		X		
High Schools That Work	1,300	$1	$50,007				X
High/Scope Primary Grades	100	$1	$135,435				X
Integrated Thematic Instruction	1,434	$1	$61,235				X
Micro Society®	200	$52,175	$67,450				X
Modern Red Schoolhouse	110	$1	$223,988		X		
Montessori	1,000	$159,723	$780,000			X	
Onward to Excellence	1,000	$12,502	$62,508				X
Paideia	100	$52,090	$100,013			X	
Roots and Wings	200	$208,361	$72,926		X		
School Development Program	600	$13,543	$33,338	X			
Success for All	1,800	$208,361	$72,926	X			
Talent Development High Schools	35	$31,254	$28,129				X
The Learning Network	200	$52,175	$32,188			X	
Urban Learning Center	29	$10,418	$165,647				X

*The four categories were based on quality and quantity of evidence and statistically significant and positive results. A compilation of findings from G. Borman, G. Hewes, L. Overman and S. Brown (Summer 2003) "Comprehensive School Reform and Achievement: A Meta-Analysis." *Review of Educational Research, 73,* 2, 125–230. Copyright 2003 by the American Educational Research Association. Reproduced with permission of the publisher.

Most lists of the more prominent efforts to improve classroom instruction include:

Accelerated Schools Project (K–8).   H. Levin. Operates on the premise that at-risk students must learn at an accelerated pace to catch up with more advantaged peers. Training and training materials provided. Phone: (860) 486-3672; www. acceleratedschools.net.

America's Choice (K–12).   NCEE. Holds students to high standards in such core subjects as language arts, mathematics, and science. Uses early identification and accelerated strategies and provides needed materials. Phone: (202) 783-3612; www.ncee.org/ac/intro.html.

Association for Direct Instruction (K–6).   Emphasizes carefully planned lessons that are designed around a highly specific knowledge base and a well-defined set of skills. Phone: (541) 485-1293; www.adihome.org.

Atlas Communities (Pre-K–12).   Seeks to coordinate a Pre-K–12 "pathway" to provide a coherent education program for each student from the first day of school until high school graduation. Materials provide authentic curriculum, instruction, and assessment. Phone: (617) 969-7100; www.edc.org/FSC/ATLAS.

Audrey Cohen College: Purpose-Centered Education (K–12).   Provides a thematic focus to education, with a secondary goal of increasing attendance and decreasing disciplinary problems. Materials and training provided. Phone: (212) 343-1234; www.audrey-cohen.edu.

The Coalition of Essential Schools (K–12).   T. Sizer. Features a set of "Common Principles" interdisciplinary instruction, authentic projects, and mastery that are intended to be used by schools to shape their own reform efforts. Phone: (510) 433-1451; www.essentialschools.org.

Community for Learning (K–12).   M. Wang. Based on collaboration with homes, libraries, museums, and community on learning, this program encourages the coordination of classroom instruction with community services. Phone: (800) 759-1495; www.temple.edu/LSS.

Co-NECT Schools (K–12).   A. Skoler. Focuses on improving student achievement by integrating technology into instruction, reorganizing schools into multigrade clusters of students and teachers, and organizing lessons around interdisciplinary projects. Print and online materials provided. Phone: (617) 995-3100; www. co-nect.net/.

Expeditionary Learning Outward Bound (K–12).   Based on two central ideas: Students learn better by doing, not listening, and developing character, high expectations, authentic projects, and a sense of community is as important as academic skills. Materials provided. Phone: (845) 424-4000; www.elob.org.

High Schools That Work (9–12).   SREB. Designed to raise the academic achievement of career-bound high school students by upgrading the academic core and combining content of college prep studies with vocational studies. Phone: (404) 875-9211; www.sreb.org.

Modern Red Schoolhouse (K–12).   Helps schools set high academic standards that are consistent with district and state assessments. Works with schools to build challenging curriculum, high standards, and technology support. Phone: (888) 275-6774; www.mrsh.org.

Paideia (K–12).   M. Adler. Changes classroom practice through three "columns" of instruction: didactic teaching, coaching, and Socratic seminars. Phone: (336) 334-3729; www.paideia.org.

Roots and Wings (pre-K–8).   R. Slavin. Used in conjunction with the Success for All reading program, Roots and Wings seeks to improve academic achievement in elementary schools, using prescribed curriculum, integrated science and social studies, cooperative learning, and support teams. Materials provided. Phone: (800) 548-4998; www.successforall.net.

School Development Program (K–8).   J. Comer. Based on the theory that children learn better when they form strong relationships with adults, this program aspires to develop personal, social, and moral strengths in students. Training, manuals, and teaching materials provided. Phone: (203) 737-4008; www.schooldevelopment program.org.

Success for All (Pre-K–8).   R. Slavin. Strives to ensure students' success in reading through nine components, such as a prescribed curriculum, cooperative learning, family support, and one-to-one tutoring. Phone: (800) 548-4998; www.successforall. net.

Talent Development High School (9–12).   Aims to reorganize students and teachers in a school and to focus instruction on students' academic needs and career interests by dividing large urban high schools into smaller units. Phone: (410) 516-8800; www.csos.jhu.edu/tdhs/index.htm.

Urban Learning Centers (Pre-K–12).   Connects an academically rigorous curriculum across grade levels and ensures the support of parents and community through teaching and learning, thematic interdisciplinary curriculum, school-to-work transition, governance and management, and learning supports. Phone: (213) 622-5237; www.urbanlearning.org.

Basic School Network.   Builds a sense of community, develops a coherent curriculum, creates a climate that supports student learning, and develops student character. Phone: (540) 568-7098; www.jmu.edu/basicschool/.

Center for Effective Schools (K–12).   PDK. Provides a structure for reform based on seven guiding principles, such as frequent monitoring of student progress and instructional leadership. Books, videos, and other materials provided. Phone: (800) 766-1156; www.pdkintl.org.

Child Development Project (K–6). Helps schools become caring communities of learning, featuring a reading–language arts curriculum based on literature, cooperative learning, schoolwide community-building activities, and more. Phone: (510) 533-0213; www.devstu.org.

Core Knowledge (K–8). E. Hirsch. Based on the premise that to function well in society, people need a common base of knowledge. Schools are responsible for providing this knowledge to students. Curriculum guidelines provided. Phone: (800) 238-3233; www.coreknowledge.org.

Community Learning Centers (Pre-K–adult). W. Jennings. Does not provide a prescribed curriculum, but instead encourages schools to act as brokers, arranging learning experiences within and beyond its walls so that the achievement of all learners is dramatically increased. Phone: (651) 645-0200; www.designlearn.net/clc.html.

Direct Instruction (K–6). S. Engelmann. Provides reading, language arts, and math curricula along with highly scripted lesson strategies, extensive writing, highly interactive lessons, flexible grouping, and frequent assessments so that by fifth grade students are at least a year and a half beyond grade level. Phone: (877) 485–1973; www.nifdi.org.

Different Ways of Knowing (K–7). Galef Institute. Advocates building on students' multiple intelligences to develop student skills in such areas as logic, mathematics, language, and the arts. Phone: (323) 525-0042; www.dwoknet.galef.org.

Edison Schools (K–12). C. Whittle. Establishes partnership schools with the school district or charter schools and provides an educational program, technology plan, Success for All, and management system. Curriculum material are provided. Phone: (212) 419-1600; www.edisonschools.com.

The Foxfire Fund (K–12). "Core Practices" guide instructional methods, materials, and strategies and encourage active, learner-centered, community-focused education. Phone: (706) 746-5828; www.foxfire.org.

High/Scope K–3 Model (K–3). D. Weibart. Works to improve children's problem-solving and independent-thinking skills; based on the belief that children should be active participants in their own learning. Manipulatives, learning centers, portfolio assessment, and so on. Phone: (734) 485-2000; www.highscope.org.

Integrated Thematic Instruction (K–12). S. Kovalik. Uses current brain research to maximize student learning by creating a "bodybrain–compatible" learning environment. Phone: (253) 631-4400; www.kovalik.com.

League of Professional Schools (K–12). Intends to democratize education by encouraging school staff, parents, students, and community members to play an active role in decision making about teaching and learning. Phone: (706) 542-2516; www.coe.uga.edu/lps/.

The Learning Network (K–8).   R. Owen. Emphasis on the Literacy Learning Model providing teacher handbooks, professional resources and development, classroom observation, and instructional dialogue in order to support schoolwide changes for improved learning outcomes for children. Phone: (914) 232-3903; www.rcowen.com.

MicroSociety (K–12).   G. Richmond. Students collaborate with parents, teachers, and community members to create a community of commerce and governance; children create and manage business ventures that produce goods and services. Phone: (215) 922-4006; www.microsociety.org.

Montessori (Pre-K–8).   M. Montessori. Incorporates the understanding of children's natural tendencies as they unfold in specific multiage group environments; curriculum is interdisciplinary and active. Phone: (440) 834-4011; www.montessori-namta.org.

Onward to Excellence (K–12).   NWREL. Builds school capacity for continual improvement through curriculum, mapping a series of workshops that help schools learn to set schoolwide goals and evaluate progress. Phone: (503) 275-9615; www.nwrel.org/scpd/ote.

QuEST (K–12).   Enables administrators, teachers, and students to build and sustain quality learning environments by improving the processes of the school. Phone: (517) 381-0917; www.ec-quest.com.

Ventures Initiative and Focus Systems (K–12).   Synthesizes applied teaching and learning methods through a step-by-step approach geared toward effective classroom management and school functioning. Phone: (212) 696-5717; e-mail: mbleich@ventures.org.

Source: Compiled from American Institutes of Research's *An Educator's Guide to Schoolwide Reform;* Northwest Regional Educational Laboratory's *Catalog of School Reform Models* (1st ed.); and J. McChesney and E. Hertling (April, 2000). "The path to comprehensive school reform," *Educational Leadership* 57, 7:10–15; www.eric.uoregon.edu. Descriptions of more reform models are available at www.nwrel.org/scpd/natspec/catalog/index/html and www.aasa.org/reform/approach.htm.

Students engage in partner reading and work in teams toward mastery and engage students in activities that enable them to apply everything. Students become active participants in scientific discovery and historical events. They use fine arts, music, computers, videos, and other technology to prepare all forms of multimedia reports. They participate in simulations that help to make what they learn immediately relevant. Students carry out experiments, investigations, and projects. An after-school program is offered to all children to further supplement regular classroom work (Slavin et al., 1996). Another possible theme is the creation of an inviting, engaging school climate that begins with teachers earning the trust and respect of their students' families and welcoming and supporting students in the classroom (Comer, Joyner, & Haynes, 1996). Schools are improved by increasing parental presence and through the use of child-centered concepts and beliefs for all students. Other factors include applying action-research; increasing instructional time and student engagement; matching curriculum, instruction, and tests; and using a developmental approach.

Generalizing, finding new examples, carrying out applications, working through understanding performances, and other activities press learners to think well beyond what they already know (Gardner, 1993). Learning is often structured around consequences, impact, dramatizations, connectability, relationships, insights, and responsibilities, which help to induce understanding.

Rubrics provide criteria for ongoing assessment throughout the learning process to support reflective activities. Portfolios are an example of ongoing assessment. The emphasis is on students' active engagement with teachers in the assessment of their own and classmates' work. Thus, use of generative topics, an understanding of goals and performances, and ongoing assessment are the core elements of all teaching for understanding (Gardner & Boix-Mansilla, 1994; Perkins & Blythe, 1994; Simmons, 1994).

Other Innovative Models and Their Benefits

This brief review provides limited information on a few of the major reform efforts existing in America today. Other efforts underway include John Goodlad's School Renewal Project, Phillip Schlechty's Leadership for School Reform, Dorothy Rich's Mega Skills, Lawrence Lezotte's Total Quality Effective Schools, Gordon Cawelti's Project on Redefining General Education, William Spady's Transformational Approach to Outcome-Based Education, character education, and Reading Recovery. In addition, many companies, such as Jostens Learning, IBM, Apple Education, Computer Curriculum Corporation, and many others, have introduced a number of new courseware systems for improving education. The Bill and Melinda Gates Foundation has invested more than $250 million in grants for the creation of new small schools and the transformation of large schools into mini-schools. The New American Schools Development Corporation tested ideas on school reform and settled on seven designs that it is broadly marketing.

Systems are being designed to review and rate these models. For example, the American Institutes for Research, based in Washington, DC, developed *Consumer Reports*–style effectiveness ratings for many of the various reform models. We will learn much from this work over the next five to ten years. The Consortium for Policy Research in Education (CPRE) has reviewed many of these systemic reforms and provides a set of criteria for evaluating improvement proposals. In evaluating some of these schoolwide reform models, Fashola and Slavin (1998) conclude that:

> it is apparent from the discussion of the currently available schoolwide reform models that much more research is needed to make available a substantial "shelf" of proven models. Yet what we do know now is that schools need not start from scratch in designing effective schoolwide plans. A wide array of promising programs are available, backed up by national networks of trainers, fellow users,

materials, assessment and other resources. . . . Once a school has chosen to affiliate with a national program, it can then work out how to implement the national model with integrity, intelligence, and sensitivity to local needs and circumstances. (p. 378)

To date, there have been five major practitioner-oriented reviews, or "catalogs," of CSR models (see Herman et al., 1999; Northwest Regional Educational Laboratory, 1998, 2000; Slavin & Fashola, 1998; Traub, 1999; Wang, Haertel, & Walberg, 1997). These publications offer information that is important for educators to consider when "shopping" for a reform model.

Modern pedagogy is a complex process requiring a delicate and insightful type of teaching. The use of preexisting models and related networks serves as an organizing tool, reduces isolation, and gives teachers the confidence to try out new ideas in their own classrooms. The network provides needed staff development, program support, and professional affiliation. Teachers can often visit other sites that have implemented the same model to learn from one another (Sizer, 1996). New successes at any one location can be quickly shared among all classrooms and schools using the same model. (For more information see: web66.coled.umn.edu.)

✳ **Select a comprehensive school reform model using the criteria developed earlier and provide a rationale for why this model was chosen.**

A Framework for School Improvement

CARL GLICKMAN, LEW ALLEN, AND JAMES WEISS • *The University of Georgia*

School leaders need to ensure that the focus, structure, and process of their work with faculty and staff is always focused on teaching and learning. In more than a decade of successful collaborations with more than one hundred K–12 public schools ("The League of Professional Schools"), we have found that a commitment to the beliefs and practices of democracy in learning and in governance is essential. This is accomplished through a three-part framework.

The framework consists of a covenant of teaching and learning, a shared governance process, and an action research process. The goal of implementing this three-part framework is to create a school that is a self-renewing, learning community that is focused on students. All three parts of the framework are of equal importance; neglect of any one will greatly compromise a school's efforts.

Covenant of Teaching and Learning
A covenant captures the beliefs that people in a school and its immediate community hold about

exemplary teaching and learning. A school's goals, objectives, activities, curriculum, and instructional practices are filtered through the question: Are they within the letter and spirit of our covenant?

A covenant of teaching and learning allows a school to embrace certain instructional practices that are consistent with the beliefs of the school community, as well as to discern practices that are not. Without a covenant to help define and clarify a school's beliefs and practices, the collective energy of the individuals in the school is often fragmented or focused on the immediate issues of the day rather than on what all would agree, in their more reflective moments, should be done to achieve the long-term goals of the school community.

It is important that a covenant of teaching and learning reflect the voices of everyone in the school. The collegial discussions and deep reflections about teaching and learning that go into creating a covenant are crucial. A covenant written in isolation deprives those not involved of the experience of participating in a collegial dialogue about their deeply held, and often unexamined, beliefs about teaching and learning. A covenant that doesn't reflect all voices in the school will not likely serve as a guide to people's work.

Shared Governance

Shared governance is the process through which people democratically decide how to bring the covenant to life in the school. The shared governance process includes agreements as to how decisions are made and which roles will be assumed by administrators, teachers, staff, students, parents, and community members. Defining the structure and composition of decision-making bodies and the process by which decisions are made are crucial components. Time and energy must be taken to ensure that everyone understands the rules so that all can benefit from them. Rules of governance must be democratically established before decisions are made, not as decisions are being made.

A clearly written shared governance model that lays out how decisions are to be made ensures that all in the school know the rules, and the processes and procedures will not change on the whims of a few or for expediency. Schools trying to implement a new decision-making process sometimes find themselves with two decision-making processes functioning at once: the old process and the new process. Creating a specific shared governance model can help a school pick its way through this difficult transition.

Action Research

Action research can first help a school identify, clarify, plan, and evaluate actions that will bring the beliefs articulated in its covenant to life. A school's ability to bring about schoolwide renewal that benefits students is closely tied to its capacity to study and reflect on how its practices are affecting students.

Staying focused on student goals is remarkably difficult. It is easier to document whether programs, new initiatives, or new structures have been put in place than it is to study what is happening to students. For example, it is much easier to study whether teachers are using more cooperative learning techniques in their classrooms than it is to gather data on the effects that cooperative learning is having on students. An action research process that is focused on students can help keep a school on track while informing the decision-making process as to what is working and what needs further attention.

Summary

A school renewal framework will provide a school with a structure that allows it to define for itself where it wants to go (covenant), how it wants to get there (shared governance), and how it will know if it is making progress (action research). Everyone in the school is systematically and collegially learning about and getting better at creating experiences for students that support this concept. Teachers are part of a community of learners working together to bring about a common vision of what their school is all about.

Harnessing Technology

The U.S. Department of Labor states that only eight of fifty-four careers, projected to have the most growth potential over the next five years, do not require technological fluency. Thus, the increasing importance of technology in the workplace and daily life makes it meaningful for students and critical in education today (Duhaney & Zemel, 2000). Studies also show that students with access to either computer-assisted instruction, integrated learning systems technology, simulations and software (that teaches higher order thinking and uses collaborative networked technologies) or design and programming technologies show positive gains on researcher-constructed tests, standardized tests, and national tests (Schacter, 1999). Although there is significant support for the need to create integrated technological programs in our schools today, research suggests that school use of technology is limited to learning games, drill and practice, and/or occasional word processing with almost no integration of technology. (For more information see: www.iste.org.)

Technology can bring resources not previously available to the typical classroom to support the teaching–learning process. In fact, teachers and students are now able to exchange their ideas and experiences with individuals anywhere on the globe, thus removing classroom walls. Teachers have the capacity to download homework and display student portfolios. Parents have the ability to schedule appointments with their child's teacher and facilitate conferences with the assistance of visual and audio aides. Administrators possess the functionality to offer curriculum tips through bulletin-board functions and deliver training through customized feedback programs. Superintendents have access to school personnel in real-time and school performance reports ranging from financial data to graduation statistics and testing data. Members of the Board of Education have the ability to monitor all schools within their district from their home computers.

Students, teachers, and others can have instant access to student work and create notes or comments or talk directly to the originator via the computer. People can create networks to participate in discussions or conferences on shared topics and interests. Volunteers in various organizations can answer students' questions, comment on their work, and pose questions for students to address. Students are also able to experience history, geography, museums, and the like through virtual learning.

Communications with parents can occur through the computer. Parents will have access to student assignments and work and be able to leave notes and schedule appointments (through distance conferencing). Parents can work with their children at home and have computer access to classroom materials twenty-four hours a day. Teachers can instantly access students' performance records to determine what students are having trouble learning. They can access a resource repository for advice on how to best reach students who are having trouble and apply specific content, curriculum, and instructional strategy.

Students can check out computer disks that allow for direct learning from faraway libraries. Students will be able to abstract information from different sources and include it in their multimedia reports and presentations. The computer becomes a window to the whole world. Students partner with children in other cities, states, and nations to complete research and reports, working together via the computer. Students in classrooms at diverse locations talk directly with other students presenting joint multimedia reports and other presentations. Constructivist types of learning accelerate as we move the limits beyond those of classrooms.

To meet these technological challenges, we will need to make profound changes in the way we prepare future administrators and teachers (www.ed.gov/teachtech/about.html). We must ensure that our future administrators and teachers are trained to enter tomorrow's schools prepared to use technology-infused methods. Technology must be integrated into subject area content and methods classes and into college students' field experiences (Moursund & Beilefeldt, 1999). In order to provide a more shared understanding of what teachers and administrators need to know about technology, the International Society of Technology Education (ISTE) created the National Education Technology Standards for Teachers (NETS-T) and The National Technology Standards for Administrators (NETS-A).

The future of education will be changed by instructional technology applications such as broadband internet access, open-source software, wireless internet access, and groupware or online collaboration. In addition, focusing on e-learning, there are at least four different categories of learning strategies—individual, assisted, collaborative, and reciprocal. For example, collaborative uses a mix of synchronous learning such as face-to-face teaching and collaborative online activities such as virtual classrooms, web seminars, coaching, conference calls, online meetings, video conferencing, instant messaging, chats, all of which take place in real time (all participants online simultaneously). Reciprocal uses a form of self-paced asynchronous learning (independent of time and space) among collaborative groups using web pages, e-mail, simulations, bulletin boards, video streaming, computer-based instructional modules, assessments, recorded events, and so on. The point is that issues surrounding the use and adoption of different learning systems, network services, and technologies are relatively complex (Khan, 2001). Administrations will be expected to acquire familiarity with the related technologies in order to be able to communicate with the experts and to implement and use these developing technologies in their schools.

In addition, there are thousands of educational sites on the World Wide Web (www or web) widely ranging in quality and reliability. Martindale, Cates, and Qian (2003, p. 47) suggest that, "this massive collection of online learning materials and activities is largely unfiltered, particularly when compared to the process of print publishing." Organizations such as the International Academy of Digital Arts and Sciences, Homeschool.com, *PC Magazine,* and the Eisenhower National Clearinghouse for Mathematics and Science Education publish lists of what they believe to be the best educational websites (www.ehc.org/weblinks/dd/; www.webbyawards.com/main/; www.pcmag.com/category20,4148,7488,00.asp; www.homeschool.com/top100/1999.htm). Also, there are nonprofit sites (www.usgs.gov/) and commercial sites (//206.166.221.131/spacecamp/welcome.jsp).

In addition, there is much administrative/instructional software to store, access and query student data, grading rubrics, staff data, assessment data, student performance data, historic data, discipline data, financial data, inventory data, and so forth. Selecting among the various administrative and instructional systems softwares can be a daunting, even overwhelming, task as is the maintenance and use of these rich data bases. These systems bring up security, privacy, liability, engagability, user-friendliness, accuracy, affordability, efficiency, accessibility, flexibility, reliability, and many other related issues. Regardless of the complexity, technology offers a rich source for improved teaching, learning, and administration that far out weigh the challenges they present to twenty-first century educators (www.ed.psu.edu/acsde/researchsummaries.htm#costbenefit).

The role of learner will be much more active, programs will be more customized for types of learners, and learning will become more learner-centered. Instruction will be reusable and shared, and learners will become more responsible for time management and progress through the instructional system. Instruction will be continuously up-to-date and assessments will provide timely feedback regarding a student's progress. Students who are ready can become involved in authentic learning and higher-order thinking.

Online instruction also appeals to most students due to the flexibility and convenience it offers. It teaches self-discipline and initiative. Certainly, these changes cannot be made overnight; however, educators must continue to build upon existing systems to develop the network and software technologies needed to support excellent teaching and learning that fully engage the mind (Allen, 2003). The bottom line is that technology should never completely eliminate the opportunity for face-to-face instruction, but it certainly provides an important resource for learning that should be integrated into almost every subject and lesson as it will be in approximately 92 percent of all jobs that these students will ultimately aspire to and be a majority component of their personal lives.

Technology does have its critics when it comes to depending too much on the computer to instruct students, particularly in the lower grades. Harvard Professor Alvin Poussaint and a number of child advocacy groups like the Alliance for Childhood argue that too much dependence on computers can damage the health and intellectual and social development of our children. Complaints include shrinking attention spans, decreasing motivation and imagination, increased loneliness and isolation, problems with risk taking and negotiating political situations, and possibly eye problems. Some of these concerns can be limited by having students work in pairs and teams when they are on the computer. The consensus seems to be that technology's and the computer's advantages far outweigh any of the disadvantages. Susan Haugland summarizes research that shows that technology can provide a very rich environment for learning, which increases intelligence, nonverbal communication skills, long-term memory, and self-esteem. (For more information see: www.childrenandcomputers.com.)

Technology Opens New Opportunities

Technology presents unprecedented opportunities for educators to create new paradigms of education that greatly expand the limited possibilities that exist in traditional schools. Technology provides access to much more and recent information, involving a greater number of people and assisting in instruction for both students and staff. The new technology will require new curricula, new instruction, and new staff development strategies. Educators must create a technology culture that parallels those students find outside schools. The key is to think technology and educational improvement, not only computers. (For more information see: www.cnet.com or www.zdnet.com.)

Multimedia technology will provide resources that have the potential to stimulate the most unmotivated learner and to allow students to expand abilities to express themselves. Interactive multimedia learning systems will allow for the better use of teacher time while students can learn at their own pace and with a style that best suits them. The potential of technology seems almost limitless; however, educators will play the critical role in making it happen.

Administrative Applications

In addition to the instruction, computers provide a tremendous resource for expanding the capabilities and efficiencies of educational leaders. These systems will allow educators to make sound decisions in a much more timely manner, allowing far greater focus on students and instructional leadership. The goal will be to connect the student data, attendance, discipline, scheduling, assessment, teacher evaluation, and other administrative systems so they can talk to one another sharing data and producing key reports, answering queries, and saving a tremendous amount of time (see project 4 in Chapter 13).

This same technology will create opportunities for altogether new ways of managing schools. Student records can be instantly accessed and updated regarding academics, attendance, behavior, achievements, and so on. Teachers, students, and parents will be able to access information regarding performance, assignments, schedules, homework, grades, historical records, newsletters, and teacher/student/parent comments. This technology will support budgeting, finance, accounting, purchasing (optimal suppliers), interviewee and employee records, inventories of books and equipment, attendance, scheduling data, to name but a few of the more immediate applications.

The school management software is usually divided into systems for student information, back-office enterprise (accounting, payroll, HR), transportation, food service, library automation, student health, special education management, curriculum management, and others. Today's educators face a dizzying assortment of choices for their school data management and analysis (DMA). Trying to determine which marketer's and vendor's system best suits the needs of a school division is a very challenging task. Some vendors provide a more comprehensive set of management software while other companies might focus on only one system.

Most systems have a data warehousing component and a data analysis and reporting component. Again, issues like comprehensiveness, affordability, reliability, and customizability become important factors to consider. The ability to store data in only one place but to be able to combine it with data across multiple domains in analysis and reporting, so as to provide comprehensive analytical capabilities, adds greatly to the future effectiveness of the school management software. This will allow for data-driven decision making, exploring relationships among data such as student achievement and attendance or expenditure, or teacher professional development and teacher effectiveness.

This new management software will allow all educators to have ready access to meaningful school system information. These data warehousing, mining, analysis, and reporting systems will support data-driven decision making at any level of education. These software systems provide internet software systems allowing easy access to multiple databases. Various data fields—class, grade, school, single student—or some combination of fields can be used to report data. The systems can also support longitudinal analysis as data is collected over time.

Predefined reports can be produced or "on demand" requests can be made for real time results to meet accountability requirements and to improve instruction. Students and parents can have improved access to information. This means that information must be delivered to the desktop computers in classrooms, schools, and homes. Online technical support will be needed to help educations and parents to obtain the information they wish to obtain. (See www.sas.com; www.escholar.com; www.etradita.com; www.admin.com; www.bearingpoint.com; www.pearsonedtech.com/sasi; www.pentamation.com; www.centryltd.com for example.)

Internet cameras in the classroom will give parents, community members, and principals access to what is occurring in the classroom. Sick students will be able to keep up from home. Tests will be taken at diverse locations and scored and reported by the computer.

The whole concept of how to use time, space, and distance in this new technological, media-oriented, self-service environment will be a challenge. The second challenge is to use technology to continuously improve instruction and administration and ultimately student performance. The third is to make sure the school is current in regard to technology and software. Those who have expertise, whether teachers, parents, students, or administrators, should be encouraged to help others in their use of computers to support better education. (For more information see: www.ncrelorg/sdrs/areas/teocont.htm.)

＊ **What types of technological systems might be incorporated at Scrivner Middle School to support administrative and instructional responsibilities?**

Wilson Elementary School District: Five Steps to a Successful Technology Program

JANE M. JULIANO, PH.D. • *Principal, Wilson Charter High School, Phoenix, Arizona*

You have just been hired as a principal of an elementary school and are charged with implementing a technology program. Although this is a daunting task, you can accomplish it if you involve a technically competent staff and key stakeholders in the school to develop and implement a long-range technology plan. The Wilson Elementary School District in Phoenix, Arizona, is an example of a school district that has successfully implemented the first five years of an eight-year technology plan. Currently, all students have their own computers and teachers are able to meet each student's curriculum goals by integrating subject-matter software activities into the classroom curriculum.

Step One: The Vision
The most important part of the technology plan is the statement of the reason for the technology program and how its success will be measured. For the Wilson District, which has a high minority, low socioeconomic population, the overriding goal for the technology program is to increase student achievement scores. It is also to give students, who otherwise would not have access to computers, the skills necessary to compete in a technological world. Of course, goals must be in line with the budget, and together these factors will set the vision for your plan and guide each aspect of the implementation.

Technology plans and budgets are never static. When you involve key stakeholders in your plan, you will obtain the support needed to implement the plan and keep it moving forward. At Wilson, following the superintendent's vision of a computer for every student, all administrators along with school board members, parents, teachers, students, and technology staff were included in the development of the plan. The technology coordinator for the district continued to hold monthly meetings with the superintendent, administrators, technology staff, and teachers to keep the plan on track.

Step Two: Design the Implementation
Next, your plan needs to specify what the implementation will look like. Will reaching your technology goals translate into installing a com-

puter lab in your school, distributing a certain number of computers in every classroom, or both? What software will you purchase to meet your goals? The software you choose will determine the hardware to purchase and whether the computers will need to be networked or stand-alone. A total software curriculum package was purchased at Wilson so teachers are able to customize activities for each student based on his or her instructional needs. This type of implementation meant that all 1,500 computers would be networked and distributed into every classroom. Teachers are able to print reports that evaluate student performance on the prescribed activities as well as track the information the district needs to measure the effect of the program on student achievement.

Step Three: "Wheeling and Dealing"
During the next stage of your implementation, you will be making all of the major purchases to get started. The technology team at Wilson learned much during this stage. They quickly realized that hardware and software continually change and that a portion of the budget needs to be reserved for updates and replacements. It also became apparent how dynamic the turnover rate of personnel is in the technology industry. Everything negotiated with a salesperson needs to be specified in your contract so agreements will stand through any changes in company salespeople, CEOs, or ownership.

Budget planning and purchasing is ongoing; be creative when you look for funding. At Wilson, two major bond elections three years apart have supported the costs of the technology program. Grants have helped finance teacher training activities. Every purchase, big or small, needs to be evaluated in terms of the big picture. For instance, although the network infrastructure at Wilson required a lot of capital up front, it was less expensive to complete the entire project than to install it piece by piece over four years' time. Student safety and hardware security also required a large portion of the budget. Customized student desks were built to house each computer. The monitor sits below a glass panel and the CPU and all wires are locked behind side and back doors. Custom shelving units were installed

in the classrooms with tubing to house the wires that connect the computer to the network. These design strategies reduce the possibility of damage, theft, or vandalism. They also increase student safety and facilitate integration of computer activities into a teacher's daily curriculum.

Step Four: Staff Development
Now, with your vendor contracts in hand, and installation imminent, a long-term teacher training plan must be set in motion. At Wilson, with a teaching staff of 100, a full-time teacher trainer became part of the technology team from the beginning of the implementation. Not only do teachers need to learn new ways of teaching, they also need to learn the new software updates, programs, and operating systems, as well as how to implement the new phases of the technology plan such as the addition of the Internet. The teacher trainer at Wilson individualizes training as much as possible so that all teachers feel successful and supported. Throughout the school year, teachers are released from their classrooms for two-hour blocks of training. In addition, the teacher trainer often works collaboratively in the classroom to model and facilitate the overall management of the classroom technology.

Mentor teachers are trained to assist their colleagues. Any annual pay incentives are given to teachers who increase their computer literacy skills by taking community college technology courses.

Step Five: Show Your Success
Finally, plan for community access to the computers at your school, and promote what you have accomplished. Evenings at Wilson are busy with adult computer classes. Parents are invited to improve typing skills and learn word processing. Elementary and high school students work on homework projects. International and national visitors tour the two Wilson District campuses on a regular basis. Members of the technology team present the district technology plan at national conferences and submit articles to national publications. Teaching with technology has become part of the district's culture, and so it can become yours, if you plan with the future in mind before you take the first step.

The Leadership Challenge

Innovations must have constituencies who support them and believe in them if they are to be successful. The chance of these innovations surviving is also increased if the constituency is broad based, including groups like parents, educators, policymakers, and business management. Communication is essential if support is to be developed and sustained. This includes stakeholders meetings, information sharing, ongoing updates, surveys, open forums, and other forms of networking.

One of the major tasks of educational leadership is to build both capacity and creativity within existing organizations. We now know that existing institutions must develop the capacity to envision a desired state of affairs that induces commitment to continuous improvement. As Drucker (1993, p. 339) points out, "We have learned to innovate because we cannot expect that the accumulated competence, skill, knowledge, product, services and structure of the present will be adequate for very long." In today's world, "staying even" usually results in "falling behind" and in many cases disappearing. In fact, "getting ahead" often results in "staying even" so organizations must constantly reinvent themselves through innovation and responsiveness. Although the process of innovation is relatively uncomplicated, that does not mean it is easy. It is hard, systematic work.

Michael Fullan (2003) talks about the need to understand "the process of change" while knowing that it is not always either understandable or predictable. There are, however, a number of enabling structures, which might facilitate innovation, entrepreneurship, and continuous improvement. Many researchers have attempted to identify what must be done to facilitate and support the implementation of innovation, what might be called "transformative change." "What this means is that we have to work directly with schools as organizations, and use school districts as local system organizers to create new contexts (led by new context leaders) which do better at student learning precisely because they provide better environments for teacher leaders and school leaders to develop in those organizations. All the way up and down the line we are talking about increasing system capacity . . ." (Fullan, 2003, pp. 105–106).

Improvement and transformation is a process made by individuals first and then by institutions. It is highly personalized as an experience and entails developmental growth in knowledge, feelings, abilities, and skills. It relates to people and capacity first and innovation and implementation second. D. H. Lawrence states, "All men dream but not equally, those who dream by night, wake in day to find it was wanting, but those who dream by day, dream with their eyes open, so to make it possible." As educators, we must be able to translate our innovation and creativity into improvements in teaching and learning. We must take the sparks of creativity and develop the capacity needed to support "actions" directed at improving our schools.

Progress occurs when we increase the number of people who conceptualize, believe in, advocate, and practice new transformational approaches. Transformation needs individuals to create them and champion their cause. Margaret Mead states: "Never doubt that a small group of thoughtful, committed citizens can change the world. Indeed, it's the only thing that ever has." Researchers tell us that these people go through different stages in the innovation and implementation process and have different needs at different stages. Table 3.2 presents a continuous improvement model, which is a good starting point for approaching challenges related to improvements within an organization. The model presents a process often required to achieve success in developing a shared vision, problem solving, action, and innovation.

The model brings significant parties together at key points in the planning process, helping them to become educated and make effective decisions and to become partners and develop a sense of ownership. This model focuses on developing and involving staff and building the needed commitment to success. It results in a great deal of development as well as a more open, comfortable, and inspiring work environment. Ultimately, it builds a consensus around a needed improvement. It is a starting point in resolving the challenges presented in the vignettes and problem-based learning activities found in this and other textbooks and, more importantly, the real world challenges of administration.

In continuous improvement and innovation, there is a natural desire to protect the delivery system and the existing culture; the normal response is to restore the old order, rather than to risk the perils of allowing a new order of things to evolve. The evolving idea creates resistance among those who want to stick with what has worked in the past. Moving from the tried-and-true to a new response to changing educational expectations requires a period of confusion, learning, and inefficiency—thus courage to move forward. Paradigm shifts involve dislocation, conflict, and uncertainty. Innovations and new paradigms are nearly always received with coolness, even mockery and hostility.

Those with vested interests will fight the changes, which only makes sense. Some of the potential costs to those with a vested interest in the status quo, if the innovation is implemented, include:

- Damage to relationships; loss of friends
- Time-consuming
- Challenges to deeply held beliefs
- Confrontations
- Feeling of guilt/burnout/negative consequence (opening "Pandora's Box")
- Giving up common practices and values
- Maintaining your identity
- Having to fix mistakes
- Requires a lot of blood, sweat, and tears
- Dissidence

A large part of the innovation process requires winning over the minds and hearts of those involved, and this need exists from the very top of the organization to the very bottom.

Continually improving any organization is a very difficult and often stressful undertaking, when compared to managing the status quo; however, anxiety and resistance can be decreased and overcome when the objectives, the frames of reference, and the reforms are clarified and have a sense of political support.

TABLE 3.2   *Steps for Success in Approaching Needed Improvements*

(Note: Gathering and dispersing information is an essential element for each of the steps discussed below)

Present Condition	Steps to Successful Innovation and Problem Solving	Typical Behavior
I. Little recognition for understanding of needs.	Awareness	• Build understanding of the challenges to be faced and open up new possibilities.
II. Lack of knowledge about the situation and/or possibilities.	Gather/Seek information	• Develop the needed knowledge base to begin the planning/renewal process. (This step has to be revisited throughout the effort.)
III. Ready to begin to look at options, approaches, and innovations.	Orientation/Deliberation	• Seek out information and learn more about the possible innovations and reforms.
IV. Need to begin pruning the options and develop a solution set.	Narrowing options/Assessment	• Develop criteria, assess options and directions to be taken, and develop a universe of acceptable alternatives and approaches
V. Concern regarding needed support for final approaches or solutions.	Political support	• Assess and work within the power structure to build required support and political allies to help to ensure the success of the innovation finally selected. (This step has to be revisited throughout the effort).
VI. Need to make a commitment to one of the options within the possible solution set.	Decision/Implementation planning	• Narrow the options to the most desirable and supportable option through consensus. Initial development of an implementation plan.
VII. All needed people are not adequately aligned toward the renewal effort that was selected.	Building shared values and goals	• Information is provided to a wide audience so that all involved understand the innovation and realize how it will affect them. The goals, values, and mission are internalized within the organizational culture.

TABLE 3.2 *Continued*

Present Condition	Steps to Successful Innovation and Problem Solving	Typical Behavior
VIII. People do not have the needed skills to successfully complete the innovation.	Development	• The organizational staff and others are readied and prepared for successful implementation of the innovation. This requires the development of staff and others.
IX. The innovation is not part of the organization because it has not yet been implemented.	Implement and integrate	• The innovation and renewal effort is implemented and obstacles and problems begin to emerge. Efforts are made to make needed modifications and to begin integrating the innovation into the organizational culture and to ensure that it works effectively.
X. The innovation has not become totally effective and is not a systemic part of the organization because it not been fully embraced.	Refinement and coordination and expanding support	• Establish a widespread pattern of use and coordinate the efforts in using the innovation and in making and sharing information regarding performance and refinements. Groups are regularly discussing the innovation as it becomes a part of routine procedure.
XI. Data has not been produced to support the effectiveness of the newly implemented innovation.	Evaluation/Reflection	• Collect and analyze data to make needed adjustment and to ensure and increase the effectiveness of the innovation. Share and celebrate successes and quickly respond to, learn from, and make needed adjustments regarding failures. (This step occurs from step IX through step XII.)
XII. There are new needs that are not being considered in the present operation of the organization.	Refocusing and renewal	• Users start to become aware of new problems, new needs, new opportunities within the very dynamic context in which they operate. The process begins anew.

Based on a model for adopting educational innovation from the Research and Development Department for Teacher Education at the University of Texas at Austin.

Everyone takes on the challenges of leadership for improvement. They mobilize the staff to obtain desired measurable results (student achievement), share a passion for continuous improvement and growth, work diligently at laying the foundation for continuous improvement, and support the actions of one another in implementing agreed upon reforms.

As will be discussed in Chapters 6 and 7 on school leadership, school improvements are more successful when school staffs and others thoroughly research and choose the types of reforms that are implemented within their schools. This means that time must be provided for teachers to study, reflect on, and apply selected reforms and to learn the new skills.

We already know enough about what future schools need to look like. The challenge is to create an educational model that addresses current knowledge and needs and that the average teacher is capable of implementing. Teachers and students also must be provided the time to conduct intensive learning experiences. Time is also needed to develop curriculum and school experiences that relate to and build on the experiences of children. Teachers need to have opportunities to network with similar types of teachers—to plan, refine, teach each other, and learn. (For more information see: www.techedlab.com/k12.html.)

✳ **Develop an implementation plan for the comprehensive school reform process and define the role of administrators, teachers, and the community in the Scrivner renewal and reform effort.**

Conclusion

Quantum physics suggests that order is inherent in all living systems, such as education. Stimulus or opportunities disturb and threaten that order or equilibrium. Under proper conditions, the system responds and evolves to a new, improved order, one that is much better suited for the new environment (Wheatley, 1992). Proper conditions suggest that (1) those within the system take advantage of the opportunities or possibilities for renewal and re-creation and (2) the entire system must be allowed to adapt and improve itself. When the system recognizes that the existing idea of organizational performance does not seem to be working, the system can resist, retreat, tune out, tighten control, create rigid structure, and return to traditions, or the system can regenerate, reform, renew, reconfigure, and re-create itself to better suit its new environment. Linda Darling-Hammond (1997) believes:

> It is critical to remember that reform is never completed because everyone continually changes and everyone continually learns, experiencing fresh insights from practices, from research, and from the synergy of teachers, administrators, students, parents, and others inquiring together. Although policy supports are essential, reform can never be enforced from the top down, because people must create change in locally appropriate ways at the school and classroom levels. The importance of both context and commitment mean that local invention must be supported by policies that provide a mix of top-down support and bottom-up initiatives. (pp. 336–337)

BOX 3.2 • *Implications for Leaders*

We need to:

Have a positive impact on student learning and the classroom.

Connect district, school, and staff development plans.

Encourage bold and creative undertakings (discourage tinkering, which wastes resources and short-circuits reform).

Provide vision and encouragement (take the long view).

Ensure adequate resources.

Rethink and re-create schools.

Keep everyone informed about research and practice.

Attract powerful constituents for support.

Make information technology a driving force (an integral part of school reform).

Measure performance.

Implement improved approaches.

Baseball Hall of Famer Casey Stengel once advised, "If the horse you're riding dies, it's best if you get off." Traditional education seems to be dying a slow death, and perhaps it is time to get off. The concern is that students will be locked into the 2000s with 1950s skills and behaviors. The call is for educators to rethink education and to create new, more effective paradigms that improve the entire system. Box 3.2 presents the implications of this call for our future leaders (see also Chapters 6 and 7).

Educational leaders need to build direction, alignment, and a culture of visionaries to encourage risk taking and experimentation, to set the pace, and to lead by example. They must discuss and translate knowledge and research for excellent schools. Schlechty (1997) concludes:

> The capacity to establish and maintain a focus on students and the quality of the experiences they are provided, the capacity to maintain direction, and the capacity to act strategically are the most crucial components to be attended to if we are serious about developing an action plan to improve the quality of America's schools. (p. 222)

We must ignite the spark of individual and group genius required to really make a difference in education. (For more information see: www.maec.org/mag-schl.html.)

Portfolio Artifacts

- Lead a school review of exemplary instructional practices (best practices) that are aligned with state standards and districtwide policy.
- Supervise a curriculum revision and/or evaluate and improve an instructional program.
- Examine state-of-the-art technology systems used to support instruction and administration.
- Articulate the rationale for implementing a curricular, instructional, or administrative reform effort. Discuss "value added" to justify use of a specific program.
- Participate and lead a group discussion of latest innovative practice focusing on the improvement of student performance.
- Develop an implementation plan for a reform effort and participate in the carrying out of the implementation plan.
- Evaluate an innovative program described in this chapter or one being implemented in a local school district.

- Select an innovative program that you believe in and join the network, collaborate and become an expert on that program, and begin to experiment with it in your existing setting. Obtain appropriate permission before beginning an innovative program in any school or district.
- Videotape innovative classrooms in your surrounding areas, and lead a group discussion

to evaluate the effectiveness of the approaches appearing on the videotape.
- Participate on a curriculum development and review committee.
- Write a proposal for curricular and instructional reform for a specific grade level.
- Integrate a current technology into your present work setting.

Terms

Accelerated learning	Implementation model	Networks
Active learning	(innovation)	Paradigm shift
Authentic learning	Interdisciplinary	Reading Recovery
Comprehensive school reform	Integrated learning	Rubric
(CSR)	technology	Site-based
Constructivist learning	Online	Sas
Distance learning	Multimedia presentations	Success for All
Direct instruction	NETS-A	Virtual reality

Suggested Readings

Comer, J. Haynes, N. Joyner, E., & Ben-Avie, M. (1999). *Child by child: The Comer process for change in education.* New York: Teachers College Press.

Darling-Hammond, L. (2001). *The right to learn: A blueprint for creating schools that work.* San Francisco, CA: Jossey-Bass.

Fullan, M. (2001). *The new meaning of educational change.* New York: Teacher College Press.

Glatthorn, A. (2000). *The principal as curriculum leader.* Thousand Oaks, CA: Corwin Press.

Gordon, D. T. (Ed.). (2000). *The digital classroom.* Boston: Harvard Educational Letter.

Hoy, A., & Hoy, W. (2003). *Instructional leadership: A learning centered guide.* Boston: Allyn and Bacon.

Johnson, S. (1998). *Who moved my cheese?* New York: Putnam.

Kohn, A. (1999). *The schools our children deserve.* Boston: Houghton-Mifflin.

LeBaron, J. F., & Collier, C. (2001). *Technology in its place: Successful technology infusion in schools.* San Francisco: Jossey-Bass.

Marsh, D. D. (1999). *Preparing our schools for the twenty-first century.* Alexandria, VA: The Association for Supervision and Curriculum Development.

Marzano, R., Pickering, D., & Pollock, J. (2001). *Classroom instruction that works.* Alexandria, VA: ASCD.

Murphy, J. (2002). *Leadership lessons for comprehensive school reform.* Thousand Oaks, CA: Corwin.

Owens, R. (2004). *Organizational behavior in education: Adaptive leadership and school reform.* Boston: Allyn and Bacon.

Owings, W., and Kaplan, L. (2003). *Best practices, best thinking and emerging issues in school leadership.* Thousand Oaks, CA: Corwin Press.

Picciano, A. (2002). *Educational leadership and planning for technology.* Boston: Allyn and Bacon.

Pounder, D. G. (1998). *Restructuring schools for collaboration: Promises and pitfalls.* Albany: State University of New York Press.

Schlechly, P. (2003). *Inventing better schools: An action plan for educational reform.* San Francisco, CA: Jossey-Bass.

Wiggins, G., & McTighe, J. (2004). *Understanding by design.* Boston: Allyn and Bacon.

Withrow, F. (1999). *Preparing schools and school systems for the twenty-first century.* Arlington, VA: The American Association of School Administrators.

4

Diversity and Community Relations

Cultures Clash in Fairhaven

The trouble didn't start in October. The brief but fierce brawls only announced it. Minutes after school let out at Fairhaven's Oakes High on October 29, hundreds of students poured into the street. The melee was on. Between twenty and thirty teenagers went at each other with shoes, sticks, belts, rocks, and canes.

Combatants were from virtually every ethnic group in attendance at the high school. "But," Assistant Principal Henry Barros suggested, "the two predominant groups were African American and Somali." It lasted about ten minutes, by the estimate of Brent O'Brien, Oakes's principal. Police and staff intervened, and a Fairhaven police helicopter ordered the crowd to disperse.

A second street fight broke out the following afternoon at the edge of Memorial Park, a few blocks away. Police cars and the vehicles of private citizens were pelted, and one motorcycle officer was struck with a rock. Tensions have receded in the last two weeks, but everyone involved has seen these lulls before. No one's offering a guarantee that this one is permanent.

For Somalis, the brawls were simply the latest eruption of an ongoing series of smaller conflicts that could be titled "Somalis versus Everybody Else." In the past, many Somalian

children in the Fairhaven neighborhood of Mesa Grande have found themselves at odds with students of various ethnic backgrounds, particularly Indochinese and Latino.

The causes for conflict are many, subtle, and complex. The Somalis' experience provides a window into exactly what difficulties can arise as a cultural group is introduced into U.S. society. It began among the children with name-calling, taunts, and bullying. In discussing these issues with Somali community members and students, Principal O'Brien learned that it started in 1993 when Somalis began arriving in Fairhaven. Thousands of miles away, their African homeland was being consumed in violent clan warfare, anarchy, and mass starvation after the collapse of the government. Somalian refugees arrived in Fairhaven in significant numbers with little or no advance notice. Such is often the case with refugee groups who are literally airlifted out of countries in turmoil and deposited in the United States perhaps a mere twenty-four hours later.

Somalian students say that practically from the beginning, other students have made fun of their cultural dress, with remarks such as "It's not Halloween." They are picked on, they say, and attacked when they pass through Memorial Park on their way to and from school.

For the most part the Somalian refugees who have come to Fairhaven have settled in Mesa Grande, an area that is often called a "Little U.N." in which more than thirty-five different languages are spoken.

Last spring, according to school district officials, Oakes High School, which draws much of its population from Mesa Grande, was 29.7 percent Indochinese, 27.3 percent Hispanic, 26.3 percent African American, 13.3 percent Anglo, 1.5 percent other Asian groups, and 1.9 percent other. Included in the African American population are 270 Somalian students.

According to Omar Jama, president of the East African Youth Center, Somalian children tend to keep to themselves at school. Somalis are relatively new to the United States and find the culture very different. In school, Somalian children form a distinct group. Most are Muslim. Women and girls wear veils and scarves that cover their hair. But, Mr. Jama argues, these are superficial differences, and the divide goes much deeper than appearance.

In Somalia few women work outside their homes or drive cars. Men generally do not take direction from women. Islamic law forbids alcohol, drugs, and premarital sex; violations incur severe penalties. Somalis do not touch members of the opposite sex who are not related to them. They follow certain dietary restrictions; for example, they eat no pork. As Muslims they pray several times a day.

These cultural differences have led other students to consider Somali students standoffish, and many take offense. Somalian parents complain to school administrators that students deliberately poke and touch Somalian girls to provoke reaction. Boys of other ethnic groups try to speak to them. "That's just not possible," comments Mr. Jama.

For school officials, police, and outside groups, issues are magnified because of communication difficulties presented by language and customs. Mr. Jama comments that Somalian parents of all clans are anguished and alarmed at the tensions their children are experiencing: "Somalis come from a country ruined by civil war. We are looking for peace."

Assistant Principal Barros believes that the public is not accustomed to distinguishing between immigrants and refugees. He maintains that how the Somalis arrive in the United States plays a role in how they are received.

Last year Somalian parents took their complaints to Rawlins Middle School, a feeder to Oakes. The Somalis expected the school to decree an end to the taunting and name-calling. The school did not do as they expected. Meetings were convened, and attended by members of the Somalian community, school staff, Fairhaven police, parents of other ethnic groups, and various interested parties. "Steps were taken," says Mr. Jama, "but they were not deep enough. The Somali parents came away very disappointed in school officials."

The Somali parents also believe the police have failed them. "The perception is that the police are only doing things against the Somali kids," says sergeant David Melholf of the Fairhaven juvenile services team. "The kids are telling just one side of the story to their parents."

Various groups such as the Urban League of African Students at Fairhaven College have offered their services to Oakes and to the Somalian community since last month's disturbances. Hardly anyone believes the troubles are over for good. "They are only over," says Mr. Jama, "until the next incident, which could be next week or next year."

✳ **If you were Principal O'Brien, how would you go about decreasing the likelihood that these incidents will recur? In what ways might parents, family members, and community groups be involved in dealing with these issues at Oakes? Is there basic content knowledge in areas of cultural diversity that all involved should have? If so, what is it?**

Diversity in Schools

Diversity is the norm in all schools. Staff and student populations are diverse, whether a school is located in North Dakota or along the border between the United States and Mexico, whether it consists predominantly of one racial or ethnic group or of a variety of cultural groups. Diversity includes differences in age, gender, sexual orientation, political beliefs, socioeconomic status, religion, physical and mental ability, language, and ethnicity. Although some schools have greater diversity than others, all schools must acknowledge and act on the diversity found in their populations, the community itself, the state, the nation, and on our planet. Staff and students need to (a) be aware of diversity, (b) have knowledge and understanding about diversity, and (c) on the basis of that knowledge take action, or *praxis.*

Many educators, when talking about diverse schools, assume that urban schools are the most heterogeneous. The words *diversity, urban,* and *minority student,* however, are not synonymous. For example, an inner-city school with a student population of all Mexican American students, who are from a low socioeconomic background, may have less diversity than a typical suburban school.

Socioeconomic Status and Social Class

Socioeconomic status (SES) refers to stratification that can be measured by factors such as economic status, family background, and job prestige. A broader term is *social class,* which involves large categories of people of similar SES who have in common such attributes as cultural identification, lifestyle, and attitudes.

SES is strongly correlated with academic success. When we talk about correlation, we are not addressing causation. Instead, researchers have found that children coming from socioeconomically low backgrounds are *more likely* to do poorly in school than children coming from high socioeconomic backgrounds. This does not mean that all children who are poor will do less well in school because they are poor. Families that are financially stable or affluent have greater access to resources, while families struggling to survive are more concerned with paying rent than buying a computer. This correlation has been found to be true in nearly every nation in the world and certainly is not a surprise to anyone. Generally, the greater the socioeconomic resources available to children, the better will be the children's educational attainment (Luster & McAdoo, 1994).

Inequities in social class intersect with other areas of difference in U.S. society (see Table 4.1). According to Parker and Shapiro (1993), "Social class plays a strong role in the struggle by people of color to achieve equal educational opportunity and vertical equity in school resources" (p. 42).

U.S. Population Demographics

As Table 4.2 depicts, it is estimated that by the middle of the twenty-first century, just over half of the U.S. population will fall into the category of white (this category includes persons not of Hispanic origin). An increase among nonwhite populations is projected for the next fifty years, with dramatic increases in the number of Hispanics.

TABLE 4.1   *Children Living in Poverty in 2000*

Ethnic/Racial Group	Percentage of Children
White	13.4%
African American	30.2%
Native American	38.6%
Asian American	11.5%
Hispanic	28.0%

Source: U.S. Bureau of Census. www.census.gov/

TABLE 4.2   *Percent Distribution of U.S. Population by Race and Hispanic Origin*

	1990	2005	2010	2015	2030
White	75.7	81.3	80.5	79.7	77.6
Black	11.8	13.2	13.5	13.7	14.4
American Indian	0.7	0.9	0.9	0.9	1.0
Asian	2.8	4.6	5.1	5.6	7.0
Hispanic	9.0	12.6	13.8	15.1	18.9
White, not Hispanic	—	69.6	68.0	66.1	60.5
Black, not Hispanic	—	12.4	12.6	12.7	13.1
American Indian, not Hispanic	—	0.8	0.8	0.8	0.8
Asian, not Hispanic	—	4.4	4.8	5.3	6.6

Source: Bureau of the Census, www.census.gov/population.

Table 4.3 indicates the change in U.S. census categories between 1960 and 2000. In 1960 Americans were asked to put themselves into two categories: white and nonwhite. By 1990 there were six major categories including "Other." We often hear reference to four ethnic or racial groups in the United States: whites, Native Americans, African Americans, and Hispanics. The terminology used to describe people is constantly changing.

Cultural Identity

In Chapter 6 we discuss organizational culture, which differs in many respects from national or ethnic group culture. Countless authors have defined the word *culture* in a variety of ways. Anthropologists Levinson and Holland (1996) maintain that emphasis should be "placed on culture as a continual process of creating meaning in social and material contexts, replacing a conceptualization of culture as a static, unchanging body of knowledge 'transmitted' between generations" (p. 13).

Anthropologist Renato Rosaldo (1989) argues that culture is open-ended, dynamic, and permeable. About a cultural group he was investigating he writes, "Immigrants and socially mobile individuals appeared culturally invisible because they were no longer what they once were and not yet what they could become" (p. 209).

TABLE 4.3 *U.S. Census Categories 1960–2000*

1960	1970	1980	1990	2000*
White	White	White	White	American Indian or
Nonwhite	Black	Black	Black	Native Alaskan
	Other	American Indian	American Indian	_____
		Eskimo, Aleut	Eskimo, Aleut	Asian
		Asian, Pacific Islander	Asian, Pacific Islander	Chinese
		Other	Chinese	Filipino
		Hispanic	Filipino	Japanese
			Japanese	Korean
			Asian Indian	Vietnamese
			Korean	Hmong
			Vietnamese	Laotian
			Malaysian	Thai
			Indonesian	Other _____
			Samoan	Black or African
			Cambodian	American
			Other	Native Hawaiian or
			Other	Other Pacific Islander
			Hispanic	Native Hawaiian
			Mexican	Guamanian or
			Puerto Rican	Chamorro
			Cuban	Samoan
			Other	Other _____
				White
				Some Other Race
				_____

*In the 2000 Census, respondents for the first time were allowed to identify one or more races to indicate racial identity.

Source: Bureau of the Census, www.census.gov/.

Rosaldo discusses the concept of *borderlands,* liminal zones where cross-cultural encounters take place, often for the first time. Public schools are certainly one of these borderlands. Children representing nearly every ethnic group on this planet can be found in U.S. public school classrooms.

Bullivant (1989) believes that in the borderlands, groups' cultural programs evolve historically as their members adapt to changes in the social environment. A growing number of classrooms typify borderlands where children and adults from diverse backgrounds influence each other. In these borderlands, students forsake some aspects of their native cultures if the cultures conflict with the values and behaviors that produce social acceptance and success in school. It is important for educators to remember that often schools are the first places in which children internalize their ethnicity as a category for describing themselves.

If we accept the definition of culture as "a continuous process of creating meaning in social and material contexts," then each of the areas included in the elements of what compose cultural identity (see Box 4.1) has the potential to change considerably over time.

> ✳ **How might issues of cultural identity be addressed at Oakes High School?**

What, then, does the borderlands concept mean for schools and school administrators? One implication is that since new "cultures" are constantly being created, educators must discard the notion that they need to *understand* children's ethnic cultures (or countries). Because (1) the culture or country a child came from two years ago is not necessarily the same today, and (2) the child himself or herself is not necessarily the same person he or she was two years ago because of entering a new culture, the notion of *understanding* or *knowing* other cultures is as complex as the notion of understanding one's own culture. Thus, although Box 4.1 discusses various aspects of cultural identity, the notion that together these factors make up cultural identity is far too simplistic. Cultural identity, too, is constantly in a state of flux, especially in the borderlands.

BOX 4.1 • *Elements of Cultural Identity*

Language
Dominant language (English) versus native language
Nonverbal communication: kinesics and proxemics
Linguistic style

Gender Roles
Male and female relationships and roles
Views of sexuality
Religious/Spiritual beliefs and practices
Religious beliefs
Religious holiday observances

Family and Kinship Patterns
How are people related?
Close versus distant relations; extended families
Familial expectations and duties

Behavioral Norms/Moral/Social Practices
Rules and norms of the culture
Appropriate versus inappropriate activities and behaviors
Dress

Diet; food and eating-related issues
Personal hygiene

Adult–Child Relationships
Acceptable/unacceptable behavior between adults and children

Learning Styles/Educational Beliefs/ Views of Intelligence
Preferred learning modality (auditory, visual, kinesthetic)
Cooperative versus competitive approaches to learning
Value of education/schooling
Country of origin education system
Ways of knowing

Cultural Traditions
Mores and customs
Holidays

View of the Individual and Life Views
"Rugged individualism" versus collectivism
Historical awareness of the culture

Gender roles differ substantially from culture to culture. We can see within the United States how the roles of males and females, as well as people's views about sexuality, are in a constant state of change. Acceptable gender roles in one culture might not be acceptable in another. Why a girl from a particular ethnic group does not speak in class might have little to do with language proficiency. The explanation for her hesitation or reluctance to raise her hand in class might be because the female role in her culture might be to always allow boys to speak first.

In recent years, a subtle change with major implications is occurring in the area of religion in the United States where the majority of citizens are Christian. Several religious populations are increasing significantly. For example, the number of people in the United States who call themselves Muslims is more than 4 million (www.worldalmanacforkids.com). Most educators know little about the Muslim faith and its beliefs. What are the implications for schools with Muslim students who are called to pray five times each day? What might be some implications of the tragic events of September 11, 2001, with regard to students' understanding, or lack of understanding, of the Muslim faith?

Another key element of cultural identity involves behavioral, moral, and social practices. Cultures differentiate themselves by dress, diet, mores, and norms. What are the implications for school policies when students, such as Sikhs, wear turbans, when the school policy states that no hats can be worn? What does it mean to a teacher or fellow students when deodorant is not typically used in a particular culture, and the group believes a student "smells"?

Family and kinship patterns differ within many cultures as well. In some cultures the extended family plays a major role in the raising of a child. This family may include a grandparent, cousin, aunt, uncle, older sibling, or a nonblood relative. These kinship patterns can have considerable implications for family involvement in schools.

Learning styles and beliefs about how people learn, as well as beliefs about what constitutes intelligence, differ widely from culture to culture within the United States. Research supports that cultural groups differ in their preferred learning style (Ramirez & Casteñeda, 1974; Stodolsky & Lesser, 1971). Additionally, children come to U.S. schools from many different educational systems. Helping families understand how the U.S. educational system is structured is crucial to obtaining their participation in their children's learning process.

Although all children deal with issues of identity, immigrant children often feel torn between worlds. One Mexican American high school student said she felt "like a jalapeño in a candy jar" (Cordeiro, Reagan, & Martinez, 1994, p. 105). One of the challenges for educators is to know how to respond, within the school environment, to the marginalization of ethnic groups in the mainstream culture.

Cultural Transitions

People experience stages as they encounter new cultures. One helpful frame for exploring these stages is Adler's (1975) five-stage model of culture shock (see Table 4.4). The stages include (1) initial contact with the culture, (2) disintegration of the familiar, (3) reintegration of new cues about the culture, (4) new identity formation

TABLE 4.4   *The Five Stages of Culture Shock*

Stage	Perception	Emotional Range	Behavior	Interpretation
Contact	Differences are intriguing. Perceptions are screened and selected	Excitement Stimulation Euphoria Playfulness Discovery	Curiosity Interest Self-Assurance Impressionistic Depression Withdrawal	The individual is insulated by her or his own culture. Differences as well as similarities provide rationalization for continuing of status, role, and identity.
Disintegration	Differences have impact, are contrasted Cultural reality cannot be screened out	Confusion Disorientation Loss Apathy Isolation Loneliness Inadequacy	Depression Withdrawal	Cultural differences begin to intrude. Growing awareness of being different leads to loss of self-esteem. Individual experiences loss of cultural support ties and misreads new cultural cues.
Reintegration	Differences are rejected	Anger Rage Nervousness Anxiety Frustration	Rebellion Suspicion Rejection Hostility Exclusiveness Opinionatedness	Rejection of second culture causes preoccupation with likes and dislikes; differences are projected. Negative behavior, however, is a form of self-assertion and growing self-esteem.
Autonomy	Differences and similarities are legitimized	Relaxation Warmth Empathy	Self-Assurance Self-Control Independent Comfortableness Confidence	The individual is socially and linguistically capable of negotiating most new and different situations; she or he is assured of ability to survive new experiences.
Independence	Differences and similarities are valued and significant	Trust Humor Love Full range of previous emotions	Expression Creativity Actualization	Social, psychological, and cultural differences are accepted and enjoyed. The individual is capable of exercising choice and responsibility and is able to create meaning for situations.

Source: Adapted from D. R. Atkinson, G. Morten, & D. W. Sue (1993). *Counseling American minorities* (4th ed.). New York: McGraw Hill.

with this new culture, and (5) biculturalism. People's perceptions, emotional ranges, and behaviors change depending on which stage they are in. These stages are not unidirectional; an event may trigger a person's returning to an earlier stage.

Adler's framework can be applied by educators to students in U.S. schools who come from other cultures. A student's ability to reach the stages of autonomy and independence in the United States is related to many factors. The culture of the school (see Chapter 5) and the school's relationship with the student's family are key factors in minimizing the negative behaviors that might result from culture shock.

✳ **If most people experience stages of cultural transition as they move from culture to culture or place to place, what implications do these stages have for students, staff, and families at Oakes High School?**

Sexual Identity

Many educators are uncomfortable in dealing with issues of student and faculty sexual identity. Whatever your beliefs and experiences are, it is absolutely crucial that you have good information about sexual identify because schools are increasingly involved in controversies surrounding this topic. For example, in 2004 a California suburban school district experienced a controversy involving gay and straight students that became highly volatile. This controversy captured the attention of the national media and continues months later and involves a series of lawsuits (Soto, 2004).

The controversy involved a student who wore a t-shirt with a handwritten anti-gay phrase including "Homosexuality is shameful." The shirt was worn on the day following the high school campus's observance of "A Day of Silence." Organized nationally by the Gay, Lesbian, and Straight Education Network, based in New York, it encourages college and high school students to take a vow of silence in opposition to anti-gay harassment. A teacher told the student that the school's dress code prohibited slogans of "hate behavior" and sent the student to the administration office. Fearing that violence might erupt on the campus, the administrators told the student to remain in the office for the remainder of the day. There are disagreements as to whether the student was suspended and chose to stay in the principal's office instead, or whether in fact he was actually suspended. This case will most likely be decided in court. This is one small example of a controversy that administrators will deal with increasingly in our schools.

At the end of this chapter we include a reference guide created by the American Psychological Association that may be helpful to you as an administrator; as with all issues of diversity it is vital that school administrators are well-informed. A school administrator has an obligation to protect all students from anti-gay harassment just as he or she must ensure protection of students from other forms of harassment. In a 1999 Supreme Court decision (*Davis v. Monroe County Board of Education*, 526 US, 629), the Court explained that "school administrators will continue to enjoy the flexibility they require" in responding to sexual harassment as long as they are not deliberately indifferent or the response is not "clearly unreasonable in light of the known circumstances." At the same time the Office of Civil Rights requires school districts to "take steps reasonably calculated to end any harassment, eliminate a hostile environment if one has been created, and prevent harassment from occurring again."

Sexual identity is a key facet of cultural identity. It is a complex and multifaceted issue. Additionally, various ethnic groups have a wide range of views on sexuality. For example, in some North African cultures it is typical for males to walk down the street with their fingers entwined. This cannot be interpreted that these men are gay. It is a cultural tradition to do this. As people prepare to become school administrators and as they practice administration, becoming knowledgeable about, and comfortable with, discussing issues of cultural identity is imperative.

Prejudice and Discrimination

Prejudice is a negative or narrow attitude or belief toward an entire group of people. It is related to the use of stereotypes—generalizations about people.

Henry Triandis (1971) differentiates between stereotypes and sociotypes. Sociotypes are accurate characterizations about social and cultural groups, and stereotypes are inaccurate and possibly dangerous beliefs about a group.

Aboud (1988) argues, "The less that is known about a group, the easier it is to assign to it negative attributes" (p. 21). Thus, one possible cause for prejudice against a certain cultural group might be lack of contact and firsthand experience with that particular group.

Gordon Allport (1979) believes that children begin categorizing and stereotyping certain kinds of differences among people at a very young age. Later, in adolescence and adulthood, they learn to modify their categories by incorporating exceptions into their stereotypes. Depending on a person's environment and experiences, however, some stereotypes may be reinforced instead of disregarded.

According to Allport, prejudices are rigid and exaggerated preferences. All people hold prejudices. Allport argues that if a prejudice is not acted on, then it does "no great harm. It merely stultifies the mind that possesses it. But prejudice expressed leads to discrimination . . . " (p. 127). Allport develops a continuum of social relationships among human groups that ranges from friendly to hostile. He believes that "we define the degrees of hostile relationships that are readily distinguishable, starting with predilection, the mildest and most normal form of group-exclusion, through active prejudice and discrimination, to scapegoating itself" (p. 127). This process could be viewed as a continuum of relationships, with cooperation at one end and scapegoating at the other extreme.

Cooperation
|
Respect
|
Tolerance
|
Predilection
|
Prejudice
|
Discrimination
|
Scapegoating

Allport refers to scapegoating as "full-fledged aggression," in which "the victim is abused verbally or physically." If, as Allport states, "No child is born prejudiced. His prejudices are always acquired" (p. 307), the focus for educators should not be on discerning *how* children acquire prejudices but, instead, on helping them to question *why* they hold these prejudices.

Discrimination occurs when people act on their beliefs. When teachers develop grading criteria that are as fair as possible and then decide that one student's paper is better than another's, they are discriminating. Discrimination is not only acceptable, it is also, in fact, necessary.

Problem discrimination arises when people's beliefs and actions are not based on evidence. For example, if a teacher has certain criteria for grading and arbitrarily changes the criteria or uses inappropriate criteria, then any resulting discrimination is harmful. When we discuss the problems of societal and educational discrimination, we should concentrate on inappropriate kinds of discrimination.

Allport identified ten sociocultural conditions that foster prejudice:

1. Heterogeneity in the population
2. Ease of vertical mobility
3. Rapid social change with attendant anomie
4. Ignorance and barriers to communication
5. The relative density of minority group populations
6. The existence of realistic rivalries and conflict
7. Exploitation sustaining important interests in the community
8. Sanctions given to aggressive scapegoating
9. Legend and tradition that sustain hostility
10. Unfavorable attitudes toward both assimilation and cultural pluralism (p. 233)

✳︎ **Which of Allport's types of sociocultural conditions may have contributed to the bias incidents at Oakes High School?**

Discrimination in Schools

It is rare in schools to find purposeful discrimination against students based on Allport's categories. For example, barring an African American child from a public school on the basis of skin color is prohibited by law. However, as Nieto (2000) argues, "Racism and discrimination are manifest in numerous practices and policies . . . for example, many studies have found that rigid tracking is most evident in poor communities with large numbers of African American, Latino and American Indian students" (p. 38). Nieto has identified nine educational structures in which prejudice and discrimination affect student learning:

1. Tracking
2. Standardized testing
3. Curriculum
4. Pedagogy

5. The physical structure of the school
6. Disciplinary policies
7. The limited role of students
8. The limited role of teachers
9. The limited role of parents and families

Bullock and Stewart (1978, 1979) identified what they call "second-generation discrimination," which includes practices that deny minority students access to education and limit integration of schools. Academic grouping and disciplining students in a discriminatory manner are examples of second-generation discrimination. In an in-depth study of Hispanic students in 142 school districts, Meier and Stewart (1991) found that second-generation discrimination exists because Hispanic populations lack the political power to prevent certain conditions that would preclude discrimination. According to their research, "School districts with greater Hispanic representation on the school board and among teaching faculty experience significantly less second-generation discrimination against Hispanic students" (p. xvii).

Educational leaders need to ask critical questions about the educational structures in schools. If a secondary school, for example, has a high dropout rate, educators must ask a variety of questions. A school administrator might ask: Who is dropping out? Are there differences in ethnicity, social class, or gender of the students who drop out? What reasons do these students report for dropping out? Are there program structures (e.g., bilingual programs, special education classes) that these students were a part of? For example, Meier and Stewart found that "Hispanic high school graduation rates are negatively associated with corporal punishment and bilingual classes, and positively associated with gifted classes. Hispanic dropout rates are positively associated with suspensions and negatively associated with gifted class enrollments" (p. 177).

Additionally they noted, "The pattern that Hispanics receive more corporal punishment, more suspensions, and more expulsions when blacks receive less, and vice versa, implies that administrators compensate for disciplining one group by lessening discipline of the other group" (p. 154).

✳ **What types of records could Oakes High School staff keep to ensure they are not guilty of various forms of second-generation discrimination?**

Competing Perspectives: Theories, Models, and Approaches to Race, Class, and Gender

Educational institutions can approach issues of cultural diversity in a number of ways. Theories, models, and approaches to learning about diversity are categorized into five areas. None of these approaches is independent of the others; each category overlaps and draws on other theoretical areas. The approaches are cultural deficiency, cultural difference, human relations, single-group studies, multicultural education, and social justice education.

Cultural Deficiency Approach

Historically, U.S. educators have viewed students from backgrounds other than the dominant culture in two ways: the deficit perspective and the cultural difference perspective (see Box 4.2). Some educators believe that students from other cultures come to U.S. schools with deficiencies. They might argue, for example, that students are *deprived* because they have minimal proficiency in the English language, or they might believe that because students are from low socioeconomic backgrounds or single-parent families, they are *disadvantaged*. Identification of students as deprived or disadvantaged implies that they have deficiencies that must be remediated. Similarly, in the 1990s the term *at-risk* became a popular label.

Educational researchers such as Beth Harry (1992) and Henry Trueba (1989) have argued that language-biased educators have incorrectly placed language-minority students in classes for the learning disabled or mentally retarded. Because language-biased educators think such students have "language deficiencies" (i.e., they are not highly proficient in English), they put them in remedial classes.

Meier and Stewart (1991) found that minority students are overrepresented among those who are expelled, disciplined, or drop out. Their research argues that Hispanics and African American students are denied access to high-quality education.

Another deficiency perception that many educators hold is that children from low socioeconomic backgrounds lack appropriate role models for their development. In a 1992 article in the *New York Times National*, Gross stated, "A mother is sometimes

BOX 4.2 • *Deficit and Difference Theories in Education*

Deficit Perspectives	*Difference Perspectives*
The child's language is considered to be a "restricted code" of the dominant language or a less developed language than the dominant language.	The child's language is considered to be different from but comparable to the dominant language.
The child's learning style is seen as an impediment to proper academic socialization and should be adapted to culturally dominant norms.	The child's learning style is an individual matter that should be seen as a tool to help the child learn.
The child's family is often seen as "broken" or dysfunctional and as a barrier to the child's success in school.	Family patterns are understood to vary, but the child's family is seen as a key player in the child's education.
The child's behavior is problematic and the child is seen as a discipline problem.	There is often a conflict between the behavioral norms of the home culture and the school culture.

Source: P. Cordeiro, T. Reagan, & L. Martinez (1994). *Multiculturalism and TQE: Addressing cultural diversity in schools.* Thousand Oaks, CA: Corwin Press. Reprinted by permission of Corwin Press, Inc.

present in these homes, but she is often a drug addict or a teenager who comes and goes. . . . Scarred by years of abuse and neglect, many of these children are angry and disruptive" (pp. 1 & 166). Many minority groups (e.g., African American males) are blamed for abandoning their families, thus causing these families to be *deprived* or *deficient*. A more enlightened way to frame these issues is to focus on access to resources and support systems instead of focusing on lack of morals or family psychological instability. The deficit perspective has been severely criticized in recent years.

Cultural Difference Approach

According to Sleeter and Grant (1993), "The main idea behind Teaching the Culturally Different Approach . . . is to ensure as much cultural compatibility as possible" (p. 44). The focus is on building bridges between the two cultures because there is a *cultural mismatch*. An example might be a child who has minimal proficiency in English. Programmatic response might be to include partial or full day ESL classes, or sheltered English classes. Providing a sign language interpreter in a regular classroom for a child who is deaf might be a programmatic response for his or her cultural difference.

As we look at ethnic minority groups, according to the cultural difference approach, some minority students fail because they do not adapt themselves to the dominant cultural style of the school or as Trueba states (1988), the schools have not provided appropriate "activity settings" to accommodate the minority student. While this approach is important because it offsets the racist *cultural deprivation* approach or *genetic inferiority* approach it ignores the historical and social factors responsible for the reproduction of "cultural differences" in schools.

John Ogbu (1992) was one of the first researchers to criticize the cultural difference approach. He argued that there has been a lack of critical analysis among educators and that this absence of critique has allowed educators to attempt to approach school conflicts in cultural styles through remediation programs.

Human Relations Approach

Sometimes referred to as *intergroup education*, the major goal of a *human relations* approach is to help *all* students develop more positive attitudes toward people who are members of different racial, cultural, and gender groups. This approach concerns the relationships that students have with one another. Another objective of a human relations approach is to help students become better communicators. Group processes and group facilitation, which are part of *cooperative learning*, are methods of achieving these goals.

A human relations approach is supported by theories and concepts developed by research that started in the 1940s. Researchers were originally interested in studying the nature of racial prejudice. Gunnar Myrdal (1944) and others such as Deutsch (1963) discovered that interaction across racial lines tended to increase racial tolerance. Several explanations were given for the finding that contact reduces prejudice.

Cognitive dissonance theory argued that dissonance occurs when an individual's behavior or experience clashes with the views he or she holds. In other words, individuals want to align their attitudes with their experiences, so they try to bring their behaviors and attitudes together. Another explanation is found in the theory of *interpersonal attraction*. This theory holds that people are attracted to others whose beliefs and values they share. Hewstone and Brown (1986) contend that contact with persons and the opportunity to learn about them will eventually "neutralize the negative relationship that formerly existed" (p. 5).

Another possible explanation for increases in racial tolerance that result when racial lines are crossed is based on the notion that contact can have an educational benefit. Interaction with others can provide more knowledge and can identify false thinking. Thus, it is argued that contact might reduce prejudice because it expands an individual's knowledge and experiences.

In his seminal book *The Nature of Prejudice*, Gordon Allport (1958) formulated a hypothesis that attitudes change most often if contact occurs between individuals of equal status. Allport made a crucial point—contact does not automatically reduce prejudice. He believed that contact across racial lines of individuals with similar educational or occupational status would have more positive effects on people's attitudes than would contact among individuals of different status. More recent work in anthropology by Levinson (1996), who studied students in a Mexican *secundaria*, found that

> students in their first and second years from the *pueblitos* [villages close to the city] . . . forge ties with one another across and within *grupos escolares* [heterogeneous cohorts who pass through the four years of middle school together]. The shared position that appears to bring them together is that of "country" or "village" dweller in relation to the school's predominantly urban culture. (p. 227)

The work of other researchers, such as Purkey and Novak (1984) and Johnson and Johnson (1975), has also contributed to our understanding of human relations. Johnson and Johnson advocate *cooperative learning*, which they believe will improve intergroup relations. Purkey and Novak have written about *invitational education*. They argue that educators and schools must be intentionally inviting.

Single-Group Studies Approach

Another approach to addressing cultural diversity in education is what Sleeter and Grant (1993) call *single-group studies*. The curriculum is the main focus of this approach. A single-group focus might be a course (Asian literature), program (women's studies), or an entire school with a particular focus on one group (Afrocentric schools). According to Sleeter and Grant, the goal in these programs is to "reduce social stratification and raise the status of the group" (p. 123). This approach was instituted in response to a curriculum that has traditionally emphasized the contributions of white, middle-class males.

Two classic books are part of the first wave of critical studies of schooling: *Schooling in Capitalist America: Educational Reform and the Contradictions of Economic Life* by Bowles and Gintis (1976) and Bourdieu and Passeron's (1977) *Reproduction: In Education, Society, and Culture.* Their authors argue that schools are not passive sites where culture is simply transmitted. To the contrary, schools actually perpetuate, or *reproduce,* the inequalities that exist in society. Instead of equalizing people, schools reproduce the inequities that separate them. Educators began to ask: What does schooling mean to children who are not members of the dominant societal group (white, middle class)?

Multicultural Education Approach

The term *multicultural education* is most often used inappropriately. Many educators who approach cultural diversity through a *cultural difference, human relations,* or *single-group* approach describe their efforts as multicultural education. Banks and Banks (1994) state that multicultural education is "at least three things: an idea or concept, an educational reform movement, and a process" (p. 3).

Davidman and Davidman (2000) have identified six interrelated goals for multicultural education:

1. Educational equity
2. Empowerment of students and their parents
3. Cultural pluralism in society
4. Intercultural/interethnic/intergroup understanding and harmony in the classroom, school, and community
5. An expanded knowledge of various cultural and ethnic groups
6. The development of students, parents, and practitioners whose thoughts and actions are guided by an informed and inquisitive multicultural perspective

Equity involves not only access to learning opportunities and physical and financial conditions within the school and district, but also "educational outcomes for both individuals and groups" (p. 4).

Empowerment requires members of the school community to take active roles, whether at the local or national level. The empowerment of students and parents is key to a multicultural education approach.

Cultural pluralism indicates an acceptance of cultural diversity as a valuable and worthwhile facet of society. Teachers who accept cultural pluralism constantly ask themselves how to help students respect and appreciate cultural diversity in the classroom, school, and society.

Social Justice Education Approach

Borrowing heavily from each of the previous approaches, the social justice education approach "deals more directly with oppression, social structural inequality based on race, social class, gender and disability" (p. 153).

In one of the most informative books on cultural diversity in education, *Affirming Diversity: The Sociopolitical Context of Multicultural Education,* Sonia Nieto (2000) states:

> Multicultural education is a process of comprehensive school reform and basic education for all students. It challenges and rejects racism and other forms of discrimina-

tion in schools and society and accepts and affirms pluralism (ethnic, racial, linguistic, religious, economic, and gender, among others) that students, their communities, and teachers represent. Multicultural education permeates the curriculum and instructional strategies used in schools, as well as the interactions among teachers and students and parents, and the very way the schools conceptualize the nature of teaching and learning. Because it uses critical pedagogy as its underlying philosophy and focuses on knowledge, reflection, and action (praxis) as the basis for social change, multicultural education furthers the democratic principles of social justice. (p. 305)

According to Nieto, multicultural education has seven basic characteristics. It is: (1) antiracist education, (2) basic education, (3) important for all students, (4) pervasive, (5) for social justice, (6) a process, and (7) critical pedagogy.

Let us examine the concepts of social justice and critical pedagogy in more detail. Figure 4.1 is a model developed by James Banks (1999) describing the levels of integration of ethnic content that can be used in curriculum reform.

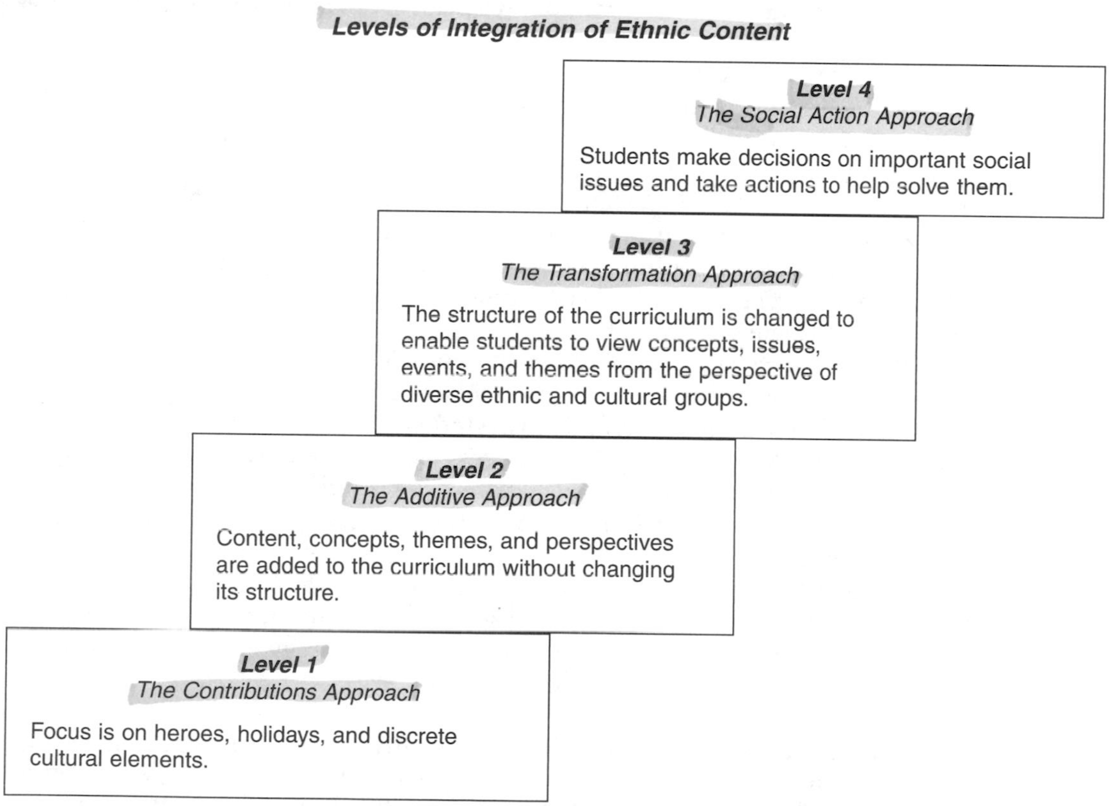

Levels of Integration of Ethnic Content

Level 4
The Social Action Approach

Students make decisions on important social issues and take actions to help solve them.

Level 3
The Transformation Approach

The structure of the curriculum is changed to enable students to view concepts, issues, events, and themes from the perspective of diverse ethnic and cultural groups.

Level 2
The Additive Approach

Content, concepts, themes, and perspectives are added to the curriculum without changing its structure.

Level 1
The Contributions Approach

Focus is on heroes, holidays, and discrete cultural elements.

FIGURE 4.1   *Banks's Approaches to Multicultural Curriculum Reform*

Reprinted with permission from James A. Banks, *An Introduction to Multicultural Education*, third edition. Boston: Allyn and Bacon, 2002, p. 30.

At the contributions level educators might celebrate Cinco de Mayo or Martin Luther King Day. The focus is on the particular contribution that a group of people (Hispanics or African Americans) or a person made toward a movement, cause, or cultural group. Most U.S. schools have a variety of activities that could fall within this approach. As Banks states, at the contributions level "students do not attain a global view of the role of ethnic and cultural groups in U.S. society" (p. 207).

The next level Banks (1999) calls the ethnic additive approach. In this approach concepts, themes, and various perspectives are added to the curriculum, but the curriculum is not restructured. Adding another perspective, however, does not necessarily enhance the curriculum. For example, if the class is studying a unit titled "Columbus's Discovery of the New World" and the teacher includes a discussion of how people indigenous to the West Indies might have responded to Columbus, an alternative perspective is not necessarily being presented. The title of the unit itself implies that it took a European to *discover* people who already had a long-standing culture. Thus, such an approach still presents only a Eurocentric perspective.

✳ **Use Fairhaven's Oakes High School to discuss alternative ways in which the lesson on Columbus might have been given a greater multicultural emphasis.**

At the transformation level, a restructuring of the curriculum occurs. Students are provided with ideas, issues, themes, and challenges from a variety of perspectives. Study of the U.S. Civil War, for example, places emphasis on how our many cultures formed the overall U.S. culture at that time. A complex weaving of diverse cultural elements (e.g., from language, music, art) originated from the wide variety of racial, gender, ethnic, cultural, and religious groups. This level is transformational because it transcends the dominant perspective and gives voice to the many cultural elements present in our society.

Banks's fourth level, social action, incorporates the three earlier levels, but the concept of social justice is the main criterion of this level. Encouraging social action and developing decision making skills in students is a key goal. Gordon (1985) includes emancipatory pedagogy. She believes that "categories such as 'critical emancipatory or liberatory pedagogy,' may work as descriptors that not only expand the narrow frames of reference, but also move them from pejorative to self-reflection, critique, and social action" (p. 29).

Some of the research and theory that informs this approach can be found in the works of Henry Giroux (1992), Michael Apple (1986), Paolo Freire (1985), John Ogbu (1992), and Jean Anyon (1980). The terms *critical teaching* and *critical pedagogy* come from critical theory. According to Giroux (1992):

> Critical pedagogy refers to a deliberate attempt to construct specific conditions through which educators and students can think critically about how knowledge is produced and transformed in relation to the construction of social experiences informed by a particular relationship between the self, others, and the larger world. (pp. 98–99)

Brazilian educator Paolo Freire (1985) maintains that critical pedagogy promotes greater understanding of this approach.

A pedagogy will be that much more critical and radical, the more investigative and less certain of "certainties" it is. The more "unquiet" a pedagogy, the more critical it will become. A pedagogy preoccupied with the uncertainties rooted in the issues we have discussed is, by its nature, a pedagogy that requires investigation. This pedagogy is thus much more a pedagogy of question than a pedagogy of answer. (Cited in Macedo, 1994, p. 102)

✳ **What are the implications of these approaches for Oakes High School? Would one approach or combinations of several approaches better match Oakes's context?**

Segregation, Desegregation, and Integration

The U.S. educational system has responded to issues of desegregation and integration in a variety of ways. Programmatic options include magnet programs, programs for "at-risk" children, bilingual programs, and Afrocentric programs or schools, to name but a few. Since *Brown v. Board of Education* (1954), school desegregation has become one of the most hotly debated education issues nationwide. Some argue that prior to *Brown,* school segregation was legal and that it is still present in the form of single-sex schools, single race and ethnic schools (i.e., Afrocentric schools), some bilingual programs, and alternative schools or programs that separate "special-education students."

It is evident that an educational leader must not only understand the programmatic possibilities and their context, but also the social and cultural factors that influence program development decisions. Clearly, the needs of the community as Tanner discusses in Chapter 8 are one of the key issues at the heart of a school's curriculum.

Magnet Schools

Magnet schools can be found at all grade levels in both private and public schools. Magnet programs are differentiated by their curriculum, special focus area, and instructional approach (e.g., Montessori, Paideia). The formats of magnet schools vary. Some programs are schoolwide, or whole-school magnets, in which all students would be involved in the "magnet" area (e.g., in a schoolwide global education magnet, all students would in some ways be involved in the global education curriculum). Another type is often called a "school-within-a-school program" (SWAS) or "program within a school" (PWS). Only some students in a particular school are involved in the magnet program. Another format might be a grade-level magnet in which only certain grade levels are offered a particular curricular focus.

Today nearly all large school districts have magnet schools. In the 1991–1992 school year, there were 2,433 magnet schools nationwide, offering 3,171 magnet programs (some schools house more than one magnet) (American Institutes for Research, 1994). Five basic factors led to the growth of magnet schools:

1. They have represented a voluntary approach to school desegregation.
2. As people call for school choice, magnet schools are alternatives to the local school with a "regular" curriculum.

3. Like a magnet they *attract* students from outside their assigned neighborhood attendance zones.
4. In recent years greater attention has been paid to the outcomes of education.
5. Magnet schools often provide knowledge that is supposed to be helpful to a particular career choice.

Language Diversity in U.S. Schools: Program Options

Although a few earlier examples of bilingual programs in U.S. history can be identified, bilingual education is a relatively recent phenomenon. In 1968 Congress passed the Bilingual Education Act (later, Title VII of the Elementary and Secondary Education Act, ESEA). The Bilingual Education Act states that "no person shall be subjected to discrimination on the basis of race, color, or national origin." School districts are required to take affirmative steps to provide children with the language skills they need to participate in school. The Bilingual Education Act and the landmark U.S. Supreme Court decision *Lau v. Nichols*, 1974, provided a legal basis for equitable treatment of limited-English-proficient children in U.S. schools. It placed non–native-English-speaking children at the forefront of an often hotly debated topic.

Bilingual Education.   *Bilingual* refers to proficiency in at least two languages, and *biculturalism* is participation in two cultures. Bilingual education usually refers to an educational approach involving the use of two languages of instruction at some point in the student's schooling.

For decades educators and policymakers have wrestled with questions related to bilingual education: What are the best ways to teach children whose native language is not English? How can the achievement of students with limited proficiency in English be enhanced? There is no debate over the issue that proficiency in English is essential to school and workplace success. Instead the debate deals with the most appropriate ways for students to learn English as a second language and what roles, if any, the first language should play.

School districts offer several types of programs to students in the United States (Box 4.3). These include ESL, sheltered English, transitional bilingual education, two-way bilingual education, maintenance bilingual education, and structured immersion.

It is important for educational leaders to determine which of these approaches is most appropriate for the children in their schools or districts. Language proficiency, the number of students whose native language is not English, the ages of children, and whether they are able to speak and read their native language proficiently are but a few of the factors that need to be examined. Most bilingual educators favor maintenance programs; the majority of existing programs, however, are transitional.

BOX 4.3 • *Program Options for Non–Native-English-Speaking Students*

English as a Second Language
A systematic, comprehensive approach to teaching English to students whose native language is not English. It is usually an important component of a bilingual program, but it can also exist by itself.

Options
- full/partial day
- pullout
- sheltered English
- English for special purposes (ESP)

Sheltered English
In what are sometimes called transition or bridge classes, students cover the same content offered in classes in which native English proficiency is assumed. The language component of these classes is adapted to suit the English proficiency levels of the language-minority students.

Transitional Bilingual Education (TBE)
The Bilingual Education Act of 1968 defined transitional bilingual education as "structured English language instruction, and to the extent necessary to allow a child to achieve compe-

tence in the English language, instruction in the child's native language." Ideally, access to a comprehensible curriculum is assured by providing basic instruction in the child's native language until the student attains English competency and comprehension in speaking, writing, and reading. The goal of these programs is for students to learn English as quickly as possible so they can exit the programs.

Two-Way Bilingual Education
Two-way bilingual programs offer a means of encouraging bilingualism in both language minority and language majority students.

Maintenance Bilingual Education
The goal in maintenance bilingual programs is to provide students with instruction that helps the development of the native language.

Submersion or Immersion
Sometimes referred to as the "sink or swim" approach, submersion (immersion) places students in a totally English-speaking environment with no use of their native language. It is not a form of bilingual education.

Promoting Linguistically Diverse Learners' Academic Success

VIVIANA ALEXANDROWICZ • *University of San Diego*

Providing comprehensible education to linguistically diverse students in the different subject areas has become a pedagogical challenge for teachers, particularly in states with a large immigrant population. In states like California, one out of four K–6 students was classified as a "Limited English Proficient" (LEP) student and of all new students who enrolled in California schools between 1998 and 2000, 71 percent were nonfluent in English. Research has shown that it can take immigrant students up to nine years to acquire the necessary language competence to successfully deal with academic tasks that are required to perform at grade level in English (Cummins, 1989). What can teachers and administrators do to help immigrant children succeed in school?

*The Importance of Understanding
Second-Language Acquisition*
Belief is widespread at all levels in the school community—from government elected officials

to school administrators, teachers, and parents—that second-language learners can acquire competence in a second language fast enough to keep up with academics within two years of arrival in the United States. This belief reflects a lack of understanding of how difficult it is to learn all the aspects of language—pragmatics, semantics, morphology, phonology, and syntax—to effectively function in academic settings. It also suggests the need for increasing educators' awareness about the factors involved in acquiring a second language.

For instance, students' prior education and literacy in their native language affects learning in a second language. Students who speak and write in a primary language that uses an alphabet and characters similar to those of English tend to acquire the English language more easily than those who do not. In addition, sociocultural factors such as family members' levels of education, parental support, living conditions, and attitudes of the host society toward the student's language and culture play a critical role in the student's motivation and academic achievement. Moreover, the student's personality and learning preferences call for a careful assessment of each child as an individual who has diverse social, affective, cognitive, and linguistic needs.

When this complex array of issues related to placement of linguistically diverse students is overlooked in U.S. schools, second-language learners often find themselves in a "sink or swim" situation. In other words, they are "integrated" in mainstream English classrooms so they can be "immersed" in authentic language environments, which supposedly allow them to "pick up" English after a period of time. As a result of these situations, we have children who, day to day, learn survival English at the expense of the rest of their education.

Usually, it is not until individuals have reached an intermediate level of language competence that they are likely to cope with and complete academic work, let alone fully participate in classroom activities in a second language. In many instances, administrators and teachers place a child who has acquired a "native-like" accent within a year in a regular English classroom because "he is doing so well in English." The same teachers and administrators are "puzzled"

when these children are "failing" in different subject areas, and a large number of second-language learners end up in special education classes.

Effective Programs Are Key to Academic Success

In "additive" programs, students add a second language to their native language in speaking, reading, and writing, becoming not only bilingual but, more important, biliterate. Examples of such programs are the "two-way" bilingual program or the "late-exit" maintenance program. In two-way bilingual programs, all students become biliterate in two languages, and in late-exit programs, students move gradually from instruction in their native language in all subject areas to instruction in transitional English until they become proficient enough to transfer to mainstream English classrooms. By the time students reach junior high school, they are receiving all instruction in English except in one subject area such as language arts, which allows them to maintain and enrich their primary language. All bilinguals know that once one has acquired knowledge and skills in the primary language, one does not have to acquire most of them again in the second language.

The programs most often implemented, which have proven highly ineffective, are those that transfer students to all-English classrooms before they are ready—for instance after two years of primary instruction in all subject areas. Tragically, in many of these "subtractive" programs, where one loses one's primary language to gain a second one, students do not receive the strong English as a second language (ESL) component that would enable them to succeed in their new all-English "sink or swim" classrooms.

Implementation of poor-quality programs has created the perception that "bilingual education" in general does not work. The "English only" movement that reemerged in the 1990s reflects this perception. Proponents of English-only classrooms tend to promote the idea that "if our grandparents made it without bilingual education, these children can make it too" (a critical question is how we define success in today's society compared with the skills people needed to succeed forty years ago). Furthermore, bilingual education (effective and ineffective programs) serves only about 30 percent of the second-language student population; therefore, other factors must account for the high dropout rates among certain culturally and linguistically diverse populations.

When effective bilingual programs are not viable for different reasons (e.g., if there is a scarcity of teachers who speak the language of their students), an alternative is to provide students comprehensible instruction using Specially Designed Academic Instruction in English (SDAIE). A SDAIE teacher may have a contained SDAIE classroom if there are enough second-language learners at that grade level, or he or she may just have a few of these students in a "mainstream" classroom. SDAIE teachers have strong professional preparation in the areas of second-language acquisition, cultural diversity, and in classroom management in classrooms with multiple levels of academic backgrounds and languages.

Effective programs employ trained teachers who go beyond "good" teaching. They know that directions, modeling, and explanations that might be clear and sufficient for most of their fully proficient English speakers are not sufficient for their second-language learners. Moreover, when they have few second-language learners who are integrated in "regular" mainstream classrooms, these teachers must assess their students' language competence and plan instruction accordingly.

These teachers hold high expectations for their students and understand that a student's ability to produce in a second language does not necessarily reflect his or her capacity to think cognitively. They also promote critical thinking early in the process of second-language development, but hold realistic expectations for their students' ability to deal with academic tasks in English.

It is imperative that educational leaders promote a community of learners where teachers, students, parents, and staff foster compassion, fellowship, and respect for others. Most important, everyone involved must sincerely believe that anyone can and should learn a second language and become biliterate and bicultural and that anyone can succeed academically in school.

English Language Learners in U.S. Public Schools

Many languages other than English have always been spoken in U.S. public schools, and this increasingly continues to be the situation. Let's examine the growth in English Language Learners (ELLs) during the last decade. From 1993 to 1994 ELL students made up approximately 5 percent of the total school population in the nation. In 1999–2000 the percentage grew to nearly 7 percent. Although the percentage increases are not the same in all regions of the nation, states in the Midwest, South, and West have all shown an increase in the ELL student population, both in total and as a percentage of the total school population. Linguistic diversity will always be a part of U.S. public education. Currently Spanish, Vietnamese, Hmong, Cantonese, Filipino, and Cambodian are the most prevalent languages spoken by immigrant children and youths. Clearly, as Alexandrowicz advocates above, the school administrator must be knowledgeable about the optimal types of programs needed for ELLs.

English Only, English Plus, and Programs for Nonstandard English Speakers

In recent years some states and organizations have called for English to be the *only* language used in state documents, in business transactions, and in schools. Other groups have pointed out the importance of being multilingual. The latter group takes a view that some call English Plus: People should not only speak English, but they also should have fluency in another language. Although these state and national debates may be important, they have not yet had a direct impact on schools.

One debate that garnered considerable attention in 1997 was the controversy surrounding a decision by the Oakland, California, School Board to offer African American speakers of Ebonics, or Black English, special instruction. Additionally, during the debate, other school districts such as that in Los Angeles were found to already be offering "Ebonics" programs. Once the issues were dissected, several common factors could be identified regardless of the voices in the debate: (1) African American students were lagging behind other ethnic groups in academic achievement, (2) something had to be done to address this lack of achievement, and (3) everyone involved (parents, teachers, students, and community members) agreed that all students must be able to speak standard English. Most linguists agree that a student who develops awareness of her or his own variety of English will make a better learner of standard English.

In volatile situations such as these, the challenges for school leaders include examining the complexity of the issues, identifying needs, identifying options, and working collaboratively to choose the best option(s).

Developing Programs of School, Family, and Community Partnerships: Administrators Make a Difference

JOYCE L. EPSTEIN • *Director, Center on School, Family, and Community Partnerships, Johns Hopkins University*

Over and again we learn that principals, district administrators, and state education policy leaders make the difference between successful and unsuccessful schools. Administrators have different leadership styles, but all effective leaders focus on important goals, encourage hard work, inspire excellence, and recognize the efforts and contributions of others. Only with outstanding support will all teachers, students, parents, community members, and others remain committed to improving schools, classrooms, and children's learning. This support is especially necessary for developing comprehensive programs of school, family, and community partnerships.

What is a comprehensive program of partnerships? First, such programs are *theory driven*. The theory of "overlapping spheres of influence" recognizes that students learn and grow at home, at school, and in their communities. Students are at the center of this model, because they are the main actors in their education. Sec-

ond, comprehensive programs of partnership are *research based*. From the results of many studies in elementary, middle, and high schools, I developed a framework of six major types of involvement:

Type 1—Parenting: Assist families with parenting skills, family support, understanding child and adolescent development, and setting home conditions to support learning at each age and grade level. Assist schools in understanding families' backgrounds, cultures, and goals for children.

Type 2—Communicating: Communicate with families about school programs and student progress in varied, clear, and productive ways. Create two-way communication channels (school to home and home to school) so that families can easily communicate with teachers, administrators, counselors, and other families.

Type 3—Volunteering: Improve recruitment, training, activities, and schedules to involve families as volunteers and as audiences at the school or in other locations. Enable educators to work with regular and occasional volunteers who assist and support students and the school.

Type 4—Learning at Home: Involve families with their children in academic learning activities at home, such as homework, goal setting, and other curriculum-related activities and decisions. Encourage teachers to design homework that enables students to share and discuss interesting work and ideas with family members.

Type 5—Decision Making: Include families as participants in school decisions, governance, and advocacy activities through school councils or improvement teams, committees, PTA/PTO, and other parent organizations. Assist family and teacher representatives to obtain information from and give information to those they represent.

Type 6—Collaborating with Community: Coordinate resources and services for families, students, and the school with community businesses, agencies, cultural and civic organizations, colleges or universities, and other community groups. Enable students, staff, and families to contribute their service to the community.

There are hundreds of practices for the six types from which elementary, middle, and high schools may choose. Each type of involvement has explicit challenges that must be met in order to turn an ordinary program into an excellent one. Each type of involvement leads to different results for students, families, teachers, schools, and communities.

From many studies, we have learned that schools make progress in home-school-community connections if plans are written and if progress is charted by an action team for school, family, and community partnerships. The team of teachers, parents, administrators, and others completes an inventory of present practices, constructs a three-year vision, and writes annual one-year action plans that address school goals with good practices from the six types of involvement.

What results will good programs of partnership produce? Many studies indicate:

• Families are important for children's learning, healthy development, and school success from preschool through high school.

• State, district, and school policy statements about partnerships are not enough. Schools need assistance, support, recognition, and ongoing guidance to develop, improve, and maintain successful programs of school, family, and community partnerships.

• All communities have resources to promote students' social and intellectual development and to assist schools and families. Community resources must be organized, mobilized, and incorporated in comprehensive programs of partnership.

• Students are more positive about school and learning and do better in school if their families and communities are involved in their education in productive ways. Specific results (e.g., improved attendance, behavior, homework completion, reading, writing, math, or other achievement) are linked to goal-oriented and subject-specific activities for family and community involvement.

• When elementary, middle, and high schools develop excellent programs of partnership, families become involved, including those who would not become involved on their own or who are typically "hard to reach."

How can administrators organize and improve their leadership on school, family, and community partnerships? Leadership for school, family, and community partnerships requires understanding, action, and persistence and includes understanding the framework of the six types of involvement, the challenges that must be met to reach all families, and the connections of involvement to specific goals and results.

Guidelines for action are available from the National Network of Partnership Schools at the Center on School, Family, and Community Partnerships at Johns Hopkins University. Members receive handbooks, newsletters, training workshops, assistance by phone, e-mail, and website, and opportunities for research and sharing best practices. There are no fees for these services, but members must invest in their own staff, identify budgets, implement annual plans, develop comprehensive programs, and share progress with the center.

Developing excellent home, school, and community partnerships is an ongoing process that takes time, organization, and effort. Progress is accelerated if efforts in school, family, and community partnerships are targeted in annual professional evaluations of teachers, principals, and superintendents.

No longer a separate topic off to the side of "real" reform efforts, school, family, and community partnerships now are seen as a central component of whole-school change and school improvement. Information for families and their involvement and input are needed for students to succeed with bilingual programs, challenging curricula, innovative instruction, and new tests and assessments. In sum, good programs of partnerships help improve schools, strengthen families, energize communities, and increase student success.

Notes: This work is supported by grants from the U.S. Department of Education and the DeWitt Wallace–Reader's Digest Fund. The ideas are the author's and do not necessarily represent the policies of either funding source. For information on the National Network of Partnership Schools or lists of related publications, contact: Center on School, Family, and Community Partnerships, Johns Hopkins University/CRESPAR, 3003 North Charles Street, Suite 200, Baltimore, MD 21218. Phone: 410-516-8818; fax: 410-516-8890; e-mail: sfc@csos.jhu.edu or Web site: www.csos.jhu.edu/p2000.

Connecting Schools and Community Organizations

In education, partnerships are either school-linked or school-based. These partnerships range in complexity from a school's forming a collaboration with one person, organization, or agency to multilayered alliances. Recent literature supports the observation that partnering is a service model that is not only useful, but in today's economic and social climate is also quickly becoming recognized as mandatory (Cordeiro & Loup, 1996; Gardner, 1993; Jehl & Kirst, 1992).

Figure 4.2 depicts the numerous human service agencies and community organizations that make up what some researchers call "cultural capital" or "sociocultural capital" (Bourdieu & Passeron, 1977, p. 90; Coleman, 1993; Cordeiro, Reagan, & Martinez, 1994). At the center is the child, encompassed first by family, then by school and school district.

A variety of other entities influence the child's school and family life either directly or indirectly. These include religious organizations, higher-education institutions, nonprofits, such as museums and local arts organizations, government agencies, the medical community, the media, social service agencies, business and industry, social and ethnic organizations, youth organizations, such as the YM/YWCA, Boys and Girls Clubs, and parks and recreation department programs, education-related organizations, and the rapidly growing outside world—the virtual community. Each of these agencies or organizations is part of a network of services available to all children. One fairly new role that schools and school districts need to play is the coordination of these many entities not only with the school, but also with the family.

Cordeiro and Monroe-Kolek (1996) identified five key factors among these organizations and schools that are preconditions for successful partnerships: leadership, trust, stability, readiness, and a common agenda. These factors interact to

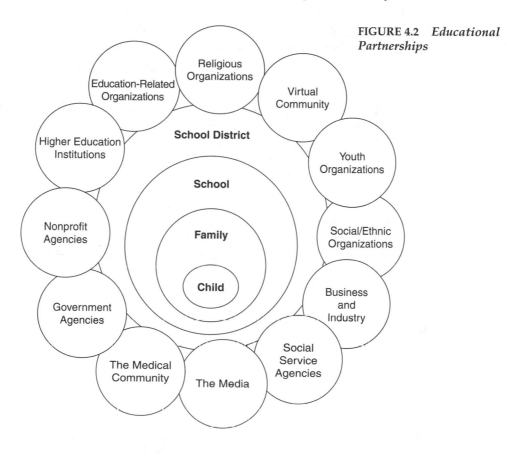

FIGURE 4.2 *Educational Partnerships*

form a foundation on which partnerships can be constructed. Without this basic framework it is doubtful that solid school-community partnerships will improve the lives of children.

Cordeiro and Monroe-Kolek's (1996) research found four conditions that support collaboration if the above preconditions exist. Crucial to any partnerships are issues of communication. The form of communication does not appear to be the key factor but rather the fact that regular and sustained communication occurs. The notion that both partners are benefiting in some way so that there appears to be reciprocity is another element in maintaining successful partnerships. Aligning and pooling of resources is another factor. Johnson and Galvan (1996) argue that the interests and transaction costs associated with such efforts suggest that certain partnerships might in fact increase the actual costs for both organizations involved. Thus, it is imperative that partners not duplicate services but instead fill in the gaps in service provision.

The final element these authors identify as crucial to maintaining and sustaining a partnership is the notion of knowing the community. One way to address this issue is McKnight and Kretzmann's (1993) concept of asset mapping. Especially in urban and low socioeconomic communities, there is a tendency to look at what is *not* present to support the growth and development of children. McKnight and Kretzman argue that poor neighborhoods have a multitude of assets, such as schools, ethnic and religious organizations, institutions of higher education, churches, and libraries, to name but a few.

✳ **What types of community partnerships should the faculty and administration of Oakes High consider developing?**

Conclusion

A number of social and cultural factors affect children's learning. Ethnicity, social class, gender, disability, family, home environment, and language are but some of the many factors that must be better understood by educators. Thoughtful consideration of these factors will assist educational leaders in analyzing issues so that prudent decisions regarding educational programming can be made. Educational leaders must create conditions for forming meaningful partnerships with families and the plethora of community agencies. These partnerships have the potential to assist educators and community members in providing services to children so that all will be better able to learn.

Portfolio Artifacts

- Revisit your educational platform. What does your platform say about your beliefs regarding issues of educational equity? How does it address issues related to multicultural education?
- Interview a person working in a community agency that partners with a school. How does this person's perspective influence your views on schools and their communities?
- Examine a curriculum. Is that curriculum reflective of the issues of diversity discussed in this chapter?
- Spend time with people who are different from you in regard to race, socioeconomic status, ethnicity, ability/disability, and reflect on the experience (e.g., switch jobs for a week with someone in a school serving a population different from yours).
- Spend a period of time riding along with a police officer in a community that is different from the one in which you live. (Many police departments have special programs for citizens.) Reflect on the experience.
- Travel to a community or country different from your own. Reflect on the similarities and differences.
- Search the Web for the National Association of Multicultural Education (www.nameorg.org). In what ways might a educational administrator find this Web site helpful?

Terms

Afrocentric schools	Cultural deficit theory	Cultural relativism
Assimilation	Cultural difference theory	Culture
Bilingual education	Cultural diversity	Culture identity/Ethnic
Critical teaching (pedagogy)	Cultural pluralism	identity

Culture shock
Desegregation
Discrimination
Ebonics
English as a second language (ESL)
English for special (or specific) purposes (ESP)
English language learners (ELL)
Equal access
Inclusive; Inclusion

Integration
Intergroup education
Language minority student
Language proficiency
Lau v. Nichols
Learning style
Limited English Proficiency (LEP)
Magnet schools
Mainstreaming
Prejudice
Race

Racism
Second-generation discrimination
Segregation
Sexual orientation
Sheltered English
Socioeconomic groups
Specially designed academic instruction in English (SDAIE)
Stereotypes

Suggested Readings

American Psychological Association. (1999). *Just the facts about sexual orientation & youth: A primer for principals, educators, & school personnel.* www.apa.org.

Banks, J. A. (Ed.). (2004). *Diversity and citizenship education: Global perspectives.* San Francisco, CA: Jossey-Bass.

Cordeiro, P. (Ed.). (1996). *Boundary crossings: Educational partnerships and school leadership.* San Francisco: Jossey-Bass.

Cordeiro, P., Reagan, T., & Martinez, L. (1994). *Multiculturalism and TQE: Addressing cultural diversity in schools.* Thousand Oaks, CA: Corwin Press.

Cushner, K. H., McClelland, A., & Safford, P. (2002). *Human diversity in education: An integrative approach.* Columbus, OH: McGraw Hill.

Epstein, J. (2001). *School, family and community partnerships: Preparing educators and improving schools.* Boulder, CO: Westview Press.

Nieto, S. (2003). *Affirming diversity: The sociopolitical context of multicultural education.* New York: Longman.

Reyes, P. E., & Scribner, J. (1999). *Lessons from high-performing Hispanic schools.* New York: Teachers College Press.

Sleeter, C. E., & Banks, J. A. (2004). *Culture, difference and power.* New York: Teachers College Press.

Media Recommendation

Cohen, R. (2004). *Going to School (Ir a La Escuela)* Venice, CA: Richard Cohen films. www.richardcohenfilms.com A documentary about inclusion, diversity, and empowering students with disabilities.

5

School District Organizational Structure and Leadership

Data Disaggregation: Building an Excellent School

You are the new principal of the 1,100 student Alta Vista School. Alta Vista was rezoned five years ago, which created a significant shift in the population attending the school. You are the third principal in this five-year period and the school has not really recovered from the changing demographics. You have had the entire summer to meet staff, disaggregate data, meet with community members, and basically learn as much as possible about Alta Vista school. Alta Vista School is listed as "Accredited with Warning." It did not made adequate yearly progress last year. In fact, the student state test scores have been declining for at least five years. The faculty insists on continuing to give the SRA standardized achievement test. Last year there were no PTA meetings scheduled due to the very low attendance in the past two years at similar meetings.

Listed below are some of the school/student demographics:

School Year	Last Year	Six Years Ago
Number of students	1,100	999
Number of assistant principals	3	2
Number of counselors	2	2

School Year	Last Year	Six Years Ago
Percent on free and reduced lunch	69%	35%
Percent eligible for special education	41%	15%
Number of office referrals	1,573	422
Number of suspensions 1–5 days	459	38
Number of suspensions 6–10 days	216	22
Number of suspensions > 10 days	55	10
Percent of white students	31	78
Percent of black students	48	22
Percent of Hispanic students	20	0
Percent of other ethnicity	1	0

Listed below are some of the SRA test data:

School Year	Last Year	Six Years Ago
Student scoring by percentile		
0–10th percentile	13%	0%

School Year	Last Year	Six Years Ago
Student scoring by percentile		
11–20th percentile	17%	4%
21–30th percentile	14%	4%
31–40th percentile	11%	6%
41–50th percentile	9%	9%
51–60th percentile	7%	14%
61–70th percentile	9%	20%
71–80th percentile	10%	17%
81–90th percentile	8%	18%
91–100th percentile	2%	8%
Percent of students reading below grade level:	62%	

Listed below are some of the faculty data:

	Current Year
Percent of conditionally licensed teachers	16%
Percent of provisionally licensed teachers	28%
Average teacher age	46 years
Average experience at the school	17 years
Percent with master's degree (or above)	10%
Percent of white teachers	87%
Percent of minority teachers	13%
Teacher turnover	11%

Only about 15 percent of the teachers showed up at the reception welcoming you to the school. The teachers have had the responsibility for assigning students to classes each summer. Ability grouping persists. Lower student teacher ratios exist in high ability classes, and higher student teacher ratios exist in lower ability classes. A large number of teachers rely on textbooks, do not differentiate instruction, and have only a sprinkling of hands-on activities. All the teachers with master's degrees teach upper-level students.

Several newer teachers approached you during the summer and expressed hope that you will change the school. They mention that the curriculum and the teaching methods have not been revised in more than twenty years, while the student body has very different needs. They ask for your help. During the first week of school, you learn that the assistant principal has been having difficulty locating substitutes and is especially concerned because your chairperson of the English department had a death in the family and will be out for over a week. You also have three emergency parent meetings and a serious discipline problem related to extreme violent behavior that may result in an expulsion hearing that requires your immediate attention. You also have a number of scheduling problems that need immediate action to get resolved and get students assigned to appropriate classes. Your bookkeeper wants to meet with you regarding a negative balance on the books that seems to be carried over from previous years that had been overlooked, since the books had not been audited for a couple of years. She also reminds you that you must attend the districtwide meeting of the health committee, which you serve on, later that afternoon. The senior custodian has been late to work, neglected his duties, has been openly critical of what he calls the "impossible expectations that you and the teachers have for the janitorial staff" and has been very harsh in dealing with his crew.

The previous principals were totally reactive and could never gain control of Alta Vista or become very proactive. You are beginning to understand the problem. The superintendent is going to be much more involved with this school at the request of the school board, who wants quarterly reports on school progress.

Source: Modified from a case study provided by William A. Owings, Old Dominion University, and Leslie S. Kaplan, Newport News Public Schools.

✳ **Do you as principal have the needed authority from the appropriate sources to begin a reform effort? Whose assistance and support might you seek?**

The Local Role

The organization depicted in an organizational chart is a structure within which individuals work to pursue identified goals and objectives. We can easily identify the formal structure of an organization and the positions within it. "In addition to defining work roles and authority relations, formal organizations also explicitly define and codify such details as the organization's channels of communication, policies and procedures, and norms and sanctions" (Loveless & Jasin, 1998).

What makes organizations unique are the people who hold these positions, people with unique personalities and unique approaches to the formal roles and structures provided. As a result, an organization always has visible and invisible aspects. The invisible aspects are often unique to the organization and time, and the visible, formal structure is fairly consistent across all organizations and thus is easier to describe and understand. The formal organization defines the structure in which people work, and the informal organization addresses the less tangible human factors and groupings within an organization.

Even though the formally defined structures do not depict total reality, being aware of them goes a long way toward helping people understand the operation of an organization. Two important aspects of formal organizational structure are norms and roles. Scott (1992) defines these two elements: "*Norms* are the generalized rules governing behavior that specify, in particular, appropriate means for pursuing goals; and *roles* are expectations for or evaluative standards employed in assessing the behavior of occupants of specific social positions" (p. 16). Scott goes on to say these are "organized so as to constitute a relatively coherent and consistent set of beliefs and prescriptions governing the behavior of participants" (p. 16). There is a constraining nature to organizational structure but also an enabling one that allows humans to accomplish more than they could through randomness and lack of structure. Each member of an organization can produce a larger outcome than he or she would be able to accomplish separately. Organization promotes the synergy effect.

Peter Blaw (1970) suggests, "Formal structures exhibit regularities that can be studied in their own right without investigating the motives of the individuals in organization" (p. 203). The focus of this chapter is the typical local school district with its bureaucratic structures and the roles of two of its key incumbents—the superintendent and principal.

The Local School Division

The primary units of structure for U.S. education are the local school divisions, which number some 15,000. Even across such a diverse system, however, some general structural patterns and issues remain fairly constant. These include authority structures, political patterns, norms, roles, and assignments. Typically, in school divisions, the major layers of responsibility within the organization are school board, superintendent, central office administration, school administration, and instructional staff.

Education is usually the largest single budgetary component of local government and, in total, employs more people than state and federal governments. The local district operates all the public schools within it and serves as the unit by which the community influences local education. The local school district is a quasi-municipal corporation that serves as an extension of state government and derives its authority from the state. It has a perpetual status, acts as an individual, survives the death of any member, and, as long as officers and employees act in good faith and fraud and collusion are absent, it has limited liabilities.

The school district is set apart from other government bodies in that it has its own board and school governance. Education is a state function, and the local board of education represents the state as well as the residents within the district. The board represents the community interests within statutory and constitutional law. A school district is either fiscally independent or it must gain approval on fiscal matters from some other governing body. Dependent boards can be appointed by the mayor (with the consent of council) or the board of county supervisors. In some cases, board members can be elected by the voting residents within the district. Independent boards must be elected. Most urban districts have dependent school boards. These boards must get prior approval from elected or appointed municipal officials to determine finally and legally the size of the local levy, the tax rate, and the size of the school division budget.

The interface between the superintendent of schools and the school board is critical to the success of the educational program within the district. Yet, only about half the states' school codes contain language defining this relationship between the board of education and the school superintendent. This lack of legislative guidance has resulted in some confusion about the status, authority, and responsibility of the superintendent of schools. In general, the board is given the freedom to determine the level of trust placed in the superintendent's judgment to guide the direction of schools.

School boards leave much of the decision making to the superintendent and school district staff as long as there is no evidence of community concern. Not that board members are powerless—since they can apply sanctions of far-reaching consequences including the hiring and firing of the superintendent.

Administrators at the central office and school level are expected to provide leadership and stewardship so as to ensure that policies, laws, and regulations are adhered to, that effective education occurs, and that desired goals and outcomes are achieved. Central office staff are typically organized around specific operational areas—finance, pupil personnel, staff personnel, curriculum and instruction, business and logistics—and are considered specialists (all discussed in later chapters). Principals, like superintendents, are generalists (line personnel) and are expected to set the tone and develop the culture for the district's schools.

The concept of line and staff responsibilities grows out of the hierarchical structure that often exists within organizations. Authority (power) and responsibility (obligation) are delegated from the very top of the organization to the bottom. Those serving in line positions are delegated the authority and responsibility required to discharge operational functions. Communications, gradation of power, and relationships are defined by the line between superior and subordinate. Staff authority comes from the need to have experts in specific areas to provide support for line officers. The staff relationship is usually a staff-to-line managerial one that can occur at any level within the school division. The staff concept gives a horizontal dimension to the organization. The line officer typically asks for the assistance of a staff person in helping with a very specific area of responsibility.

＊ **What are the most pressing issues that need to be addressed? How can you as principal of Alta Vista School be proactive when there are so many immediate problems that develop each day and must be addressed (reactive) to keep the school operating efficiently?**

The School Board

Over 95 percent of the nation's school board members are elected officials chosen by the voters to govern the some 15,000 school districts. A third of the nations' districts have five-member boards. Most of the other two-thirds are evenly divided between seven and nine members. Some large districts have over twenty board members. There are more than 100,000 school board members who are entrusted by the electorate to govern organizations spending many billions of tax dollars. School boards are required to adhere to state statutes and federal laws and regulations. As long as they do so, they remain in office unless turned out by the electorate at the polls. School boards who violate the dictates of public opinion for a period of time are generally removed when levels of dissatisfaction become pronounced.

Diversity is a term that appropriately applies to U.S. school boards. Over 4,000 school districts have fewer than 400 students and about 170 have more than 25,000. The greater number of school districts still remain in rural and small-town America. However, a majority of minority children attend school in one of the twenty-five urban districts. Board members themselves are becoming more diverse. The traditional board member has been a white male between 40 and 50 years of age, married and with a college degree. This is changing as more women and minorities seek board positions, especially in metropolitan areas (Glass, 2000).

In theory, the board of education is the policy making body, and the superintendent and school staff execute policies. In practice, however, boards sometimes micromanage schools and educational administrators sometimes develop policy statements. The "fuzziness" of the demarcation of responsibilities often causes discontent, which can erode the effectiveness of the school division. School boards in fact are empowered to provide strategic planning and policy for the school system, and most board members take this civic responsibility quite seriously.

The powers of local boards are: (1) those expressly granted by statute, (2) those fairly and necessarily implied in the powers expressly granted, and (3) those essential to the accomplishment of the objectives of the school district. The board has no choice but to comply with the statutes of the state. It can, however, work through established legislative channels to amend, abolish, or modify statutes that it finds are not in the best interest of the school district. The laws provide a great deal of opportunity for board members to exercise individual discretion and judgment. School boards answer to the citizens in their local communities and provide an effective mechanism through which communities can address their concerns. Public schools can, however, become the political arena in which ideological, social, economic, and religious differences are reconciled, sometimes actually at the expense of student needs. Serving on the Board can be a stepping stone to a higher-level political position.

All boards have legal authority to determine salary and working conditions within the school division. They almost always hire and fire the superintendent of schools and approve the hiring of all other staff. They must approve the final budgets for schools and assist in obtaining needed resources. They also make decisions related to the financing of capital purchases. They resolve issues that are closely related to interpretation of community values, like family life and sex education, religious issues, acceptable moral behavior, character education, and other issues of community concern. They keep the community informed about the general condition of schools and help to build local support for school systems. They approve all policies by which the schools are governed.

School boards are involved in determining school sites, selecting architectural designs and contractors, determining attendance boundaries, entering into contracts, and bargaining with employee groups. Much of a board's time is spent interpreting rules made at other levels of government. The board provides minutes from all meetings, which serve as the official record and are open to examination by taxpayers. All board meetings must be open to the public except for special "executive sessions" in which school personnel matters are discussed. Even though meetings are open, past research suggests that fewer than 6 percent of Americans have ever attended a school board meeting (Boardman & Cassel, 1983, p. 740). No state currently requires that the performance of individual board members or entire boards be subject to evaluation on a formal or regular basis.

If the board does not feel involved in the thought process, or the superintendent overwhelms the board with information or is domineering, there is alienation. Problems the board causes include interference in management functions (micromanagement); the presence of single-issue, single-region, or single-interest members; the leaking of discussions from executive sessions; involvement in personnel matters; attempts to get favorable treatment for friends and relatives; lack of skill, knowledge, and experience; and the pursuit by board members of political power, careers, and activism.

Many researchers have suggested that board turnover is a major reason that superintendent/board relationships deteriorate. New members on a board might not support the initiatives underway or the personal qualities that previous board members felt were important. The turnover of board members is often cited as a main reason that school initiatives are abandoned and mistrust develops. This situation is especially difficult when a new member has a mandate from constituents that she or he pursues with significant energy.

Very active political board members' decisions are viewed, in the opinion of many superintendents, as "more with an eye to what will gain the support of voters rather than what is best for the children." Tough decisions that alienate voters can result in loss of support from the Board, even if the decisions are best for the school system over the long haul. Educational leaders have learned that they must have board support if they or their initiatives are to weather the heat that accompanies almost every decision.

Superintendents suggest that the balance has shifted to a point where political astuteness matters more than job performance. "Absolutely, politics plays a big role," said Dr. Frank Petruzielo, then superintendent of the Houston Independent School District. "Competency in many instances is not the issue, and that's what makes these jobs more difficult to perform than any other in public or private sectors" (Carter & Cunningham, 1997, p. 104).

Recently, U.S. school boards are being criticized by state governments, education experts, and the public in general. Reports from the Institute for Educational Leadership (IEL), the Committee for Economic Development, and the Twentieth-Century Fund have all recommended changing school boards into education policy boards or children and youth coordinating boards, improving relationships with local government, improving involvement in school board elections, and setting state-established performance criteria to hold boards accountable. Kentucky, West Virginia, and Massachusetts have enacted laws that have modified the responsibilities of local school boards. Danzberger (1998) states:

> The Institute for Educational Leadership has worked hard to raise general reform higher on states' reform agendas and among national leaders of education reform. . . .
>   State policy makers avoid tackling comprehensive local governance reform, even though it is critical to achieving states' own education reform objectives. The political risks appear too great. . . . There certainly is not broad grassroots pressure to reform local school boards, but there are those who would organize quickly, or use existing organized networks, to fight any change perceived to weaken the power of a representative body close to the people and strengthen the power of professional educators. (p. 208)

In the early 2000s, mayoral control over school boards increased. The political rhetoric has compared school boards to "dysfunctional families" and questioned whether they still serve a useful purpose. Others argue that school boards are "dynamic democratic institutions that go along way toward making public schools public." This contention is being challenged in that vying for school board positions has become out of reach for potential candidates who are unable to raise needed campaign funds, secure political allies, and run a political campaign that can compete against large organized groups. Citizens argue for a need to "rebalance the governance equation in favor of lay citizens while diminishing the power of the state and of educational professionals" (Murphy, 1999).

Yet, citizens have become largely uninvolved in school governance, with only 10 to 15 percent voting in school board elections. Those with economic, political, and social power dominate educational policy, with little of the public dialogue, debate, and participation that are so important to democracy and citizenship. The results are declining participation in education and distrust of policymakers and bureaucrats (Land, 2002). Price (2001) suggests that as a result boards and communities have become polarized, thwarting progress and frustrating parents and citizens. As a result, mayors and governors are staging takeovers in such cities as Baltimore, Boston, Chicago, Cleveland, Oakland, New York, Philadelphia, Detroit, Newark, and Washington.

In a study funded by The Educational Commission of the States, Thomas Glass (2001) found that 52 percent of the 175 superintendents judged as outstanding by their peers believed that the school governance structure needed to be seriously restructured. Indeed, most research on the superintendency over the past decade has raised serious concerns about various aspects of school board governance. Thus, the once secure and cherished tradition of the U.S. school board is being challenged. There is little current evidence suggesting that "mayoral" takeovers have resulted in higher test scores; however, there are reports of better management, better maintained buildings, greater budgetary control, and more efficient management.

Policy formation and overseeing schools is a very difficult job, and most school board members deserve a great deal of credit for being willing to serve the schools. They serve as the decision makers among conflicting ideologies, political pressures, and shifting economic and social conditions. They work with business, government, and community organizations to continuously improve the schools and promote student welfare. There are many opportunities for missteps in a highly public forum. In fact, many board meetings today are televised to the local community and receive full media attention. Board members are peppered with questions by critics and supporters alike and feel the same pressures that superintendents do.

✳ **What responsibilities does the school board have in supporting the administrators, teachers, and program at Alta Vista School given its present condition? How can the school obtain the board's support, and is that feasible and/or important?**

The School Division Superintendent

The superintendent is the chief educational leader and spokesperson for the school district. The AASA (1993) Commission on Standards for the Superintendency has stated:

> To a great extent, the quality of America's schools depends on the effectiveness of school superintendents. These executives of our nation's schools have complex leadership responsibilities, and those who hold the position must be among the brightest and best our society has to offer. Their vision and performance must focus on creating schools that will inspire our children to become successful, caring Americans, capable of becoming contributing citizens of the world. (p. 3)

The superintendent has become the chief executive officer for the board, serving as the professional advisor to the board, leader of reforms, manager of resources, and communicator to the public. Thus, the superintendent has become the most visible, most vulnerable, and potentially most influential member of the organization. Educational decisions are usually made in an environment of strong pressure from various segments of the community, state, and nation. A major responsibility of the superintendency is to deal with conflicting expectations, multiple political agendas, and varying ideas without unduly creating enemies or distrust. The superintendent's success as chief executive officer is determined largely by his or her ability to deal with these pressures while running an effective and efficient school system.

Larry Cuban (1988) defined the core roles of the superintendent to be instructional, managerial, and political. Superintendents are expected to meet with a burgeoning constituency who want to influence school policy and to be able to influence people and groups. A reality that many superintendents recognize is that the job also represents a dizzying array of complex business units that must be effectively managed.

The superintendency has been studied in relation to reform and restructuring, centralization versus decentralization, acting as change agent, effectiveness, instructional impact, politics and political strategy, critical challenges, qualifications and access, leadership styles, context, and many social and economic factors. Grogan (2000a) suggests that recent interest is in ethics and leadership and the notion of the superintendency as a position with moral responsibility and an expectation to act morally and wisely. Often, the factors that are considered important in the superintendency emerge or become dormant as the social, political, and economic dramas of a community unfold.

Traditionally, the superintendency has been filled by white males. This has probably influenced both access to and the administrative style of this position. Glass, Bjork, and Bruner (2000, pp. 1–2) state:

> The number of women and superintendents of color has increased since 1992. Women superintendents increased from 6.6 percent in 1992 to 13.2 percent in 2000, and superintendencies held by persons of color moved from 3.9 percent to 5.1 percent during the same period. Although these data indicate progress, they also confirm a dramatic underrepresentation of these two groups in relation to white males. (NSBA, 1990).

Major functions of the superintendency, in descending order of time commitments devoted to the activities, are instructional leadership, finance and business management, general planning, personnel administration, school plant management, communication and public relations, and pupil services. Many superintendents have difficulty scheduling their day and often find themselves reacting to issues and crises that seem to occur on a daily basis. The majority of superintendents' interactions are with members of the school organization and board members, but there is an increasing demand from a wide variety of community groups—parents, vendors, mass media, chambers of commerce, city officials, special interest groups, civic leaders, business community, ministers and church members, police, and others.

As such, one of the most important challenges to the superintendent is maintaining the confidence of the school board members while providing needed attention to systemwide employees, the community, and ultimately teaching and student learning. One crucial element in all of this is to establish positive relations with the local media who are often in a position to set a tone to everyone's view.

Factors creating the "crisis" mentioned in Thomas E. Glass's study titled *Superintendent Leaders Look at the Superintendency, School Boards, and Reform* (2001) and other recent reports are (1) viability of the board governance model, (2) board relations, (3) inadequate funding, (4) stress, (5) lack of emotional support, (6) a plethora of insignificant demands, (7) mandated demands to meet standards and achieve higher district test scores, and (8) lack of gender and ethnic balance in the profession (Cooper, Fusarelli, & Carella, 1999; Glass, Bjork, & Brunner, 2000; Hodgkinson & Montenegro, 1999).

The AASA and the National School Board Association (NSBA) met in 1980 and again in 1992 and 1994 to develop jointly approved guidelines regarding roles and responsibilities of the superintendent. These guidelines (AASA–NSBA, 1994, pp. 11–12) are presented in Appendix 5.A at the end of this chapter.

To further define the superintendency as a profession, the AASA Commission on Standards for the Superintendency developed a set of professional standards (AASA, 1993). The commission stated, "All superintendents should be held accountable for the eight professional standards." The Professional Standards for the Superintendency are as follows:

- Standard 1: Leadership and District Culture
- Standard 2: Policy and Governance
- Standard 3: Communications and Community Relations
- Standard 4: Organizational Management
- Standard 5: Curriculum Planning and Development
- Standard 6: Instructional Management
- Standard 7: Human Resources Management
- Standard 8: Values and Ethics of Leadership

At the same time that they are balancing conflicting expectations and responding to mandates, superintendents are asked to empower teachers so they can both design and carry out the curriculum. Greater decentralization has resulted, as well as involvement of school administrators, teachers, and parents in determining what will work best in the schools. They are also being asked to respond to the statewide standards-based reforms and assessment. This state focus on what young people are learning and how well they are learning it has become a driving force in school divisions across the United States. The report Quality Counts '99 (*Education Week*, January 11, 1999) states: "The pressure is on. After years of exhorting and cajoling schools to improve, policy makers have decided to get tough. States are taking steps to reward results and punish failure in an effort to ensure that children are getting a good education and tax dollars aren't being wasted" (p. 5). From 53 to 77 percent of employers and parents "agree" with these standards/assessments/accountability approaches; 64 to 76 percent of teachers, however, "disagree."

In the past, superintendents typically talked more about the budget, finance, legal considerations, and things of that nature. Today the conversations are much more focused on instruction and student performance. Closing the achievement gap, without limiting the education of students at the high end, has become a huge issue of concern. Where needed resources will come from, given economic conditions, baby boomer retirements, widespread anti-tax sentiment, and federal and state priorities is still an important issue, however, it does not receive primary attention. The high-stakes environment coupled with chronic shortage of resources makes the superintendency a very challenging job.

Staying focused on the core business of instruction and student learning in an environment rampant with special interest groups, political distractions, conflicts, media coverage, and governance pressure is not an easy task. This environment requires lots of communication so everyone is informed and has confidence in the direction in which the school district is moving and speaks with a common voice. Mutual respect, common goals, and a concern for professionalism guide decisions. The success of the district is largely determined by the quality of the staff and the alignment of staff, board, and community toward the school vision of achieving improved student performance. Recent research by the Council of Greater City Schools show that this "district-level leadership provided by school boards and superintendents is much more critical than previously imagined in improving outcomes for all children" (Carr, 2003).

The superintendents' evaluation systems are often based on professional competencies and job duties, like those described in the AASA standards. According to DiPaolo and Stronge (2001), 89 percent of the states employ some variation of MBO in their performances evaluations, 1 out of 42 used portfolios, while 26 percent featured duties-based evaluations. Most states provide information to school boards on how to evaluate the superintendent, and several state school board associations offer training for board members. There is, however, a growing use of state and other standardized tests to evaluate school districts and superintendents. An increasing number of legislatures have decreed that compensation and contract renewal must be tied to student achievement. Some are suggesting to protect the viability of the superintendency, they should be granted at least a six-year renewable contract to provide some level of security. The 2000 AASA Superintendent Survey found that the board's primary expectations for the superintendent was: 40.1 percent as educational leader; 36.4 percent as managerial leader; 12.7 percent as political leader; 2.8 percent as reform leader; and 8 percent as other. A widely held opinion is that, in the end, it is questionable what evaluations really mean because if the board doesn't like you they probably will not rehire you.

✳   **How can the superintendent best support the administrators, teachers, and programs at Alta Vista School? How can the school obtain the superintendent's support?**

Central Office Operations

The titles of those in central office administration include deputy superintendents, assistant superintendents, directors, coordinators, and supervisors. The central office staff emphasizes planning, compliance, development, and accountability. Most staff in the central office provide expertise to those serving at the school level. Although central office staff personnel do not have direct control over the school, they have considerable power through their positions, knowledge, time, and resources.

The central office staff is usually broken up into various divisions or departments based on their operational responsibility and school division size. Departmentalization is used to subdivide tasks among the central administrative staff.

Organizational charts, available in almost all school districts, portray a rough description of this departmentalization. When a person is assigned to a position, she or he should report to only one boss (unity of command), and authority should always be equal to her or his responsibility.

Departments typically include various combinations of human resource management, curriculum and instruction, administrative and logistical services, finance, technology, pupil personnel services, information and community relations, transportation, and planning, assessment, and developmental services. Most are staff positions providing support to such people in line positions as superintendent, deputy superintendents, principals, and teachers. Individuals in staff positions usually help in the handling of details, locating data requirements and offering expertise in specific areas.

The line officer is typically a generalist, while the staff person is a specialist. The authority over operations is given to line officers, with staff officers providing advisory and consultant services. Those working in central offices complement the work of those working in the schools. The main duties of central office staff are to:

1. Provide technical expertise
2. Recommend courses of action
3. Discuss plans with others in the organization to promote the exchange of information and collegial decision making
4. Prepare written documentation to support work efforts
5. Explain and interpret decisions made by supervisors
6. Conduct evaluations and research, and assemble, summarize, and interpret results
7. Provide assistance to line position personnel
8. Inform and advise others what is occurring in the field

One of the more recent roles is monitoring school compliance with federal and state law and local policy. The NCLB legislation has greatly expanded this role as staff produce reports and analysis of school system–wide test data and recommend needed changes. Central offices become more directly involved in schools that do not reach their performance targets.

In theory, central office staff should depend on expert knowledge, persuasion, and prestige to influence the decisions of those responsible for operations; however, they are taking on more of a command and control role.

Because of the superintendent's busy schedule, he or she often has to depend on central office administrators to keep the school district running smoothly. Superintendents often have little time to supervise central office administrators directly and have to depend on their staffs' ability to follow up on the vision established by the superintendent and board. It is important that the board, superintendent, and assistant superintendents focus on the strategic objectives of the school, allowing the central office staff to support operational areas and the deputy superintendent(s) and school personnel to be responsible for day-to-day operations (Glass, 1992).

Central office personnel often feel caught in the middle, between state authority and local autonomy (Crowson, 1988; Elmore & Fuhrman, 1994; Murphy &

Hallinger, 1993). "The central office must come to see itself not as a regulator or initiator but as a service provider. The function of the central office must be to ensure that individual schools have what they need to be successful" (Carlson, 1989, 1996). Central office staff members focus on helping schools achieve their improvement goals. Success at the central office is now dependent on educational leaders' ability to create new knowledge together with colleagues at the school sites.

Central office administration can greatly assist school staff, and their support can be key to a school's success in its continuous improvement efforts. These connected central office administrators can present ideas in palatable terms and gain the needed support and resources for local school efforts. They can also help address certain school challenges that only they have the authority to remedy. Central administrators have a much better understanding of federal and state rules and how they will support or inhibit school plans. They can help schools to interpret these rules. Obviously, this is much less likely to occur if the central office staff have limited school site knowledge and there is a disconnect between schools and central administration.

That means it is very important that good relationships be developed between central administration and the school sites and that the communication flows freely in both directions. The quality of these interactions is largely determined by the level of trust that exists between central administration and the schools. Effective policy development requires an understanding of individual site needs and practices so that they can enable these practices. That means that central office administrators need time on site.

Frontline central office administrators tend to have stronger site knowledge and senior central office administrators, who have systemwide knowledge, defer to frontline administrators to answer site-specific questions. School administrators, in some districts, call frontline administrators several times a week to discuss various opportunities and challenges. Therefore, it is very important that these frontline offices have a strong understanding of systemwide knowledge and provide accurate information, avoid confusion, and support local responsiveness as well as central office understanding of site needs. That means that frontline central office administrators must be in frequent contact with their senior colleagues. Senior colleagues will share systemwide knowledge and be willing to listen to school issues. The "Don't bring me any school messes" approach will not work. Frontline administrators will not allow the majority of their time to be diverted to central office administration and away from working with the sites (Honig, 2003; Leithwood et al. 2001).

Central office educational leaders create learning communities to illuminate the knowledge that will be needed in the new millennium. Brown (1995) reports that

> Central office personnel must embody the best in current practice and research. More than any other body of workers within a school system, they should be informed about the latest research in educational trend literature. In turn, they should make efforts to articulate this body of information to schools in such a way that school staffs can understand and use this data. . . . Supervisors and central office specialists must become knowledge workers if they are to survive and prosper. (p. 116)

Other ways in which the central office administrators can coordinate and provide support and assistance to schools is by (Glickman, 1993):

- Defining the district's core beliefs about teaching and learning;
- Defining the goals and objectives of an educated student;
- Providing the money, technical services, and human consultation to allow schools to figure out how to get the job done;
- Providing information and identifying common needs; and
- Coordinating and linking resources. (For more information see: www. mcrel.org.)

Central administrative staff are being called on in a number of districts to work directly with principals and teachers to improve students' test scores. The responsibility for improving test scores is being placed solidly on the principal and teachers, calling on central administration for needed financial and technical support. A key will be working together to attain high-quality professional development that is focused on improving student achievement. Expectations for low-performing schools include developing plans for improvement, imposing sanctions for failure to implement improvement plans, developing partnerships for improving schools, and supporting the state's accountability systems (*Quality Counts '99,* January 11, 1999).

✳ **Define the role of the central office staff in supporting the administrators, teachers, and programs at Alta Vista School. How can the school obtain the central office staff support? How much responsibility do the central office administrators have for this school and does such responsibility create problems related to micro-management?**

Local School Structures and Arrangements

MARILYN TALLERICO • *Syracuse University*

Future educational leaders face a number of challenges related to how schools are structured and the arrangement among local schools and their school districts. These arrangements affect where and how key decisions are made that touch the core functions of schools: teaching and learning.

One issue that school leaders must grapple with is how to balance needs for autonomy at the local school level against coordination or standardization among schools at the district level. Scholars often refer to this as a tension between centralization and decentralization of authority over decision-making processes.

School arrangements that structure these decisions can be better understood if we look at them from a variety of perspectives. One perspective views schools as bureaucracies, characterized by formal organization based on a hierarchy of authority, multiple divisions of labor, specializations of functions, an overall impersonal orientation, and rules and regulations. While some see these features as important means of maximizing rational decision making and efficiency, others emphasize the potential dysfunction of such a system (e.g., when chains of authority become unbreakable or when regulatory controls are excessive).

From another perspective, local school structures are viewed as loosely coupled, open to a variety of internal and external influences, and more like organized anarchies than tightly connected hierarchies. In this view, schools are characterized by unclear and diffuse goals, uncertain technologies of teaching and learning, nonrational decision-making behaviors, loosely connected structural elements, and fluid participation of teachers, administrators, students, parents, and community members. Thus, in the bigger picture, school districts are more like federations of largely autonomous schools, which in turn represent federations of autonomous individual classrooms. An assumption underlying this perspective is that administrators and teachers, as professionals, have broad discretionary decision-making power within existing school structures.

From a more eclectic perspective, school structures may be understood as having aspects of: (a) hierarchical order and bureaucracy; (b) collegiality, personal autonomy, and professionalism; (c) political features, such as conflicts among different interests; and (d) cultural and symbolic dimensions. An assumption underlying the latter is that shared beliefs, values, symbols, rituals, and traditions drive human behavior and may be the "glue" that holds together loosely or variably coupled school structures.

What does this all mean for you as a school leader? First, it's important not to limit your sights to just one perspective on whatever school structure in which you find yourself. Second, it is highly likely that dual decision-making systems will coexist in your school and district, some centralized and some decentralized, with relative dominance of each dependent on the particular context. Third, as a school leader, you can and will both affirm and shape your school's culture. It's important to use this influence wisely and intentionally. Fourth, it is equally important to be aware that distinct constituent (e.g., teachers', students', administrators') and department *sub*cultures will likely constrain the development of a schoolwide culture. It will be important for you to understand—and exercise leadership through—both the information organization and formal school structures.

Whether schools and school districts are tightly coupled bureaucracies or loosely knit confederations, the reality remains that principals stand at a pivotal point of interchange between central office—school board decision makers, teachers, parents, and students. Because of this critical positioning, an important role of principals is to buffer teachers and students from the dysfunctional aspects of large, impersonal school organizations and to use the system's structures effectively to acquire resources for the school's learning priorities.

Recent literature emphasizes the moral and ethical responsibilities of school leaders, including teachers, principals, and other educational administrators. Whatever the particular cultures and organizational systems you might inherit, it is important to continually question those cultures and structures. More specifically, I suggest raising and attending to at least two questions: (a) Who benefits from the way this school is structured and (b) who occupies the positions of leadership within those structures?

The assumptions underlying the first question are that not all students or adults in schools benefit equally from extant organizational arrangements. A significant leadership challenge is to uncover and remedy such inequities. Which students are put at a disadvantage, for example, by how schools are organized by grade levels or special programs? Which gain an advantage from certain labels or course-taking tracks?

You will also have to consider the limited integration of many educational leadership roles when analyzed by gender, ethnicity, race, and other variables. Why is this so? What evidence of improvement has there been in recent years? What needs to happen to ensure diversity and the optimization of all talent pools for leading our schools? Although these certainly are not the only questions that might be raised in the course of providing moral and ethical leadership of schools, they are ones that are directly related to the topic of local school structures. And they challenge us all to think about taken-for-granted organizational arrangements.

The School Administrator

Each school building is staffed by a principal and, as size warrants, any number of assistant principals, teachers, and a number of others in staff and clerical positions. The principal carries out all the duties necessary to run an effective school. Generally, these duties include administering all policies and programs; making recommendations regarding improvements to the school; planning, implementing, and evaluating the curricular and instructional programs; hiring, coordinating, and developing staff; organizing programs of study and scheduling classes; maintaining a safe school environment; providing stewardship for all school resources; and providing for cocurricular and athletic activities. Principals usually serve in elementary (K–5), middle (6–8), or high (9–12) schools. It is generally agreed that the high school principalship is the most demanding job, followed by the middle school, and then the elementary principalship, and this is reflected in the difference in principal pay scales.

Research has shown that the principal is the single most important individual to the success of any given school (Edmonds, 1979; Lezotte, 1988; Miller, 1995). School effectiveness research in the 1980s pointed to the importance of the principal and teachers as the main determiners of school success. Allan Glatthorn (1994) states that principals play a very active part in developing special curricula for their school within district constraints. Regardless of the committee structure used for curriculum work at the school, there will be a need for strong leadership, which is typically provided by the principal. (In some schools, however, the assistant principal or another individual assumes major responsibility for curriculum leadership.) (p. 66)

The principal is at the very heart of school improvement. In the report *America 2000: Where School Leaders Stand* (1991), the AASA states: "Effective schools have at least one thing in common: sound leadership. School administrators have never had a more crucial role in American society; they must be the ones who stimulate the debate and help develop a vision of what our schools should become in communities across the nation" (p. 6). Management functions and clerical chores must not be allowed to dominate the work of the principal. In fact, the most important responsibilities focus on vision and developing and motivating staff to achieve optimum student learning outcomes.

Both the National Association of Elementary School Principals (NAESP) and the National Association of Secondary School Principals (NASSP) have established proficiencies that they believe to be critically important to principals' leadership. It is generally agreed that these proficiencies are constantly evolving to fit the context in which schools operate.

Ubben, Hughes, and Norris (2001) believe that the perception of the principal has changed from the traditional view of a manager who implements policy within the bureaucratic hierarchy. They believe:

> Instead, today's school principals have been charged with the task of shaping their schools to become outstanding beacons of productive learning. They are challenged to clarify their own values, beliefs, and positions and to engage proactively with others in the redesign and improvement of their schools. They are expected to establish

conditions that foster personal empowerment and enhanced development of organizational members and to orchestrate shared power and decision making among an array of individuals both internal and external to the school setting. At the same time, they are encouraged to build a community of leaders and learners who will effectively shape the school environment to champion increased productivity among students. (p. 3)

Changing Roles

The perceptions and expectations of the school principal have changed dramatically given the changing context of education over the last fifteen years. The traditional roles and responsibilities of ensuring a safe environment, managing the budget, and maintaining discipline are still in force, however, there are many new demands. While programming and associated auxiliary activity are expanding, needed resources and support have not been forthcoming. In looking at the role of the principal as instructional leader, The National Center for School Leadership (NCSL) identified five key aspects of the role of effective principals:

- Defining and communicating a school's educational mission
- Coordinating curriculum
- Supervising and supporting teachers
- Monitoring student progress
- Nurturing a positive learning climate

A major theme of the new changes is that principals are paying more attention to instructional leadership. This includes development and evaluations of curriculum and instruction, use of instructional time, disaggregation of data, analyzing classroom practices, faculty and staff development, and curriculum alignment with standards. The principal also has to deal with more outside groups, thus serving as a conduit for communication and understanding (Shen & Crawford, 2003).

The conflict between management-related tasks and leadership initiatives is at an all-time high, which can deplete the emotional and physical energy from the individual in this position. This condition is not helped by the layering of responsibilities placed on the schools along with major concerns related to accountability, multicultural awareness and understanding, special education/inclusion, and moral values. The mantra is "I must do more." Principals are more on call than ever with e-mail, cell phones, and pagers to an ever-expanding constituency. Most principals are also spending significantly more time on paperwork.

The conflicts abound and include role conflict, conflicting expectations (inclusion, diversity needs, and accountability); autonomy and mandates; and efficiency and support for needed assistance. More home–school communication is required. It is truly a very challenging time to be a principal, but as always it is an exciting time, and principals can be influential and make a difference in the lives of kids.

In a study completed by Kochan, Spencer, and Matthews (2000), principals perceived the major challenges to the job as "insufficient financial resources," "control of financial matters," "being overloaded by the demands placed on them," "controlling and dealing with teacher apathy (male principals)," "building a climate of trust and enhancing morale (female principals)," "dealing with school discipline and handling conflicts," and "safety issues related to deteriorating facilities (female principals)." Themes regarding the most important skills fell into the categories of organizational, interpersonal-relational, curricular and instructional, technical and administrative, and personal attributes (concern, flexibility, and personal strength).

Brown-Ferrigno (2003) asked teachers to describe their understanding of the roles and responsibilities of school principals. Different views developed in relation to respondents' teaching experience. Table 5.1 displays the role descriptions used by four subgroups based on years of experience (p. 480). These differences in age and experience appeared to influence staff perceptions regarding principal responsibilities. Perhaps this means that teachers with different levels of experience require different types of support from the principal.

One of the evolving roles of the principals is to oversee the procurement and integration of technology. This includes the integration of technology into both the curriculum and school management. It can result in many efficiencies and new opportunities when technology becomes an integral part of the daily operations of the school. This will require the spelling out of competencies for staff, faculty, and students providing appropriate training, education, and support. Computers have tremendous potential for simplifying many clerical aspects of the work and opening up opportunities to create new innovative approaches that would be unheard of without the tremendous capabilities that computers offer. Along with advanced technology comes an increasingly important theme: Areas that have computers

TABLE 5.1 *The Principalship: Comparison of Role Conceptions*

Role Descriptors Used by Teachers in Four Subgroups Based on Years of Experience			
5 or fewer years	*6 to 10 years*	*11 to 20 years*	*More than 20 years*
A Principal Is a(n)	*A Principal Is a(n)*	*A Principal Is a(n)*	*A Principal Is a(n)*
Assessor	Advocate	Communicator	Decision maker
Decision maker	Coach	Evaluator	Facilitator
Disciplinarian	Communicator	Facilitator	
Educator	Director	Friend	
Facilitator	Educator	Implementer of	
Goal setter	Evaluator	new programs	
Leader	Facilitator	Instructional	
Organizer	Leader	leader	
Resource person	Mediator	Motivator	
Role model	Organizer	Visionary	
Visionary	Problem solver		
	Role model		
	Supporter		
	Visionary		

Brown-Ferrigno, T. (2003). "Becoming a principal: A role conception, initial socialization, role-identity transformation, purposeful engagement." *Education Administration Quarterly, 33*(4):468–503. Copyright © 2003 by Sage Publications, Inc. Reprinted by permission of Sage Publications, Inc.

and other expensive equipment must be maintained secure. This includes special security equipment on all doors, proper air-conditioning, and the use of closed-circuit cameras that can be easily observed.

The 2003 NCPEA Morphet Dissertation Award went to a study that described the changing role of the secondary principal (Goodwin, 2002; Goodwin, Cunningham, & Childress 2003). The general conclusion is that the role of the principal is in transition and conflicted at the same time. Goodwin (2004, p. 19) states: "The findings of this study illustrated the breadth of the interactions related to the principalship. Interactions with people in the school, in the district, in the community, the interaction of social changes with school expectations, the interaction of politics and bureaucracy with daily school life, the interaction of standards and accountability with the social and emotional needs of students, and the interaction of the expectation to be an effective instructional leader and an efficient manager are all evidence of the complexity of the position."

There is still a disconnect between the principal's changing role and what demands his or her daily attention. Instructional leadership has become the principal's primary role; however, there has been an erosion of authority. The principal needs to be an expert in so many more things—special education, standards, data-based decision making, testing, high technology, dropouts, tight budgets, lobbying, student diversity, brain research, teaching, learning, nutrition, safety, distance learning, litigation, legislation, court cases, paperwork, and the list goes on. "The role of the principal has increased in complexity, and the principal's perceived linear conflicts between being inclusive and meeting high standards, between accountability and meeting the diverse needs of students, between being responsive to mandates and being autonomous, and between and among the roles of strategic leader, instructional leader, organizational leader, and political and community leader" (Goodwin, 2004, p. 19).

Critical Incidents

Principals must be prepared to handle critical incidents that typically occur with little or no advance warning. Difficult issues such as racial disharmony, sexual misconduct, religious freedom, educational equity, drugs, anti-American sentiment, and violence have found their way into schools across the United States. Principals can misjudge the nature, direction, and scale of the conflict resulting in the underestimation or exaggeration of existing conditions. How effectively the principal deals with *critical incidents* ultimately determines his or her effectiveness and that of the school.

Principals also need an instinct to recognize potential "time bombs." Many principals who lose their jobs have experienced some form of critical incident that turned the tide against them. Drs. Donald Thomas and Gene Davis offer us an example of a critical incident in their PDK fastback titled *Legal and Ethical Bases for Educational Leadership* (1998). As the principal of a high school, you are confronted with a number of challenges related to an incident that had occurred the previous day. The headline of the morning newspaper, in an article about your school, reads "Teacher Steps on Flag." The superintendent has already left an e-mail directing you to suspend the teacher involved, immediately and without pay. Parents, requesting that their son be returned to the teacher's class, and a policeman, to serve a warrant on the teacher, are waiting to see you. This critical incident has a number of "red flag" characteristics that could embroil the principal and the entire school system in destructive conflict and embarrassment. Red flag issues are those that (1) endanger the health, safety, and security of students and/or employees; (2) are escalating in intensity; (3) fall under close media or community scrutiny; (4) interfere with the normal operation of the school; and (5) jeopardize the positive public image of the school district. Violence, racial discrimination, sexual misconduct, and other such issues are automatic red flags needing immediate attention.

The previous day a student in Mr. Calisch's class showed up wearing a swastika, a Nazi symbol, on a necklace. The teacher requested that the young man put the necklace in his pocket. The student admittedly refused and the teacher asked the student to go to the assistant principal's office and discuss it with the assistant principal. The student and some others in the class asked for an explanation. Mr. Calisch explained that he was Jewish and several of his relatives had been killed in concentration camps during World War II. In trying to help the students to understand, Mr. Calisch took out his handkerchief and asked: "What is this made of?" "Cloth," responded the class. He dropped the handkerchief to the floor and stepped on it. "Does it bother you that I stepped on this piece of cloth?" "No," was the unanimous answer.

Then Mr. Calisch took down the American flag. "What is this made of?" he asked. "Cloth," responded the class. He then proceeded to drop the flag on the floor and stepped on it. The class was offended. The responses were quick and direct:

"You can't step on the flag, it is a symbol for our country."

"The flag is sacred, it is a symbol of democracy and all the values held by our nation."

"It's wrong to desecrate the flag; you could go to jail for stepping on it."

At this point, all class members, except one, agreed that the Nazi symbol held sufficient symbolism to offend the teacher. The boy wearing the necklace disagreed and left the room. The rest of the class period went on as usual.

How the principal handles this situation has the potential to affect not only his future career and his relations with a number of key individuals, but also student's and teacher's respect for the beliefs of others, the reputation of the school, and the level of conflict related to this issue that will develop in the community. The potential dangers make this an example of a critical incident.

The principal's first duty is to educate the students, manage the school, and make decisions that do not disrupt the educational process. Although the superintendent ordered suspension without pay, the principal is also governed by the rights of the teacher and due process and the principal will be responsible, not the superintendent. The principal must balance individual student rights with his obligation to provide an education without disruption, including overt disruption, potential disruption, disruption caused by symbols of immoral or illegal acts contrary to prevailing community values, and nexus disruption. The decisions the principal makes this day regarding this critical incident has tremendous implications for everyone's future. This can become a smooth positive learning experience, or it can become a catalyst for volatile and cataclysmic events in which the principal will be in the middle.

The examples are endless: A health teacher tells middle-school students that they "are going to experiment with sex and that her own child had at the age of 15"; a complaint from a high school girl that she wanted the derogatory and sexually explicit graffiti about her removed from the boys' bathroom; a teacher falsified a student's individualized education plan; a teacher assaulted my child; a teacher propositioned my child for sex; a student said he is going to kill teachers and students; drugs are being sold in school; or there are increasingly violent racial tensions.

When reasonable norms of behavior are breached, there is a demand for quick action and control and the development of appropriate sanctions. This is even more pressing when the health, safety, and security of students and/or employees are endangered. The best approach to a crisis is to have developed a plan for the crisis during a noncrisis period, and to have built good relations with those who you might need in a crisis—teachers, students, parents, lawyers, police, media, ministers, social services. As the flow of events escalates, the key is to maintain control and not to panic. This is much easier if you are already prepared for the possibility of such events. Take charge and communicate, communicate, communicate! Then rebuild, recover, and heal.

Politics of the Principalship

School administrators often operate in a contentious arena and vie for ways of balancing, directing, controlling, manipulating, managing, and surviving their edgy environments (Lindle & Mawhinney, 2003). Interested parties exert various forms of power over others in order to achieve their self-interests. Decisions are based on who is able to apply the greatest pressure or create the worst damages as opposed to what might be the larger good for all involved. Politics is sometimes used to determine who will participate or be heard.

Parents, teachers, community members, and others can become alienated as they see inequality in the opportunity to influence their schools. The national concern is whether schools are operating for the public good as powerful groups are taking on an unprecedented role in school decision making. Questions begin to arise as to whether educational administrators are motivated by the general welfare and/or by the interests of powerful individuals and groups. This concern has crated distrust and a "crisis of confidence" in the schools.

Who gets to make what kinds of decision is at the very core of politics and educational governance. This evolves into an issue of who gains and who loses when the political model is used. "Whose personal beliefs and values are raised to become public beliefs and values, which all are asked or forced to accept, is what makes debate of governance so contentious" (Cooper, Fusarelli, & Randall, 2004). Educators are responsible to ensure that the voices of the diverse stakeholders are heard and carefully considered. The overarching goal is to develop decision-making processes that incorporate teachers, parents, community members, researchers, business and civic leaders, and policymakers.

This inclusiveness is difficult when coalitions form around specific interests, and decisions are made through bargaining, negotiation, coercion, and compromise. The quality of decisions is influenced by the political skill and acumen of the leader to be able to channel power toward the most desirable outcomes. Those who have a stake in the outcome build power bases in order to influence the decision. For example, a principal may establish strong relationships with parents and community members in order to build a power base. That principal, at some risk, can then call upon that power base to influence the superintendent or school board to support a schoolwide program that is not presently supported by the board and/or central administration.

One's position also provides a sense of power as long as the position holder is recognized as appropriately holding that position. The ability to have some control over another position holder's professional life also creates power. Mutual respect, high status, expertise, expressive ability, wealth, popularity, and so on can allow an individual to dominate the political process. The principal needs to know how to work through this political process in order to achieve desired outcomes.

Principal: Instructional Leader or School Manager?

Instructional leadership is focused on curriculum and instructional development; staff development; instructional supervision; program, teacher, and student evaluation; research and experimentation; provision of resources; and the continuous improvement of teaching and learning. The school manager focuses more on facilities, equipment, supplies, schedules, discipline, procedures, stewardship, critical incidents, and general compliance with efficient behavior and practice, and district policies, procedures, and programs. Management is associated with planning, coordination, control and operations of the school. Research tends to suggest that principals must first and primarily be the instructional leader, but not at the expense of effectively managing the school (Pounder & Merrill, 2001). Drake and Roe (1999) state:

> very often principals feel as if they face a dilemma as management duties interfere with educational leadership. This concern is real because role expectations of the school and community may often shape the principal's activities, with emphasis on managing people and things. However, a carefully selected principal candidate, properly prepared and motivated, can run a well-managed school and still consider/effect educational leadership as his or her major function. (p. 38)

Some practitioners argue that principals cannot do both jobs and tend to get drawn into general management at the expense of instructional leadership (Richards, 2000). Smith and Andrews (1989) found that effective principals were more likely to communicate about instructional matters, to pay attention to test results, to discuss curriculum and instruction, to focus on how well learning objectives were mastered in communication to students, teachers, and parents, and to be a visible presence in and around the school. Achilles and Smith (1999) conclude:

> The stimulation of pupil academic performance is a continuing challenge for the principal. Improvement will not occur without the principal's time and attention, for

"as is the principal, so is the school." The principal is the coordinator of the learning environment and must demonstrate a commitment to pupil performance. The principal, the teachers, and the pupils are a learning team. (p. 242)

Principals express their commitment to improved student performance through words, focus, and actions (see Chapter 7). They will be visible throughout the school expressing interest in instruction and learning—their presence felt and seen by everyone. They are involved in planning for instruction and know what is to be taught and make sure it is being taught. They often meet with teachers, chair persons, lead teachers, specialists, and others collaboratively discussing various aspects of the curriculum, observed instruction, assessment, student progress, what's going well and what is not, ultimately shaping the vision for an improved school. It is the shared vision that energizes and inspires faculty to put in the needed effort that will result in the highest probability of students' academic success. The vision is influenced by research (articles, books, studies, and so on) as well as best practices.

As an instructional leader, staff development and providing for teacher's instructional needs become a primary focus of the administrators' work so that teachers are able to do their best for children. This requires effective evaluation and monitoring of both teacher and student progress to provide the needed information for planning appropriate developmental activities (Pollard & Durodola, 2003).

Another related area of debate and discussion is whether curriculum and instructional reform should be centralized or decentralized. The difference lies in where the primary power, information, and decision-making capacity exists. As has been suggested, school districts are moving more toward a decentralized approach. It is important that the board and superintendent be clear about what authority has been delegated if decentralized instructional leadership approaches are to work. The approach selected has a profound effect on the organizational structure, the type of demands placed on the principalship, and the school's effectiveness. Drake and Roe (1999) found that

one serious way we can improve schools is by revamping their structure. Structure must be developed that keeps citizens in close communication with schools and allows individual schools to be more responsive to students and parents. Greater decentralization can bring schools closer to the people so that the schools may make decisions that will immediately affect the local area and provide the opportunity for their "customers" to have a reasonable impact on the decision-making process. (p. 111)

Recent research (Shen & Crawford, 2003) suggests that principals are still heavily engaged in managing resources and maintaining physical security. There is still pressure to run an orderly school.

✳ **What do you see as your role as principal of Alto Vista school? How will you marshal the needed resources to gain control of this school and ultimately improve student performance? What will be the major challenges that you will face both personally and professionally?**

School Safety Audit

School safety is the responsibility of everyone—administrators, staff, students, parents, and the community. Kenneth Trump (2002) states:

> The safety of your students and staff members might very well depend upon your ability to evaluate, plan, and implement a comprehensive school safety program. As many school administrators struggle to learn about drug trafficking trends, gang identification, stranger danger, and the prevention of aggressive and violent behavior, even newer challenges have arrived at the schoolhouse doorway. (p. 11)

Homemade bombs, anthrax scares, concealed weapons, and other "new crimes for new times" now present school administrators with the formidable task of developing security and crisis preparedness guidelines at both building and district levels. Along with the "traditional" security threats, recent shifts in school violence are driving administrators in even the safest of schools and communities to realize that "it could happen here." And staff members, students, parents, politicians, lawyers, and the media want to know what you, as a school administrator, have done to prevent these things from happening.

Most states require all schools in the state to conduct a building level school safety audit. This is an internal inventory of exsisting practices, policies, and procedures as they relate to school safety. For best results and credibility, assessments should be performed by individuals with expertise in professional school security in cooperation with other key school staff and community members. A comprehensive safety audit provides a useful basis for faculty and staff in-service, as well as for recommendation for and needed modification of current policies, practices, and procedures that relate to issues of student, faculty and staff health, safety, and well-being. This proactive process helps to ensure that students maximize their learning potential within a safe and secure environment.

The audit is a written assessment designed to assess the safety conditions in each public school, identify and if necessary develop solutions for physical safety concerns, including building security issues. The assessment helps to identify and evaluate student safety concerns occurring on school property or at school-sponsored events. The audit should provide guidelines for improving school security and safety (Flanary, 1997).

Each school should conduct a complete safety audit every three years. Prudent school administrators should annually review the progress on the recommendations set forth in the report, update policies, and maintain a written copy of the audit in the principal's office. Appropriate personnel should meet regularly during the school year to discuss problem areas and address needed improvements and refinement.

The following ten domains provides an example of what might be assessed annually for school safety:

- Development and enforcement of policies
- Procedures for data collection
- Development of intervention and prevention plans

- Personnel security
- Level of staff development (education and training)
- Opportunities for student involvement
- Level of parent and community involvement and linkages
- Role of law enforcement
- Standards for safety, security personnel, and police staffing
- Safety and security of buildings and grounds
- Development of emergency response plans (crisis preparedness)

A copy of a school safety audit protocol and an example of a form for the above domains may be viewed on the Virginia Department of Education homepage: www.pen.k12.va.us (click site index and scroll down to school safety audit guidelines; see also www.schoolsecurity.org).

Putting "Cs" into the Village

PAUL C. HOUSTON, ED.D. • *Executive Director, American Association of School Administrators*

Many leaders are currently caught in the trap of trying to emulate the success achieved by earlier generations of "command and control" administrators. Today, you cannot command the staff or community—you can't even get them to take a number.

Rather than try to lead by command, administrators must develop and nurture relationships. I am fond of reminding my colleagues that if you stand in the middle of the road, you get hit by traffic going in both directions. However, that is also the best place from which to direct traffic. You can either get the plate number of the truck that just ran you down, or stand up and wave your arms to move the flow in a positive direction.

Educators are particularly fond of saying "It takes a village to raise a child," but the real question for school leaders is "What does it take to raise a village?" The villages of yesterday are gone and must be rebuilt in the new era we face. Schools are the connect points for communities. They can, and must, play the role of creating the needed network of support for children. School leaders must be the connectors, the bridge builders who bring diverse elements of the community together to support children.

School leaders must move from the "Bs" from past days of school administration (bonds, building, buses, budgets—the "stuff" of education) to the "Cs" (connections, collaborations,

communication, children—the building of relationships). School system leaders must create a balance between being courageous champions for children and communities and collaborative catalysts who use their pivotal roles to bring people together to make things happen. I have called this shifting role as moving from being a superintendent of schools to being a superintendent of education. It implies reaching out beyond the traditional walls of schools and school districts to embrace a broader set of responsibilities and relationships.

School leaders will of necessity behave very differently from the way they do today. Proactive leadership is required that initiates contact and issues and demands both human and political sensitivities. Changed attitudes and new skills will be required as well as change in the organizations supporting schools such as district offices. District offices must reduce their oversight and monitoring role and replace it with the building of capacity for schools. Schools need guidance and support; they do not need control. Savvy school district leaders will make it their business to transform district offices into places of support.

School management in the next century will be the management of relationships: the relationship of child to learning, child to child, child to adult, and school to community. There can be no barriers. It is all interconnected. Education is organic in nature and the pieces cannot be mechanically separated. The role of school leadership will be to foster and nurture the old relationships and to create new ones necessitated by the changing social conditions facing children and schools.

I have always thought that leadership comes from the ability to comfort the afflicted and afflict the comforted—helping the public understand that schools are more effective than they think and helping staff understand that they are not as effective as they think. Successful leaders find the balance between the demands and expectations of those working on the problems, and those who depend on the problems to be solved. Like a performer at a sea park who rides a pair of dolphins, you must have one foot on the back of the community and the other on the back of the staff. If you lean too far in either direction, you fall off.

There is one final relationship that must be fostered—the relationship with the board of education. In essence, the real role of school boards is to translate the values of the community into policy for the system. It is a crucial role that, too often, is not being played appropriately. School boards are often not asked to focus on the very thing that they are there to provide—insight into what the community hopes and dreams for its children. Boards need to be helped to move away from a preoccupation with the "stuff" of education to its higher purposes. School superintendents must use their positions to help school boards play this role if any success is expected.

Successful school district leaders are moving from acting like sharks to behaving like dolphins. The role is no longer one of the lone predator, swimming menacingly through the water in search of the next meal. It is one where sophisticated communication and sonar are used, where collaboration and cooperation are stressed, and where a bit of playfulness doesn't hurt. For all those people who would hold on to the shark behavior out of fear of being swallowed up in the dangerous waters of the next century, it is good to remember that dolphins kill sharks. You do not have to be a predator to be successful. Swimming fast and not taking yourself too seriously also do not hurt.

Parental Involvement

When asked how families are involved in a child's education, educators typically respond that parents are invited to a variety of school functions—open houses, parent conferences, school assemblies, sports activities—and to participate as classroom volunteers. Many educators believe that schools need to increase the numbers of parents who attend school-based activities, even though many parents cannot, and do not, participate at the school site. Often educators comment:

> We hardly ever get very many parents from juniors and seniors attending open house.
>
> The parents who attend parent conferences are not necessarily the ones we need to see.
>
> [Racial/ethnic group's name] don't value education.

Families are not directly involved in their children's school activities for many reasons. In order to alter the paradigm of parent involvement, we need to begin by talking about *family* involvement. Given the changing demographics of families, schools can no longer think only about mom and dad. Simply by expanding our definition of *family,* as we think about involvement, the possible participation net is enlarged. In many families, older siblings, a grandparent, or an aunt or uncle have primary responsibilities of child care.

A second part of the paradigm needing change is the relationship between schools and families. Schools need to think of family member as *partners.* Two or more independent agents agree to work together to accomplish a common purpose that is mutually beneficial. For schools and educators, partnership means that family and school share power. Family members are given opportunities to provide ideas and advice just as educators are. Both partners are obliged to be committed and are responsible for doing their part.

Another part of the old paradigm requiring change is the way educators have traditionally viewed involvement—attendance of parents at school functions and volunteering at school. If educators continue to think about involvement in these limited ways, little will change in the relationship between schools and families.

Epstein (2001) describes a typology of parent involvement. The six types of family involvement include:

1. Parents as providers of the child's basic needs
2. Communication between the school and the home
3. Parents as volunteers at the school
4. Parents as instructors in the home
5. Parents involved in school governance
6. Parents working in collaboration with the entire community

Research shows that when families are involved in their children's education, grades are higher, attendance is better, homework completion improves, and students are more motivated (Epstein, 2001; Epstein et al., 2002; Henderson & Mapp, 2002; Sheldon, 2003; Van Voorhis, 2001). Epstein and Jansorn (2004) states, "Every school needs a purposeful, planned partnership program that creates a welcoming environment and engages families in activities that contribute to students' readiness for school, academic success, and positive attitudes and behaviors" (p. 10). The first step in increasing family involvement is to create a welcoming environment—positive handling of phone calls and drop-in visitors, a clean school, visible student work, a parent's space for meeting, welcoming attitudes, and so on. Next is providing needed information through a school newsletter, teacher–parent conferences, and scheduled activities for parents. Parents want to get a feel for the values, beliefs, and attitudes of those who surround their children each day (www.partnershipschools.org; www.finenelwork.org).

The 6.5 million member national Parent Teacher Association (PTA) has developed standards to encourage parent involvement in their children's education. The six factors identified by the National PTA are:

- Regular, two-way, meaningful communication between home and school
- Promotion and support of parenting skills
- Active parent participation in student learning
- Parents as welcome volunteer partners in schools
- Parents as full partners in school decisions that affect children and families
- Outreach to the community for resources to strengthen schools

Other organizations, such as the National Coalition for Parents' Involvement in Education (NCPIE), work to create meaningful family–school partnerships in every school. They have been further supported by the NCLB Act, which requires schools to have well-planned programs of family and community involvement to support student achievement and to communicate clearly with parents.

Principals have unique responsibilities to support family and community involvement in the education of students. This includes daily schedules, clear expectations, curricular plans, safe learning environments, guidance and support for parent participation, information about school and their children's success, fair and constant discipline, homework policies, and involving parents in decisions. The principal shows that parents are valued by frequently letting teachers and students know that parents are valued at this school. Their involvement on action teams further stresses their importance. Only with the principal's ongoing support will parents, teachers, students, and others work closely together for the benefit of schools and the children they serve.

The response and needs of parents can be different based on their experiences and socioeconomic level, and principals need to be prepared to assist all parents. Some parents felt inadequate or unable to assist their children with school work and/or may not have had a particularly good experience at school. Horvat and colleagues (2003) found that middle class and above parents react collectively or at least threaten the possibility of collective involvement, which essentially trumps or neutralizes the authority of educators, thus creating a more open environment. They also seem to have closer ties to those who can provide needed information, expertise, and authority needed to effectively participate.

The working-class and poor parents tend to undertake individual response and do not receive support through broader networks. They do not have the same trappings of authority, community response, information, or expertise. They tend to be the easiest to ignore and marginalize, which can become a problem if the principal does not put in a greater effort to ensure that the staff values their participation beyond discipline and negative school experiences (www.familysupportamerica.org).

✳ **How would you involve the parents at Alta Vista School to help turn this school around? How might you make this happen?**

Assistant Principal

Principals are in desperate need of more assistant principals if they are to meet the expanded expectation of their role. They can keep their "hands on" central responsibilities while keeping their "fingers on" those delegated to the assistant principals. Some principals will assign a very limited, narrow set of responsibilities to assistant principals so that they become single-facet administrators. Assistant principals (APs) should be provided a well-rounded set of experiences to better prepare them to take on full responsibility for the school and to deepen their understanding of the school.

The traditional roles of the AP have been "operations manager" and "disciplinarian" where they administer discipline, buses, attendance, schedules, student activities, and other noninstructional roles. The changing role of the principal requires them to share greater power and create an instructional leadership team.

There is strong pressure to upgrade and expand the role of the AP. Two-thirds of principals (DiPaola & Tschannen-Moran, 2003) reported that they did not have enough assistants to fulfill the expanding role of the principalship. This study found that 65 percent of elementary assistant principals, 41 percent of middle school assistant principals, and 34 percent of high school assistant principals indicated they would seek a position as principal. Fifty-six percent planned to retire in the next eight years.

Assistant principals hold the keys to the type of instructional leadership being called for in schools today. The AP responsibility for teacher evaluations could be expanded to include that of a mentor/coach who actively assists teachers to improve their performance, gain skills and confidence, implement best practices, interpret feedback data, and deal with a wide range of students (Kaplan & Owings, 1999). They can use conferencing, observations, modeling, professional development, and direct instruction to improve teachers' performance. APs would meet regularly with department heads/grade leaders to address the school instructional concerns. This may require an increase in the number of administrative assistants or deans within the school; however, some division of labor will be required. In this expanded role, assistant principals will learn the same skills that make principals effective, thus preparing them to be principals.

The assistant principalship is an excellent source of professional development for the principalship role. Principals listed the assistant principalship role as one of their most valuable experiences in preparing for the responsibilities of the principalship. This experience should allow for development in all areas with major emphasis on instructional leadership. In this way, assistant principals will be prepared to take on the changing role of the principal.

Conclusion

The basic operating unit of U.S. education is the local school. It is at this level that teaching and learning occur and that services are provided. The role of the school board and school division staff is to support and facilitate the development of outstanding schools. At the same time, parents and other community members are seen as partners in this process.

Existing school division structures tend to be bureaucratic with rigidly coded roles, rules, and procedures. Studies (Johnson, 1996) suggest that leaders who use these structures to encourage initiatives, the free flow of ideas, and information have been more successful in promoting improvements than those who restrict access and encourage centralized control. As a result, many school divisions are shifting the roles of all those within the district, freeing the superintendent to work more closely with the board and community power structures, sharing greater authority and responsibility with local schools, and expecting the central office staff to provide the needed support for both. The superintendent is in the most important position for establishing the tone for the local school district. The principal holds a similar position for the individual school.

As the demands on education have increased, the roles of those responsible for education have shifted. The desire to develop schools that are responsive to student and family needs has resulted in a move toward greater decentralization and responsiveness. The principal and teachers within the school are expected to be more entrepreneurial, having the power and authority to come up with needed school improvements and seeing them through to success. The central office administrators are to facilitate, support, and assess these efforts. The superintendent and board are to articulate core values and outcomes, obtain political support, develop alignment, provide resources, and maintain accountability for results. This entire process works best when it is open, allowing for input from parents and community members as well as public, nonprofit, and private organizations.

Becoming a school principal is a transformative process. Much of the day-to-day work of the principal remains somewhat reactive. The principal must deal briefly but effectively with the rapid events that occur and communicate in brief encounters and unscheduled meetings. The principal places high priority on current "emergencies" and problems that occur on a daily basis. The principal also spends a good deal of time on management of school matters, instructional and curricular leadership, pupil control, teacher development, and community relations. The principal understands the need to be sensitive to parents and strives to gain strong community support. The principal also is concerned with staff issues and recognizes how necessary it is to have staff support to succeed. The biggest principal concern is how often urgent matters (crises, pressing problems, deadline-driven activities) have gotten in the way of what is important (planning, preparation, empowerment, development). Principals recognize how difficult it is to be a proactive instructional leader rather than a reactive manager. Finally, what underlies a principal's successful leadership is the creation of a school culture that promotes and sustains the continuous improvement of the school. Fullan (1997) concludes:

> People change organizations. The starting point is not system change or change in those around us, but taking action ourselves. The challenge is to improve education in the only way it can be—through the day-to-day actions of empowered individuals. This is what's worth fighting for in the school principalship. (p. 47)

The role of educational leadership is to prepare students for the twenty-first century and to encourage continuous improvement in our schools.

Portfolio Artifacts

- Ask to serve as "principal for a day." Note the various roles, responsibilities, obligations, time commitments, and issues that occur in this single day.
- Attend a superintendent's administrative meeting.
- Prepare reports that will be reviewed by central office administrators, school board members, and/or state and federal department of education staff.
- Study districtwide school policies and relate policies to an existing issue at your school.
- Conduct a safety audit. Sustain a safe, efficient, clean, well-maintained, and productive school environment.
- Determine what sustains cohesion among the stakeholders in a school district and how equitable decisions, in the interest of all involved, are achieved.
- Leverage and marshal school resources to support an instructional program.
- Promote equity, fairness, and respect among all members of the school community.
- Generate support for two-way communication among all those who have a stake in the effectiveness of student learning.

- Work with the governing board, district, and local leaders to influence policies that benefit students and support the improvement of teaching and learning.
- Interview a school board member.
- Become a member of a school planning or curriculum review team.
- Review and update your school system's organizational chart, job descriptions, or policy manual.
- Search the web for organizations such as:

    AASA—www.aasa.org
    AASPA—www.aaspa.org
    NAESP—www.naesp.org
    AERA—www.aera.net
    NASSP—www.nassp.org
    NPBEA—www.npbea.org
    NMSA—www.nmsa.org
    CCSSO—www.ccsso.org
    NSBA—www.nsba.org
    NCPEA—www.ncpea.net
    ASCD—www.ascd.org
    UCEA—www.ucea.org

Who are their target audiences? What do they offer to members?

Terms

Accountability	Instructional leadership	Politics
Authority and responsibility	Leadership and management	Principal skills and
Coalitions	Line and staff	proficiencies
Decentralization and	NSBA, AASA, NASSP,	Role conflict
delegation	NAESP, NMSA, ASCD	School safety audit
Dependent and independent	Operational areas	Stewardship
school board	Policy and procedures	

Suggested Readings

Bernhardt, V. (2004). *Data analysis for continuous school improvement.* Larchmont, New York: Eye on Education.

Blasé, G., & Blasé, J. (2004). *Handbook of instructional leadership.* Thousand Oaks, CA: Corwin.

Bottoms, G., & O'Neill, K. (2001, April). *Preparing a new breed of school principals: It's time for actions.* Atlanta, GA: Southern Regional Education Board.

Carter, G. R., & Cunninghan, W. G. (1997). *The American school superintendent: Leading in an age of pressure.* San Francisco: Jossey-Bass.

Drake, T. & Roe, W. (2003). *The principalship.* Boston: Allyn and Bacon.

Epstein, J. (2002). *School, family and community partnership*. Thousand Oaks, CA: Corwin Press.

Glanz, J. (2004). *The assistant principal's handbook*. Thousand Oaks, CA: Corwin.

Glass, T., Bjork, L., & Brunner, C. (2000). *The study of the American school superintendency 2000: The superintendent in the new millennium*. Arlington, VA: American Association of School Administrators.

Glatthorn, A. A. (2000). *The principal as curriculum leader*. Thousand Oaks, CA: Corwin Press.

Matthews, L. J. (2003). *Being and becoming a principal: Role conceptions of contemporary principals and assistant principals*. Boston: Allyn and Bacon.

Rallis, S., & Goldring, E. (2000). *Principals of dynamic schools*. Thousand Oaks, CA: Corwin Press.

Sergiovanni, T., Kelleher, P., McCarthy, M. & Wirt, F. (2004). *Educational governance and administration*. Boston: Allyn and Bacon.

Sergiovanni, T. G. (2001). *The principalship: A reflective practice perspective*. Boston: Allyn and Bacon.

Short, P. M., & Green, J. T. (1997). *Leadership in empowered schools: Themes from innovative efforts*. Upper Saddle River, NJ: Merrill.

Tallerico, M. (2000). *Accessing the superintendency*. Thousand Oaks, CA: Corwin Press.

Tucker, M., & Codding, J. (Ed.) (2002). *The principals' challenge: Leading and managing schools in an era of accountability*. San Francisco, CA: Jossey-Bass.

Ubben, G., Hughes, L., & Norris, C. (2004). *The principal: Creative leadership for excellence in schools*. Boston: Allyn and Bacon.

Weller, L. (2001). *The assistant principal*. Thousand Oaks, CA: Corwin.

APPENDIX 5.A

The Joint AASA–NSBA Superintendent Guidelines

- To serve as the school board's chief executive officer and preeminent educational adviser in all efforts of the board to fulfill its school system governance role.
- To serve as the primary educational leader for the school system and chief administrative officer of the entire school district's professional and support staff, including staff members assigned to provide support service to the board.
- To serve as a catalyst for the school system's administrative leadership team in proposing and implementing policy changes.
- To propose and institute a process for long-range and strategic planning that will engage the board and the community in positioning the school district for success in ensuing years.
- To keep all the board members informed about school operations and programs.
- To interpret the needs of the school system to the board.
- To present policy options along with specific recommendations to the board when circumstances require the board to adopt new policies or review existing ones.
- To develop and inform the board of administrative procedures needed to implement board policy.
- To develop a sound program of school/community relations in concert with the board.
- To oversee management of the district's day-to-day operations.
- To develop a description for the board of what constitutes effective leadership and management of public schools, taking into account that effective leadership and management are the result of effective governance and effective administration combined.

- To develop and carry out a plan for keeping the total professional and support staff informed about the mission, goals, and strategies of the school system and about the important roles all staff members play in realizing them.
- To ensure that professional development opportunities are available to all school system employees.
- To collaborate with other administrators through national and state professional associations, to inform state legislators, members of Congress, and all other appropriate state and federal officials of local concerns and issues.
- To ensure that the school system provides equal opportunity for all students.
- To evaluate personnel performance in harmony with district policy and to keep the board informed about such evaluations.
- To provide all board members with complete background information and a recommendation for school board action on each agenda item well in advance of each board meeting.
- To develop and implement a continuing plan for working with the news media.

Leadership Theory and Practice

Failing Health

You are in the second year of your first principalship at Atlas Shrug High School. Atlas Shrug has an enrollment of 1,600 students and 65 full-time teachers. This old school has had a number of problems, and you were brought in to take command. The new superintendent of the district has given you considerable freedom in determining how to turn Atlas Shrug around so as to be more responsive to student needs and the district's new reform agenda.

Recent standardized test scores indicate that the students, most from middle-class homes, are scoring slightly below the national and state averages. Only 52 percent are performing at or above grade level in mathematics and science, two areas of particular concern. The superintendent has noticed that a much higher percentage, over 65 percent of the students, receive As and Bs in their course work, and 90 percent earn Cs or above. The teachers explain away these inconsistencies. One highly influential teacher states, "The tests do not measure the skills that we have traditionally believed to be important at Atlas Shrug. We have prepared students for a long while and know a lot more about these students and their parents than can be learned from any tests." In general, there are few complaints from either the teachers or the community about Atlas Shrug High School.

Few improvements have been made in the school, and teachers often express concern at how difficult and traumatic it is to try anything new at Atlas Shrug. A number of innovative teachers have requested transfers. The new superintendent has charged the Office of Research to help the district gain a better understanding of the overall health of the schools within the district and their readiness for renewal efforts. The Research Office is beginning with the Organizational Health Instrument (OHI), developed by Dr. Marvin Fairman and associates (Fairman et al., 1979; Hardage, 1978; Johnston, 1988; Lucas, 1978; 1982), to look into the critical dimensions of school health. The following ten dimensions focus on the preparedness and probable success of any improvement effort within the schools:

1. *Goal focus* measures the degree to which members of the organization clearly perceive and share system goals and objectives.

2. *Communication adequacy* refers to the extent to which information flows freely and without distortion, vertically and horizontally, within the organization.

3. *Optimal power equalization* relates to the distribution of influence between subordinates and superiors within the work group.

4. *Resource utilization* measures the extent to which resources within the organization, particularly personnel, are obtained and used effectively.

5. *Cohesiveness* measures the extent to which members of the organization feel attracted to and wish to remain with the organization.

6. *Morale* measures the degree to which members of the work group experience feelings of well-being, satisfaction, and pleasure in being part of the organization.

7. *Innovativeness* relates to the extent to which members of the work group believe the organization to be open, responsive, innovative, diverse, and supportive of creative thinking and risk taking.

8. *Autonomy* refers to the ability of the organization to deal with external pressure while maintaining its ideals and goals.

9. *Adaptation* relates to the degree to which the organization can tolerate stress and maintain stability while coping with the demands of and responses to the external environment.

10. *Problem-solving adequacy* measures the members' perceptions of the organization's ability to solve problems completely and efficiently.

The results were reported by dimension percentile score, a measure from 0 to 100 percent of the degree to which each characteristic exists in a school as compared with a normal set of schools (70 percent and above is an acceptable score). The results for Atlas Shrug High School are as follows:

Dimension	Percentile Score
Resource utilization	88
Goal focus	83
Problem-solving adequacy	80
Communication	74
Innovativeness	35
Cohesiveness	32
Autonomy	30
Morale	27
Adaptation	25
Optimal power equalization	17

"These can't be right!" responds Guy Francon, your assistant principal, who has been at the school more than seven years. The director of research assures Francon that the data were collected very carefully and have been double-checked and that these in fact are the perceptions of the teachers. Francon continues, "I don't mean that your figures are wrong but that the teachers are wrong. We are able to cope with external demands, the teachers do have influence, there are clear school expectations, and the morale is much higher than this shows. They say they want to be involved but they seem very passive and unwilling to put in the time. They seem satisfied with existing programs. Sometimes their recommendations are unacceptable, and we have to be accountable that good decisions have been made. After all, the administration is responsible for this school." The director of the research department explains, "The teachers' responses are not right or wrong. This is an expression of their perceptions of the school. If you don't think these perceptions are correct, it is important to find out why the teachers hold these perceptions. It is important that the profile is interpreted, along with other information regarding your school."

Other data suggest that very little change has taken place at Atlas Shrug High School over the past ten years. Test scores are still low, grade inflation is still high, teacher evaluations and development are uninspiring, curriculum and instruction have not changed, community involvement is limited, and although there have been few complaints, morale is not good. There is no spirit or responsiveness in this school. Although no one makes waves and there are no obvious problems, the school seems to lack energy or excitement, and, worse, it seems to produce mediocre results, with little being done to improve them. You begin to ask yourself, "What is wrong in this school?"

✻   **What might explain the wide range in the percentile scores on the ten dimensions of organizational health? Are teachers' perceptions of their organizations' health, ethos, and culture important? Why or why not?**

Assessing Leadership Characteristics

Success in administration depends on one's overall leadership ability. The National Policy Board for Educational Administration describes educational leadership as

> giving purpose and direction for individual and group processes; shaping a school culture and values; facilitating the development of a strategic plan and vision for the school; formulating goals and planning change efforts with staff; and setting priorities for the school in the context of community and district priorities and student and staff needs. (Matthews, 1994, p. 11)

Clark and Clark (1996) provide a definition of leadership that emphasizes working together:

> Leadership is an activity or set of activities, observable to others, that occurs in a group, organization, or institution and which involves a leader and followers who willingly subscribe to common purposes and work together to achieve them. (p. 25).

An administrator's leadership to a large extent determines how successful his or her organization will be in delivering appropriate services and winning community support.

Although the meaning of administration, management, and leadership is often debated, there is some agreement that *administration* is the broadest term related to organizational responsibility, *management* focuses on efficient use of resources, and *leadership* focuses on organizational direction and purpose. Leadership is doing the right things, management is doing things right, and administration is responsible for both. Administrators are expected to be effective leaders and efficient managers.

Leadership concentrates on vision, the direction an organization should take. It draws others into the active pursuit of the strategic goals. Management focuses on the nuts and bolts of making the organization work, such as hiring, distributing resources, and enforcing policy and procedures (Hanson, 1991). Northhouse (1997) states, "Management is about seeking order and stability; leadership is about seeking adaptive and constructive change" (p. 8). Researchers (Cunningham, 1982; Lewis & Miles, 1990; Sergiovanni, 2001) suggest that leadership relates to vision, mission, purpose, direction, and inspiration and management to implementing plans, arranging resources, coordinating effort, and generally seeing that things get done. You can have strong leaders who are weak managers and vice versa. Strong administrators are good at both leadership and management.

Leadership, by far the most studied aspect of administrative behavior, is especially important because we have entered a time of transformation. Reform in education is a continuous process of improvement to meet the needs of a dynamic society. Leadership in this new "era of change" requires the ability to envision an improved school and the spark to energize and lead staff to bring it about. Improvement requires perseverance, nurturance, and problem solving. Leaders must be entrepreneurial in the sense that they empower employees to meet new challenges.

Research has begun to provide a more complete knowledge base regarding effective leadership. Frederick W. Taylor (1947), often called the father of scientific management, is given credit for developing a scientific approach to the study of leadership. Since Taylor's day, thousands of studies have been completed on leadership. What follows is a brief review of some of the seminal works.

✳ **Do the conditions at Atlas Shrug High School suggest more of a manager or a leader? On what basis did you draw this conclusion?**

Paradigms of Leadership: A Growing Knowledge Base

A person brings a personal style to any administrative position that permeates all that he or she does within the organization and serves as the screen through which he or she views organizational activity. Style influences and is influenced by the way leaders view people, tasks, and organizations. These three factors have been extensively studied, discussed, written about, and taught to help leaders improve their style.

The qualities of leadership are similar whether your discipline is education, business, health, government, criminal justice, higher education, engineering, or any other field. Frederick Taylor's theories are classic examples of the scientific rational approach to administration (see Chapter 1). This scientific rational approach views people as interchangeable parts of a machine (the bureaucracy) and studies physiological aspects and organizational structure, such as time and motion, human engineering, policy, procedure, tasks, delegation, control, and specialization (Fayol, 1949; Taylor, 1947; Urwich, 1937; Weber, 1947). These ideas are all important, but today it is widely recognized that they are by no means an adequate explanation of organizational leadership and productivity.

Mary Parker Follett (1942) was among the first to critique the mechanistic interpretation of organizations and the disregard of the human factor in the structuralist approach to leadership (see Table 6.1). She was particularly concerned with the scientific belief that there is no place for debate, conflict, ambiguity, and perhaps chaos within organizations. Follett (1924) stated that these were "not necessarily a wasteful outbreak of incompatibilities, but a normal process by which socially valuable differences register themselves for the enrichment of all concerned" (p. 300). Her work was later to influence the critical feminist and postmodernist theories of leadership.

Follett's and others' concern spawned the human relations and organizational behavior movement. The development of this movement is usually traced back to Elton Mayo and the studies completed in the Hawthorne plant of the Western Electric Company in Chicago (Roethlisberger & Dicksin, 1939). Perhaps the most important achievement of these findings was the tempering of the focus on organizational structure and the realization that the classical scientific theorists did not have all the answers.

Mayo's work directly challenged the concept that human beings could be viewed as passive cogs in a machine. One set of experiments held all other condi-

TABLE 6.1   *Benefits and Problems with Empirical Positivist Theory*

Classical Theories	Benefits	Problems
Division of labor	Expertise	Boredom
Unity of command	One immediate supervisor	None
Hierarchy of authority	Disciplined coordination of power	Communication blocks
Operating procedures and regulations	Continuity and uniformity	Rigidity and lack of responsiveness
Standardization of tasks	Rationality	Lack of morale
Impersonal, objective orientation	Competition, incentive to produce	Conflict, lack of teamwork

Source: W. Hoy & C. Miskel (1991). *Educational administration: Theory and practice.* New York: McGraw-Hill. Reproduced with permission of McGraw-Hill.

tions constant and changed the frequency and duration of rest periods. The classic theories suggested that if people took more rests, the level of their output would go down because they would have less time to spend on the task. These experiments indicated, however, the actual productivity (output) of the employees went up when their rest pauses were increased. These puzzling findings later led to a number of other such discoveries that one by one established the importance of the study of organizational behavior. Behavioralism is concerned with psychological satisfaction, social interaction, motivation, job satisfaction, climate, ethos, group dynamics, interpersonal relations, empowerment, and organizational culture.

＊   **Which paradigms (see Chapter 1)—those of scientific rational and scientific and structuralist theory; those of organizational behavior, human relations, and behavioralistic theory; those of values, ethics, and control; those of political, critical, constructivist frames; those of critical-contextual, gender, and race; or those of broad poststructural and postmodernism—best describe the perceived qualities at Altas Shrug High School? On what basis did you draw this conclusion?**

Leadership Instrument Analyses

You may wish to review the discussion of Administrative Platforms in Chapter 1 prior to proceeding. The instruments that follow are to be used as self-reflection tools in order to enhance reflection on your own leadership style in relation to the theories presented. They are to stimulate self-awareness, self-evaluation, as well as discussing, rethinking, and sometimes even changing practice. This process is referred to as "guided reflection" by Hole and McEntee (1999).

Following are some of the most popular theories of leadership among educational administration practitioners along with some associated self-diagnostic instruments. Complete the instruments first, and analyze your results. Be advised, however, that people tend to record their intentions rather than their actual behavior (Argyris & Schon, 1978; Blake & McCanse, 1991). The purpose of instrument analysis is to lay the groundwork for people to initiate discussions about values and attitudes and to stimulate reflective thinking about personal behavior. Reflections should include examples that support the responses you and colleagues provide, examples that frame behaviors first and then describe the effects of the behavior. This technique will help you see yourself while revealing how you and others view leadership.

McGregor's Theories X and Y

Douglas McGregor (1960) perceived an administrator's style as closely associated with his or her fundamental beliefs about human beings. He devised two contradictory views of human behavior, which he described as theory X and theory Y (Box 6.1). [Please respond to the X–Y scale presented in Box 6.1 to determine your X–Y beliefs about people (the scoring key appears in Appendix 6.A at the end of this chapter)]. Box 6.2 presents the properties of X–Y belief patterns, which have been related to autocratic and democratic styles of leadership. The *autocratic style* is based on theory X assumptions in which leaders announce decisions, sell decisions, and invite questions about what is expected of others. In some cases they might even test their ideas to learn how subordinates will respond, in order to plan a strategy for forcing compliance. This approach relies heavily on the institutional authority of bureaucracy by carefully controlling the workforce, structuring the work, following standard operating procedures, emphasizing the importance of respect for positions of authority, threatening economic and professional harm to those who do not follow directives, and praising those who do. The leader is granted the power to force followership.

The *democratic style* is based on theory Y assumptions, in which leaders delegate authority and responsibility and permit subordinates to function within defined limits. This form of leadership is collaborative; it encourages team effort to narrow possibilities and make final decisions. Leadership based on theory Y beliefs structure organizations and use leadership to facilitate and support efforts of subordinates to develop and express themselves and to act in the best interests of the organization. Theory Y leaders emphasize self-control and development, motivate through encouragement and recognition of achievement, and expect quick response to and correction of any failures that occur (Tannenbaum & Schmidt, 1958). Organization members develop themselves and prepare for and accept ownership of their jobs. The leader shares power, provides evaluative data, develops staff, and expects continuous improvement.

Leadership style may, in fact, influence the behavior of subordinates in such a way that the subordinates' behavior actually supports the use of the leader's preferred style, becoming a self-fulfilling prophecy. Thus, the leader's assumptions about a person and the way she or he treats that person may actually create the behavior—the Pygmalion effect—rather than vice versa. Autocratic approaches ac-

BOX 6.1 • *The X–Y Scale*

DIRECTIONS: As an administrator (manager, leader) you may engage in various types of behavior in relation to subordinates. Read each of the following items carefully, and then put a check mark in the appropriate column to indicate what you would do: 1 = make a great effort to do this, 2 = tend to do this, 3 = tend to avoid doing this, 4 = make a great effort to avoid this.

	1	2	3	4
1. Closely supervise my subordinates to get better work from them.				
2. Set the goals and objectives for my subordinates and sell them on the merits of my plans.				
3. Set up controls to ensure that my subordinates are getting the job done.				
4. Encourage my subordinates to set their own goals and objectives.				
5. Make sure that my subordinates' work is planned out for them.				
6. Check with my subordinates daily to see if they need any help.				
7. Step in as soon as reports indicate that the job is slipping.				
8. Push my people to meet schedules if necessary.				
9. Have frequent meetings to keep in touch with what is going on.				
10. Allow subordinates to make important decisions.				

The scoring instructions for the X–Y scale appear in Appendix 6.A at the end of this chapter.

Source: D. McGregor (1960). *The human side of enterprise.* New York: McGraw-Hill. Reprinted with permission of McGraw-Hill.

tually cause individuals to move toward immature behaviors, and democratic approaches cause people to move toward mature behaviors, whatever their initial starting points (Meyer, Kay, & French, 1965). Box 6.3 presents a continuum of immature and mature behaviors. Autocratic styles might actually trigger the lazy, indifferent, and intransigent reactions that are described as type X behaviors. Democratic leadership styles might motivate the more active, responsive, and self-directed approaches described as theory Y behaviors.

✻   **Are the perceived behaviors at Atlas Shrug High School more related to Theory X or Theory Y beliefs? What causes you to believe this?**

BOX 6.2 • *McGregor's Two Major Belief Patterns*

Theory X	Theory Y
1. People dislike and will avoid work if they can.	1. People find work as natural as play and prefer it to doing nothing.
2. People will shirk responsibility, are inherently lazy, lack creativity, and are unreliable, and therefore a leader must coerce, direct, and threaten them to make them work.	2. People are capable of self-direction and self-control; are naturally creative and strive for excellence; and therefore will make personal commitments to shared organizational goals.
3. People desire security, external direction, and rigid structuring; resist change and avoid responsibility; and have little ambition.	3. People seek and accept greater self-direction and new challenges and can be trusted with both authority and responsibility.

Source: D. McGregor (1960). *The human side of enterprise.* New York: McGraw-Hill. Reprinted with permission of McGraw-Hill.

NREL Behavior Matrix

There is a great deal of diversity in the personal styles that people bring to their organization. As mentioned earlier, these styles serve as screens through which the individual views people, tasks, and organizations. Dr. Susan Sayers-Kirsch and the Northwest-Regional Educational Laboratory (1985) developed an instrument to help people identify their own behavior style and to identify and understand the basic styles of others. The following abbreviated version helps individuals to

BOX 6.3 • *Continuum of Immature and Mature Behaviors*

(Type X) Immaturity _____ Maturity *(Type Y)*

Passive _____	Active
Dependent _____	Independent
Limited skills _____	Diverse skills
Erratic, shallow interest _____	Well supported, strong interests
Short-term perspective _____	Long-term perspective
Unempowered, subordinate mentality _____	Empowered, equal position
Lack of awareness of potential _____	Awareness and control of self

Source: Chris Argyris (1993): *The Individual and the Organization: Some Problems of Mutual Adjustment.* New York: Irvington.

achieve these outcomes. As you think about the four descriptors below, place yourself along the continuum near the description that best describes you (stay off the midpoint):

Dominant —————————|————————— Easygoing

Informal —————————|————————— Formal

The lines are next reorganized in order to develop four quadrants. Box 6.4 presents the reorganized lines in the form of a Behavior Matrix. Convert your marks to these axes and draw a horizontal and vertical line through your marks and determine the point where the two lines intersect. This will place you into a quadrant on the Behavior Matrix. After you have completed the interpretation of the Behavior Matrix using Appendix 6.B, hopefully you will draw the same conclusion that is supported by research, which is that successful people come from all quadrants of the matrix and an organization needs all four types of people to be successful. It is important for leaders to be reflective and to think through their strengths and weakness and the types of people who will best complement their ability to lead and those with whom they might be most likely to be in conflict (look at the "Working Relationships: A Worksheet" in Appendix 6.B).

✳ **What seems to be the personal style and what impact is it having on teachers who are working at Atlas Shrug High School?**

BOX 6.4 • *The Behavior Matrix*

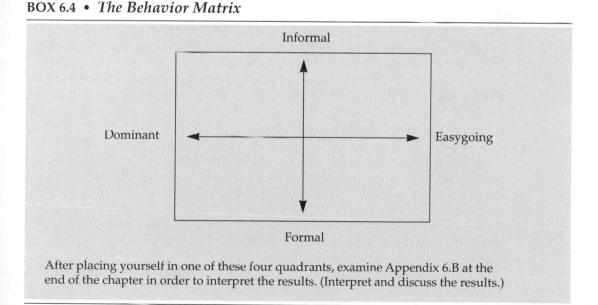

After placing yourself in one of these four quadrants, examine Appendix 6.B at the end of the chapter in order to interpret the results. (Interpret and discuss the results.)

Early Studies

Among the earliest of the vast research completed on leadership was *The University of Iowa Studies* (Levin, Lippet, & White, 1939), which suggested that leadership be classified on the basis of how the leader handles several decision-making situations—authoritarian, democratic, and laissez-faire. They found that subordinates preferred democratic styles, were aggressive or apathetic under authoritarian styles, and that laissez-faire produced aggressive behavior. Productivity was slightly higher under authoritarian than democratic leaders and was worse under laissez-faire leaders.

Path-Goal theory (House, 1971; House & Boety, 1990) is one of the original contingency theories. This theory suggests that by increasing the number and kinds of subordinate payoffs for the attainment of goals and by establishing paths to these payoffs (by clarifying the paths, reducing roadblocks and pitfalls, and increasing the opportunities for personal satisfaction along the way), the group will be able to achieve its goals. Employees work toward goals if they can see a source of satisfaction, and effective leaders make these sources contingent upon subordinates' efforts. This can be achieved through one of four distinct leadership behaviors: directive, supportive, participative, or achievement orientation. Each is appropriate under certain conditions but not in others. Subordinate characteristics include ability, locus of control (whether the individual or others control the environment), and needs and motives. The environmental conditions include tasks, work group characteristics, and authority systems. Leader behaviors moderated by subordinate characteristics and environmental conditions result in effective performance and job satisfaction.

Compliance theory (Amitai Etzioni, 1975) creates a typology of power and how subordinates respond. The types of power are coercive, enumerative, and normative, and the three types of responses are alienation, calculation, or commitment. Coercive power uses force and fear to control subordinates and usually generates alienation among the more mature workers. Utilitarian power uses extrinsic rewards that are based on an external locus of control (giving others responsibility for one's own self-worth), which works best with a calculative response based on the utility of the rewards to the individual who is motivated in this way. The normative power uses intrinsic rewards based on an internal locus of control (taking full responsibility for oneself) in which the value of the work itself, to the individual, serves as the motivator and the response is commitment. Obviously, problems can develop when there is a mismatch of styles.

Theory Z (William G. Ouchi, 1981) is an extension of McGregor's theory X and Y and focuses on culture. The theory Z culture exhibits trust, cooperation, collective decision making, career orientation, and teamwork. These characteristics create a sense of security, commitment, and loyalty to the organization. The employee is focused on career development and sees the organization as a community of equals who work cooperatively toward a common goal. Employees see their careers as investments over the long term that will be appreciated and rewarded.

Chris Argyris (1993) questioned the benefits of bureaucracy on the basis that it hindered employees from using their full potential. He viewed individuals as progressing along an immaturity to maturity continuum (see Box 6.3). As people mature they require a greater level of independence, which bureaucracy and autocratic leadership do not support. As a result, these approaches can decrease the person's ability to reach his or her full level of development and thus make a maximum contribution to the organization. This can result in this person's becoming either aggressive or apathetic. Argyris supports a more participatory style of leadership that results in greater maturity and development.

The Ohio State Studies

The *Ohio State Studies* (Fleischman & Hunt, 1973; Hemphil & Coons, 1950; Stogdill, 1974, 1981) helped shift thinking away from a single-axis paradigm of leadership, often with democratic and autocratic at either ends of the continuum, to a two-dimensional paradigm of leadership that includes two continuums: consideration and initiating structure. *Consideration* includes behavior indicating mutual trust, respect, and a certain warmth and rapport between the administrator and the work group. This dimension appears to emphasize a deep concern for group members and their development. It stresses such behavior as participation in decision making, encouraging communication, developing staff, supporting independent thinking, and keeping staff informed about the quality of their output.

Initiating structure includes behavior in which the supervisor organizes and defines group activities. The leader defines the role she or he expects each member to assume, assigns tasks, plans ahead, establishes work methods, pushes for improved productivity, emphasizes deadlines, encourages use of procedures, keeps staff informed of what is expected of them, and follows up to ensure that staff is working up to capacity. These two dimensions were found to be independent of one another; thus, a person could operate in one of four different quadrants—high on both dimensions, low on both, or high on one and low on the other. Previous research had suggested that these two approaches were opposed to one another on a single continuum, but Halpin and others showed how they were complementary in effective leadership approaches.

Well over 100 studies of leadership have examined this model. The general findings suggest that consideration and initiating structure are positively related to various measures of group effectiveness, cohesiveness, and harmony. A leader who scores high on both of these dimensions would be considered more effective based on traditional values held by organizations. For example, Andrew Halpin (1956, 1966) completed a study of superintendents and found that the most effective were described as being high on both of these dimensions; Box 6.5 presents a leadership behavior instrument based on this research. (Complete the instrument before you examine the scoring instructions, which appear in Appendix 6.C at the end of this chapter.) The most desirable approach to leadership, according to these researchers, is to stress both the importance of the individual and the importance of the task.

✳   **In which of the four quadrants defined by the Ohio State Studies do you believe the administration at Atlas Shrug High School would fall? Why? What benefits and what problems might this style cause?**

BOX 6.5 • *Leadership Behavior Survey*

Instructions: Place a check mark in the column that most closely describes your behavior in group activities. Scale: 5 = always, 4 = often, 3 = occasionally, 2 = seldom, 1 = never

Behavior	1	2	3	4	5
1. I make my attitude clear to the group					
2. I do personal favors for subordinates					
3. I try out my new ideas with the group					
4. I do little things to make it pleasant to be a member of the group					
5. I rule with an iron hand					
6. I am easy to understand					
7. I speak in a manner not to be questioned					
8. I find time to listen to subordinates					
9. I criticize poor work					
10. I mix with subordinates rather than keeping to myself					
11. I assign subordinates particular tasks					
12. I look out for the personal welfare of individuals in my group					
13. I schedule the work to be done					
14. I explain my action to subordinates					
15. I maintain definite standards of performance					
Column Total					

Behavior	1	2	3	4	5
16. I consult subordinates before taking action					
17. I emphasize the meeting of deadlines					
18. I back up subordinates in their actions					
19. I encourage the use of uniform procedures					
20. I treat all subordinates as equals					
21. I make sure that my part of the organization is understood					
22. I am willing to make changes					
23. I ask that subordinates follow standard rules and regulations					
24. I am friendly and approachable					
25. I let subordinates know what is expected of them					
26. I make subordinates feel at ease when talking with them					
27. I see to it that subordinates are working up to capacity					
28. I put suggestions made by my group into action					
29. I see to it that the work of subordinates is coordinated					
30. I get group approval in important matters before acting					
Column Total					

Source: A. Halpin, *Theory and research in administration.* © 1966. Adapted by permission of Prentice Hall, Upper Saddle River, New Jersey.

The New Managerial Grid

Although both were completed independently, the managerial grid (Blake & McCanse, 1991; Blake & Mouton, 1964, 1978) is a two-dimensional model that closely resembles the one in the Ohio State Studies. The Grid, which was the popularized version, includes various phases of training to help leaders become proficient in both dimensions of leadership. For these researchers, initiating structure was a "concern for production" and consideration was a "concern for people." Blake and McCanse (1991) identified seven different leadership styles, which they believe encompassed all the most important differences among leaders. These styles are:

1. *Control and Dominate (Dictatorial).* A 9,1—oriented person demonstrates a high concern for results and a low concern for people. The resulting style is autocratic; the person comes across like a steamroller, pushing for results without considering how his or her behavior influences others. "People" concerns, such as benefits, training, flexible work hours, and career paths, are given a low priority. Human qualities of relationships are seen as issues that slow down or impede the main focus of achieving sound results. The 9,1 does not mean to attack people, but he or she truly believes this is the only way to get the job done—and "all that other stuff is frills, anyway" that distract people from working hard.

2. *Yield and Support (Accommodating).* The 1,9 person demonstrates a low concern for results with a high concern for others. The resulting style comes across as warm and friendly, but lacking in strength and purpose. This leader is the "nurturer" who is genuinely concerned about what people think and feel, and sees her or his role as generating enthusiasm and building morale rather than generating results. The 1,9 and 9,1 styles are diametrically opposed. While they both understand the difference in the two perspectives, they are unable to appreciate that these styles are equally harmful. Each of these orientations leads in a narrow and single-focused manner. The Achilles' heel in the 1,9 thinking is that "as long as I'm keeping people happy, results will follow." The evidence shows the opposite: Because there are never any serious consequences for poor performance, people respond by not really caring about personal or team effectiveness.

3. *Balance and Compromise (Status Quo).* The 5,5 style is located in the middle of the Grid figure with a medium level of concern for both results and people. Like the 9,1 and the 1,9, the 5,5 person believes there is an inherent contradiction between the two concerns. This contradiction is resolved by balancing the needs of people with results, through compromises and trade-offs rather than trying to achieve the soundest possible results. The objective is not to strive for excellence but to play it safe and work toward acceptable solutions. The 5,5 is often very informed, but his or her efforts are weakened by the objective of fitting in with popular trends. Information gathered is not used for challenging standards and searching for creative solutions but is used to reduce or suppress controversy.

4. *Evade and Elude (Indifferent).* The 1,1 indifferent evade and elude style, located in the lower left corner of the Grid, represents the lowest level of concern for both results and people. This is the least visible person in a team; he or she is a "follower"

who maintains a distance from active involvement whenever possible. The key word for this style is *neutral*. Such a person goes through the motions of work rituals, doing enough to get by and rarely making a deliberate effort to do more. 1,1 survival is possible in structured workplaces where the boundaries of effort are clearly defined and communication is minimal. This sort of workplace allows the 1,1 to blend in without attracting attention.

5. *Prescribe and Guide (Paternalistic).* The (1,9; 9,1), or paternalism style, results from the coming together of two individual Grid styles in a way that produces a unique, joined style. Relationships with the paternalists are like parent to child where reward comes from the 1,9 influence and punishment comes from the 9,1 influence to dictate behaviors. The resulting style is a controlling and dominating person who also seeks approval and admiration. A person who complies receives rewards in the form of praise, advantage, and benefits that are more characteristic of the 1,9 style. This person is still expected to maintain the high standards of performance, but receives more support, guidance, encouragement, forgiveness, and overall "help" from the paternalist along the way. A person who does not comply receives more of a 9,1 treatment as seen in increased scrutiny, "prove to me you are worthy of my support," and "this is for your own good" attitude regarding expectations for performance.

6. *Exploit and Manipulate (Opportunistic).* The opportunist is a person who uses whatever Grid style is needed to advance his or her personal goals. This person has little concern for what is best for others or the company and instead is driven by the ever-present question "What's in it for me?" The opportunist uses whatever Grid style is needed to help her or him along. The 1,9 is appealed to with 1,9 values, and the 9,1 is appealed to with 9,1 values. The opportunist succeeds by using and deceiving people in order to gain trust and support and move on. Since people learn fast; the opportunist cannot make a lasting impact without being exposed as self-serving.

7. *Contribute and Commit (Sound).* The 9,9 demonstrates a high concern for both results and people. 9,9 leadership is based on examining "what's right" not "who's right?" The 9,9 leader rises above politics and fears to constantly evaluate actual effectiveness against standards of excellence. These leaders utilize feedback and criticism to develop shared understanding of objectives, to learn from experience, and to find ways to strengthen team performance. Every member is encouraged to contribute to and challenge ideas without fear of retaliation. This attitude of openness generates strong commitment to results because members feel a personal stake in outcomes. The candor present in 9,9 teams also builds a high degree of mutual trust and respect where people are not afraid to take risks and test the limits of creativity.

(*Source: The Grid Style Summaries,* Copyright © 1998 by Scientific Methods, Inc. Reproduced by permission of the owners.)

Blake and Mouton's and Blake and McCanse's findings are very similar to those of the Ohio State studies with the "contribute and committed" management style being positively associated with productivity, profitability, and success. Tables 6.2 and 6.3 on pages 168 and 169 illustrate the various approaches used in these seven leadership styles. (Box 6.6 on page 170 provides an instrument that can be used to suggest which of these seven management styles you would most naturally apply in practice. Complete this instrument and then check your responses using the scoring key in Appendix 6.D at the end of the chapter.) Research suggests that it is important to become a team-participation (contribute and committed) manager.

＊ **Which of the Blake and Mouton and Blake and McCanse leadership styles should be used at Atlas Shrug High School in planning, organizing, activating, directing, and controlling? Why?**

Situational and Contingency Leadership

Fiedler (1967) found that a leader's effectiveness in a given situation depends on the fit between his or her style and the task, authority level, and nature of the group. The interactions between these various combinations yield different results in different situations. A key condition is the maturity level of the followers. Immature followers need more structure and task behavior; as maturity increases, they need less structure and more human-relations-oriented behavior. In the most favorable situation, relations between leader and followers are good, when tasks are well defined and the leader is in a position of power.

Fred Fiedler and Martin Chemers (1974, 1984) suggested that leadership style is a fixed personality-based trait that no amount of training will modify. They state that the relationship between leadership style and effectiveness depends on several factors in the situation. These factors are good or bad leader–member relations, structured or unstructured tasks, and high or low position power. The combinations create a range of situations from high control to low control. These "leader match" models became known as contingency theories of leadership. Leadership is, to a large extent, determined by characteristics, such as relationships, structure, and power, that are vested more in the position and in the leader's personal ability to establish effective relations with appropriate people within the organization. Contingency theory suggests that both high- and low-power and control positions call for task-oriented leaders. Moderate power and control positions call for human-relationship-oriented styles (Fiedler & Garcia, 1987). These researchers expanded the study of leadership to include the qualities of the leader, the group, the task, and the situation.

Fiedler and Chemers maintain that one cannot change her or his style, but Hersey and Blanchard (1977, 1982, 1993; Hersey, Blanchard, & Johnson, 1996) suggest that leaders are expected to readily modify their styles to cope with changes in the follower readiness. The situational style of leadership is influenced by the maturity and development of the work group and the individual subordinates, and it varies from subordinate to subordinate. Their four leadership styles are telling, selling, participating, and delegating. Figure 6.1 on page 175 shows the relationship between subordinate readiness and the appropriate leadership behavior to be used given that readiness level. There are four appropriate styles of leadership determined by various combinations of relationship and task behavior. Once you have

TABLE 6.2 *Grid Styles Description Table*

Grid Style	Integrated Level of Concern	Leadership Approach	Creates a Team Culture Where . . .
1. Control and dominate (Dictatorial)	Concern for results: High (9) Concern for people: Low (1)	I expect results and take control by clearly stating a course of action. I enforce results that support production and do not permit deviation.	Members are suppressed, hidden, and sullen. People become resentful and antagonistic and feel little motivation to do more than they are told. Tensions and low commitment are obvious.
2. Yield and support (Accommodating)	Concern for results: Low (1) Concern for people: High (9)	I support results that strengthen happy, warm relations. I generate enthusiasm by focusing on positive and pleasing aspects.	Members are complacent but also insecure and solicitous. People are friendly and accommodating as long as problems don't arise.
3. Balance and compromise (Status quo)	Concern for results: Medium (5) Concern for people: Medium (5)	I endorse results that are popular but caution against unnecessary risk taking. I test my opinions with others involved to ensure ongoing acceptability.	Members are accessible and outgoing but cautious and guarded when controversy arises. Creativity is inhibited by an overdependence on protocol, procedures, and bureaucracy.
4. Evade and elude (Indifferent)	Concern for results: Low (1) Concern for people: Low (1)	I distance myself from taking active responsibility for results to avoid getting entangled in problems. If forced, I take a passive or supportive position.	Members are apathetic and prefer working in isolation whenever possible. Members feel little or no personal commitment to results.
5. Prescribe and guide (Paternalistic)	Concern for results: 9 and 1 Concern for people: 1 and 9	I take control of results by defining initiatives for myself and others to take. I offer praise and appreciation for support and discourage challenges to my thinking.	Members are polarized by the favoritism in place. Favored members are not held up to the same high standards as others, which causes resentment, antagonism, and lower mutual trust and respect.
6. Exploit and manipulate (Opportunistic)	Concern for results: Inconsistent Concern for people: Inconsistent	I persuade others to support results that benefit me personally. If they also benefit others, that's even better in gaining support. I rely on whatever approach is needed to ensure collaboration.	Members operate independently with little to no mutual trust and respect. People resist sharing resources for fear of losing personal gain. Destructive competition is high.
7. Contribute and commit (Sound)	Concern for results: High Concern for people: High	I demonstrate my commitment to sound results by initiating team action. I explore all facts and alternative views to reach a shared understanding of the best solution.	Members demonstrate high levels of mutual trust and respect with each other, and creativity flourishes. Members feel high levels of commitment to results.

Source: Grid Style Description table, Copyright 1998 by Scientific Methods, Inc. Reproduced by permission.

TABLE 6.3   *Summary Preferred Management Styles*

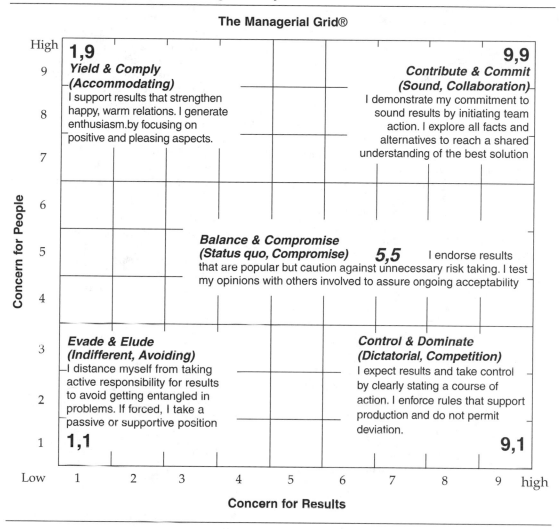

The Managerial Grid®

1,9
Yield & Comply
(Accommodating)
I support results that strengthen happy, warm relations. I generate enthusiasm.by focusing on positive and pleasing aspects.

9,9
Contribute & Commit
(Sound, Collaboration)
I demonstrate my commitment to sound results by initiating team action. I explore all facts and alternatives to reach a shared understanding of the best solution

Balance & Compromise
(Status quo, Compromise)   **5,5**   I endorse results that are popular but caution against unnecessary risk taking. I test my opinions with others involved to assure ongoing acceptability

Evade & Elude
(Indifferent, Avoiding)
I distance myself from taking active responsibility for results to avoid getting entangled in problems. If forced, I take a passive or supportive position

1,1

Control & Dominate
(Dictatorial, Competition)
I expect results and take control by clearly stating a course of action. I enforce rules that support production and do not permit deviation.

9,1

Concern for People — High / Low axis values: 9, 8, 7, 6, 5, 4, 3, 2, 1

Concern for Results   Low 1 2 3 4 5 6 7 8 9 high

identified the follower's present level of readiness, you can identify the appropriate combination of task and relationship behavior appropriate for that individual. Hersey, Blanchard, and Johnson (1996) state,

> to use this model, identify a point on the readiness continuum that represents follower's readiness to perform a specific task. Then construct a perpendicular line from that point to a point where it intersects with the curved line representing leader behavior. This point indicates the most appropriate amount of task behavior and relationship behavior for that specific situation.

BOX 6.6 • *Measuring Preferred Management Styles*

Leader Behavior

Name _____ Date _____

The Managerial Grid

Please complete the attitude survey below before turning to Appendix 6.D for scoring instructions.

Instructions: For each of the statements below select the alternative (A or B) that is more characteristic of your attitude or actions. You are to distribute a total of 3 points across the two alternatives in each question according to your preference. If you would always choose A you would assign A, 3 points and B, 0 points. If you would most often select A but sometimes select B you would assign A, 2 points and B, 1 point. This same logic applies to selecting B. Indicate your answers in the spaces provided. Remember the responses to each question should total 3.

1. When a subordinate disagrees, the executive should
   _____ A. shift to another position to maintain cooperation.
   _____ B. see to it the subordinate follows orders.

2. When an executive is planning an operation and gets some of the ideas from subordinates, the executive should include
   _____ A. the suggestions that are thought to be acceptable, remembering to thank all contributors for their interest.
   _____ B. all suggestions in some modified form, whether initially good or not.

3. When a subordinate presents a new idea that goes against the boss's convictions, the boss should
   _____ A. listen but reinforce the soundness of his or her own convictions.
   _____ B. let the subordinate know that the boss will solicit ideas when needed.

4. When direct reports are in conflict, an executive should
   _____ A. stand aside as far as possible unless he or she anticipates gaining personal benefit from a successful outcome when intervention is critical.
   _____ B. let them work it out alone; everyone should be responsible for himself or herself.

5. When a subordinate runs into trouble carrying out a job, the boss should
   _____ A. give support and encouragement; the subordinate should learn that the boss can be relied on.
   _____ B. work with the subordinate for a common understanding of the problem so that the difficulty can be corrected and eliminated in the future.

6. The executive who gets best results is one who tells subordinates what is expected
   _____ A. and holds the line.
   _____ B. but realizes that since people are people, they won't be able to meet full expectations.

7. To keep within budget, the boss should
   _____ A. try to maintain a balance between cost considerations and meeting subordinates' desires.
   _____ B. continually remind subordinates of cost considerations and thank them for compliance.

8. When planning a new project not previously undertaken, an executive should
   _____ A. seek input from others before decision making while maintaining a vigilant attitude toward new information that might modify previous plans.
   _____ B. avoid making decisions until the positions of others are evident, then adopt plans that are likely to be supported and that also reflect favorably on her or his executive expertise.

9. When an executive and a subordinate disagree, the executive should
   _____ A. not force the issue unless it becomes a crisis.
   _____ B. bring the disagreement into the open and seek to resolve the subordinate's reservations to achieve understanding and agreement.

10. An executive who really understands people will plan a job by
    _____ A. giving subordinates the overall picture—encouraging them to handle the task in the way they would be most comfortable.

_____ B. checking with each subordinate individually to get ideas and then pull these together to make a plan.

11. In planning the boss should

_____ A. establish the plan but make a positive effort to see that subordinates embrace it in a positive manner.

_____ B. solicit cooperation of subordinates to establish a plan that keeps work flowing at a level congruent with good feelings.

12. When promoting new ideas or procedures it is important to

_____ A. gain in advance the support of those likely to embrace the ideas and circumvent those who might offer opposition.

_____ B. help people accept that these ideas have been carefully thought through by those responsible to act in the best interests of the corporation.

13. An executive should recognize that if people try to do as little as possible

_____ A. they should be pushed hard, even if it generates dissatisfaction.

_____ B. there is not much that can be done about it except to live with it.

14. To get highest respect when reporting to a boss, a subordinate should relate

_____ A. matters that the boss needs to know in depth, whether things are going well or not.

_____ B. only things that are out of line and require direct action from the boss.

15. Executives should exercise control in such a way that

_____ A. subordinates are more or less on thier own unless chronic problems become crises.

_____ B. detailed reporting is expected with expressions of approval for those who cooperate.

16. When making decisions that might be resisted by others, the executive should

_____ A. meet with those affected to gain their points of view; implementation can then be adjusted to accommodate dissenting opinions.

_____ B. let people know that in this give-and-take world their support on this issue will be repaid at a later time.

17. Production should be

_____ A. high even though it places demands on subordinates.

_____ B. whatever it takes to keep oneself out of trouble.

18. When a subordinate disagrees with the boss, the boss should listen to understand the

_____ A. points of agreement as well as disagreement; then reach a sound agreement with the subordinate to establish the best course toward the goal.

_____ B. points of disagreement, then after explanation persuade the subordinate that the boss's approach to the goal is sound.

19. When exercising authority, the boss should

_____ A. be direct but gracious, persuading doubters that those in higher positions have thought it through and know what is best for the organization.

_____ B. reach decisions by gaining the involvement of those who can contribute to quality of implementation.

20. When reviewing an operation that has a number of recurring problems, an executive should

_____ A. leave no stone unturned in getting to the bottom of a mistake and pinpointing the responsible party, then make clear that there is no room for any more mistakes.

_____ B. be cautious so as not to offend those whose future support might be critical; it is better to downplay problems than to create enemies who can undermine future operations.

21. A boss can avoid trouble by

_____ A. accepting, without comment, the work tempo subordinates set for themselves.

_____ B. asking subordinates to set their own work tempo in order to create positive feelings toward their jobs.

(continued)

BOX 6.6 • *Continued*

22. When dealing with a difficult colleague in a situation that might provoke conflict, it is
    _____ A. more productive to avoid direct confrontation and to work around him or her.
    _____ B. better to back off rather than to run the risk of creating hostile feelings.

23. To promote best effort, important decisions should be developed
    _____ A. in a team made up of both the executive and subordinates to ensure coordination of effort.
    _____ B. on a one-to-one basis between executive and subordinates to ensure efficiency and accountability.

24. When asked for an opinion on a difficult matter, the executive should
    _____ A. review past practice or precedent in an effort to offer a tried-and-true position that accommodates different points of view.
    _____ B. avoid spontaneous reactions to gain more time to assess where others stand and what response is likely to engender their support for his or her position.

25. When a special assignment is given to a subordinate, the executive should
    _____ A. outline the job for completion within a predetermined time schedule and tolerate no deviations or excuses for failure to deliver.
    _____ B. assign the project a part at a time so that progress can be praised and the executive can introduce corrections as needed.

26. Where there is conflict, an executive should
    _____ A. offer to help ease the disruptive tension.
    _____ B. not get involved if possible.

27. When a new project is to be undertaken, an executive should
    _____ A. gather the relevant information and seek ideas from those who will carry out the project.

_____ B. analyze the facts and request recommendations from subordinates, then present a solution to subordinates, gaining their commitment to it by showing how the boss has taken their ideas into account.

28. When dealing with bosses on a high-stakes issue
    _____ A. it is important to find out what they want and to tailor one's actions and responses accordingly.
    _____ B. one should remain on the sidelines and let those in positions of authority make the final decisions.

29. When evaluating performance, it is necessary for the executive to
    _____ A. keep a constant watch on subordinates in their own best interest to help them avoid repeating mistakes and errors.
    _____ B. offer praise for positive performance while withholding demoralizing criticism.

30. After a difficult job has been completed, an executive should
    _____ A. show appreciation by easing off to relieve whatever tensions might have been generated.
    _____ B. have plans made for the next job and move people on to it as fast as they finish the previous task.

31. The way to handle suggestions is to
    _____ A. defer reacting to them, either positively or negatively, until your boss has evaluated them, then pass her or his reactions along to your subordinates.
    _____ B. listen to them with a positive attitude and pass those on to your boss that imply no serious criticism; sit on the rest.

32. When approving training and development activities for subordinates, an executive should
    _____ A. permit subordinates to choose the path they prefer since it is more likely to motivate them.

_____ B. encourage subordinates to move in directions that are likely to forward the executive's objectives.

33. When communicating with subordinates an executive should

_____ A. see that official information passes through organizational channels and use informal channels to communicate unofficial information.

_____ B. pass through organization channels what it is in the best interest of others to know and use informal channels to deal with the rest.

34. An effective way for a boss to handle mistakes and errors on the part of a subordinate is to

_____ A. get the mistake fixed by influencing third parties to put pressure on the erring subordinate.

_____ B. seek out the underlying causes for the problems and work with the appropriate parties to gain understanding and commitment to correction.

35. When planning, an executive should call in the people affected

_____ A. but let them arrive at their own plan, since they are more likely to follow it.

_____ B. and work with them until the best plan is devised.

36. Quality standards are

_____ A. a reflection of the boss's values, which team members are expected to embrace wholeheartedly.

_____ B. given tongue-in-cheek recognition; actions might not be consistent with words.

37. When an executive and a subordinate disagree on a decision, the executive should

_____ A. explain reasons for the decision and affirm apologetically that the decision must stand.

_____ B. tell the subordinate that the decision will stand.

38. When unable to resolve a disagreement with a subordinate's decision, the executive should

_____ A. disengage by tabling the discussion.

_____ B. make the decision and let the subordinate know that her or his acceptance of it is appreciated.

39. Effective coordination among subordinates can be achieved through

_____ A. actively engaging them in solving problems of work.

_____ B. letting them know that people come first.

40. One way to spur performance of subordinates is to

_____ A. encourage competition among them to increase the effort of each.

_____ B. pressure individuals to put forth maximum effort.

41. In reviewing a subordinate's performance, an executive should realize

_____ A. that it is important for the subordinate to understand how he or she is performing.

_____ B. that since most formal appraisals are touchy and can lead to hard feelings, experience on the job is the best teacher for correcting poor performance.

42. When conducting a meeting an executive should

_____ A. listen to subordinates to gain their support, while reserving the right to make final decisions.

_____ B. see to it that decisions are based on shared understanding and agreement.

Note that the curved line never goes to either the lower left or the lower right corner. In both quadrants 1 and 4 there are combinations of both task and relationship behavior. Style 1 always has some relationship behavior and style 4 always has some task behavior. (p. 200)

Situational theories answer the question "What is excellent leadership?" with the reply "It depends." They believe that there is no one best way to influence others.

Contingency and Situational Leadership® theorists reject the conclusion that there is one best approach to leadership. They suggest that time available, task specificity, competence and maturity of the staff, need for involvement, authority, and dynamics of the situation determine what style should be used. Other contextual factors include group size, rewards, leader status, method of appointment, and technical background. For each level of development among the workforce the leader should adopt a specific style of leadership; thus, leaders demonstrate a strong degree of flexibility regarding approach.

Vroom and Yetton (1973) developed yet another relatively complex model for determining different situations and their relationship to subordinate participation in leadership. Decision making is on a continuum that runs from unilateral at one end to a shared model in which all group members participate in the decision at the other. Factors such as quality requirements, potential conflict, acceptance, information availability, and structure are used to determine which approach should be applied in a given situation.

Vroom and Jago (1988) presented a decision tree to help leaders determine the "best" approach under different combinations of circumstances. Ubben and Hughes (1997) expanded the factors involved and stressed the importance of time available as a consideration to leadership approach.

Yukl (1989) differentiated the situational approach on the basis of whether the requirement was for a "leader" or a "manager." In the capacity of leader a person needs an advanced repertoire of skills, and different skills are used in different situations. Participation of the workforce is important to the development of knowledge, skills, and a shared vision. Also important are gaining subordinate understanding and commitment and encouraging experimentation. In the capacity of a manager, that person is more directive, sending messages, establishing channels of command, and closely monitoring work. Followers comply with the perceived legitimacy of the leader to manage the organization. Yukl strongly argues that no single approach will suffice for all situations.

The formulas devised for matching these variables are not simple. Many argue that the nature of leadership does not vary with each situation. Critics of the situational model suggest that its unpredictable aspects provoke suspicion, distrust, deceit, and confusion. What contingency and situational approaches ignore is the Pygmalion effect—the power that expectations and treatment have on the behavior of others. People often become what their leader expects them to become. Berlew and Hall (1988) found that what higher-level managers expected of lower-level managers determined the lower-level managers' subsequent performance and success. These findings are corroborated by the work of Dr. Edward Deming (discussed later in this chapter). Another matter of concern is that

LEADER BEHAVIOR

Task Behavior—

The extent to which the leader engages in defining roles, i.e., telling what, how, when, where, and if more than one person who is to do what in:

- Goal-Setting
- Organizing
- Establishing Time Lines
- Directing
- Controlling

Relationship Behavior—

The extent to which a leader engages in two-way (multi-way) communication, listening, facilitating behaviors, socioemotional support:

- Giving Support
- Communicating
- Facilitating Interactions
- Active Listening
- Providing Feedback

(Supportive Behavior)
Relationship Behavior

(HIGH)

(LOW)

S3
Share ideas and facilitate in decision making

Participating

S2
Explain decisions and provide opportunity for clarification

Selling

| Hi. Rel. Lo. Task | Hi. Rel. Hi. Task |
| Lo. Rel. Lo. Task | Hi. Rel. Lo. Task |

Delegating

Telling

S4
Turn over responsibility for decision and implementation

S1
Provide specific instructions and closely supervise performance

(LOW) ⟵——————⟶ (HIGH)

Task Behavior
(Guidance)
Follower Readiness

HIGH	MODERATE		LOW
R4	**R4**	**R4**	**R4**
Able and Willing or Confident	Able but Unwilling or Insecure	Unable but Willing or Confident	Unable and Unwilling or Insecure

Follower Directed   Leader Directed

DECISION STYLES

1
Leader-Made Decision

2
Leader-Made Decision with Dialogue and/or Explanation

3
Leader- and Follower-Made Decision or Follower-Made Decision with Encouragement from Leader

4
Follower-Made Decision

Ability: has the necessary knowledge, experience, and skill

Willingness: has the necessary confidence, commitment, motivation

When a Leader Behavior is used appropriately with its corresponding level of readiness, it is termed a High Probability Match. The following are descriptors that can be useful when using Situational Leadership for specific application:

S1	**S2**	**S3**	**S4**
Telling	Selling	Participating	Delegating
Guiding	Explaining	Encouraging	Observing
Directing	Clarifying	Collaborating	Monitoring
Establishing	Persuading	Committing	Fulfilling

FIGURE 6.1 *Expanded Situational Leadership® Model.* Paul Hersey, *Situational Selling.* Escondido, CA: Center for Leadership Studies, 1985, p. 35.

Source: Hersey, P., Blanchard, K. & Johnson, D. (1996). *Management of Organizational Behavior: Utilizing Human Resources.* Upper Saddle River, NJ: Prentice Hall, p. 208.

Situational Leadership® is a registered trademark of the Center for Leadership, Inc. Copyright © 2002, Center for Leadership Studies, Inc. All Rights Reserved.

leaders can create situations that demand their preferred styles. For example, a leader can place short time constraints on decisions to justify more autocratic approaches.

University of Michigan Studies

Another series of studies originated with Rensis Likert (1967) at the University of Michigan Social Research Center. He was able to identify the four types of leadership styles described below.

> *System 1 (Exploitative authoritative).* Management does not trust subordinates, who are not free to discuss matters with supervisors and whose opinions are not sought in solving problems. Motivation comes from fears, threats, occasional rewards. Communication comes down from higher management. Goals are ordered from on high, where all decisions are made.

> *System 2 (Benevolent authoritative).* Management and employees exist in a master–servant relationship. There is some involvement of employees; more rewards than in system 1; slightly better communications up. This is a paternalistic organization, not giving much latitude to employees to "do their thing."

> *System 3 (Consultative).* Management controls things, but employees are consulted before solutions to problems and decisions are made by management. Communication upward is better, but is still cautious. Unpleasant or unfavorable information is not offered freely. Employees feel they will perform some roles in preliminary stages of decision making and policy setting but that their contributions might not always be taken seriously.

> *System 4 (Participative group).* Management trusts employees, regards them as working willingly toward the achievement of organizational objectives. People are motivated by rewards and are involved at all levels in discussing and deciding issues that are important to them. Communication is quite accurate and goes up, down, and across. Goals are established with the participation of the people who will have to work to achieve them.

The ideal style was identified by Likert as system 4, the participative style, which was consistently associated with more effective performance. System 3 was next best and so on, with system 1 being the least effective. (Table 6.5 provides an instrument that can be used to determine which of the four styles is most characteristic of an organization.) The University of Michigan studies complement the Ohio State Studies and those completed by Blake and Mouton and Blake and McCanse.

✳ **Use the ten dimensions of the Organizational Health Instrument to characterize the leadership system that now exists at Atlas Shrug High School.**

TABLE 6.5 *Leadership Style That Is Most Characteristic within an Organization*

Organizational Variable	1	2	3	4
How much confidence and trust does management place in subordinates?	Virtually none	Some	Substantial amount	A great deal
How free do subordinates feel to talk to superiors about the job?	Not very free	Somewhat free	Quite free	Very free
How often are subordinates' ideas sought and used constructively?	Seldom	Sometimes	Often	Very frequently
Is predominant use made of (1) fear, (2) threats, (3) punishments, (4) rewards, 5) involvement?	1, 2, 3, occasionally 4	4, some 3	4, some 3 and 5	5, 4, based on group
Where is responsibility felt for achieving organization's goals?	Mostly at top	Top and middle	At most levels	At all levels
How much cooperative teamwork exists?	Very little	Relatively little	Moderate amount	Great deal
What is the usual direction of information flow?	Downward	Mostly downward	Down and up	Down, up, and sideways
How is downward communication accepted?	With a great deal of suspicion	With some suspicion	With caution	With a receptive mind
How accurate is upward communication?	Usually inaccurate	Often inaccurate	Sometimes inaccurate	Almost never inaccurate
How well do superiors know problems faced by subordinates?	Not very well	Rather well	Quite well	Very well
Are subordinates involved in decisions related to their work?	Almost never	Occasionally consulted	Generally consulted	Fully involved
What does the decision making process contribute to motivation?	Not very much	Relatively little	Some contribution	Substantial contribution
How are organizational goals established?	Orders are issued	Orders are issued, some comments are invited	After discussion, by orders	By group action (except in crisis)
How much covert resistance to goals is present?	Strong resistance	Moderate resistance	Some resistance at times	Little or none
Is there an informal organization resisting the formal one?	Yes	Usually	Sometimes	No—same goals as formal
What are the cost, productivity, and other control data used for?	Policing, punishment	Reward and punishment	Reward, some self-guidance	Self-guidance, problem solving

Source: R. Likert (1967). *The human organization: Its management and values.* New York: McGraw-Hill.
Reproduced with permission of McGraw-Hill.

Recent Works on Leadership

The elusive concept of leadership can perhaps never be fully grasped, but knowledge of its properties carries one a long way toward being an effective leader. It is beyond the grasp of a single volume to be exhaustive, much less definitive. There is too much theoretical and empirical literature to cover in a survey of this subject; however, a number of studies provide the overall recent themes in the popular literature. Much of it builds on the studies already presented in this chapter.

To judge by the best-seller lists, there is a growing interest in the topic of leadership. The success of the twenty-six books of Peter Drucker (1954, 1974, 1980, 1992, 1998, 2002), a leading management and leadership philosopher, attests to the prominence of this subject. One of Drucker's works (1992) contains essays from leadership experts around the world. The books focus on the importance of core values—integrity, respect, tenacity, curiosity, learning, standards, friendliness, resilience, convictions, and courage. Leaders need to respect diversity, see the potential in all employees, and communicate persuasively. They must model a commitment to continuous education and self-growth. Effective executives believe in shared decision making. They also must have advanced computer skills.

Search for Excellence

Tom Peters and Robert H. Waterman's *In Search of Excellence* (1982) was the leadership and administrative book of the century based on marketplace success, with more than 5 million copies sold in fifteen languages. The sequels, *A Passion for Excellence* (1985), *Thriving on Chaos* (1987), *The Pursuit of Wow!* (1994), and *Circle of Innovation* (1997), have also done extremely well, although none has had the impact of the first book. The basic theme of this body of work is familiar—to succeed leaders must attend to both the hard and soft components of the organization (the tasks and the people). The eight attributes of successful leadership as described in these books are presented in Box 6.7.

Peters promotes the importance of organizations being responsive to customer needs and supporting experimentation, initiative, and risk taking to accomplish goals and satisfy highly visible customers. Slogans like "ready, fire, aim" support the try-it-now, fail, learn, shift, interact, and modify approach to leadership. Because of the rapidly changing times he has recently modified this slogan to "fire, fire, fire." Another related slogan is "fail faster, succeed sooner." "Paralysis in analysis" suggests that emphasis on long-term planning be reduced so the organization can be more spontaneous in response to quickly evolving conditions. The research stresses the importance of rich, informal communication, open forums, management by walking around (MBWA), positive reinforcement, better listening, constancy of innovation, and responsiveness to customer and employees. Mistakes are always viewed as progress, although they must be identified and corrected quickly. The bedrock of Peters's message is listening, trust, respect, innovation, and whatever else results in "turned-on" and "in-touch" people. Leaders must love change (instead of fighting it) and instill and share an inspiring vision.

BOX 6.7 • *Lessons from* In Search of Excellence

---

1. *Bias for Action.* A preference for doing something—anything—rather than sending an idea through endless cycles of analyses and committee reports.
2. *Staying Close to the Customer.* Learning customer preferences and catering to them.
3. *Autonomy and Entrepreneurship.* Breaking the corporation into small companies and encouraging them to think independently and competitively.
4. *Productivity through People.* Creating in all employees the awareness that their best efforts are essential and that they will share in the rewards of the company's success.
5. *Hands-On, Value-Driven.* Insisting that executives keep in touch with the firm's essential business and promote a strong corporate culture.
6. *Stick to the Knitting.* Remaining with the businesses the company knows best.
7. *Simple Form, Lean Staff.* Few administrative layers, few people at the upper levels.
8. *Simultaneous Loose-Tight Properties.* Fostering a climate in which there is dedication to the central values of the company combined with tolerance for innovation from all employees who accept those values.

Source: Attributes of leadership as specified from *In Search of Excellence* by T. J. Peters and R. H. Waterman, Jr. Copyright © 1982 by J. J. Peters and R. H. Waterman Jr. Reprinted by permission of HarperCollins.

✳ **Use the eight lessons from *In Search of Excellence* to describe an effective work culture for Atlas Shrug High School.**

The 7 Habits of Highly Effective People

Stephen R. Covey's book *The 7 Habits of Highly Effective People* (1989) is similar to the works of Peters in its homey approach and has been phenomenally well received. It was a best-seller for fourteen months. There is considerable debate among academicians as to whether this book is a study of leadership or a self-help book. Covey described the 7 Habits of Highly Effective People as:

Habit 1: Be Proactive®. Take the initiative, responding and making things happen. Realize you have freedom to choose, be aware of self, develop knowledge and integrity in choices.

Habit 2: Begin with the End in Mind®. Start with an image or paradigm of the end in mind. Have a clear understanding of where you are going, where you are, and what it is going to take to get to the destination.

Habit 3: Put First Things First®. Practice effective self-management day in and day out. All truly successful people make present decisions that help achieve desired outcomes.

Habit 4: Think Win/Win®. Have a frame of mind that always seeks to have all parties feel as though they have won—the benefits to be mutually shared. Cooperation is the key.

Habit 5: Seek First to Understand, Then Be Understood®. Practice empathetic listening skills so that you understand other people from their frame of reference. Listen with not only ears, but with eyes and hearts. Then, present your ideas logically, clearly, specifically, and in the context of understanding the other person.

Habit 6: Synergize®. Create new alternatives. Leave your comfort zones to confront new and unknown challenges. Value differences, respect them, and use them to build on strengths. Develop unity and creativity with others. Unleash new powers, create new, exciting alternatives.

Habit 7: Sharpen the Saw®. Leading people requires a tremendous amount of energy. Make a constant effort to manage health needs. Model good self-help techniques. Convince others that they are valued and should value others. Enjoy and celebrate accomplishment.

(*The 7 Habits of Highly Effective People* and the 7 Habits respectively are all registered trademarks of Franklin Covey Co. Used with permission.)

Vision is the fundamental force that drives everything else in our lives. It empassions us with a sense of the unique contribution that's ours to make. It empowers us to put first things first, compasses ahead of clocks, people ahead of schedules and things (Covey, Merrill, & Merrill, 1994, p. 116).

Many researchers have identified core values, enduring purpose, and vision as the most distinguishing characteristics of the more successful organizations. Such organizations understand the difference between what should and what should never change. In discussing vision, Collins and Porras (1994) state:

If you do this right, you will spend only a small percentage of your time articulating the vision. The vast majority of your time will be spent bringing the organization into alignment. Yes, it's very important to stop and think about vision. But even more important, you have to align the organization to preserve the core ideology and stimulate progress toward the envisioned future, not merely write a statement. Keep in mind that there is a big difference between being an organization with a vision statement and becoming a truly visionary organization. (pp. 238–239)

Successful organizations move toward visions and practices that reinforce their core ideologies and values.

Organizations build trust and collegiality, develop people and align them toward a shared vision, and then release their creative energies to work in cooperation and harmony to achieve desired results (see the illustration at the top of the next page).

Communication is at the heart of successful leadership and begins by understanding what others are saying through effective listening skills. Take time to un-

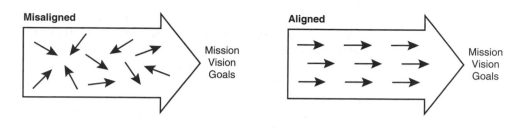

derstand others; it is far less than the time needed to back up and correct misunderstandings. Do not offer suggestions until you are completely clear on what the person you are talking to means. Present ideas clearly, specifically, visually, and most important contextually so that others can understand you and your beliefs and interest in the matter, knowing you have considered all facts and positions.

✳ **How might the staff at Altas Shrug High School be aligned so that they are working toward a common shared vision for the school?**

The Learning Organization

The "learning organization" concept developed by Peter Senge (1990) is a generative process that enhances and extends an organization's ability to create. The concept of responsiveness is an important organizational behavior, but the real payoffs come from being generative. Clarify what is important by continually learning how to see the current reality more clearly and developing abilities to move beyond it. This new learned knowledge permeates the organization and gives coherence to diverse activities. A shared vision provides the focus and energy for learning and creates commitment (not compliance). Commitment to the vision fosters risk taking and experimentation. It is central to the daily work of those within the organization.

Vision grows out of opportunities to communicate, learn, experiment, be held accountable for results, and most of all to shape the future. Although this process can be chaotic, it most often "converges on a conclusion or course of action" (Senge, 1990, p. 247). Senge stresses the importance of having teams develop fluency in the language of systems thinking. The system provides the unifying principles that serve to integrate the diverse activity occurring within the organization. Successes in one classroom influence the entire system. Like Peters, Senge stresses the importance of being able to "forgive" and "forget" mistakes and knows how hard it is to provide the needed time to allow this process—understanding complexity, clarifying vision, and learning—to occur.

Max DePree (1989) believes that although it is clear that leaders draw their inspiration and spiritual reserve from their sense of stewardship, much of the leverage leaders actually have lies in helping people achieve more accurate, more insightful, and more empowering views of reality. According to DePree, success requires that employees feel needed, involved, cared for, and rewarded with fair wages and benefits. The DePree model respects the diversity of people's gifts, talents, and skills. People, relationships, information, and communication—not structures—build organizational effectiveness. "Information is power but it is pointless power if hoarded" (p. 104). Effective leaders help their employees to understand the systematic forces that shape change and to see current reality. Effective leaders instill the confidence in their employees that together "We can learn whatever we need to learn in order to achieve the results we truly desire" (Senge, 1990, p. 399).

Another book that is a great success based on popularity and sales is Jim Collins's *Good to Great* (2001). The author's research team completed a study to determine what distinguished "good-to-great companies" from their competitors. This is a fun book to read, rich in stimulating ideas like first who, then what; don't worry about who got credit; rigorous, not ruthless; disciplined people, thought, and action; buildup followed by breakthrough; manage the system, not the people; harness technologies; and let the truth come out (confront brutal facts). This book challenges some conventional wisdom such as putting in much time in motivating and aligning people, instead, allow the infectious momentum to do that.

✳ **How would you create a learning organization at Atlas Shrug High School?**

The New Science of Leadership

Margaret G. Wheatly (1992; Steinberg, 1995) suggests a fundamental shift in thinking in which leaders look for order rather than control in organization. Order is inherent in living systems. It does not evolve from avoiding different or disturbing information, smoothing turbulence, defining situations, standardizing approaches, writing procedures, and telling people what to do. Discomfort is a part of greater understanding, motivation, and satisfaction as new approaches are made successful. Order is inherent—people naturally seek to make their conditions coherent. A small change can disturb and threaten order or equilibrium and result in chaos throughout a system. But even that chaos will act within specific parameters with order and predictability. Chaos has boundaries beyond which it will not go.

Disequilibrium creates growth, and under proper conditions the system will respond and evolve to a new, improved order. Successful organizations adapt and change and are free to interact with a turbulent, changing environment in such a way that it is open, free, and capable of responding and regenerating—a viable, living, adaptive, well-ordered organization. Successful organizations take advantage of the opportunities or possibilities for renewal and enhancement. Such opportunities involve longer, more thoughtful conversations, greater participation, more risk taking, more tolerance of mistakes, more openly shared information, more acceptance of chaos, more volatility of politics, and more effort toward figuring out what works and what doesn't. The foundation of leadership is a welcoming of diverse and rich viewpoints, inclusion of many different people in the process of thinking together in self-renewal, and continuous improvement.

Leaders often become wary of periods of turbulence and clamp on controls, retreat, tune out information, and create rigid structure to calm the waters. Some administrators focus on holding all the pieces together and smoothing the political and ideological debate. Unfortunately, this "circle the wagons" mentality short-circuits the learning and improvement process that is needed for success and excellence by cutting off the uncertainty, debate, disagreement, confusion, and conflict. Administrators who react this way stop the organization from learning, responding, and regenerating itself and force it back into equilibrium—the status quo. A principal, for example, seeing that test scores are falling, might abandon a new program and go back to simpler, more basic past standard practices to avoid the debate, concern, and confusion that result. "We'll go back to the basics in order to make sense out of all of this."

This effort to gain control cuts off learning and shuts down the natural, life-enhancing processes of responding and improving. The problem cited above might in fact be with the instructional strategy that worked for the old program but doesn't work for the new one. Organizations cannot become more fit in their present environments unless leaders are willing to risk the perils of the path through chaos, which leads to knowledge, growth, order, and regeneration. Leaders help the system to reform, renew, reconfigure, and recreate itself to better suit the new demands and environment. Dr. Rexford Brown, from the Education Commission of the States, is fond of saying:

> Educational improvements will require new kinds of leadership. We need leaders to create conversations, to change the levels and kinds of discourse going on in and around schools, and to stimulate inquiry, questioning, problem solving, and a focus on learning for everyone in the system, not just students. . . . The primary conditions for this type of thoughtfulness are mystery, uncertainty, disagreement, questions, ambiguity, and curiosity.

✳ **Characterize what is happening at Atlas Shrug High School using Margaret Wheatley's theories regarding disequilibrium, chaos, order, and improvement. What needs to be happening?**

Total Quality Management (TQM)

Advocates of total quality management (TQM) established a foothold in Japan in the 1950s and the effects of their philosophy have been growing and spreading ever since. The fundamental messages of TQM are to improve quality, serve the customer, satisfy customer requirements, encourage employee innovation, provide for the free flow of information, attack the system (not the employees), instill pride and teamwork, and create an atmosphere of innovation and continuous improvement. Henry Mintzberg (1987) argues that organizational success is less a rational plan than an "emergent phenomenon." Successful organizations "craft strategy" according to Mintzberg, as they continually learn about shifting conditions and inclusively determine "what is desired" and "what is possible." The job of leader is to create and improve the system so that more is possible. The potential for continuous improvement lies with the staff. It evolves from their work.

Edward Deming (1986, 1991, 1993), the father of TQM, stated, "Workers are responsible for only 15 percent of the problems, the system for the other 85 percent."

He then added that the system is the responsibility of management. The heart of Deming's approach to improving the organization is teamwork and collaboration among managers and workers. The leader provides core values, consistency of purpose, information, support, training, integration, common language, continuing feedback, improved systems, alignment, integrity, time, trust, and resources. Employees are responsible for improving themselves and the work process in such a way that the outcomes of the organization continuously improve.

Individual performance appraisals and merit raises are eliminated (they ruin morale and force workers to kiss up to bosses), and work team performance is evaluated and rewarded instead. Other TQM tenets include eliminating numerical goals, tearing down walls between work groups, and sharing information; reducing or eliminating micromanaging; and letting work teams tackle the inefficiencies and outcome problems. Matrix teams draw workers from several departments to study something in addition to their regular work; project teams pull workers for temporary work on a project; process teams look into the way work is being completed; and vertical teams take a diagonal slice through the organization so as to include people at different levels to create organizational vision and expand abilities. Regardless of the type of team, the members work together to develop one another and thus the organization.

Fear is eliminated so that people feel free to ask questions, take a stand, make suggestions, experiment, and take risks. Leaders must build the culture within the organization to support the needed transformation. The focus of everyone's work in the TQM model is excellent, quick, high-quality, and flawless service. Quality improvement is the goal of every single individual within the organization. Deming provides a number of statistical models and theories to organize and present information in order to improve and streamline communication:

Tools for Quality Improvement

Action plan	Force field analysis
Block diagram	Graphs: bar, line, pie
Brainstorming	Histogram
Cause and effect analysis	Interviewing
Checklist	Pareto diagram
Consensus	Problem selection matrix
Control charts	Problem statement matrix
Cost estimation	Quality indicators
Cultivating	QIC review form
Customer needs analysis	Requirements solution selection matrix
Customer/Supplier model data gathering	Stratification
Fishbone diagram	Target and goals
Flowchart	Team project planning worksheet

✳ **Graph the percentile scores on the ten dimensions of organizational health for Atlas Shrug, using a bar graph. How might this graphical representation of the data help?**

School-Based Management (SBM)

School-based or site-based leadership follows many of the same principles as total quality leadership. It empowers staff to create conditions in schools that facilitate improvement, innovation, and continuous professional growth (David, 1989). It gives the school principal and professional staff members the widest possible latitude in sustaining efforts to continuously improve the effectiveness of the teaching and learning process. Teachers would be encouraged to introduce improvements that directly affect teaching and learning and that require genuine authority over budget, personnel, curriculum, instruction, and program evaluations. This change in roles and responsibilities affects the entire school organization (Elmore, 2000). The factors that affect success are the provision of opportunities for professional development and training, adequate information to make informed decisions, the institution of a reward system to recognize improved performance, and the allotment of enough time to each person to participate in shared planning and development (Odden & Wohlstetter, 1994).

Site councils and subcommittees within schools are used to disperse power to a broader range of stakeholders. Information is disseminated broadly to both the schools and the community, and time is provided to meet and discuss the information. This approach intensifies the need for effective leadership from the principal and others serving in leadership roles. Principals must be strong supporters of their staffs as the people who introduce innovation and move the reform agenda forward. They are constantly involved in outreach efforts, development, facilitation, support, and infrastructure.

The probability of success is increased when school staff are provided guidelines and have time to acquire new knowledge and skills, to discuss and share ideas, and to formulate, implement, and evaluate ideas to improve student learning (Cunningham & Gresso, 1993). Participants are rewarded for the progress they make toward the shared goals and vision. Rewards include extra compensation for defined responsibilities, money for professional development, money for materials, reimbursements for extra time expended, stipends for council membership, and nonmonetary benefits such as notes of appreciation, recognition meals and banquets, plaques, public recognition, reduced teaching loads, and prestige of leadership. Often the process requires some kind of waiver from district authority, state rules, and collective bargaining agreements to be effective. Schools that have been provided these kinds of waivers from state and local policies are often called "charter" schools. The school charter sets out its unique character and defines its mission, policy, priorities, and standards and ultimately describes the school's program and practices.

✳ **Would a school-based management approach work at Atlas Shrug High School? Why or why not?**

Cultural Leadership

Schein (1985) suggests that the most important thing that leaders do is help shape an effective culture in which people will complete their work. He talks about shared beliefs that define basic views of an organization and its environment. He contends that culture "influences the ways in which group members perceive, think, and feel about the world thereby serving to stabilize that world, give meaning to it, and thereby reduce the anxiety that would result if we did not know how to categorize and respond to the environment" (p. 312). In fact, culture is often defined as "the way we do things around here." Deal and Kennedy (1982) suggest that culture gives meaning to work, providing an understanding of how the organization moves from desired values and outcomes to work performance and finally to actual results. It is the internal system of organizational integration. Lee G. Bolman and Terrence E. Deal (1991) believe that

> Culture is both product and process. As product, it embodies the accumulated wisdom of those who were members before we came. As process, it is continually renewed and re-created and new members are taught the old ways and eventually become teachers themselves. . . .
>
> Our view is that every organization develops distinctive beliefs and patterns over time. Many of these patterns and assumptions are unconscious or taken for granted. They are reflected in myths, stories, rituals, ceremonies, and other symbolic forms. Managers who understand the power of symbols have a better chance of influencing organizations than do those who focus only on other frames. (p. 231)

They go on to say, "Beliefs, values, practices, and artifacts define for . . . members who they are and how they do things" (p. 250).

Our culture is important because it shapes the different ways we recognize and react to events, gives meaning and purpose to our work, and unites people (Deal & Peterson, 1998). According to Deal and Kennedy, the goal of leadership is to make something as ill-defined as culture work for leaders and for the improvement of educational performance. Bolman and Deal (2003) discuss the importance of being able to reframe or reconceptualize situations in order to gain varying perspectives regarding key issues. They discuss structural, human resource, political, and symbolic frames of reference; it is the symbolic that provides the cultural frame of reference.

Perhaps the cultural glue that holds organizations together is *trust.* In examining the effects of organizational structure and team behavior on the level of trust exhibited by educators, Henkin and Dee (2001) suggest that

> Trust benefits from the flexibility and adaptive features that distinguish organizations that operate within fluid social environments. Strong, coherent, mechanistic organizational forms, in contrast, may actually deter the development of high levels of trust. Underregulated forms of organization, we suggest, may be more effective, though less efficient, in producing and sustaining high levels of trust. . . . Individuals and school constituencies can expect to derive benefits from collective trust only as long as it can be sustained. Collective trust can endure as long as teachers, administrators, parents, and community members work together under the assumptions that collective behaviors are rational and their collective fate and interests are coupled. (p. 59)

The process of developing improvements, interacting about needed improvements, considering alternatives, and developing plans are as important to the improvement of the school as is the substance of the change (Cunningham & Gresso, 1993; Lieberman, 1991; Sarason, 1996; Sashkin & Walberg, 1993; Schein, 1991). Bennis (1983) found that culture can give an organization transformative power to continuously improve itself. Bennis states:

> In sum, the transformative power of leadership stems less from ingeniously crafted organizational structures, carefully constructed management designs and controls, elegantly rationalized planning formats, or skillfully articulated leadership tactics. Rather, it is the ability of the leader to reach the souls of others in a fashion which raises human consciousness, builds meanings, and inspires human intent that is the source of power. Within transformative leadership, therefore, it is vision, purposes, beliefs, and other aspects of organizational culture that are of prime importance. (p. 70)

Bolman and Deal (1995) stressed this theme when they identified courage, spirit, and hope as the enduring elements of leadership. This is the heart of leadership. Leaders put the organization in touch with what gives it passion, purpose, and meaning. They discovered that

> Heart, hope, and faith, rooted in soul and spirit, are necessary for today's managers to become tomorrow's leaders, for today's sterile bureaucracies to become tomorrow's communities of meaning and for our society to rediscover its ethical and spiritual center. Leading with soul requires giving gifts from the heart that breathe spirit and passion into your life and organization. Seek new sources of vigor, meaning, and hope to enrich your life and leave a better legacy for those who come after you. (p. 12)

✳ **How would you characterize the organizational culture at Atlas Shrug High School? What cultural characteristics of the organization are having a positive impact? What characteristics are having a negative impact?**

Transformational Leadership

Burns (1978) proposed "transactional" and "transformational" leadership. "Transactional" leadership is based on defining needs, assigning clear tasks, rewarding congruent behavior, and having a command-and-control mentality. Followers are willing to trust the leader because they need to have problems solved and they believe the leader can solve them. "Transformational" leaders develop followers, help map new directions, mobilize resources, facilitate and support employees, and respond to organizational challenges. They see change as necessary and strive to cause it. In describing transformational leaders, Burns concluded: "Leaders engage with followers but from higher levels of morality; in the enmeshing of goals and values, both leaders and followers are raised to more principled levels of judgment. . . . Much of this kind of elevating leadership asks from followers rather than merely promising them goods" (p. 455).

Transformational leaders create the incentives for people to continuously improve their practices and, thus, those of the organization. Although the idea of transformational leadership was proposed by Burns (1978), Kenneth Leithwood (1992; 1999; Leithwood & Duke, 1994; Leithwood, Steinbach, & Raun, 1993) and his colleagues have added greatly to our understanding of it and have examined the benefits of this approach to school reform. According to these researchers, transformational school leaders are in continuous pursuit of three fundamental goals:

1. Helping staff members develop and maintain a collaborative, professional school culture,
2. Fostering teacher development, and
3. Helping teachers solve problems together more effectively.

Transformational leaders provide the mechanisms by which solutions are transferred into subsequent practice by building the capacity of the individuals and the group.

Transformational leadership is a process to shape and elevate goals and abilities so as to achieve significant improvements through common interests and collective actions (Bennis & Nanus, 1985). Successful leaders expend extraordinary efforts to achieve goals through:

Vision—knowing your desired outcomes and methods of achievement through lots of idea development and the creation of vision.

Communication—expressing your ideas through various forms of presentation, including symbolic actions and shared meaning.

Trust—being predictable, accountable, persistent, and reliable and having integrity.

Deployment—knowing and nurturing of strengths, compensating for weaknesses, evaluating in relation to job requirements, and focusing on positive goals not problems.

Transformational leaders ensure the existence of collaborative goal setting, shared power and responsibility, continued professional growth, resolved discrepancies, teamwork, engagement in new activities, a broad range of perspectives, validated assumptions, periodic reflection, monitored progress, and intervention when progress stalls. School personnel are inspired to rise above self-interest goals, make commitments to continuously improve student learning, and take responsibility for instructional innovation. Bill Gates, chairman and CEO of Microsoft Corporations states, "People like to have a sense of purpose, to feel that they're doing something unique and to actually see the impact their work is having." Effective leaders encourage experimentation and risk taking to meet the challenges posed by changing social conditions. The research on transformational leadership is limited but uniformly supportive of this approach as being effective in school leadership (Leithwood, 1992). Studies by Blase (1990) and Thurston, Clift, and Schacht (1993) support transformational leadership as an effective approach for the school principalship.

Leadership Traits or Skills

The study of leadership traits and skills that emerged in the second half of the 1980s represents an important departure from the theoretical perspectives. The driving forces behind it were many and diverse (Murphy, 1993), including practitioners, professors, commissions, professional associations, and legislatures. Perhaps one of its defining moments was a highly influential address titled "Leaders for American Schools" given by Daniel E. Griffiths at the 1987 annual conference of the American Educational Research Association (AERA). Dr. Griffiths provided a comprehensive analysis of the qualities required in school leaders. Around the same time, the National Association of Secondary School Principals (NASSP) under Dr. Paul Hersey had identified twelve skills that were used in their Principal Assessment Center for principal selection and development. The American Association of School Administrators published guidelines for administrators in 1983, which became standards in 1993. A number of other professional associations also looked into the skills of effective school leadership (NAESP, AACTE, NCEEA, UCEA, ASCD, and NCATE).

The University Council of Educational Administrators (UCEA), worked to develop the National Policy Board of Educational Administration (NPBEA). The NPBEA, created in 1988 under the leadership of David L. Clark, forged a union among ten groups interested in school administration. In 1993, the NPBEA, with its new executive director, Dr. Scott Thompson, published *Principals for Our Changing Schools: Knowledge and Skill Base,* which was written by a number of teams under the direction of Wayne K. Hoy.

The early 1990s produced more than fifteen different widely accepted lists of leadership skills, including one from each of the different professional associations. In 1994, Dr. Joseph Matthews, working in conjunction with the NPBEA, completed an analysis of seven frameworks of educational leadership, combining all the domains into a revised list of twenty-one (revisions of the National Policy Board domains), which are presented in Appendix 6.E. As discussed in Chapter 1, the Interstate School Leadership License Consortium (ISLLC) crafted standards (see Box 1.1) in 1996, which have been the model most states have used in developing administrative endorsement and licensure requirements.

There are many more conceptions of leadership that might be included; however, those presented are among the most widely discussed. Hopefully they also create greater clarity and enlightenment on the crucially important activity called leadership.

Conclusion

The call to duty is a challenging one: providing better futures for students, over-hauling outdated systems, knocking down barriers, altering culture, broadening leadership, and developing highly effective schools. The decades ahead will offer many new challenges and opportunities and require what Michael Fullan (1991) calls "a new ethos of innovation." He states:

> It is time to produce results. Individual and institutional renewal, separately and together, should become our *raison d'être*. We need to replace negativism and Pollyanna-ish rhetoric with informed action. Armed with knowledge of the change process, and a commitment to action, we should accept nothing less than positive results on a massive scale—at both the individual and organizational levels. (p. 354)

Effective leadership has a long tradition of research and successfully integrated ideas. Many luminaries (Campbell, 1987; Campbell, Cunningham, Nystrand, & Usdan, 1980; Culbertson, 1981; Griffiths, 1959, 1979; Halpin, 1958; Hanson, 2003; Hoy & Miskel, 2005; Kimbrough & Nunnery, 1983; Knezevich, 1975; Lunenburg & Ornstein, 2000; Murphy & Lewis, 1999; Owens 2001; Razik & Swanson, 2001) have made significant contributions to the practitioner's understanding of leadership in educational administration. In addition, many outstanding books are now available on the principalship and superintendency.

Research and literature on leadership will always be a growing body of understanding. The body of literature is not so much a sampling of existing work and widely accepted beliefs as it is a lifelong struggle for understanding. The "search for knowledge and truth" presented in this book depends on the perspective of those conducting and presenting the research. Bill Foster (1998) stated:

> I think postmodernism allows us to acknowledge the concern that knowledge is contested and that often in the contestation, some win and some lose. In educational administration, for example, there have been, since its history, competing ways of knowing, but many of these ways have been subjugated. It is to our credit, of course, that many of these ways of knowing have been recognized, but we need also ask, "What other ways are there?" (p. 296)

Leadership is shifting from a role of directing and controlling to one of guiding, facilitating, supporting, and coordinating efforts on behalf of schools. A wider population is now envisioned as having leadership potential, and we are flattening organizations, empowering more people, and decentralizing decision making (Hill & Ragland, 1995). Hoy and Miskel (2005) conclude:

> Leadership in schools is a complex process. It involves more than the mastering of a set of leadership skills or matching the appropriate leader behavior with a specific situation. Useful methods to improve school leadership are selecting and educating leaders, assuming new leadership positions, engineering the situation, and transforming schools. Leadership is not only an instrumental and behavioral activity but also a symbolic and cultural one. (p. 420)

We are at a watershed in our history. How we function as a school system, how we exchange ideas, and how we learn will affect how we continuously improve our schools. Leaders will be expected to have a leadership framework (see administrative platforms in Chapter 1) expressing their primary philosophy, beliefs, and attitudes regarding leadership, learning, and teaching. Platforms will need to accommodate working together with people, focusing on issues in common, being inclusive, setting ground rules, setting attainable goals, implementing and evaluating programs, celebrating victories, and using modern technology.

Most of all, the new leadership will require open communication and the realization that we must work together. Research (Little, 1986) suggests that successes are more likely to occur when people talk together regularly and frequently, work together, and teach one another about new ideas and possibilities.

H. G. Wells stated, "Civilization is a race between education and catastrophe." Many historians certainly agree. In explaining his great hockey play, Wayne Gretsky stated, "You always skate to where the puck is going, not to where it's been." The call is for educators to move toward where education needs to be to improve the entire system, not regress to where it's been.

✳ **As principal of Atlas Shrug High School, describe your philosophy of leadership and state how that philosophy will inspire needed school reforms.**

Portfolio Artifacts

- Plan and supervise a school-sanctioned event.
- Organize and facilitate data analysis and long-range planning activity with staff.
- Revisit your leadership platform as a framework for administrative action.
- Collaborate with teachers in identifying students at risk of not meeting grade level standards and help create plans to accelerate and track the student's progress.
- Work with staff to order materials that will support classroom instruction.
- Plan, coordinate, and lead committee meetings such as Parent Teacher Association (PTA/PTSA), Individual Educational Plan (IEP) Self-Study Team, Student Appeals, Curriculum Revision, faculty meeting, and/or building maintenance.

- Assist in the development of a relationship between the school and its business partners providing the agenda, minutes, and so forth.
- Brainstorm a list of what skills you will need as a school leader (reflect upon what skills you already possess, what skills you will need to improve upon, and how you will improve upon skills).
- Take on a leadership role within your school division, the surrounding community, or a professional organization.
- Shadow a leader within the school division, another organization, or the community.
- Actively participate in educational administrative or professional leadership associations.
- Volunteer to help administer a summer school program.

Terms

Alignment	Cultural leadership	Leadership and management
Bureaucracy	Delegation	Leadership platform
Chaos theory	Facilitation	Learning organization

MBWA
Organizational health
Participatory team
   management
Pygmalion effect

School-based management
   (SBM)
Situational leadership
Synergy

Total quality management
   (TQM)
Transformational leadership
Vision
X–Y theory

Suggested Readings

Bolman, L., & Deal, T. (1995). *Leading with soul: An uncommon journey of spirit.* San Francisco, CA: Jossey-Bass.

Collins, J. (2001). *Good to great: Why some companies make the leap . . . and others don't.* New York: HarperCollins.

Cunningham, W. G., & Gresso, D. W. (1993). *Cultural leadership: The culture of excellence in education.* Boston: Allyn and Bacon.

Deal, T., & Peterson, K. (2003). *Shaping school culture: The heart of leadership.* San Francisco, CA: Jossey-Bass.

Donaldson, G. A. (2001). *Cultivating leadership in schools.* New York Teachers College Press.

Educational Testing Service. (2000). *School leadership series school leaders licensure assessment: Practice and review.* Princeton, NJ: ETS.

Hanson, E. M. (2003). *Educational administration and organizational behavior.* Boston: Allyn and Bacon.

Hoy, W., & Miskel, C. (2004). *Educational administration: Theory, research and practice.* New York: McGraw-Hill.

Leithwood, K. A. (1999). *Changing leadership for changing times.* Bristol, PA: Taylor Frances Incorporated.

Lunenburg, F., & Ornstein, A. (2004). *Educational administration: Concepts and practices.* Belmont, CA: Wadsworth/Thomas Learning.

Razik, T. A., & Swanson, A. D. (2001). *Fundamental concepts of educational leadership and management.* Englewood Cliffs, NJ: Prentice Hall.

Short, P. (2002). *Leadership in empowered schools.* Columbus, OH: Prentice Hall.

APPENDIX 6.A

Directions for Scoring Box 6.1: The X–Y Scale

The column in which you placed a check mark on the X–Y scale determines whether you operated with X or Y beliefs on that particular question. Record an X or Y in the blank column at the end of the question based on the column that you checked. When you have scored all ten questions, count the total number of Ys you have recorded (see page 160 for interpretation of results).

	1	2	3	4	X/Y
1. Closely supervise my subordinates to get better work from them.	X	X	Y	Y	
2. Set the goals and objectives for my subordinates and sell them on the merits of my plans.	X	X	Y	Y	
3. Set up controls to ensure that my subordinates are getting the job done.	X	X	Y	Y	
4. Encourage my subordinates to set their own goals and objectives.	Y	Y	X	X	
5. Make sure that my subordinates' work is planned out for them.	X	X	Y	Y	
6. Check with my subordinates daily to see if they need any help.	X	X	Y	Y	
7. Step in as soon as reports indicate that the job is slipping.	X	X	Y	Y	
8. Push my people to meet schedules if necessary.	X	X	Y	Y	
9. Have frequent meetings to keep in touch with what is going on.	Y	Y	X	X	
10. Allow subordinates to make important decisions.	Y	Y	X	X	
				Total Y =	

$10 \geq Y \geq 9$	Strong Y beliefs	$4 \geq Y \geq 3$	X beliefs
$8 \geq Y \geq 7$	Y beliefs	$2 \geq Y \geq 0$	Strong X beliefs
$6 \geq Y \geq 5$	Mild X beliefs		

APPENDIX 6.B

Directions for Interpreting Box 6.4: The Behavior Matrix

Below are the descriptors for each of the quadrants in the Behavior Matrix:

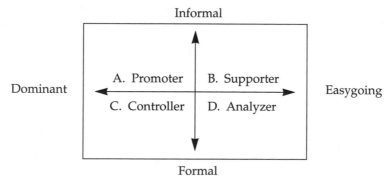

The description of the characteristics of individuals falling in each of these four quadrants starting with the upper-left quadrant (promoters) are:

A. *The Promotional Style.* Promoters get involved with people in active, rapidly changing situations. These people are seen as socially outgoing and friendly, imaginative and vigorous. Because people react to behaviors as a result of their own value biases, some see the promotional style as dynamic and energetic while others perceive the same behavior as egotistical.

In a work situation, promoters can get things going but might sometimes settle for less than the best in order to get on to something else. When faced with a task, these people can generate creative ideas for work, but are less likely to follow through to get the task done. If a group or organization can accommodate this style, it will benefit from enthusiasm, but must tolerate a lack of concern for details. Promoters are frequently highly competitive and might need to learn to work with others in a collaborative manner.

B. *The Supporting Style.* Supporters value interpersonal relations. These people try to minimize conflict and promote the happiness of everybody. Some people see the supporting style as accommodating and friendly, while others describe it as "wishy-washy" and "nice."

In a work situation, supporters might find it difficult to say "no," therefore frequently finding themselves overcommitted. They can be counted on to do what will please others. Supporters are people-oriented and nonaggressive. They will rely on others to give direction about how to get the tasks done.

C. *The Controlling Style.* Controllers want results! They love to run things and have the job done in their own way: "I'll do it myself" is a fre-

quent motto of the controller. These people can manage their time to the minute. Some see them as business-like and efficient, while others refer to them as threatening and unfeeling.

In a work situation, controllers will make sure the job is done. They will get impatient with long discussions about "the best way" or "the way to please everybody." Controllers are confident in their ability, take risks, and push forward.

D. *The Analyzing Style.* Analyzers are problem solvers. They like to get all the data before making a decision. Some say they are thorough, but others complain that they're slow. These people are frequently quiet and prefer to work alone.

In a work situation, analyzers bring valuable conceptual skills. They ask the difficult, important questions. Interpersonally, they might seem aloof and cool. Analyzers might miss deadlines, but they'll have all the reasons to support the delay.

To explore your style more in depth, join together with people of the same style and create two lists. The first list should include what you like about your selected operating style, its strengths, what it does well. The second should include what you dislike about your selected operating style, behaviors that get in the way, its weak points. Discuss your lists with individuals who fall in the three other different quadrants. Discuss which behaviors are most important to an organization and leadership.

Complete the Working Relationships Chart, thinking of two people (preferably different behavior matrix styles) with whom you have a working relationship. Complete the questions regarding your relationship with these two individuals. Review and reflect on the implications of the information in regard to leadership.

Working Relationships: A Worksheet

My style is: _____

My strengths are: _____

	FIRST PERSON	*SECOND PERSON*
1. Identify two people closely associated with you (i.e., superintendent, principal, spouse, etc.) and his or her style.	Name: Style:	Name: Style:
2. Identify his or her strengths.		
3. Identify what you can do to supplement/ assist him or her.		
4. Identify your most likely conflict.		
5. Identify ways you can manage the conflict.		

Source: S. Sayers-Kirsch (1985). "Understanding Behavioral Style." *NREL Behavioral Matrix.* Portland, OR: Northwest Regional Educational Laboratory. (Reproduced with permission of NREL.)

APPENDIX 6.C

Directions for Scoring Box 6.5: Leadership Behavior Survey

The columns on the left side of the survey represent the initiating structure values. The right side columns represent consideration values. Record the column totals in the initiating structure and consideration boxes below. (Total the number of checks you marked in each column of Box 6.5, the Leadership Behavior Survey, and enter the totals in the square below for the appropriate column.) Multiply each of these totals by the weighted factors indicated. Add weighted factor totals for a grand total, representing the initiating structure grand total and consideration grand total. Chart both of these grand total values on the Charting Leadership Style Matrix to determine the quadrant of your selected leadership style.

Initiating Structure (left-hand column)

	Column Totals		Weighted Factor Totals
Always (5)		× 4 =	
Often (4)		× 3 =	
Occasionally (3)		× 2 =	
Seldom (2)		× 1 =	
Never (1)		× 0 =	
I.S. Grand Total	⨯	⨯	

Consideration (right-hand column)

	Column Totals		Weighted Factor Totals
Always (5)		× 4 =	
Often (4)		× 3 =	
Occasionally (3)		× 2 =	
Seldom (2)		× 1 =	
Never (1)		× 0 =	
C. Grand Total	⨯	⨯	

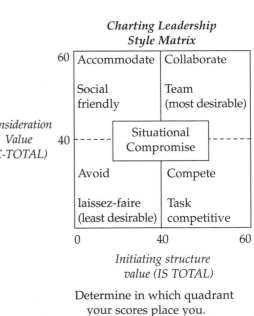

Charting Leadership Style Matrix

Determine in which quadrant your scores place you.

Source: A. Halpin, *Theory and research in administration.* © 1966. Upper Saddle River, NJ: Prentice Hall. Adapted by permission of the publisher.

APPENDIX 6.D

Directions for Scoring Box 6.6: Measuring Preferred Management Styles

Fill in the "answer number" from Box 6.6, Measuring Preferred Management Styles, in the blanks below: Transfer the three points that you distribute across the two alternatives. For example, on number 1, if you placed a 3 by alternative A, and a 0 by alternative B, then you would fill in a 0 under B, column 9,1, and a 3 under A, column 1,9 in the answer key. Then go to Question 2. Please pay particular attention to the way the alphabetical letters are listed under each column. Sum up each column to come up with a final point total, which helps to define the leadership style you selected. When all 42 answers are transferred and each of the 7 columns is totaled, the column with the highest total (number response) represents the grid style you most value. The next highest number is the back-up style. In some cases there might be ties among columns, which could suggest belief in more than one style.

A Comparison Study of Leadership Values

	9,9 (7)	9+9 (5)	9,1 (1)	5,5 (3)	OPP (6)	1,9 (2)	1,1 (4)
1			B____			A____	
2				A____		B____	
3		A____	B____				
4					A____		B____
5	B____					A____	
6			A____	B____			
7		B____		A____			
8	A____				B____		
9	B____						A____
10				B____		A____	
11		A____				B____	
12		B____			A____		
13			A____				B____
14	A____		B____				
15		B____					A____

(continued)

A Comparison Study of Leadership Values   *(Continued)*

	9,9 (7)	9+9 (5)	9,1 (1)	5,5 (3)	OPP (6)	1,9 (2)	1,1 (4)
16				A____	B____		
17			B____				A____
18	A____			B____			
19	B____	A____					
20			A____		B____		
21						B____	A____
22					A____	B____	
23	A____		B____				
24				A____	B____	A____	
25		B____	A____				
26							B____
27	A____			B____			
28					A____		B____
29		A____				B____	
30			B____			A____	
31				B____			A____
32					B____	A____	
33		B____		A____			
34	B____				A____		
35	B____						A____
36		A____			B____		
37			B____	A____			
38		B____					A____
39	A____					B____	
40			B____		A____		
41				A____			B____
42	B____	A____					

							= 126

Total Each Column

(See pages 165–169 for an explanation of results.)

Source: An Evaluation of Organizational Culture, Copyright 1991 Scientific Methods, Inc. Reproduced by permission.

APPENDIX 6.E

Twenty-One Combined Domains of Effective School Leadership

Domains	Definition
Leadership	Giving purpose and direction for individual and group processes; shaping a school culture and values; facilitating the development of a shared strategic plan and vision for the school; formulating goals and planning change efforts and setting priorities for the school; understanding leadership theory and organizational theory.
Problem Analysis	Identifying the important elements of a problem situation by gathering and analyzing data, facts, and impressions, identifying possible causes; seeking additional needed information; devising possible solutions, being creative in solving problems; applying conflict management techniques when needed.
Decision Making	Reaching logical conclusions founded on ethical and moral standards (judgment); making high-quality, timely decisions; analyzing alternative approaches; giving priority to significant issues.
Planning	Planning and scheduling one's own and other's work so that resources are used appropriately and short- and long-term priorities and goals are provided; managing change; establishing timelines and scheduling projects.
Implementation	Putting programs and change efforts into action; facilitating coordination and collaboration of tasks; supporting and monitoring those responsible for carrying out projects and plans.
Delegation	Assigning projects, tasks, and responsibilities together with clear authority; following up on delegated activities.
Supervising and Motivating Others	Planning and encouraging participation; facilitating teamwork and collegiality; supervising and treating staff as professionals; providing feedback and coaching on performance; providing intellectual stimulation; supporting innovation; serving as a role model.
Interpersonal Sensitivity	Perceiving the needs and concerns of others; embracing diversity; recognizing multicultural differences; dealing tactfully with others; obtaining feedback.
Oral Communication	Making oral presentations that are clear and easy to understand; utilizing appropriate communicative aids; adapting to audiences; using effective counseling skills with staff, students, and parents.
Written Communication	Expressing ideas clearly in writing; writing appropriately for different audiences such as students, teachers, and parents; preparing brief memoranda, letters, reports, and other job-specific documents.
Instruction	Creating instructional programs for the improvement of teaching and learning; recognizing developmental needs; ensuring appropriate instructional methods; accommodating differences in learning styles and achievement.

(continued)

Domains	Definition
Curriculum	Understanding major curriculum design models; initiating needs analyses; aligning curriculum with anticipated outcomes; monitoring social and technological development as they affect curriculum; adjusting content as needs and conditions change.
Student Guidance and Development	Understanding and accommodating student development; providing for guidance, counseling, and auxiliary services; utilizing and coordinating community organizations; responding to family needs; planning student activities.
Staff Development	Working to identify professional needs; planning, organizing, and facilitating programs that improve faculty and staff effectiveness; arranging for remedial assistance and development activities; initiating self-development.
Research, Measurement, and Evaluation	Determining what diagnostic information is needed about students, staff, and the school environment; conducting needs assessments; drawing inferences; interpreting measurements or evaluations for others; designing, conducting, and evaluating research and evaluation studies; designing accountability mechanisms.
Resource Allocation and Management	Procuring, apportioning, monitoring, accounting for, and evaluating fiscal, human, material, and time resources; planning and developing the budget process with appropriate staff; managing all fiscal responsibilities.
Philosophical and Cultural Values	Understanding the role of education in a democratic society and accepted ethical standards; recognizing philosophical influences and values in education; understanding the values of the school and community, including current social and economic issues related to education.
Legal Policy and Political Applications	Acting in accordance with federal and state constitutional provisions, working within local rules, procedures, and directives; recognizing standards for civil and criminal liability and intentional torts; administering contracts and financial accounts; examining and effecting policies individually and through professional groups; addressing ethical issues.
Public Relations	Responding to the electronic and printed news media; initiating and reporting news through appropriate channels; managing school reputations; enlisting public participation and support; forming collaborative relationships to promote school programs.
Technology	Advocating and using computers and other information systems as curriculum and instructional tools; applying technology in the management of school office business; promoting technology use among faculty and staff.
Personal Development	Practicing self-reflection; improving leadership and management skills; attending workshops, conferences, and so forth; reading current literature; belonging to appropriate professional organizations.

Source: J. Matthews (January 19, 1994). *Analysis of seven frameworks of educational leadership.*
Paper presented to the National Policy Board for Educational Administration.

7

Successful School Leadership

Donna Tobin has served the last three years as an assistant principal in a high school in a small suburban school district. She recently applied for a principalship at Packer Middle School that is located in an urban district. At this moment she is being interviewed by a group comprised of an assistant superintendent, a central office curriculum specialist, the district's director of special education, one elementary and one middle school principal, two teachers from the school, and one parent. They have given her the following scenario to respond to.

It is July and you are appointed as a principal in a middle school. The school has had three principals in the last five years. In addition, the achievement levels in all core areas for students are either flat or have slightly dropped. Most faculty have been teaching at the school for a minimum of fifteen years; however, seven new teachers out of a total staff of forty-two need to be hired. In the last five years a large number of families from Somalia, Sudan, Mexico, and Cambodia have moved into the area. As you develop a work plan for the school, what would be your starting points and how would you proceed?

✳ **How might you respond to this scenario? What topical areas do you need to consider in order to frame your response?**

Leadership Matters

In the previous chapter, we provided an overview of several of the much researched as well as the more recent theories and models of leadership and management. Those generic leadership and management theories and models are the backdrop for thinking about the unique context of school leadership. This chapter explores the context of schools and what is unique in leading learning in schools.

The recent research in education has focused on how to improve teaching and learning. This book (see Chapters 3 and 8) describes some of the recent school reform efforts. They include programmatic reforms, whole school reforms, greater diversity of teaching strategies, among other things. Clearly, in order to improve teaching and learning, successful leadership is a prerequisite. Galvanizing and supporting colleagues (teams) to improve learning for children and youths are crucial ingredients for school reform. But what do we know about successful school leadership? A meta-analysis conducted by Waters, Marzano, and McNulty (2003) found a "substantial relationship between leadership and student achievement . . . the average effect size between leadership and student achievement is .25" (p. 3). Thus, a quarter of the total school effects on student learning can be attributed to leadership. Another key finding of their analysis is that principals can have a negative impact on student achievement as well. "When leaders concentrate on the wrong school and/or classroom practices, or miscalculate the magnitude or 'order' of the change they are attempting to implement, they can negatively impact student achievement" (p. 5). Their study concludes that there are two key variables that determine whether leadership will have a positive or a negative impact on learning: (1) the focus of the change and (2) the magnitude of the change.

A review of the literature conducted by Leithwood, Seashore Louis, Anderson, and Wahlstrom (2004), found that "research also shows that schools that demonstrated effects of successful leadership are considerably greater in schools that are in more difficult circumstances . . . there are virtually no documented instances of troubled schools being turned around without intervention by a powerful leader" (p. 3). So, what do these powerful school leaders do to turn around troubled schools? Are there differences in the skills needed by administrators leading 'troubled' schools compared with schools that have demonstrated success based on multiple indicators? The research literature is beginning to provide some clarity in identifying school leadership models and practices needed by administrators in order to lead successful schools.

Based on their review of the research literature, Waters, Marzano, and McNulty found that there were certain practices associated with greater student achievement. Figure 7.1 lists school and teacher practices as well as student factors that influence student achievement. A school leader must drill down in each of these areas. Let's take one area in Figure 7.1, "instructional strategies." By drilling down we are referring to the need to understand not only what instructional strategies are being used in all classrooms in the school, but also what the research tells us about the impact of certain instructional strategies. Are there certain instructional strategies that should be used to teach a child whose native language is not English? What do we know about children who are literate in their first language versus those who come to us without being able to read and write fluently in their native language? Or, what about a child who enters first grade without having attended preschool or kindergarten and has little experience with print literacy? What might it mean for the learning of a math teacher if she or he knew that in a high school math classroom the research literature finds a strong positive correlation between the types of problems used by teachers and the achievement scores of their students? What does it look like if teachers use authentic intellectual work in order to raise math achievement scores?

Many school administration books and articles use the metaphor of principal as instructional leader. Although it is an interesting metaphor, we really have little

FIGURE 7.1 *School and Teacher Practices and Student Factors Influencing Student Achievement*

School	1. Guaranteed and viable curriculum
	2. Challenging goals and effective feedback
	3. Parent and community involvement
	4. Safe and orderly environment
	5. Collegiality and professionalism
Teacher	6. Instructional strategies
	7. Classroom management
	8. Classroom curriculum design
Student	9. Home environment
	10. Learned intelligence/background knowledge
	11. Motivation

understanding of what being an instructional leader looks like in different types of schools and at different levels. Clearly, a principal of a small elementary school leads instruction in different ways from the principal of a large comprehensive high school. Additionally, a high school principal cannot be an expert in mathematics, chemistry, English, etc.; however, an administrator who is an instructional leader must know what good teaching in mathematics looks like compared to poor teaching, and she or he must know what effective learning for students in any classroom looks like. Let's use a high school math classroom as an example. When an administrator who is an instructional leader visits math classrooms, he or she is looking at: student time on task, student–teacher interactions, what "big" mathematical idea(s) is being taught; what materials were prepared in order to teach this particular lesson; what skills the teacher wanted the students to learn that day; what routines or warm-ups were provided; how the teacher launched the lesson. Was the purpose and rationale of the learning understood by the students? Was the purpose connected to prior learning? Were the tools and materials available identified? Were expectations set (e.g., learning outcomes, time, and structures)? Was there whole group instruction, individual, pairs, or small group instruction? At the conclusion of the lesson, did the teacher provide opportunities to make public the learning that was accomplished by students by sharing what was learned? Did the teacher provide opportunities for students to analyze, share, discuss, extend, clarify, connect, and record thinking strategies? Was a summary of the learning articulated and connected to the lesson's purpose? Can the students articulate the learning/understanding of the mathematical concept being taught? And finally, is meaningful practice in the form of homework assigned to extend the learning? These are some of the key areas and questions that an instructional leader will note when she or he observes a class.

Whatever the teaching background of the principal, these practices are part of what makes good teaching and can be applied to math or any other subject area. If an administrator is to be an instructional leader then she or he must ensure that all teachers continuously have opportunities to fine-tune their practice. We know from the adult learning research that attending professional development workshops a few times per year, which has been one of the primary mechanisms afforded to teachers to improve their practice, is not necessarily the most effective way of doing so. Learning transfer is a key issue, and no study has found that more than 10 percent of what is learned in one-session workshops, without any follow-up, is actually transferred into the workplace (Detterman, 1993). According to adult learning theorist Sharan Merriam (2001) "the learning process is much more than the systematic acquisition and storage of information. It is also making sense of our lives, transforming not just what we learn but the way we learn, and it is absorbing, imagining, intuiting, and learning formally with others" (p. 96).

Adult Learning

In order to be an effective school leader, one must have a deep understanding of how adults learn. Two of the most important jobs of the school administrator are: (1) recruiting and hiring teachers, and (2) ensuring that all teachers continue to have optimal opportunities to learn so they can improve their teaching practices. There is no one theory of adult learning; however, there are various models and sets of practices that will prove most helpful as school administrators increase their own understanding of how to lead a successful school. According to Mezirow (1991), central to the process of adult learning is critical reflection. He argues that it is our work as adult educators "to assist adults to learn in a way that enhances their capacity to function as self-directed learners" (p. 137). So, perhaps instead of using the adjective "instructional" to describe principal leadership, we need to think of the principal as adult educator being a more apt metaphor.

According to Merriam (2001), two goals of self-directed learning include developing the learner's capacity to be self-directed and deepening the critical reflection done by the learner. If we examine the typical learning opportunities afforded to teachers (workshops, professional development conferences, university coursework, etc.), increasing one's capacity for self-direction and deepening critical reflection are not often the goals. Therefore, designing learning opportunities for teachers is the core of the role of the school leader. Whether the administrator herself actually leads the professional development is not the important point. The key issue is that she should be involved in designing the opportunity. Too often an outside expert is brought into a school or district to present on a particular topic. She or he knows little about the context in which they are presenting, has not held critical conversations with school leaders in order to contextualize the work for this school, and, after delivering the workshop, does not return for follow-up. Chapter 8 discusses declarative (factual), procedural (practical or strategic), and contextual knowledge. If school leaders do not plan with the consultant on how to address procedural and contextual knowledge issues, then, at best, teachers may learn some declarative knowledge. However, again, we have evidence that, at most, only 10 percent of what is learned in this type of professional development format is transferred to the classroom (see Chapter 8 for a discussion of learning transfer). This fact alone has major learning and fiscal implications.

The following research-based findings were synthesized from the adult learning literature:

- Critical reflection is essential to adult learning (Mezirow, 1991).
- Learning can be gradual or it can result from sudden, powerful experiences (Clark, 1993).
- Learning is an interdependent relationship built on trust; thus relationships are of key importance (Taylor, 2000).
- Action learning and collaborative learning are important strategies resulting in sustained changes in organizational culture (Yorks & Marsick, 1999).
- Power dynamics are a crucial part of learning and people seen as authority figures must state their values and "model questioning their own values" (Cranton, 1994, p. 201).
- Contextual factors that influence the ability to learn well enough to implement the desired solution include: the availability of appropriate sources (time, money, people from whom to learn . . .); willingness and motivation; and, "the emotional capacity to take on new capabilities in the middle of what could be a stressful challenge" (Marsick & Watkins, 2001, 30).

✳ **How might Donna Tobin use the above findings to inform her response to the questions posed by the interview team?**

If the school leader were to take these findings from the adult learning literature and apply them to learning opportunities in his or her school, then what might teacher professional development opportunities include? Throughout the history of the United States, from the one-room schoolhouse to many of today's schools in which classroom doors are closed until bells ring and visitors are infrequent, teaching has been, and still too often continues to be, lonely and isolated work. If a key ingredient of adult learning involves collaboration, then clearly school administrators must develop expertise in identifying powerful learning strategies that will allow teachers to engage in collaborative activities. In the next section, we list several learning practices that can operationalize the adult learning research findings discussed above.

Effective School Leadership Practices

Our work as principals is to improve instruction for every child, in every single classroom in the school. (Elaine Fink, 2002, p. 5)[1]

In the previous section we briefly examined some of the key findings from the adult learning research literature. Now let us examine the practices that the educational research literature has identified as the practices of effective school leaders.

- Are directly involved with teacher selection (Maryland State Dept. of Education 1978).
- Closely monitor student progress (Venezky & Windfield, 1979).
- Influence aspects of instructional strategies (Venezky & Windfield, 1979).

- Encourage risk taking (Berman & McLaughlin, 1977).
- Are attentive to details focusing on connecting routine decisions and actions within the school to a larger strategy of instructional leadership (Bossert, Dwyer, Rowan, & Lee, 1982).
- Focus on student assessment (Purkey & Smith, 1983).
- Possess an explicit, mutually shared, concrete vision for the school (Cunningham & Gresso, 1993)
- Believe that "relational" trust is key to urban school improvement (Bryk & Schneider, 2002)
- Are expert at diagnosing and analyzing complex problems (Portin, Schneider, DeArmond, & Gundlach, 2003).
- Set directions, develop people, and redesign the organization so that learning conditions are optimal (Leithwood, Seashore Louis, Anderson, & Wahlstrom, 2004).

The principal must be the lead learner in the school. This means that she or he is modeling what it means to be a good learner: relentlessly asking questions, continuously seeking assistance in strategizing how to solve problems, constantly examining his or her own practices, inviting and receiving feedback on his or her own behavior and decisions, and so forth. Clearly, in order to be a good learner, a school principal must know what she or he believes about education and its many complexities. This is why we began in Chapter 1 with a focus on values and beliefs and the importance of creating your educational leadership platform. We cannot lead others if we don't know what we believe about learning and leading. Our beliefs cannot merely be opinions; instead, they must be based on practice (experience), educational values, research data, and reflection. Effective school leadership places adult and student learning at the center of the school. We know quite a bit about how students learn and what conditions are optimal for that learning. What we must pay far more attention to is the role that school leaders need to play in helping the adults in the building to learn.

Figure 7.2 illustrates the steps in leading a school through the improvement of instruction. Once the school leader has developed a "voice," that is, she or he can clearly articulate what educational beliefs they hold, then it is crucial that administrators hold conferences with teachers, visit classrooms, and engage in meetings with parents. School leaders need to understand and articulate instructional practices not only in regular education settings, but also they must understand what is good practice for children with special needs and for those whose native language is not English. Being expert at assessing the quality of instruction is crucial. This involves diagnosing problems and analyzing solutions (Portin et al. 2003). Some problems may require what Waters, Marzano, and McNulty (2003) call first-order change, while others may need second-order changes. First-order change is an extension of the past. It is focused, bounded, incremental, and solution oriented. It is consistent with the prevailing values and norms of the school. "A change becomes second order when it is not obvious how it will make things better for people with similar interests, it requires individual or groups of stakeholders to learn new approaches, or it conflicts with prevailing values and norms" (p. 7). They maintain that

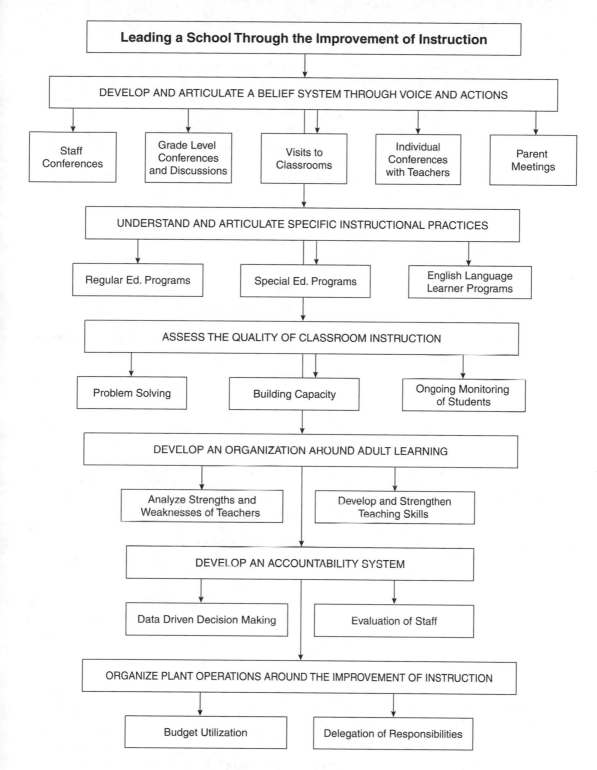

FIGURE 7.2 *Leading a School Through the Improvement of Instruction*

Adapted from the University of San Diego's Educational Leadership Development Academy handbook.

recognizing whether a change is first or second order helps school leaders to select leadership practices and strategies that are appropriate. "Doing so enhances the likelihood of sustainable initiatives and a positive impact on achievement. Failing to do so will just as likely result in the negative impact on achievement" (p. 8). Another key aspect of learning instruction is adult learning. In order to provide structures to develop and strengthen teaching skills, school leaders must analyze teacher strengths and weaknesses. Finally, developing an accountability system is a crucial component for leading a school. The school leader needs to have timely and accurate data so that instructional and budgetary decisions will support student learning.

Leadership and the Change Process

MICHAEL FULLAN • *University of Toronto*

What makes the principal's role so critical in the change process stems from the conclusion that neither top-down nor bottom-up strategies are effective by themselves. It is only when bottom-up and top-down forces interact and are mediated in purposeful directions that improvement occurs. The principal is the one person ideally placed to play this mediating role.

It has always been said that the principal is key to change, but only recently has research given a detailed understanding of what that role means in practice. We set forth a rationale and framework for the role of the principal in our *What's Worth Fighting For* trilogy (Fullan, 1997; Fullan & Hargreaves, 1992; Hargreaves & Fullan, 1998). I also illustrate the role in practice from the evaluation of the Chicago schools reform (Bender, Sebring, & Bryk, 1998).

We wrote *What's Worth Fighting For* to provide principals and teachers guidelines for action to enable them to take greater control over the change process in a system that is fragmented and overloaded—one that places them in dependent positions. In the first book, *What's Worth Fighting for in the Principalship* (Fullan, 1997), we argued that the starting point for reform is not to hope for or wait for "systemic change" but to look for actions that we ourselves could take. We formed a number of guidelines for action for school principals such as:

- Avoid "if only" statements, externalizing the blame, and other forms of wishful thinking.

- Practice fearlessness and other forms of risk taking.
- Build a vision in relation to goals as well as change processes.

In the second book, *What's Worth Fighting for in Your School* (Fullan & Hargreaves, 1992), we widened the problem to focus on the culture of the school. We suggested there are at least four cultures in schools—individualized, balkanized, contrived collegiality, and collaborative. Only the last one really makes a difference in school improvement. Since the publication of that book our analysis has been confirmed precisely in Neuman and Wehlage's (1993) careful study of school restructuring in over 800 schools. All schools were engaged in reform, but some were especially successful in increasing student performance.

The three intraschool factors that distinguished the successful schools were (1) the existence of a professional learning community (none other than the collaborative culture), (2) continual review and refinement of instructional practice, and (3) evaluation of student progress. These professional communities constantly examined student work and achievement and revised their teaching accordingly. Neuman and Wehlage concluded, as we had, that the role of the principal was to foster and shape collaborative cultures that focus on student achievement using strategies that will accomplish that goal—focused professional development, organization of teaching, use of data, school improvement plans as a tool of developing new school cultures and the like. We said in short that "reculturing" (creating professional learning communities) was the main goal of principals and teachers.

In the third book, *What's Worth Fighting for Out There* (Hargreaves & Fullan, 1998), we extended the analysis even further to say that the context for schools has radically changed and that the "out there" in the form of community, technology, media, government policy, and so on, is now "in here." Therefore, the roles of principals (and teachers) are extended even further. They must in this new environment not only help contend with external forces, but also *form alliances* with many of them. We acknowledged that this was dangerous terrain, but that there were inevitable, indeed sound, reasons for "moving toward the danger." The reasons were inevitable because the outside forces were relentlessly in the school anyway and sound because the job could not be done in the absence of new partnerships with the outside. Our guidelines for principals included:

- Steer clear of false certainty (don't look for the silver bullet, but create your own change models drawing on external ideas).
- Respect those you wish to silence (learn new things from resistance).

- Move toward the danger in forming new alliances.
- Fight for lost causes (be hopeful when it counts).

Our analysis has been corroborated recently by the Chicago schools' reform evaluation. Bender, Sebring, and Bryk (1998) found that "the quality of the principal's leadership is a critical factor in determining whether a school moves forward to improve learning opportunities for students" (p. 1). More particularly, they found that principals who are most effective (1) focus on student learning, (2) use support and pressure to enable others to act, and (3) attack incoherence through planning that provides continuity. Moreover, effective principals moved forward on two big issues: promoting stronger social ties between school staff and community and creating a viable professional community among the school staff (p. 5).

School leadership has never been more critical. It is essential in these complex times because of the need to mediate and integrate bottom-up with top-down forces. There will be tremendous turnover in teachers and principals over the next five to ten years. This will be a difficult time for new leaders, but also an enormously exciting period with a real opportunity to make a difference in the life of students, teachers, and parents.

Structures That Provide Opportunities for Teacher Collaboration

Organizing a school around adult learning, a key element in leading instruction that is depicted in Figure 7.2 means that certain structures are built into each school. Key structures that operationalize the findings from the adult learning research include study groups, teacher conferences, school visitations, and district and/or instructional conferences.

Study Groups

Study groups can reinforce, clarify, and deepen teacher learning by providing opportunities for teachers to teach each other. They can vary in size, content, and length. Ideally, they would not be too large so that all involved will have ample opportunity to discuss and critically reflect on practice. Study groups work best when the participants themselves decide what they need to focus on. For example, if teachers believe they need to learn better ways to monitor and assess student learning, then they might decide to invite a colleague whom they believe has strong skills in this area to work with them. How long and how often they meet and over what time period, are other factors to consider.

For example, what might it look like if a group of math teachers had a study group? It might mean that they, as self-directed learners, would decide if they will visit each others' classes. It might include deciding what kind of feedback they would like to receive after those visits. It also could include what they might jointly read and reflect on. Perhaps it would include what lessons plans they would share and critique. One teacher might ask someone to videotape her lesson, and then she might take the study group through key parts of the tape, soliciting their input on what and how she taught the particular mathematical concept. Study groups work best when teachers set their own agenda, as well as the schedule they will follow and activities they will conduct. The central focus is always on what teachers can do to improve student achievement. They may use resources such as websites, videos, professional books, and presenters (experts).

Instructional Walk-Throughs

Walk-throughs are being used in many schools throughout the nation and can take various forms. They usually involve small groups and a facilitator spending time in classrooms looking for evidence of good instructional practice. Often walk-throughs involve using an observation guide that has general components of quality teaching. Participants focus their observations in those identified areas and may record items during the observation. The main reason for conducting walk-throughs is to help improve the teaching skills of the staff. Methods seen as effective can then be shared with other teachers at the school. Often it is the school principal, or others who coach teachers, who conduct the walk-throughs. However, a study group might decide they would like to conduct walk-throughs of the classroom of the teachers in their group and then meet to discuss what they observed. Walk-throughs could include the same concept being taught in different classrooms so that teachers can see the impact of different strategies being used.

Walk-throughs help to keep the school staff focused on instruction. These informal walk-throughs promote meaningful dialogue about instruction and inspire inquiry as teachers and administrators learn about best research-based practices as they are incorporated into practice in the context of individual lessons. The walk-through should be very focused with the overall purpose being to improve student achievement as an instruction team. The observer looks at specific activity, students' work, teacher plans, lessons, and so on and assembles the information in a way that it helps to better portray what students have learned. This provides "bite-sized pieces" that can be more easily discussed and shared. They might focus on instructional modalities, assignments, instructions, questioning, instructional strategies, and so on. The principal's presence is viewed as a sign of support for instructional improvement.

Teacher Conferences

After an administrator, staff developer, or a master teacher (a peer coach) has observed a classroom, then the feedback process needs to follow. Teacher conferencing can be a powerful vehicle for teacher learning if conducted appropriately. A strong relationship built on trust is key to supervisor–supervisee conferences in order for optimal teacher learning to occur. Instructional leaders need to know what each individual teacher needs in order to improve learning in his or her classroom. Ideally, teacher conferencing would take place both before and after the classroom visit. Teacher conferences should not be sessions in which the supervisor is telling the teacher what to do. Instead, the administrator might begin with a statement such as "Tell me about the class I observed." Or, "Tell me what you have been doing since I last visited your class." Or, "Tell me where in your lesson you were having difficulty and what you are doing to problem solve how to change that." Or, "Tell me what you want me to focus on when I visit your class." Or, "What do you think I am going to see when I visit your class?" Teacher conferencing can be difficult work. Administrators must be in teachers' classrooms on a regular basis, and they need to know what they are looking at. Knowing what is happening in classrooms is the core of the school leaders' work. If administrators are unwilling to visit classes on a regular basis, and if they do not know what aspects of instruction they need to focus on, then they might want to consider a different job.

School Visitations

Visits to other schools by administrators and teachers should be a normal part of professional development. During those visits educators can visit classrooms to observe specific teaching practices, or they may want to examine particular approaches to learning or models being implemented in a school. It's crucial that school visits be focused and that educators have opportunities to discuss what they observed and learned from the visit. During the visit they need to be able to ask questions and probe for deeper understanding. Needless to say, carefully choosing the school for the site visit is crucial. If a teacher or administrator is to critically and constructively examine a practice, then she must first be sure that the site itself has good practice. Seeing effective practice and then having the opportunity to critically reflect upon what was observed, so that learning can then be transferred to the observer's classroom, are key to ensuring that the visit resulted in teacher or administrator learning.

District and/or School Instructional Conferences

For many years school districts have been offering in-services. Often this means teachers either choosing from a list of offerings (e.g., a two-hour workshop in cooperative learning or working with second language students, etc.) or all teachers (or administrators) being required to attend a workshop that, at best, was conducted by a knowledgeable and engaging speaker. If a school district's central office is going to regularly offer professional development conferences, then those conferences or workshops should be highly focused and tied to the district's instructional goals.

The content of professional development conferences should always be on improving instruction and tied to specific district or school goals. Instructional conferences should be carefully planned and structured so that teachers are engaged throughout, and they should provide opportunities for teachers to practice what is being taught. Finally, two other vital ingredients are evaluation and follow-up. What evidence exists that what was taught in the instructional conference was learned and that it was appropriately transferred to the classroom?

In order for learning to be deep, teachers need to have multiple opportunities to practice and receive feedback. Study groups, walk-throughs, teacher conferences, school visits, and instructional conferences are five structures that school leaders can provide for the adult learners in their building in order to improve practice. In his thoughtful book on professional development, Bredeson (2003) discusses the importance of creating professional learning communities. He maintains that in order for professional development to be effective it must involve "teachers and principals in the identification and design of learning experiences to meet individual and collective needs" (p. 14). Thus, active involvement of the school administrator in professional development is crucial to creating a professional learning community.

Principals as Instructional Leaders: Modeling and Supporting Teaching and Learning

PAUL V. BREDESON • *University of Wisconsin–Madison*

Given the nature of schools and professional work in them, highly successful principals have learned to be selective in their professional work, balancing what others expect them to do (role taking) with their own work priorities and goals as educational leaders (role making). Thus effective leadership requires balancing many conflicting activities and responsibilities. Through their work, principals create, nurture, and sustain successful and healthy teaching and learning environments for teachers as well as students. The principal's primary role is in modeling and supporting the learning of others, the essence of instructional leadership.

Play the Ball
From the sidelines, a softball coach yells advice to the players on the field. "Play the ball. Don't let the ball play you." In other words, the players need to make the plays, not let the ball determine how they should move or play the game. This advice is as useful on the ball field as it is for principals in schools. Like players facing a number of possibilities to field balls, principals daily face countless events, some predictable, others not. What's important is that principals use their expert knowledge and skills in ways that support the primary teaching and learning goals. On a daily basis principals must deal with sick children, conflicts among staff, student discipline problems, unexpected visits by parents, telephone calls, piles of paperwork, emergencies, central office meetings, bus and cafeteria duties, and student records. In addition, let's not forget about instruction, curriculum, staff development, and school improvement initiatives. The sheer number of activities can overwhelm even the most experienced principal.

To cope, successful principals keep in mind the big picture, nurturing and supporting a healthy and successful teaching and learning environment, while simultaneously attending to the details of all of their administrative responsibilities. Principals influence student learning outcomes directly and indirectly by what they do, what they believe, and how they use symbols. By viewing their work through the lens of instructional leadership, principals "play the ball," knowing that what they do has the potential to ripple across the school, amplifying its effect on teaching and learning processes and on student and organizational outcomes.

Instructional Leadership in Action

For principals, keeping the focus on teaching and learning is more than the application of technical knowledge and expertise. How principals choose to spend their time, what they do substantively and symbolically, and what they believe are steeped in values, intentions, and understandings about teaching, learning, and educational outcomes for children. The fact that principals pay attention to some things in schools while ignoring or deemphasizing others infuses the continuous stream of actions, substantive and symbolic, with clarity, consensus, and commitment to what's important, in teaching and learning. Ordinary routines become expressions of values and purpose.

To illustrate how principals' behavior, values, and purposes come together, let's examine one common instructional leadership behavior: principals' visits to classrooms. For instructional leaders, classroom visits are more than opportunities to monitor teacher work. They become occasions for principals to clarify the primary mission of the school (teaching and learning), validate this mission for others (students, teachers, and parents), engender excitement and high expectations for teaching and learning, and infuse the daily routines of students, teachers, and support staff with meaning and significance.

Principals as Teachers and Learners

In addition to exercising their influence as instructional leaders on teaching and learning, principals are themselves teachers and learners. "Principals as teachers need not be omniscient paragons of pedagogy. Rather, they are coaches and facilitators who help students, teachers, and other staff understand the mental models and basic assumptions about teaching and learning in particular schools and communities" (Hart & Bredeson, 1996, p. 137). Principals are also learners.

As Edgar Schein (1985) reminds us in his discussion of leadership and organizational culture, if you want to know what's important and valued in a school, watch what the principal pays attention to and does, rather than what he or she *says* is important. For example, principals who greet staff at the beginning of a planned in-service and then give their apologies for not staying because they have other work to do send a clear, albeit negative, message regarding the use of time and learning. If learning is important in a school, the principal will model the behaviors of an active learner. Principals who read broadly and remain knowledgeable in their fields, who participate actively in professional development opportunities, and who see their own learning as an important part of their professional work are modeling the beliefs and behaviors they espouse for others in schools.

Challenges for Instructional Leaders

Many challenges await principals as instructional leaders in the twenty-first century. Here I describe three in particular. The first centers on clarifying and articulating the values and principles that will guide you as an instructional leader. Understanding and being committed to the values will guide you and your school colleagues as you work together to meet such challenges as inclusive education for children with disabilities, charter school competition, new state and national curriculum standards, public school choice, and bilingual education, to name a few.

A second challenge for principals in the future will be to determine work priorities. As described earlier in this piece, there is no shortage of activity and responsibility for principals. There will always be unexpected and routine tasks that need to be carried out. The question is whether you as leader let the flow of events and activities define you as an instructional leader or whether your values and beliefs about teaching and learning set the tone and substance of your work. Finally, principals as instructional leaders are confronted with the perennial paradox of continuity and change. The certainty of change may be the most predictable factor in your future work, yet the certainty of change brings anxiety and ambiguity.

Supporting the Change Process

Earlier we discussed what Waters, Marzano, and McNulty (2003) referred to as first-order and second-order change. Some changes are incremental or technical (first order) and other changes are second-order changes that require what Heifetz (1994) calls *adaptive change*. School leaders need to define problems, and using these two categories can be helpful in determining how one might best respond. Adaptive change is needed when the problem cannot be solved with one's existing knowledge or skills. Adaptive change requires people to make a shift in their expectations, attitudes, values, or habits of behavior.

The Concerns-Based Adoption Model (CBAM), developed by Hall and Hord (1987), provides tools and assistance for those involved in the implementation of change in schools. The model includes six dimensions referred to as Stages of Concern that are the feelings and perceptions that people involved in the change or innovation experience. Additionally, the model has eight Levels of Use describing the various levels that users of an innovation experience as they move from becoming oriented to the innovation and then preparing to use it, to later focusing on developing effectiveness in using the innovation (see also pp. 86–87). In the final level the user is seeking even more effective alternatives to the original use of the innovation.

Whether you use a framework of technical and adaptive change, or a model such as CBAM, the key point if that the school leader needs to develop knowledge about the change process. Fostering the growth of a professional learning community may be a long and challenging process in some schools; however, it has enormous potential to result in greater teacher and student learning.

The Teacher Selection Process

Earlier in this chapter we discussed two of the most important jobs of the school administrator: (1) recruiting and selecting teachers and (2) ensuring that all teachers continue to have optimal opportunities to learn so they can improve their teaching practices. We have not yet discussed teacher recruitment and selection. Clearly, the work of ensuring that all teachers continue to learn is far easier if teachers begin the position with the disposition that lifelong learning is a requirement for being an effective teacher. Most of the literature about selecting teachers is procedural and deals with what types of questions should be asked in the interview, or how to best conduct the interview (see Chapter 10). But let's step back for a moment. How does the district recruit teachers? Can you as a school leader influence that process? Does the district or the principal contact university faculty and ask who are their best graduates? Is the district involved with college students studying to be teachers from the time of their admittance to the teacher education program? If the answer is no, then why not? Does it not behoove school district leaders to try and shape who enters the teaching profession? What induction and support does the district have for beginning teachers? Are new teachers assigned mentors? Do local college and university programs partner with the district in supporting new teachers? Of course, the interview is a key part of the selection process and some questions that might be asked include the following: What were some strengths of your teacher education program? What were some of the weaknesses? What actions have you taken to learn about students' cultural backgrounds? Give an example of a key idea in your subject matter and how you developed a lesson to teach it. Tell us about a difficult instructional problem you have worked on. Using your experience, how do classroom management and discipline differ from the beginning of the year compared to later in the school year? What experience do you have in working with classroom volunteers, parents in the room, or classroom aides? Describe a time when you learned something about teaching or an individual student by listening to a parent. Describe some teacher-led organization, support group, or network from which you have benefited. How can this school help you to become a better teacher? How do you think this interview went?

The interview itself, although very important, is only one part of the selection process; it should not be the entire process. Is the prospective teacher asked to teach a lesson or submit a video of a lesson? What criteria does the committee use to evaluate the lesson? Is a portfolio required? What criteria does the committee use to evaluate the portfolio? These are a few of the key issues that must be considered in the recruiting and selecting of teachers. Teacher selection is one of the most important decisions administrators will make. Identifying well-prepared novice teachers and providing mentoring and support will result in a much greater likelihood that student achievement will increase significantly. Selecting teachers who do not have the disposition for lifelong learning and are ill-prepared for teaching will result in a much greater likelihood that student achievement will not improve. An administrator who is an educational leader knows that teacher recruitment and selection are crucial ingredients for an effective school.

> ✳ **How might Donna Tobin use some of these ideas to talk about the seven new teachers she would need to hire according to the scenario presented in her interview?**

Conclusion

This chapter provided a brief overview of some of the literature on effective school leadership and adult learning. We believe that two of the most important aspects of effective school leadership are the recruitment and selection of teachers and then providing support for their continued learning. We offered five structures that can help to provide that support: study groups, instructional walk-throughs, teacher conferences, school visitations, and instruction conferences. These structures allow for building and strengthening teacher capacity. The research tells us that school leadership matters. Along with teaching, leadership is the most important school-related factor impacting student learning.

*Endnote*_____

1. Quote taken from interview transcripts conducted by educational sociologist Lea Hubbard (2002) with Elaine Fink, former New York City District Two superintendent and recently retired executive director of the Educational Leadership Development Academy (ELDA) at the University of San Diego.

*Terms*_____

Action learning
Adult learning
Collaborative learning
Contextual knowledge
Critical reflection

Declarative knowledge
Disposition
Effect size
Instructional conferences
Learning transfer

Procedural knowledge
School visitations
Study group
Teacher conferences
Walk-through

*Suggested Readings*_____

Bredeson, P. V. (2003). *Designs for learning: A new architecture for professional development in schools.* Thousand Oaks, CA: Corwin Press.

Bryk, A. S., & Schneider, B. (2002). *Trust In schools: A core resource for improvement.* New York: Russell Sage Foundation.

Detterman, D. K. (1993). "The case for prosecution: Transfer as an epiphenomenona." In D. K. Detterman & R. J. Sternberg (Eds.), *Transfer on trial: Intelligence, cognition and instruction.* Norwood, NJ: Ablex Publishing Corporation.

Leithwood, K., Seashore Louis K., Anderson, S., & Wahlstrom, K. (2004). *How leadership influences student learning (executive summary).* Minneapolis, MN: Center for Applied Research and Educational Improvement.

Merriam, S. B. (2001). (Ed.). *The new update on adult learning theory.* San Francisco, CA: Jossey-Bass.

Sparks, D. (2005). *Leading for results.* Thousand Oaks, CA: Corwin Press.

Teske, P. E., & Schneider, M. (1999). *The importance of leadership: The role of school principals.* Arlington, VA: Pricewaterhouse Coopers Endowment for the Business of Government.

Tichy, N. M. (2002). *The cycle of leadership: How great leaders teach their companies to win.* New York: Harper Collins Publishers.

Waters, T., Marzano, R. J., & McNulty, B. (2003). *Balanced leadership: What 30 years of research tells us about the effect of leadership on student achievement.* Aurora, CO: McREL.

Program Development, Delivery, and Assessment

Program Improvement

A parent approached Principal Rich Newman of Linton Elementary School regarding the second-grade health curriculum. This parent believed the curriculum taught by the school psychologist was inappropriate for second-graders; he indicated that several other parents shared his views. The principal listened to the parent's complaints and wrote down the specific concerns.

Although in his third year as principal of Linton, Newman was not familiar with the details of this second-grade health curriculum. Following the meeting with the parent, Principal Newman asked the opinions of the three second-grade teachers. All three agreed that the curriculum was of value and well received by the students. In speaking with the school psychologist, Principal Newman discovered that the curriculum had been introduced by the psychologist's predecessor. The incumbent was in her first year at Linton, her first position in an education setting. The psychologist stated that like the parent, she had similar reservations concerning the curriculum. Because of her lack of experience, however, she had not surfaced the concerns.

Principal Newman immediately asked the assistant superintendent for curriculum and instruction when the school board had approved this particular curriculum. The assistant superintendent could not recall approval during her four-year tenure; eventually it was discovered that the curriculum had never been presented to or approved by the school board.

Board policy stated that the decision to retain or reject curriculum materials would be based on specific criteria, including whether the material represented life in true proportions, whether circumstances were dealt with realistically, and whether the materials had literary or social value. Policy required that factual material be included in all instructional material collections.

✳ **How do you assess the "value and worth" of a curriculum? This school district's board policy had guidelines for choosing this curriculum. Does your school district have board policy in this area? What does it say? How does it compare with the policy in Principal Newman's district?**

Conceptions of Academic Achievement

According to Cole (1990) there are currently two major conceptions of academic achievement. The first, called basic skills and facts, grew out of the 1950s and 1960s when behavioral psychology dominated the way educators viewed learning. The second conception of achievement involves the notion of higher-order thinking skills, problem solving, and advanced knowledge. These achievement skills could be regarded as a progression described in Bloom's (1984) taxonomy (knowledge, comprehension, application, analysis, synthesis, and evaluation).

As Cole maintains, "Conceptions of educational achievement change with the times, are influenced by many factors, and take different forms for different people" (p. 2). Cole finds the two conceptions of academic achievement inadequate in helping us to think about learning, concluding that educators need to formulate an alternative conception that integrates divergent views of achievement, carries clear instructional implications, and focuses on long-term educational goals. Choices are related to what is valued, what is teachable, how it is organized, how much time should be devoted, who should be involved, what best communicates intentions, and what goals are served, to name but a few of the elements of these alternatives (Costa, 1997).

Theories of Intelligence

In recent years, two theories of intelligence have proved particularly useful to educators: Robert Sternberg's triarchic theory, and Howard Gardner's multiple intelligence (MI) theory.

Robert Sternberg (1996) maintains that intelligence, defined by its underlying components, can be altered through instruction. Sternberg's triarchic theory of intelligence comprises three parts—synthetic, analytic, and practical—each of which is related to creativity.

The *synthetic* part of intelligence generates ideas and redefines problems. "Synthetic" relates to a person's internal thinking and consists of three processes. The first process is used in planning, monitoring, and evaluating performance of a task. The second governs behavior in the performance of the task itself; Sternberg maintains that a person can become more, or less, intelligent, by learning what to attend to and what to ignore. The final internal component of intelligence controls the previous knowledge a person brings to a new situation. According to Sternberg, it is this previously acquired knowledge a person brings to the new situation that is more important than the mental speed or memory skills a person uses.

The *analytic* part of intelligence recognizes ideas, structures, themes; allocates resources; and evaluates the quality of ideas. It addresses the basics of problem solving. The *practical* part of intelligence makes ideas work. It promotes and refines ideas based on how the learner critiques the information she or he gets from others.

A key aspect of Sternberg's theory is that intelligence depends heavily on how people learn to cope with the world around them. He believes that "academic intelligence of the kind measured by IQ tests matters, but really it doesn't matter that much" (p. 22). Sternberg (1996) argues that his concept of successful intelligence is of paramount importance because it is the type of intelligence that is used to achieve important goals and is needed in the twenty-first century.

In his 1983 seminal book on intelligence, *Frames of Mind,* Howard Gardner groups people's broad range of abilities into seven categories of intelligence: linguistic, logical-mathematical, spatial, bodily-kinesthetic, musical, interpersonal, and intrapersonal. In recent years Gardner added an eighth intelligence: a naturalist intelligence, which allows people to recognize and discriminate among living things (Checkley, 1997).

Gardner's theory is referred to as Multiple Intelligence (MI) theory. He maintains that each person possesses all eight intelligences to varying degrees. Within each category are multiple ways to be intelligent. Each of these intelligences interacts with other intelligences, and the context of learning is crucial. Gardner disavows the notion that knowledge and ability in one area (e.g., musical intelligence) is less important than knowledge in another area (e.g., logical-mathematical). Table 8.1 summarizes the core components of seven of Gardner's intelligences (Armstrong, 1994).

Acceptance of the idea that (1) intelligence comprises multiple forms and that (2) it can be altered through instruction challenges the traditional school curriculum, which emphasizes linguistic and logical-mathematical forms of intelligence. One need only examine the allocation of time in schools to see which disciplines are most valued. Little learning time is devoted to spatial, bodily-kinesthetic, musical, interpersonal, and intrapersonal intelligences, compared with the amount devoted to the areas of linguistic and logical-mathematical intelligences. It is a rare U.S. elementary school that does not begin the school day with reading or language arts. If, as Armstrong suggests, teaching activities, materials, and instructional strategies were to incorporate all of the intelligences, then students with "less intelligence" in one area than another would not be left out of the learning loop or made to believe they are "dumb." Confusion sometimes exists between mismatches in styles of teaching and learning being mistakenly described as poor teaching and/or lack of student ability (teachability grouping).

The traditional school curriculum also includes the notion that intelligence can be measured by an instrument. This reification of intelligence through IQ tests has had a detrimental effect on thousands of schoolchildren throughout the last century. If there are numerous forms of intelligence, our goal should be to determine how people best learn certain types of knowledge.

Both Sternberg's and Gardner's theories of intelligence have important implications for teaching and learning. If people possess varying degrees of intelligence in different areas and if intelligence can be altered through instruction, then a school's curriculum can influence the degree of student learning significantly.

Types of Knowledge

What does it mean for a person to learn something? Are some ways to learn superior to others? Is a person's learning style defined by what he or she is learning? Researchers (Leithwood, Begley, & Cousins, 1994; Sternberg & Caruso, 1986; Sternberg & Frensch, 1993) suggest that there are various types of knowledge: declarative knowledge, practical and procedural or strategic knowledge, and contextual

TABLE 8.1 *MI Theory Summary Chart*

Intelligence	Core Components	Symbol Systems	High End-States
Linguistic	Sensitivity to the sounds, structure, meanings, and functions of words and language	Phonetic languages (e.g., English)	Writer, orator (e.g., Virginia Woolf, Martin Luther King Jr.)
Logical-Mathematical	Sensitivity to, and capacity to discern, logical or numerical patterns; ability to handle long chains of reasoning	Computer languages (e.g., Pascal)	Scientist, mathematician (e.g., Marie Curie, Blaise Pascal)
Spatial	Capacity to perceive the visual-spatial world accurately and to perform transformations on one's initial perceptions	Ideographic languages (e.g., Chinese)	Artist, architect (e.g., Frida Kahlo, I. M. Pei)
Bodily-Kinesthetic	Ability to control one's body movements and to handle objects skillfully	Sign languages, Braille	Athlete, dancer, sculptor (e.g., Jesse Owens, Martha Graham, Auguste Rodin)
Musical	Ability to produce and appreciate rhythm, pitch, and timbre; appreciation of the forms of musical expressiveness	Musical notational systems, Morse code	Composer, performer (e.g., Stevie Wonder, Midori)
Interpersonal	Capacity to discern and respond appropriately to the moods, temperaments, motivations, and desires of other people	Social cues (e.g., gestures and facial expressions)	Counselor, political leader (e.g., Carl Rogers, Nelson Mandela)
Intrapersonal	Access to one's own feeling life and the ability to discriminate among one's emotions; knowledge of one's own strengths and weaknesses	Symbols of the self (e.g., in dreams and artwork)	Psychotherapist, religious leader (e.g., Sigmund Freud, Buddha)

Source: T. Armstrong (1994). *Multiple intelligences in the classroom.* Alexandria, VA: Association for Supervision and Curriculum Development. Reprinted with permission.

knowledge. Declarative knowledge is factual; it is knowledge about something. Sternberg and Caruso (1985) define practical knowledge as "procedural knowledge that is useful in one's everyday life" (p. 134). Leithwood and colleagues (1994) add the descriptor "strategic." They maintain that practical knowledge is "concerned with *how* to solve problems rather than knowledge *about* problem solving" (p. 192), which they term declarative knowledge. Contextual knowledge is knowledge that depends on context.

Learning Transfer

Transfer has been defined as "the degree to which a behavior will be repeated in a new situation" (Detterman, 1993, p. 4). Educators are often perplexed when they have a student who learned something in the recent past but is unable to transfer that learning to a similar situation. For example, in Spanish class, a student might have spent considerable time learning the past tense form of a verb and might demonstrate that knowledge on a written and oral test. Yet the student is often unable to remember the correct verb form when required to use it in a conversation. Are there mechanisms that will increase the likelihood that learning in one situation will be transferred to another situation?

According to Sternberg and Frensch (1993), the degree of transfer from one situation to another depends on four mechanisms. First, there must be *encoding specificity*. The degree of transfer depends on the original encoding of the knowledge. Retrieval of knowledge depends on how the learner has encoded it. If students are not taught (in the classroom) how to apply information, then the likelihood of their being able to transfer information to a situation is reduced. For example, most educators are well versed in adolescent development but could be unable to transfer such knowledge to raising their own children.

A second mechanism that influences transfer is *organization*—how information is originally organized in a person's memory. Sternberg and Frensch believe "that organization of information from old situations can either facilitate or impede transfer to new situations" (p. 26). When we learn something in a particular way (e.g., memorizing verbs by conjugation), we must reorganize the information to apply it.

A third mechanism involves *discrimination*, in which information is retrieved depending on whether it was tagged or stored as relevant to a new situation in which it might be applied. Discrimination occurs frequently, of which tagging is the key process. What makes a learner tag one piece of information and not another? Reinforcement and review of information might make it more likely that certain knowledge will be tagged by the learner.

Sternberg and Frensch (1993) label the fourth mechanism for transfer the *mental set*. Whether a person "sees a useful way of doing something depends in part upon the mental set with which he or she approaches the task" (p. 26). In most schools, academic subjects are taught in isolation. Subjects such as algebra are infrequently made relevant to real-world use. Yet educators expect students to transfer the knowledge of the algebraic formula to practical applications. Many students study algebra for two years in high school and perceive little relevance other than that it is usually required for college entrance.

One day while sailing, a person tried to explain to one of the authors how to plot a course and stated, "This is just basic algebra." This statement enabled the author to transfer what had been learned in algebra class to an actual situation. If the learner has an appropriate mental set, transfer is more likely to occur.

Each of these mechanisms has implications for teaching and learning. Current research on teaching and learning calls for approaches that recognize students' transfer of learning and that make sense of what they learn.

✳ **What criteria should be used to evaluate Linton's second-grade health curriculum and how it is being taught?**

Constructivism: A New Conception of Learning

By the mid-1980s the educational community was beginning to talk about a "constructivist" way of learning. Constructivist literature calls for a marked departure from behaviorist theory, which continues to drive much educational practice today. Different theories of learning such as behavioral, cognitive, and constructivist approaches have both advantages and disadvantages, but these theories have much to offer educators in improving student learning.

Behaviorist theory of learning includes measurable behavioral objectives (e.g., by the end of this unit the student will have . . .) and sequenced curricula. In language texts before the mid-1980s, for instance, students were taught language structure sequentially; the present tense followed by the past tense. Many language teachers believed a natural progression existed that was the best way for people to learn. Conditionals such as "can" and "may," for example, were not often presented until midway through a course or toward the latter part of a text, if at all. Requesting something—May I go to the restroom? May I borrow a pen?—are language statements required by beginners. A behavioral approach to language learning, however, with its tight control on presentation of grammar and vocabulary, precludes a beginner's ability to make such requests.

Behaviorist approaches segment knowledge and skills into small pieces, with an overall idea that if each of these small pieces can be mastered, they will, taken together, result in acquisition of complex language skills. It pays little attention to conceptions and misconceptions that students might hold about the knowledge or skills being introduced. We now understand that, like thinking, learning a language is more than the sum of its parts. It is possible to know all grammar tenses and possess a large vocabulary and still be unable to speak a language.

According to Woolfolk (2001), "Cognitive theories of learning deal with thinking, remembering, and problem solving" (p. 2). The focus with cognitive theory is on how learners process information. Teaching techniques such as strategies to improve memorization, graphic organizers, or note-taking skills are examples of cognitive theory in action.

Constructivism, by contrast, is based on the belief that students learn best when they acquire knowledge through exploration and active learning. Individuals construct knowledge rather than receive it. According to Airasian and Walsh (1997), constructivism is a theory about how people learn. "Constructivism is based on the fundamental assumption that people create knowledge from the interaction between their existing knowledge or beliefs and the new ideas or situations they encounter" (p. 445).

Constructivist theory posits that students learn by actively constructing knowledge, comparing new information to previously learned information, thinking about and working through discrepancies, and ultimately reaching new understandings. Constructivist views have strongly influenced the movement toward national standards. Constructivism reminds us that ordering of information takes place in the minds of individuals, so when we as teachers impose our order on students, we rob them of the opportunity to create knowledge and understand themselves.

Building a Culture of Learning

Throughout the 1970s numerous studies explored variables that showed high correlations with increased academic achievement (Bossert, Dwyer, Rowan, & Lee, 1982; Brookover & Lezotte, 1979; Lezotte, Edmonds, & Ratner, 1974; Rutter, Maughan, Mortimore, Ouston, & Smith, 1979; Spartz, Valdes, McCormick, Meyers, & Geppert, 1977). These factors include:

- A safe and orderly environment
- An academic focus on basic skills
- Close monitoring of instruction by testing and supervision
- Strong instructional leadership from the principal
- High expectations and clear goals for students

The 1970s research findings, however, oversimplified the notion of effectiveness, and little attention was paid to the contexts in which these studies were conducted. What might be a successful practice in one context does not necessarily transfer to another. Programs often do not travel well to other locations regardless of how meticulously they were originally crafted.

In more recent studies that longitudinally examine academic achievement, other factors related to achievement present a more comprehensive picture (Cunningham & Gresso, 1993; Duke, 1987; Lipsitz, 1984; Reyes & Scribner, 1999; Wimpelberg, Teddlie, & Stringfield, 1989). These researchers discuss the broad-based conditions necessary for successful schools. Themes include leadership and management, changing school culture, and implementing challenging curricula and instruction. According to a study by Binkowski (1995), higher-performing schools include the following themes: participative leadership and management, communication and collaboration between central office and school staff regarding district and school goals, parental involvement, and staff development tied to curriculum and instruction.

In a provocative study of a school using site-based management, Beck and Murphy (1996) identified four imperatives for successful schools. These include:

- A consistent and powerful focus on learning;
- Strong, facilitative leadership;
- A commitment to nurturing a sense of internal and external community; and
- Resources aimed at building the capacity of people within the community to lead, learn, and teach. (p. ix)

Beck and Murphy observed that staff members were highly motivated to increase learning in schools that have site-based management. "We found a school where promoting learning was a clear priority and, for some teachers and the principal, a consuming passion" (p. 43). They noted that more attention was paid to student learning than to adult education. Additionally, they discovered that certain instructional strategies worked well in a particular school. These strategies matched students' interests and needs.

Beck and Murphy noted that the principal and a number of teachers exercised leadership. Additionally, parents contributed to children's success "by actively and enthusiastically supporting the work of educators" (p. 79). Finally, they found that site-based management provided more opportunities for parents to take leadership roles.

Beck and Murphy's third imperative for successful schools refers to the role of the community. Site-based management of schools creates opportunities for collaboration with organizations and agencies in the community. This comprehensive focus on children was a crucial factor in academic success.

Beck and Murphy's fourth imperative deals with capacity building. They found that site autonomy "encouraged a sense of agency on the part of teachers and parents" (p. 114). Site-based management allows teachers greater freedom to control their professional lives. Autonomy and a degree of budgetary control allows teachers to more quickly make decisions regarding curriculum, program innovations, and professional development.

A strong focus on learning, sufficient resources, strong facilitative leadership, and human capital from the school, district, and community are essential conditions for learning. Once these optimal learning conditions exist in a school, then attention must be given to the most appropriate teaching and learning approaches for the various types of knowledge that are part of the curriculum.

✳︎   **What conditions must exist at Linton Elementary School to ensure that an effective health curriculum is being taught?**

Teaching and Learning Approaches

A multitude of teaching and learning approaches can be used to optimize learning, and it is important to keep in mind Wiggins's (1989) idea of the futility of trying to teach everything of importance. He maintains, "Students cannot possibly learn everything of value by the time they leave school, but we can instill in them the desire to ask questions throughout their lives" (p. 44).

A number of different constructs can be used to analyze and determine what and how students should learn. Glatthorn (1994) believes that "some knowledge and skills seem to have high importance for all students, and they are the essential learning that all students need to master" (p. 27). They include major concepts, principles, ideas, and skills of a subject. Glatthorn also maintains that the structure of learning should be analyzed: "Understanding the principles of genetics is learning of high structure; it must be explicitly planned, taught, and tested. But developing scientific curiosity seems to be learning of low structure." He argues that teachers should nurture students' developing curiosity when possible, rather than simply spout facts that are taught "and then forgotten" (p. 27). Content raises questions and provides answers as it moves the learner from a basic grasp to a sophisticated and systematic view.

In this section we briefly describe learning and teaching models embedded in a constructivist approach to learning and in multiple intelligence and triarchic intelligence theories.

Apprenticeship Learning

Much has been written about apprenticeship, one of the oldest models for learning. Researchers have recently revisited the potential of this model. As Gardner (1991) states, "Apprenticeships may well be the means of instruction that builds most effectively on the ways in which most young people learn" (p. 124). He posits that "the best chance for an education leading to understanding lies in the melding of certain features of apprenticeships with certain aspects of schools and other institutions" (p. 125).

Why are a growing number of educators and researchers (Gardner, 1991; Lave & Wenger, 1993; Moffett, 1994) advocating apprenticeship learning? One major reason might be that in addition to situating learning in context, apprenticeships provide interaction, which is a key part of psychologist Lev Vygotsky's (1978) *zone of proximal development*. This "zone" is the space between what a student can do when working alone, compared with what he or she can do when working with an experienced adult or peer. Learning and mastery occur through active joint participation. This zone represents the gap between the individual learner's problem-solving ability and the total capacity demonstrated by those with whom the learner interacts.

According to Moffett (1994), natural learning methods such as witnessing, attuning, imitating, helping, collaborating, interacting, experimenting, transmitting, and investigating are all combined into the educational practice of apprenticing. Apprenticeships, however, are not the only learning formats that involve interaction in the zone of proximal development.

Cooperative Learning

Over the last twenty years professionals in education have become increasingly familiar with the practice of cooperative learning. Students are arranged in groups of heterogeneous ability levels in which they work together to accomplish shared goals. Cooperative learning can be used in any level class and subject area.

A substantial body of research documents the effectiveness of cooperative-learning strategies (Slavin, 1990; Stevens & Slavin, 1995). Children learn by piggybacking on the ideas of others through collaboration; they serve as instructional agents for one another. Work is carefully structured; students work in cooperative groups and thereby obtain a sense of positive interdependence.

Cooperative learning fosters problem solving and works best if there are five or fewer in a team. It promotes cooperative interpersonal behavior, mutual encouragement, and individual responsibility and accountability. Cooperative learning has been found to improve student achievement, intergroup relations, and self-esteem (Slavin, 1996). Cooperative learning is a sturdy platform for problem-based learning.

Problem-Based Learning

Problem-based learning (PBL) is widely used in medical education, and in recent years it has found a place in a variety of disciplines, including engineering, law, architecture, social work, and educational administration (Boud & Feletti, 1998; Bridges & Hallinger, 1995; Clarke et al., 1998). In the early 1990s PBL was introduced in elementary and secondary schools.

PBL begins with a practical problem that the student is likely to encounter in the real world. Problems are selected to illuminate core concepts in the school's curriculum. Subject matter is organized around the problem rather than around a discipline, and students have considerable responsibility and autonomy for directing their learning. Most learning is done in dyads or small teams (cooperative learning groups). Students must demonstrate their learning through a product or performance. Clearly the role of the teacher in PBL differs considerably from that of the teacher as expert. In PBL the teacher challenges, facilitates, and questions. In small groups, students work on PBL projects that are situated in a learning context and have multiple opportunities to work within the zone of proximal development.

Students are required to struggle with complicated real-world issues within the classroom setting. Problems should provide just enough information to guide investigation and student-directed inquiry. Students grapple with open-ended problems and are expected to propose solutions. They gain experience in self-direction, reasoning, problem solving, and collaboration. Teachers become facilitators, helping students understand their own thinking and guiding them as they search for new information. Students interact with others and acquire information before deciding how they will deal with the problem.

Apprenticeship learning, cooperative learning, and problem-based learning are three approaches embedded in constructivist philosophy. It is important that the school administrators understand the various approaches to learning and how to implement them in the curriculum. Other approaches related to constructivism are thematic, authentic, and differentiated instruction.

Thematic Instruction. In a thematic instruction approach, various related disciplines are brought to bear on a theme, issue, problem, topic, or experience. It is best when the themes or problems emerge from the student's world. Teachers and students are engaged in a learning partnership to examine a specific area in-depth and from multiple perspectives. Teachers in separate disciplines are united to team-teach around a selected set of issues. Information is viewed in a holistic manner. This orientation offers a way to show how different subject areas relate, thus affirming their relevance.

Authentic Instruction. Students learn best from actual experiences rather than from simulations. Authentic instruction requires the teacher to work with students in choosing a topic on which to focus and in obtaining needed information.

Information-gathering might include contacting expert practitioners, students from another culture, and authors as well as collecting data from researchers, foundations, governments, and others. Technology is often used in obtaining, organizing, manipulating, and displaying information. The teacher serves as a coach, providing structure and actively supporting students. Some educators refer to certain types of problem-based learning as a form of authentic instruction.

Differentiated Instruction. The approach called differentiated instruction is based on a diagnosis of student readiness, interest, and learning profile. All students are engaged in a continual progression of challenging work. Use of time, space, and groupings is flexible.

Research indicates the importance of meeting varying learning needs, even though in practice the process has proved difficult. This type of study allows students to pursue topics of interest in a direction or depth that might not be suitable for or likely to be pursued by the class as a whole. Students ready for independence from teacher direction will be released from persistent supervision, and those requiring assistance are provided greater structure. Differentiated instruction involves such strategies as curriculum compacting, independent study, interest centers or interest groups, tiered assignments, flexible grouping, mentorships and apprenticeships, learning contracts, and anchoring activities. Other types of curricular and instructional approaches include brain-based, discovery, interdisciplinary, and whole language.

  ✳ **What instructional model(s) might work best for health education at Linton Elementary? Explain why.**

Curriculum Design and Educational Programming

According to Glatthorn (1997), "principals can best discharge their leadership role if they develop a deep and broad knowledge base with respect to curriculum" (p. 3). What is it that school administrators need to know about curriculum?

Functions of Curriculum

Textbooks on curriculum development traditionally discuss four curriculum levels: state, district, school, and classroom. Box 8.1 lists the functions for each level, which is embedded in the preceding level. For example, one role of the teacher is to develop units of study. Those units of study emanate from one of the school functions— developing a program of studies. This program in turn is embedded in a district function—identifying a common program of studies. At the state level, administrators develop frameworks embodying broad goals and general standards. Thus, there is a connection, an alignment, among the functions at the various levels.

A fifth curriculum level should be added to Glatthorn's four: the emerging roles played by national professional organizations, national and international research groups, and the U.S. Department of Education in Washington, DC. These

BOX 8.1 • *Summary of Curriculum Functions*

State functions
Develop state frameworks, including broad goals, general standards, and graduation requirements.
Develop state tests and other performance measures in required academic subjects.
Provide needed resources to local districts.
Evaluate state frameworks.

District functions
Develop and implement curriculum-related policies.
Develop a vision of a quality curriculum.
Develop educational goals based on state goals.
Identify a common program of studies, the curriculum requirements, and subject time allocation, for each level of schooling.
For each subject, develop the documents for the core or mastery curriculum guides.
Select instructional materials.
Develop district curriculum-based tests and other performance measures to supplement state tests.

Provide fiscal and other resources needed at the school level, including technical assistance.
Evaluate the curriculum.

School functions
Develop the school's vision of a quality curriculum, building on the district's vision.
Supplement the district's educational goals.
Develop its own program of studies.
Develop a learning-centered schedule.
Determine nature and extent of curriculum integration.
Align the curriculum.
Monitor and assist in the implementation of the curriculum.

Classroom functions
Develop yearly planning calendars.
Develop units of study.
Enrich the curriculum and remediate learning.
Evaluate the curriculum.

Source: A. Glatthorn (1997). *The principal as curriculum leader.* Thousand Oaks, CA: Corwin Press. Reprinted by permission.

groups can be described not only as influencing local curriculum, but also as being major players in the creation of frameworks and in the development of national tests and standards.

Principal as Curriculum Leader

ALLAN A. GLATTHORN • *University of East Carolina*

When I told a friend that the title of one of my books was *Principal as Curriculum Leader*, she responded, "That's an oxymoron if I ever heard one." Her reaction is understandable: Most principals do not believe that they have any role in setting curriculum. However, I believe that they do have a key part to play in this essential component of schooling.

Curriculum development and implementation are nested processes: The state, the school system, the school, and the classroom all have legitimate roles to play in learning enhancement. The state should identify curriculum standards for each subject; the school district should use those standards in developing coordinated curricula for grades K–12, with appropriate benchmarks.

The school should develop its own program of studies, within district guidelines. The classroom teacher should operationalize the district curriculum guides in several ways: develop long-term plans, write units of study, enrich the district curriculum, and adapt it so that it responds to individual student needs.

School-level leadership functions with respect to curriculum, as follows:

1. Influencing district curriculum guides
2. Developing the school's program of studies
3. Developing a learning-centered schedule
4. Determining the nature and extent of curriculum integration
5. Aligning the curriculum
6. Monitoring the curriculum
7. Helping teachers make long-term plans
8. Helping teachers develop curriculum units
9. Helping teachers provide enrichment and remediation
10. Evaluating the curriculum

This list does not mean that the principal must do all the work. Instead, I encourage principals to play an active role but to use a team-leadership approach that recognizes the strengths and needs of classroom teachers.

While educators need to strengthen curricula at all levels, I believe that the most important challenge is to develop curriculum competence at the school and classroom levels. In responding to this challenge, principals are the key agents in curriculum reform.

The Standards Movement

In recent years a variety of national and state agencies and professional organizations have been involved in the development of curriculum standards or frameworks. Almost all states have standards of learning in English, language arts, history/social studies, mathematics, science, and writing. Many of these frameworks have influenced the development of local school curricula. Certainly an administrator should carefully consider the standards developed by these organizations when setting curriculum at the local level.

Standards are norms for quality control. They tell us what students should know and be able to do. According to Diane Ravitch (1995), there are three types of standards: content standards, performance standards, and opportunity-to-learn (OTL) standards. Content standards are the descriptions of the knowledge and skills desired for students to learn. Performance standards refer to the level of proficiency, or degree of mastery, at which the knowledge or skill is to be displayed. OTL standards have to do with the availability of resources. The premise of OTL standards is that schools, districts, and states must provide the necessary programs, staff, and other resources to meet the basic needs of students.

Currently, national curriculum standards documents are available (online and on paper) in the following areas: arts (dance, music, theatre, visual arts), civics, economics, English/Language Arts, foreign languages, geography, health, history, mathematics, physical education, science, social studies, and technology. Each document is organized differently but many include the knowledge, skills, and dispositions that students need to have in order to achieve. Some of these standards documents, such as those for technology, have student, teacher, and administrator standards.

✳ **What is the role of the principal and teachers at Linton Elementary School regarding the health curriculum, and how might standards help in this effort?**

Curricular and Instructional Change

Whether curriculum is based on national, state, or locally developed standards, the process of change is key to understanding curriculum implementation and program innovation. Fullan (1993) argues, "It is probably closer to the truth to say that the main problem in public education is not resistance to change, but the presence of too many innovations mandated or adopted uncritically and superficially on an *ad hoc* fragmented basis" (p. 23). The successful development and implementation of programs thrives on abundant opportunity for dialogue that encourages educators to critique the curriculum. This dialogue will more than likely involve conflict. If we think of conflict in terms of "conflict with civility," then it is not only healthy, but a necessary ingredient in curriculum and program development.

Several researchers have discussed the stages of change in schools (Cordeiro, 1998; Fullan, 1991; Kilmann, 1989). A model for program development including four approaches to change, and the stages inherent in each, is particularly appropriate to this discussion.

As Figure 8.1 shows, there are four overarching types of approach to change: a top-down approach ("This district will use computer technology in all courses"); a model adoption approach ("We are considering adopting the Accelerated Schools model"); a change agent approach ("Several teachers have piloted the Success for All curriculum and are recommending that it be used by the school"); and a catalytic events approach ("After this terrible racial incident we must consider a multicultural approach to our curriculum").

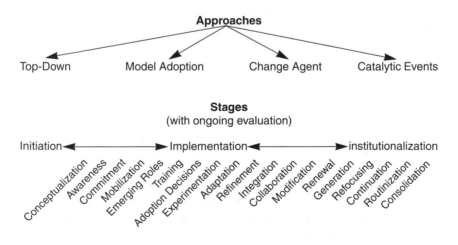

FIGURE 8.1   *A Model of Program Development*

Whatever the approach, all innovations pass through a series of stages. Change proceeds along a continuum. Initiation might involve conceptualization, awareness, and commitment. Implementation might include development, experimentation, adaptation, and refinement. Finally, institutionalization might involve refocusing, continuation, routinization, or possibly consolidation.

Modification of a curriculum and educational program begins in a specific proposal to modify what already exists. Curriculum change focuses on what will be taught, and instructional change focuses on the way the curriculum will be taught. The proposal grows from the staff's knowledge of the goals, standards, and research as well as of the students and community. Participants can become knowledgeable by reading, visiting other schools, experimenting, discussing, and consulting. The formal proposal includes a rationale for change and an analysis of the change's potential impact on resources.

The proposal should be presented to all concerned, including faculty and parents, for final review before it is submitted through the school system's review process. Those involved might choose to join one of the networks to help develop the curriculum and provide needed support (see Chapter 3). The final step after approval is determining how the curriculum will be organized and delivered.

✳ **What steps should Linton Elementary School staff take to develop and refine the existing health curriculum?**

Developing Curriculum and Programs

According to Elliot Eisner (1995), all schools teach three curricula: explicit, implicit, and null. The explicit curriculum is the actual curriculum the school uses to teach pupils. The explicit curriculum usually takes the form of curriculum guides, but all too often it consists of textbooks. The implicit curriculum is not a formal part of the curriculum, yet it is taught in school. For example, the importance of punctuality and respect for others is part of many schools' implicit curriculum. Eisner maintains that "the implicit curriculum of a school is what it teaches because of the kind of school it is" (p. 97). Eisner's thesis is that "what schools do not teach is just as important as what they do teach" (p. 97).

Eisner defines the null curriculum in two dimensions. First, educators need to look at the subjects or content areas that may or may not be present in the curriculum. Teachers might ask such questions as: Why do we teach pre-algebra? Why do we have five tracks for English classes? Why are no advanced placement courses offered? Why do so few female students enroll in advanced math classes? What should students be expected to know as part of U.S. literature?

The second dimension involves the intellectual processes that the school emphasizes or neglects. Eisner maintains that "not all thinking is mediated by word or number, nor is all thinking rule-abiding" (p. 98). Critical questions educators might ask include: What forms of knowing (i.e., visual, metaphoric) are absent or marginal? In what ways do we cultivate students' imaginations?

Asking questions such as these is not only helpful in curriculum development and implementation, but also in evaluating curriculum and programs. Clearly many factors affect curriculum development.

Designing and Managing the Curriculum

A variety of policies and factors are associated with effective programs. Whether a curriculum is based on a national, state, or local framework, the goal of curriculum development is to create a coherent educational program. Regardless of the design of the curriculum, important issues to consider are curriculum *congruity, integration, sequence,* and *access.* Administrators must foster a school environment that continuously raises questions related to these four areas. Following are some of these questions:

Curriculum Congruity
- How consistent is the curriculum across grade levels and schools?
- What criteria are used to determine whether a student has achieved mastery of a concept?
- What enables the student to understand the interpretation of knowledge and how it is used to examine authentic problems?

Curriculum Integration
- Is the curriculum socially relevant?
- Which is more important—breadth or depth of subject matter?
- Should additional time be given to a specific subject?
- Is the program balanced between essential knowledge and special interests?
- What requirements and standards should be established?

Curriculum Sequence
- Should certain topics precede other topics?
- Should a topic be taught chronologically?
- Should a topic be taught from a developmental viewpoint?
- Should a topic be taught inductively or deductively?

Student Access
- What program options are available to students?
- How are students assigned to classes and teachers?
- How do policies regarding promotion, required courses, and the like affect students?
- How is the program of studies responsive to the special needs of the students served?
- What information is provided to students and families about course and program options?
- How are students grouped or tracked into courses?
- What are the enrollments by gender and race or ethnicity in courses?

These are but a few of the questions that address issues of curriculum congruity, integration, sequencing, and access. These questions and a variety of critical factors must be investigated in the design and development of curriculum and programs. Critical factors include nature and scale of the program, community expectations, resources needed, stakeholders involved, the utilization of time, community and school demographics, incentives for teachers, timeline implementation, and program monitoring. Once a curriculum is developed or a program or model adapted to a school, the work of program improvement has begun. And it is an ongoing process.

✳   **What are some of the questions that need to be asked regarding Linton Elementary's health curriculum?**

Seeing the Curriculum Whole: The Function of a Real Educational Leader

LAUREL N. TANNER • *Temple University*

The school administrator's task, of course, involves the entire curriculum. Nowhere is the task more beautifully set forth than in Lawrence Cremin's *The Genius of American Education*. "Someone must look at the curriculum whole and raise insistent questions of priority and relationship" (1965, p. 58). No individual, he writes, can or ought to have the sole responsibility for this concern, but it certainly must be the main business of anybody who sees himself or herself a principal, superintendent, or president of a school board.

Specialists do not look at how the parts must relate to the whole. Principals must have a larger vision and see the entire curriculum. Because we lack such a vision, schools are wrestling with some intractable problems that might have been avoided. In the famous curriculum reform movement of the 1960s, priority was given to science, mathematics, and modern foreign languages because these subjects were deemed essential for our national defense. Daniel Tanner and I found, as a result of the reforms that were instituted, that the schools were left with problems stemming from misguided curriculum priorities, curriculum imbalance, and failure to articulate the curriculum with the nature of the learner (Tanner & Tanner, 1995).

Two of our most difficult problems—discipline and dropping out—are due in no small way to the failure to look at the curriculum whole. For example, some school districts that reduced their offerings in the studio and industrial arts experienced an increased dropout rate (Tanner, 1997). The loss to individual students was tremendous. Unable to develop in the one area in which they excelled, they decided to leave school. The literature is filled with references to the "strong" educational leader.

The principal's strength derives from professional knowledge and experience in working out problems by using theoretical principles. It is in no sense an arbitrary thing. Three constructs provide strength for a principal to see the curriculum as an entirety.

The School's Philosophy
First, the curriculum and how it is taught must be governed by a statement of philosophy and goals—a theory of what the school hopes to achieve. Tyler (1949) suggests that a school have seven to fifteen broad educational goals. Without a goals statement a school is susceptible to whatever schemes are fashionable at a given time and the whims of individual faculty members.

Hoy and Tarter (1995) provide an interesting example of a high school principal who denied a member of the English faculty's request to offer an elective in Latin American literature. The department chair had already turned down the request because it was inconsistent with the thrust of the program. The school had a statement of philosophy and goals and tried to make decisions that were consistent with it.

As Cremin warned, "To refuse to look at curricula in their entirety is to relegate to intraschool policies a series of decisions that ought to call into play the most fundamental philosophical principles" (1965, p. 58). The strong educational leader derives her or his strength from a statement of philosophy and goals developed collaboratively with the faculty. No philosophy, however, should be a barricade against change. "Any person who is open-minded and sensitive to new perceptions, and who has concentration and responsibility in connecting them has, in so far, a philosophic disposition," observed Dewey (1916, p. 380).

What a Whole Curriculum Looks Like

The second source of strength is knowledge of what the entire curriculum looks like. Such a comprehensive vision is a difficult thing for any one person, because there are so many knowledge categories. It is little wonder that administrators regard the curriculum as specialized and compartmentalized knowledge over and beyond their domain of expertise. But there is a manageable way of looking at the macrocurriculum, in terms of five inclusive functions (Tanner & Tanner, 1995):

1. General education or the common understandings and competencies necessary for responsible citizenship in a free society.
2. Specialized education that enables the learner to become a productive earner as well as a lifelong learner.
3. Enrichment education—avocational instruction that enriches the life of every individual.
4. Exploratory education that stimulates the individual to extend his or her reach into untried realms.

5. Special-interest education that provides for intensive learning experiences beyond one's vocational and avocational pursuits.

Like the fingers of a hand, these five functions are interdependent. Equipped with a comprehensive view of the curriculum, the administrator can help faculty develop a shared vision and put it into practice as an ongoing operation.

A good leader asks what Cremin called "insistent questions of priority and relationship" (1965, p. 58). The point is that a good school is always involved in curriculum development and better teaching methods. Interestingly, even top-scoring countries, with which the United States is told to compare itself, are dissatisfied with their practices in teaching science and mathematics and "are investing large sums to change" (Atkin & Black, 1997, p. 28). There is a big difference between the reform movement of the 1960s and the present one: Teachers are involved in working out the curriculum at the classroom level.

Putting the Vision into Practice

Third, how does the administrator orchestrate the vision of a whole curriculum? How does he or she bring the specializations into relationship? The best answer is an approach pioneered by Ralph Tyler (1949). It concerns what happens—or should happen—immediately after a school has firmed up its goals statement. The faculty has already answered Tyler's question "What educational purposes should the school seek to attain?" (p. v). Tyler shows the way a high school English department might use these broad goals to open up the question, How do we in the English department not just teach literature but also help achieve our school's seven or nine or twelve educational goals? Every teacher has a responsibility to deal with the school's goals—academic, social, personal, and vocational. Attention to the goals is key. The strong leader uses the goals, not just to test and screen curriculum proposals but to bring the specializations together.

Program Improvement and Evaluation

The notion of evaluation is integral to the change process. Too often it is an afterthought and is tacked on to a completed or near-completed program. Genuine program improvement requires that evaluation be built into the curriculum or program from the beginning. Program improvement may be conducted by those involved in the program itself or by an outside organization such as an accrediting agency. Regardless of the approach used, evaluation is an ongoing part of the improvement process of the school.

CRESST, the UCLA Center for Research on Evaluation, Standards, and Student Testing (www.cresst.org), proposes six steps for guiding evaluation (see Table 8.2). Two of the six steps include the involvement of key constituencies. Guba and Lincoln (1989), in their book *Fourth Generation Evaluation*, maintain that "the claims, concerns and issues of stakeholders [should] serve as organizational

TABLE 8.2   *Principles of Sensible Evaluation*

Step	*Sensible Actions*
Focus the evaluation	Involve significant constituencies Include improvement and accountability concerns Look at long- and short-term targets of change Look at relationships between processes and outcomes based on your theories of action Look for unanticipated side effects
Identify tracking strategies	Use strategies well aligned with school goals Use multiple indicators Build in checks for validity of inferences Build measures on existing information
Manage instrument development and data collection	Consider accountability mandates Match instruments with specific evaluation questions
Score and summarize data	When appropriate, use scoring sessions for staff development Assure valid inferences by choosing appropriate scores
Analyze and interpret information	Involve key constituencies Examine progress over time Consider and refine your theories of action Be alert to unanticipated side effects Corroborate findings by using multiple indicators
Act on findings and continue program monitoring	Use the principles guiding focusing activities to monitor actions based on your findings

Source: Sensible evaluation. (1997). Los Angeles: Center for Research on Evaluation Standards and Student Testing. Reprinted with permission.

foci (the basis for determining what information is needed" (p. 50). Therefore, an initial step in any approach to evaluation involves identification of stakeholders.

Fenwick English (Frase, English, & Poston, 1995) developed a curriculum auditing process that is widely used by school districts and is part of an auditing approach sponsored by the American Association of School Administrators. A key concept in curriculum auditing is the alignment of goals and objectives, curriculum content, and testing. The audit determines the degree to which the written, taught, and tested curricula are aligned. The audit provides information for curriculum and instructional planning by validating what currently exists within a school district. The results of an audit are used to improve the quality of the curriculum and instruction and ultimately to improve the quality of learning.

✳ **How might the health curriculum at Linton Elementary School be evaluated?**

Utilizing Time

Perhaps the two most important jobs of a school administrator are recruiting and hiring faculty and deciding how time in a school year will be allocated. The length of the school year, day, and class session, as well as their organization, have significant impact on teacher–student and student–student relationships. In recent years there has been renewed interest in various types of scheduling. Additionally, the notion of looping—teachers moving with students over a two- or three-year period—is growing in popularity.

Year-Round Education

Year-round education (YRE) is not a new idea in the United States or in other nations. The literature on year-round education in the United States first appeared with some degree of regularity in the 1970s. Most of the discussion, unfortunately, focused on the importance of utilizing the school building, rather than on efficiency and effectiveness as has been done more recently. YRE is being revived, and it is estimated that "nearly 1.5 million students in more than 25 states now attend elementary and secondary schools that function on a year-round schedule" (Levine & Ornstein, 1993).

YRE involves a reorganization of the school calendar into instructional blocks, with vacations (or special inter-sessions) distributed throughout the calendar year, rather than concentrated in the summer. Learning opportunities need to be continuous throughout the year. School districts can operate on single-track or multitrack schedules. The most common year-round schedule is the single-track, 45–15 day plan. Students attend school for 45 days, followed by 15 days with no school. This pattern is repeated four times. According to the research literature the several advantages to year-round education include:

- Increased attendance of teachers and students
- Lower student dropout rates, greater flexibility in instruction, greater retention of learning

- Greater flexibility in teacher planning, student assessment, and curriculum development
- Additional opportunities for remedial and accelerated classes during the intersessions (Ballinger, 1988; Doyle & Finn, 1985; Gee, 1997; Peltier, 1991; Quinlan, George, & Emmett, 1987; White, 1988)

Block Scheduling

Canady and Rettig (1995) estimated that more than 50 percent of U.S. high schools use some form of block scheduling. There are numerous formats for block scheduling. Two widely used models include the 4/4 semester plan and the alternative day or A/B schedule. In a 4/4 semester block schedule, each semester students attend four classes a day, completing the course during this time. In the alternative day, or A/B schedule, a course meets every other day for the entire school year. Figure 8.2 on page 238 depicts a typical A/B block schedule.

A powerful variation of block scheduling is the Copernican Plan (Carroll, 1994). In this scheduling model, class periods are longer so that teachers have fewer students each semester. Students have two 85- to 90-minute classes each day, lunch, and either one or two electives. Classes meet for ninety days and then another class is scheduled. In the Copernican Plan credit is awarded for mastering course objectives, and students graduate at the end of the semester in which they complete the required number of credits.

There are many reasons secondary schools are experimenting with allocating time differently from seven- or eight-period schedules. Criticisms of these schedules are numerous: Time is lost passing in hallways, hallway time increases discipline problems, students are overwhelmed by having seven or eight teachers each day, teachers are overwhelmed with having 120–150 students per day, an impersonal assembly-line atmosphere is created, far too many subjects might be assigned homework for the same evening, and so on.

In a study of 820 high schools Glickman (1998) found that activity-learning methods, which are more likely to be found in schools with longer class periods, led to higher achievement. Additionally, fewer class changes resulted in fewer discipline problems and a less stressful school setting. The research data describe several advantages to block scheduling:

- Reduction in disciplinary referrals and suspensions (Carroll, 1994; Einedar & Bishop, 1997; Glickman, 1995; Meadows, 1995; Reid, 1995)
- Positive effects on school climate (Carroll, 1994; Glickman, 1998; Reid, 1995)
- Lower dropout rates (Carroll, 1994; Hottenstein & Malatesta, 1993; Reid, 1995)
- Improved student attendance (Cameron, 1995; King et al., 1995; Schoenstein, 1995)
- Improved student attitudes (Carroll, 1994; Einedar & Bishop, 1997; Hottenstein & Malatesta, 1993; Meadows, 1995)
- Improved teacher attitudes (Carroll, 1994)

Varying the structure of the school day and the school year can provide numerous academic benefits. In a study that focused on block scheduling and its

Monday	Tuesday (even)	Wednesday (odd)	Thursday (even)	Friday (odd)
Period 1 7:27–8:14	**Block 1** 7:27–9:06 Period 1	**Block 2** 7:27–9:06 Period 2	**Block 1** 7:25–9:04 Period 1	*Block 2* 7:25–9:04 Period 2
Period 2 8:20–9:07	**Block 3** 9:13–10:53 Period 3	**Block 4** 9:13–10:53 Period 4	**Block 3** 9:13–10:53 Period 3	**Block 4** 9:13–10:53 Period 4
Period 3 9:13–10:07				
Period 4 10:13–10:53				
Lunch Period—A 11:00–11:30 5 **Class Period—B** 11:00–11:49	**Block 3** 11:00–11:30 5 Class Period—B 11:00–11:49	**Block 3** 11:00–11:30 5 Class Period—B 11:00–11:49	**Block 3** 11:00–11:30 5 Class Period—B 11:00–11:49	**Block 3** 11:00–11:30 5 Class Period—B 11:00–11:49
12-Minute Overlap				
Class Period—A 11:37–12:26 5 **Lunch Period—B** 11:56–12:26	Class Period—A 11:37–12:26 5 Lunch Period—B 11:56–12:26	Class Period—A 11:37–12:26 5 Lunch Period—B 11:56–12:26	Class Period—A 11:37–12:26 5 Lunch Period—B 11:56–12:26	Class Period—A 11:37–12:26 5 Lunch Period—B 11:56–12:26
Period 6 12:33–1:20	**Block 4** 12:33–2:12 Period 6	**Block 4** 12:33–2:12 Period 7	**Block 4** 12:33–2:12 Period 6	**Block 4** 12:33–2:12 Period 7
Period 7 1:26–2:12				
After School	**After School**	**After School**	**After School**	**After School**

FIGURE 8.2   *Example of a Block Schedule*

effect on math instruction, Kramer (1997) noted that transitioning to block schedules can lead to achievement gain, given sufficient staff development, planning time, and curriculum modification. It is evident that when transitioning to a block schedule, the major role of the school administrator is to provide faculty with adequate support.

Looping

Perhaps one of the most important strategies for affording students more contact time with the same teacher, and additional opportunities for group learning, can be met through the concept of looping. *Looping*, or multiyear interactions between cohorts of students and a single teacher is common practice in many countries. In

Spain, for example, students in kindergarten and grades 1 and 2 have the same teacher for all three years. Beginning in grade 3 the student cohort has a different teacher for the next three years (grades 3–5). Finally, this student cohort has another new teacher for grades 6, 7, and 8. Similarly, in Mexico, the heterogeneous grouping of students into cohorts facilitates students' passage through the curriculum. These *groupos escolares* remain together for three years. A growing body of research supports the notion that long-term relationships with teachers and multiyear relationships with peers can increase student learning (Cordeiro, 1990; Liu, 1997).

Time on Task

According to Stallings (1980), efficient allocation of time spent on a task can increase student achievement. The research literature has identified three levels of time: allocated time, engaged time, and academic learning time. *Allocated time* is the amount of time that is actually assigned for a class. *Engaged time* is the amount of allocated time in which the student is actively engaged in the learning activity. *Academic learning time* is a refinement of engaged time and reflects the quality of the learning (e.g., high, moderate, or low degree of success; appropriateness of the instructional materials).

Research indicates that the allocation of time, including models that examine the school year, day, multiple years, and time in the classroom, is an important approach that enhances learning opportunities.

Assessing Student Progress

Considerable discussion and debate centers around the best ways to assess student progress. Some of the most common forms of student assessment include standardized achievement testing (norm-referenced tests), criterion-referenced testing, and performance or alternative assessment.

Standardized tests, which are designed to compare the performance of students to the performance of a normative group, inspire much debate (Kean, 1986; Neill, 1997). The National Forum on Assessment, which included a group of eighty education and civil rights organizations, concluded that multiple-choice testing (e.g., true or false, selecting one item among several) should be only a small part of any assessment program (Marzano & Kendall, 1997; Popham, 1997). Criterion-referenced tests are meant to ascertain a learner's status with respect to a learning task. They are used to see if a student has mastered specific material.

Performance assessment is a relatively new method that provides more appropriate indicators of student learning than do multiple-choice tests. Performance assessments are sometimes referred to as *alternative assessments* and can assume many forms. Herman, Aschbacher, and Winters (1992) define alternative assessments as measures with common characteristics. Such assessments (a) ask students to perform, create, or produce; (b) tap higher-level thinking and problem-solving skills; (c) use tasks that represent meaningful instructional activities; (d) involve scoring; and (e) require new instructional and assessment roles for teachers.

Some educators maintain that assessments must be authentic. Wiggins (1990) defines authenticity as the extent to which a test, performance, or product in an assessment bears a relationship to a real-world referent.

Portfolios

A portfolio is a collection of individual students' work that results from participation in a developmental process. Decisions related to what is collected depend on the purpose of the portfolio—assessment, culmination, display, future study, to name a few. Through reflection students can become increasingly aware of themselves as learners. Portfolios tend to focus attention on what students are learning, how well they are learning it, how well they demonstrate learning, and how well they reflect on this work.

Portfolios and other types of performance assessments are a relatively recent phenomenon in education, except in arts education. Some teachers specify what goes into a portfolio, whereas others allow the student to select what will be included. This work should exhibit to the student, teacher, and others the student's progress and achievement in a particular area. A portfolio should show the various stages through which a project has passed. For example, a portfolio could contain a series of drafts of a paper. Or, it might contain video clips from different time periods showing how a dance performance has improved as the student practiced.

Assessing Student Performance

GRANT WIGGINS • *President and Director for the Center on Learning Assessment and School Structure (C.L.A.S.S.)*

Assessment should be educative, not merely a quick audit of performance as is now too often the case. Students and teachers need useful and timely feedback, not arcane item analysis provided in the summer when school is out. Educative assessment thus requires an approach and schedule very different from what is typically found in classroom, district, and state testing.

Assessment should be educative in two senses: It should teach students (and teachers) what kinds of performance tasks and standards are most valued. It should reflect situations in the wider world—real problems, real situations, real audiences, and real purposes. Assessment should also provide timely, ongoing, user-friendly feedback to make possible the slow but steady mastery of such tasks (as opposed to one-shot testing and ranking).

The use of such feedback—the student's ability to self-adjust—should become increasingly central to what and how we assess. As is true of Little League, Nintendo games, karate, or cooking, the assessment system should provide ongoing feedback using standards and measures of progress over time. It should also provide opportunities to use the feedback as part of what we assess—the assessment of self-adjustment.

Four maxims about reform follow from this idea of educative assessment:

1. Assessment must be grounded in authentic tasks if it is to inform and improve performance. To improve and not just audit student performance, we need assessment based on what adults actually do in the world. Although tests and quizzes have a place in rounding out the performance picture, they must be made secondary to more "authentic" tasks.

An assessment is authentic if it:

a. replicates or simulates the ways in which a person's knowledge and abilities are "tested" in real-world situations;

b. requires the student to use knowledge and skills wisely and effectively to solve complex, multistep problems (where the solution involves more than just following a set routine or procedure or "plugging in" knowledge);

c. asks the student to "do" the subject—to *do* science or history, not just recite or replicate through demonstration what was taught or is already known.

d. replicates the *contexts* in which adults are "tested" in the workplace, in civic, and in personal life. By "context," we mean the situations, purposes, audiences, constraints, and the "messiness and murkiness" so common to life's challenges—but so typically absent from neat-and-clean school tests;

e. tests the student's ability to use a repertoire of knowledge and skill to solve complex, multifaceted performance challenges. By contrast, most test items are "plug-in" questions—similar to the sideline drills in athletics (as opposed to the actual game, which requires integrated use of all the drills). While there is, of course, a place for drill tests, *performance is always more than the sum of the drills*; and

f. allows for *appropriate* opportunities to rehearse, practice, consult resources, get feedback on and refine performances and products.

Only by ensuring that the assessment system *models* genuine performance challenges, requirements, and feedback will student performance and teacher instruction be improved over time. This model makes teaching more appropriately like coaching athletic, artistic, and intellectual performance.

2. Assessment must do more than *audit* performance. It must be designed to *improve* per- **formance.** This principle exposes the weakness of one-shot typical tests. Students, teachers, and administrators need timely, ongoing, user-friendly feedback about the key performance challenges of learning and adult performance. As in athletics and the arts, students need clear, worthy, and recurring tasks that can be slowly mastered over time.

By contrast, all current testing typically "audits" student performance once. Tests use a small number of relatively simplistic indirect "items" that can be easily and quickly scored. A more direct assessment of performance would look at whether students can use knowledge in real-world ways and judge whether they can improve over time on known tasks and standards.

Consider an analogy with athletics. Imagine if basketball season consisted of one game, played on the last day of the year, in which the players did not know which plays they would be asked to make. Imagine further that they would not know if their shots went in the basket until weeks later. Imagine further that if instead of playing the game of basketball, teams of measurement experts each year invented an arcane series of drills to test with—valid to measurement experts, but unconnected to basketball playing in the minds of players and coaches. Finally, imagine a scoring system fully understandable only to the assessors and not the players and coaches. Who would improve at the game under these conditions? Yet state testing consistently provides feedback that can't easily be deciphered or used on tasks that do not mirror real performance, where the test is unknown until test day, and where the feedback comes at the end of the school year, when it cannot be used to improve the performance of the student or the cohort.

3. Assessment must be credible and open if genuine reform is to occur. Accountability occurs only when adults not only are *responsive* to results but also feel *responsible* for them. Genuine accountability thus requires credible assessment tasks. As in athletics and the arts, where teachers typically work overtime to enable students to meet high standards, that sense of responsibility is attributable to the fact that (1) the standards and tasks are credible and worthy and (2) the assessment system (and the results generated) are open and defensible as a system. No coach complains that the "test" of the game or recital is somehow unfair or unknown; there are many opportunities to improve performance over time. A system of assessment must meet the test of local credibility if we are to get beyond local excuses for poor performance.

Assessment must not rely solely on secret test items and performance standards and one-shot tests. Although simplistic test items (kept secure until test day) are relatively inexpensive to use and easy to measure, implementing them as standard policy is counterproductive to student, teacher, and school improvement. How can anyone improve his or her performance if what specifically is going to be tested is kept secret?

4. An effective assessment plan must build *local* **high-quality assessment capacity.** An assessment system should be deliberately designed to improve the quality of local tests, standards, grading, and reporting.

Consider another analogy. The district's or state's goal should not be that of a narrow-minded doctor who merely forces patients to have an annual physical exam based on a handful of simple tests. Rather, the physician's goal should be to promote daily healthfulness. As things now stand, however, the state "doctor" seems interested only in seeing whether schools "pass the physical."

The unintended but powerful effect of the current system causes the school "patient" to fixate on the simple tasks of the physical exam rather than on attaining daily standards of health and fitness. As a result, few teachers understand how to test for genuine intellectual "health" and "fitness." Fewer still see that their own testing need not mimic the *form* of state testing. Teachers do not need to "teach to the (simplistic) test" for their students to do well on it. Teachers become (wrongly) convinced that the only way to get good test results is to teach to and practice the checkup, ignoring the fact that a multiple-choice test is based on a reverse logic: If you are "healthy" and meet high standards day in and day out, your health will show on the checkup.

The goal of improving local intellectual "fitness" thus requires a system that models good assessment practice as it audits local fitness, so that local assessment improves. Tests teach teachers and students what we value, irrespective of an intent merely to measure. The district (and the state) should provide models of "health" (good performance) and "physical fitness standards" (exemplary tests) in its assessment system. And incentives should be provided to ensure higher-quality local assessment, grounded in clear policies about design and use.

Note: A thorough discussion of these points can be found in G. Wiggins. *Educative assessment: Designing assessment to inform and improve student performance* (1998). San Francisco: Jossey-Bass.

Reporting Student Progress

Of the many formats used for reporting student progress, letter grades (A, B, C, D, F) are the most common. Numbers (percent correct), symbols (S = Satisfactory, N = Needs Improvement, U = Unsatisfactory), or descriptors (Emerging, Developing, Maturing) are sometimes used at the elementary level.

Another format is a dual marking system. The student gets two marks in a subject—one for the student's level of achievement and the other perhaps the student's achievement in relation to personal ability (student improvement).

Pass–Fail, or Pass–No Pass, is another option for reporting student progress. One advantage to this option is that students will be more likely to explore new areas of knowledge if they know they will not receive a poor grade. A disadvantage is, some educators argue, that students will do the minimum to receive a "pass," rather than being motivated to do better by receiving a letter grade.

Some schools report success with narrative reports. A letter grade may or may not be included. This narrative is a description of the student's progress in a particular subject area and may be developed from a listing of characteristics related to the student's progress. Computer programs are often used to print out selected comments.

Presenting Student Outcomes to the Community

Who are the stakeholders in the assessment process? Parents, students, teachers, administrators, state officials, and community members—all of whom are stakeholders—have potentially differing expectations of program and student assessment.

Administrators must also ask what kinds of information each stakeholder needs and how that information will be used. The answers to these questions will help administrators communicate more effectively and efficiently with each stakeholder.

In his book *Student-Centered Classroom Assessment* (1994), Stiggins provides a helpful way to evaluate the users and uses of assessment results (Table 8.3). Stiggins lists the various stakeholders, the key questions that need to be answered, and the information needed to answer those questions. Staff should be informed first and oriented to the results of testing programs. Then the community should be informed through the appropriate means. Special meetings should be held to discuss and explain test results.

There has been a national trend to move toward high-stakes student assessment, attaching real consequences to low performance. Students who do not perform well on assessment tests are required to go to summer school, are retained, or are awarded less than standard high school diplomas. Research has not provided evidence that such consequences improve student performance. As a result, a number of districts are looking at smaller class sizes, enriched and more rigorous curriculum, focusing on areas of weakness, and enrichment programs. Some states want to hold principals and teachers accountable by tying their evaluations and salaries to assessments of student progress.

Some argue against high-stakes assessment, suggesting that it works best when it is a central part of teaching, influencing the way we think about curriculum, teaching, and learning. Assessment is to "educate and improve" performance, not merely to audit it. Assessment establishes clear linkage between state and district standards and local testing and grading of students' work. Wiggins (1998) tells us that assessment is central to instruction; that authentic tasks anchor assessment, which anchors teaching; and that performance improvement is locally achieved.

A partial list of Wiggins's (1998) strategies for the future includes:

- Turn tests into prompts and prompts into performance tasks;
- Change typical contextual constraints or limits on resources available during a test;
- Redefine passing to ensure that a grade is standard-based;

TABLE 8.3   *Users and Uses of Assessment Results*

Users	Key Question(s) to Be Answered	Information Needed
Classroom Level		
Student	Am I meeting the teacher's standards? What help do I need to succeed? Are the results worth my investment of energy?	Continuous information about individualized student attainment of specific instructional requirements
Teacher	Which students need what help? Who among my students should work together? What grade should appear in the report card? Did my teaching strategies work? How do I become a better teacher?	Continuous information about individual student attainment of specific program requirements. Continuous assessment of group performance
Parent	Is my child succeeding in school? What does my child need to succeed? Is my child's teacher(s) doing the job? Is this district doing the job?	Continuous feedback on individual students' mastery of required material
Instructional Support Level		
Principal/Vice Principal	Is instruction in particular areas producing results? Is this teacher effective? What kinds of professional development will help? How shall we spend building resources to be effective?	Periodic assessment of group achievement
Lead Teacher (mentor, support teacher, dept. chair)	What does this teacher need to do the job?	Periodic assessment of group achievement
Counselor/ Psychologist	Who needs (can have access to) special support services such as remedial programs? What student should be assigned to which teachers to optimize results?	Periodic assessment of individual achievement
Curriculum Director	Is our program of instruction effective?	Periodic assessment of group achievement

TABLE 8.3   *Continued*

Users	Key Question(s) to Be Answered	Information Needed
Policy Level		
Superintendent	Are programs producing student learning? Is the building principal producing results? Which programs need/deserve more resources?	Periodic assessment of group achievement of district curriculum
School board	Are students in the district learning? Is the superintendent producing results?	Periodic assessment of group achievement
State department of education	Are programs across the state producing results?	Periodic assessment of group achievement of state curriculum
Citizen/legislator (state or national)	Are students in our schools achieving in ways that will allow them to be effective citizens?	Periodic assessment of group achievement of valued achievement targets

Source: Student-Centered Classroom Assessment by Richard J. Stiggins (Columbus, OH: Merrill, 1994). A teacher's handbook distributed by the Assessment Training Institute, 50 SW Second Ave., Suite 300, Portland, OR 97204.

- Get colleagues to "own" the problem of quality;
- Go for scoring consistency;
- Establish a set of R & D task forces;
- Make self-assessment and self-adjustment more central to the job; and
- Provide opportunities, incentives, and criteria that allow each teacher to engage in more careful research into what constitutes effective practice. (pp. 327–329)

School districts should devise a plan for conducting assessments to provide all stakeholders understandable and accurate information about student achievement.

Conclusion

The curriculum provides a statement of what knowledge, skills, and moral principles students will be expected to acquire during their time at school. Program development and delivery "is a decision-making process—constantly balancing the emerging and ever-changing needs of students, society, and the content to be taught. As research adds to the knowledge base, as political systems change, as trends in society change, as technology advances, as we learn more about learning, and as we gain greater insight into the functioning of the human brain, so too must the curriculum change" (Costas, 1997, p. 49).

It is important to realize that one's perspective will determine how the results of program and student assessment will be perceived. Spring (1998) states:

> A newspaper headline reads "Lower Test Scores in City Schools." A religious-right group might give a spin that "lower scores exemplify the lack of instruction in traditional moral values." Another group might spin an interpretation that "lower scores are the result of low academic standards." Or another interested party might respond, "Poor-quality instruction is causing test scores to decline." A spokesperson for a teacher union might put the following spin on the story, "Low teacher salaries make it impossible to keep good teachers, causing test scores to fall." And a union spokesperson might blame "inadequate school funding causes a decline in test scores." A spokesperson for a group representing a cultural minority might provide the following spin: "Culturally biased curriculum causes low test scores." This means that it is very important that the school division take control by characterizing the causes for the scores and actions to be taken in the future regarding curricular and instructional changes. Otherwise they become the fuel for future ideological battles and limited improvement in student performance. (p. 24)

Portfolio Artifacts

- What does your educational platform say about teaching and learning? Developing curriculum? The allocation of time in schools? Developing assessments?
- Analyze and critique a variety of different secondary-school schedules. What are the strengths and weakness of each? What are the implications for teachers in each of these schedules?
- In collaboration with others, devise a schedule using a computer program.
- Participate on a curriculum development or auditing team at the state or local level.

- Write a curriculum for a specific grade or subject level.
- Disaggregate testing data for a school. Use different variables such as grade level, gender, native language, and so forth.
- Implement a curriculum change at your school that has an impact on children from more than one classroom.
- Apply for a grant for an innovative new program.
- Work on a curriculum team focused on improving test scores.

Terms

Adequate yearly progress (AYP)	Curriculum audit	Performance assessment
Apprenticeship learning	Curriculum maps	Portfolios
Authentic instruction	Differentiated instruction	Problem-based learning
Backward instructional design	Hidden curriculum	Thematic instruction
Constructivism	Learning transfer	Triarchic theory
Cooperative learning	Looping	Zone of proximal development
Curriculum alignment	Multiple intelligence theory	
	National standards	
	OTL standards	

Suggested Readings

Beck, L., & Murphy, J. (1996). *The four imperatives of a successful school*. Thousand Oaks, CA: Corwin Press.

Glatthorn, A. (2000). *The principal as curriculum leader: Shaping what is taught and tested* (2nd ed.). Thousand Oaks, CA: Corwin Press.

Jacobs, H. H. (1997). *Mapping the big picture: Integrating curriculum & assessment K–12*. Alexandria, VA: Association for Supervision and Curriculum Development.

Marzano, R., Pickering, D., & Pollock, J. (2001). *Classroom instruction that works: Research-based strategies for increasing student achievement*. Alexandria: VA: Association for Supervision and Curriculum Development.

Payne, R. K. (1996). *A framework for understanding poverty*. Highlands, TX: aha! Process.

Popham, W. J. (2004). *Classroom assessment: What teachers need to know* (4th ed.). Pearson Education.

Wiggins, G., & McTighe, J. (2001). *Understanding by design*. Boston: Allyn and Bacon.

9

Pupil Personnel Services

Special Education

Edgar Allan Poe Middle School currently houses 1,134 students in grades 6 through 8. Poe is comprised of 3 administrators, 38 classroom teachers, 3 guidance counselors, 2 gifted and 2 special education resource teachers, and 1 computer teacher, in addition to other staff. The teachers in the school feel pushed to the limit with large class loads, discipline problems, attendance issues, student apathy, an increase in the special education population, inclusion, and accountability. The teachers are being asked to do more and more, when in reality, the teachers have extended all resources beyond the limit and are having great difficulty dealing with existing responsibilities. The general feeling is that they have been "pushed over the edge."

You as principal of this school are very proud of the IEP process and inclusion model used in this school. Your assistant principal (AP) typically chairs these IEP meetings, but you sat in because the AP was absent and you felt it to be a good opportunity to get a first-hand sense of how the process was working. The first student to be discussed at today's IEP meeting is Natasha, who has a recent history of behavior problems. Natasha was found eligible for special education services in the fourth grade under the category of Learning Disabled (LD) while attending Calcutta Elementary School. She was referred for a re-evaluation in the sixth grade, and her category was changed from LD to Emotional Disturbance (ED). This change in category was initiated because of escalated incidents of verbal and physical aggression. During the sixth grade, Natasha was suspended seven times for a total of twelve days of absences. Natasha's suspensions were for spitting in the teacher's face, hitting and kicking other students, running out of the classroom without permission, and disrupting class.

Natasha, a black female, receives instruction in a special education resource class for Reading/Language Arts. Instruction for Science, Math, Health, and Social Studies are provided in an inclusion classroom. She also receives Speech/Language Therapy twice a week for thirty minutes. Natasha is performing well below grade level and is receiving failing grades. She is experiencing difficulty following directions and acquiring basic skills. She frequently refuses to attempt class assignments even though her class work is on her current achievement level. Her distractibility, impulsiveness, and short attention span has adversely affected her academic achievement. Natasha has been diagnosed with ADHD, Bipolar Disorder, and Oppositional Defiant Disorder. Natasha is currently taking the following medication: Zoloft, Wellbutrin, and Prozac.

The IEP meeting involving the annual review of her daughter's educational program was barely under way when Natasha's mother starts yelling at you. She calls her daughter's classroom teacher and the rest of the staff in the school, including you, uncompassionate. She is very unhappy with the planned IEP modification, to place her daughter at Behavior Horizon, which serves students who are unable to maintain appropriate behavior, and with the way her daughter is being treated by the regular classroom teacher within her inclusion class. She could not be calmed down and got up and said she was going to the superintendent's office to report you, the student's regular classroom teacher, and others for totally neglecting her special education student's welfare. The mother was very aware of the laws related to special education and said she was also going to contact her lawyer since the first IEP was never implemented and her daughter never received the services spelled out in the IEP, which she had consented to.

After the mother left, you discuss this case with all those involved. The classroom teacher immediately became very defensive and stated that the expectations in this school were ridiculous and that inclusion put the responsibilities over the top. The special education resource teacher felt that the environment in the classrooms did not support good instruction for the diverse populations and behaviors within the classroom and that most teachers seemed to be struggling with inclusion and basically ignoring student IEPs and her efforts in their behalf.

The school psychologist questioned the lack of active participation and planning for IEP meetings, the development of behavior improvement plans (BIP), and the resistance that her suggestions met regarding the needs of specific students, and the refusal to adhere to the IEP team's recommendations, and the guidance counselor concurred. It was further discussed that the school often used a somewhat standard IEP and BIP that were completed prior to the meetings. The staff believed that this was efficient and that everyone involved was very pressed for time and the IEP meetings were best if they were quite short. They also mentioned that parents did not understand the pressure that teachers are under and that the meetings were not cordial and had become a real chore. The classroom teacher said, "She was tired of so-called experts telling her what she had to do all the time."

You had sensed a decline in the culture of the school as a result of increases in discipline problems, parent and teacher complaints, and, of course, the fall in scores on state standard tests. You believed that this was caused by the increase in special ed students but that it would work its way out. Obviously, the situation is not getting better. You are now quite concerned about this parent's meeting with the superintendent.

　✳ **How will you determine if students and teachers in Edgar Allan Poe Middle School are struggling with inclusion? How might this be relevant to Natasha's case?**

Pupil Personnel–Student Service Team

Pupil personnel services are an essential component of an effective, modern school system. It is readily acknowledged that children's emotional, social, physical, and mental conditions and their out-of-school experiences are powerful influences on their in-school performances (The Center for the Future of Children, 1992; Children's Defense Fund, 1991; National Commission on Children, 1991). Most all now agree that schools should address the root causes of youth disability and special needs. This service typically requires collecting pupil information, assessing pupil needs, and planning and developing comprehensive programs to ensure that all students are receiving needed service. When exceptionality lowers a student's chances of success and is environmentally caused, the student is described as "at risk." When the causes of exceptionality are organic in nature they are described as handicapping conditions or disabilities.

The pupil personnel services team consists of professionals who specialize in fostering the healthy, career, educational, social, emotional, and intellectual development of all students. Specialists serve as counselors and as guides and provide psychological services, special education, and remedial instruction. They are concerned with child accounting and school safety, school health, speech and hearing therapy, pupil appraisal, testing and diagnostics, and school-court liaison. They also function as social workers and visiting teachers. Figure 9.1 lists the essential services that are part of pupil personnel.

FIGURE 9.1 *Essential Services to Facilitate Student Success*

Three Stages of Enrollment

Preenrollment—the period when one is preparing to enroll in a school.

Enrollment—the period when a student is enrolled.

Postenrollment—the period when a student has left the program whether he or she has advanced to the next level or withdrawn.

Source: C. Maddy-Berstein & E. S. Cunanan (1995). Improving student services in secondary schools. *Office of Student Services Briefs.* 7(2), 3–6. Adapted with permission.

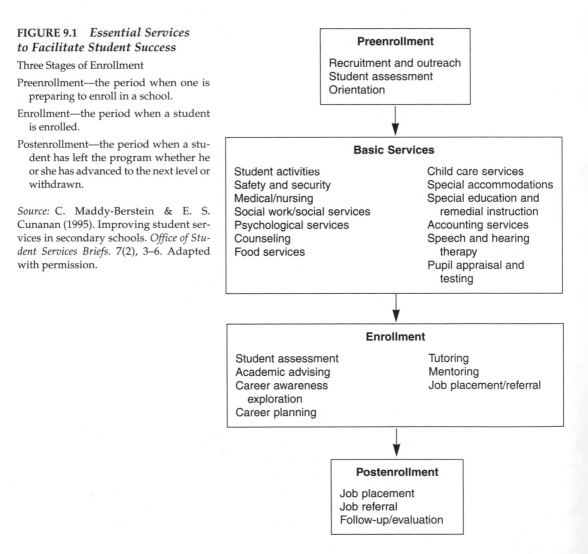

Preenrollment

Recruitment and outreach
Student assessment
Orientation

Basic Services

Student activities
Safety and security
Medical/nursing
Social work/social services
Psychological services
Counseling
Food services

Child care services
Special accommodations
Special education and
 remedial instruction
Accounting services
Speech and hearing
 therapy
Pupil appraisal and
 testing

Enrollment

Student assessment
Academic advising
Career awareness
 exploration
Career planning

Tutoring
Mentoring
Job placement/referral

Postenrollment

Job placement
Job referral
Follow-up/evaluation

Teachers (although parents and students can request services) typically arrange to consult with a specialist to discuss needs for intervention and then make arrangements to discuss the referral with parents and to complete referral forms. This referral often results in a child's being screened by the child study team, followed by a decision regarding formal evaluation. Once a child has been determined to be eligible for special education services, an individualized educational plan (IEP) is written that outlines the specific pupil personnel services a student will begin receiving. Public Law 94-142, the Education for All Handicapped Children Act of 1975, and now called the Individuals with Disabilities Education Act (IDEA), ensures the rights of children with disabilities to a free, appropriate public education, an IEP, special education services, due process procedures, and the least restrictive learning environment.

The 1997 amendments to IDEA have specifically addressed the issue of discipline for students with disabilities. In the case of a child with disabilities whose behavior impedes her or his learning or that of others, the IEP team shall consider strategies and supports to address that behavior. A behavioral intervention plan (BIP) detailing the interventions and supports must be included as part of the IEP for such students.

> ✳ **Whom might you call upon to assist in determining if appropriate programs and services were in place to meet the needs of all students, including Natasha? Describe how they might help.**

Counseling, Guidance, and Psychological Services

The major role of counseling and psychological services is to facilitate wise choices and to promote positive adjustment, mental health, learning abilities, and development. Students' personal, social, educational, and career needs are the focus of the work of guidance counselors and school psychologists. These professionals assist in orientation, provide information, analyze and interpret results, increase possibilities and create new ones, help with decisions and commitments, remove obstacles, and identify emotional problems and learning disabilities, including reading problems. Their role, however, in addressing severe abnormalities should be very limited. Such conditions should be referred to an external professional who is an expert in the treatment of human behavior problems.

School counselors and psychologists work with students individually and in groups and consult parents, teachers, and a diverse group of community service providers. They make recommendations regarding curriculum, instruction, and classroom management to meet the needs of the child. They suggest ways in which parents can work with the school to help their children. They also provide various forms of education programs for parents, children, teachers, and administrators. School psychologists and counselors often assist in compiling significant information, which becomes part of the student's school cumulative record. Quasi-administrative duties such as compiling student records, counting credits, keeping track of attendance, and testing programs tend to get in the way of the performance of duties related to assisting teachers, students, and parents.

Certification for counselors and psychologists is required in all states, although the requirements vary. The school counselor's professional organization is the American School Counselors Association (ASCA), which is a division of the American Counseling Association. The National Association of School Psychologists (NASP) is the professional organization for school psychologists (Neukrug, 2003).

The main function of school psychologists is to provide testing and consultation for special education students. Because the training in school psychology tends to be in testing, human development, and system change, school psychologists are usually not licensed by the state to do counseling or psychotherapy. They are experts in identifying learning disabilities, developmental disorders, physical impairments, or other special needs including the gifted. Many special-needs students are eligible to receive services under IDEA.

The school psychologist works with a team to design a program of services. It blends the best methods of teaching and the most conducive learning environment for the child into a remedial plan to be implemented within the classroom. Although school psychologists spend most of their time on child study activities, they are also involved in consultation, individual and group counseling, research, and program development. They share and interpret results at parent conferences and with child-study teams and write final reports. They follow up on the progress of students and work with others to make needed adjustments for the student (for more information see www.schoolcounselor.org).

School counseling includes developing an active public relations program for staff and the community through newsletters, local media, and school community presentations (Sears & Coy, 1991). Counselors provide a diverse array of services to help students, including advising in academic, social, emotional, and behavioral matters. They address a wide array of issues such as course selection, vocational placement, college selection, parental divorce, dating, loneliness, study habits, controlling aggressiveness, violence, depression, bullying, and many other developmental issues.

✴ **What role do counselors have in helping students like Natasha with their problems, even going back to earlier grades?**

Special Education and Remedial Instruction

The 1975 passage of the Education for All Handicapped Children Act, later known as the Individuals with Disabilities Education Act (IDEA), stressed the placement of services in the least restrictive environment. IDEA defines *special education* as specially designed services and instruction to meet the unique needs of students with disabilities. Turnbull, Turnbull, Shank, and Leal (1995, p. 53) outline five principles for educators in implementing the law.

Principle	Command to Educators
Zero rejects (nondiscriminatory evaluation)	Enroll the student. Determine if the student has a disability and, if so, whether the student needs special education and related services.
Appropriate education	Provide beneficial special education and related services.
Least restrictive environment	Include the student with children who do not have disabilities.
Due procedural process	Check to determine if schools and parents are complying with IDEA.
Parent participation	Collaborate with parents.

To remove barriers presented by a disability, students who will require some modification or accommodations in the environment or the instructional methodology will have a document called a 504 plan. Students who have a disability requiring special education services will have an IEP. The 1997 IDEA lists the following as disabilities that must be addressed by an IEP:

Autism, deaf-blindness, deafness, hearing impairment, mental retardation, multiple disabilities, orthopedic impairment, other health impairment, serious emotional disturbance, specific learning disability, speech or language impairment, traumatic brain injury, and visual impairment.

In addition, the following conditions are to be covered under section 504:

attention deficit disorder—ADD (also attention deficit hyperactivity disorder—ADHD); chronic medical conditions (such as cancer, Tourette syndrome, asthma, or epilepsy); communicable diseases; some temporary medical conditions; physical impairment; and disorders of emotion or behavior. To qualify, there must be a demonstrated and substantial limitation of a major life activity.

There are many possible disabilities, but almost 90 percent of students identified with disabilities typically are categorized as specifically learning disabled, speech or language impaired, mentally retarded, or emotionally disturbed.

Recent Court Revisions (*Cedar Rapids Community School District v. Garret F.*, 1999) suggest that all services necessary by a child with complex health needs are also covered under IDEA as long as a physician does not provide the services. If you knowingly do not provide needed accommodations it can be viewed as discrimination and you can be personally liable for legal action.

When evidence of an exceptionality appears, the psychologist conducts a complete diagnosis of the student to pinpoint strengths and weaknesses and to plan a comprehensive IEP. The diagnosis and classification of children is based on a comprehensive set of assessments in the areas of behavior, achievement, and functioning profiles as measured through interviews, examining records, observation, a battery of psychoeducational assessment instruments, and IQ scores. The functional assessment identifies the abilities, accomplishments, conditions, potential, and full range of challenging behaviors. The results are used to develop complementary strategies that provide the greatest potential for success.

The IEP addresses evaluative information, curriculum plans, and appropriate special education placement and related services. After determining the student's educational program, placement, and need for related services, the team then determines long- and short-term objectives and specific support plans for students in general education placements. These plans meet the individual student's needs while maintaining the integrity of lessons for classmates without disabilities (Giangreco et al., 1993). The students' progress is reevaluated periodically, and specialists work with the classroom teacher to obtain maximum success.

Students might need many different, related services. *The school-community worker, visiting teacher, or school social worker* provides a link between the school, home, and community, rendering interpretation, support, assistance, coordination, advocacy, and investigation services. He or she also assists in the proper enforcement of all laws pertaining to juveniles. *Speech, hearing, and learning specialists* address problems such as sensory loss, speech and language delays, academic achievement delays, writing difficulties, and other communication disorders. These experts provide remediation and compensation and should be certified specialists in their respective fields.

The special education teacher helps identify basic disabilities and develops instruction, lesson plans, materials, and tests. He or she also tests approaches to determine if they are successful and transfers the procedure and materials to the classroom teacher. The main function is to adapt curriculum materials such as assignments, tests, worksheets, reading books, and tests for individual students. Sometimes the special-ed teacher works as a coteacher, jointly planning and team-teaching lessons with the regular classroom teacher. Other times, the special-ed teacher may work with small groups or individual special-needs children within the regular classroom to provide tutorial or remedial assistance.

The special-ed teacher may also pull students out of regular classrooms for intensive individualized and small-group instruction. Children with severe disabilities are sometimes placed with a special-ed teacher in a self-contained classroom and also are included in the mainstream. Special-ed staff provide consultation and training for regular classroom teachers in alternative assessment, instruction, and discipline strategies. These teachers receive specialized training and licensing to work with the special-needs population of students. Some of the additional services from which special education students can benefit are audiology, medical and health services, occupational therapy, physical therapy, recreation, transportation, and assistive technology services (for more information see www.cec.sped.org).

Administrators must advocate the rights of all children to receive needed services and to promote inclusive school practice. An enormous responsibility for a school administrator is to establish and maintain a learning environment that meets the needs of a diverse student body. Administration and leaders will be under continuous pressure to ensure that applicable regulations regarding students with disabilities are observed and that all students achieve success in their schools.

A number of new issues are occurring regarding special education students. One such decision is whether and how to include a special education student in state testing and to ensure such policies are not seen as a way to maneuver students out of state testing so as to raise schoolwide scores. In addition, there is a continuous need to train administrators and teachers so they are prepared to provide leadership for special education programs.

Inclusion

In 1992, the National Association of State Boards of Education (NASBE) published a report titled *Winners All: A Call for Inclusive Schools* (NASBE, 1992), which supported a massive but controversial inclusive schools movement in the United States. Inclusive classrooms place students with exceptionalities in general classrooms, and special education resource teachers work with general classroom teachers in team-teaching modes. Children in inclusive classrooms can take advantage of cooperative learning, curriculum adaptations, classroom aides, environmental accommodations, cooperation between regular and special education teachers, proactive behavior plans, and peer tutoring. In this way the general education of all students is improved while exceptional students receive necessary supports and services in the context of general education (Goodlad & Lovitt, 1993; Turnbull et al., 1995). Requirements for educating students with disabilities in the least restrictive environment are specified in the IDEA amendments of 1997 as follows:

> To the maximum extent appropriate, children with disabilities, including children in public or private institutions or other care facilities, are educated with children who are not disabled. Special classes, separate schools, or other removal of children with disabilities from the regular educational environment occurs only when the nature or severity of the disability of a child is such that education in regular classes with the use of supplementary aids and services cannot be achieved satisfactorily [(sec. 612.(a)(5)].

Initial research suggests that such programs do not have negative effects on either general education or special education students and might actually be a positive experience for both (Salisbury et al., 1993; Walsh & Snyder, 1994; Wang, Reynolds, & Walberg, 1995).

The research suggests that the setting itself is less important than the quality of the program and the transformation within the school to support what is going on in the setting. Effective best practice teaching strategies and an individualized approach are the critical ingredients in special education (Zigmond, 2003). The NCLB Act of 2001 emphasized the addition of effective instructional strategies based on scientific research since special education students' needs are rarely met through general education instruction alone. Teachers will need to implement best practices to meet the needs of their increasingly diverse student population in regular classrooms.

Inclusion is not about differences; it is about our responses to differences. General education classes are the placement of first choice for all learners including disabled learners and all special services and supplemental supports are brought into the classroom, as opposed to removing students from general education class-rooms to receive services. As a result, the number of students with disabilities included in general education classes have dramatically increased. The number of students with disabilities spending 80 percent or more of their time in general education classes went from 25 percent in 1985 to 47.4 percent in 1999. That percentage has increased, in the first half of the 2000s, to greater than 50 percent. However, disparities exist among schools, districts, and states. For instance, these percentages range from a low of 18 percent in Hawaii to a high of 82 percent in Vermont (U.S. Department of Education, 2003).

Inclusion requires the elimination of two separate systems—general education and special education—and the development of only unified general education that includes all students. This includes subjects, school-based programs, curriculum, clubs, sports, extracurricular activities and transportation. The planning of whole-school approaches involves five steps:

- Establish a diverse school planning group
- Conduct a school self-assessment
- Develop the school plan
- Implement the school plan
- Evaluate outcomes and revise the program accordingly (Lipsky, 2003).

Generally, the following characteristics can be found in inclusive schools:

- Programs and procedures are planned to meet the needs of all students, not a one-size-fits-all approach.
- Classrooms are differentiated and use a wide range of curricular materials and instructional strategies.
- Curricular materials are accessible to all and not retrofitted after the fact.
- Peer learning and cross-age tutoring support classroom learning.
- Instructional technology is infused into the curriculum.
- Collaboration between and among school personnel brings greater expertise to instruction and allows for professional development.
- Accommodations and modifications in testing are used to measure what students know and can do.
- Superintendents and principals assume responsibility for the planning, implementation, and outcomes of the education of all their students (Lipsky & Gartner, 2003).

The bottom line is that curriculum and instruction, leadership practices, and school structure might need to change to meet the needs of students of all abilities (Copper, Frattura, & Keyes, 2000; Bartlett, Weisenstein, & Etscheidt, 2002).

According to Villa and Thousand (2003), the degree of administrative support and vision was the most powerful predictor of general educators' attitudes toward inclusion. They stress the importance of meeting the needs of a diverse student population by using, "initiatives and organizational best practices to accomplish this aim, including trans-disciplinary teaming, block scheduling, multi-age student grouping and looping, school wide positive behavior support and discipline approaches, detracking, and school-within-a-school family configurations of students and teachers. These initiatives facilitate the inclusion and development of students with disabilities within general education" (p. 20). They also stress approaches like parallel teaching, supportive teaching (support personnel provide needed assistance), complimentary teaching, co-teaching, alternative teaching, model interactive teaching, and station teaching. Other important best practice elements include cooperate learning, constructivist learning, differentiation instruction, partner learning, authentic learning, demonstrations, whole language, phonics instruction, thematic/interdisciplinary approaches, curriculum overlapping, and technology support (www.imsglobal.org/accessibility/index.cfm;hcam.wgbn.org/webaccess/magpie/). These approaches require scheduling time for planning teams to work and teach each other and to collaborate with parents.

✳   **What evidence will be needed to support the decision to remove Natasha from Edgar Allan Poe Middle School and send her to Behavior Horizon? How might this case influence the service delivery model and the use of proactive strategies for students?**

Leadership for Special Services

JUDY MANTLE • *University of San Diego DeStrunk Endowed Chair in Special Education*

School leaders of special service programs frequently face a multitude of issues and challenges when attempting to orchestrate programs for those who manifest disabilities or other learning needs. When students have needs that depart from those who are served in the *"mainstream,"* discussions can quickly intensify around who should get what types of services and how those services should be provided. This phenomenon appears to become even more evident in times of fiscal restraint. Even the best of school leaders can be challenged by circumstances posed by various students and sometimes from among their family members. Leaders in this capacity are charged with meeting the laws that govern the provision of special services while helping these students realize their maximum potential. In spite of these challenges, school leaders must assure that all students are given the resources and supports needed so that these individuals can access their educational environments and realize their maximum potential.

Fundamental to performing these duties and responsibilities is an introspective examination of one's own attitudes and beliefs about those persons with disabilities and special needs. Reaching a comfort level and becoming truly empathetic toward this population will greatly enhance one's capacity to help those with special needs achieve full access to the curriculum so that they may strive for maximum level of independence and realize the highest quality of life possible given their respective limitations and challenges. Perhaps the most important prerequisite to leading special service programs is a deep and sincere willingness to respect these students as *"persons first"* who happen to have a disability or special need. Then the school leader can engage the appropriate parties who have the talents, skills, and capacity to address these needs while honoring the rights guaranteed by IDEA and other pertinent legislation.

Educational leaders who oversee special services will have an opportunity to greatly enhance their effectiveness in this capacity if they incorporate the following principles into their practice.

1. *Acquire knowledge about the laws* that apply to school aged special needs populations and their families and become clear about everyone's role and responsibilities in providing these services.

2. *Engage directly with those individuals who manifest special needs and their families* so that you can gain an understanding of perspectives about their educational interests first hand. Hopefully it will be possible to learn about factors that hinder one's educational pursuits as well as factors that facilitate the educational progress of these students.

3. Embrace and model a *genuine commitment to serve every aspect of diversity* inherent in the student body under your leadership umbrella, and reward others for doing the same. The message that is sent by a leader's sincere actions that portray a clear advocacy for all students can be extremely powerful.

4. *Explore research-based models of inclusive practice* and engage others in the creative process of brainstorming with you about new possibilities for your school or district. Gather baseline data and monitor results over time to determine whether better results are gleaned from student outcomes data as a result of shifts in service delivery practices.

5. Assure that *expectations for students are appropriate and challenging* given individual strengths and needs. If instructional targets are too high, students become even more at risk for failing. If the instructional targets are too low, the self-fulfilling prophecy may be what becomes actualized, and consequently, students are not challenged to reach their full potential.

6. Utilize a *collaborative model of engagement* with others since effective teamwork is vital for assessing and providing the full range of special services to meet all students' needs. Skills and talents among those who organize and provide a full range of special services must be explored and cultivated by leaders. The capacity and expertise of key individuals in the service delivery process must be understand and communicated so that everyone involved gleans a complete appreciation of the strengths possessed by various personnel who provide services in this arena.

By acquiring the appropriate *knowledge, skills, and dispositions,* school leaders will be able to positively impact persons with disabilities and special needs, their families, teachers, specialists and other support personnel who are concerned with providing quality special service programs for this population. In this way, school leaders can serve as a great inspiration to many and they can make a significant difference in the lives of those who require special support to achieve their education goals.

School Health Services

The school nurse is often the first representative of pupil personnel services to have contact with the child and her or his parents. Parents can inform the school of any unique medical problems, learning disabilities, or emotional problems that might affect the student's educational progress.

The school nurse additionally performs a large number of other services including screening for hearing and visual problems, head lice, tuberculosis, and heart defects; checking teeth and throat; teaching units on human development and personal hygiene; providing emergency first aid; consulting about health problems with teachers and students; and assisting in homebound instruction and in referring children to physicians and social workers. Physicians periodically visit schools to provide medical screening, immunization, diagnosis and referral, and health education and as medical advisers to athletic teams.

An emerging consensus indicates that present health care delivery systems do not meet the needs of children and families (National Commission on Child Welfare and Family Preservation, 1990; Zepeda & Langenback, 1999). School administrators are expected to determine whether the health services provided within the school meet the needs of students. That means periodically assessing the current state of health delivery in the school by reviewing with the school nurse the numbers of students and teachers served, types of services being offered, and services needed.

Child Accounting and School Safety

A significant amount of data is collected and stored on each student, including directory information, demographics, attendance, courses taken, grades, test scores, extracurricular activities, individualized educational plans, deportment, disciplinary action, health, recognitions, and so forth (see Project 4, Chapter 13). The Family Education Rights and Privacy Act (FERPA) restricts accessibility to student records and provides for the removal of inaccuracies. FERPA protects the privacy of students' educational records. Parents and students who reach the age of 18 have the right to inspect and review the student's education records, request that records be corrected when inaccurate or misleading, have the right—after a panel hearing—to place his or her view of contested information within the record, and to approve the release of any information from a student's education record. The school can disclose those records to the following parties without consent:

- School officials with legitimate educational interest
- Other schools to which a student is transferring
- Specified officials for audit or evaluation purposes
- Appropriate parties in connection with financial aid to a student
- Organizations conducting certain studies for or on behalf of the school
- Accrediting organizations
- To comply with a judicial order or lawfully issued subpoena
- Appropriate officials in case of health and safety emergencies
- State and local authorities, with a juvenile justice system, pursuant to specific state law

Schools may also provide some directory information without consent. Schools must notify parents and eligible students annually of their rights under FERPA (www.ed.gov/policy).

Parents do not have the right to inspect counselor, psychologist, and teacher records unless these are part of the student's cumulative records. Many associated activities, such as compulsory attendance, class scheduling, follow-up services, school reports, student eligibility, and dropout prevention depend on accurate student data.

To focus on one example, attendance records can be used to ensure that the child's right to receive a free public education up to a certain age is being enforced. School attendance and other student rights are usually covered in *Students Rights,*

Responsibilities, and Disciplinary Rules pamphlets each family receives, which must comply with school system policy and procedures. Good attendance habits should be established early so problems related to academics, deportment, drop-out rates, and later employment do not develop. Irregular attendance, frequent tardiness, and low achievement are strong predictors that a child might drop out of high school and have later social and economic problems (Achilles & Smith, 1994; Kaplan et al., 1997). The attendance clerk provides monitoring and communication and triggers intervention strategy involving attendance problems.

Although not often used (Schwartz, 1995), the most frequent interventions by school personnel are counseling, remedial education, peer tutoring and mentoring, adult-student mentoring, training, special placement, student advising, safe and disciplined school programs, family partnership, and comprehensive support systems. These programs have proven successful for early intervention for attendance problems, discipline problems, and delinquency prevention.

School Security

Research and experience suggest that much violence in schools is motivated by teasing, being left out, threats, stealing, prejudice, harassment, intimidation, aggression, slurs, taunts, derogatory remarks, and being hit or kicked by one or more other students. Research suggests that as many as 4.8 million U.S. students are victimized and bullied by other students. Bullying does seem to occur more often based on a student's race or ethnicity, religion, disability, gender, or sexual orientation. Bullies enjoy harassing certain types of children—provocative and passive—gaining satisfaction from the pain of their victims.

This bullying is unacknowledged, underreported, and too often ignored. Bullying can be reduced by local, state, and national campaigns to reduce bullying. Harris, Petrie, and Willoughby (2003, p. 11) believe:

> Bullying is part of the daily life of the students in this study. Nearly three out of four students observe some type of bullying at their school. Although most of the bullying is confined to teasing and name-calling, such treatment is still hurtful and cruel, and one in four bullied students feels anger or sadness. Victims are most likely to tell their mother or a friend; they rarely tell a teacher. However, telling is likely to not change anything; it might even make things worse for the victim. In general, students do not feel administrators or teachers support a stop to bullying. Who students tell about being bullied, what happens when they tell, and their perceptions of teacher and administrator support are critical, given that one of the main components in intervention programs is encouraging students to tell someone in authority.

All schools should have policies that prohibit the expression of hate and/or violence against others. (For more information see: www.ed.gov/offices/OSERS/IDEA.) These policies can include:

- Restricting attire that (1) is linked to disruption, (2) is lewd, or (3) presents a safety hazard.

- Allowing random searches of lockers by school personnel and personal searches of students, given reasonable grounds (for example, if detectors are set off or dogs detect drugs).
- Questioning students about violations (police officials involved when there is a breach of the criminal code).
- Prohibiting possession of written or printed material that is divisive or creates hatred; preventing all types of disrespectful behavior.

The challenge in all of this is creating the delicate balance between protecting individual rights and ensuring general welfare.

McCarthy and Webb (2000) discuss this delicate balance:

> Some limitations on student behavior are necessary to prevent violence in public schools, but students' rights must be protected in imposing such restrictions. Student handbooks should clearly describe the rationale for any conduct regulations and the consequences for noncompliance. Disciplinary rules should be discussed with the students, their justification should be debated, and rules should be eliminated if they lack a sound educational or safety rationale. Any constraints imposed on students' freedom must be necessary to protect the general welfare and advance the school's educational mission. Students should feel safe, but they should not view schools as prisons where they have lost all personal liberties.
>
> Moreover, school authorities' emphasis should be on the prevention of antisocial and illegal behavior rather than on punitive action. Schools need to make every effort to encourage students to engage in civil conduct and healthful living and to use mediation to resolve conflicts. Student assemblies and group and individual counseling sessions can assist students in learning to treat others with respect and to expect such treatment in return. Various programs, some of which include simulations and role-playing exercises, are available to help students acquire mediation skills so they can resolve conflicts without resorting to violence and can empathize with individuals who are the victims of disrespectful or harassing behavior. (p. 43)

Another aspect of school security is to lock doors, install video cameras and metal detectors, and assign police to patrol the school. These signal a fear of violence, however, and certainly do not make students feel safe. Today's children need to be respected and helped to feel secure within their schools. Students need to have a clearly defined forum in which they can express their concerns. That requires an active counseling staff, teachers who care about students, and administrators who are welcoming, and have an open door to students and their parents. Educators should invite and welcome both written and verbal expression of student concerns and feedback and be prepared to address those concerns. Most of all everyone within the school should take harassment of any form very seriously and put procedures in place to prevent disrespectful behavior (see School Safety Audit in Chapter 5).

Student Discipline

Most schools have codes of student conduct that are to be enforced by the teachers, administrators, and pupil personnel workers. Administrators are responsible for

reinforcing teacher disciplinary actions and taking responsibility for the more difficult or unusual behavior problems. Discipline and safety have been linked to
pupil achievement and student attendance. Traditional methods (Kimbrough &
Burket, 1990, p. 277) for correcting student behavior include (1) corporal punishment, (2) reprimands, (3) detention, (4) enforced duties, (5) suspension from school,
(6) in-school suspension, and (7) expulsion from school. The disciplinarian must be
consistent, tough, deliberate, fair, just, and compassionate and perceived as such.
Youth, and particularly inner-city youth, want the security and predictability that
accompany clear codes of conduct and consistent, clear, and firm discipline. Inner-
city youth seek the concern and security conveyed by strong discipline as long as
they perceive the discipline as swift, certain, and fair (McLaughlin, Irby, & Longman, 1994).

In order of teachers' perceived frequency of occurrence, school problems over
the past decade include:

- Physical conflict among students
- Conflict and abuse involving teachers and other staff
- Student use of alcohol
- Student use of illegal drugs
- Vandalism of school property
- Robbery and theft
- Student possession and occasional use of weapons

Teachers also suggest that the nature of each of these school problems is more serious than in the past (Shen, 1997). All of these problems are much more serious in
secondary schools than in elementary schools. Shen (1997) suggests, "When we discuss school violence, students are usually the center of concern. But given the increasing severity of verbal abuse of teachers, educators also deserve our attention"
(p. 20).

The 1989 U.S. Supreme Court decision in *Honig v. Doe* found that students
with disabilities cannot be unilaterally suspended or expelled for more than ten
days without provisions for due process. This triggered many new procedures.
Functional Behavior Assessment (FBA) is a systematic process for identifying the
causes for problem behaviors and developing an effective plan to reduce the severity or eliminate the problem behaviors. The purpose of an FBA is to collect information to explain the relationship among associated environmental factors and the
problem behavior. The problem behavior can then be addressed through the IEP
process and behavior intervention plan (BIP).

The FBA addresses the relationship between precipitating conditions, the behavior, its consequences, and the function of the behavior. The precipitating conditions identify specific triggers related to the behavior such as setting, time, cause,
provocation, who's in the environment, and so on. The specific behavior describes
the pattern of behavior that the student has demonstrated including a specific description of what the student does or does not do. The consequences describe the
responses or events, both situational and personal, that typically follow the behavior. The function of the behavior allows professionals to hypothesize about the

purpose the behavior serves such as avoidance, gaining attention, anger, frustration, vengeance, control, intimidation, anxiety relief, and so on. Assessment techniques (e.g., observation, rating, interview, taping) and related information (e.g., academic, social/peer, family) are also provided (Fad, Patton, & Polloway, 2000).

Section 612 (a)(1) of the IDEA amendment of 1997 and the 1999 IDEA final regulations state that free, appropriate public education (FAPE) shall be available to all children with disabilities, ages 3–21, and restrict suspensions to ten school days and interim alternative education settings (IAES) to ten days except in cases involving weapons or illegal drugs. Weapons or drug violations warrant suspension for not more than forty-five days. The expulsion and discipline provision requires a hearing to determine whether there is a manifestation (disability causes behavior). The manifestation hearing must be held in cases of (a) weapons, (b) drugs, (c) dangerous behavior, or (d) any discipline for more than ten days. If the school has not already conducted a *functional behavioral assessment* (FBA) and implemented a *behavioral intervention plan* (BIP) before disciplining the student, the IEP team must do so. If the school, however, has conducted a functional behavioral assessment and developed a behavioral intervention plan, the IEP team must review and modify the plan, "as necessary, to address the behavior."

The purpose of the BIP is to provide appropriate responses, including strategies for improving the student's behavior, in order to complement the IEP. Appropriate practice suggests that BIPs include the following components: specific goals, proposed interventions, person(s) responsible, methods, evaluation criterion, and the timelines to be followed. Table 9.1 provides a list of possible intervention strategies for improving student behavior.

According to Johns (1998), success lies in a series of action steps that school administrators should implement. First and foremost is the establishment of total staff commitment to the process. School discipline policies and procedures must be established with input from all parties. Plans should treat students with respect, place responsibility on students, encourage appropriate choices, and teach social skills. School personnel need in-depth training, the opportunity to practice behavioral management, and technical support in these applications. Students must know what is expected of them in all school settings. Staff must recognize students who follow the rules and must establish logical consequences for those who do not. For instance, it is illogical to only suspend a student for property damage; a logical consequence is for the student to pay for or repair the property.

Those involved in disciplining students are often in an ideal position to identify troubled students who might be in the need of special services. This requires the use of computer systems to capture all disciplinary action and concerns regarding a student, along with formal review procedures for monitoring and assessing these student needs. Ultimately, parents and community agencies will need to be involved to get students the right kind of help.

Horner, Sugai, and Horner (2000) suggest, "Too often efforts to remove or contain the small number of the most disruptive students simply results in identification of an ever-increasing number of these students" (p. 22). They found that functional behavior assessment and implementation plans resulted in problem behaviors being reduced. They also suggest that zero tolerance and get-tough

TABLE 9.1 *Intervention Strategies for Improving Student Behavior*

A. Restructuring Precipitating Conditions (Antecedents)
1. Remove distracting materials
2. Provide quiet, separate seating area
3. Modify academic requirements
4. Use visual cues/signal/advance organizers
5. Provide written or visual schedule
6. Use proximity cues
7. Provide choices related to assignments
8. Use gestures, physical cues
9. Minimize transition time
10. Other: _____

B. Instructional Techniques
1. Teach class rules and establish expectations/ set limits
2. Model desirable behavior
3. Use strategic placement
4. Role play
5. Coach through use of corrective feedback
6. Provide literature-based lessons
7. Monitor and provide written feedback
8. Develop student–teacher contract
9. Develop student–parent contract
10. Teach self-monitoring
11. Show and discuss videotapes
12. Use team-building activities
13. Provide social skills games
14. Organize group discussions
15. Other: _____

C. Consequences for Positive Behaviors
1. Use frequent, consistent, specific verbal praise
2. Provide positive social reinforcement
3. Establish point system
4. Establish in-class or in-school reward system
5. Establish home-school reward system
6. Establish token economy
7. Provide consumable reinforcement
8. Provide tangible reinforcement
9. Refer to other adults for praise
10. Use privileges/responsibilities
11. Use private praise
12. Other: _____

D. Consequences to Reduce Misbehavior
1. Use nonverbal signals
2. Provide vergal reminder/reprimand
3. Set up system of planned ignoring
4. Use a structured warning system
5. Assign essays/writing assignments
6. Use cost response procedures
7. Provide time to cool off at desk or other area
8. Implement loss of privileges
9. Arrange student–teacher conference
10. Implement previously agreed behavior contract
11. Refer to counselor or mentor
12. Telephone parent(s)
13. Use lunch detention
14. Use after school detention
15. Implement in-school suspension for _____ periods/days
16. Contract parent and send student home for remainder of day
17. Set up in-school suspension up to 10 school days without committee meeting
18. Suspend up to 3 consecutive days without committee meeting
19. Place in Alternative Educational Placement up to 10 school days without committee meeting
20. Other: _____

Evaluation Methods
1. Behavior monitoring forms (e.g., contracts, point sheets)
2. Grades on assignments recorded in grade book
3. Anecdotal records
4. Attendance records
5. Tally sheets or hand-held counter of the frequency of target behavior(s)
6. Tape recordings (audio or video)
7. Progress reports/interim notices
8. Portfolios/work samples
9. Student self-assessments or ratings
10. Teacher/parent rating scales
11. IEP review forms
12. Parent feedback forms
13. Time totals on stopwatches
14. Graphing behavioral performance
15. Other: _____

Source: K. Fad, J. Patton, & E. Polloway (2000). *Behavior intervention planning.* Austin, TX: Pro-ED.

punishment and exclusion policies without proactive approaches to improvement "is associated with increases in aggression, vandalism, truancy, and dropouts" (p. 22). They conclude that "administrators, in particular, need to define school wide discipline as a major goal within their school, build disciplinary systems to complement traditional reactive systems and establish assessment and intervention programs. (www.pbis.org; www.ed.gov/offices/osers/osep/earlywrn.html.)

＊ **If Natasha was to stay at the Middle School, what might be some proactive strategies to give her and the teacher greater support? What is Natasha's impact on school safety and security and how might discipline policies help in this case?**

Pupil Appraisal, Testing, and Diagnostics

Testing and diagnostic programs are often organized schoolwide or systemwide for administering standardized tests. These programs supplement the wide variety of teacher-made tests prepared for use in a single class or school. Tests are used to diagnose difficulties, identify aptitudes and discrepancies, appraise achievement, group students, identify needs, assess competencies, and create accountability. They are also used to inform the public. A major part of most testing and diagnostic programs is achievement testing. A common approach is a standardized norm-referenced test. Other types of tests include criterion-referenced, objective-referenced, domain-referenced, intelligence, minimum competency, and performance assessment.

Testing helps school staff, students, and parents in assessing learning and planning educational programs and helps school students in making educational and life choices and plans. Testing is also used to compare schools and districts, plan curriculum, assess effectiveness, stimulate reform, and provide recognition. The demand for greater accountability and higher standards is increasing the importance of assessment (Hymes et al., 1991, p. 32).

A major area of concern in testing and appraisal, as a result of the NCLB legislation, is "how are our students, teachers, and administrators doing and are things improving in our schools?" As a result, high-stakes testing is being used to determine if students are promoted and will graduate (26 states by 2003) and to provide a "school report card" for the teachers and administrators. The data collected is used to both facilitate instruction (a diagnostic tool) and to make comparisons and hold administrators, teachers, and students accountable (communicating with parents and community).

Data-driven decision making is a major theme in educational leadership today. The major data used today is the state student performance test, which reports the percentage of students in the school who answered questions correctly and meet state standards. The focus is placed on maintaining progress in areas of success and focusing additional attention on the weak content or skills areas (did not meet state standard or average yearly progress).

The idea of the analysis is to identify problem areas that stand out by comparing scores to standards, to previous years' performance, to resources available and time devoted, to supporting materials and textbooks, to other schools and leaders, and to curriculum and instructional strategies in order to identify and target areas needing attention. The analysis should focus on causes of poor performance such as alignment issues, changes from year-to-year, problems with special ed or at-risk students, reading problems, differences among teacher or schools, ineffective use of time, resources and/or supporting materials and so on.

Figure 9.2 provides an illustration of the type of data that might be used to track performance in an elementary school. This data can be used to track the performance/progress of the student, teacher, program, school, and district. The data is most helpful when it is in a sequence and format that disaggregates the data in such a way that problems, trends, comparisons, etc. can easily be made. This can become more complex for standards, and related assessment, that cover a number of different grade levels, not just the tested grade level, where skills are developed and built up over time. Figure 9.3 provides a simple example of how data might be aggregated for fifth-grade students for one school. The discipline data for the school appears in Figure 9.4.

Whether tests really measure what students need to be able to do to succeed in the twenty-first century is a growing concern. Many believe that performance assessment and demonstrations are better suited to measure the skills and abilities that students will need to be successful in a world that is undergoing significant transformation (see Chapter 2). Given the debate, testing and research experts must determine the role of testing within their school districts. Perhaps the single best resource for gaining greater understanding of these and other related complex concerns is the American Educational Research Association (AERA). (For more information see: www.aera.net.)

It is clear that test scores and what to do to improve them will occupy significantly more time in the administrator's future. This will include choosing assessments, determining how to interpret them, providing incentives and sanctions to encourage improvement, and developing programs that will allow students to be successful on assessments. The curriculum, the standards, and the assessment must all flow together. The general purpose of all final reports is to summarize, organize, and interpret test results so that a meaningful picture of the school or the individual emerge. (For more information see: www.nces.ed.gov/nationsreportcard.)

✳ **What will be the sources of data used in an inquiry-oriented data-driven approach when working toward the success of Natasha and other such students at Edgar Allan Poe Middle School?**

Extracurricular Activities

Athletics tends to be the most prominent of all extracurricular activities. Through athletics students set personal goals, learn to be responsible, develop self-discipline, learn to work with others, adjust to the many personalities and situations that arise, learn dedication, sacrifice, and patience, and develop lifelong physical fitness habits. Studies suggest that participation in sports contributes to better academic

FIGURE 9.2   *Core Data Elements to Track Yearly • Elementary Schools*

Key Performance Indicators—For Each Content Area (Language Arts/English, Mathematics, Science, History/Social Science)

- Number/percent of students passing each of the SOL* tests (grades 3 and 5)
- Number/percent of students failing each of the SOL tests (grades 3 and 5)
- Number/percent of students requiring remediation for each of the SOL areas
- Number/percent of students successfully completing remediation for each SOL area
- Number/percent of 4th grade students scoring above the 50 th percentile on the Stanford 9 achievement tests.
- Number/percent of the 4th grade students scoring in the first Quartile on the Stanford 9 Achievement Tests
- Number/percent of students meeting or exceeding expectations of SOL objectives in grades K–3 (score of 3 or 4 on a 1–4 scale)
- Number/percent of students in grades 3–5 with satisfactory report card grades
- Number/percent of students reading on grade level
- Number/percent of students promoted to the next grade.

*Standard of Learning

Demographic Indicators

- Number/percent of minority students passing each of the SOL tests (grades 3 and 5)
- Number/percent of mobility (transfer) students passing each of the SOL tests (grades 3 and 5)
- Number/percent of special education students participating in SOL tests
- Number/percent of students (by disability category) participating in SOL tests

Community Indicators

- Number/percent of parents in PTA
- Number/percent of parents satisfied with quality of education students are receiving at school

School Characteristics Indicators

- Number/percent of teachers with advanced degrees
- Number/percent of students attending school on a daily basis—missing 10 or fewer days per year
- Number/percent of students on free or reduced price lunches
- Number of student referrals for discipline

Use this space to list other school data you want to track yearly.

- Percent of teachers meeting state licensure requirements.
- Percent of staff involved in professional development activity.

Source: Core Data Elements to Track Yearly, copyright 2000 by Successline, Inc.
Reproduced by Permission of Deborah Wahlstrom.

FIGURE 9.3   *Percentage of Students Passing SOL Tests—Seaside Elementary School*

Subject Grade 5	Previous Year			Current Year			Below Average	Average	Above Average
	Non-White	White	Total	Non-White	White	Total			
English/ Reading	28.08	34.80	62.88	25.08	35.73	60.81*			
Math	16.01	23.21	39.22	20.08	28.10	48.18*			
Science	28.04	35.00	63.04	30.15	40.18	70.33			
History	15.81	18.07	33.88	10.61	14.07	24.68*			
Writing	20.70	24.27	44.97	28.04	30.40	58.44*			

*Did not meet state requirement of a 70% pass rate

▬▬▬▬ Comparison to District Averages

▬ ▬ ▬ ▬ Comparison to State Averages

Evidence of Need: SOL testing showed that Science was the only subject area with a pass rate higher than the standard score for the state. The scores in English/Reading and writing were a particular concern since they may be affecting other areas, and they are much closer to the needed pass rate. The noteworthy weakness in the areas of mathematics and history were particularly troubling since the students answered a majority of the questions with the same answer choices that were the wrong choices. There was discouragement in that English/Reading and history scores actually declined from the previous year. This is a school with a majority of free/reduced lunch students whom has particularly low scores on the SOL assessment as did the large population of special education students.

School-Based Goals: The school will implement writing across the curriculum and reading recover strategies to improve SOL test scores from the 60.81 and 58.80 percentiles to at least the 70 percentile in both English/Reading and writing. Math and history teachers need to visit other schools that are having greater success on SOL tests to discuss appropriate and additional instructional strategies to raise pass rates for each subgroup. Increase the participation rate of economically disadvantaged and special education populations in special remediation and support programs. We will also increase the use of manipulates in all math programs and remediation. We will expand on the number of computer-based programs available to help these students, afterschool-based training programs for teachers, and remediation programs for students.

performance, serves to keep many students in school, and inspires greater involvement and leadership (Holland & Andre, 1991; Reith, 1989).

Athletics are magnified by the press and it is quite important to operate an honest, well-organized, and safe program. Schools typically must follow the athletic rules and regulations that are established for the region and state. Student-athletes should put academics first and should model exemplary behavior. An athletic director typically reports to the principal and is responsible for the entire athletic program. The coaches and assistant coaches report to the athletic director. The athletic trainer also reports to the athletic director and is responsible for medical coverage for

FIGURE 9.4   *Seaside Elementary School Student Referral Report—All Students*

	Previous Year	Current Year	Change from Previous Year
Assault	13	4	−9
Bus referrals	166	206	+40
Disorderly conduct	128	173	+45
Drug/Tobacco violations	0	3	+3
Fighting	4	19	+15
Robbery/Theft	12	12	0
Sexual offenses	1	8	+7
Threat/Intimidation	6	3	−3
Weapons	3	5	+2
Vandalism	2	6	+4
TOTAL	335	439	+104

Evidence of Need: With an enrollment of 628 students there is a .16/1 incidence ratio for the current year compared to a .12/1 incident ratio last year, which is of serious concern. Eighty-two percent of the referrals come from 2nd, 4th, and 5th grade students. Eighty-seven percent of all referrals were male. Seventy-six percent were students receiving free/reduced lunch and 62 percent were black. Fourteen percent of the same students represent 70 percent of the student referrals. The following disciplinary consequences were prescribed: 149 in-school suspension, 62-out-of-school suspensions, 4 alternative-education placements, 149 bus suspensions, 70 written warnings.

School-Based Goals: The administrators will implement a high administrative visibility program visiting every classroom once or twice on a daily basis as a strong deterrent to student misconduct. An intervention program will be designed and implemented by the guidance counselors and the physical education teacher and others will informally mentor struggling and multi-referral students (special time will be made available to proactively impact student behavior).

all athletics. In addition, good managers are critical to running an efficient program. Coaches along with the athletic director are responsible for schedules, uniforms, player eligibility, tryouts, parental contacts, coaching, team travel, safety, discipline, recognition, and many other aspects of athletic programs.

Sports are not the only extracurricular activities within schools. Many different honorary, service, class related, and special interest clubs exist as well as various types of field-trips and school activities. The primary purpose of all of these programs is to provide unique learning experiences while developing a positive school climate, school spirit, and fellowship, which add to the overall morale of the school. Susan Gerber (1996) found that the amount of participation in extracurricular activities also was positively related to academic achievement.

These programs depend on the commitment of school staff to provide a comprehensive range of student activities that meets the needs and interests of all students. The faculty sponsor and the treasurer of each organization participate in the management of finances according to the policy of the state board of education, school board, and superintendent. Itemized day-by-day receipts and expenditures are recorded with the school bookkeeper. In many schools the student cooperative association (SCA) has a responsibility to oversee and to disseminate information about school activities. Extracurricular activities also receive support from student services, parent–teacher associations, and a number of community sponsors.

The goal is to provide a wide variety of extracurricular activities to meet the needs and interests of as many students as possible. Students involved in these kinds of cocurricular activities find opportunities to shine and are less likely to become disengaged from school. A Gallup survey showed that participation in cocurricular activity is positively correlated with high school and post–high school academic achievement as well as occupational status after graduation.

Usually, one person is designated in each school to coordinate extracurricular activity. Sometimes students must meet specific criteria to be allowed to participate in an extracurricular activity. Written and well-understood rules and regulations for the governance of these activities are important. Issues sometimes develop around adult interference, broken rules, overcompetitiveness, overemphasis, interference with academics, irrelevance, financial problems, faculty supervision, equitable treatment, transportation, and prejudice.

Extracurricular activities are becoming even more important as safe spaces for children are shrinking as those for adults are expanding—restaurants, health clubs, tennis clubs, golf courses, sports and entertainment complexes, resorts. Many argue that technology as well as television is further privatizing lives and making needed human interactions even less available to children who desperately need them.

✳ **Should students like Natasha participate in extracurricular activities? Why or why not? What policies and supporting activities should exist regarding student participation in extracurricular activities? How would you respond to Natasha's mother's right to challenge the appropriateness of educational services being planned for her daughter?**

Conclusion

Many programs are needed to address the social, emotional, and affective needs of students and to balance them with their educational needs. If such programs are not developed, schools will continue to experience high drop-out, failure, and expulsion rates. These failures take a high toll on the future use of society's resources for remediation of social problems. The challenge to educators, then, is to achieve the difficult and sometimes shifting balance between academics and successful human development and thus produce productive citizens.

Pupil personnel services help schools confront difficult issues that keep students from achieving academic success. All the professionals within a school are encouraged to contribute their unique knowledge and skills to the goal of achieving competent, well-educated, and well-adjusted students, and, ultimately, self-sufficient adults.

With the support of public policy, more and more special-needs students are receiving assistance and being accommodated in regular classes. The inclusion of a pupil personnel plan to complement classroom activity has proven absolutely essential to student success. The focus of pupil personnel services is to help remediate developmental issues within a student's life and to enable the student to reach his or her full potential. When pupil personnel services are well organized and integrated into the culture of the school and community, they make a substantive contribution to student achievement by better preparing students to participate in the academic work and by improving their lives. Professionals who provide these services have a formidable responsibility to adhere to the highest professional and ethical standards. Changes within a variety of disciplines, judicial decisions, legislation, societal changes, child development research, technological and other advancements, and many other forces will continue to have enormous impact on pupil personnel practices. Keeping up with the trends and issues in the decades ahead will be an exciting, challenging, sometimes frustrating but always rewarding endeavor.

Portfolio Artifacts

- Prepare a BIP or FBP for a chronically disciplined student.
- Decide the fate of an appeal for a student.
- Discuss a discipline referral with a teacher, hold a conference with person(s) involved, and assign appropriate disciplinary action.
- Develop strategies for creating inclusive learning communities that promote equity and learning for all students.
- Contact community resources to provide enrichment for students in need and their families (mobilize and leverage community support services).
- Determine how a school supports high expectations for student behavior in a context of care.
- Develop some proactive strategies for students who need more intense support.
- Identify a variety of curriculum accommodations and teaching techniques that respond to a wide range of individual differences.
- Develop concrete anti-harassment policy and strategies.
- Conduct/oversee a child-study team and oversee an individualized educational plan (IEP) causality meeting.
- Visit a home with a school social worker and write a report on your experience.
- Participate in a group counseling session with a small group of people and keep a reflective journal of your experiences.
- Work with a school psychologist in administering and interpreting tests.
- Spend a day with a social worker, juvenile court judge, pediatrician, surgeon, law enforcement officer, mental health worker, health department worker, or park and recreational worker (check insurances and protect your safety).
- Shadow the director of pupil personnel services.
- Serve as a faculty sponsor for an extracurricular activity.

Terms

Behavior intervention plan	Data-driven decision making	Extracurricular activity
Differentiated instruction	The Education for all	Functional behavior
Data disaggregation	Handicapped Children Act	assessment (FBA)

Individualized educational plan (IEP)	In-school suspension	School counseling
Individuals with Disabilities Education Act (IDEA)	Learning disability (LD)	School psychologist
	Mainstreaming and inclusion	504 plan
	Norm-referenced test	

Suggested Readings

Bartlett, L., Weisenstein, G., & Etscheidt, S. (2002). *Successful inclusion for educational leaders.* Upper Saddle River, NJ: Merrill/Prentice Hall.

Burrello, L., Lashley, C., & Beatty, E. (2001). *Educating all students together: How school leaders create unified systems.* Thousand Oaks, CA: Corwin Press.

Capper, C., Frattura, E., & Keyes, M. (2000). *Meeting the needs of students of all abilities.* Thousand Oaks, CA: Corwin Press.

Center for Effective Collaboration and Practice. (1998, January 16). *Addressing student problem behavior.* Washington, DC: American Institutes for Research.

Doyle, L. H. (2002). "Leadership and special education: A study of powershifts," *Journal of School Leadership.* 12, 1:23–56.

Dryfoos, G. (1994). *Full-service schools.* San Francisco: Jossey-Bass.

Dryfoos, G. (1998). *Safe passage: Making it through adolescence in a risky society.* New York: Oxford University Press.

Duke, D. L. (2002). *Creating safe schools for all children.* Boston: Allyn and Bacon.

Fad, K. M., Patton, J. R., & Polloway, E. A. (2000). *Behavioral intervention planning.* Austin, TX: Pro-Ed.

Hughes, F. P., & Noppe, L. D. (1991). *Human development: Across the life span.* New York: Macmillan Publishing Company.

Newkrug, E. (2003). *The world of the counselor.* Pacific Grove, CA: Brooks/Cole.

Strange, J., & Tucker, P. (2003). *Handbook on educational specialist evaluation: Assessing and improving performance.* Larchmont, NY: Eye On Education.

Tomlinson, C., & Allan, S. (2002). *Leadership for differentiating schools and classrooms.* Alexandria, VA: ASCD.

Turnbull, A. P., Turnbull, R. H., Shank, M., & Leal, D. (1995) *Exceptional lives: Special education in today's schools.* Englewood Cliffs, NJ: Prentice-Hall.

Turnbull, R., & Cilley, M. (1999). *Explanation and implementations of the 1997 amendments to IDEA.* Upper Saddle River, NJ: Merrill.

Zepeda, S. J., & Langenbach, M. (1999). *Special programs in regular schools.* Boston: Allyn and Bacon.

10

Human Resource Management

Staffing Problems

You are a new principal, newly appointed to Lincoln Elementary School. The assistant superintendent for human resource development (HRD) is Dr. Fred Henry, with whom you have an excellent working relationship and rapport. Dr. Henry is totally collaborative in his management style and has full confidence in you as principal. You and he agree on how to handle almost all HRD situations.

Two weeks ago, your school district announced plans to assign and bus students to Lincoln Elementary School because of its low enrollment. This is not an unprecedented action in your district. One week ago, the district held open hearings to discuss this decision. Three days ago the board reaffirmed their position. Since the busing order, you have been very aware that many parents, teachers, and children are concerned, apprehensive, and angry. Busing will begin at Lincoln in the next academic year. It is January, and staffing plans and student assignments will need to be completed over the next three months. This new plan is described as the capacity adjustment program (CAP).

Yesterday you received a call from Brad Brakeman, the school advisory chairman, and Elena Lopez, the building representative (who is the teacher elected by the faculty to represent them). They have asked that you meet with both of them to consider and address the concerns of

parents, teachers, and children and to discuss your short- and long-range implementation plans regarding the busing order.

You know that you and others must address the concerns of parents, teachers, and children and gain their support for short- and long-range plans to make the change a positive experience for affected parties. You know that the school advisory chairperson and building representative share many of the parents' concerns. You are very aware that it is of utmost importance that you as a new principal gain the support and confidence of these individuals.

The Receiving School: Lincoln Elementary School

Lincoln Elementary School is located in a wealthy and stable area of the city. The school's enrollment has been declining over the last four years, as citizens in the immediate community have become older. The building can hold 1,200 students; currently only 875 children are enrolled in the school. Lincoln prides itself on its academic achievements and school spirit. It has very active parent groups and a large number of parent volunteers. It has won beautification awards and Junior Achievement awards. Many of its students go on to graduate from college.

Lincoln has a magnet program in mathematics. About 200 high-ability math students from adjacent schools are bused to Lincoln. This program has always been controversial, as parents from all schools involved are concerned about their children's safety and social acceptance at Lincoln. Others complain that the magnet program takes the best and brightest students from the sending schools.

The magnet math program has attracted a minority ratio slightly higher than the number that live in the school attendance zone. The student population is 1 percent Asian, 18 percent African American, 21 percent Hispanic, and 60 percent white. On standardized tests, Lincoln students score in the 75th percentile in reading, the 72nd percentile in oral language, and the 82nd percentile in math.

The Sending School:
Washington Elementary School
The students that will be identified as CAP students to attend Lincoln will come from Washington Elementary School, which is now severely overcrowded. It was selected as the sending school because of its overcrowding and proximity to Lincoln. The neighborhood around Washington can be characterized as "the wrong side of the tracks" compared with Lincoln's. The neighborhood is economically very poor and somewhat transient. It is not uncommon for children to come from single-parent families or homes where both parents work. There is a high rate of juvenile crime, child abuse, and child prostitution. Washington is not considered a good school. Those parents who can afford it send their children to private schools.

The school population at Washington is 55 percent Arabic, 12 percent African American, 25 percent Hispanic, and 8 percent white. Most of the Arabic students don't speak English very well, since their parents recently immigrated from countries such as Lebanon, Iran, Saudia Arabia, Kuwait, and Jordan. Arabic children come from the poorest families. There is animosity among the students in these neighborhoods, especially in the junior high and high schools.

On standardized tests, Washington students score in the 25th percentile in reading, the 27th percentile in oral language, and the 15th percentile in math.

The table presents the school capacities, staffing patterns, and student enrollment this year, at the two schools. To simplify this vignette, all teachers and students will return at both schools, and all students will pass to the next grade. In addition, next year, student enrollment will grow by 210 at Washington and 65 at Lincoln, as shown in the table. The data presented in this table represent the planned pattern before the CAP decision to transfer students and implement the student busing plan. The total for kindergarten next year will be 232 for Washington and 50 at Lincoln, before the CAP decision is made. You have been asked to reconfigure both students and staff to meet the superintendent and school board's objectives regarding the transfer of Washington students to Lincoln.

The Complaints and Concerns
Listed below are the concerns of parents, parent groups, and teachers that have been brought to your attention by Brad Brakeman and Elena Lopez:

1. Lincoln has an excellent academic environment; the bused students will lower educational standards. A third-grader in Washington is not equivalent to the third-grader in Lincoln. They use different textbooks. The Washington school is so poor that the better students go to private schools. Lincoln will lose its famous school spirit.

2. There is too much busing. Why do so many young children's lives have to be disrupted? The values of a community school are being lost.

3. Teachers will not be able to effectively instruct children with such diverse abilities, and everyone concerned will suffer.

4. The communities of sending and receiving schools are complete opposites, and people in these neighborhoods have always disliked one another. Children from these communities have totally different experiences and family environments. It will be impossible for teachers to relate their instructional objectives to children with such different life experiences.

School Capacities, Staffing Patterns, and Student Enrollments for This Year and Next Year Prior to the New Student Transfer Capacity Adjustment Plan (CAP)

Washington		Lincoln	
Capacity:	960 Students	Capacity:	1,200 Students
Total Enrollment:	1,160 Students	Total Enrollment	875 Students
Total Classrooms:	37	Total Classrooms:	50
Student/Teacher Ratio:	29/1	Student/Teacher Ratio:	24.3/1
+3-year Target:	25/1	+3-year Target:	25/1

	Washington				Lincoln			
Grade	Teachers	Teacher Aides	Present Year Student Enrollment	Projected Additions Next Year	Teachers	Teacher Aides	Present Year Student Enrollment	Projected Additions Next Year
6	6	3	146	+40	8	8	200	+25
5	6	3	146	+30	7	7	179	+10
4	6	3	174	+25	7	7	174	+10
3	5	3	145	+25	5	5	118	+10
2	5	3	145	+25	4	4	91	+ 5
1	6	3	202	+35	3	3	68	+ 0
K	6	6	202	+30	2	2	45	+ 5
	40	24	1,160	210	36	36	875	65

Washington	Lincoln
1 Principal	1 Principal
1 Assistant Principal	1 Assistant Principal
1 In-School Suspension Coordinator	1 Gifted-Program Coordinator
2 Special-Education Coordinators	1 Bilingual-Program Coordinator
1 Title-1 Coordinator	1 Special-Education Coordinator
2 Counselors	1 Resource Specialist
2 Secretaries	1 Counselor
2 Nurses	2 Secretaries
	1 Nurse

5. Busing will require the development of a bilingual program for children who speak Arabic, and no one on the staff at Lincoln can effectively implement such a program. The Hispanic bilingual program is just beginning to be effective after years of effort.

Informing the Teaching Staff
It is essential that the teachers at both schools fully understand the background, purpose, and goals of the capacity adjustment plan (CAP).

They should also be informed of changes that will occur in the existing staff, student configuration, and school program and be given the opportunity to ask questions. They should be told what will be done to help with the transition for teachers, students, and their families.

Additional Program Funding
A dollar amount is allocated to the receiving school for each CAP student. Additional adjustments are periodically made to account for the

increased enrollment. For this reason, it is imperative that the number of CAP students be identified and reported.

CAP funds, which are in excess of regular funds, can be expended only to serve the needs of CAP students. Activities for which funds may be budgeted include, but are not limited to, the following:

- Instructional materials to address needs of incoming students.
- Teaching assistants and aides for enrichment and skill building.
- Coordinatorships to assist nonresident students.
- Preschool counseling and programming for nonresident students.
- Additional nonresident student counseling.
- Clerical relief and overtime pay.

Instructional materials necessary to meet the educational needs of Limited English Proficient (LEP) students transported to relieve overcrowding are also available.

The Capacity Adjustment Plan

The plan should result in enrollment numbers that place both schools close to capacity or only slightly over capacity. (Since there will be 2,211 students at these two schools next year and there is a capacity of 2,160, one or both schools will be slightly over capacity.) You have total freedom to configure the schools in such a way as to cause the least possible concern and debate among teachers, students, and families. Because of the proximity of the two schools, all students in both attendance zones can easily attend either school. Your plan should describe how students will be selected to attend which school and how decisions will be made regarding needed staff transfers. You do not have to consider the busing plan, which will be devised by others after you have decided how you will configure the two schools and which students and staff will be assigned to each school.

You must provide opportunities to encourage the parents of pupils affected by CAP to participate in school affairs. You should develop a plan that will facilitate the transition for students, parents, and staff and provide lots of support during this important first year. You should consider the training and development needs of staff and propose ideas that will help the staff to make this transition a success.

Balance

Consistent with school policies, resources, and programs, classes should be organized so that (1) an ethnic balance appropriate to the school population is maintained in each classroom and (2) CAP students are assigned to all rooms to avoid isolation. These factors are in addition to all the other criteria normally considered when organizing classes and assigning staff.

✳ **Write two needed policy statements: one for voluntary transfer and the other for involuntary transfer. Explain how decisions will be made regarding which students will attend each school. Explain how decisions will be communicated.**

Source: Development Dimensions International. (1995). *Assistant principal elementary school policy simulation* modified by permission. Development Dimensions International, Inc., is a world leader in providing human resource training programs and services. For more information contact DDI at 800–933–4463 (U.S.), 800–668–7971 (Canada), via e-mail info@ddiworld.com or at its Web site, www.ddiworld.com.

Taking Care of the Staff

The investment in human capital or human resources is the most important one made within any organization. The focus is on creating an organization that serves its own goals while meeting the personal needs of the school system's employees.

Human resource functions run throughout the organization from top to bottom; however, employees who are first entering their profession have needs that are very different from those of seasoned employees. Regardless, the focus at all levels is the achievement of school district objectives by helping individual members of the staff to reach the highest possible level of achievement and performance. Webb and Norton (1999) suggest that

> the quality of education programs in large part depends upon (1) the quality of human resources within the system; (2) the extent to which productive human relationships are realized; and (3) the development, motivation, and utilization of existing human qualities. Whereas a positive organizational climate depends upon a variety of factors, the human resource function assumes a major responsibility for providing a high quality of work life in the school system by focusing upon goals of the system in relation to its human resources. (p. 70)

The American Association of School Personnel Administrators, founded in 1940, is the national professional association for human resource professionals in the United States and Canada. (For more information see: www.aaspa.org.)

Rebore (1998) states, "The goals of the personnel function are basically the same in all school systems—to hire, develop, and motivate personnel in order to achieve the objectives of the school district, to assist individual members of the staff to reach the highest possible levels of achievement, and to maximize the career development of personnel" (p. 11). Typically, human resource management is broken into three major functions as shown in Figure 10.1. Young and Castetter (2004) suggest:

> Evolving models of the human resource function extend well beyond traditional tasks or recordkeeping, social work, and collective bargaining. Today's designs consider the human resources function to be a vital unit in any organizational entity. The organized and unified array of system parts interact through human performance to establish a productive public institution. (p. 27)

✳ **Which of the various HRD functions might be involved in helping make the transition of staff and students as successful as possible? Explain how these human resource functions might benefit this situation.**

Job Analysis, Classification, and Staff Planning

The various functions of human resource management (HRM) can be viewed as sequential beginning with job analysis, job classification and staff planning, and ending with employee record keeping. This linear flow of personnel functions aids in organizing thinking about HRM functions; however, in practice, such an orderly flow seldom exists and functions are not discrete but integral aspects of a systematic process. The HRM process begins with an educational plan that has attained consensus. Implementing a new educational plan often requires a rethinking of policy and changes in the allocation of work duties and responsibilities, as well as the structure of the organization (Sredl & Rothwell, 1987).

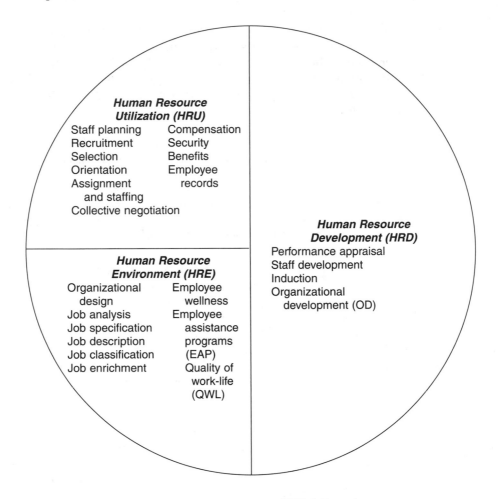

FIGURE 10.1 *Human Resource Management (HRM) Functions*

Policies are written to provide guidance regarding acceptable practice. Policy proposals can come from any department, but those regarding employees are typically routed to the human resource department for consideration and recommendation to the superintendent's office. Ultimately, the policy will be submitted to the school board for adoption and, if adopted, will guide all future actions. Policies must be complete, concise, clear, changeable, and distinctive (Clemmer, 1991, p. 107). Since policy is legally binding for all district personnel, it often becomes an issue in the negotiation process with teacher associations and others. Following is an example of a typical policy statement:

• In the event that it is necessary to make reductions among teachers who have attained tenure, such reductions shall be made on the basis of total seniority, which shall be determined by the total number of years under contract with the school district.

The job analysis and classification systems break down the work, group the activities into an organizational structure, define the duties and requirements for each position, and rank the position in relation to all other positions. An organizational chart is often used to visualize the total organization, including major functions, relationships of positions, lines of authority and communication, relative authority and power, channels of supervision, and other general organizational patterns. Box 10.1 provides some classical principles for the creation of organizational structure and the assignment of duties. An important function of HRM is to stipulate the duties, authority, and responsibilities related to every position within the organization. The completion of a job analysis and job description is an essential part of the personnel activity (Webb & Norton, 1999).

Figure 10.2 on page 280 illustrates how these various elements interact. The carrying out of these important functions requires extensive knowledge of both the nature of the work organization and the workforce.

BOX 10.1 • *Definitions of Classical Organizational Structure*

Organizational channels—Channels of supervision and communication; considered the formal lines of authority that transmit information throughout the organization.

Line authority—The major line of authority from the very top to the bottom of the organization; employees in line positions make day-to-day decisions regarding the substantive operation of the organization.

Staff authority—Those who provide advisory, specialized services to line administrators; staff duties include interpreting, recommending, discussing, explaining, evaluating, and promoting but not making line decisions.

Unity of command—The arrangement by which each individual within the organization reports and receives direction from one superior.

Delegation—The concept that authority should be given to the lowest-level individual who has the needed information, knowledge, and ability to make a decision.

Span of control—The factors that affect the number of individuals a single administrator can effectively control: time, mental capacity, complexity, number of duties, stability, capability, leadership style.

Coequality of authority and responsibility—The concept that the power (authority) and obligation (responsibility) to make and enforce decisions related to assigned duties should always be equal. Responsibilities tend to increase or decrease to the level of authority when they are not equal, thus frustrating the position holder and her or his subordinates.

Fixed responsibility—The concept that the obligation to successfully complete one's duties should be placed squarely on the subordinate to help the subordinate develop, get work accomplished, identify areas needing action, and minimize buck-passing.

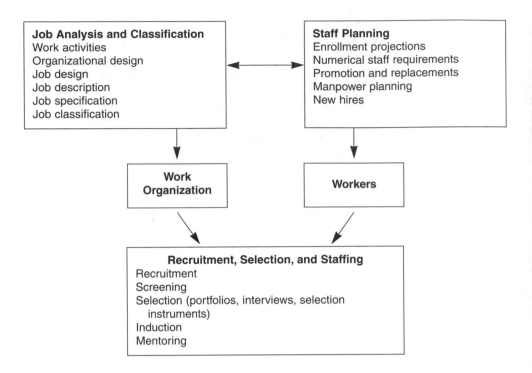

FIGURE 10.2   *Creating and Defining the Needed Organization*

Job Analysis

Job analysis is the process of gathering and analyzing information about the principal work activities in a position and the qualifications (knowledge, skill, abilities, and other attributes) necessary to perform those activities. It is the first step in creating and updating job descriptions for all organizational positions. People must know what they will be doing, the qualifications they must possess to be able to do it, and what they will be paid in order to feel comfortable in their hiring and employment decisions. Classifying positions into jobs and jobs into families; setting wage and salary rates; articulating standards to guide employee selection, appraisal, and training; and developing employees are all based on information collected in the job analysis. Equal employment opportunity laws also require employees to determine whether individuals with disabilities are qualified for a job.

Job analysis can be completed in several different ways. These methods include observation, work sampling, interviewing, questionnaires, structured approaches, or commercial methods. A comprehensive review of existing documents and possible external sources such as the *Dictionary of Occupational Titles* can also be helpful. The job analysis results in a job description (i.e., title, status, relationships, nature of job, duties, tasks, and responsibilities) and a job specification (minimum qualifications).

✳ **Obtain job descriptions for a bilingual program coordinator, a special-education coordinator, and a principal. Determine how they were created and whether they fit the needs at Washington and Lincoln Elementary Schools.**

Job Classification

Once jobs have been analyzed, they are grouped, according to similar work requirements, into common classes or pay grades. Henderson (1985) defines pay grades as convenient groupings of a wide variety of jobs that are similar in a number of critically important ways, even though they have little else in common. Pay grades are used to determine appropriate salary levels for each position, regardless of who holds it at present. In this way, the job classification system appraises the relative value of a position in regard to all other positions. In contrast, the performance appraisal system evaluates the merits of a position holder in relationship to others holding the same position. If an employee challenges the pay that his or her position receives in relation to other positions, it is important to have sound and rational justification for the pay scales in order to maintain effective morale and productivity. For example, if you decide to pay higher salaries to high school principals than you do to middle school principals, you will need to have sound justification to avoid harmful conflicts.

Most HRM departments use a technique that is often described as a "factor-point system" of job classification. The school system must first determine the factors that it believes are most important in determining the relative worth of all positions within the organization. Factors selected by the Virginia Beach Public School system are "education; experience; policy, methods, or procedures; program development; supervision; assets; records and reports; community contacts; student and personnel welfare; and job stress." The system establishes and defines degrees and assigns points for each of the factors. Numerical point values are assigned for each degree of each factor to reflect the relative importance of each. The following definition of degrees and point values relates to the responsibility for development and execution of "policy, methods, or procedures."

Points	Definition of Degrees
5	Requires execution and interpretation of existing operational policies, instruction methods, or procedures.
10	Requires development of intraschool operational policies, instructional methods, or procedures.
15	Requires development of intradivision or interschool operational policies, instructional methods, or procedures.
20	Requires development of operational policies, instructional methods, or procedures affecting the entire school district.

The total points awarded for all respective factors represent the value of the job in relation to all other jobs. Typically, a diverse committee is charged with reviewing available factors and properly weighing all positions within the organization. A salary range is set for each pay grade or classification, using both internal and external comparisons to ensure that the salary schedule is internally consistent and externally competitive. It is recommended that all jobs be classified at least once every ten years.

* **Consider a proposal that teachers in the magnet mathematic program should be paid higher wages than all other teachers. How would you resolve this question?**

Staff Planning

Prerequisite to any efforts to recruit and select employees is an assessment of the organization's needs for employees. Staff planning is a forecast of the number and kinds of employees the organization will need in each position over a given period of time. Questions that must be answered include:

- How many and what kinds of students will be served?
- What kinds of educational programs will be needed to serve those students?
- Where will these students be located, and what existing staff will be available to serve them?
- What support services will be needed to serve the students and for the programs to be operated?
- What level of funding will be available?
- What types and how many people will need to be hired?

Once the educational program has been determined, it is necessary to prepare enrollment projections. An error in enrollment projections will result in expensive and disruptive overstaffing or understaffing of the school system. Most assignments are based on the number of students expected to enroll in each school. Based on projected enrollments, U.S. Census Bureau statistics suggest that between 1997 and 2007 at least 190,000 new teachers will be needed in the United States.

Minimum personnel-to-student ratios are often controversial and established by state boards of education. A school system with 20,000 total enrollment of which 1,610 are third-graders and a teacher staffing ratio of 23 students per certified third-grade classroom teacher would require 70 (1,610/23) third-grade teachers. Staff requirements are calculated for all grade levels, all schools, and the school district office. Adjustments are made for special programs and special student needs. Final hiring requirements are determined by comparing the school district's future human resource needs with the numbers of those already employed who will remain with the school district. Retirements, resignations, sabbatical leaves, dismissals, and deaths affect the number of personnel to be replaced. The totals help pinpoint needed new hires, highlight areas of overstaffing (reduction in force—RIF), identify employees for possible intrasystem movement (promotions, transfers, demotions, and so on), identify needs to support an ever increasingly diverse work force, and ultimately identify the number and kind of individuals who must be recruited to satisfy future needs.

✳ **Develop a proposal for reconfiguring and assigning all students to Washington and Lincoln Elementary Schools. Once you know how many students will be attending each school, determine how many teachers and aides will be required for each grade level at each school. How many new hires will be required at each of the grade levels based on the +3-year target? How will teacher-transfer decisions be made?**

Recruitment

The effort to successfully match human resource demands with human resource supply is one of the most important efforts educational leaders make. The process begins with developing ways to attract qualified people to apply for open positions within the school district. Vacancy announcements, advertisements, employment agencies, university visits, professional organizations, employee referrals, job fairs, incentive programs, and other school systems are all potential sources. Perhaps the single most important factor in attracting qualified candidates is the reputation and image of the school division and community. Other factors that influence any recruitment plan are affirmative action and equal employment opportunity, professional negotiations, salary and fringe benefits, school system policy, employment continuity, employee relations, staff development, availability of opportunity, and the work itself.

Both equity and excellence must be goals for recruiting and hiring teachers. Career opportunities for minorities and women have increased in business, medicine, law, and engineering, causing a decline among this population in education. Some recruiters have anticipated the decline and have begun to develop programs to encourage high school students to become teachers, have expanded their geographical recruiting areas, and have worked with state departments of education to develop alternative certification programs.

There is projected to be a shortage of educational personnel over the next ten to fifteen years. Those presently in teacher preparation programs are far less than what is needed to fill the projected demand—especially in key subject areas such as math, science, special education, and bilingual education. In fact, the pipeline will fill only slightly more than half of those that will be needed in a few states. This problem is partially caused by the 30 to 50 percent of the new teachers who leave education within the first five years. As a result, most states have developed emergency licensing procedures and alternative routes to teacher licensing such as Military Career Transition Program (MCTP), Troops to Teachers (TTT), and career switcher programs that are being funded by the federal government.

A brochure published in April 2002 by the Defense Activity for Non-Traditional Education (DANTES) states:

> The Troops to Teachers (TTT) program enriches the quality of American education by helping to place mature, motivated, experienced, and dedicated personnel in our nation's classrooms. Thousand of retiring military and Reserve Component personnel are discovering new and rewarding careers in teaching, helping to build and sustain our nation's communities, starting with our children.

The program has been successful in producing quality teachers, a high percentage of whom are men and minorities. In addition, they have experience beneficial to successful teaching in high-demand fields, such as mathematics, science, and special education, and are teaching in high-demand areas, such as inner cities and outlying rural areas. Historically, military veterans are highly successful public school teachers. More than 4,000 participants have been hired in our nation's public school systems. Experienced TTT teachers value community, responsibility, training and teamwork.

Many agree that these second-career people in education are essential to fully staffing the schools.

Some challenge that the minimal training received in emergency licensing procedures and alternative certification programs do not properly prepare teachers for the challenging tasks of teaching. This argument is based on findings like those of Darling-Hammond and Ball (1998) that teacher knowledge and skill accounts for between 40 and 90 percent of the variation in student achievement. Teachers' knowledge of subject matter, student learning, and teaching methods are all very important to student learning. Linda Darling-Hammond (2003) states, "Although no state will permit a person to write wills, practice medicine, fix plumbing, or style hair without completing training and passing an examination, these states fill nearly 100,000 vacancies a year with teachers who do not meet basic requirements" (p. 78). She goes on to suggest the problem is compounded by minimal, one-shot professional development activities.

The shortages that exist can be better turned around with creative staffing and use of time; aggressive recruitment; hiring of well-prepared, committed, and diverse staff; high quality professional development; career ladders; teacher assessment, mentoring, and support; active involvement in internships; reallocation of time (so teachers can work intensively with students and collaboratively with each other); incentives; and competitive salaries.

Recruiters are also working to determine the factors that are causing education to lose many of the best and brightest students. Higher salaries, stock option plans, and other lucrative benefits outside the public domain, although a main reason, are not the only reasons—another, for example, lack of teacher respect. Obviously, the quality of the application pool is only as good as those who choose to enter the profession.

School districts will want to use technology for online job vacancies, recruitment materials, applications, electronic evaluation forms, portfolios, and electronic ordering of transcripts, teaching certificates, and so on. A number of groups have developed educational databases, to link school divisions with candidates and include California State University (www.cateach.com), the American Association for Employment in Education (www.aaee.org), National Teacher Recruitment Clearinghouse (www.recruitingteachers.org), and the Regional Education Application Placement System (www.gary@info.csd.org).

Successful recruiting includes getting the word out and collecting application materials necessary to make initial screening decisions. Although recruitment and screening can be centralized, it is best that selection be decentralized to the unit in which the individual will work. It is important to follow up quickly, particularly with strong candidates who are probably being recruited by other systems.

The process of recruitment, selection, and development are receiving increased attention as a result of the NCLB legislation, which states that by 2006 teachers be "highly qualified" in the subjects they teach. The law defines that "highly qualified" teachers must demonstrate competence by passing a rigorous subject exam or possess an academic major or equivalent coursework or certification or credential in the subject taught. This may change the hiring pool for teachers and create a challenging goal. There is some evidence (Jerald & Ingersoll, 2002) that more than 25 percent of present teachers lack training (33 percent in high poverty schools) in core academic classes (www.edtrust.org/main/documents/ALLTalk.pdf).

This legislation also waives the use of hiring teachers on emergency, temporary, or provisional basis. One idea for increasing the application pool in high-need poverty areas and subjects that have shortages, like math, science, and special education, is to pay bonuses in those positions or even higher salaries in order to induce more applicants to enter the job pool in these areas of greatest need. The federal government is considering a teacher tax deduction of up to $400.00 for training and other education expenses. This also opens up the possibility for career switchers to enter the job pool if they can successfully pass national tests (Rotherham & Mead, 2003). This might eliminate the need to raise salaries since anyone who could pass the test would be allowed to teach.

✳ **What qualities might be especially helpful for the new teachers that will be hired for these two schools? What will be the best source for teachers having these qualities, and how might you recruit them?**

Selection

The selection process involves matching applicants' qualifications to the selection criteria, job description, specifications, and work unit. The determination to hire is related to technical skills (*can* he or she do the job?) and motivation (*will* he or she do the job?). Those involved in the interview process should be trained in its use and familiar with all legal requirements that govern employee selection. Regardless of whether a single individual or a number of staff members jointly perform the tasks of interviewing, the steps remain basically the same. The six typical steps to the structured interview process (Arons, 1999) are:

1. Introduction and welcoming
2. Obtaining information
3. Providing information
4. Responding to questions
5. Concluding the interview
6. Evaluating the candidate

The *introduction and welcoming* step begins by setting the environment and schedule for the interview. Schedule enough time for the interview, and no disruptions should occur. The interviewer should form a positive relation with the interviewee while collecting all needed information and retaining control of the interview. Study information on the applicant before the interview, checking appropriate experiences and their sequence; the quality, attitude, style, and tone of the materials; and the strength of supporting documents. Make notes on items to follow up in the interview. Background investigations are very useful, but all legal requirements must be followed. The interview should begin by putting the applicant at ease and setting up ground rules related to time frame, people to be seen, use of note-taking or recording devices, and the time when interviewee's questions will be answered.

Obtaining information is the heart of the interview, with success resting on the interviewer's skills in questioning. Good interviewing is the process of getting valid and complete information related to the interviewee's ability and motivation to perform the job. A prime objective is to get the applicant to be honest and forthright during the discussion. It is best to have thought through questions in advance of the interview. Questions should be specific, probing the individual's ability to carry out the responsibilities of the position and assessing the specific characteristics sought. Questions should be open-ended, giving the applicant an opportunity to provide a fair amount of information.

Hiring is the most important activity in administration and most problems can be avoided by hiring the best people up front. It is not always teaching ability that becomes the serious problems but personal characteristics like intentions, tone of voice, respect, perseverance, honesty, dedication, work ethics, and character that cause the difficulties in education. The interviewer needs to be aware of these important personal characteristics during the screening and hiring process. Interview questions that are particularly good at revealing a person's character place candidates in situations and ask them how they would handle values that are presented in opposition to one another: loyalty to a supervisor versus a staff member; truth to a parent versus silence for a child's welfare; justice versus kindness. Ask if you might call the person who worked next to him or her if no one was included as a reference (Slosson, 1999).

The interviewer should not lead the response with any form of directive or point of view. For example, "We use cooperative education in this school. Do you think this is an effective approach?" is an ineffective question, because it is both a leading and close-ended question. A number of questions are also not in compliance with federal legislation and most state human rights laws. It is best only to ask questions that are directly related to the job. Effective listening is important to the interview process. Some common suggestions for improved listening skills are:

- Get the respondent to clarify, elaborate, and reflect (e.g., tell me more, turn a statement into a question, silence).
- Summarize or restate key points (e.g., summary bridges).
- Look at the person (good eye contact).
- Get the main points and test for understanding (e.g., paraphrase).

- Control your desire to mentally argue.
- Avoid making assumptions.
- Recognize your own prejudices.
- Do very little of the talking.
- Be accepting, there are no wrong answers.
- Watch your body language.

It is best to make brief notes during the interview to help remember what was said. Then immediately after the interview, record your observations.

In the *providing information* stage, the interviewee needs information about the nature of the position, the community, and the school system itself. Key concerns are typically about salary, benefits, working conditions, policies and procedures, colleagues, reporting relationships, opportunities, staff development, and community support. Brochures, manuals, fact sheets, and promotional materials can provide needed information to the candidate. Information allows the candidate to make better decisions regarding his or her fit within the organization. For this reason, it is very important to set a positive environment and put the best possible face on the organization, without being deceptive or overselling. Always allow time for the interviewee to ask any questions and keep notes on the questions asked. Keep responses to questions brief, always maintaining control of the interview.

Concluding the interview is important to inform the candidate what happens next and give time frames in which decisions will be made and when and how the individual will be notified. Everyone who is interviewed, whether he or she receives the job or not, should receive a letter of appreciation or a telephone call indicating that the decision has been made. It is very important to successfully close the interview before showing the applicant out.

Evaluating the candidate results in the recording and rating of significant attributes of the candidate that contribute to the effectiveness of final selection. It is best to have an interviewer rating form so that information on all candidates is similarly recorded for easier comparison. Some interviewers find it helpful to construct a matrix on which to compare applicants in terms of their responses to job-related questions. Selecting employees is among the most important decision any administrator makes because an organization can be no better than the people it employs. Recording information helps in making appropriate final decisions and provides a clean audit trail against charges that decisions were based on discrimination, bias, or favoritism (Avery & Campion, 1982).

✳ **What criteria will you use to select teachers for these schools? New hires? Transfers? How will you determine whether teachers meet these criteria?**

Alternative Selection Approaches

Packaged, structured interviews ask the same series of questions of all candidates for a position, and their responses are scored. Interviewers are trained to "listen for" very specific types of statements in regard to each question. The interviewer might ask, "What is your mission? What are your beliefs about the significance of education?" The "listen for" is "the development of students, civilization's survival, or democracy depends on education." Some school systems have designed their own standard sets of questions and responses or "listen fors." Research suggests that candidates who score higher on perceiver systems are more effective in their jobs than those who have lower scores.

Assessment centers are geared more for promotion decisions and provide an opportunity to observe candidates for administrative positions in an environment that simulates situations the individual will face as an administrator. A team of trained assessors observes and rates the candidates as they participate in various activities. The candidates are evaluated on a set of relevant skills or dimensions based on the evidence collected to identify and measure their management potential (Bynham, 1971, 1978; Richardson, 1988; Schmitt et al., 1983).

The NASSP Assessment Center model typically generates behavioral data relevant to the critical skill dimensions presented in Table 10.1 (Hersey, 1994; NASSP, 1988, 2003). The NASSP has developed a set of "21st Century School Administrator Skills," which are detailed in the "21st Century School Administrator Skills Self-Assessment and Observer Assessment" (for more information see: www.Principals.org/training/04.html).

The courts have upheld selection/promotion decisions based on assessment centers (*Berry, Stokes and Lant v. City of Omaha*). The final report on each candidate

TABLE 10.1 *NASSP Administrative Skill Dimensions*

Principals		Superintendents	
Skills	*Dimensions*	*Dimensions*	*Skills*
Educational leadership	Set instructional direction Teamwork Sensitivity	Encourage innovation Serve the need of diverse constituencies Plan strategically	Take educational initiative
Resolving complex problems	Judgment Results orientation Organizational ability	Collect and interpret data Make decisions judiciously	Analyze and judge educational problems
Communication skills	Oral communication Written communication	Empower teams Communicate expectations	Build and maintain educational teams
Develop self and others	Development of others Understanding own strengths and weaknesses	Facilitate action Model continuous professional development Foster continuous professional development in others	Expanded leanings

Source: Reprinted with permission of NASSP.

describes strengths and weaknesses, skills needing improvement, recommendations for professional development, and comparison of the candidate's performance with others.

Other possible alternatives for selection are requesting videotapes, portfolios, and other forms of evaluative data.

✳ **What questions would you ask an individual interviewing for a bilingual program coordinator position? What criteria would most influence your evaluation and final decision to hire a specific person for this job?**

Performance Appraisal and Evaluation

Performance evaluation is one of the hardest jobs in education and one of the most important. The primary goal of performance appraisal is the professional improvement of employees and thus the instructional process. It has two purposes: Formative evaluation identifies areas for improvement and designs developmental plans. The second, summative evaluation accumulates records regarding the overall quality and degree of improvement in an employee's performance in order to make and support decisions regarding the individual's continued employment, salary, and promotion potential. In this way evaluation is a continuous process throughout ones entire career in education. Its use in granting tenure is quite important since once granted, the court assumes the teacher is competent.

Human resource management is more involved in the design, development, and maintenance of the appraisal process, which will be used by line administrators in the appraisal, development, and supervision of employees. The performance appraisal process shown in Figure 10.3 emphasizes the three major phases (modified from Ellena & Redfern, 1972).

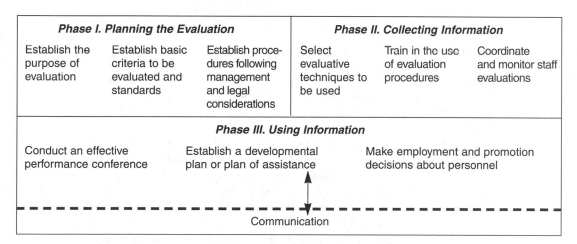

Phase I. Planning the Evaluation			Phase II. Collecting Information		
Establish the purpose of evaluation	Establish basic criteria to be evaluated and standards	Establish procedures following management and legal considerations	Select evaluative techniques to be used	Train in the use of evaluation procedures	Coordinate and monitor staff evaluations

Phase III. Using Information		
Conduct an effective performance conference	Establish a developmental plan or plan of assistance	Make employment and promotion decisions about personnel

Communication

FIGURE 10.3   *The Three Phases of Performance Appraisal Process*

Planning the Evaluation

Employees typically make needed adjustments if they are made aware of required performance improvements. The absence of such feedback will result in more, longer, and larger errors in their work. In this way, the purpose of the evaluation process is always related to continued improvement of employee performance. The appraisal includes a feedback delivery system on employee progress along with an effective means of communication on performance and development. The system must have integrity if employees are to trust and act on the results (Joint Committee on Standards for Education Evaluation, 1988). Unless skillfully conducted, the appraisal process often results in ill feelings and misunderstandings for both parties and probably does more harm than good.

Performance appraisal planning covers the philosophy, purpose, criteria, objectives, methods, and skills needed for the appraisal process. Some of the most compelling reasons to pursue it are to:

- Help the employee assess and improve performance.
- Motivate the employee to improve knowledge, skill, and methods.
- Make the employee accountable for performance expectations.
- Recognize and reward outstanding performance.
- Identify and remediate ineffective performance.
- Terminate incompetent employees.
- Plan professional development and training.
- Support organizational credibility.

Evaluations provide an opportunity for employees to discuss their professional growth and ways they and the organization might improve curriculum, instruction, and student learning.

There have been a number of efforts to link teacher evaluation, teacher development, teacher pay, and teacher promotion to national and state standards. In earlier chapters, we discussed sanctions that resulted because of student's poor performance on high-stakes standardized tests. There is an effort by the National Board for Professional Teaching Standards (NBPTS), Education Testing Service (ETS), and the Interstate New Teacher Assessment and Support Consortium (INTASC) to advance standards of practice and methods of measuring teaching excellence. Many states and districts reward teachers with bonuses and/or salary increases if they obtain National Board Certification. (For more information see: http://www.wcer.wisc.edu/cpre/teachercomp.)

The National Board for Professional Teaching Standards creates incentives to become better by recognizing teachers for improving their competence and documenting their student's achievements. The hope of such efforts is to improve the quality of the teaching force and its capacity to succeed in meeting high standards for student achievement. Similar efforts have occurred for educational administrators. The ISLLC standards for administrators have been used to design preparation and training programs and evaluation systems for administrators. Some are suggesting that to be considered for the principalship an individual should first be a national board certified teacher, especially to close that option off to people who may never have been in the classroom. Others suggest that leadership requires a different set of characteristics than teaching and administrators should be selected because they have that knowledge and skill and have displayed the characteristics in their jobs.

Collecting Information

Future relationships and ability to influence one another depends on the accuracy and quality of information regarding performance. Although multiple assessment methods may be used to appraise performance, most school systems have a specific evaluative form that evaluators complete as they observe the employee's performance on the job. Both evaluator and evaluatee assume responsibility for collecting and exchanging a variety of performance data. The most common techniques are the checklist and rating scales, but recently essay approaches have gained in popularity. The essay method requires the evaluator to describe in writing how well each employee has performed. The instrument usually spells out evaluation criteria as a cue for the rater who checks, rates, or describes the level of performance.

Supervisors usually complete the instrument, but 360-degree systems, for which supervisor, colleagues, and subordinates all complete performance appraisals on an individual, have proved to improve the quality of information provided (Church & Bracken, 1997; Lepsinger & Yukl, 1995; Manatt, 1998). The researchers suggest the 360-degree feedback process is more reliable, valid, and credible than any other performance assessment process. Employees achieve an increased self-awareness of their strengths and weaknesses.

Other techniques, such as portfolios, self-evaluation, cognitive coaching, parent and student evaluation, structured simulations, videotaping, test scores, transcripts, interaction analysis, and action research, are also used to provide information. Some states have legislature specifying that student performance on state-mandated achievement tests will be used as a basis for evaluating teacher and principal performance.

Student scores on standard-based performance tests are being used by an increasing number of school divisions and states as a part of the teacher-evaluation process. In Dallas, Oregon, Colorado, and Tennessee, test results are part of the teacher evaluation and are used to guide feedback, instructional improvement planning, and staff development. James Stronge and Pamela Tucker (2000) support the use of student achievement information in teacher and administrative evaluation if the following nine practices are followed, in order to reduce bias and increase fairness:

1. Use student learning as only one component of a teacher evaluation.
2. Consider the context in which teaching and learning occurs.
3. Use measures of students' growth.
4. Compare gains from one point in time to another for the same student.
5. Recognize gain scores have pitfalls that must be avoided.

6. Allow a time frame for patterns of student learning to be documented.
7. Use fair and valid measures of student learning.
8. Align assessment measures and the curriculum.
9. Don't narrow the curriculum and limit teaching to fit a test.

New education approaches—constructivist, authentic learning, for instance—will require the gathering of more diverse data to get an accurate picture of performance (Darling-Hammond 1997; Millman & Darling-Hammond, 1990; Wiggins, 1998). Teachers being evaluated might include portfolio artifacts such as samples of student work over time linked to evidence of teaching plans and activities, teacher feedback to students, and analyses of student needs and progress. The focus is on how student learning grows out of specific teaching actions and decisions and emphasizes effective performance assessment employed to measure high-level knowledge and skills (Darling-Hammond, 1998).

There are a number of other related issues. For example, school employees hold "safety-sensitive" positions in schools and may be subjected to urinalysis or blood tests under certain circumstances. Reports of innuendo and inappropriate remarks, gestures, or touching of a co-worker or student must be investigated and corrective action taken immediately. Certainly these are not what might be considered part of a typical performance appraisal; however, the supervisor is responsible for having broad knowledge of the behavior of his or her staff and its impact on others.

Using Information

In the using-information phase, evaluator and evaluatee jointly diagnose, analyze, and discuss evaluative data and plan and agree on follow-up action. Some suggest that this collaborative process is made easier by using a clinical supervision (Goldhammer, 1969; Cogan, 1973) five-step type of process. The process involves a preobservation conference (to focus the observation); the classroom observation (focus on items selected in preobservation conference); analysis of the evaluative data collected; postobservation conference; and postconference analysis (evaluation of process and outcome). The emphasis is on specific areas in which the evaluator and evaluatee have the greatest interest in order to discuss and develop ideas and activities for improvement regarding these areas of interest. An alternative to clinical supervision is collegial supervision by which teachers work with one another as colleagues in a more informal process. They can use the clinical supervision process or a less intense informal process. The National Education Association favors the concept of peer review and assistance. This process can also complement peer coaching and mentoring.

If the employee's performance meets minimum standards, a "development plan" is constructed to build on the individual's performance. If performance falls below standards, the individual is placed on a "plan of assistance" to help him or her improve performance and thus remain employed. Unless an evaluation conference is completed, a performance appraisal has not occurred.

The postobservation conference is the crucial step in which the evaluator provides useful information for reflection, discussion, and development. Some suggestions for providing useful feedback are:

1. Be descriptive rather than judgmental.
2. Be specific rather than general.
3. Concentrate on things that can be changed
4. Consider your own motives.
5. Focus on things that can be reasonably documented.
6. Show respect for the other's opinions and use good listening skills.
7. Don't overload the person being evaluated with information or developmental efforts.
8. Ask open questions.
9. Discuss both strengths and areas to focus on for improvement.
10. Check to ensure that all parties are clear on what was communicated and there are no discrepancies.

The feedback is used to help individuals see how they can continuously improve their performance and better achieve the organization's and their own goals.

The first step in discussing evaluative information is identifying where increased levels of performance might occur. It begins with good communication about how things are going, moves through things that are going well, and leads to areas that might benefit from further improvement. Disagreements are expected and are resolved through discussion and mutual problem solving. Performance improvement might require changes in policy, performance expectations, resource availability, or job skills, or it might require increased performance on the part of the employee.

Participants actively listen to one another and discuss each idea thoroughly, agreeing on specific action to be taken by all parties and establishing a date for formal follow-up. Feedback is focused on specific situations and exploration of alternatives to improve future performance and develop potential. The final developmental plan should:

- Protect the individual's pride.
- Show how evaluation and developmental plans are credible.
- Consider the urgency relative to the area being developed.
- Think about feasibility and the impact of the plan.
- Consider reasonableness and manageability.
- Consider sufficient duration.
- Think about costs involved in the plan.

All evaluations, performance improvement and developmental plans, supportive documents, and validating data are placed in the employee's personnel file along with comments, recommendations, or rebuttals of all parties. Due process requires the existence of substantiative written documentation and credible judgments, establishment of plans of assistance, and disciplinary action that is consistent and reasonable. A hearing and appeals procedure must exist, and all law must be followed. James Stronge (1997) states: When evaluation is treated as less than it deserves (i.e., superficially, with little or no resource allocation, invalid evaluation systems, and flawed implementation designs), the school, its employees, and the public at large are deprived of opportunities for improvement and the benefits that accountability can afford. All of us, whatever our relationship to the educational enterprise, deserve high-quality evaluation. (p. 18)

   ✱ **How might the performance appraisal system be used to increase the probability that students will have successful experiences at Washington and Lincoln Elementary Schools?**

Staff Development

Shakespeare's famous line tells us, "We know what we are but not what we may be." Staff development is any activity or process intended to improve skills, attitudes, understandings, or performance in present or future roles (Fullan, 1990). Educators recognize that training is critical in helping schools to achieve the high standards that are expected of them. Development should address both individual learning and organizational improvement. According to Ernest Boyer (cited in Cunningham & Gresso, 1993), past president of the Carnegie Foundation for Advancement of Teaching:

> The only way we're going to get from where we are to where we want to be is through staff development. . . . When you talk about school improvement, you're talking about people improvement. . . . The school is the people, so when we talk about excellence or improvement or progress, we're really focusing on the people who make up the building. (p. 173)

Successful organizations promote and demand continuous professional development throughout one's career.

The National Staff Development Council Executive Director, Dennis Sparks, suggests that 10 percent of the school budget and 25 percent of teachers' time be used for professional learning. The council also recommends the creation of teacher teams, sharing responsibility for students, improving student performance, reducing teacher isolation, and providing opportunities to learn from each other.

The National Commission on Teaching and America's Future (1996) found that some of the more recent and powerful learning approaches have been built on the importance of creating networks, collaborations, teacher academics, National Board Certification, teaching teams, action research, subject matter associations, and learning communities where continuous and ongoing staff development and sharing can occur.

There are a number of teacher networks other than those mentioned in Chapter 3 that provides total development to build the capacity of school faculties. Among the best known are the National Writing Project, the Urban Mathematics Collaborative, and the Collaboratives for Humanities and Arts Teaching. They also see such opportunities as ways of circumventing professional isolation while learning new perspectives and ways to teach. In examining recent research, Scribner (1999) identified a growing consensus of guiding principles as "(a) ongoing professional learning that is tied to new standards for curriculum, assessment, and student performance; (b) professional development connected to teacher work; (c) school communities that foster shared learning; and (d) professional development that is integrated into the school schedule" (p. 240).

Effective programs are ongoing, collaborative, and collegial, highly connected to what teachers are doing in their classrooms (tied to actual classroom practices). Concrete, hands-on activities, meaningful applications and simulations, linked to concrete teaching tasks, reflecting current research, and including coaching, collaboration, and conversation are examples of effective approaches that can be more practical and relevant. Self-assessment and reflection is also quite important for effective professional development (Kaplan & Owings, 2002).

Specifically, teachers are interested in developing/improving pedagogical skills and classroom management strategies. The major function of administrators is to create school cultures that value professional development and involve teachers in planning, learning activities, that best support teachers. The challenge remains in creating schedules that allow time for teachers to participate in continuous development.

Prawat and Peterson (1999) suggest that staff development points: "towards the importance of encouraging members of an organization to learn and develop, realizing that goal is apt to be met when members of the organization work together to make it happen. Administrators . . . play a key role in establishing and nurturing the organizational arrangements that enable learning to occur." (p. 223)

A number of different groups have published lists to help educators to improve the quality of professional development activities. Table 10.2 shows the results of an analysis (Guskey, 2003) of thirteen different lists, identifying characteristics that were common among the various lists. The numbers in the body of the table represents the identifying number of a characteristic as it appeared in each of the original thirteen lists. Results shown on Table 10.2 illustrate that some items, like numbers 18 through 21, only appear on one of thirteen lists of important characteristics for staff development. Items 14, 16, and 17 only appear on two of the lists. All the other items, except number 8, appear on 5 or more of the different lists and therefore are interpreted as more of a consensus among researchers as an effective characteristic of staff development for teachers.

Guskey (2003) concludes:

> The characteristics that influence the effectiveness of professional development are clearly multiple and highly complex. For this reason it may be unreasonable to assume that a single list of effective professional development characteristics will ever emerge, regardless of the quality of professional development research. Nevertheless, by agreeing on the criteria for effectiveness, considering the unique contextual elements of each school and the community of learners in that environment, and continually directing efforts toward improvements in student learning outcomes, visionary school leaders can do much to guarantee sure and steady progress in educators' and researchers' efforts to improve the quality of professional development endeavors. (p. 16)

TABLE 10.2 *Characteristics of Effective Professional Development Cited by Various Sources*[a]

Characteristic/principle	References												
	1	2	3	4	5	6	7	8	9	10	11	12	13
1. Enhances teachers' content and pedagogic knowledge	3	1,2		2	5	7,15	1	4	5	1	7	2	11
2. Provides sufficient time and other resources	7	7			8	11	2,3	2	3		4	1	3
3. Promotes collegiality and collaboration	5		4	4	7			3	7	5	8		9
4. Includes procedures for evaluation		5	6	7	10	16			10	7			5
5. Aligns with other reform initiatives			8	6	9	4,9		6	2	9	5		1
6. Models high-quality instruction	4	6		3				5	8		2		7,8
7. Is school or site based	1		3			14	5			4	6		
8. Builds leadership capacity				5	3	5			4				
9. Is based on teachers' identified needs	6	8	2			13				3			2
10. Is driven by analyses of student learning data			1			1,16			1	2	1		4
11. Focuses on individual and organizational improvement	2	3			1,2	3			9				
12. Includes follow-up and support	7		5			12	4			6			
13. Is ongoing and job-embedded	8				6	2					3		10
14. Helps accommodate diversity and promote quality						10						3	
15. Is based on best available research evidence		4			4	6							6
16. Takes a variety of forms		9						1					
17. Provides opportunities for theoretical understanding			7							8			
18. Is driven by an image of effective teaching and learning				1									
19. Provides for different phases of change						8							

TABLE 10.2   *Continued*

Characteristic/principle	*References*												
	1	*2*	*3*	*4*	*5*	*6*	*7*	*8*	*9*	*10*	*11*	*12*	*13*
20. Promotes continuous inquiry and reflection									6				
21. Involves families and other stakeholders												12	

[a]Numbers in Table 10.2 correspond to the references listed below.

1. Corcoran, T. B. (1995). *Transforming professional development for teachers: A guide for state policymakers.* Washington, DC: National Governors' Association.
2. American Federation of Teachers. (1996). *Principles for professional development* (Item NO. 176). Washington, DC: Author.
3. Hawley, W. D., & Valli, L. (1996, Fall). The essentials of effective professional development: A new consensus. *Professional Development Newsletter—ASCD Human Resource Development Program,* 1–2.
4. Louks-Horsley, S., Stiles, K., & Hewson, P. (1996). Principles of effective professional development for mathematics and science education: A synthesis of standards. *NISE Brief, 1*(1), 1–6.
5. U.S. Department of Education. (1997). *Achieving the goals: Goal 4. Teacher education and professional development.* Washington, DC: Author.
6. Educational Research Service. (1998). *Professional development for teachers: Challenges and trends.* Arlington, VA: Author.
7. Kennedy, M. M. (1998). *Form and substance in inservice teachers education (Research Monograph No. 13).* Madison, WI: National Institute for Science Education, University of Wisconsin.
8. Birman, B. F., Desimone, L., Porter, A. C., & Garet, M. S. (2000). Designing professional development that works. *Educational Leadership, 57*(8), 28–33.
9. Kent, K., & Lingman, C. (2000). California's course. *Journal of Staff Development, 21*(3), 31–36.
10. National Partnership for Excellence and Accountability in Teaching. (2000). *Improving professional development.* Retrieved February 15, 2001, from *www.npeat.org/strand2/pdprinpdf*
11. Terzian, M. (2000). *Design principles for effective professional development: A research synthesis.* Newton, MA: Educational Development Center.
12. Wenglinsky, H. (2002). How schools matter: The link between teacher classroom practices and student academic performance. *Education Policy Analysis Archives, 10*(2). Retrieved May 13, 2002, from *www.epaa.asu.edu/epaa/v10n12*
13. National Staff Development Council (2001*). Standards for staff development.* Retrieved March 26, 2001, from *www.nsdc.org/educatorindex.htm*

Source: Reprinted from T. Guskey "Analyzing Tests of the Characteristics of Effective Professional Development to Promote Visionary Leadership." *NASSP Bulletin, 87*(637):4–20. With permission from the *NASSP Bulletin.*

Development activities can eliminate differences, introduce new programs, induct new staff, assist new personnel, promote continuous improvement, improve competence, reform schools, extend interests, prepare for changes in position, and provide many other benefits. Development efforts can be geared toward board members, administrators, teachers, noncertified personnel—all who are a part of the education process. Most important, training must be proactive and closely tied to school values, priorities, goals, and strategies.

And with a severe teacher shortage being projected over the next ten years, it is going to be more important than ever to remediate weak teaching and save weak teachers. Tucker (2001) defines the components of a focused plan of assistance as evaluator and evaluatee work together to develop: (1) a definition of the problem, (2) a statement of objectives, (3) intervention strategies, (4) a timeline, (5) a procedure to collect data, and (6) a final judgment. She believes:

> Plans of assistance can help administrators formalize the communication process with teachers around the issue of instructional improvement. Such plans offer structure, clarity of purpose, and assistance that go beyond traditional supervision. The remediation process requires a substantial investment of effort by both the teacher and the administrator, but has the potential to yield substantial benefits for all concerned parties, especially students. (p. 55)

Electronic learning technologies to deliver information and facilitate the development of skills and knowledge will revolutionize staff development activities. Teleconferencing, for example, allows development activities to occur at multiple locations within the same time frame. The Internet can provide on-demand multimedia training at any time within a 24-hour day. Distance education programs will provide new ways in which staff development can be delivered. Computer-based training (CBT) and CD-ROM have been and will continue to remain top choices in developmental activities. Keeping pace with the rate of change will be the biggest challenge.

✳ **Draft three or four specific staff development activities that might improve the transition of students and teachers between schools or that will improve the staffs' ability to succeed after the capacity adjustment plan is implemented.**

Employee Assistance and Wellness Programs

All school systems have employees whose health or personal problems adversely affect their performance, productivity, and job satisfaction. Now employers are providing assistance to these employees as an alternative to poor performance appraisals, plans of assistance, and termination. This emphasis on employee assistance occurs because organizations recognize that helping otherwise good employees is much less expensive and much more motivating than replacing them. Employees who exhibit excessive absenteeism or tardiness, decreased work performance, inconsistent behavior, loss of interest, accidents, depression, physical illness, temper or substance abuse might have personal problems that cannot be resolved by disciplinary action and warrant intervention through an employee assistance program (EAP).

EAP is a free, confidential, voluntary program providing a formal structure that helps employees get counseling and clinical services for health and personal problems. It provides a method for disentangling an employee's problems from her or his performance ability. An important part of this program is selecting effective community service providers and maintaining a liaison with them. The program typically allows for self-referral, peer referral, or referral by supervisor, but it is the employees who decide whether they will participate in an EAP. Directed referrals are often used as a management tool to assist the supervisor and employee in improving unacceptable job performance that could be resulting from personal problems. According to school districts, participants reported substantial increases in functioning in work and nonwork settings, and their supervisors reported sharp increases in employee work performance. Over 90 percent of participants reported they would recommend the program.

Statistics show a significant decrease in medical care costs and employee absenteeism as a result of wellness programs (Health Insurance Association of America, 1986). The idea of a wellness program is to stimulate health-enhancing behaviors in areas such as smoking, alcohol and drug abuse, nutrition, physical fitness, safety, stress, and environmental sensitivity. Myriad wellness programs stress taking responsibility for a healthy lifestyle, practicing preventive health habits, and educating employees regarding the control of risk factors.

✳ **What assistance or wellness programs might be especially helpful to the staffs at these two schools?**

Human Resource Administration in the Third Millennium

RONALD REBORE • *St. Louis University*

The administrator who has overall responsibility for the human resource function must be committed to continual evaluation of this function and make changes in human resource practice to meet future needs. The signs are already vivid as to the future challenges facing human resource administration in public school districts. Humanizing school districts, the institutionalization of technology and decentralization of functions are all possible examples.

Humanizing school districts has become a necessity, given the following symptoms: increased stress on faculty and staff, lingering inequities, the pluralistic composition of staff, unrealistic demands from parents and taxpayers, and disruptive pupil behavior. Stress is certainly related to job ambiguity, which leads to contradictory or unrealistic expectations for employees on the part of supervisors. Ambiguity is the product of ever-changing circumstances that require teachers, administrators, and staff members to assume responsibilities that were not originally part of their job descriptions. Another factor that is equally distressing to employees is an inadequate match between a person's abilities and the responsibilities of his or her job. Stress results because the person is *under-* or *overchallenged.*

Human resource administrators must focus attention on the symptoms of job-related stress identified by supervisory staff members. Remedies for this situation can be found in *employee assistance programs* for those people who are experiencing such stress. Further evaluation of administrative practices can point out systemic problems that also can be sources of stress.

The *institutionalization* of technology presents human resource administrators with many options that can enhance the human resource function. Computerization means less shuffling of paper and more effective use of staff members. Available software enable a single employee to process hundreds of applications in a timely and efficient manner. Computers can complete skills inventories for existing staff and applicants to create lists of possible candidates for new positions and promotions.

A group of school districts in a certain location or region might decide that collaboration is the most effective way to implement human resource planning and hiring. The Internet allows a potential employee the opportunity to fill out one application that can be viewed and considered by multiple school districts. Staff can scan the contents of paper applications and résumés into a network computer. Through the Internet a potential employee can apply from home via his or her computer. Employer's can review computer network files to identify possible candidates. Interviews can occur using distance communication technology. Thus, human resources planning and forecasting meld with the recruitment and selection processes to result in the more timely hiring of candidates.

Of course, security is a major consideration not only through the unauthorized viewing of applications and related information but also in regard to the integrity of the information.

The institutionalization of technology as set forth above will necessarily decentralize certain aspects of the human resource function. No longer will it be necessary for principals, teachers, and other staff members to travel to central office to review applications and supporting documents. Selection criteria can be transmitted by fax or printed out from a computer. The observation, comments, and rating of candidates by interviewers can be transmitted through the computer. As previously stated, the institutionalization of technology in human resource administration will accelerate the personnel function, will be more cost effective, will decentralize certain aspects of this function, and might even reduce stress for those involved in the selection process.

Finally, the result of these changes and modifications to the human resource function should enhance decentralization. Decisions should be made and tasks should be performed at the most immediate level within an organization. The use of computers and decentralization will allow people at various levels within the organization to complete HRD tasks that previously were centralized.

Of course, implementing the changes outlined here will require staff development, but even implementation can be enhanced through technology.

Organizational Development

Organizational development (OD) is a planned process directed toward building and maintaining the health of the organization and increasing the productivity of work groups. It is a process of change in the organizational culture through the use of behavior science technology, research, and theory. Kurt Lewin's (1951) model is used to provide support for the challenging of old attitudes, values, beliefs, behaviors, or performance patterns to open the mind to new possibilities. Lewin described this prelearning process as "unfreezing." The learner is much more open to "processing" new ideas and learning as a result. "Refreezing" occurs as new attitudes, beliefs, and behaviors are stabilized in such a way that the organization reaches a new, improved equilibrium state. This three-stage change process provides the general framework for all OD approaches.

Most OD requires collecting data, diagnosing the situation, providing an appropriate intervention, and monitoring and stabilizing results. The basic approach is described as action research (Lippit, Watson, & Westley, 1958). Appropriate interventions are derived from careful diagnosis and are meant to resolve specific problems and improve particular areas of organizational functioning. A consultant uses the information to work with the top administrative team first and then moves through the organization's hierarchy. The action-research process often creates self-assessment (unfreezing) with the hope that learning (processing) will occur, resulting in improved functioning for the organization (refreezing). Many OD consultants believe that this is the only way improvements occur (Schmuck & Runkel, 1994).

* **How might an organizational development model be used to resolve a problem that could develop as a result of the capacity adjustment plan program?**

Wage and Salary Considerations

The job classification system, as discussed earlier, groups jobs into classes or grades that represent different pay levels, ranging from minimum to maximum for a particular grade of jobs. The compensation system determines the way salary payments are allocated between and within levels. The ultimate objective is to establish proper compensation for positions as well as for individuals holding the positions. The plan should attract, retain, and motivate qualified and competent employees; remain consistent with pay plans in other industries; and meet the acceptance of the taxpayers. The compensation system takes the form of wages, salaries, and benefits.

Consistent debate has occurred over the amount of money paid to educators (Bennett, 1988; Carter & Cunningham, 1997) compared with the salaries of those in comparable positions in business, industry, and commerce. The Educational Research Service in 1998–99 indicated the average compensation of superintendents (25,000 or more students) was $133,702 and for high school principals was $64,010. The comparable compensation for business and commerce Chief Executive Officers (CEOs), including salary, stock options, and bonuses, is $2,583,000 and for middle-level managers is $107,800. In other words, CEOs earn $2,449,298 and middle-level managers earn $43,790 more per year than do their counterparts in education. At an 8 percent return, this means educators in administration give up approximately $264,000,000 to be a superintendent and $4,800,000 to be high school principal over a thirty-year career. When compared to business, the number of employees and size of budget managed is often very comparable or even larger in education (Cunningham & Sperry, 2001a, 2001b). Better candidates tend to gravitate toward higher salaries. A major responsibility of human resource management professionals is to work with superintendents and school boards to ensure that salaries are competitive and attract competent individuals to their school districts.

The first step in creating a compensation system is to establish the economic value of each of the various job classifications or pay grades. One way to do this is to establish a base rate and to index each of the pay grades to the base figure. Within a pay grade, a salary range provides an opportunity to recognize variations among individuals for factors such as preparation, experience, and performance according to legal requirements and ethical obligations. The salary schedule with its accompanying rules, regulations, and procedures is an expression of the district's salary policy. The single salary schedule typically allows equivalent salaries for equivalent preparation and experience and automatic progression through the salary range within each of the pay grades. In many cases, these single salary schedules form a matrix structure of dollar salary amounts by columns and rows. The columns, commonly referred to as "scales," usually correspond to differences in academic levels or professional preparation, and the rows, commonly referred to as "steps," correspond to number of years of experience.

There are a number of different ways to plan a salary schedule, including fixed dollar increments, variable dollar increments, simple index, and compounded index. The choice of these methods depends on how you want to allocate pay increases within the pay grade. Some methods provide a higher percentage increase for less senior employees, whereas others, such as the compounded index, ensure that everyone receives the same percent increase from step to step, regardless of level of seniority. Other compensation issues include pay for additional duties, pay intervals, and pay for performance.

The problem with some compensation plans is that they do not consider performance. The most competent and the least competent teacher in the school system will be paid the same throughout their professional careers as long as they have the same preparation and number of years of experience. Some believe that this system results in lack of motivation and lower-quality performance and is inherently unfair (National Governors Association, 1986). Performance pay plans factor in merit to the automatic step increases found in most single salary schedule pay plans. Performance pay plans include merit pay, differentiated staffing, performance contracting, and incentive pay.

Merit pay is paying an educator, at least in part, according to the quality of his or her work. Merit adjusts salaries to recognize different levels of job performance. It is based on the belief that individuals should be rewarded in proportion to their contributions and, more pragmatically, that sustaining productivity requires a close link between performance and rewards. The performance appraisal system is the key to a successful merit pay plan. If employees trust the appraisal plan, they often will be able to support merit pay.

In its simplest form performance increments—for rating from unsatisfactory to exceptional—are added to the single salary schedules. More complex approaches include point or unit systems and salary performance formulas. The arguments against merit pay include the creation of jealousy, envy, distrust, and conflict; breakdown of collegiality, cooperative spirit, and teamwork; places discretionary power in the hands of the evaluator; failure because of weak performance appraisal systems and insufficiently qualified evaluators; and, inequitable pay for the same job.

Differentiated staffing, or career ladders, create different roles that permit educators to assume responsibilities, initiative, authority, and pay commensurate with their interests, talents, abilities, and performance. In general, differentiated staffing plans require as many promotion channels and layers as possible so as to provide for advancement in responsibility and pay. For example, positional advancements and pay incentives do not reinforce teaching as a career; they reinforce educational administration. All promotion channels in teaching lead away from the classroom. At the same time, all teachers are treated as interchangeable parts, regardless of talent, experience, or performance because there are no structural provisions for differences among them.

Possible promotion channels within teaching might include associate teacher, staff teacher, senior teacher, and master teacher. Master teachers might work on curriculum, instruction, testing, and student support, spending only 40 percent of their time in the classroom. Master teachers would be paid comparably to assistant principals. In 1998, Massachusetts created a master teacher corps for high-performing teachers certified by the National Board of Professional Teaching Standards. Arthur Wise (2001) states:

> In a differentiated staffing structure, with corresponding levels of compensation, qualified teachers would supervise those without proper qualifications.... A staffing structure could include board-certified teachers, fully licensed teachers, beginning interns, teacher candidates and those with little or no preparation. Individuals would have distinct titles and different pay scales. This structure would provide a career ladder for highly qualified teachers by encouraging them to stay in teaching and it would give school districts a way to fulfill staffing needs with integrity. (p. 37)

Incentive pay and performance contracting are salary supplements or bonuses paid for fulfilling specified conditions. This approach was particularly popular in the 1960s and 1970s; however, there seems to be a resurgence of interest in the late 1990s. The general theme of these plans is to pay people according to how much pupils actually learn. (For more information see: www. wcer.wisc.edu/cpreteachercomp.). Despite their survival, most incentive plans are considered controversial, have mixed results, and fail to receive support from teacher unions that favor guaranteed annual salary increases for all employees, regardless of their performance.

✳ **How might wage and salary compensation be used to support and reinforce the changes that will need to occur at Washington and Lincoln schools? Do you support these ideas? Why or why not?**

Benefits

Fringe benefits provide assistance and protection to all employees and are not contingent on performance. They have risen in cost to represent approximately 35 percent of total compensation paid to employees. Under the provisions of law, school districts as employers are required to provide benefits related to social security, retirement insurance, health insurance, unemployment compensation, long-term care, and worker's compensation. These six along with a minimum paid vacation are often considered core benefits in a flexible-benefit, sometimes called a cafeteria, or market-basket, program.

Other possible fringe benefits include leaves of absence, safety and security, duty-free lunch periods, periodic health screening, dental insurance, savings incentive plans, newsletters, legal services, wellness and health consultants, travel awards, tuition assistance, paid holidays, suggestion awards, recreation programs, and extended core coverage. Fringe benefits are an important part of all compensation programs and influence recruitment, hiring, and employee motivation.

✳ **How might teachers be rewarded for outstanding student performance?**

Collective Bargaining

Collective bargaining is the process of negotiating an agreement between an employer and an employee organization, usually for a specific term, defining the conditions of employment, the rights of employees and their organization, and the procedures to be followed in settling disputes. States have legislated regulations in areas such as unfair practices, administration of labor law, determination of bargaining units, impasse procedures, and prohibiting teacher strikes in order to create a more orderly negotiation process. In addition, school boards have tightened up on the scope of negotiations with teachers. As a result, many see a decrease in the power of professional associations in the collective bargaining process. However, this condition varies by state and school district.

If there is a persistent contract disagreement between the employee organization and the employer and an agreement has not been worked out approximately 90 days before the due date for the budget, a district is automatically at impasse. In the *meet-and-confer process,* the bargaining unit is advisory in capacity and the school board, which has legal responsibility for the contract, writes the contract with the teachers' input. Teachers' input might have minimal impact because it can be ignored.

A significantly greater number of items reach impasse under a meet-and-confer agreement than in situations in which an appeals process exists. An appeals procedure permits the employee organization, the employer, or both to seek assistance in resolving impasses through mediation, fact-finding, arbitration, or other forms of assistance from a third party. *Mediation* is voluntary and advisory in order to come up with a nonbinding compromise solution. In *fact-finding* situations, a neutral panel gathers data, studies the impasse, publishes a report of the facts and issues involved, and makes a recommendation for settlement. Fact-finding is not binding, but it has significant power in that the results are generally published and known by all parties and may carry considerable political weight.

Arbitration is a process whereby the disputing parties at impasse submit their differences to a third party, sometimes from the American Arbitration Association, for a decision. The decision can be advisement and voluntary or compulsory and binding as agreed on by both parties. Final steps such as sanctions and strikes must follow the laws that govern the collective-bargaining process. Court-ordered injunctions can be obtained to keep individuals or groups from committing acts that the court determines to be illegal or harmful. When strikes are legal it is important for the district to have a strike plan. The most important part of this plan is a communication component to provide information, notification, and quick response to news media, parents, staff, safety and security officials, and others in the community. The plan will also identify specific spokespersons and a decision-making center.

The collective-bargaining process generally addresses issues such as teacher workload, duties, evaluation, and development assignments; salary and fringe benefits; the school calendar; curriculum content and quality; management rights; a grievance procedure; a no-strike provision; a zipper clause (when negotiation will be reopened); reduction-in-force; class size; and check-off (collection of dues) procedures (Hoyle et al., 1990). An obvious problem that develops is determining what is negotiable and what falls under the policy responsibilities of the school board. A written agreement regarding all the issues is essential because it serves to formalize the basic rights governing the parties to the agreement and prevent controversies later.

✳ **How do collective bargaining considerations complicate or facilitate the planned changes at these two schools?**

Employee Records and Reports

Effective personnel management requires collecting, maintaining, analyzing, and reporting large amounts of employee information in each of the functions of human resource management previously discussed. Recording and reporting is a routine responsibility of all staff personnel offices. It begins with job analysis, recruitment, affirmative action, and application information and covers all information through exit interviews, unemployment insurance claims, and retirement. Technology has made the collection, storage, and transmittal of information more efficient and thereby the quality of decision making has improved. For example, a skills inventory system allows position requirements to be entered into the computer, which generates a list of all present employees who meet the qualifications for a specific position. Information is more likely to be credible if it is maintained in a single automated personnel file. All updates are made to this single integrated file (see Project 4, page 380).

A number of laws address the importance of protecting employee privacy rights, which must be considered in record keeping and reporting. This is a relatively perfunctory task, but it is essential to the smooth operation of the school system. Accurate information is required to successfully respond to every aspect of the organization from educational planning to defending against litigation.

Employee Litigation

Among the issues that affect human resource development perhaps none is greater than the litigious nature of society. Rebore (1998) states, "Over the last decade, school districts have experienced an increase in litigation. In addition, personnel administrators are far more vulnerable today to judicial review of their actions than personnel administrations of a decade ago" (p. 333). Personnel administrators must carefully evaluate all decisions to ensure that they are ethically responsible and legally defensible (see Chapters 1 and 11). They must also maintain all needed records to support HRD decisions. Rebore continues, "Personnel policies are the key to effective human resource management. Boards of education should take a deliberate approach to policy development that will ensure defensible personnel operations" (p. 334).

✳ **What information might be collected and used to make staff transfer decisions and to protect the school system from any future litigation regarding staff transfers?**

Conclusion

Kaplan and Owings (2002, p. 63) suggest: "We know what constitutes good teaching, and we know what factors contribute to being a better teacher. If principals, superintendents, and other instructional leaders are going to meet the challenges facing them, they need to recruit high-quality teachers and support high-quality teaching in their schools."

Research shows that when an organization voluntarily acts to benefit members, it signals a value placed on employees and concern for their well-being, which pays off through greater productivity and loyalty. Effective HRM efforts offer a wide array of resources to attract competent workers, to develop and reward them, and to foster a relationship that retains them.

Assimilating school system employees by socializing them into the school culture continues to be a essential organizational practice. Diverse forms of support—compensation; development and other inducements; effective hiring practice; respected, fair, and helpful evaluation procedures; and other well-established HRM functions—all contribute to a high-performance school system. Such efforts have been linked to high trust and attachment, continued organizational learning, greater responsiveness, acceptance of change, and greater organization productivity.

Portfolio Artifacts

- Approve faculty/staff leave.
- Plan, develop, and coordinate professional development activities to meet the needs of teachers and improve instruction (organize multiple opportunities in order to accomplish this goal).
- Explain how the principal can protect the rights and confidentiality of staff.
- Participate in a daily walk through with the principal to calibrate observations of instructors.
- Design, implement, and teach whole and small groups to improve some aspect of the school program based upon relevant data and research about effective teaching and learning.
- Provide ongoing coaching and feedback to an individual or group (informal observations,

write-up findings, provide feedback, including one-on-one and small group).
- Write for the weekly bulletin and/or staff newsletter.
- Develop a staffing plan for a school and determine how many new staff will be required.
- Pair up with someone and interview one another for the position to which you both aspire. Write up the results of your interview and discuss the effectiveness of the interviewee and interviewer.
- Pair up with someone and complete a performance appraisal on one another. Write up the results of the appraisal and discuss the effectiveness of the appraisee and appraisor.

- Compare a salary and fringe benefit plan for a school system with that of another organization.
- Help the personnel records manager to update records and produce an affirmative action report for the school district.

- Shadow the assistant superintendent for human resource management.
- Write staff personnel policy.
- Participate in the interview, selection, hiring, and induction of new employees.

Terms

Assessment center	Human resource utilization (HRU)	Perceiver academies
Clinical supervision	Job classification	Performance appraisal
Differentiated staffing	Line and staff	Personnel-to-student ratios
Due process	Open-ended questions	Plan of assistance
Employee assistance program (EAP)	Organizational development (OD)	Professional negotiation and meet-and-confer
"Highly qualified" teachers	Pay grade and single salary schedule	Troops to Teachers (TTT)
Human resource development (HRD)		Unity of command

Suggested Readings

Glickman, C., Gordon, S., & Ross-Gordon, J. (2001). *Supervision and instructional leadership: A development approach.* Boston: Allyn and Bacon.

Guskey, T. R., & Huberman, M. (1995). *Professional development in education.* New York: Teachers College Press.

Pandiscio, H. (2004). *Job hunting in education: An insider's guide to success.* Lanham, MD: Scarecrow Education.

Rebore, R. (2004). *Human resource administration in education: A management approach.* Boston: Allyn and Bacon.

Sayfarth, J. (2005). *Human resource management for effective schools.* Boston: Allyn and Bacon.

Stronge, J., & Tucker, P. (2000). *Teacher evaluation and student achievement.* Washington, DC: National Education Association.

Webb, L. D., & Norton, M. S. (2003). *Human resource administration: Personal issues and needs in education.* Upper Saddle River, NJ: Prentice Hall.

Young, I., & Castetter, W. (2004). *The human resource function in educational administration.* Boston: Allyn and Bacon.

11

Laws and Policies

Not Following School Board Policy

It was 7 A.M. and Principal Ginger Blackmon was sitting at her desk contemplating her next step. Yesterday, high school teacher Glenn O'Brien had chosen not to follow school board policy on field trips. The policy required that parents give written permission prior to their children going on a field trip. O'Brien knew what the policy was, but in his own mind the circumstance was different and justified deviation from the policy. Clearly it wasn't. He had chosen not to get prior permission, and the car he was driving with the four students had been involved in an accident around 5 P.M. No permission slips, a clear violation.

Principal Blackmon knew that O'Brien was not incompetent. She had worked with him for nearly fifteen years. Before she became principal, Blackmon had been a teacher in this school. Blackmon and O'Brien had spent hours discussing education and how to improve schools for kids. In fact, O'Brien was one of the top teachers in the building. Two years before he had received the district's "Outstanding Teacher"

award. He just hadn't thought about the possible implications of his field-trip decision.

The previous afternoon Principal Blackmon and her assistant principal had tried to find out as much as possible about the situation. One of the students was still in the hospital and was scheduled to be released the next day. O'Brien and the three other students had suffered minor injuries and were released from the hospital that same night. Blackmon called the superintendent to inform him of what had occurred. Since he was out of town, she left a message at his hotel.

Last night, after arriving home around midnight from a work-related dinner, Blackmon had found a long message on her answering machine from Mike Canavan, the Board president. Outraged by what had happened, he demanded that O'Brien be fired, tenured or not. "This is gross negligence," he clamored. There was also a message from her superintendent asking her to call him first thing in the morning. He had spoken to Mike Canavan and was very concerned about the situation.

❋ **If you were the principal, what would you do next? Obtain a copy of your state's policy regarding the dismissal or suspension of teachers. What does it say?**

Legal Responsibility

Every week federal and state courts hand down decisions that have the potential to affect every school in the nation.

It is important for educational leaders to learn about current legal issues and their potential impact on schools. School districts are involved in a number of major litigation areas, and knowledge of several key concepts in school law are essential. It is also important for administrators to understand compliance with policies and procedures and risk management.

Learning about Schools and Legal Issues

One way to begin to acquire a basic understanding of the legal system and the laws and statutes that pertain to schools is to take a basic course in school law. Although such a course provides a foundation, keeping up to date must become an ongoing part of professional development. School leaders should have an understanding of and appreciation for the legal rights of teachers and students.

Educators need a basic understanding of the federal Constitution and Bill of Rights as well as their state constitutions and statutes. Common law is a general, overarching statewide or nationwide precedent that derives from earlier legal controversies. It prescribes social conduct enforced by courts by the doctrine of the supremacy of law.

One of the functions of school boards is to adopt policies in accordance with state legislation. Thus, educational leaders must understand school district policies. Many professional organizations, such as the National Association of Secondary School Principals (NASSP), publish monthly updates regarding current issues in school law (see *Cases in Point; A Legal Memorandum* at the NASSP Web site, www. NASSP.org). Educational newspapers and journals have special sections pertaining to legal issues (e.g., see Kappan, PDK's monthly magazine with a special department titled "Courtside"). Other resources include Web sites and publications that serve as guides to federal and state cases. The official newspaper of the U.S. government, the *Federal Register* (available online as well as in paper format) is the vehicle through which all federal agencies publish their regulations and legal notices.

A graduate-level university course in school law and professional reading on a regular basis will help administrators stay current about issues related to school law. For interpretations of court decisions, which can sometimes be difficult to follow, a telephone call to the school district's lawyer (most districts have legal counsel) might be appropriate.

The U.S. Legal System

Federal Role in Education

Education is not specifically discussed in the U.S. Constitution. Box 11.1 lists those amendments that are particularly relevant to typical school legal issues. The Tenth

BOX 11.1 • *Selected Amendments of the U.S. Constitution*

Amendment I (1791)

Congress shall make no law respecting an establishment of religion, or prohibiting the free exercise thereof; or abridging the freedom of speech, or of the press; or the right of the people peaceably to assemble, and to petition the Government for a redress of grievances.

Amendment IV (1791)

The right of the people to be secure in their persons, houses, papers, and effects, against unreasonable searches and seizures, shall not be violated, and no Warrants shall issue, but upon probable cause, supported by Oath or affirmation, and particularly describing the place to be searched, and the persons or things to be seized.

Amendment IX (1791)

The enumeration in the Constitution of certain rights, shall not be construed to deny or disparage others retained by the people.

Amendment X (1791)

The powers not delegated to the United States by the Constitution, nor prohibited by it to the States, are reserved to the States respectively, or to the people.

Amendment XIV (1868)

Section 1. All persons born or naturalized in the United States, and subject to the jurisdiction thereof, are citizens of the United States and of the State wherein they reside. No State shall make or enforce any law which shall abridge the privileges or immunities of citizens of the United States; nor shall any State deprive any person of life, liberty, or property, without due process of law; nor deny to any person within its jurisdiction the equal protection of the laws.

Amendment states, "The powers not delegated to the United States by the Constitution, nor prohibited by it to the States, are reserved to the States respectively, or to the people." This does not mean that the federal government has little influence on schools—in fact, the amendments to the Constitution, U.S. Supreme Court decisions, and congressional acts have considerable influence on both public and private educational institutions.

Federal Courts

The three levels of federal court are shown in Box 11.2. Each state has at least one federal district court; some have several, depending on population density. Appeals from federal district courts can go to the next level, the U.S. circuit court or the U.S. court of appeals.

The procedures and functions of intermediate and the highest appellate courts differ from those of trial courts. These courts do not conduct trials, nor do they hear any new evidence or conduct fact-finding. Their function is to review records of lower courts to determine whether any errors of law have occurred. Errors of law might include procedural mistakes, misinterpretations of the Constitution or statutes, and incorrect instructions to juries, to name but a few.

BOX 11.2 • *The Federal Court System**

U.S. Supreme Court
(highest court of the country)

U.S. Circuit Courts of Appeals (Appellate Courts)
(thirteen intermediate appeal courts)

U.S. District Courts (Trial Courts)
(eighty-nine district courts)

*For more information see: www.uscourts.gov/

There are thirteen circuit courts of appeal (see Table 11.1). One, the Federal Circuit Court of Appeals, has jurisdiction to hear special claims such as those related to taxes, patents and copyrights, customs, and international trade. The remaining twelve are those to which an education-related case would be appealed.

Decisions rendered in a federal appellate court are binding only in the states that fall within that circuit's jurisdiction. For example, the first Circuit Court of Appeals includes Maine, Massachusetts, New Hampshire, Puerto Rico, and Rhode Island. A decision rendered in the first Federal Court of Appeals pertains to these states and territory only; however, the decisions rendered by individual courts of appeals often *influence* the decisions of other courts dealing with similar issues.

TABLE 11.1   *Jurisdictions of the Federal Circuit Courts of Appeal*

Circuit	Jurisdiction
1st	Maine, Massachusetts, New Hampshire, Puerto Rico, Rhode Island
2nd	Connecticut, New York, Vermont
3rd	Delaware, New Jersey, Pennsylvania, Virgin Islands
4th	Maryland, North Carolina, South Carolina, Virginia, West Virginia
5th	Louisiana, Mississippi, Texas
6th	Kentucky, Ohio, Michigan, Tennessee
7th	Illinois, Indiana, Wisconsin
8th	Arkansas, Iowa, Minnesota, Missouri, Nebraska, North Dakota, South Dakota
9th	Alaska, Arizona, California, Guam, Hawaii, Idaho, Montana, Nevada, Northern Mariana Islands, Oregon, Washington
10th	Colorado, Kansas, New Mexico, Oklahoma, Utah, Wyoming
11th	Alabama, Florida, Georgia
DC	Washington, DC
Federal	Three specialized courts, Washington, DC

The U.S. Supreme Court is the court of highest appeal on questions of federal law. The Supreme Court has heard numerous education cases dealing with particular provisions of the U.S. Constitution. In particular the Fourteenth Amendment's *equal protection clause* (e.g., *Plessy v. Ferguson*, 163 U.S. 537, 16 S. Ct. 1138, 41 L. Ed. 256 [1896] and *Brown v. Board of Education*, 347 U.S. 483, 74 S. Ct. 686, 98 L. Ed. 873 [1954]); the Fourteenth Amendment's *due process clause* (e.g., *Meyer v. Nebraska*, 262 U.S. 390, 43 S. Ct. 625, 67 L. Ed. 1042 [1923]); and the First Amendment's *establishment clause* (e.g., *Board of Education v. Allen*, 392 U.S. 236, 88 S. Ct. 1923, 20 L. Ed 1060 [1968]) are cited more often than other amendments in school law cases.

Understanding Court Decisions

PERRY A. ZIRKEL • *Lehigh University*   **KATHLEEN A. SULLIVAN** • *Lehigh University*

Published court opinions form an important body of law that fills in the gaps and resolves the interactions between other sources of law, such as the Constitution and legislation, in relation to specific factual situations. Not all court decisions result in published opinions. Generally, the proportion of published opinions is higher in federal than in state courts and in appellate than in trial courts.

Citations provide identifying information for published court decisions. This sample citation illustrates the key elements:

Yankton School District v. Schramm, 93 F.3d 1369 (8th Cir. 1996). The first element, the name of the case, is customarily underlined or italicized and contains the names of at least one party on each side of the case. Inasmuch as many of the published opinions, including this one, are at the appellate level, the order of the names does not necessarily convey who was the plaintiff, or suing party. Instead, at the appellate level, the first of the two names (here "Yankton") is the appellant, or the party who lost at the level below and, as a result, has brought the appeal.

The second element consists of numbers and an abbreviation that tell where to find the case. The central piece of information, here "F.3d," signifies the reporter, or set of volumes for a particular group of courts. The *Federal Reporter*, originally abbreviated as "F." and now in its third series, contains published decisions of the intermediate, appellate courts in the federal system. The number in front of the abbreviation, here "93," is the volume in that series, and the number

after the abbreviation, here "1369," is the page in that volume where the court's opinion starts.

The final element, which is in parentheses, contains the year in which the decision was issued and, if not indicated by the reporter abbreviation, an abbreviation for the court that issued the decision. Since only Supreme Court decisions appear in the alternative Supreme Court Reporters, "U.S." and "S. Ct.," no additional notation beyond citation to the reporter is necessary to identify the court. As in the sample citation, the United States circuit courts of appeal, the level below the Supreme Court, are identified by circuit number. An opinion rendered by the highest state court will contain only the state's abbreviation in parentheses, and opinions from lower levels will contain further abbreviations for the name of the court.

The court opinion also has identifiable elements that help the reader understand the import of the decision. The first part, which follows the name of the judge who authored the opinion, typically contains the facts that were distilled from the evidence in the case. The facts include who did what to whom, giving rise to the specific controversy. At the appellate level, this section also includes the disposition of the case in the lower court(s).

The central element of the opinion, which might take several readings to accurately identify, is the issue of the case. Usually a single question answerable by "yes" or "no," the issue poses the relevant facts in a sufficiently generalizable form. In the *Schramm* case, for example, the issue may be stated as follows: "Whether instructional accommodations fulfill the 'special education' criterion for eligibility under the Individual with Disabilities Education Act (IDEA)."

The court's answer to this question, along with the basis, or legal source, and rationale for the decision provide the final part of the court's opinion. The court's answer is called the rule or holding in the case. In *Schramm*, the Eighth Circuit Court of Appeals answered the question affirmatively, based on the definition of "special education" in the IDEA. The rationale was that the plain meaning of the words in the definition, such as "specially designed instruction" to meet individual needs, conveyed a congressional intent to include instructional accommodations for otherwise qualified students. Usually the court presents its rationale through a logical discussion and application of the law to the facts of the case.

Opinions also often contain statements made by the court that are not necessary for the "holding," such as a comment on how the decision might change if the facts were different. These comments, known as "dicta," should not be confused with the holding. Only those state-ments or observations essential to the judge's decision form the holding in the case and may be relied on for guidance.

Usually a court's decision applies both to the immediate parties and to future cases that have the same circumstances. These past cases and their effect on future cases is called prece-dent. Precedent is binding on courts at the same or higher level within a jurisdiction. Since our legal system contains both federal and state branches, each with different boundaries of au-thority, not all decisions are binding on all other courts. Decisions from outside jurisdictions, al-though not binding, might be persuasive to other courts.

Judicial opinions offer insight into the prob-able outcome of similar cases and establish boundaries to guide future conduct. Deciphering the elements of not only of the citation but, more important, of the opinion, enables school leaders to locate and use court decisions. Because they cannot afford to leave such matters entirely to lawyers, school leaders can benefit by knowing how to find and understand court decisions to an-swer as well as ask key questions.

In addition to federal courts, the federal government enacts legislation (fed-eral statutes) that directly affects educational institutions. Statutes are regularly up-dated, supplemented, and revised by successive legislatures (see the *Federal Register*). Courts determine the validity and meaning of these legislative acts. These acts are binding for all citizens as long as they satisfy constitutional requirements. Civil rights legislation such as the Education of the Handicapped Act (EHA) and the 1975 amendment, Education for All Handicapped Children Act, Section 504 of the Rehabilitation Act of 1973, and Title VII of the Civil Rights Act of 1964 (Title VII) are examples of federal statutes.

One example of federal legislation that has affected nearly all school districts in the country is Goals 2000. This legislation was introduced by President George Bush Sr. in 1989 and later passed by Congress and signed by President Bill Clinton in 1994. Consisting of eight goals, it appropriates federal money each year for states that adopt voluntary standards. These standards must meet federal guidelines for student achievement. It is not required that a state apply for the funding, but, if it does, it would then make subgrants to local education agencies (LEAs may include school districts, regional service centers, and others). This legislation also estab-lished two other acts: The Gun-Free Schools Act and the Safe Schools Act. (For more details about federal involvement in education, see Chapter 2.)

The Department of Education's (DOE) role is to implement the administra-tion's policies regarding education. The chief executive officer of the DOE is the secretary of education. The Department of Education maintains a home page on the World Wide Web. (For more information see: www.ed.gov/index.html.)

The operationalizing of the administration's policies can be seen in the federal education budget. (Chapter 12 provides an example of how federal monies are distributed to certain program areas for use in local school districts.) The federal government can penalize or sanction local education agencies that do not adhere to federal policies. Additionally, guidelines and policies from federal agencies, such as the Equal Employment Opportunities Commission (EEOC), are often cited in employment discrimination claims.

✱   **What federal laws are relevant to addressing issues related to O'Brien, the injured students, and the field trip?**

The State's Legal Role in Education

Although state court systems vary, most state courts have three levels: trial courts, intermediate appellate courts, and the state supreme court (see Box 11.3).

The majority of education-related cases are heard at the state level because education is a function of the state, rather than the federal government. A state supreme court case can be appealed to a federal court only if it involves a question of federal law. Appellate courts, whether at the federal or state level, do not review an entire case. Instead, they take appeals only on questions that the lawyers properly "preserve" for appeal. The narrowness of the appeals process explains why some school law cases are litigated several times before all the important issues are finally settled. Examining one state education case will be illustrative.

Sheff v. O'Neill was filed in 1989 on behalf of seventeen Hartford, Connecticut, schoolchildren. Milo Sheff was a fourth-grade African American student at the time (sixteen other white and Hispanic children living in the city of Hartford and the suburbs were also plaintiffs). William A. O'Neill, the defendant, was then governor of Connecticut. The plaintiffs argued that it was up to the state to alleviate the educational deprivation associated with living in a racially and socioeconomically isolated urban area such as Hartford. The case was originally filed in the lowest court in the state—the superior court. This district court ruled against the plaintiffs, Milo Sheff

BOX 11.3 • *State Court Systems*

State Supreme Court
(highest state court)

State Appellate Courts
(intermediate appellate courts)

Trial Courts
(district, circuit, or county courts)

and the other children. The superior court ruled that because the state did not create the segregation that now held sway, it need not take measures to dismantle it.

The case was appealed by the plaintiffs to the state appellate court. The appeal was granted and in 1995 the case went to the Connecticut State Supreme Court. In 1996 this court ruled in favor of the plaintiffs. It declared that the state constitution's education and equal protection clauses require the legislature to ensure that students in the Hartford public schools are provided with integrated and equal educational opportunities. Although this case is not binding outside Connecticut, it has the potential to influence similar claims in other states.

State Legislatures, Administrative Agencies, and Local Boards of Control

States have the power to enact statutes within the limitations of state and federal constitutions. Valente (1997), in his text on school law titled *Law in the Schools*, maintains that within the realm of education

> legislative power includes authority to (1) create, alter, and abolish school districts; (2) alter the structure and powers of school boards; (3) remove incumbent school board members and abolish offices; (4) prescribe the school calendar and curriculum; (5) determine the sources and procedures for raising school revenue and school spending; (6) fix the appointment, term, and qualifications of teachers; (7) require local schools to admit children of nontaxpayers; and (8) revoke charters of public schools for noncompliance with state regulations. (p. 17)

For example, a Connecticut statute (Sec. 46b-56) regarding the rights of noncustodial parents reads:

> Sec. 46b-56. (Formerly Sec. 46-42). Superior court orders re custody and care of minor children in actions for dissolution of marriage, legal separation, and annulment. Access to records of minor children by noncustodial parent. (a) In any controversy before the superior court as to the custody or care of minor children, and at any time after the return day of any complaint under section 46b-45, the court may at any time make or modify any proper order regarding the education and support of the children and of care, custody, and visitation if it has jurisdiction under the provisions of chapter 815o. Subject to the provisions of section 46b-56a, the court may assign the custody of any child to the parents jointly, to either parent, or to a third party, according to its best judgment upon the facts of the case and subject to such conditions and limitations as it deems equitable. The court may also make any order granting the right of visitation of any child to a third party including but not limited to grandparents.

Some statutes are designated as education statutes. For example, Sec. 10-221 of the Connecticut statutes pertains to rule prescription by boards of education:

> Sec. 10-221. Boards of education to prescribe rules. (a) Boards of education shall prescribe rules for the management, studies, classification, and discipline of the public

schools, and, subject to the control of the state board of education, the textbooks to be used; shall make rules for the control, within their respective jurisdictions, of school library media centers and approve the selection of books and other educational media therefore, and shall approve plans for public school buildings and superintend any high or graded schools in the manner specified in this title.

All states have a *state superintendent of instruction* or *state commissioner of education*. This person is the chief state school officer and serves as the chief executive of the state department of education. (For more information see: www.CCSSO.org/.) State education departments typically comprise a variety of divisions, such as teaching and learning, educational programs, vocational-technical schools, finance and administration, and so forth. The size of the department often depends on the state's population as well as whether there are regional or county departments of education. For example, Texas has regional service centers with appointed directors, whereas California has county service centers that fall under the aegis of the county board of education, an elected board with an elected superintendent. The roles of these service centers vary but often include providing direct services to school districts such as special-education services, adult education programming, family service coordination, and cooperative purchasing programs, to name but a few. (See Chapter 2.)

Administrative agencies include not only the state department of education but also other state and regional agencies that might have jurisdiction over all or some schools in a given state. In some states boards of education are referred to as *school committees* and in others they are called *school boards*. States cannot implement the general supervision of schools, so it is delegated to local boards of education. (Hawaii is an exception because it is composed of a single school district.) Since local school boards have the authority to enforce federal and state policies, their actions must be within federal and state constitutions and statutes. (See Chapter 5.)

The statutes of each state contain provisions that concern certain aspects of teachers' and administrators' behavior. Statutes dealing with a variety of topics can be found in the state's education statutes, including information regarding teacher and administrator certification; discipline; dismissal; the denial, revocation or suspension of certification; and contract termination, for example. The school administrator must be familiar with the statutes in the state's education code and refer to them when needed.

✳ **What specifically does your state's education code say regarding the tenure, nonrenewal, or dismissal of teachers? What implications, if any, does this have for Glenn O'Brien?**

School Districts and Litigation

According to a study conducted by Underwood and Noffke (1990), the number one cause for school district litigation was employee-related issues. Table 11.2 displays the percentage of total cases initiated in three categories: employee issues, districtwide issues, and student issues.

TABLE 11.2   *Issues That Land Schools in Court*

Issues	Percentage of total cases initiated	Percentage of times district prevailed
Employee issues (total)	42.6	81.4
Dismissal/nonrenewal	14.2	93.3
Contract negotiations/implementation	11.6	75.0
Discipline	10.5	88.8
Other	1.6	33.3
Hiring	1.0	100.0
Districtwide issues (total)	37.4	67.5
Negligence	22.6	63.1
District property	4.7	60.0
Desegregation	3.2	66.7
Curriculum	2.6	0.0
Finance	2.1	50.0
Other	2.1	90.0
Student issues (total)	20.0	65.4
Special education	8.9	50.0
Discipline practices	6.8	87.5
Discrimination	2.1	33.3
Grades and promotion	1.0	100.0
Constitutional issues	.5	100.0
Other	.5	33.3

Source: J. Underwood & J. Noffke (1990). School law news: You're winning. *The Executive Educator, 12*(3), 18–20. Reprinted with permission.

Negligence is the primary reason for litigation. However, as Underwood and Noffke (1990) point out, "It's most likely to be settled by the parties, rather than being litigated in court" (p. 20). The authors identify the second-highest litigation area as employment-related issues. Under the category of student issues, special education ranked highest. According to the authors, litigation in this area is on the upswing.

Legal Issues and Schools

Common law, statutes, and constitutional law touch on such issues as tenure, contracts, student rights, civil rights, collective bargaining, finance, property, desegregation, intergovernmental relations, instructional programming, and teacher rights. These and other issues are governed to some extent by law. A few important issues that educational administrators might face are due process, freedom of expression, student discipline, records, and tort liability.

Due Process

According to the Fourteenth Amendment a person cannot be deprived arbitrarily of "life, liberty, or property, without due process of law." Before the state can damage these rights, due process must be afforded. According to Data Research Inc. (1991), an organization that publishes law texts, "There are many variations, and the courts do not always agree on what constitutes due process of law" (p. 92).

Of the two types of due process, substantive and procedural, substantive due process deals with the entire process of being fair. According to Strahan and Turner (1987) substantive due process includes the necessity for a rule not to be unduly vague, and that discipline should be based on written rules. Further, decisions should be supported with evidence, the identity of a witness should be revealed, an impartial hearing must be afforded each person, and if the accused so requests, a public or private hearing should be offered. Procedural due process involves providing notice and fair hearing so that an impartial and just settlement of a conflict between parties can be reached; thus, procedural due process is an established system.

Notice refers to making the rules orderly and ensuring that the party involved is aware of them and how they should be followed, as well as possible penalties for their violation. Inherent in this notion is that people have a right to know the standards by which they are to be judged. It would be unreasonable and unfair to hold people accountable for meeting expectations if they are ignorant of those expectations. For example, if a school system has a teacher-evaluation system and the procedures and standards involved in that system are not explained to teachers, then it would be unfair and unreasonable to expect teachers to be evaluated using that system. Similarly, if there is a student discipline code, including the procedures and penalties for certain behaviors, and the code is not explained to a student, it is unreasonable to punish the student for not following it. Standards must be known in advance, and they should be clear so that a person knows that what he or she has done counts as meeting, or not meeting, the standards.

Fair hearing includes several aspects: a written statement of the charges and the type of evidence that should be given to the individual; explanation of procedural right; adequate time to prepare a defense; and an opportunity for a formal hearing. According to McCarthy, Cambron-McCabe, and Thomas (1997), in cases where a teacher is terminated, the following procedural elements must be afforded:

- Notification of charges
- Opportunity for a hearing
- Adequate time to prepare a rebuttal to the charges
- Access to evidence and names of witnesses
- Hearing before an impartial tribunal
- Representation by legal counsel
- Opportunity to present evidence and witnesses
- Decision based on evidence and findings of the hearing
- Transcript or record of the hearing
- Opportunity to appeal an adverse decision (pp. 381–382)

✷ **What implications do these procedural elements have for Principal Black-mon's decisions?**

Freedom of Speech and Expression

The First Amendment covers written, oral, and symbolic forms of expression, including:

- Academic freedom (e.g., *Keyishian v. Board of Regents of New York*, 1967)
- Censorship (e.g., *Planned Parenthood v. Clark County School District*, 1991)
- Community service programs (e.g., *Steirer v. Bethlehem Area School District*, 1993)
- Defamatory expression, which includes slander (oral) and libel (written) (e.g., *Scott v. New-Herald*, 1986)
- Symbolic expression (e.g., *Tinker v. Des Moines Independent School District*; the Supreme Court in 1985 ruled that a rule prohibiting students from wearing black arm bands in school as a protest against the Vietnam War was invalid)
- Hate speech (e.g., *Doe v. University of Michigan*, 1989)
- Obscene, vulgar, or inflammatory expression (e.g., *Miller v. California*, 1973; *Fenton v. Srear*, 1980)
- Freedom of the press (e.g., *Hazelwood School District v. Kuhlmeier*, 1988)
- Distribution of religious materials (e.g., *Stone v. Graham*, 1983)
- Dress and hair codes (e.g., *Farrell v. Dallas Independent School District*, 1968)

Numerous controversies over freedom of speech erupted starting in the 1960s. Many educators argue that schools should not tolerate student speech and expression that is inconsistent with the school's basic educational mission. Given a compelling purpose, speech can be regulated; but no one can be prohibited from speaking simply because her or his ideas differ from those of the administration or staff.

Discipline and Students with Disabilities

In the expert inquiry, school law Professor Charles Russo discusses the expanded rights of students with disabilities. As previously noted in Table 11.2, for litigation areas related to students, Underwood and Noffke rank special education highest. They maintain that litigation in special education is on the upswing. Discussing the disciplining of regular and special education students, legal expert Perry Zirkel (1996) recommends that policies and practices be "in accord with federal constitutional requirements and any procedural safeguards under state law" (p. 21).

Substantive and procedural due process must clearly be kept in the forefront as regards disciplining students. Nathan Essex (1999) states, "It has long been held that children with disabilities may not be punished for conduct that is a manifestation of their disability. . . . In situations where certain types of discipline are warranted, an effort must be made to ensure that the punishment does not materially and substantially interrupt the child's education" (p. 80). Exercise caution and work with the district's legal counsel to protect your schools and district from legal costs and liability awards. (See Chapter 9.)

School district personnel make many common mistakes when dealing with families with children with special needs. Often these mistakes result in litigation that could have been avoided if due process had been followed. First, parents must be informed and their consent obtained. They need to be notified of all due process procedures and be given lists of all procedural safeguards upon the initial referral for evaluation. Additionally, parents should once again be informed at each IEP meeting about due process procedures and procedural safeguards. Another common mistake involves improper or insufficient evaluations. Evaluations must be administered by knowledgeable and trained personnel and must be in accordance with any instructions provided by test produces. Also students should be assessed in all areas of suspected disability, including, if appropriate, health, vision, social and emotional status, hearing, academic performance, general intelligence, and motor abilities. The findings from these evaluations need to be translated into a single coherent view of the child. The document should be easily understood, detailed, and should have realistic and concrete recommendations.

Another common mistake made by school personnel is to deny an independent educational evaluation. If the parent disagrees with the district's evaluation *and* the district's evaluation is not appropriate, the parent, at public expense, has the right to an independent evaluation. Another error often made is that there is an insufficient or incomplete IEP. This may include not including measurable objectives: omitting current levels of performance based upon recent data; failing to summarize discussions at IEP meetings such as areas of concern, agreement, disagreement, and the length of the meeting, among others; and failing to get partial consent when parents disagree or refuse to sign the document. Another common mistake is to deny services based on cost considerations. Districts are required to provide Free Appropriate Public Education (FAPE) without regard to the funds they receive. Costs can only be considered when the choice is between two equally appropriate educational programs.

Another common mistake is a conducting a deficient IEP meeting. It is crucial that the mandatory people be present. In some states such as California this includes at least one regular education teacher if the student has regular education classes [see Education Code 56341; 1414(d)(1)(B)]. Other issues that may mean an IEP meeting is deficient are the need to video or tape-record, needing an attorney present, and attempting to exclude persons. There also may be a need to have note takers, sign language interpreters, English language interpreters, etc. Another common mistake is to give in to parent demands. Educators are the experts, and since they are trained to conduct IEPs, they should provide guidance for parents. FAPE is a student right that parents cannot waive. Another common error is to deny access to student records or not to protect confidentiality. It is crucial that school personnel are knowledgeable about what their state education code asserts on this topic. In many states teachers must be informed of who commits suspendable or expellable offenses. Finally, a common mistake that leads to litigation is procrastination. Neglect and indifference are often reasons for litigation. It is imperative that school personnel follow though on mediated agreements and due process decisions. It is easy to become busy and allow time lines to pass and services to be ignored.

The Confidentiality of Student Records

The Family Educational Rights and Privacy Act (FERPA, Public Law 93-380), enacted by the U.S. Congress in 1974, established a student's right to privacy. Also included in this act is the requirement that schools adopt and publicize the procedures for accessing and obtaining school records as well as explaining how information can be removed. FERPA stipulates that a parent's written consent is required for a third party to obtain access to a student's record. An amendment to this act, the Buckley amendment, threatens the withdrawal of federal funds if parents are prevented from seeing their children's complete records.

Administrators should formulate guidelines regarding student records that include developing procedures for allowing access to the files, keeping a log of all people who have obtained access to the records, allowing parents and students to submit outside materials to the record, and developing procedures to obtain informed consent from students and parents before data in the student's record can be released to a third party. Clearly the issue of the privacy of records is an important one, and the development of clear guidelines is not only an important legal issue but also an ethical one as well.

Student Rights

CHARLES J. RUSSO • *University of Dayton*

The legal landscape of American public education has changed greatly over the past forty-five years. The catalyst for this dramatic metamorphosis was the U.S. Supreme Court's 1954 ruling in *Brown v. Board of Education*, which struck down separate but equal educational facilities as inherently unequal. In the decades after *Brown*, the combination of judicial and legislative action has not only protected the rights of children of color, female students, and those with disabilities to equal educational opportunities, but has also defined the range of constitutional rights available to all school children.

Tinker v. Des Moines Independent Community School District (1969), decided in the middle of the civil rights era that was ushered in by *Brown* and the social unrest of the 1960s, did much more than uphold the rights of students to wear armbands as a protest against American involvement in Vietnam. The Court's often quoted words, "[i]t can hardly be argued that students or teachers shed their constitutional rights to freedom of speech or expression at the schoolhouse gate" (p. 506), signaled the dawn of a new day in student rights.

Congressional passage of Title IX of the Educational Amendments of 1972 protected female students by prohibiting discrimination based on gender in educational programs receiving federal financial assistance. The Supreme Court has since expanded the scope of Title IX to cover students who have been victims of sexual harassment (*Franklin v. Gwinett County Public Schools*, 1992).

The Court further defined the rights of students in *Goss v. Lopez* (1975). In *Goss*, the Court ruled in favor of students who did not receive procedural due process before being suspended from school for ten days. The Court found that since a suspension of ten days (or longer) is more than a minimal deprivation of the rights of students to education, they "must be given some kind of notice and some kind of hearing" (p. 738). Although it stopped short of mandating hearings for all disciplinary infractions, the Court suggested that longer suspensions or expulsions may require more formal procedures.

Perhaps the most significant expansion of student rights occurred in special education. The passage of the Education for All Handicapped Children's Act in 1975, now the Individuals with

Disabilities Education Act (IDEA, 1997), opened the door for millions of children with disabilities. Along with ensuring that all students with disabilities are entitled to free, appropriate public education in the least restrictive environments, the act includes substantive and procedural protection to assist children and their parents in safeguarding their rights.

The judicial expansion of student rights ended in 1985. In *New Jersey v. TLO,* the Court upheld the warrantless search of a student's purse because the administrator who did so satisfied its two-part test. According to the Court a search is permissible; first, as long as there is reasonable suspicion (a lower standard than probable cause, which applies to the police) to believe that a student has violated or is violating school rules or the law. Second, the Court maintained that the area being searched has to be reasonably related in scope to the circumstances that justified the interference in the first place. Following *TLO,* school officials have won all but a handful of the approximately forty cases involving searches of students, including a decision by the Supreme Court (*Vernonia School District 47 J. v. Acton,* 1995) that permits the drug testing of interscholastic athletes.

The Court cut back on the free speech rights of students in *Bethel School District v. Eraser* (1986). In *Eraser* the Court ruled that educators could discipline a high school student who delivered a nominating speech at an assembly because it contained sexual innuendoes. The Court distinguished *Eraser* from *Tinker* on the basis that the nondisruptive, passive expression of a political viewpoint in the latter case intruded on neither the work of the school nor the rights of other students.

The Court went full circle in a 1988 decision involving a dispute over a student newspaper. In *Hazelwood School District v. Kuhlmeier,* the Court concluded that "educators could exercise reasonable editorial control over the style and content of student speech in school-sponsored expressive activities so long as their actions are reasonable related to legitimate pedagogical concerns" (p. 273). As such, the Court permitted educators to exclude an article on pregnancy at the high school from the newspaper, along with one about the divorce of a student's parents because they believed that these topics were inappropriate.

How today's educational leaders answer challenging questions will go a long way in determining the kinds of students and schools that the United States will have in the twenty-first century.

Cases and Legislation Cited

Bethel Sch. Dist. No. 403 v. Eraser, 478 U.S. 675 (1986).

Brown v. Board of Educ., 347 U.S. 483 (1954).

Franklin v. Gwinett County Pub. Schs., 503 U.S. 60 (1992).

Goss v. Lopez, 419 U.S. 565 (1975).

Hazelwood Sch. Dist. v. Kuhlmeier, 484 U.S. 260 (1988)

Individuals with Disabilities Education Act, 20 U.S.C.A. 1400 et seq. (1997).

New Jersey v. TLO, 469 U.S. 325 (1985).

Tinker v. Des Moines Indep. Community Sch. Dist., 393 U.S. 503 (1969).

Title IX of the Educational Amendments of 1972, 20 U.S.C.A. 1681 (1997).

Vernonia Sch. Dist. 47 J. v. Acton, 515 U.S. 646 (1995).

Torts

A tort is a civil (not a criminal) wrong, not including contracts, for which a remedy in damages can be sought. According to Valente (1997), tort liability is created by federal and state law. Actions alleging failure of schools to protect students against sexual harassment and violence are being brought against schools under federal law. According to state tort law, "A person who causes injury to another through violation of some legal duty is liable to pay compensatory money damages to the injured party" (p. 443). Claims are usually covered by a district's group insurance; minimizing the potential for tort litigation, however, should be of much concern to educational leaders.

A basic concept of tort law is *fault*. Torts may be intentional, or may result from negligence or carelessness. According to Taylor (1996), three factors must be met in order for a party to be liable for negligence: (1) there must be a duty on the part of the defendant toward the victim either to act or to refrain from acting in a particular way, (2) this duty must be breached through failure to exercise a reasonable standard of care, and (3) there must be injury caused by this breach (p. 66).

All school employees are required to carry out their duties in a reasonable manner so that no damage or injury is incurred. Typical tort liability settings include laboratories, shops, playgrounds, field trips, spaces for physical education, and classrooms.

With regard to negligence:

- School employees have a duty to protect students in their care (*in loco parentis*).
- School employees must act with a reasonable standard of care.
- Once a cause of injury is established, the school leader must ask if the employee failed to act with a reasonable standard of care.
- There must be evidence that damage to the plaintiff was the result of the injury.

✳ **What implications does the discussion about torts in this chapter have for the students involved in the accident and their parents?**

Monitoring Compliance with Policies and Procedures

How can the school administrator ensure that the policies of the school district are followed and that teachers and students understand them? What systems can be put in place to monitor compliance? As schools continue developing partnerships and collaborations with individuals and community organizations, complying with state and district policies is crucial to risk management. According to Shoop and Dunklee (1992), "Risk management is a coordinated, effective pre-event and post-event response to a school district's liability exposure, developed through planning, organizing, leading, and monitoring a district's activities and assets" (p. 307).

Risk management is a concept that started in the insurance industry, and the business manager of a school district should be keenly aware of its importance. It includes areas such as safety, security, transportation, and health. Given the growth of litigation against school districts and the simultaneous decentralization of management from the district to the site level, risk management is a concept with which all administrators should have familiarity. A key way of operationalizing the myriad issues involved in risk management is the development of clear and succinct policies and procedures, which are then explicated to students and teachers in school handbooks.

Another important concept is the *legal audit*. In the case of school districts, this refers to a *professional* review of the legal affairs of the district, carried out on a periodic basis and reported to the school board. Shoop and Dunklee (1992) cite two advantages of a legal audit:

1. The likelihood is increased that significant, but preventable, legal problems will come to the attention of district administrators and the board of education.
2. The flow of information to district administrators and the board of education is increased, with the assurance that the parties are receiving accurate facts on which to base preventive action.

Part of the legal audit involves examining the policies the school board has developed and the procedures for informing school district personnel and students of those policies. School-based administrators should be aware that the central office arranges for legal audits to be conducted and that these reports might have implications for the daily operations of their schools.

Box 11.4 exemplifies a school district policy regarding the acceptable use of electronic information systems. Plainville Schools in Plainville, Connecticut, has community relations, business, instruction, personnel, and student policies that appear not only in student handbooks, but also on the district's website. The policy in Box 11.4 is for students. Note that a policy on "acceptable use" was originally approved in 1997, then it was revised in 2002 and again in 2003. One of the first things an administrator new to a district needs to do is become familiar with all district policies and where to find them.

To ensure that students are familiar with district policies that pertain to them, it is typical for the student handbook to include all such policies. Usually, there is a signature sheet in the student handbook that must be signed by the student and his or her parent acknowledging that they have indeed read the policies.

It then becomes imperative that the school site administrator develop mechanisms to monitor that all such forms are returned and filed. This is part of what is referred to as *preventive law*. Shoop and Dunklee (1992) define it as "a branch of law that endeavors to minimize the risk of litigation or to secure, with more certainty, legal rights and duties" (p. 308).

✳ **How might the school system make sure that problems like the one caused by O'Brien's negligence do not occur in the future?**

Legal and Ethical Dimensions of Educational Leadership

MARTHA McCARTHY • *Indiana University*

An important purpose of public education in our nation is to instill core values for citizen-ship—values that form the foundation of a democratic society, such as love of liberty, justice,

BOX 11.4 • *Board of Education Policies Policy Detail View*

Section	(5000) Students
Policy Name	Acceptable Use Policy (AUP)
Policy Number	5131.8
Date Approved	04/14/1997
Date Revised	01/14/2002
Date Revised	10/14/2003
Date Revised	
Date Revised	
Policy	Plainville Community Schools provides electronic information systems for improving teaching, learning, and managing. These systems shall be used by members of the school community in accordance with policy and procedures established by the school district and laws enacted by state and federal governments. The following acceptable use policy (AUP) applies to supervised and independent use of all forms of technology. It does not attempt to articulate all access scenarios and user behaviors.
	For the purposes of this AUP, the definition of information systems is any configuration of hardware and software that provides users access to information stored electronically. The configuration can be a single unit or multiple units networked together. Networks include computer hardware, operating system software, application software, and stored text and data files, regardless of source and content.
	Users shall be defined as any person who utilizes these information networks. Users include all students, district employees, and members of the Board of Education. It may also include other persons outside of these groups who, in the course of using district facilities, require access to the systems.
	The Plainville Board of Education expects all users of its technologies and electronic information systems to demonstrate responsible, courteous behaviors. Responsible behavior includes abiding by the law and the terms of the AUP with regard to privacy, confidentiality, security, and intellectual property.
	Computers, computer files, the e-mail system, software furnished to users, and other pieces of the school's information network are school district property. Students should not consider any of their use of computers to be private, including all electronic communications. Use of passwords to gain access to the school's information systems does not imply privacy in that use. The school district has the right but is not required to monitor any and all aspects of its information systems, including all materials students create, store, send or receive.
	The Superintendent of Schools or his/her designee will be responsible for implementing this policy, establishing procedures and guidelines, and supervising access privileges. Such guidelines shall be used to enforce the measures to block or filter Internet access and to preserve the students' and staff's rights to examine and use information to meet the educational goals and objectives of the Plainville Community School District.
	Violations of this policy may result in revocation of access to and privileges relating to use of the information systems and networks. Encouraging, allowing, or ignoring student use of the computer resources in a manner contrary to this policy is strictly prohibited. Violations of this policy by students may result in disciplinary action, up to and including suspension and/or expulsion. Violations may also result in civil and criminal liability. Students will be responsible for any losses, costs or damages incurred by the school district as a result of unauthorized use or intentional destruction of its information network or pieces.
	Legal References: Public Law 94-553, Title 17, The Copyright Act of 1976 Family Education Rights and Privacy Act (FERPA), 20 U.S.C. §1232g 20 U.S.C. §1232h 20 U.S.C. §1400 et. seq., Individuals with Disabilities Education Act C.G.S. §10-15b C.G.S. §53a-182b through §53a-183, as amended by Public Act 95–143, An Act Concerning Harassment by Computer and the Possession of Child Pornography.

democracy, equality, and fairness and freedom of thought (Etzioni, 1993; McCarthy, Bull, Quantz, & Sorenson, 1993). A related function of public schools is to teach how our legal system and ethical codes protect these values. Many school administrators, however, currently are hesitant to engage teachers and students in reflecting on legal and ethical concerns. Legal discussions are sometimes avoided because school leaders are uneasy about their own knowledge of the law and consequently fear that such discussions will identify legal problems or make schools more vulnerable to legal challenges. Ethical deliberations may be avoided because they frequently surface value conflicts. Public schools have been faulted by some conservative citizen groups for encouraging students to clarify their values (Cohen, 1990).

Educators should not fear the law, apologize for exploring ethical concerns, or try to eliminate value-oriented material from the public school curriculum (an impossible feat). On the contrary, school leaders have an obligation to encourage their staff members and students to examine their values and the fundamental values undergirding the Constitution and laws in our nation.

All actions of school leaders have legal and ethical dimensions, yet many school administrators hold the erroneous impression that law and ethics simply set boundaries for their behavior (Bull & McCarthy, 1995). Indeed, the law is often viewed as a bothersome, external constraint—a prescriptive limitation—imposed on administrators' discretion and creativity. And some view ethical considerations as more concrete and settled—a precise list of "correct" behaviors—than they are.

Prospective school leaders should be encouraged to embrace a broader view of law and ethics. The law provides the basic framework for all interactions in an ordered society, and it specifies mechanisms for conflict resolution. The law emanates from experience, is constantly evolving, is designed to facilitate individual and collective activities, and reflects political and social changes over time. Thus, understanding the law is not simply a mechanical process of locating rules and regulations that govern our behavior. When educators do not understand the law, they often have unfounded fears of legal sanctions and they focus solely on the legal directives rather than on the process of developing, interpreting, and applying the law. Increased awareness of fundamental legal principles and the tensions between individual and collective interests leads to greater respect for the responsibilities that accompany legal rights.

Ethical deliberations also are more complex than school leaders often perceive them to be. Ethics is a social process of justifying human actions and exploring the validity of reasons for actions. By examining school situations through the lens of ethical behaviors (e.g., what is considered "just" and why), individuals can acquire a deeper understanding of their own values and biases as well as those of society. One's ethical code is more than a list of virtuous behaviors; it involves an examination of the concept of "virtue" and other concepts (e.g., "good," "moral"). To gain an understanding and appreciation of ethics, one must explore various ethical perspectives on a range of issues.

Although there are similarities between law and ethics, the commonalties should not be overstated. Some actions may be considered ethical but violate the law and vice versa. Individuals continue to be willing to suffer legal consequences for breaking laws they consider morally wrong (civil disobedience). Also, practices that some view as unethical, such as misleading a colleague regarding a professional matter, have no legal ramifications. This is why many professional organizations have developed codes of ethics in an effort to regulate behavior for which legal sanctions are not available.

If school leaders are to develop a deep understanding of law and ethics and translate such knowledge into action, these topics must be approached differently in educational leadership preparation programs. The notion is no longer widely supported that school administrators should be taught to deal with school situations as objective problems to be solved in a scientifically rational manner. Many now believe that preparation programs should guide school leaders in exploring complex, messy school situations that have no concrete answers and in understanding that personal beliefs influence what they do on the job (Beck, Murphy, & Associates, 1997).

Yet most preparation programs still do not encourage future school leaders to think critically about the legal and ethical aspects of their roles or to challenge their own values and worldviews. Preparation programs should expose future school leaders to scholarship in law and ethics and provide them ample opportunities to practice legal and ethical discourse and engage in intense personal reflection and critique (McCarthy et al., 1993; Starratt, 1994). Moreover, if school leaders become comfortable with legal and ethical deliberations during their prepara-

tion programs, their comfort level should carry over into their professional roles.

Whereas law has been a part of the educational leadership curriculum for several decades (although often too technically focused), only recently has ethics received systematic attention in some programs (Beck et al., 1997). Both law and ethics lend themselves to problem-based instruction and the exploration of legal and ethical implications of real and simulated school situations. By identifying and exploring dilemmas and considering alternative perspectives in formulating responses, school personnel can ask penetrating questions and make thoughtful decisions.

Conclusion

It is critically important that educational leaders keep abreast of school law issues. Administrators need a comprehensive knowledge of both education and law to make prudent judgments. Consulting professional publications and, when appropriate, contacting the district's legal counsel are important preventive measures for protecting your school from litigation. Follow these guidelines:

- Schools may regulate speech only when it is necessary to achieve a compelling purpose and when regulations are no more extensive than necessary.
- Schools cannot prohibit speech simply because the ideas expressed differ from those of the administration or staff.
- The prohibition of speech can occur only when it disrupts the school's educational purpose or if it invades the rights of others.
- Students must be given an opportunity for a hearing before exclusions from school for disciplinary purposes.
- Students with disabilities, as well as limited-English-proficient students, must be afforded an education from which they may reasonably be expected to benefit.
- State statutes establish the only acceptable bases for termination or nonrenewal of contract of a teacher after that teacher has passed a probationary period.
- It is imperative that all school personnel act reasonably with regard to the rights of others.

In the *International Handbook of Educational Leadership and Administration* (1996) Ann Shorten reminds readers, "Prudent administrators will establish operational mechanisms which enable the changes in the law to be brought to their notice as soon as it is possible to do so, and have in place an adequate communication system to enable that information to be disseminated to those who need to know it" (p. 83). This is sound advice, and the prospective educational administrator must be keenly aware of the importance of this type of communication system.

Portfolio Artifacts

- Explore the following website for the Plainville Public Schools in Connecticut (www. Plainvilleschools.org/boepolicies/). Notice how the manual is organized. Note the types of sections and policies found in the manual. How does this compare with your school district?
- Some states produce one (or several) document(s) referred to as the education code. Does your state have such a code book? If so, review a copy. Examine one topic, such as teacher evaluation and dismissal. What is the essence of the code? How many times has it been revised?
- Interview a school principal and ask questions related to legal issues in schools. The

ISLLC standards (see Chapter 1) can be used to create your questions. See Standards 3, 5, and 6 in particular.
- Spend a day observing cases in family and domestic relations court or follow an educational case through the courts.
- Identify an issue within a school and research the laws that relate to the issue developing a legal brief arguing for, or against, the issue.
- Spend a day with a juvenile or family court judge.
- Find and read the published report on a court decision listed in this chapter or of interest to your school division.

Terms

Circuit court
Defendant
Desegregation
Due process
Equal protection clause
Establishment clause
Family Educational Rights and
    Privacy Act (FERPA—1974)

FAPE (free appropriate public
    education)
IDEA (Individuals with
    Disabilities in Education
    Act)
IEP (individualized education
    program)
in loco parentis

Libel
Negligence
Plaintiff (complainant)
Slander
Statute
Tort

Suggested Readings

Alexander, K., & Alexander, M. D. (2004). *American public school law.* Belmont, CA: The Wadsworth Group.

Alexander, K., & Alexander, M. D. (2003). *The law of schools, students, and teachers in a nutshell.* Belmont, CA: West Group.

Kemerer, F., Sansom, P., & Kemerer, J. (2005). *California school law.* Palo Alto, CA: Stanford University Press.

LaMorte, M. W. (2004). *School law: Cases and concepts.* Boston: Allyn and Bacon.

Rothstein, L. F. (1999). *Special education law.* Boston: Allyn and Bacon.

Smithson, M. J., Russo, C. J., & Osborne, A. G. (2003). *Special education and the law: A guide for practitioners.* Newbury Park, CA: Sage.

Sperry, D. J. (1999). *Working in a legal and regulatory environment: A handbook for school leaders.* Princeton, NJ: Eye on Education.

Court Cases

Board of Education v. Allen (1968), 392 U.S. 236, 88 S. Ct. 1923, 20 L. Ed 1060

Brown v. Board of Education of Topeka (1954), 347 U.S. 483, 74 S. Ct. 686, 98 L. Ed. 873

Brown v. Coffeeville Consolidated School District (1973)

Doe v. University of Michigan (1989), 721 F. Supp. 852

Fenton v. Stear (1976), 423 F. Supp. 767 (W.D. Pa)

Farrell v. Dallas Independent School District (1968), 392 F. 2d 697

Hazelwood School District v. Kuhlmeier (1988), 484 U.S. 260

Keyishian v. Board of Regents of New York (1967), 385 U.S. 589

Meltzer v. Board of Public Instruction (1977)

Meyer v. Nebraska (1923), 262 U.S. 390, 43 S. Ct. 625, 67 L. Ed. 1042

Miller v. California (1973), 413 U.S. 15

Planned Parenthood v. Clark County School District, 941 F. 2d 871 (9th Cir. 1991)

Plessy v. Ferguson (1896), 163 U.S. 537, 16 S. Ct. 1138, 41 L. Ed. 256

Stone v. Graham (1983), 449 U.S. 39

Scott v. New-Herald (1986), 655 F. Supp. 1353 (S.D. Ohio)

Sheff v. O'Neill (1996), 211 Conn. 627 A. 2d. 518

Steirer v. Bethlehem Area School District, 987 F. 2d. 989 (3d Cir. 1993)

Tinker v. Des Moines Independent School District (1969), 393 U.S. 503 (1985)

12

Resource Allocation and Management

Identifying Funding Sources for Meadows High

Oceanview School District is located adjacent to a large city in the West. It comprises seven elementary schools, two middle schools, and a high school with nearly 3,000 students. Meadows High School (MHS), like many of its counterparts throughout the nation, is experiencing problems with an aging facility.

MHS, originally built in 1926, nearly doubled its size in 1980 by means of an addition. Although the facility has been well maintained, it needs retrofitting. Referring to the science and computer labs the faculty have often told Principal Lamont Jackson that although safety requirements have been met, the facilities are in a "deplorable condition." The faculty say they are "completely embarrassed" about the lack of equipment, particularly when visitors pass

through the rooms. A typical high school class has twenty-five students, but the computer lab has only ten computers. In science labs, students have to share microscopes and other equipment.

Principal Jackson has discussed these concerns with the central office; however, they have informed him that in the foreseeable future no additional money will be available. Jackson has requested that the school-site council include discussion of these issues on the next agenda. The school-site council comprises five teachers, one student, the principal, two parents, and two community members. Because Oceanview District has decentralized authority in recent years, MHS has considerable control in budget planning and expenditures.

✳ **If you were formulating next year's budget, what approach might you use to help reallocate funds within the existing budget? How can money be identified so that additional resources will be available to students in the science and computer laboratories?**

Financing Schools

To address fiscal issues in operating a school and to speak knowledgeably with school community members, administrators should have an understanding of school finance.

Taxes

Tax revenues are used to finance many public services, including social service agencies, police departments, fire departments, transportation systems, and schools. Public schools are primarily funded through the revenues generated from property, consumption, and state income taxes. Each of these taxes has advantages and disadvantages when evaluated on such criteria as equity, yield, tax base, economic impact, and compliance.

The *equity* of a tax refers to fairness. One of the basic assumptions since the inception of American taxation has been progressivity. The belief is that an equitable tax is one that takes a higher percentage from those whose net worth increases the most because they are gaining the most from society and that such taxes do not take away from the basic necessities of life but only from luxuries. Former Secretary of Labor Robert Reich (1997), expressing concerns about recent policies that have lowered the taxes of the wealthiest income earners, stated, "I find this trend deeply disturbing. We have the most unequal distribution of income of any industrialized nation" (p. 32). This trend of lowering taxes for the wealthiest Americans occurred as part of the Tax Reform Act of 1986 and became an issue again at the turn of the century.

Yield refers to the revenue produced by a tax. Questions such as the following are asked with regard to yield: With this type of tax is a high yield generated at a low tax rate? Does the income from this tax increase as the economy improves and decrease as the economy downturns?

The *tax base* refers to the particular category to which a tax rate can be applied. Typical tax base classifications include income, wealth, property value, consumption, and privilege.

Economic impact is another factor used to evaluate taxation systems. Key questions to ask are: Is the tax a disincentive to the U.S. business owner or worker? Does this tax produce any negative impacts on the economy?

The *administration of taxes* can be highly cumbersome. The question to ask is: How can maximum revenue be generated while keeping tax administration costs to a minimum?

Finally, *compliance* involves ensuring that taxes are actually paid. One example is the automatic nature of withholding of income taxes. In some countries the worker pays income taxes on a quarterly or yearly basis and the taxes are not deducted from the paycheck; thus, compliance becomes an important issue.

In recent years the federal government has moved more toward a proportional or flat tax, which reduces the taxes on the wealthy and increases the taxes on the middle class, if the expenditure remains constant.

As states examine their school finance legislation, there is a trend toward reducing the reliance on property taxes and increasing the amount of revenue from other types of taxes (e.g., consumption taxes such as the revenues generated from state lotteries). Property taxes and some other types of taxes are often regressive—that is, they ask middle-class taxpayers to pay a higher percentage of their wages in taxes than higher-income groups. Knowledge of taxation for education and its effect on citizens is important since taxes provide much of the revenue stream for public education.

Federal Involvement in Financing Schools

Although education is a state rather than a federal responsibility, the federal government plays a role in financing specific education programs supported by the government. The federal government's role as a source of revenue has changed little since 1970. The percentage of a local school budget contributed by the federal government is usually less than 10 percent. This figure varies according to the type of school.

For example, large urban school districts are more likely to have federally financed initiatives such as bilingual programs, magnet schools, migrant programs, Headstart, and school-to-work programs. Thus, the percentage of their budget contributed by the federal government is larger than that in districts not offering these programs.

Table 12.1 depicts a budget outlay for a variety of programs supported by the U.S. government. Aid is usually distributed to school districts as block grants, categorical aid, or as general aid. These monies are usually sent to the state office of education, which distributes funds to local education agencies.

State Involvement in Financing Schools

Most states have complex systems of funding; however, one particularly important concept is what is called the foundation program. The *foundation program* refers to the

TABLE 12.1 *Where Do School Dollars Go?*

A breakdown of average per-pupil spending by category in nine selected districts in 1967, 1991, and 1996.

Program Area*	1967	1991	1996
Regular education	80.1%	58.5%	56.8%
Special education	3.6%	17.8%	19.0%
Food services	1.9%	3.3%	4.8%
Compensatory education	5.0%	4.2%	3.5%
Pupil support (attendance and counseling)	2.1%	3.5%	3.2%
Transportation (regular education)	3.6%	3.9%	3.1%
Vocational education	1.4%	2.8%	2.7%
Bilingual education	0.3%	1.9%	2.5%
Desegregation	0.0%	1.9%	1.5%
Regular health and psychological services	1.4%	1.0%	1.1%
After school athletics	0.4%	0.7%	0.6%
"At risk" youth education, alternative education	0.1%	0.6%	0.6%
Security and violence prevention	0.1%	0.5%	0.6%
Total	100.0%	100.0%	100.0%

*Programs listed in order of 1996 share of total per pupil spending.

Source: Economic Policy Institute, 1996.

established minimum of financial support that a district receives for each enrolled student. School districts are reimbursed by the state on an average daily membership (ADM) or average daily attendance (ADA) basis. The amount, sometimes called a per-pupil allotment, might be affected by several factors, including the amount of local fiscal effort, the number of special, vocational, and bilingual education students, and the number of students from families below the poverty level. Figure 12.1 depicts the increases in per pupil expenditures from 1991–2001.

In addition to the foundation concept, other approaches to financing public schools include a flat-grant model, power-equalizing plan, guaranteed tax base plan, and a weighted-student model. Several states use more than one method for financing schools.

With a *flat-grant model*, state aid to local school districts is based on a fixed amount. This amount is then multiplied by the number of students in the district. Many people argue that this approach to funding schools is unequal because it is more expensive to educate some children than others. For example, a child requiring special education services or bilingual education would cost a school district more to educate than a child not needing these services.

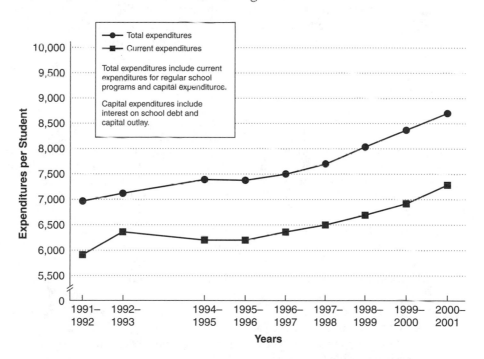

FIGURE 12.1 *Total Expenditures per Student:* Total and current public school district expenditures per student (in constant 2000–01 dollars): 1991–92, 1992–93, and 1994–95 to 2000–01.

Source: U.S. Department of Education, NCES, Common Core of Data (CCD), "Public School District Universe Survey," 1991–92, 1992–93, and 1994–95 to 2000–01; "Public School District Financial Survey," 1991–92, 1992–93, and 1994–95 to 2000–01; and Geographic Cost of Education Indexes (GCEIs) available from the Education Finance Statistics Center (http://nces.ed.gov/edfin/).

A *power-equalizing model* pays a percentage of local school expenditures in an inverse ratio to the school district's wealth. The wealthier the district, the less matching state monies it receives. The goal is an equalization between wealthier school districts and those of less wealth. Since those living in wealthy districts can pay a much lower percent of their income and yet raise considerably more money for the education of every child in average daily membership, the state tries to make adjustments for these inequities.

In a *weighted-student model* of financing public education, students are weighted in proportion to their special needs. For example, students requiring bilingual education, special-needs classes, or vocational classes, would be allotted additional money according to the costs of those services. One of the problems with this model is the complexity involved in assigning weights. For example, some children receive not only special education services but also bilingual program services. Calculating weights for special programs can become highly complex.

The school financial issue that has received the greatest sustained court attention is the alleged inequities in financing public education. The issue is inequality of educational opportunity caused by educational funding that is "a function of district property wealth; whether or not a disputed financial scheme provides each child with at least a basic or adequate education; the importance of local control; and the extent, if any, of courts' involvement in providing remediation" (LaMorte, 1999, pp. 351–352).

A related issue is providing choices of educational services at public expense. LaMorte (1999) goes on to say:

> Unfortunately for discussion purposes, the notion of choice does not describe a single, well-defined plan but is an umbrella term for a host of programs. . . . Its proponents argue that bringing a concept—consumer choice—to education will break the alleged monopolistic stranglehold of the educational bureaucracy by introducing the necessary ingredient of a measure of needed competition, with all the positive connotations that term implies, to the public schools. (p. 374)

Charter schools are a form of choice that encourages innovative educational ideas.

Charter schools, which are public schools that have many of the characteristics of independent schools, are also financed through taxes. Typically, certain per-pupil allotment is given by the district or state directly to the charter school for each child enrolled, rather than to a district central office. If a student chooses to leave a school, she or he takes the funding away from that school. (For more information see: www.nationalcharterschools.org/.)

Let us examine the sources of funding for schools in one state, using California as an example (see Table 12.2). Approximately 13 percent of the K–12 education budget for a California school district is from federal government funds. These monies are allotted through categorical or block grants. About 53 percent of the funding comes from the state's budget. These monies come from business, corporate, and personal income taxes as well as sales taxes and other special taxes. Local property taxes make up about 27 percent of the funding. This varies depending on the state's overall budget for a given year. There are other local revenues as well.

TABLE 12.2   *Sources of Revenue for California Schools*

	1994–95	*1998–99*	*2003–04*
Federal aid	8.3%	9.6%	13%
State aid	53.2%	54.0%	53%
Property tax	29.1%	28.0%	27%
Local miscellaneous	7.2%	7.0%	6%
Lottery	2.2%	2.4%	1%

Making up approximately 6 percent of the funding, these sources might include: fees on commercial or residential construction; contributions from parents, businesses, and foundations; interest on investments by local school districts; and cafeteria sales, to name but a few. Finally, approximately 1 percent of the funding for schools comes from the California Lottery (about $125 per student annually). As Table 12.2 shows, these sources of funding vary slightly from year to year.

Local Involvement in Financing Schools

Because school districts do not generate revenue from profits on sales, they have been granted by their state government the power to tax individuals and companies. The main revenue source for public schools is the local property tax. The property tax is a function of three variables: the tax base, the assessment practice, and the tax rate. The tax base includes all taxable property in the district except that owned by the federal government, public hospitals, state parks, churches, and nonprofit entities, which are not taxable.

States vary as to how they assess property. Usually a percentage rate, established by the taxing authority, is applied to the property's market value. The market value is the amount the owner would receive on selling the property. Depending on the state, the tax rate is expressed in a variety of ways: per thousand dollars of assessed valuation, dollars per hundred dollars of assessed valuation, and mills. According to William Sharp (1994), "The school district's tax rate is multiplied by the assessed value of the tax base of the community to yield the amount of money the school will receive" (p. 2).

Let's look at an example for a single home. If the market value of a home is $120,000 and the taxing authority's assessment practice is 80 percent, the assessed value of the home would be $120,000 × .80 or $96,000. This is the amount on which the homeowner would be taxed. If the rate were $2.00 per $100.00 of assessed value, the property tax on this house would be $96,000 × .02, or $1,920.00. Keep in mind, however, that the homeowner's overall tax rate includes other taxes in addition to school taxes (e.g., water district, hospital district).

This is a simplified version of the tax process. Often homeowners and businesses are eligible for certain types of exemptions. Additionally, when a community is trying to lure businesses into town, it often offers tax abatements (a lesser amount of taxes in the first few years).

Here is a typical formula for a school district's income:

General purpose (Revenue limit × ADA)
+ Special purpose (categorical aid)
+ Miscellaneous local and other (i.e., sale of assets, investment income)
+ Lottery
_____
= Total District Income

Vouchers

In the mid-1950s economist Milton Friedman proposed that every family be given a voucher of equal worth for each child attending public schools. Under his plan, a family could choose any school meeting the basic requirements set by government. Parents could add their own resources to the voucher, and schools could set their own tuition level and admission requirements.

Throughout the last forty years, various versions of a voucher system have been debated at local, state, and national levels. Vouchers have been tied to the concept of school choice, with a voucher program being proposed as one form of schooling that should be made available to children and families.

School choice has become a major policy issue affecting schools throughout the nation. At present no state has a voucher system. Several cities, however, are utilizing voucher systems (e.g., Milwaukee, Chicago, Cleveland) with limited measures of success. In 1998, the Wisconsin Supreme Court upheld the use of vouchers, and the U.S. Supreme Court declined to review the case. Florida Governor Jeb Bush proposed a voucher plan providing up to $4,000 for each student attending a failing school (based on the school's test scores) that can be used to attend public, private, or religious schools. The school choice movement includes ideas such as vouchers, magnet schools, and charter schools. These movements have the potential to change the allocation of revenues and have implications for revenue generation for schools.

Nontraditional Revenue Sources

To expand services many school districts have begun to look at a variety of nontraditional sources of revenue. Meno (1984) identified three categories for nontraditional funding sources: donor, enterprise, and cooperative. Table 12.3 depicts these three categories as well as various kinds of revenues assigned to each category. According to the research of Garnos and King (1994), superintendents and principals believe that nontraditional revenues are viable ways to enhance public school budgets. As the charter school movement expands nationwide, these sources will become more commonly used. Additionally, much can be learned from independent schools (both private and religious) about alternative sources of revenue generation; in order to exist these institutions have had to utilize a variety of funding strategies. School administrators must be skilled in fostering partnerships, securing donors, and establishing enterprises.

TABLE 12.3 *Sources of Nontraditional Funding*

Donor	Enterprise	Cooperative
1. Cash gifts from individuals 2. Real property from individuals 3. Private foundation grants 4. Corporate gifts 5. Gifts from nonprofit organizations 6. Donated services 7. Donated supplies 8. Donated equipment 9. Fundraisers to support educational programs. 10. Fundraisers to support cocurricular activities.	1. Services leased to other school districts or organizations 2. Facilities leased to other school districts or organizations 3. User fee payments (community education, drivers education, etc.) 4. Rental of school facilities or equipment 5. Sale of school access (vending machines, advertising, etc.) 6. Sale/lease-back arrangements	*Local Agencies* 1. Programs shared with other districts 2. Activities shared with other districts 3. Cooperative programs with universities 4. Programs or activities sponsored by service clubs or organizations *Governmental Agencies* 1. Joint facility maintenance programs with city, county (property, equipment, etc.) 2. Joint use of buses 3. Joint use of athletic facilities or swimming pool *Business and Industry* 1. Work-study programs 2. Youth job placement programs 3. Career guidance

Source: M. L. Garnos & R. A. King (1994). *NASSP Bulletin 78,* 566. Reprinted with permission.

School Foundations

A school foundation is similar to a university's development office. A foundation has a tax-free status; thus, donors can benefit from their gifts. Foundations allow community members to raise funds through gifts from individuals and corporations. Funds can be used to pay for field trips, special projects, scholarships, and awards.

Thayer and Short (1994) maintain that the principal must be a key player in forming a foundation. They recommend the following steps in creating a foundation:

- Organize a team to study the feasibility of such a move.
- Obtain 501(c)(3) status and authorization to transact business, subject to all applicable state and federal laws.
- Inform stakeholders why a foundation is needed and of the history behind the process.
- Set specific, reasonable goals.

Revenue Sources for Independent Schools

Independent schools include both religious and private schools located in the United States and overseas. Independent schools are primarily funded through tuition and gifts. Alumni are among the largest sources of gifts for independent schools. One difference between independent private schools and religious schools is that for the latter, religious institutions usually support a portion of the school budget.

Much can be learned from independent schools, not only regarding their fundraising strategies, but also in how they market their programs.

✳ **What implications do funding mechanisms have for the plans of the school-site council of Meadows High?**

Obtaining Funding for Educational Programs

HARVEY B. POLANSKY, PH.D. • *Superintendent of Schools, Southington, Connecticut*

Funding has become an intricate part of district and school management. Strategies in the development, procurement, and public approval of school funds vary greatly but have one common strand: accountability. Accountability is less a process of bookkeeping and more one of intense taxpayer scrutiny of what value the public receives for its educational dollars. With the new millennium comes even greater scrutiny and criticism of school funding. Administrators will be forced to defend funding strategies and seek alternative and creative means to obtain funds. They will have to manage the funds with greater competency and preparation. Many of us started our educational journey in the spend-free 1980s. Since then a quasi–tax revolt has diminished educational dollars.

Where Do School Funds Come From?
Nationally, over 80 percent of all school funds come from local and state funding, entitlements, and tax revenue. Tax revenues have decreased, placing both tax revenues and entitlements in jeopardy. School districts seek other means to develop strategies in obtaining funds for worthwhile programs. No longer can administrators expect the municipality to cover all expenses. Creative strategies to find school funding include the following five.

Development of Educational Enterprise Zones
Schools can no longer sit back and expect tax dollars to cover the costs of innovative programs. In many cases, school must put up an "open for business" sign. Fees for extended-day programs, day-care programs, and enrichment programs often come from consumers. Principals must learn how to market and create fiscal systems of accountability to manage these programs. School will be open from 6 a.m. to 6 p.m., and the fees earned can be used for staff, materials, and building initiatives. Governance teams and building improvement teams must be coordinated to get the full "bang for the buck."

Preschool Programs
Schools will have to compete with private day-care providers. Are preschool programs educationally sound, providing the students fewer transitions? Can they be an economic cash cow? Effective preschool programs will enhance feeder programs, engage parents at early ages, and offer community outreach to a population that is politically strong. Funds can be used for schoolwide initiatives. In addition, research suggests that the experience of children in the first four years has a strong influence on their future development.

Resource Sharing

School districts tend to view their existence in isolated management camps. Regional service centers attempt to develop resource sharing but are often in the market themselves. School districts should learn to share business and support side functions, such as transportation, substitute teachers, food service, custodial service, bidding services, and innovative technological and curricular programs across district lines. Sharing will diminish personnel costs and enhance district funding. Cooperative arrangements with museums, corporations, and businesses will also bring needed services to schools. Most corporate giving has ceased or is part of a competitive grant program.

Grant Writing

School administrators must turn to the Internet and find grants. Entitlements are drying up and competitive categorical grants are becoming increasingly available. Dream a little. Put your thoughts on paper, go online, and find out what grants are available. The National School Boards Association (www.nsba.org) and the U.S. Department of Education (www.sdoe.org) have Web sites and periodicals listing available grant programs. Local organizations might also list grant opportunities. Some administrators are hesitant to submit a grant proposal. Remember, the worst that could happen is that they reject it. You'll still be learning a great innovative approach to finding alternate funding.

Distance Learning

While some teacher unions oppose the concept of distance learning, satellite, interdistrict distance-learning programs can decrease costs (thereby allowing administrators to use funds elsewhere) and offer opportunities to charge for programs. Latin 4, French 6, and esoteric math and science courses can be taught via interactive distance-learning programs. Equipment is expensive but does tend to attract grant funding. Universities also offer programs that can reduce costs and provide much-needed studio facilities.

We can no longer rely on traditional funding sources. It is the entrepreneurial administrators who will find funds that best meet the needs of their schools and programs.

Grant Writing

Given the increase in the need for schools and school districts to obtain funding from nontraditional sources, skills in understanding grant writing are now requisite for school administrators. Ruskin and Achilles (1995) summarize the grant-writing process as follows:

1. Identify a philanthropist or foundation interested in your type of project.
2. Develop a comprehensive and individualized plan to interest this person.
3. Design a short-term strategy and a long-range plan for support.
4. Make personal contact with the funder.
5. Devise a plan to enlist support of other key people.
6. Send a letter of inquiry and interest.
7. Submit the required proposal.
8. Establish ongoing dialogue with the funder.
9. Steward the funder through various phases of your project to ensure that the funder becomes a stakeholder. (p. 30)

Not only do school administrators have to understand the process of applying for grants, but they also need to understand what information is typically found in any grant. Ruskin and Achilles (1995) provide eleven suggestions for grant writers to use when supporting their case in a grant proposal:

1. Provide a clear picture of your school site—demographics, curriculum, special programs, best features, and the problem.
2. Clearly present the needs you are attempting to meet, with supporting data about the impact of needs on the quality of education provided to students.
3. Articulate the plan you are proposing to meet these needs, including how the plan was developed. Provide a comprehensive picture of the reasons this plan is the best means to address the educational needs. Support your ideas with other successful models, and provide a timetable for implementation.
4. Outline direct and indirect educational benefits derived through successful implementation of your plan. Emphasize the impact of your project on the quality of education and its implications for the individual student.
5. List funder costs for your plan. Depending on what the funder is seeking, you may need to convince the funder that you have given careful attention to costs and that you can complete the project within your budget.
6. Provide an evaluation design for your plan as part of your implementation timeline. Tie it to measurable objectives.
7. Provide a convincing argument about the professional and personal qualifications of the proposed project director.
8. Delineate future funding needs and a strategy to secure needed resources.
9. Develop a plan to continue the project after initial funding is completed. How will you institutionalize the grant?
10. Provide appropriate support information in appendixes.
11. Develop a calendar with your agenda for grant follow-up. Specify important targeted grant deadlines and appointments on this calendar to ensure ongoing contact with the funder. Details of stewardship activities could be added here. Make it easy for the grant manager to take one glimpse at the calendar and anticipate any significant deadlines. (pp. 53–54)

Budgeting, Accounting, and Facility Management

The receipt of the budget provides that moment of truth when the administration learns the type of educational program that the community can afford or is willing to support. Budgeting ensures that required resources will be available at the right time and in the right amount to accomplish the educational plan. It is a financial plan that needs to be interpreted to the school board and community so that it can be approved.

The Budgeting Process

The budgeting process involves planning, formulating, presenting, administering, and evaluating. Many states follow a calendar that determines when certain stages of a school district's budget must be met. Often the process begins in September, and the budget is adopted the following June or July.

Planning. The academic program should drive the budget; therefore, in the planning stage of the budget process, factors such as needs, program goals and objectives, alternatives for achieving goals, and selecting cost-effective alternatives must be considered. In Figure 12.2 NASSP presents the specific components of the instructional and implementary costs of education.

Formulating. To formulate the budget it is crucial to have input from the many constituencies of the school. Schools can no longer jealously guard the budget, keeping secret how and why money is spent. Teachers are being asked to assume a greater role in the budget process in many school districts, especially in schools that are site managed. Creating and detailing the budget should involve input and discussion from faculty, staff, and other groups who are part of the school's community.

Box 12.1 displays a checklist for developing a school budget. It includes the process, the organizing of the budget document, and the types of data needed to compile the budget.

Presenting. A crucial part to presenting a school budget is the development of a rationale. In most school districts, principals meet with superintendents and other

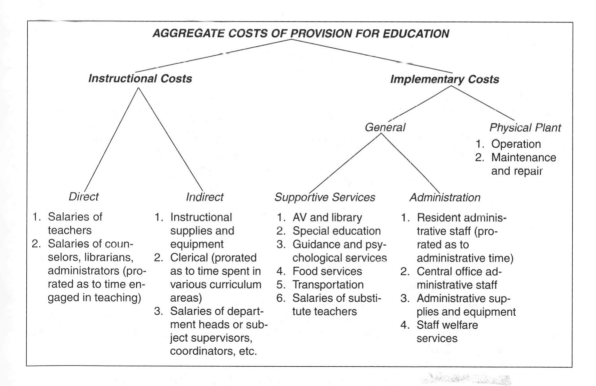

FIGURE 12.2 *Aggregate Costs of Provision for Education*

Source: Sanders, K. P., & Theimann, F. C. (1990). Student costing: An essential tool in site-based budgeting and teacher empowerment. *NASSP Bulletin, 74*(523), 95–102. Reprinted with permission from NASSP.

BOX 12.1 • *School Budget Development Checklist*

Process: Procedures for Conducting Hearings

___ Roles of board and superintendent clearly defined

___ Board finance policies updated regularly

___ Financial data accurate and timely

___ Staff adequately in budget request

___ Public hearing held with citizen participation

___ Budget document (or summary) widely distributed

___ Process complies with legal requirements

___ Community/political support generated for budget

___ Contingency strategy (budget options) exists

___ Efficient accounting/financial reporting system used

Format: Preparing the Document

___ Cover, title page, appearance attractive

___ Table of contents or index; number pages

___ Board members and officers' names included

___ Organizational chart and school administrators listed

___ Budget message or transmittal letter included

___ Graphics/artwork, charts, figures, tables

___ Clarity of style; avoidance of technical jargon

___ Manageable size and shape of document

___ Glossary of key terms

___ Concise executive summary (budget in brief)

Contents: Data Compilation

___ Feasibility of bottom-line requests

___ School system goals and objectives

___ Budget guidelines or priorities

___ Object budget summary (e.g., salaries, supplies)

___ Site budget summary (e.g., individual campuses)

___ Budget history (expenditures for previous five years)

___ Unit cost analysis (per-pupil expenditures)

___ Estimated revenue summary (all sources)

___ Explanation of tax rate impact

___ Explanation of major cost factors (contracts, inflation)

___ Budget coding system explained (account charts)

___ Performance measures included (test data)

___ Pupil enrollment projections by grade

___ Staffing history and projections

___ Long-range plans (five years) for district

___ Major decisions justified (layoffs, closings)

___ District or state comparisons

___ Capital budget summarized (improvement projects)

___ Budget detail (line-item expenditure data)

Source: H. Hartley (1990). Boardroom bottom line, with permission from the *American School Board Journal* 177(2):31.

central office personnel involved with the budgeting process to discuss their budget. The final school district budget is presented to the school board and, in the case of dependent school districts, to the city council or board of county supervisors. It is crucial that an administrator be able to articulate a strong rationale for budget priorities.

Administering. One way to administer the budget is to allocate money to each program or department and allow staff to spend as they wish as long as they stay within the assigned amount. The responsibilities related to purchasing and accounting, however, are very important. Often it can take several months between the time an item is ordered and the time the bills actually arrive (encumbrances). The money that will be used is encumbered until the bill is actually paid. Thus, although the money is technically available, it should not be used. A multitude of computer programs are available to help school administrators manage the school budget and ensure that encumbered monies are not used and that the budget is not overexpended.

Evaluating. The school budget is usually organized into categories such as programs (early childhood, bilingual, language arts), functions (instructional, transportation, facilities management), and objects (supplies, salaries, staff development, travel). These areas can be evaluated separately or in combination. Questions such as the following need to be asked: How well did the budget serve the goals it was meant to accomplish? How will we determine whether the goals and objectives were achieved? Were the goods and services purchased actually used? Should the program be expanded? Should the program be eliminated? As programs are evaluated, school administrators should ask if the approach used was the most effective as well as most efficient way to accomplish the goals.

Types of Budgeting

The following four types of budgets are not mutually exclusive; each can provide useful and needed information. One might become more important depending on the organizational needs and situations. If the computer system used is sophisticated enough for financial records and the data are properly organized, the computer program can prepare cost and budget information in a number of different formats.

Line-Item Budgeting

An *object budget* is a listing of the objects of expense, such as salaries, supplies, equipment, services, insurance, travel, professional improvements, postage, maintenance, utilities, fringe benefits, rents, debt reduction, and so forth. A *function classification* lists estimates of expenditures in terms of the purposes for which they are made—administration, instruction, health service, pupil transportation, food service, operation, fixed charges, summer school, adult education, and so on. Today's general line-item budget has evolved from a combination of these two organizational categories.

The wide variety of classification systems used to account for school expenditures and revenues complicate the process, along with the consequent difficulties involved in securing expenditure and revenues. Additionally, the difficulty involved in securing comparable data concerning the financial operation of the school systems impelled the U.S. Office of Education to issue a handbook, *Financial Accounting for Local and State School Systems*, which is periodically updated. The handbook provides recommendations regarding expenditure and revenue accounts to be used in budgeting and accounting. For the most part, state requirements and local school budgets have followed the basic recommendations made by the U.S. Office of Education.

Budget estimates are typically made from one year to the next by adding a percentage increment of the previous year's budget. The typical procedure is to record expenditures for a given budget classification for one or two years prior, enter the request for the future year, and note the additional amounts requested. Then the budget director, superintendent, and school board arrive at a final figure by taking a fixed percentage cut (or addition) in the school's requests. This is the basis of stability in the appropriations process and provides an excellent mechanism for control.

Planning, Programming, Budgeting System (PPBS)

Typically the line-item budget deals primarily with the functions and objects of expense but not with the programs. A program-budgeting system provides a method of determining the costs of programs. Sometimes called PPBS and at other times referred to as PPBES, with the *E* referring to evaluation, this approach to budgeting requires that the budget be organized around program goals and the processes to accomplish these goals. Although it originated in the 1940s, PPBS did not gain momentum until the 1960s.

According to Ubben and Hughes (1997), PPBS involves five steps:

1. Establish the general goals to be achieved.
2. Identify the specific objectives that define this goal.
3. Develop the program and processes that it is believed will achieve the objectives and goals.
4. Establish the formative and summative evaluation practices.
5. Implement a review and recycle procedure that indicates whether or not, or the degree to which, the program and processes resulted in the achievement of the objectives and the goals, and, if not, to help determine other procedures, processes, and programs. (p. 308)

Program budgets are not increased incrementally, but require leadership to decide how much to spend on achieving program goals and objectives. The administrator might select a more favorable alternative for one program and a less favorable one for another based on cost-and-benefit analysis. Candoli, Hack, Ray, and Stollar (1984) maintain that PPBES is a cyclical process that constantly requires feedback. The two-way arrows in Figure 12.3 depict the recursive nature of this budgeting approach. One disadvantage of PPBES is that it is far more time-consuming than other budgeting approaches and might not provide as efficient fiscal control; it is, however, excellent for planning purposes.

Zero-Based Budgeting

Zero-based budgeting requires administrators to justify all expenditures on an annual basis. Thus, starting with a zero amount, current and new expenditures must be fully justified so that monies can be allocated for them. Zero-based budgeting also requires yearly evaluations so that priorities based on program evaluation data can be set.

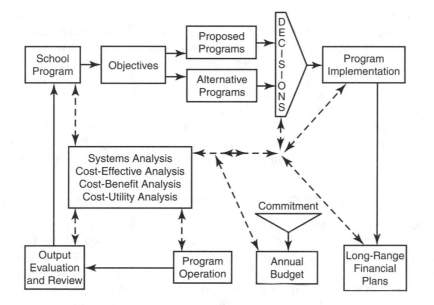

FIGURE 12.3 *Illustration of Way in Which Planning, Programming, Budgeting, Evaluation System (PPBES) Might Work*

According to Bliss (1994), zero-based budgeting involves five steps:

1. Identify decision units (defined as any programs that consume resources).
2. Analyze decision packages (documents that describe a decision's objectives, activities, resources, and costs).
3. Rank decision packages.
4. Allocate funds.
5. Prepare official budgets.

One of the key benefits is that functions or programs can be ranked as to desirability and marginal activities can be identified. Administrators can reassess their operations from the ground up and justify every dollar spent in terms of current goals. However, the major focus is typically on those program increments that are just above or below the projected funding level. The heart of zero-based budgeting is, therefore, the ranking process. This ranking procedure establishes priorities among the decision packages. One disadvantage to zero-based budgeting is its time intensiveness. A major advantage is the elimination of expenditures that were valid in the past but are no longer relevant.

Incremental Budgeting

The most common budgeting in schools is incremental budgeting, which involves adding to or subtracting from the current year's budget. Budget development for the current year begins with the previous year's budget. An assumption is made that the upcoming year's budget will be similar to the current year's. Last year's programs are regarded as a base and allowed to grow by some fixed percent; whatever resources are left over are then assigned to new or improved programs.

Incremental budgeting does not include formal evaluation of needs and programs. Often programs that do not necessarily fulfill existing needs continue to be allocated monies, while more effective, newer programs might go underfunded. These are serious problems for a nation calling for greater accountability. Items such as special programs and facility renovations are handled separately. Additionally, money coming from federal sources is usually addressed separately.

Trends in Budgeting and Management

In recent years various types of organizations have been calling for performance-based budgeting, results-based budgeting, or mission-based budgeting and management. Results-based budgeting is based on the premise that managers should seek to obtain control over human and financial resources by developing budget systems that fund outcomes rather than inputs. Advocates of results-based budgeting maintain that it is a vehicle for moving beyond short-term increments to a long-term view of strategies to address priorities. A results-based budgeting system defines the mission and the outcomes, but it does not directly link dollars spent to the quality of the outcomes.

Performance-based budgeting requires strategic planning regarding the organization's mission, goals, and objectives and a process that requires quantifiable data that provides meaningful information about program outcomes (Willoughby & Melkers, 1998). Performance-based budgeting may also require that an organization assess its progress toward specified target goals.

Gaining considerable popularity in universities and colleges, and to a lesser degree in schools, is mission-based management and mission-based budgeting. Mission-based management refers to introducing a new reporting system that tracks revenues and expenses and measures faculty activities and contributions on a mission-specific basis. It also involves the implementation of a new management and decision-making structure and processes that are enabled by these new reporting systems. A key issue in mission-based management is allocating resources based on a better understanding of the distribution of faculty effort.

Whatever approach to budgeting is used, identifying concrete district and school goals is crucial. For example, if one districtwide goal is to improve student achievement in mathematics, then this may result in a request to add a part or full-time math instructor at a particular school. Recent years have seen an increase in the use of metrics to measure student and school performance; thus, there will continue to be greater focus on quantifying teacher and administrator performance in relation to student achievement data.

✳ **What budgeting approach(es) might help the school-site council at Meadows High School in reallocating funds for the science and computer labs? In what way?**

Activity Funds

Typical student activity funds include accounts for student organizations (e.g., sports clubs, student council), profit earnings (e.g., concessions and school pictures), special-purpose accounts (e.g., field trips, hospitality), and others. Monitoring accounts is essential to a well-managed school.

The Association for School Business Officials (ASBO) has recommended twelve guidelines for managing student activity accounts (Box 12.2). Additionally, most school districts have policies regarding activity funds as well as soliciting funds (Box 12.3).

BOX 12.2 • *ASBO Guidelines for Managing Student Activity Accounts*

1. All money received should be acknowledged by issuing prenumbered receipts or prenumbered tickets to the person from whom the money is received.
2. Deposits should be made daily if possible. Cash should never be left in the school over the weekend or holidays.
3. Receipts should be issued to the person making the deposit. Deposit slips should be retained by both the depositor and the school accountant or bookkeeper.
4. Purchase orders or requisitions should be initiated by the person in charge of the activity fund.
5. Payments should be made by check, prepared and mailed from the business office to the payee.
6. The principal should designate two or more persons in addition to himself or herself who will be authorized to sign checks. Two of the three authorized signatures should also be required for all withdrawals.
7. No payment should be made unless supported by a written purchase order and by a signed invoice certifying receipt of merchandise and accuracy of prices.
8. Student-activity funds should not be used for any purchase that represents a loan or accommodation to any school district employee or other nonstudent. Emergency loans may be made to students for lunches, carfare, and the like on written permission of the principal. Individuals may not make purchases through the student body in order to take advantage of better prices.
9. Student bodies may enter contracts for the purchase of supplies, equipment, and services from an approved vendor provided the term of the contract is within the tenure of the students of the school (usually three years).
10. The student body should operate on a budget reflecting past experience and future plans; like the school and school district budget, the student budget should serve as a guide for the year's financing activities.
11. Student activity books and financial procedures should be subjected to periodic internal and external audits. An annual examination by outside, independent accountants is also recommended.
12. Regular reports (monthly and annual) should be prepared and submitted to the principal, business office, or any others responsible for the supervision of student activity funds.

BOX 12.3 • *Board of Education Policy: Soliciting Funds from and by Students*

Section	(1000) Community Relations
Policy Name	Soliciting Funds from and by Students
Policy Number	1324
Date Approved	10/10/1989
Date Revised	01/13/2003
Date Revised	
Date Revised	
Date Reviewed	
Policy	School personnel shall educate students about services performed by humanitarian agencies and shall encourage student participation in financial support of agencies as a social and community project, but fund-raising on school grounds or at school sponsored activities shall not be conducted by non-school agencies or for non-school activities among students except as provided by law and approved by the board of education.
	Organizations or persons not under the control of the board of education shall not use school children in any fund-raising programs on school grounds or at school-sponsored activities. Any child engaged in such enterprises must not in dress or speech indicate that the school department has any part in the canvass or sale.
	Fund-raising should be kept to a minimum, purely for economic reasons. Any fund-raising activity shall first have the approval of the principal before any direct planning. Approval shall be based on, but not limited to, such factors as need, type of activity, and frequency.
	Athletic requests should obtain the approval of the athletic director and the assistant principal or principal.
	<u>General Guidelines</u> Whenever school personnel and/or students are involved in any such activity, the school principal shall have full responsibility and final control. Guidelines and applications for fund-raising activities are available in each principal's office. -An attempt will be made to rotate all fund-raising. -All funds must be turned in to the school account for proper deposit. -All items or monies must be equally shared by the group or team, not individuals. -No student or athlete or team should be pressured or embarrassed into donating or solicitation. -No fund-raising activity will include gambling or the use of alcohol or drugs.

Reprinted with permission of Plainville Community Schools, Plainville, Connecticut.

Fiscal Accounting

Fiscal stewardship is of the utmost importance and is a responsibility that no administrator should take lightly. The funds an administrator allocates each day are public funds, and there is an inherent expectation that they will be accounted for properly.

Once the budget for the school district has been approved, it is the responsibility of the administration to ensure that the money that has been appropriated is expended properly. Fiscal accountability is maintained through the district's accounting system and its reporting, auditing, and inventory procedure.

Administrators must maintain accurate records of all money spent and received during the fiscal cycle and provide an accurate accounting at the end of the budget year. Administrators must be knowledgeable and skilled in maintaining accounts for revenues and expenditures as well as for inventories of materials and equipment. The accounting system must adequately control requisitions, purchase orders, contracts, payments, claims, payrolls, and other actions influencing the assets of the organization. The expectation is that all records will be accurate and provide assurance to the board that its financial policies are being observed.

The typical accounting system is described as a double-entry system. For example, the most common entry would be to increase (purchase) an asset and to decrease capital (money) or to increase a liability (debt to creditors). Transactions are entered into the accounts as debits and credits. A debit typically increases an asset or decreases a capital or liability account. The debits and credits in all the school system's accounts must be equal, and all assets, resources, and liabilities must be accounted for in the financial records. The books in which financial records are maintained are called journals and ledgers. The *journal* provides a historic record of all transactions, and the *ledger* provides all transactions made to a given account.

Each school system has its own procedures for maintaining fiscal accountability, but the administrator or his or her designee is expected to code expenditures properly and follow accounting system procedures to accurately maintain ledger accounts and a cash receipt and payment journal. One of the most important decisions an administrator makes is selecting financial officers and bookkeepers to help maintain the financial records. Nonetheless, the administrator is ultimately responsible and should understand accounting procedures.

The Audit

Checking for accuracy in accounting is referred to as auditing. Internal and external audits should be conducted regularly, and reports should be prepared. Most states require that a certified public accountant conduct an external audit on an annual or bi-annual basis. It is in the best interests of the school that audits be conducted regularly to maintain credibility and accountability. An administrator should ensure that an audit has been completed before taking responsibility for a budget.

✳ **What accountability procedures need to be addressed at Meadows High?**

Acquiring, Allocating, and Accounting for Resources

RICHARD A. KING • *University of Northern Colorado*

Acquisition of adequate resources to attain performance goals challenges educational leaders at all levels. Finding funds for desired programs entails several aspects of school finance: (1) gathering resources, which is often referred to as a *revenue* dimension; (2) directing appropriate resources to educational programs, which forms an *allocation* dimension; and (3) ensuring that resource use makes a difference in program outcomes, which entails both a *management* function (to be sure resources are directed where intended) and an *accountability* dimension (to relate allocations to school performance measures).

Balancing Uniformity and Local Control

Many state courts concluded that wealth-based spending inequities violate state constitutions' equal-protection provisions or articles mandating "uniform" or "thorough and efficient" educational systems. Other courts upheld finance policies, finding that revenue variations do not deny equal protection, since they are a consequence of legitimate state interests in maintaining local control over schooling. State legislatures responded to judicial and political pressures to equalize resources, and in the 1990s the average state share rose to 48 percent—exceeding the local contribution of 45 percent—with the remainder financed by federal revenue.

Partnerships with businesses, educational foundations, and sales of advertising space on facilities and buses have promised new resources. These funds, however, account for but a small portion of total revenue, and, like property taxation, they raise questions about resulting inequities when opportunities to generate new resources differ greatly from community to community.

Leaders will be increasingly pressed to secure more revenue to expand programs, obtain essential instructional materials and technologies, finance necessary professional development, and be competitive with private schools and charter schools. Educational leaders will address such questions as: Will our school community be satisfied with the level of resources provided through traditional channels, or will we aggressively seek additional resources to meet parental demands and student needs despite resulting inequities among schools?

Deciding Priorities When Allocating Resources

Planning and budgeting frameworks help school personnel determine goals and objectives, the most cost-effective mix of human and material resources to reach goals, the funds necessary to deliver programs, and evaluation of outcomes in relation to resources as new budget cycles begin. These budget development processes raise questions about priorities. The difficulty of reaching consensus about priorities among stakeholders makes the allocation dimension highly political. For this reason, it is tempting to adopt an incremental approach and thus ease tensions by increasing all prior budgets by a given percentage. However, as new instructional approaches and technologies emerge, as program demands shift along with a school's demography, and as the productivity of traditional programs is challenged, discussions about resource priorities are inevitable.

In the context of school-based decision making, budget decisions will increasingly be made at building levels. Allocations among existing and proposed programs will challenge educational leaders to address many questions, including: Will we incrementally raise all current program budgets, or will we examine which instructional approaches and consequent resource allocations best enable school personnel to meet changing student needs and improve student performance?

Accounting for the Use of Financial Resources

Budget management and accounting functions within central offices and schools are concerned primarily with ensuring the lawful use of public money within designated funds. This dimension of school finance has been expanded in recent years to embrace a broader accountability function, that of relating resource decisions to improvements in program outcomes.

Relationships between human and financial inputs and resulting outcomes define a traditional view of school productivity and efficiency. Another perspective on efficiency calls for maximizing the satisfaction of consumers—parents, students, employers, and legislators—at the same or perhaps at an even lower investment of society's resources.

An emerging policy direction is to induce school improvement and greater efficiency through performance-based school finance. This entrepreneurial restructuring of schools aligns resources, as well as potential sanctions, with state standards and assessments. By rewarding those schools or districts whose students' performance meets desired standards or whose performance improves toward such targets, this approach is intended to stimulate school leaders and teachers to redesign curriculum and instruction in ways that achieve educational reform goals. There are concerns, however, that "high-stakes" accountability brings unintended consequences (see Chapter 2).

To the degree that program and financial accountability relates future school resources to performance, educational leaders will address questions such as: Will budget management be primarily concerned with proper accounting for revenue and expenditures within designated funds, or will we also lead schools in ways that help all personnel to maximize the results of programs financed by those resources—and ultimately strengthen public accountability and support for public education?

Managing School Supplies and Equipment

Managing school supplies includes purchasing, storing, distributing, and accounting. Computer programs can be particularly helpful in managing supplies and equipment. Table 12.4 describes the process of purchasing and control and enumerates those responsible for the process (see Project 4 on page 380).

Maintaining School Buildings and Grounds

Creating a meaningful and appropriate learning environment for students is a challenge for educators. It demands not only an excellent curriculum but also designing and maintaining the school building and grounds. Anne Bullock and Elizabeth Foster-Harrison (1997) describe twelve requisite factors of the school environment: furniture, color, aesthetics, carpet, building and grounds maintenance, decorating detail, comfort, space and design, lighting, classroom elements (e.g., ceiling fans, sinks), instructional items (e.g., areas for displaying student work), and professional items (e.g., access to a telephone).

   ✱ **How will you include needed improvements for the building and grounds in your proposal?**

Conclusion

School administrators must have at least a basic understanding of how schools are financed. There are various sources for school revenues, and some sources have a more important role than others in revenue generation. As the next century begins, issues in generating revenue and allocating resources for schools will continue to dominate the discussion at both the state and national levels.

In addition to the acquisition of resources, budgeting, accounting, and maintenance are vital to a well-managed school. Planning, management, and control each play their own distinctive part in the complete budgeting and accounting

TABLE 12.4 *The Supply Process and Its Control*

Process of Purchasing and Control	Staff Member or Department Involved
1. Develop standard list of supplies and equipment	1. By users in cooperation with business manager
2. Stock catalogs refined from standard list; includes all possible supplies normally handled with necessary ordering data	2. Business office
3. Annual supply and equipment request (detailed statement of requirements for year)	3. Entire staff, including teachers and custodians
4. Budget document (listing, in general, supplies and equipment authorized and money available)	4. Supply and equipment budget developed by business office, approved by superintendent and board of education
5. Requisition and approval	5. Initiated by individual approved by designated administrative officer
6. Purchase order	6. Designated purchasing office
7. Note of receipt in good order	7. Receiving clerk
8. Spot-checks made on weight, quality, and quantity; notations made	8. Business office
9. Material placed in supply or equipment accounting ledger	9. Supply clerk
10. Bill paid by accounting office	10. Sent to accounting office by purchasing officer
11. Distribution records material sent to accountable individual buildings, based on annual requests and periodic requisitions	11. Principal of school
12. Building distribution personnel records each teacher who gets basic supplies at beginning of year and periodically as requested	12. Principal administers, may be coordinated with central office computer
13. User accountability: user signs for supplies	13. Users (teacher, custodians, etc.) and equipment in room at beginning of year; list provided by supply clerk
14. User "use" chart: materials checked off as used; form provided by supply, appraisal may be computerized	14. User (teacher, custodian, etc.)
15. Spot-checks and inspections	15. Business office and principal
16. Yearly inventory of all areas of supply storage	16. Business office (supply)
17. Use charts, reports, summaries	17. Business office (supply)

process. One does not operate at the expense of the other; rather, they all coexist as multiple purposes of fiscal stewardship.

Portfolio Artifacts

- Compare and contrast the school budgets of two comparable schools within the same district and between two different districts.

- Collaborate with colleagues in your school or in your internship site school in writing a small grant. When you have completed the project, describe in writing what you learned.
- Investigate a school that has a foundation. Interview some of the people on the foundation's committee. How did the foundation first begin? How does it currently operate? Describe in writing what you learned about school foundations from your interviews.
- Examine a safety plan for a school. What is included in the plan? Who is involved in implementing it?

- Work with the bookkeeper to make entries in a school's accounting records or follow a purchase order through the system.
- Attend a school board meeting at which the budget is discussed.
- Explore the following Web sites to learn more about: charter schools (www.ncsc.info/); U.S. independent schools (www.nais.org/); independent schools abroad (www.aaie.org/); and (www.academyish.org/).

Terms

Americans with Disabilities Act (ADA)	Mission-Based Budgeting (MBB)	Planning, Programming, Budgeting & Evaluation System (PPBES)
Charter schools	Per pupil allotment	School foundation
Flat-grant model	Power-equilizing model	Vouchers
Foundation concept	Planning, Programming,	Weighted-student model
Independent schools	Budgeting System (PPBS)	

Suggested Readings

Brewer, E. W., & Achilles, C. M. (Eds.). (2001). *Finding funding: Grantwriting from start to finish.* Thousand Oaks, CA: Corwin Press.

Burrupe, P., Brimley, V., & Garfield, R. (1999). *Financing education in a climate of change.* Boston: Allyn and Bacon.

King, R. A., Swanson, A. D., & Sweetland, S. R. (2002). *School finance: Achieving high standards with equity and efficiency.* Boston: Allyn and Bacon.

Levenson, S. (2001). *How to get grants and gifts for public schools.* Boston: Allyn and Bacon.

Owings, W. E., & Kaplan, L. (2006). *American public school finance.* Belmont, CA: Wadsworth Publishing Company

Peterson, S. L. (2000). *The grantwriters' internet companion: A resource for educators and others seeking grants and funding.* Thousand Oaks, CA: Corwin Press.

Ray, J., Hack, W., & Candoli, I. (2001). *School business administration: A planning approach.* Boston: Allyn and Bacon.

Schools in the middle. (1997, November/December). NASSP middle level education (entire issue devoted to facilities design and management).

13

Problem-Based Learning Projects

This chapter contains five problem-based learning (PBL) projects. It is recommended that only one project be used in a typical 3-credit university course. The instructor and students might decide to use the same PBL project with more than one group, or different groups could complete different projects at the same time. Project selection might depend on the interests of students and the level of school (elementary, middle, or high school, or school district) in which they would like to focus their learning. Table 13.1 lists the main features of each project.

Problem-Based Learning

Problem-based learning (PBL) is an instructional approach that uses typical problems of practice as the context for an in-depth investigation of core content. According to Bridges and Hallinger (1995) PBL has five elements:

1. The starting point for learning is a problem.
2. The problem is one that students are apt to face as future professionals.
3. The knowledge that students are expected to acquire during their professional training is organized around problems rather than disciplines.
4. Students, individually and collectively, assume a major responsibility for their own instruction and learning.
5. Most of the learning occurs within the context of small groups rather than lectures. (p. 6)

A key part of PBL involves the nature of the problems used in a project. Leithwood, Begley, and Cousins (1994) categorize problems that confront educational leaders into two types: high ground and swampy. They discuss the characteristics of preparation programs for developing expert school leaders and urge programs to focus on "swampy" problems. High-ground problems are those "of a more technical nature, where a well-rehearsed procedure for solving [is] available" (p. 53).

TABLE 13.1 *Main Features of PBL Projects*

Project Name	Grade Level	Related Chapters	Related Topics and Concepts
Safe Havens	K–8	1, 3, 5, 6, 9, 10, 11	Service integration Partnerships Grant writing Site-based management Transformational leadership Facilities management and allocation Change
A Jalapeño in a Candy Jar	Middle school	3, 4, 6, 7, 8, 9, 10, 11	Cultural diversity Change Staff development Curriculum Learning theory Equity, student rights Central office and board roles
Atoms and Bits	High school	2, 3, 4, 5, 6, 8, 10, 11, 12	Technology Staff development Change Curriculum Program evaluation Instruction
Data Management, Analysis, and Decision Making	High school	2, 3, 4, 5, 9, 10, 11	Data-driven decision making Assessment and accountability Technology Curriculum and instructional development Diversity and ethics
Marveling at the Results	School district	1, 2, 3, 5, 6, 7, 8, 10, 11, 12	Reform Leadership style Staff development School improvement Organizational structure Reform

Swampy problems are complex, at least to the person who has to solve them. The authors explain that problems are swampy when "one only vaguely understands the present situation, has no clear way of knowing what solutions would be superior, and lacks procedures for addressing the obstacles or constraints in the situation" (p. 43). Given the vast array of constituents and needs that face school administrators, it is crucial that the preparation of future educational leaders focus on solving swampy, ill-structured problems.

At the same time, educational administration students need to have conversations with experts to probe how effective practitioners solve identical or similar problems. Working with real audiences for the culminating activity of the PBL project, as well as people use to developing solutions to problems, affords students opportunities to learn how experts engage in problem solving and reflection. The goal of such reflection is for the learner to examine swampy problems by analyzing, exploring, gathering data, and critiquing.

Leithwood (1995), for example, discusses the high level of reflection that was an integral part of the problem-solving practice of reputationally effective superintendents he studied. Similarly, Schön (1987) advocates "reflection-in-action through which practitioners sometimes make new sense of uncertain, unique, or conflicted situations of practice" (p. 39). Schön maintains that if instructors encourage reflection, students will not assume "that existing professional knowledge fits every case nor that every problem has a right answer" (p. 39). Reflective thinking is crucial to helping educational leaders improve their problem-solving expertise.

In the real world of schools, problems are not solved independently. The complexity of the problems addressed by school leaders requires collaboration. Collaboration requires learning to listen to others, collectively reviewing outcomes, and responding to and partaking of relevant discussion. Vygotsky's (1978) concept of the "zone of proximal development" may be particularly relevant to PBL. This zone is the gap between a person's individual capacity for problem solving and the capacity of the group or peer with whom the learner is working. The group processes of discussing and critically reflecting afford the individual learner opportunities to internalize the group's problem-solving capacities. Ultimately, the ability to show good judgment, take control of situations, and communicate effectively will determine the success of solutions to problems, pinpoint perceptions, rank options, and resolve the issue at hand. The leader's future effectiveness depends on how well he or she handles problems, whether they are high ground or swampy (see Table 3.2, Chapter 3, page 86).

Because learning group-processing skills is essential to problem-based learning, peer and instructor feedback are integral components of projects. Students are usually asked to reflect on their role in the group with peers, and instructors provide feedback to students about those roles. Part of a discussion might include exploring why certain decisions have been made and how other factors might be involved. Thus, opportunities for what Argyris (1982) calls *double-loop learning* can be built into the feedback and assessment process.

Problem-Based Learning in Educational Leadership

ED BRIDGES • *Stanford University*   **PHILIP HALLINGER** • *Vanderbilt University*

Problem-based learning (PBL) provides a context in which participants can develop various leadership skills, acquire the knowledge needed to deal with problems of leadership, and experience what it means and feels like to be a leader. PBL develops leaders who solve problems through thoughtful deliberation with people who have a stake in the outcome and, in the end, are committed to implementing the group's decision.

When people first encounter PBL, they often initially feel "lost at sea." The sea can become rough as the group struggles with defining the problem and agreeing on what should be done about it. If a lot of wheel-spinning occurs and deep divisions develop within the group, the experience can be less than satisfying, result in a shoddy product, and thwart learning. Over the years we have learned that these undesirable consequences can be minimized or avoided by using particular methods and techniques. In this brief commentary we share some of what we have learned with you.

Group Size
Through experimenting with various group sizes, we have discovered that groups of six or seven members are ideal and are large enough to permit members to occupy and learn different roles (e.g., leader, facilitator, recorder, group member). Moreover, groups of this size afford opportunities for everyone to participate and contribute ideas. Three-person groups are especially troublesome because there is an inherent tendency in these groups for two people to form an alliance against the third. As groups increase in size beyond seven, they constrain the amount of "airtime" each member can have. The potential for problems to develop that interfere with group functioning increases unless an extremely skilled facilitator guides the discussion.

Method for Conducting Effective Meetings
The vast majority of people have worked in groups; some have undoubtedly wasted time and accomplished little, and others have worked much more efficiently and effectively. When groups go awry, people tend to attribute their difficulties to personality clashes. While these clashes might account in part for troubles in the group, more often discord is due primarily to a lack of methods for conducting effective meetings.

In our search for ways to assist groups in functioning more effectively, we have introduced them to the interaction method (Doyle & Straus, 1982). Groups that use this method initially find it too constraining; the discomfort gradually disappears, however, as group members begin to in-

ternalize the method and acquire the skills and tools. Occasionally, after trying it once or twice, groups abandon the method on the grounds that they function well together and do not need such a method. Typically, these groups run into difficulty and revert to the interaction method with a greater appreciation of the contribution it makes to effective group functioning.

Criteria for Problem Framing and Analysis
Learning in PBL, as the term implies, begins with a problematic situation. Some problems are fairly well structured, and others are ill-structured, messy, complex, and multifaceted. Identifying and stating the problem concisely poses a challenge for most people. The vast majority of PBL groups rush to solve the problem without fully understanding it. Yet, as Dewey (1910) and others have taught us, "A problem well-defined is half solved." Unless the problem is well-defined, problem solvers may follow a path that fails to remedy the existing situation while creating additional difficulties in the process because they fail to consider an adequate range of alternative courses of action.

To facilitate the problem-framing phase of the problem-solving process, we have found it beneficial to provide PBL groups with two criteria for evaluating the adequacy of a problem statement. The first criterion underscores the importance of stating the problem without embedding a solution in it. Groups commonly incorporate a solution into their statement of the problem, thus shutting off consideration of solution alternatives. A brief example might help to clarify this point.

In a Desert Survival exercise we use in our leadership program, groups either bypass the problem-framing stage or frame the problem as "Should we stay at the crash site, or should we leave and walk to safety?" Either of these formulations of the problem contains a solution to the "real" problem: "How can we survive?" The choice the group makes, to stay or leave, has profound consequences on its chances of survival. Groups that identify the "real" problem are much more likely to make the right choice of whether to stay or leave.

In addition to the solution-free criteria for judging the adequacy of a problem statement, we encourage PBL participants to look for facts in the problem scenario that support their definition of the problem. By testing their definition of the problem against the facts contained in the description of the problem, participants have a basis for evaluating their particular definition of the problem.

Use of Resources

With many PBL projects, the instructor supplies a list of resources that might have relevance to the problem; in some instances, the instructor also includes a copy of the suggested readings. Group members often decide to assign each person a different set of readings. At the next meeting of the group, members take turns providing brief synopses of what they have read. Having completed their reading "assignments," they turn to attacking the problem. By following this procedure, group members are apt to focus simply on the knowledge without regard to its application and might compromise their own in-depth knowledge of the content.

Because knowledge and application are of equal importance in PBL, we encourage group members to postpone reading the pertinent resources until they agree on a formulation of the problem. As individuals proceed to read the material, they ask themselves a question such as, "How does what I read apply to the problem we are facing?" When reporting back to the group, members discuss how what they have read may apply to their problem. If two members read the same material, they can share their perspectives on the same issue. We have learned that group members are much more likely to use the knowledge in solving the problem if they study the resources after, not before, they have framed it.

Facilitating Groups

The Institute for Development of Educational Activities, Inc. (I/D/E/A) has been involved in a number of projects that require the development of effective facilitator skills. The following discussion of group facilitation is based on the I/D/E/A projects.

The success of the group in solving problems is interrelated with the facilitator's ability to help the group work as a productive team (Cunningham & Gresso, 1993). The facilitator works with the group to establish a climate of mutual understanding, trust, and commitment to work together as a team to develop the best possible solution to the problem at hand. Facilitation requires a sensitivity to and appreciation of the diverse talents on the team and the skill to value each person's unique contribution to the group. The ability to model positive reinforcement of members but also to stick to a reasonable plan of action is essential for a successful group leader. The facilitator must be nonthreatening, supportive, and positive.

Group members clarify their thinking by expressing their perspectives and attaining consensus relative to the solution to the problem. One of the key decisions a facilitator makes is when to keep quiet and when to intervene in the group.

The major role of the facilitator is to:

- Build the capacities and stature of group members.
- Nurture diverse values and perspectives among group members.
- Create ownership among group members.
- Nurture creative thoughts of others.
- Ask questions that help members rethink positions.
- Ensure that team members identify resources, outside information, and ideas needed to address the problem.

- Use effective, solid, time-tested group processes to maximize the efficacy of the group and its individual members.
- Demonstrate effective listening, processing, and communication skills.
- Encourage goal-directed behavior and foster a patient and encouraging environment.

Depending on the approach used for the division of duties for team members playing various roles, the facilitator's tasks might include working with team members to develop schedules, agendas, and assignments in regard to solving the problem. The facilitator should begin by establishing mutual understanding of why the group exists and setting forth what will happen. Members should be encouraged to be open, take risks, share expertise, stay focused, and suspend judgment until the problem has been solved.

To be successful, group members need to be able to solve problems together and make effective decisions to which they are all committed. Cunningham and Gresso (1993) state, "The role of the group facilitator is to provide support by serving as a catalyst during the consideration, discussion, and resolution phase of team deliberation" (p. 23). The facilitator should help the group to be aware of the needs of the individual members and assist the group to focus on its purpose. "The facilitator models appropriate forms of participation and assists the individual to be as effective as possible. The main function of the facilitator is to continuously encourage and support human development, resulting in individual, team, and organizational improvement" (p. 243).

Understanding Group Process

CHERYL GETZ • *University of San Diego*

Unlike traditional learning, problem-based learning (PBL) is an instructional approach that affords participants opportunities to examine real-life problems, while at the same time gaining knowledge about group process, group dynamics and leadership in groups. My comments herein are drawn from emerging perspectives of "experiential learning groups" (Gillette & McCollom, 1995), which are heavily influenced by previous work in experiential group instruction at the National Training Institute (NTL) (www.ntl.org/index.html) that focuses primarily on interpersonal skills in relation to the group, and by scholars and consultants working at the A. K. Rice Institute (www.uvm.edu/mkessler/akrice/index.html), whose focus is on the study of social systems and group relations. Both offer valuable perspectives about groups and how they function.

Typically, candidates in educational administration programs bring with them a wealth of knowledge, skills, and experiences, with which all members can apply to their own learning. However, those attempting to complete PBL projects often lose sight of the process, due to a variety of factors such as time constraints, a strong desire to focus primarily on outcomes, and differences of opinion or personalities present in the group. Given this scenario, the valuable learning that can occur by examining the *process* of getting to the final product is often lost.

At this juncture, one might ask, "what can we learn from the *process* of working on a PBL project?" To answer this question, I begin with a typical example that I will use throughout to demonstrate the powerful learning that can transpire by reflecting on the group process. A group of six administrative candidates are assigned

Project 2: "A Jalapeño in a Candy Jar" (p. 368). The group consists of three men and three women. The task of the group is to prepare an action plan to address issues in multicultural education.

In the initial phase of the PBL group, members are encouraged to identify formal roles for members of the group. Generally, the group designates roles such as facilitator, recorder, and timekeeper, recognizing that this will contribute to the overall effectiveness of the group. In this phase of a group's life, members are seeking safety and a certain level of comfort with each other. The identification of specific roles helps members feel more secure about the process, as they work together to accomplish the task at hand.

Using the example above, one of the males asks to be the facilitator and suggests that one of the women be the recorder. She agrees, and one of the other women volunteers to be the timekeeper. There is no discussion about the reason for the assignments, and the group spends the next couple of meetings discussing the PBL project and trying to outline a plan of action. The first two meetings of the group seem to go very well, but as the group enters the next phase of the life of the group, differences of opinion arise, and the group cannot seem to agree on a direction. Five members of the group agree on a direction to take, but one of the women strongly opposes the direction the group is taking. She thinks discussions about cultural differences are divisive, and she proposes an alternate plan to the direction the group had been taking. After the meeting, the other five members "blame" the sixth member; after all, she is the one who "just doesn't understand the value of multicultural education." The sixth member now becomes the "scapegoat" for everything that goes wrong in the group, because other members project (on her) their own hidden fears and doubts about multicultural education but are unable, unaware of, or not willing to confront their hidden anxieties. Members of the group quite naturally bring expectations with them, and each member of the group will act in accordance with the expectations and the valences that they bring. It is in this phase that these expectations begin to influence the *life of the group*.

The *life of the group* can be defined in two ways; first as the beginning and end of the group, which is bounded in time (the beginning and end of each group meeting and the entire time allotted for completion of the project) and space (where the meetings are located); and the second, is ways in which the group recreates the social systems that are present in our everyday lives.

Consider again our example. During the next meeting, the facilitator (speaking on behalf of the five members who are aligned against the six member) confronts the sixth member. He tells her that the group has decided to stay with their original plan, since the majority of the members agree, and it seems impossible to reach any consensus. With tears in her eyes, she angrily responds, "Sure, this is how the group has been going all along, you decided you would be the facilitator, and I would be the recorder, so I'll just be quiet and take notes." The comment frustrates the group, some members think the facilitator was too harsh, and they feel empathy for her. Others are secretly glad that she remains quiet for the remainder of the meeting. A new alignment emerges, informal roles shift, but the group continues to work.

Careful observation of any group reveals the numerous roles that members take up or are drawn into by the group, often without their conscious awareness. For example, the formal roles that were designated by the group, and informal roles, that surfaced and may change at any time. As previously mentioned, in PBL groups, designated roles, such as facilitator, recorder, and timekeeper serve important functions and keep the group "on-task." However, informal roles also emerge, such as silent observer, dissenter, scapegoat, and so forth that often threaten group members and prevent the group from completing the assigned task. What happens then? Members try to "patch things up," further conflict is avoided, people take sides, judgments are made that further diminish the possibility of some members ability to contribute to the groups work, and usually two or three members take on the major responsibilities of task completion.

What *could* happen, if members discussed in advance the possibility (and probability) of the various roles emerging? Recognizing that during the life of any group members will take on a variety of roles, and without making judgments members can give and receive feedback on the roles they find themselves and others taking up during the life of the group. As the group's life unfolds over time, the results will be discussions that provide all members with critical feedback as each grapples with what it means to be a leader. Some questions that might surface include how the formal roles were determined or negotiated. Whose voice is heard more often and why? Whose values are received positively or negatively by the group and why? How are individual and group biases and prejudices played out in the group? How do societal expectations of individuals and the roles they bring influence the group?

This observation of self and others and the difficult discussions that follow often creates an onerous task, one that can illuminate differences, and instigate conflict. Yet, much can be learned about exercising leadership by examining the group and the role each member experiences during the time the group is together. The individual and group observation includes reflecting on ones own attitudes, behavior and roles in relation to the various attitudes, and behaviors and roles present in members that together form the *life of the group*. Groups operating at this level are more likely to uncover the root causes of the conflict by examining their own role in undermining the group's process.

When exploring the dynamics of any group, understanding and discussing the concept of boundaries (physical, task, time, and role) can serve as a starting point. Some boundaries are less permeable than others, for example, the *physical* boundary (membership and location) and the *task* of the assigned PBL group are generally quite impermeable because neither is likely to be altered in any way. The *task* of the group has several levels worth considering, such as the task of completing a final product, the task of each member (usually assigned by the group) in between meetings, and the various tasks of the group during designated meeting. However neither is completely impermeable, for example, intrusions on the physical boundary often affect the group. For instance, if the group wants to

meet at a coffee shop or a member wants to bring a pet or child to a meeting. The boundaries should be renegotiated to ensure that this does not negatively affect the group.

In contrast to the physical and task boundaries, boundaries such as *time* and *role* are much more permeable and are likely to change over the life of the group. When working in a PBL group, setting time limits on the group's work contributes to the groups' effectiveness. Time limits can be set for each group meeting, for a discussion about a specific topic during a group meeting, as well as for the completion of the final product. While time boundaries should be closely monitored to ensure that the group stays on task, groups that are able to make adjustments to the agreed upon time boundaries, as a result of a changing task, are likely to benefit from their ability to accept this flexibility.

The most complex boundary is that of *role*. The various *roles* that members participate in during the life of the group can change frequently or not at all, depending on the group and its members. Some roles may be familiar roles that members are accustomed to outside of the group, other roles that members find being placed on them by the group, are less familiar. Back to our example: Suppose at the very first meeting, the male member who offered to be the facilitator and suggested that one of the women be the recorder, asked himself why he made that suggestion, and then shared his perspective with the group. This might open a dialogue about all of the roles that needed to be assigned, and the tendency for each member to take on specific roles. Perhaps the woman, who "agreed" to be the recorder, would then speak to her frustration of agreeing to this role because she was often the note taker in previous settings, and this restricted her ability to bring her ideas forward. Both might still agree to take on these roles, but the individual and group awareness has been elevated.

When conflicts arise, such as when the woman could not agree with the plan, the group can benefit from looking at her dissention, from a *group* perspective versus an individual or *interpersonal* one. Group members typically respond to each other on an interpersonal level, that is, they attribute conflicts within the group to *individual* personalities, behaviors, or attitudes. However, groups are much more complex! A more effective, parallel reflective process includes a dialogue that considers the interpersonal aspects of group members and an awareness of the group as a social system. The group might ask: What is she representing for us? Who are the constituents in our schools that she represents? Individuals, at various points throughout the group's life might also ask themselves the same question: What am I representing for the group? If the group can move away from making judgments on an interpersonal level, members will be more apt to see that dissention offers the group powerful learning. An individual may embody a strong sentiment in the entire group, as well as in other social systems, such as the school communities that each member is associated with.

As a leader, one can imagine the difficulties that might arise when attempting to adopt a new policy or advance a strategic plan when the leader does not notice or pays little attention to the dynamics present in the groups she or he will be leading. The value of the PBL process is the opportunity for participants to gain awareness of group dynamics, including an awareness of self and others. Like high-performing teams, group members who understand themselves and each other and work together in the service of learning, are more likely to produce work that represents the integration of ideas from all members, and a culmination of the groups ideas are likely to be reflected in the final product.

References
Gillette, J., & McCollom, M. (Eds.). (1995). *Groups in context. A new perspective in group dynamics.* New York: University Press of America.

PROJECT 1

Safe Havens: Developing School-Based Health Clinics

ELLEN SMITH SLOAN • *Southern Connecticut State University*

Not unlike much of the public discourse today, health care for underserved children became a topic that provoked differing viewpoints and often heated conflict (Raftery, 1992) in social and political discussions (Cortese, 1993; Jehl & Kirst, 1992). "Activist writers like Jacob Riis . . . cast a bright light on the suffering of children—the wasting of a generation—and cried out for action" (Tyack, 1992, p. 20). Strong recommendations that the public school act as the vehicle for remedying these ills became an increasingly popular notion in the country (Wollons, 1992; Zigler, Kagan, & Klugman, 1983).

Today many public schools still find themselves faced with children's unresolved health issues. Social, emotional, and physical health problems all present themselves at the doorways of America's public schools. Aware of the political and fiscal realities of trying to assume total responsibility for these health concerns, schools and other community agencies have become creative in their strategies for meeting children's needs. An emerging phenomenon across the country has been the development of school-based health centers or clinics (SBHC), a type of interagency collaborative. Spurred on by recommendations from child advocacy groups urging schools and communities to collaborate in linking families with health and human service providers (Anne E. Casey Foundation, 1993; Children's Defense Fund, 1992), more than 570 SBHCs have been formed in over thirty-three states (*Education Week*, February 2, 1994), and the number continues to grow annually.

Great variety exists among present models of collaborative services for children; and within the generic categories of these models (school-based, school-linked, neighborhood-based, community-based) are widespread differences (Kirby & Lovick, 1987; Raftery, 1992). Indeed, most people feel that these differences in interagency initiatives are healthy and allow those at local levels to be creative with networking, needs, and resources. Many eschew creating "cookie-cutter" designs for others to recreate. Knapp (1995) acknowledges the complexities (and the dangers) of labeling specific models and chooses to phrase the interagency process as "comprehensive, collaborative services for children and families" (p. 5).

Another dimension comes into play when these services are school based or school linked, as teachers and principals become integral players in an interagency collaborative comprising very different professions. Hooper-Briar and Lawson (1994) illuminate some of these interprofesional issues as they describe the "well-intentioned language of 'collaboration'—in reality most groups are cooperatives facing the challenge of working together" (p. 28). As Dryfoos (1994) quipped, collaboration is "an unnatural act between non-consenting adults" (p. 149).

Learning Objectives

- To develop specific strategies for the implementation of a school-based health center.
- To reflect, through group discussions, the extent to which deep beliefs and assumptions shape our "ways of doing and thinking" and hence play an important role in the decisions we make as educational leaders (see Chapter 1).
- To gain expertise in the art of discussing controversial and emotionally charged issues facing a school and its community.

- To prepare short- and long-range plans for the development of a school-based health center.
- To heighten the productivity of meetings through the strengthening of group interaction skills (see Chapter 6).
- To strengthen ability to conduct productive and inclusionary meetings (see Chapter 5).

Guiding Questions

1. If your school has a school-based health center (SBHC), reflect on the ways your school has involved the social worker or the school nurse in faculty meetings, social events, classroom activities, and other educational functions. Are they included? Do they feel a part of the school? Why or why not? How do you reach out to these adults from different professions? (see Chapter 9).
2. Thinking as a principal, what organizational processes, in your building, support and strengthen the work of the school nurse or social worker? What processes or structures impede their work?
3. How would you involve parents and caregivers in the very early discussions of implementing an SBHC? Has your school involved parents and caregivers in other initiatives? Why or why not? (see Chapters 5 and 9).
4. Have you ever developed or considered developing a partnership with an outside

   agency? Has your school? Does the school already have a solid, albeit informal, relationship with the juvenile system or a hospital or shelter in your community? What works? What doesn't?
5. As you read this problem and gain insights from the readings and conversations with people from other professions, where do you think it best to initiate a health center for children: In the school building? On the school grounds but not inside the building? In the neighborhood or community? Explain your choice.
6. Issues always arise pertaining to what specific services should be offered to children in a health center. Reflect on your beliefs and assumptions. Learn your district's policies on what school nurses can and cannot do in regard to treating children for physical, social, or emotional needs.

The Problem

As you begin your third year as principal of A. M. McCabe School (K–8), increasing numbers of students are referred to the school nurse, the social worker, and your office. The lines of children with physical or social health concerns waiting outside these three office doors remain a persistent image in your head. Not only do you wonder how the nurse and social worker are handling it all, but you worry about the students' welfare, the academics they may be missing, and the disruptions to your teachers' classrooms. And what happens when the nurse and social worker are not in school? (Working hours for both the nurse and social worker are Monday, Wednesday, and Friday.)

The superintendent, extremely sympathetic to and supportive of your concerns at McCabe, did increase the hours of both the social worker and the nurse to the present level of three days a week. In addition, she redistributed monies to provide the K–3 grade levels with teacher aides. These improvements have mitigated teacher anxiety levels somewhat. Everyone realizes that these changes, though gratifying, barely tip the balance in favor of children. The superintendent has also broached the concerns of McCabe with the board of education, but the board cannot reach agreement on how to better meet the health needs of students.

Coupled with the discussions of scarce financial resources and the existence of twenty-five other schools in the district with similar issues is the belief many hold that schools are not in the business of resolving the serious physical and mental health needs of children; these people believe the school's focus ought to remain strictly on academic issues. Opponents also remind you that there is a community health center downtown to which all families can and should go. You've checked out that avenue as well and discovered that there are myriad reasons people do not use the city's community health center, including lack of transportation, erratic city bus schedules, its four-mile distance from the housing development where most students reside, presence in the home of infant siblings who cannot be left at home, complicated bureaucratic procedures and forms, and the absence of a concerned parent or caregiver.

Cognizant of the realities of what the district can actually do, you decide to take a grassroots approach and involve your faculty in the problem-solving process. A year ago you all met and voted to create a Faculty Council (eight of your thirty-four faculty members, the nurse, and the social worker). In addition to tackling academic issues facing the school, you encouraged the council to focus on children's unmet health needs. In the initial problem-solving sessions focusing on health issues, teachers talked about creating a business partnership with the school, with the ultimate goal that the partnership would lead to a short-term grant for additional health and human service personnel.

The pursuit of that line of thinking came up dry. Coupled with the fact that most business and industry had moved out of the city was the reality that the remaining companies were already committed to other programs and charities. Discussion also included exploring private philanthropic sources, providing children with transportation to the city's community health center, requesting pro bono work from community medical professionals, and writing to nationally based foundations. Despite roadblocks and unfamiliar territory for the council, you have felt continually buoyed up by the group's optimism, energy, and commitment to helping kids.

Two months ago you became aware of state grants to be awarded to schools and their local city boards and departments of health for the development of school-based health centers. (City boards and departments of health would actually oversee the administration of the centers.) The grant would be available for three years in the amount of $150,000 per year, per school. In addition to serving students who attended the school, the SBHC would also treat students' younger non–school-age siblings residing at home (birth to 5 years old).

After making the council aware of this opportunity, you requested the application materials. They arrived three weeks ago. You and the council shared the idea and application process with the entire faculty, who subsequently voted to have the school proceed with the idea.

You have approached the superintendent and city board of health about the grant, and they have encouraged you to pursue this path. The superintendent was impressed with your involvement of the council and faculty and believes that this ownership is a crucial step. To assist you with budgetary items and grant-writing language, she has asked the assistant superintendent to step into the process whenever you feel it appropriate. In addition, you have invited the nurse from the city's board of health, the agency that technically will be responsible for the SBHC's administrative structure, including the hiring and firing of personnel.

Only the nurse and social worker have some knowledge of what an SBHC is. This is new territory for your eight teachers on the council, as well as for you. The application guidelines are comprehensive, rigorous, and due in four weeks. Will the group be able to meet the deadline and do it well? Will individuals feel overwhelmed with the task or uncomfortable that the nurse and social worker know so much more than they? And in the back of your mind you are wondering whether you are leading the school down the "wrong" path. After all, you're just beginning to learn about SBHCs and haven't even had time to visit one. You also recognize a strong interest in the improvement of student performance on state assessments. If awarded the grant, how will you then deal with all the controversial health issues that are sure to arise with the board and other city taxpayers? Will you be able to gather board support? How will the sensationalizing local newspaper deal with the news? How will this affect other school initiatives?

You've just taken a deep breath. It's 3:15 and you walk into the workroom. These questions will not stop whirling around in your head.

Grant Application: Questions and Areas to Address (Product Specifications)

1. Submit a written rationale for the creation of a school-based health center in your educational setting.
2. What children's health and human service needs will be addressed by the SBHC? Be specific about why the school has selected these needs.

3. List the people who will be involved in the development of the SBHC, including those involved in the preparation of this written application. (List people by profession and community role, not by name.)

4. Using the annual grant allocation of $150,000, outline the specific types of personnel (including hours and salaries but not names) who will be employed in the SBHC for each of the three years of the grant's duration. (*Special information for PBL participants:* Each SBHC must by law include the services of a medical doctor for at least three hours per week to oversee all medical procedures.)

5. What processes does the school plan to put into place to allow new health and human services personnel to interface with the current school nurse and social worker?

6. What processes and procedures will be initiated to encourage interprofessional understanding between the teaching faculty and health and human services professionals? How will the success of this effort be monitored over the three-year cycle?

7. Describe the process(es) by which teachers, parents and caregivers, and the media will be introduced to the concept of an SBHC.

8. What specific role(s) will the building administrator play in implementing, integrating, and sustaining the SBHC?

9. Where will the SBHC be located? Be specific about why its location is the most appropriate decision for your school. What is your rationale? (*Pertinent information for PBL participants:* The school has three options, all of which have the same square footage. The options are: (1) the room that adjoins the current school nurse's office, (2) the room that adjoins the principal's office, and (3) a modular unit on the school campus that is not accessible from the school building. Renovation costs for all three would be the same.

Profile of A. M. McCabe School

1. Grade Levels
K–8 (two classes per grade level)

2. Total School Enrollment: 457
Race/Ethnicity Breakdown

Asian	10
Black	112
Hispanic	218
Native American	1
White	118

Sex

Male	207
Female	250

3. Average Class Size

Kinder/Grade 1	24.5
Grades 2 and 3	25.0
Grades 4 and 5	26.5
Grades 6, 7, 8	25.0

4. Special Program Enrollment (by number)

Bilingual Education	180
ESL	9
Extended-Day Kindergarten	49
Special Education	
0.5 or fewer hours per week	40
0.5–15 hours per week	25
15 or more hours per week	27

5. Other Student Needs (by percentage)

Free or reduced-price meals	72.8%
Home language non-English	45.0% (approx.)

6. Percentage of Students Returning to McCabe Each Year

Approximately 92%

7. Levels of Absenteeism

Grades K–4—Approximately 10% of class per week

Grades 5–8—approximately 13% of class per week

8. Staffing

Total Teaching Staff	34
Regular classroom	18
Art, Music, PE	5
Special education	5
Special programs (ESL, bilingual)	6
Total administrative staff	1
Noncertified staff (aides)	8
Secretarial staff	1
School nurse (part-time)	1
Social worker (part-time)	1

9. Gender and Ethnicity of Teaching Staff

Female	
Asian	1
African American	3
Hispanic	5
White	22
Male	
Hispanic	1
White	2

10. Documented Reasons for Visits to the School Nurse

(Number per eight-month period)

Temporary illness	272
Chronic medical problems (ear, stomach, throat, eyes, bowels)	175
Asthma related	52
Dental pain	160
Reproductive questions	32

Special Note: Many children with medical problems were referred to the community health center physicians or a family doctor (if the child had one). These other serious medical issues included children in need of: lead level tests, immunizations, physical examinations, cardiovascular care, respirators, ear infections leading to deafness, dental check-ups and related surgery, eye impairments, and physical injuries occurring at home or at school.

11. Documented Reasons for Visits to the School Social Worker

(Number per eight-month period)

Reproductive questions	25
Counseling issues with peers	180
Family problems	225
Substance abuse	56
Academic issues	129

12. Family Involvement

McCabe has traditionally enjoyed family support for the school's mission of educating children, but actual involvement of parents and caregivers (e.g., conferences, volunteers, open house, PTO) has been limited. The limited involvement is due to the fact that 45 percent are from non–English-speaking homes as well as home- and job-related responsibilities. Two years ago the faculty, principal, and a small but energetic PTO developed a plan to address these issues. A room adjacent to the entrance of the school was designated the "family room." Coffee and tea are always available, magazines and books are there for browsing, and children's work covers the walls. The principal, who also speaks Spanish, often stops in to chat with visitors. Judging from the guest book, parent/caregiver visits have become more frequent, and teachers report higher comfort levels and increased attendance in conferences.

13. Children in Single-Parent/Caregiver Homes

With mother	212
With father	18
With grandparent	38
Other caregivers	18
TOTAL	286

14. McCabe's External Community

McCabe is a neighborhood school, and most children walk to school every morning. Homes include single-family low-income dwellings and two federally funded low-income housing developments.

The percentage of taxpayers in the city without children in school is 35 percent and the majority of this population is over 55 years old.

15. McCabe's School Governance Structure

School governance was very traditional for the twenty-five years preceding the arrival of the new principal. With the advent of the faculty council, decisions are beginning to involve the whole faculty. The principal hopes to involve parents in the near future.

Resources

To obtain specific statistics and policies and procedures concerning health and related issues in your state, contact the appropriate agencies; also refer to appropriate chapters within this book. Their data and other resources will strengthen knowledge and productivity levels of PBL project participants.

PROJECT 2

A Jalapeño in a Candy Jar: Addressing Cultural Diversity

PAULA A. CORDEIRO • *University of San Diego*

One of the greatest challenges facing schools today is the diversity of the children at our doorsteps. The demographics of the United States are shifting in important ways. American families are rapidly becoming more diverse— the definition of what is meant by "family" is being reconceptualized. Increasing numbers of single-parent families, more families with stepchildren, more fathers raising children alone, and more mothers in the labor force are all factors. The cumulative effect of a significant influx of immigrants in the last thirty years promises to be both profound and interesting. Many of our recent immigrants represent cultural groups that have never immigrated to the United States before in significant numbers. These immigrants fall into three categories: refugees, legal immigrants, and undocumented immigrants. In absolute numbers, this migration is among the largest in U.S. history.

Most teachers and administrators have not been trained to deal with the unique needs these children bring to schoolhouse doors. The structural aspects of local governments in many cities and towns do not lend themselves easily to linking services that might be available to other community members and schoolchildren. Additionally, racism rises to the surface as jobs are lost and financial constraints on local governments increase.

Learning Objectives

- To collaboratively develop a plan incorporating knowledge from research in multicultural education.
- To develop specific strategies for the implementation of multicultural programming.

- To examine personal beliefs and assumptions about language and cultural issues.

Guiding Questions

1. Reflect on the ways in which your ethnic and racial background, gender, religion, ability or disability, and sexuality affect your beliefs. Share with your team some of your basic beliefs. How have they changed over time? Why?
2. What should a school administrator know about issues related to cultural diversity? Do you know these things? If so, how did you learn them? If not, how might you learn them?
3. What should a teacher know about cultural diversity? If a teacher has had little training in this area, what are the best ways for him or her to learn more?
4. What roles, if any, should parents, families, school boards, and community members play in working with schools? In the case of Seaview School District, and Silvermine Middle School in particular (see below), how might they be actively involved in multicultural educational programming?
5. How might Banks's (1999) (see Chapter 4) "Approaches to Multicultural Curriculum Model" be applied to this situation?
6. Chapters 7, 9, 10, and 11 discuss legal and ethical considerations, learning, learning transfer, pupil services, and staff development. What implications do these readings have for the development of your team's plan?

Seaview School District

Seaview School District is adjacent to a large city in the northeastern part of the United States. Seaview has approximately 2,970 students. Until the mid-1990s the demographics of the district were relatively stable. Seaview had been a predominantly white, middle-class community. However, since that time the African American and Hispanic (Puerto Rican and Mexican American) populations have steadily increased. Additionally, two local organizations have sponsored Laotian and Vietnamese immigrants. One of these groups also has plans in the near future to sponsor Hmong immigrants.

Silvermine Middle School

Silvermine Middle School has approximately 520 students and thirty certified staff members. Currently, there are no bilingual programs, but as the Spanish-speaking population increases steadily, the assistant superintendent has begun discussing the need to consider some type of bilingual (Spanish/English) program. The district employs two full-time ESL teachers and six aides. One ESL teacher covers the middle and high schools, and the other teacher works in three elementary schools that have the highest proportions of non–native-English-speaking students. Each of the aides works in a different elementary school "tutoring" students and helping those elementary teachers who have non–native-English-speaking children in their classes.

All Silvermine staff members (certified and noncertified) are white. Twenty-seven percent of the students are currently receiving free or reduced-priced meals; this percentage has doubled in the last ten years.

Silvermine offers the typical content areas found in a middle school. The staff and students are especially pleased with their technology education program. The school has a strong library information center as well as a computer lab. It does not offer any language classes except English and ESL.

The Problem

You are the new principal of Silvermine Middle School. One day last fall after your first two weeks on the job, a serious racial incident occurred on school grounds. The incident involved students from your school and from another middle school in a nearby city. Several students had black eyes and were badly bruised from having been hit with baseball bats. These students required medical attention. After a complete investigation, which included community groups, eleven students from the two schools were suspended. Two parents claimed that their children were unfairly punished. They argued that because there was a lack of evidence to prove that their children were involved and that suspension was too severe a punishment.

During the investigation you discovered that numerous racial, ethnic, and religious incidents have occurred over the last five years. Numerous "minor" incidents also have taken place throughout your first year. After exploring the curriculum and talking with your assistant principal and staff members during the school year, you have seen little evidence that issues of cultural diversity are being addressed. Additionally, you have found that more than half your staff and your assistant principal do not feel that these "incidents" were bias-related incidents. They believe them to be "typical problems encountered by adolescents."

Several African American and Spanish-speaking families have complained to you and the central office staff, both formally and informally, that their children are being treated unfairly by some teachers at Silvermine. In your observations this year, you have seen some evidence of such discrimination as well. Also, at the last school board meeting, several African American parents called these issues to the attention of the board. The school board promised to investigate and report back to the parents.

More than 60 percent of the teachers have been at Silvermine for more than seventeen years. You believe that many of these staff members are dissatisfied with the "different" kinds of children the district has now, as compared with fifteen years ago. Although most staff members have had little experience working with children from non–native-English-speaking backgrounds or with children representing racial and ethnic groups other than white, several faculty members do have teaching experiences with LEP students and students from culturally diverse backgrounds. Mrs. Sasse recently told you a story of a Hispanic student who confided in her that at Silvermine she felt "like a jalapeño in a candy jar."

As a result of the information collected during the investigation of the fight as well as through exploring the curriculum, you are keenly aware that Silvermine Middle School cannot continue to be reactive in its approach to dealing with racial, cultural, and religious incidents. Meanwhile, the superintendent has sent a memo to all administrators in the district (see the following memorandum).

Memorandum

June 2

To: All Principals, Assistant Principals, and Instructional Leaders
From: Valerie Blandy, Superintendent
Re: Multicultural Education

As you may be aware, the population of Seaview school district is rapidly changing. Additionally, we are seeing an increase in serious confrontations among students. There is increasing evidence of the inability of all of us in the schools to understand the nature of the new, diverse population of students in our schools.

These changes make it imperative that schools at all levels begin addressing issues in multicultural education. Multicultural education is not solely a racial issue. Rather, the focus of multicultural education is on those cultural groups that experience prejudice and discrimination in our society. The purpose is to reduce discrimination against them and to provide equal educational opportunities for all. To meet this goal, the district will:

- Nurture lifelong respect and compassion in students for themselves and other human beings regardless of race, ethnic origin, gender, social class, disability, religion, and sexual orientation;
- Remain steadfast in guaranteeing equal opportunity for high-quality education for all students, and not unlawfully discriminate;
- Endeavor to secure equal opportunities for all students.

Multicultural education is a major concern, and we encourage all schools to begin to address this issue through curriculum and staff development. By beginning the process now, we can eliminate problems at a later date.

Each school is to develop a three-year plan to address these issues starting in the following school year. I will be contacting each school in the next few weeks to set up a meeting in which you will present an outline of your plan.

Your Challenge

Today is June 3, and the superintendent has scheduled a meeting with you at 10 A.M. on June 29. You have been working with a team of staff members on the plan requested by the superintendent. She has asked you to present a draft outline of the written plan at that meeting. She and the assistant superintendent would like to familiarize themselves with what your team is proposing for your school so that they can marshal district resources.

Seaview School District

School	Grade	Enrollment	School	Grade	Enrollment
Unity Elementary	K–5	380	Seaview Middle School	6–8	468
Hope Elementary	K–5	438	Silvermine Middle School	6–8	522
Praxis Elementary	K–5	291	Seaview High School	9–12	870

Silvermine Middle School

Total certified staff	25	Total noncertified staff	14
Regular classroom teachers	20	Instructional	4
Special-program teachers	2	Noninstructional	10
Administration	2		
Pupil personnel services	1	Average class size	26

Silvermine Middle School

		School enrollment		
			Percentages	
			Now	In 3 Years
	Numbers		100%	(approx.)
Total	522			
Race-ethnicity				
Asian American	34		7	10
African American	62		11	15
Hispanic	60		12	20
Native American	5		1	1
White	361		69	51

Product Specifications

Prepare an action plan that reflects your solution to the superintendent's request for Silvermine Middle School. Your plan should include the following sections:

1. *A definition of the problem* as you view it at Silvermine. If your team identifies more than one problem, please prioritize what you choose to address.
2. *A three-year draft plan* for addressing the important components of the problem. The plan should include sample activities, the sequence in which you intend to proceed with them, and a rationale for the selection and sequence.
3. Your *strategy* for gaining the support of faculty, staff, students, and families. It should include how you will overcome the potential obstacles you will face in implementing the plan.

(Please refer to appropriate chapters in this book as a resource.)

Four Silvermine Middle School Staff Members

Kathy Collins has been teaching social studies at Silvermine for seventeen years, and she currently serves as a team leader. Before working at Silvermine, Kathy taught for five years at an International American School in Spain. Kathy usually spends her summer vacations in Spanish-speaking countries (Mexico, Spain, Guatemala). She has a keen interest in Latino cultures and is well respected by many of the Spanish-speaking families.

Scott Newkirk is in his eighth year of teaching English. Before coming to Silvermine he taught in New York City for ten years. Scott has spoken with the principal several times about his concerns with the LEP students. He believes that he cannot adequately meet their language needs because the ESL teacher has to cover both the middle school and high school, and many students have only one class of ESL each day.

Helen Sasse has been teaching ESL at Silvermine and Seaview High School for the last four years. Before that time she taught English three-quarter time and ESL one-quarter time at Silvermine. Helen has a master's degree in teaching English as a second language (TESOL). Last summer she attended her third special weeklong workshop, which focused on LEP students from specific language backgrounds.

Jaime Romo is a guidance counselor who has been at Silvermine for eleven years. Jaime has been particularly adept in working with students involved in some of the racial and ethnic incidents in the last few years. He is married to a woman who is African American and has strong ties with the black community.

PROJECT 3

Atoms and Bits: A Technology Project

BARBARA S. CAMPBELL • *Assistant Superintendent, Wolcott Public School, Connecticut*

Microchip technology's power to store, manage, and transmit large amounts of information rapidly has transformed all aspects of living and working in our society. Information mediated by microchips is the commodity of the future. In the past, the mission of education was to equip students with competencies that would serve as their stock in trade (e.g., in agriculture, industry) to live a productive, high-quality life. Schools currently are information-based institutions charged with the same mission, so one would expect them to be aggressive adopters and users of technology.

They have not, however, been successful in adopting and integrating technology. The reasons frequently cited are:

- Insufficient hardware
- Inappropriate and or insufficient software
- Lack or inadequacy of technical support
- Lack or inadequacy of teacher training and staff development
- Lack of administrative support
- Mismatch between the technology and educational need
- Lack or inadequacy of initial and continuing funding.

If schools are to be successful in preparing productive, informed citizens for the twenty-first century, they will have to overcome the problems they have had with integrating technology into the teaching and learning process. Administrators, who are responsible for program development, must meet this challenge.

Learning Objectives

- Define the opportunities and challenges associated with technology integration.
- Collaboratively design a plan for adopting and implementing technology in a school that incorporates prior learning, field experiences, and best-practice models gleaned from available resources.
- Prepare the plan, using available computer technologies.

Guiding Questions

1. Whom will you involve in developing the plan? In implementing it? What role will you play? (See Chapter 7.)
2. Which technology is "right" for your building's initial experience? What kinds of implementation challenges are associated with the technology? (See Chapters 11 and 12.)
3. What potential leverage points do you have for developing and implementing the plan?
4. What elements constitute an exemplary building technology plan?
5. Based on what you have learned about change, staff development, curriculum/instruction, and school reform, how will you address the issues that have caused previous attempts at integrating technology to fail? (See Chapters 2, 3, 7, and 10.)

The Problem

As the new principal of Marietta High School, you have spent most of the year gathering information about the school's culture. Even though many of the problems are characteristic of comprehensive high schools in the area, you are beginning to feel frustrated and overwhelmed by the way in which each issue compounds another.

Marietta is the only high school in the Mountjoy district of 2,800 students. Its enrollment of 730 students is beginning to increase as larger classes make their way through the system. The district seems to be a buffer zone. It is surrounded by affluent suburban districts on one side and a large urban district on the other. From your conversations with other district principals, you sense a tension between the achievement levels of the suburban schools and having to deal with more at-risk students from the inner city whose parents have moved into Mountjoy. Data show that your minority, free or reduced lunch, and special-education numbers are increasing annually.

The faculty (fifty-five certified) are a veteran staff who, for the most part, view themselves as content experts. The head of the social studies department summed up their beliefs, "We cover our content in the limited time we have. That stuff (e.g., learner-centered methodologies, alternative assessments, technology, any of the literacies) is for the elementary and middle school teachers, anyway!" They note that the only ongoing "fad" has been the district's commitment to technology. However, since the initiative started at the elementary level, they believe that money and commitment will run out before the technology gets to them.

Feedback from students is conflicting. You are disturbed by the "listlessness" you feel as you walk down the halls during passing times and that you observe in class. Many students respond to your questions regarding issues affecting them with "I don't know" or a shrug. On the other hand, a few students have come to you with complaints about boring classes, the lack of computers, and the absence of student input into decision making.

You suspect that student experiences in the lower grades might be a significant contributing factor to negative student behavior and attitudes. Your conversations with other principals lead you to believe that the expectations of incoming freshmen have been dramatically changed by the success of the district's technology initiative at the elementary and middle school levels. By the time students leave the elementary schools, they are accustomed to generating their assignments using word processing, graphics, and charts in fully networked environments. Their experiences at the middle school build on this expertise. Students are used to working with a team of teachers in long blocks of time. They are accustomed to being in charge of their learning. Confronted with the technology wasteland of Marietta and lecture-style teaching delivered in 42-minute segments, students seem to respond with behaviors that rapidly degenerate into apathy or disciplinary issues.

The school's crumbling physical infrastructure compounds all these problems. It is poorly designed and poorly equipped for implementing more effective programs. Electrical wiring is inadequate; blueprints are almost nonexistent. You suspect that any facilities monies in the district have been consumed in attempting to respond to ever-increasing enrollments at the elementary and middle levels.

There is no area with computers that can accommodate a class of more than fourteen, and the average class size is twenty-three. The few computer areas in English, business, and technology education are considered exclusively for the use of those respective departments. The computers themselves are a hodge-podge of Apple IIes and GSs, DOS machines ranging from 286s–486s, and Macintoshes. Some of the DOS machines run Windows; others don't. Of the mini-networks in the building (office, technology education, and business), none connects with the others. There are no connections to the Internet.

Marietta's parents seem to be divided into two camps. One group wants to perpetuate the status quo; the other argues strongly in favor of raising levels of academic performance and expanding the program of studies. The president of Marietta's Parent Group, Karen Strong, belongs to the former. She has not found her participation in the newly formed district parent council (whose membership consists of the presidents of all of the school parent councils) worthwhile. She has told you that the group is made up of parents who think that Mountjoy schools are private technology academies. Her recommendation to drop out of the group was overturned by high school parents interested in academics and increased use of technology.

At your last meeting with Superintendent Garcia, you learned that monies will be available during the next budget year to begin the process of making Marietta High School a technology-rich environment. She has asked you to develop the first part of a three-year plan for the project and informed you that she will send you a memo outlining details.

Product Specifications

1. Develop Marietta's technology-based plan. The plan must include:
   a. a brief description of how the plan was developed (e.g., who was involved, when they met, how they organized their task, what the principal's role was);
   b. a list of the technology(ies) chosen for initial adoption and implementation with a brief rationale for the selection;
   c. an outline of the adoption and implementation stages and strategies, with a brief rationale for each major stage and strategy;
   d. a description of how you will monitor the progress and success of the plan.
2. Prepare the plan, using computer applications.
3. Prepare for and participate in a review of the plan by the administrative council. *Note:* The review will not include a formal presentation, since the purpose of an administrative review is to refine a plan before it is finalized and implemented. The council will read your plan in advance. During the review, you must be prepared to answer questions about it.

Plan Due: _____

Memorandum

April 15

To: Deborah Carroll
From: Esmeralda Garcia, Superintendent
Re: Technology initiative

At our last meeting, I reviewed our district's technology initiative with you and asked you to begin developing a technology plan for your building. We will review your plan at the September administrative council meeting the following year. Final adoption is scheduled for the October meeting. To assist you with plan development, I am providing these conditions and guidelines:

- Consider the district's goals for technology—improved teaching, learning, and leading with technology.
- Our corporate partners and the Board of Education have been willing to provide generous funding for well-thought-out plans. Therefore:
  —the network infrastructure will be provided for your building.
  —funding to cover plan development costs (e.g., summer work by staff, consultant fees, visitations, training, materials) is readily available.
  —cost should not be a primary decision-making criterion when selecting technology(ies).
- Think long-range but develop the plan *only* for Marietta's first year of adoption and implementation. You should list "next steps" for years two and three.
- Technology coordinators and principals from other buildings stand ready to assist you at any point in your plan development.
- Please send a copy of your plan to me by September 15, so that we can duplicate and distribute it before the meeting.

Selected Readings from the Principal's Journal

May 1

I toured my building today. Reality hit me in the face. What an ugly monster of a place! Ceiling tiles stained, floor tiles mismatched, walls painted in awful institution colors. . . . And those awful chairs with arms placed in rows.

According to Frank, the head custodian, Marietta has antiquated heating and intercom systems and problems with asbestos and electricity. He also informed me that he does not have enough staff to manage a building of its size.

My assistant Elaine interrupted the tour because the computer network had crashed while she was running schedules. The level of anger was incredible. I learned from Fred and Carol [assistant principals] that the network spends most of its time crashed. When I asked what we do about a crashed network, I unleashed the office staff's frustration. The contracted service responds on its time schedule, not on the basis of our needs.

May 24

When I got back to the building, I ran into Kelly, our library media specialist. As we chatted, I gathered some valuable information. Although her budget is not adequate, it seems that she has been working with Fred, Nancy, and Pat to move away from textbooks to resource-based learning. Kelly implied that I might see some kind of proposal from the group. I assured her I look forward to reviewing it. She asked whether I thought funding would be available to automate Marietta's library media center in the near future. It seems the other buildings have online circulation and catalog systems, CD-ROM reference materials, and telecommunications!

May 28

Here are my initial impressions about the department leaders:

Fred Gollner (English): Articulate, seems to know the latest buzzwords. Peers tease him about being the "bleeding edge" of education; wants more computers for writing.

Nancy Heisey (Science): Believes her staff is doing some interesting things. Hinted at issues related to the district policy that every course must have an approved textbook. Seems to know how to help her colleagues to compromise. Listens in a group more than she speaks. Has jerry-rigged computers that others don't want; used to form a small computer-based learning lab.

Hank Keller (Social Studies): Has he read or thought about anything since the early 1960s?! Seems attached to the expression "If it ain't broke, don't fix it." Complains about all the work he has to do as department head, but has been in the position ten years.

Terry Rankin (Health and Physical Education): Apparently he has been used to excusing himself regularly from these meetings, since his area isn't an "academic" subject. Body language during the meeting ranged from apathy to hostility.

Carl Groff (Mathematics): Behaves like Hank's yes-man. Informed me that the high school has enough technology and that his math teachers are experts. How does he explain our low test scores in math? Hedges on responding whenever I bring up NCTM standards.

Jose Gomez (Foreign Language): Seems to know his stuff! Desperately needs and wants additional staff and some computer setup so that kids can interact with native language speakers. Great sense of humor.

Sally Ball (Combined Arts): What a powerhouse! Two years ago she single-handedly persuaded the BOE to fund Arts Propel and a graphics computer for kids to use and then proceeded to have kids earn all kinds of awards. She seems to value Fred's input.

George Crandall (Vocational Studies): When asked what changes he'd like to see, he replied that all students should take keyboarding. He informed me that he will not entertain revision of the home economics or automotive programs, because they meet the needs of Marietta's nonacademic kids.

Pat Green (Special Services): Seems ostracized by the group—sat alone, no one greeted her. Several times she was addressed indirectly by the phrase "your kids" or "Green's kids." She seems pleasant and knowledgeable. I wonder whether she is shunned because of the district's unpopular inclusion initiative.

May 29
Although I had met many of the staff earlier, this was the first time I had them together. I've formed some initial hypotheses: (1) New staff are regarded as outsiders; (2) most of the staff do not link what they do instructionally with student performance; (3) many staff believe that only some students can achieve at high levels; (4) staff identify strongly with their respective departments. It is amazing that some of these people don't know the names of recent hires in other departments! This is a staff of 55 teachers, not 200.

My initial categories: the movers and shakers (a smattering of teachers across departments, Kelly, and Pat); the middle majority; and the "guys" as they call themselves, a group made up of Hank, Carl, George, and Terry. They took their lunches to the AV area to watch a baseball game.

June 3
I suppose I shouldn't be disappointed with the list the faculty brainstormed, but I am. Vision is absent but need is apparent. Imagine 4–5 intercom interruptions to class, an intercom system that doesn't work in some classrooms (liability), and having only one copier that serves administrative and instructional needs in a school this size! Another big issue is that the teachers feel that many of the meetings they are contractually obligated to attend are meaningless.

I think I made some allies when I promised no intercom announcements during class time and rotation of events like pep rallies.

I also asked them to form a committee to make recommendations for their copying and intercom needs. Dead silence was followed by a maelstrom of complaints regarding the absence of any kind of technology in sufficient numbers and condition. Finally, Kelly offered to provide me with an inventory of most of the AV equipment. Apparently no one has kept computer and software inventories.

Then Mary, the teacher association president, sarcastically noted that many of the meetings are contractual. I see some room to use time more effectively, but wasn't ready to make my ideas public. So I proposed that the teachers who volunteered to serve on the copier/intercom committee hold their first meeting during the faculty meeting, which contractually must be scheduled at the end of the school day (whose crazy idea is that?!). That went over well, and the meeting ended.

Harry (science) and Kelly, who had volunteered to co-chair the committee, came up to ask whether I would consider letting a secretary meet with the committee, since office staff also use the technologies. I agreed—much to their surprise.

June 5

I'm in trouble with Dr. Garcia. (One of the staff must be an informant.) By the time I arrived at school this morning, I had a note to call the superintendent after 9:00. When I did, I was told very firmly that I was to hold teachers to their required meetings. After I explained my rationale and plan (use the time flexibly for staff development, small study groups, etc.), she seemed to accept the idea "because you need to build a relationship with the staff" but warned me about the importance of "holding their feet to the fire." Hmmm . . . this is a potential area of conflict.

June 10

Harry and Kelly met with me today on the copier recommendations. I agreed to budget for their copier and telephone requests. Their report also raised some important issues regarding other technologies. The AV inventory is ancient and inadequate for our needs. There is no building inventory of computers and software because of intense department territoriality.

June 12

How depressing! Seven of the last eight observations have shown me that teachers lecture and students sit; worksheets, questions at the end of the chapter. No student engagement, no ties to their lives or current events.

I think I'll mix my observations from now on. I balance this last bunch with some of the really gifted educators I have on staff—veteran and new. I have to find a way to get the traditional teachers to see some of their techniques.

The topic of discussion was the state mastery test scores—(low, low, low!). I had asked the chairs to analyze the results to see what we could do to improve our students' performance. I don't think I was prepared for their responses.

> Marietta kids are all good kids.
>
> Some Marietta kids can learn because they are motivated.
>
> We can help the motivated ones. (A group they think comprises approximately 20 percent of the student body. Like improving their scores will significantly impact our results!!)
>
> Their teachers work hard but will try even harder. (Doing what??)
>
> It's the middle school's fault for coddling kids rather than teaching them.

Only Fred and Nancy had even discussed the test results with their departments. Nothing I said or did could move most of the group toward linking instruction and curriculum and student achievement.

June 13

I finished my initial meetings with students and student groups. I am deeply troubled by what I heard and observed. Apathy and anger co-exist. Students feel outside the decision-making process. The present clubs and athletic programs do not seem of interest to many. On the other hand, a small group of students expressed interest in building "school spirit." This group wants to restructure everything from the extracurricular program to the number of computers available during the day.

I reviewed my findings with both vice principals. They were defensive, citing no time to deal with the issues because of the increasing amount of time they have to spend on discipline.

I am surprised how many teachers have, in casual conversation, wanted to know whether Marietta will ever be able to have the kinds of technology-rich environments other schools in the district have. It seems they have heard from students about what other buildings have, but many have never been to the buildings themselves!!

Reference

Negroponte, N. (1995). *Being digital.* New York: Alfred A. Knopf.
    (Also refer to appropriate chapters within this book.)

PROJECT 4

Data Management and Analysis (DMA) and Decision Making at Madison High School

WILLIAM G. CUNNINGHAM • *Old Dominion University*

Madison High School is currently required to collect, file, and summarize millions of data elements that directly relate to school operations and student and teacher performance. There has literally been an explosion of data within the schools and the district. This data includes operational data such as financial, inventory, schedules, employee records, performance appraisal, school climate, maintenance, and so on. The student data includes performance on standardized tests, attendance, discipline, progress reports (report cards), IEP plans, and so on. Although this data can be analyzed and reported in various ways, it has been underutilized by Madison staff for any decision-making purpose and is mainly used to meet local, state, and federal reporting requirements. The question is how to best use the wealth of data that is now available.

There is a growing demand within the school community to broaden the use of this data for diagnostic and improved decision-making purposes, highlighting and interrelating information in reports to teachers, administrators, and others. Such reports could help school personnel to define strengths and weaknesses in all aspects of the schools instructional programs and operational support (www.eschoolnews. com).

The development of information/diagnostic reports are based on a recent ability to access, interrelate, and process data from computer-based systems. These systems allow school districts to combine data from all files using various data hierarchies, such as student, teacher, department, grade level, performance appraisal categories, budget size, school, and so on (see www.sifinfo.org; www.opengroup.org).

The primary focus at Madison is to select a computer-based, data-driven decision-making system, along with related reports that can be used by school personnel. The recent explosion in the amount of data available is due to the data-oriented culture in which staff collect the needed information but it does not get integrated into a DMA. The proposed computer system is also to be used to free up some administration and teacher time by producing reports, forms, and other documents that teachers and administrators have completed by hand in the past. The local school board has created a challenge for Madison High School administrators and staff to begin to use the extensive technology now available within the district to organize and analyze data in such ways that it will lead to the improvement of the educational process.

They have backed this vision with a significantly increased budget for a data management and analysis (DMA) software system that has yet to be selected. There is a significant amount of research that suggests such data-based decision-making systems provide a notable opportunity for administrators to improve schools (Thornton & Perrault, 2003; Creighton, 2001; Sparks, 2000; Holcomb, 1999; Bernhardt, 1998).

Learning Objectives

- To develop an understanding of applied database systems, possible databased reports, and needed databased work cultures
- To develop an understanding of how to efficiently manage and analyze large quantities of student and operational data and make it useful and an integral part of educational efforts
- To develop an ability to process, analyze, interpret and report data so as to continuously improve curricular, instructional, and related factors in order to increase student academic success
- To obtain knowledge of the capabilities of vendor-provided K–12 educational data management and analysis software systems and the criteria needed to effectively evaluate and select/develop the optimal system, ultimately, to lead the way toward data-based leadership.

Guiding Questions

1. How can data available be reported in such a way that it becomes useful in effective data-based decision making?
2. What data-based reports might be used to diagnose opportunities for school improvement?
3. How can a process and culture be developed that will support and expand the use of data in continuous school and program improvement?
4. How can program and student assessment, pupil personnel information, human resource information, and finance systems be linked to improved performance and efficiencies?
5. What criteria should be used to assess the capabilities of leading vendors delivering data management and analysis technologies and services in order to select a vendor that best meets your districts/school needs?

Madison High School

Regal City is considered one of the more diverse public school districts in the Southeast. What was once considered a secluded seaside tourist getaway during the summer and a home for a diverse number of farmers year round has now become an urban city with a diverse population, due to an influx of varied businesses and tourist attractions. The once-small, close-knit community now encompasses a wide variety of student populations. The school community now consists of 43 percent white, 35 percent African American, 14 percent Hispanic, 3 percent Asian, and 5 percent other. Madison High School serves the lowest socioeconomic community with 58 percent of children attending Madison coming from low-income families. The focus on high-stakes testing has forced the Madison school community to rethink its vision and strategies.

The teacher–pupil ratio at Madison is one to twenty-four. Teacher diversity is consistent with the makeup of the student population, although in the past five years the teacher turnover rate has increased by 22 percent. Sixty-one percent of the current teachers have a master's degree. Teachers and administrators willingly participate in varied workshops and conferences in order to enhance professional skills and knowledge. Overall, they are committed to the success of the students and often create and support innovative ideas.

School staff and community members are concerned that the improvement efforts so far have been add-on, stopgap approaches, because no one knows what is really going on at the school. Although diverse data elements are being collected on the school, teachers, and students, this information is not readily available to the staff. The PTA president commented: "The school seems to be flying by the seat of its pants with no data analysis and reporting capability beyond student grade cards and standardized assessment reports that often contradict one another. Too many reports are being hand developed, and the schools' and districts' computer technology is underutilized." The teachers are complaining about the amount of paperwork that they are completing.

The community has one Fortune 500 company that is high technology–oriented, and thus the lack of automated, integrated database reporting and decision-making systems has been an area of contention throughout the community and more recently at school board meeting. The push is to link information in ways to help analyze problem areas and support needed improvements.

The superintendent of schools in Regal City was hired last year partially because of his technological literacy and his support for databased decision systems. The superintendent spent the first year in the district expanding technology capability, screening possible software DMA vendors, and developing the school technology and support teams. Expectations are now high that the culture at Madison High School and all of the community's schools will soon be based on data-driven decisions and continuous improvement.

You, as principal of Madison High School, are starting to get questions as to, "Why is databased leadership missing from Madison High school?" The staff are technology competent. The answer, however, is the lack of integrated data management and analysis software within the district and school. This includes the lack of systems and data analysis and design skills among the staff, the lack of time caused by the present effort at stopgap measures to improve high-stakes test scores, and worry about what the data might reveal. The staff realizes the system would save them time in the long run but can't find time in the short run to specify their needs and to participate in selecting a system. The superintendent believes that such participation is essential.

The K-12 management and analysis systems under consideration for use within the school and district are:

Edmini:Virtual Education (www.edmin.com/)
IBM Education (www-1.ibm.com)
SAS (www.sas.com/)
BearingPoint (www.bearingpoint.com)
Tetra Data (www.tetradata.com/)
eScholar (www.escholar.com/)
School Net (www.schoolnet.com)
SASIx;(www.pearsondigital.com/sasi/ or www.pearsonedtech.com/sasi/)
Sungard Pentamation (www.pentamation.com)
Star Base School Suite (www.centuryltd.com)

Your Challenge

Many man-hours are now used to scour and compile data from multiple spreadsheets, databases, and manual systems in order to draw conclusions regarding student and/or operational performance. Computers could complete the task in minutes.

The computer-based systems and reports selected will be used by staff to better understand the effects of current procedures and practices on both operations and student performance and to identify areas needing modification or replacement in order to improve performance. Information is to be reported at the right time and in an integrated format allowing for improved decisions. Reports and analysis must be useful in solving building and classroom problems, helping to improve instruction and student performance, supporting meaningful decision making, and providing for needed educational monitoring.

Product Specification

You have been asked to specify data about individuals, groups, and programs, and other information that will be needed to plan for the enhancement of teaching and student achievement (www.iste.org). The data and other information is to be used to identify strengths and weaknesses in the programs and practices in order to ensure continuous improvement in the high school program. You have also been asked to develop recommended criteria to be used in assessing the various vendors' data management and analysis software in order to select the one that would be most beneficial for Madison High School.

More specifically, you have been charged with developing criteria to evaluate the technologically supported K–12 integrated management, analysis, and data-driven decision-making systems that are now under consideration for Regal City Schools. You will be expected to involve your staff and key stakeholders. Your and their participation in the selection/development process is very important to the superintendent.

You will need to explain what data management and analysis software will be helpful and why. How can the vast information now available be organized, combined, collated, and reported by this system so as to be most useful? What criteria should be used to select a vendor's product that most closely meets the schools needs? You have a strong technological team to provide the software support once a software product has been selected. You also do not have to be concerned with the finance and the economic elements of this issue. Some of the specific questions you might address:

- **How will the various data management and analysis software systems be assessed and what criteria will be used?** What criteria will be used to determine which of the data-driven decision-making system to select? What framework will be used for comparing DMA systems and what criteria should serve as the basis for this comparison? What data organization, analysis, and reporting will be most helpful for Madison High School? In other words, what are the appropriate uses of data and how can data best be presented and used to drive student and operational improvements? Ultimately, which DMA vendor's product should be selected to support the data-driven decision making at Madison High School and why?

- **What is the plan (vision)?** What are the goals for the data-based decision-making system? What are the hard operational and performance questions that should be asked and what data will be needed to answer them? How might the way the data is organized and categorized on reports—by student, teachers, departments, funding levels, performance appraisal, demographics, and so forth—and the way patterns emerge among the data suggest possible opportunities to improve practices? How might the reports simplify work efforts and free up valuable resources? Who will receive the data reports and analysis, how often, and how will they be used to improve decision making? What additional data might be useful in the future? How might the data-driven decision-making system help the staff and policymakers to improve practice and increase student performance? How do the reports free up administrator, teacher, counselors, and others time for focus on improved student learning?

- **What is the design for implementation?** How will the data-based reports and decision-making system be implemented? How will reports be analyzed, by whom, and for what purposes? What are the benefits and the drawbacks of the DMA systems under consideration?

PROJECT 5

Marveling at the Results: Power, Roles, Relationships, and School Reform

WILLIAM G. CUNNINGHAM • *Old Dominion University*

Expectations of staff to learn from and work with one another have increased. Linda Darling-Hammond in a background paper for the National Commission on Teaching and America's Future (1996) states, "Current efforts at school reform are likely to succeed to the extent that they are built on a strong foundation of teaching knowledge and are sustained by a commitment to structural rather than merely symbolic change." Dennis Sparks, executive director for the National Staff Development Council, concurs: "Significant changes in the daily work lives of teachers must be at the core of reform efforts that are truly intended to create schools in which adults feel competent in their work and all students develop to their full potential."

Those who have opportunities for growth, development, and promotion often raise their aspirations, value their own skills, engage in improving performance, form political alliances with an improvement orientation, and actively participate in and support reforms. Those without such opportunities lower their aspirations, undervalue their skills, disengage from work

improvements, form protective peer groups, and resist passively. Positive attitudes are encouraged by the ability to influence others within the organization. If the individual has very limited power, his or her knowledge and ability will not be respected. Powerlessness leads to petty domination, not leadership, reform, or improved performance.

Powerlessness usually manifests itself as focusing on means, not the ends, and adherence to standard operating procedures and past practices. How can leaders provide school personnel the development, opportunity, and power needed to encourage ambitious, committed staff who willingly put in the kind of work that reform efforts require? How can teachers share their knowledge so that it can be synthesized in improved practice?

Learning Objectives

- To acquire an understanding of the complexity of achieving school reform.
- To examine the types of organizational structures that will promote staff development and curriculum and instructional improvement.
- To analyze the types of leadership styles that will best promote successful school reform and the types of support these styles will need to be successful.
- To examine methods by which the knowledge and ability of very different groups of

people may be brought together in an ongoing, mutually beneficial way; to determine how groups can share their talents, knowledge, and resources, thus supporting each other in relationships that merge their abilities for the purpose of improving the school.
- To distribute power and responsibility in such a way that it encourages mutual respect and willingness to work together to jointly improve schools.

Guiding Questions

1. How can you get staff members to develop their full potential and encourage their full participation in a school-improvement process? What are the characteristics of a job that provides and supports opportunities for development and advancement?
2. If power means the capacity to mobilize resources, influence others, and "get things done," how can different staff members be given power so they can develop the credibil-

ity needed to be respected and ultimately "get school reform done"?
3. What are the sources of order, power, and purpose within the school?
4. What types of efforts will facilitate complex learning, creativity, experimentation, and continuous improvement of the school?
5. How will you know that you are nurturing potential and capacity?

Hickory Ridge High School

Hickory Ridge High School is a large urban school of approximately 1,800 students, 15 percent exceptional or special-needs students, 46 percent white, 40 percent African American, 12 percent Hispanic, and 2 percent Asian, of whom many are recent immigrants. The mean composite score on standardized tests such as the Iowa Test of Basic Skills have improved from the 45th to the 49th percentile, but some students score in the bottom quartile.

The faculty and school community have sought to meet the needs of the students, but those needs have significantly changed over the past four years and the system has been unable to keep pace. During the past year, the Hickory Ridge faculty, staff, parents, and business partners worked toward a variety of reform initiatives but achieved very limited success. The district's reform efforts allowed a core of Hickory teachers to participate in activities. They took technology-based industry tours and attended forums on the implementation of pilot programs to reform the schools. Although Hickory has formulated a new mission statement and vision for the school, the teachers and administrators are in conflict about how best to proceed. The school is generally viewed as unable to meet new reform guidelines, out of date, and in serious conflict.

The makeup of the teaching staff at Hickory Ridge High School is illustrated in Table 13.2. There was concern over standardized test scores that, having fallen slightly over the past three years, had risen last year.

All rooms at the high school were wired and each had at least fifteen computers. The district was seen as a leader in obtaining the needed equipment to make the schools technological centers. The actual use of the computers by both teachers and students, however, was disappointing and major pressure was put on the system to incorporate the computers into the curriculum and daily instruction. Even though the scores and performance of the students on standardized tests were disappointing, the school board and community believed that these changes would result in "better teaching and learning for all kids," and "give their children a head start by providing them with critical thinking and technological skills."

Hickory High has a very supportive parent group who are civic minded, young, technically advanced, and middle class. The turnover in this neighborhood is high because it is considered a stepping-off point to greater affluence. The central administrative staff and you hold the teachers at Hickory High in high regard.

The Problem

You are the superintendent for Wingfield School District. You were hired four years ago to help the school district achieve its newly established vision of becoming a technologically driven, innovative school district. The focus of the reforms was to be school based, beginning at Hickory Ridge High School and spreading to other schools.

The faculty at the high school are aging and many have been teaching for twenty years or longer. Jim O'Connor, the principal, was a teacher for eight years

TABLE 13.2 *Makeup of the Teaching Staff at Hickory Ridge High School*

Faculty Demographics	All Teachers (percentage)
Total	100.0
Sex	
Male	35.0
Female	65.0
Age	
Under 26 years old	21.4
26–30 years old	16.4
31–35 years old	2.1
36–40 years old	4.5
41–45 years old	10.0
46–50 years old	11.3
51–55 years old	20.0
56–60 years old	8.0
61 or more years old	6.3
Race/Ethnicity	
Asian or Pacific Islander	0.0
Hispanic, regardless of race	1.3
African American, not of Hispanic origin	20.6
White, not of Hispanic origin	75.6
Native American	2.5
Highest academic degree	
High school diploma	0.0
Business/technical school certificate	0.0
Associate degree (2 years or more)	0.0
Bachelor's degree	38.3
Master's degree	56.9
Education specialist or professional diploma	2.4
Doctorate	1.2
Professional degree	1.2

at the middle-school level before moving to the assistant-principal position. He served as an assistant principal for thirteen years before being promoted last year to his present job of principal at Hickory Ridge High.

Jim O'Connor is not seen as an individual who would go any further than high school principal. He is the keeper of the history and, although he relates well to children and their parents, he lacks understanding of their needs in the twenty-first century. No one, however, is more knowledgeable about the community, people, and existing programs and policies within the school district. You called on him to gain perspective on reactions of both internal and external publics to issues being considered within the school district. His staff see him as knowledgeable but not well respected and unable to understand the school district's vision for Hickory Ridge High School. He has a lot to offer, particularly to younger staff, in perspective and understanding the community; however, younger staff see him as having limited power, importance, and as not being able to help them to gain desired promotions.

Over the last four years you have placed twenty-seven new teachers at Hickory, all of whom are identified as having very high potential, although still relatively young. They have all been in the top 10 percent in their programs of study. They have been well prepared regarding the desired school reforms and are experts in technology. These new high-potential people are highly likely to become administrators themselves someday—they are "fast-trackers."

You placed these "fast-trackers" at Hickory in hopes that O'Connor and the aging teaching staff would learn from them regarding new, innovative programs. At the same time, you hoped that the "fast-trackers" would learn more about the community, families, and children and the school district's past successes from O'Connor and the more experienced teachers. You hoped that the younger and older staff would share their talents, resources, knowledge, and skill and support each other and the school in the achievement of needed reforms. This respect and appreciation of each others' abilities and knowledge never developed, however.

Two of the top fast-trackers, Michael Scott and Kerri Beth, have recently requested to be taken off the site-based planning team for the school. Many of the new teachers have been complaining about O'Connor's management and the attitude of a number of older teachers on the staff, first to O'Connor and then, more delicately, to Sandi Walchek, the associate superintendent O'Connor reports to, and even to you. They told Walchek that O'Connor is always looking over their work, second-guessing how they teach their classes and what they say to parents, and is endlessly critical.

They are beginning to raise questions about whether Jim and a few of the older teachers can really do their jobs. They see Jim and the older teachers as being out of touch with modern times, too bureaucratic, and too concerned about the parents and the community. They are concerned that the principal and staff will hold back their careers and are not in touch with the power base within the district. The principal measures performance by adherence to routine procedures and community relations, not accomplishments, responsiveness, or reform efforts. Walchek, concerned, has asked O'Connor about this situation without, of course, identifying the people involved.

O'Connor explains that he has a lot of experience and sees the new hires as not understanding the community or kids or appreciating the significant progress we have made in this school district. He complains that they seem to look down on him and everything the experienced teachers have to say. As a result, they don't understand the culture, the children, or the community and are trying to make too many changes that will not work. This requires that he pay very close attention to their work and that educating children and maintaining the good relations with the community is simply too important to take chances. "Anyhow," he says, "they're not as smart as they think. It takes time, experience, and an understanding of the school's heritage and community to develop the skills you need to be a good educator." Although O'Connor doesn't say so, Walchek can tell that he is also very angry.

You now find yourself under some pressure from the board. You do agree with the direction that the board has established for the schools and you are empathetic with their frustration with what is occurring at Hickory Ridge High School. You have won the trust of the board, staff, and community, and you do not want to lose it. You also realize that the staff and parents at Hickory seem to be beginning to divide themselves in support of either the older or the younger staff. You also know that O'Connor has many friends within the community, including some board members. You are frustrated that this perfect marriage between the younger staff, who are so technologically competent and so knowledgeable about needed reforms, and the older staff and principal, who have so much knowledge about Wingfield children, programs, services, and families, is not working. You do not want to give up on this idea, because you see no other option that has a higher probability of succeeding.

In reflecting on the situation, you believe that perhaps you have not structured the plan properly for success or that you can do something to get these groups to respect one another and work together on reforming the school. You believe that the principal and teachers have the right combination of knowledge, experience, and ability to be successful if only they would work together. You are now going back to the drawing board to come up with ideas to make this plan work.

Some of the problems that you see as holding back the reform efforts at Hickory High include lack of trust, confidence, and power; misunderstanding about roles; insufficient communication; lack of respect for each other and the important knowledge each has to share; the principal seen as lacking power with central administration and the superintendent; neither side feels involved or important; the juniors regret the lack of opportunity for powerful mentorship; the seniors feel disrespected and lack motivation to change what already exists.

Your Challenge

You, as superintendent of Wingfield school district, realize that the organizational culture at Hickory Ridge High School is actually hindering the needed school reform efforts. All parties need to work together to achieve the desired curriculum and instructional improvements. The staff, from O'Connor to the newest teachers, now seem to feel a sense of helplessness and powerlessness. They are unable to act at a time when they are absolutely essential to needed reform efforts. You realize that you must identify ways to give the principal and teachers a sense of purpose, direction, responsibility, power, respect, optimism, and mission.

You have been given a free hand by the board to see that all Hickory staff develop a plan of action and have a common direction, are working together and supporting one another, and have the time and power "to develop needed reforms and then deliver on those plans." The idea is to develop respect for each person's unique talents as an important resource so she or he can work together to create and implement a plan of improvement for the school.

The board chairman has challenged you: "Free up the energy, creativity, and commitment in individual schools, then step back and marvel at the results." You now realize the full meaning in the challenge of this statement. Everything you ask staff to do appears to be an add-on. They seem incapable of working together. There is a lack of respect for the principal. Energy and focus gets lost; stress and anxiety are running high.

The plan should address the following elements:

1. Helping Jim O'Connor to gain the respect of the new faculty.
2. Developing collegiality, honest and open communication, and support among all the faculty.
3. Creating a structure and sense of direction for the development of school improvement and reform.
4. Encouraging more design and greater experimentation and risk taking.
5. Providing tangible support and empowerment for all members of the staff.
6. Encouraging them to reach out to the extensive research and knowledge pertinent to the desired reforms and to look into promising innovative programs.
7. Protecting what is important and good about Hickory High while reforming it to better meet the needs of twenty-first-century students.

You have been told that "it takes a few mistakes before you get it right." You want to get it right this time.

Product Specifications

You realize you must, in a way, remake Hickory High so it is better prepared to meet the demands for school reform. As one board member warned, with a smile on his face, "You can't bludgeon people into greatness." The initial focus of your plan will be building the needed relationships and exploring structural, process, and cultural changes. You need to give O'Connor greater symbolic power so he will be seen with greater respect. You need to see that teachers work together to share knowledge and expertise. You must create a catalyst for needed reform at Hickory Ridge High School. You will want to help the school staff in their development of a sense of direction and to support the development and implementation of needed improvements.

You are to create conditions whereby purpose, values, information, and relationships are meaningfully connected and aligned around the school system's desire to develop an integrated, technologically supported curriculum. You are to address the conditions that must be created at Hickory High School if the school is to be successfully reformed. You are to create a process at this high school that builds on the capacity of everyone in the school, so as to develop the school's collective intelligence. The plan should create continuous generative learning and staff engagement for the purpose of school reform and improvement. The plan should encourage experimentation and implementation. Your plan should build the school's capacity for participation, engagement, interconnectedness, development, and resilience. You should examine creative ways to distribute power throughout the school district so as to improve respect and each person's opportunity to make a difference. The point is that you truly have been given a free hand to solve this very "swampy" problem and to begin developing an effective integrated, technologically supported curriculum.

The process by which the school personnel create needed reforms is an important element in relation to its ultimate success. You will be asked to make an oral presentation to the board on your written plan. The plan should address short-term initiatives (first year) and long-term initiatives (two to five years) and include a chronological sequence of steps to be taken.

(Please refer to appropriate chapters within this book as a resource.)

Suggested Readings

Ashbaugh, C., & Kasten, K. (1991). *Educational leadership: Case studies for reflective practice.* New York: Longman.

Bridges, E. (1992). *Problem based learning for administrators.* Eugene, OR: ERIC.

Hanson, K. (2001). *Preparing for educational administration using case analysis.* Upper Saddle River, NJ: Merrill Prentice Hall.

Hoy, W., & Tarter, C. J. (2004). *Administrators solving the problems of practice: Decision making concepts, cases and consequences.* Boston: Allyn and Bacon.

Kowalski, T. (2005). *Case studies of educational administration.* Boston: Allyn and Bacon.

Short, P., & Scribner, J. (Eds.) (2000). *Case studies on the superintendency.* Lancaster, PA: Tecnomic Publishing Co.

References and Bibliography

Aboud, F. (1988). *Children and prejudice.* New York: B. Blackwell.

Achilles, C. M., & Smith, P. (1994, 1999). Stimulating the academic performance of pupils. In Larry W. Hughes (Ed.), *The principal as leader.* New York: Merrill.

Adams, J. E., & Kirst, M. W. (1999). New demands and concepts for educational accountability: Striving for results in an era of excellence. In J. Murphy & K. Seashore Louis (Eds.), *Handbook of research on educational administration.* San Francisco: Jossey-Bass.

Adler, P. (1975). The transitional experience: An alternative view of culture shock. *Journal of Humanistic Psychology, 15*(4), 23–40.

Airasian, P., & Walsh, M. (1997). Constructivist cautions. *Phi Delta Kappan, 78*(6), 444–449.

Alam, D., & Seick, R. (1994). A block schedule with a twist. *Phi Delta Kappan, 9,* 732–733.

Alexander, L. (1986). Chairman's summary. In National Governor's Association, *Time for Results.* Washington, DC: National Governor's Association.

Allen, M. (2003, November-December). "I had no idea": How to build creative e-learning experiences." *Educational Technology, 43* (16), 15–20.

Allison, G. (1971). *Essence of decision making: Exploring the Cuban missile crisis.* Boston: Little, Brown.

Allport, G. (1979). *ABC's of scapegoating.* New York: Anti-Defamation League of B'nai B'rith.

Allport, G. (1958). *The nature of prejudice.* Cambridge, MA: Addison-Wesley.

American Institutes for Research. (1994). *Educational innovation in multiracial contexts: The growth of magnet schools in American education.* Palo Alto, CA: Prepared for the U.S. Department of Education.

American Association of School Administrators. (1993). *1994 Platform and resolutions.* Arlington, VA: American Association of School Administrators.

American Association of School Administrators. (1991). *America 2000: Where school leaders stand* (Report No. ISBN-0–8762–172–3). Arlington, VA: AASA (ERIC ED 344 325).

American Association of School Administrators. (1988). *School-based management* (AASA Stock Number 0221–00209). Washington, DC: American Association of School Administrators, National Association of Elementary School Principals, National Association of Secondary School Administration.

American Association of School Administrators. (1981). *Statement of ethics.* Arlington, VA: American Association of School Administrators.

American School Counselor Association. (2003). *The ASCA national model: A framework for school counseling programs.* Alexandria, VA: Author.

Anderson, G. (1991). Cognitive politics in principals and teachers: Ideological control in an elementary school. In J. Blase (Ed.), *The politics of life in schools: Power, conflict, and cooperation* (pp. 120–138). Newbury Park, CA: Sage.

Anderson, L., & Shirley, R. (1995). High school principals and school reform: Lesson learned from a statewide study of project. Re: Learning, *Educational Administration Quarterly, 31*(3), 405–423.

Anderson, R. S., & Reiter, D. (1995). The indispensable counselor. *The School Counselor, 42,* 268–276.

Andrade de Herrera, V. Education in Mexico: Historical and contemporary educational systems. In J. LeBlanc Flores (Ed.), *Children of La Frontera.* Charlestown, WV: ERIC Clearinghouse.

Anyon, J. (1980, Winter). Social class and the hidden curriculum of work. *Journal of Education, 162,* 67–92.

Apple, M. (1986). *Teachers and texts: A political economy of class and gender relations in education.* New York: Routledge.

Archer, J. (1994, February 2). School-based health centers. *Education Week, 3,* 7.

Argyris, C. (1993). *The individual and the organization: Some problems of mutual adjustment.* New York: Irvington,

Argyris, C. (1982). *Reasoning, learning, and action.* San Francisco: Jossey-Bass.

392

Argyris, C., & Schön, D. (1978). *Organizational learning: A theory of action perspective.* Reading, MA: Addison-Wesley.

Argyris, C., & Schön, D. (1974). *Theory in practice: Increasing professional effectiveness.* San Francisco: Jossey-Bass.

Arias, B. (1986, November). The context of education for Hispanic students: An overview. *American Journal of Education,* 26–57.

Aristotle. (1962). *Nicomachean ethics.* Trans. Martin Ostwald. Indianapolis, IN: Bobbs-Merrill.

Armstrong, T. (1994). *Multiple intelligences in the classroom.* Alexandria, VA: Association for Supervision and Curriculum Development.

Arons, E. L. (1999). *Successful interviewing techniques.* Mimeographed sheet, p. 18. Rockville, MD: Montgomery County Public Schools.

Association of School Business Officials. (1986). *Guidelines for managing student activity accounts.* Reston, VA: Association of School Business Officials.

Atkins, J. M., & Black, P. (1997). Policy perils of international comparisons. *Phi Delta Kappan, 79*(1), 22–28.

Avery, R., & Campion, G. (1982). The employment interview: A summary and review of recent research. *Personal Psychology, 35*(2), 281–322.

Bacharach, S. B., & Mundell, B. (Eds.). (1995). *Images of Schools: Structures and roles in organization behavior.* Thousand Oaks, CA: Corwin Press.

Baker, E. T., Wang, M. C., & Walberg, H. J. (1995). The effects of inclusion on learning. *Educational Leadership,* (4), 33–35.

Ball, S. (1987). *The micropolitics of the school, Toward a theory of school organization.* New York: Methuen.

Ballew, A., & Prokop, M. (1994). *Earthquake survival.* San Diego: Pfeiffer.

Ballinger, C. (1988). Rethinking the school calendar. *Educational Leadership.*

Bamburg, J., & Andrews, R. (1990). School goals, principals and achievement. *School Effectiveness and School Improvement, 2*(3), 175–191.

Banks, J. A. (1999). *An introduction to multicultural education.* Boston: Allyn and Bacon.

Banks, J. A. (1995). The historic reconstruction of knowledge about race. *Educational Researcher, 24*(2), 15–25.

Banks, J., & Banks, C. (Eds.). (1994). *Multicultural education: Issues and Perspectives.* Boston: Allyn and Bacon.

Banks, J. A. (1993). The canon debate, knowledge, construction, and multi-cultural education. *Educational Researcher, 22*(5), 4–14.

Bardwick, J. M (1997). Emotional leadership. In K. Shelton (Ed.), *A new paradigm of leadership* (pp. 191–194). Provo, UT: Executive Excellence.

Barker, J. A. (1992). *Paradigms: The business of discovering the future.* New York: Harper Collins.

Barnett, B. G. (1991). The educational platform: Articulating moral dilemmas and choices for future educational leaders. In B. G. Barnett, F. O. McQuarrie, & C. G. Norris (Eds.), *The moral imperatives of leadership: A focus on human decency.* Memphis, TN: National Network for Innovative Principal Preparation.

Bartlett, D., & Steele, J. (1994). *America: Who really pays the taxes.* New York: Simon & Schuster.

Bartlett, L., Weisenstein, S., & Etscheidt, S. (2002). *Successful inclusion for educational leaders.* Upper Saddle River, NJ: Merrill Prentice Hall.

Bass, B., & Avolio, B. (1989). Potential biases in leadership measure: How prototypes, lenience, and general satisfaction relate to ratings and rankings of transformational and transactional leadership construct. *Educational and Psychological Measurement, 49*(3), 509–527.

Beck, L. (1994). *Reclaiming educational administration as a caring profession.* New York: Teachers College Press.

Beck, L., & Murphy, J. (1997). *Ethics in educational leadership programs: Emerging models.* Columbia, MO: University Council for Educational Administration.

Beck, L., & Murphy, J. (1996). *The four imperatives of a successful school.* Thousand Oaks, CA: Corwin Press.

Begley, P. (1996). Cognitive perspectives on values in administration: A quest for coherence and relevance. *Educational Administration Quarterly, 32*(3), 403–426.

Bell, C. (1997). Passionate leadership. In K. Shelton (Ed.), *A new paradigm of leadership* (pp. 195–198). Provo, UT: Executive Excellence.

Bell, T. H. (1993). Reflections: One decade after a nation at risk. *Phi Delta Kappan, 74*(8), 592–598.

Bellah, R., Madsen, R., Sullivan, W., Swindler, A., & Tipton, S. (1991). *The good society.* New York: Knopf.

Bellah, R., Madsen, R., Sullivan, W., Swindler, A., & Tipton, S. (1985). *Habits of the heart.* Berkeley, CA: University of California Press.

Bender, W., Sebring, P., & Bryk, A. (1998). *School leadership and the bottom line in Chicago.* University of Chicago, Consortium on School Research.

Benham, M. (1997). The story of an African-American teacher–scholar: A woman's narrative. *Qualitative Studies in Education, 10*(1), 63–83.

Benham, M., & Cooper, J. (1998). *Let my spirit soar! Narratives of diverse women in school leadership.* Newbury Park, CA: Corwin Press.

Bennett, C. I. (1998). *Comprehensive multicultural education: Theory and practice.* Boston: Allyn and Bacon.

Bennett, K. P., & LeCompte, M. D. (1990). *How schools work: A sociological analysis of education.* New York: Longman.

Bennett, W. J. (1988). *American education: Making it work.* Washington, DC: U.S. Government Printing Office.

Bennis, W. G. (1983). *The chief.* New York: Morrow.

Bennis, W., & Nanus, B. (1985). *Leaders: The strategies for taking charge.* New York: Harper & Row.

Berlew, T., & Hall, F. (1988). Pygmalion effect of first time bosses. *Harvard Business Review, 62*(3), 150–168.

Berliner, D., & Biddle, B. (1995). *The manufactured crisis.* Reading, MA: Addison-Wesley.

Bernard, C. I. (1938). *The functions of the executive.* Cambridge, MA: Harvard Press.

Bernhardt, V. (1998). *Data analysis for comprehensive school improvement.* Larchmont, NY: Eye on Education.

Bernstein, B. (1964). Elaborated and restricted codes: Their social origins and some consequences. *American Anthropologist, 66,* 55–69.

Berman, P., & McLaughlin, M. (1977). *Federal programs supporting educational change, Vol. VIII: Implementing and sustaining innovations.* Santa Monica: Rand.

Berube, M. R. (1994). *American school reform: 1883–1993.* Westport, CT: Praeger.

Bilingual Education Office. (1986). *Beyond language: Social and cultural factors in schooling language minority students.* Sacramento, CA: Bilingual Education Office.

Binkowski, K. (1995). *Factors contributing to school improvement in high performing elementary schools.* Unpublished doctoral dissertation. University of Connecticut.

Birdwhistell, R. (1970). *Kinesics and context.* Philadelphia: University of Pennsylvania.

Bjork, L. G., Lindle, J. C., & Van Meter, E. J. (1999, October). A summing up. *Education Administration Quarterly, 35,*4:658–664.

Blake, R. R., & McCanse, A. A. (1991). *Leadership dilemmas—Grid solutions.* (Formerly *The managerial grid* by Robert R. Blake and Jane S. Mouton.) Houston: Gulf Publishing.

Blake, R. R., & Mouton, J. S. (1978). *The new management grid.* Houston: Gulf Publishing.

Blake, R. R., & Mouton, J. S. (1964). *The managerial grid.* Houston, TX: Gulf Publishing.

Blanchard, K. H., & Peale, N. V. (1988). *The power of ethical management.*

Blase, J. G. (1993). The micropolitics of effective school-based leadership: Teachers' perspectives. *Educational Administration Quarterly, 29*(2), 142–163.

Blase, J. G. (1990). Some negative effects of principals' control-oriented and protective behaviors.

American Educational Research Journal 27(4), 727–753.

Blau, P. M. (1970). A formal theory of differentiation in organization. *American Sociological Review 35*(2), 201–218.

Bliss, W. (1994). Managing budgets. *NAASP Bulletin, 78*(566), 327–344.

Block, P. (1993). *Stewardship: Choosing service over self-interest.* San Francisco: Berrett-Koehler.

Bloom, B. (1956). *Taxonomy of educational objectives: A classification of educational goals. Handbook I:* Cognitive domain. New York: David McKay.

Bloom, B., & Krathwohl, D. R. (1984). *Taxonomy of educational objectives.* Boston: Addison-Wesley.

Bloom, L., & Munro, P. (1995). Conflicts of selves: Nonunitary subjectivity in women administrators life history narratives. In J. Hatch & R. Wisniewski (Eds.), *Life history and narrative* (pp. 99–112). Washington, DC: Falmer Press.

Blount, J. (1993). One postmodern perspective on educational leadership: And ain't I a leader? In S. Maxcy (Ed.), *Postmodern school leadership* (pp. 47–59). Westport, CT: Praeger.

Blumberg, A., & Greenfield, W. (1980). *The effective principal: Perspectives on school leadership.* Boston: Allyn & Bacon.

Boardman, G. R., & Cassel, M. (June, 1983). How well does the public know its school board, *Phi Delta Kappan 64*(10), 739–744.

Bolman, L. G., & Deal, T. (2003). *Reframing organization: Artistry, choice, leadership.* San Francisco: Jossey-Bass.

Bolman, L. G., & Deal, T. E. (1995). *Leading with soul: An uncommon journey of spirit.* San Francisco: Jossey-Bass.

Bolman, L. G., & Deal, T. E. (1993). Everyday epistemology in school leadership: Patterns and prospects. In P. Hallinger, K. Leithwood, & G. Murphy (Eds.), *Cognitive perspectives on educational leadership.* New York: Teachers College Press.

Bolman, L. G., & Deal, T. E. (1991). *Reframing organizations.* San Francisco: Jossey-Bass.

Bonsignore, F. N. (1997). People leadership. In K. Shelton (Ed.), *A new paradigm of leadership* (pp. 55–58). Provo, UT: Executive Excellence.

Borman, G., Hewes, G., Overman, T., & Brown, S. (Summer, 2003). Comprehensive school reform and achievement: A meta-analysis, *Review of Educational Research 73,* (2), 125–230.

Bossert, S., Dwyer, D., Rowan, B., & Lee, G. (1982). The instructional management role of the principal. *Educational Administration Quarterly, 18*(3), 34–64.

Boud, D., & Feletti, G. (1998). *The challenge of problem-based learning.* New York: St. Martin's Press.

Bourdieu, P., & Passeron, J. (1977). *Reproduction: In education, society, and culture.* Newbury Park, CA: Sage.

Bowles, S., & Gintis, H. (1976). *Schooling in capitalist America.* New York: Basic Books.

Boyan, N.J. (Ed.). (1988). *Handbook of research on educational administration.* New York: Longman.

Bracey, G. W. (2003, January). Investing in preschool. *American School Board Journal,* 32–35.

Bracey, G. W. (2003, October). The condition of public education. *Phi Delta Kappan, 85* (2), 148–164

Bracey, G. W. (1995, October). The fifth Bracey report on the condition of public education. *Phi Delta Kappan 77*(2), 149–160.

Brandt, R. (1992, September). On building learning communities: A conversation with Hank Levin. *Educational Leadership, 50*(1), 19–23.

Brandt, R. (1992, February). On rethinking leadership: A conversation with Tom Sergiovanni. *Educational Leadership, 49*(5), 46–49.

Bredeson, P. V. (2003). *Designs for learning: A new architecture for professional development in schools.* Thousand Oaks, CA: Corwin Press.

Bredeson, P. (1995). A journey toward community in educational administration. *UCEA Review, 36*(1), 1, 13–17.

Brewer, D. (1993). Principals and student outcomes: Evidence from U.S. high schools. *Economics of Education Review, 12*(4), 281–292.

Bridges, E. M. (1986). *The incompetent teacher.* Philadelphia: Falmer.

Bridges, E., & Hallinger, P. (1995). *Implementing problem-based learning in leadership development.* University of Oregon, ERIC Clearinghouse on Educational Management.

Brookover, W. B., Brady, C., Flood, P., Schwirgen, J., & Wisenboter, J. (1979). *School systems and school achievement.* New York: Praeger.

Brookover, W., & Lezotte, L. (1979). *Changes in school characteristics in coincidence with changes in student achievement.* East Lansing, MI: Michigan State University.

Brown, F. (1995). Privatization of public education: Theories and concepts. *Education and Urban Society, 2*(2), 116.

Brown, K., & Anafara, V. (June, 2003). Paving the way for change: Visionary leadership in action at the middle level. *NASP Bulletin, 87,* (635), 16–34

Brown-Ferrigno, T. (2003). Becoming a principal: Role conception, initial socialization, role-identity transformation, purposeful engagement. *Educational Administration Quarterly, 39,*(4), 468–503

Bryk, A. (1993, July). *A view from the elementary school: The state of reform in Chicago.* Chicago: Consortium on Chicago School Research.

Bryk, A., & Schneider, B. L. (2002). *Trust in schools.* Newbury Park, CA: Sage.

Bull, B. L., & McCarthy, M. M. (1995, November). Reflections on the knowledge base in land and ethics for educational leaders. *Educational Administration Quarterly 31*(4), 613–631.

Bullivant, B. M. (1989). Culture: Its nature and meaning for educators. In J. Banks & C. A. McGee Banks (Eds.), *Multicultural education: Issues and perspectives* (pp. 27–45). Boston: Allyn and Bacon.

Bull, B. L., & McCarthy, M. (1995). Reflections on the knowledge base in law and ethics for educational leaders. *Educational Administration Quarterly, A,* 613–631.

Bullock, L., & Gable, R. (1998, February 21). *Implementing the 1997 IDEA new challenges and opportunities for serving students with behavior disorders.* Reston, VA: Council for Exceptional Children.

Bullock, A., & Foster-Harrison, E. (1997, November/December). Making the best decisions: Designing for excellence! *Schools in the middle: NASSP, 7*(2), 37–39, 60–61.

Bullock, C. S., & Stewart, J. (1979). Incidence and correlates of second-generation discrimination. In M. L. Palley & M. B. Preston (Eds.), *Race, sex, and policy problems* (pp. 115–129). Lexington, MA: Lexington Books.

Bullock, C. S., & Stewart, J. (1978). *Compliant processing as a strategy for combating second generation discrimination.* Paper presented at the annual meeting of the Southern Political Science Association, Atlanta.

Burillo, R. C., & Reitzug, U. C. (1993). Transforming context and developing culture in schools. *Journal of Counseling and Development, 71*(6), 669–677.

Burns, J. M. (1978). *Leadership.* New York: Harper and Row.

Bynham, W. C. (1978, November). How to improve the validity of an assessment center. *Training and Development Journal, 32*(11), 4–6.

Bynham, W. C. (December, 1971). The assessment center as an aid in management development. *Training and Development Journal, 25*(12), 10–22.

Callahan, R. E. (1962). *Education and the cult of efficiency.* Chicago: University of Chicago Press.

Cameron, T. (1995, October). Block scheduling one year later, or, what's your schedule done for you lately? *Oklahoma Association of Secondary School Principals Newsletter.*

Campbell, C. A., & Dahir, C. A. (1997). *Sharing the vision: The national standards for school counseling programs.* Alexandria, VA: American School Counselor Association.

Campbell, R. (1987). *A history of thought and practical educational administration.* New York: Teachers.

Campbell, R. F., Cunningham, L. L., Nystrand, R. O., & Usdan, M. D. (1980). *The organization and control of American schools.* Columbus: Merrill.

Campion, J., & Arvey, R. (1989). Unfair discrimination in the employment interview. In R. Eder & G. Ferris (Eds.), *The employment interview: Theory, research and practice.* Newbury Park, CA: Sage.

Canady, R. L., & Rettig, M. (1995). *Block scheduling: A catalyst for change in high schools.* Princeton, NJ: Eye on Education.

Candoli, I. C., Hack, W. G., Ray, J., & Stollar, D. H. (1984). *School business administration: A planning approach.* Boston: Allyn and Bacon.

Capper, C. A. (1991). Educational administration in a pluralistic society: A multiparadigm approach. In C. A. Capper (Ed.), *Educational administration in a pluralistic society.* Albany: State University of New York Press.

Carlson, R. (1996). *Reframing and reforms.* White Plains, NY: Longman.

Carlson, R. (1989). *Restructuring schools: International memorandum.* Washington, DC: District of Columbia Public Schools.

Carnegie Forum on Education and Economy. (1986). *A nation prepared: Teachers for the twenty-first century.* New York: Report of the Task Force on Teaching as a Profession.

Carnegie Task Force on Meeting the Needs of Young Children. (1994, August). *Starting points: Meeting the needs of our youngest children.* New York: Carnegie Corporation of New York.

Carr, N. (2003). Leadership: The toughest job in America. *American School Board Journal,* 14:20.

Carroll, J. M. (1994). The Copernican plan evaluated: The evolution of a revolution. *Phi Delta Kappan, 76*(2), 105–113.

Carroll, J. M. (1990). The Copernican plan: Restructuring the American high school. *Phi Delta Kappan, 51,* 358–365.

Carson, C. C., Hiwelskamp, R. M., & Woodall, T. D. (1992, April). *Perspectives on education in America.* Albuquerque, NM: Sandia National Laboratories.

Carspecken, P., & Cordeiro, P. (1995). Being, doing, and becoming: Textual interpretation of social identity and a case study. *Qualitative Inquiry, 1*(1), 87–109.

Carter, G. R. (1993). Revitalizing American's public schools through systemic change. In Stanley Elam (Ed.), *The state of the nation's public schools.* Bloomington, IN: Phi Delta Kappan.

Carter, G. R., & Cunningham. W. G. (1997). *The American school superintendent: Leading in an age of pressure.* San Francisco: Jossey-Bass.

Castetter, W. B. (1996). *The human resource function in educational administration.* Englewood Cliffs, NJ: Prentice-Hall.

Center for the Future of Children. (1992, Spring). *The future of children.* Los Altos, CA: The David and Lucile Packard Foundation.

Center for the Future of Children. (1992, Spring). School linked services. *The Future of Children,* 2(1), 31–43.

Center for Mental Health in Schools. (1999, Spring). Expanding school reform. *Addressing Barriers to Learning, 4*(2), 1–9.

Cetron, M., & Cetron, K. (2004, January). A forecast for our schools. *Educational Leadership, 61,* (4), 22–29.

Chapman, J., Sackney, L., & Aspin, D. (1999). Internationalization in educational administration: Policy and practice, theory and research. In J. Murphy & K. Seashore Louis (Eds.), *Handbook of research on educational administration* (pp. 73–98). San Francisco, CA: Jossey-Bass.

Chase, S. (1992). *Narrative practices: Understanding power and subjection and women's work narratives.* Paper presented at the qualitative analysis conference. Carleton University, Ottawa.

Checkley, K. (1997). The first seven . . . and the eighth: A conversation with Howard Gardner. *Educational Leadership, 55*(1), 8–13.

Children's Defense Fund. (1991). *The state of America's children.* Washington, DC: Children's Defense Fund.

Chung, K., & Miskel, C. (1989). A comparative study of principals administrative behavior. *Journal of Educational Administration, 27,* 45–57.

Church, A., & Bracken, D. (1997, June). Advancing the state of the art of 360-degree feedback. *Organizational Management, 22*(2), 149–162.

Cibulka, J. G. (1997). Two eras of urban schooling: The decline of the old order and the emergence of new organizational form. *Education and Urban Society, 29*(3), 317–341.

Clark, K. E., & Clark, M. B. (1996). *Choosing to lead.* Greensboro, NC: Center for Creative Leadership.

Clark, M. C. (1993). Transformational learning. In S. B. Merriam (Ed.), *An update on learning theory.* New Directions for Adult and Continuing Education, no. 57. San Francisco: Jossey-Bass.

Clarke, G. H. (1998). *Real questions, real answers.* Alexandria, VA: Association for Supervision and Curriculum Development.

Clemmer, E. F. (1991). *The school policy handbook: Primer for administrators and school board members.* Boston: Allyn & Bacon.

Clinchy, E. (1995, January). Sustaining and expanding the educational conversation. *Phi Delta Kappan, 77*(5), 352–354.

Cogan, M. (1973). *Clinical supervision.* New York: Houghton Mifflin.

Cohen, D. K., & March, J. G. (1974). *Leadership and ambiguity: The American college president.* New York: McGraw-Hill.

Cohen, D. K., & Spillane, J. P. (1992). Policy and practice: The relations between governance and instruction. In G. Grant (Ed.), *Review of research in education.* Washington, DC: American Educational Research Association.

Cohen, J. J. (Ed.). (1990). *The fundamentalist phenomenon.* Grand Rapids, MI: William B. Eerdmans.

Cohen, J. M., & March, J. G. (1977, September). Almost random careers: The Wisconsin superintendency, 1940–1972. *Administrative Science Quarterly, 22,* 79–92.

Cohen, J. M., March, J. G., & Olsen, J. P. (1972). A garbage can model of organization choice. *Administrative Science Quarterly, 17,* 1–25.

Cole, N. S. (1990). Conceptions of educational achievement. *Educational Researcher, 19*(3), 2–7.

Coleman, J. (1993, March). *Family involvement in education.* Paper prepared for The Milken Family Foundation, National Education Conference. Los Angeles.

Coleman, J. (1990). *Foundations of social theory.* Cambridge, MA: Harvard University Press.

Coleman, J. S., & Hoffler, T. (1987). *Public and private high schools: The impact of communities.* New York: Basic Books.

College Board. (1986). *Keeping the options open: Recommendations.* Final report of the Commission on Precollege Guidance and Counseling. New York: College Entrance Examination Board.

Collins, G. C., & Porras, G. I. (1994). *Build to last: Successful habits of visionary companies.* New York: Harper-Collins.

Collins, J. (2001). *Good to great: Why some companies make the leap . . . and others don't.* New York: HarperCollins.

Comer, J. P. (1991). *A brief history and summary of the school development program.* New Haven, CT: Yale Child Study Center.

Comer, J. P., Joyner, E. T., & Haynes, N. M. (1996). Lessons learned. In J. P. Comer, N. Haynes, E. Joyner, & M. Ben-Avie (Eds.), *Rallying the whole village.* New York: Teachers College Press.

Commission on the Skills of American Workforce. (1990). *America's choice: High skills or low wages?* Rochester, NY: National Center on Education and the Economy.

Commission on Standards for the Superintendency. (1993). *Professional standards for the superintendency.* Arlington, VA: American Association of School Administrators.

Committee on Labor and Human Resources, United States Senate Report to the Chairman. (1993).

School-linked human services: A comprehensive strategy for aiding students at risk of school failure. (GAO/HRD-94–21). Washington, DC: General Accounting Office.

Constas, M. A. (1998, March). The changing nature of educational research and a critique of postmodernism. *Educational Researcher, 27*(2), 26–32.

Cooper, B., Fusarelli, L., & Carella, V. (1999). *Career crisis in the superintendency.* Arlington, VA: American Association of School Administrators.

Cooper, B., Fusarelli, L., & Randall, E. (2004). *Better policies, better schools.* Boston: Allyn and Bacon.

Cooper, J., & Heck, R. (1995). Using narrative in the study of school administration. *Qualitative Studies in Education, 8*(2), 195–210.

Copland, M. A. (2001, March). The myth of the superprincipal. *Phi Delta Kappan.*

Copper, C., Frattura, G., & Keyes, M. (2000). *Meeting the needs of students of all abilities.* Thousand Oaks, CA: Corwin Press.

Cordeiro, P. (1999). The principal's role in curricular leadership and program development. In L. W. Hughes (Ed.), *The principal as leader* (2nd ed.). Upper Saddle River, NJ: Prentice-Hall.

Cordeiro, P. (1998). The principal's role in curricular leadership and program development. In L. W. Hughes (Ed.), *The principal as leader.* New York: Merrill.

Cordeiro, P. (1996). *Border crossings: Educational partnerships and school leadership.* San Francisco: Jossey-Bass.

Cordeiro, P. (1990). *Growing away from the barrio: An ethnography of high achieving, at-risk, Hispanic youths at two high schools.* Dissertation Abstracts International. University of Houston, Houston, TX.

Cordeiro, P., & Loup, K. (1996). Partnering changes the roles of school leaders: Implications for educational leadership preparation programs. In P. Cordeiro (Ed.), *Border crossings: Educational partnerships and school leadership.* San Francisco: Jossey-Bass.

Cordeiro. P., & Monroe-Kolek, M. (1996). Connecting school communities through the development of educational partnerships. In P. Cordeiro (Ed.), *Border crossings: Educational partnerships and school leadership.* San Francisco: Jossey-Bass.

Cordeiro, P., Reagan, T., & Martinez, L. (1994). *Multiculturalism and TQE: Addressing cultural diversity in schools.* Newbury Park, CA: Corwin.

Corey, M., & Corey, G. (1987). *Groups: Process and practice.* Pacific Grove, CA: Brooks/Cole.

Cortese, P. A. (1993). Accomplishments in comprehensive school health education. *Journal of School Health, 63*(1), 21–23.

Costa, A. L. (1997). Curriculum: A decision-making process. In A. L. Costa & R. M. Liebmarin (Eds.), *Envisioning process as content.* Thousand Oaks, CA: Corwin Press.

Covey, S. (1997). Leading by compass. In K. Shelton (Ed.), *A new paradigm of leadership* (pp. 83–88). Provo, UT: Executive Excellence.

Covey, S. R. (1989). *The 7 habits of highly effective people.* New York: Simon & Schuster.

Covey, S. R., Merrill, A. R., & Merrill, R. R. (1994). *First things first.* New York: Simon & Schuster.

Craig, R. (1999). Ethical frameworks to guide action. In L. Hughes (Ed.), *The principal as leader.* Upper Saddle River, NJ: Prentice-Hall.

Craig, R. (1994). Ethical frameworks to guide action. In L. Hughes (Ed.), *The principal as leader.* New York: Merrill.

Cranton, P. (1994). *Understanding and promoting transformative learning: A guide for educators of adults.* San Francisco: Jossey-Bass.

Creighton, T. (2001). Data analysis in administrator's hands: An oxymoron? *The School Administrators, 58* (4), 6–11.

Cremin, L. (1965). *The genius of American education.* New York: Vintage.

Crosby, P. B. (1996). *The absolutes of leadership.* San Diego, CA: Pfeiffer.

Crowson, R. (1988). Editor's introduction. *Peabody Journal of Education, 65*(4), 1–8.

Cuban, L. (1989). *The urban school superintendency: A century and a half of change.* Bloomington, IN: Phi Delta Kappa.

Cuban, L. (1988). *The managerial imperatives and the practice of leadership in schools.* Albany: State University of New York Press.

Cuban, L. (1976). *The urban school superintendency: A century and a half of change.* Bloomington, IN: Phi Delta Kappa Education Foundation.

Cubberly, E. (1909). *Changing conceptions of education.* Boston: Houghton Mifflin.

Culbertson, J. A. (1981). A century's quest for a knowledge base. In N.J. Boyan (Ed.), *Handbook of research on educational administration.* New York: Longman.

Cummins, J. (1989). *Empowering minority students.* Sacramento: California Association for Bilingual Education.

Cunningham, L., & Hentges, G. T. (1982). *The American school superintendent.* Arlington, VA: American Association of School Administrators.

Cunningham, W. G. (December, 1994). The way we do things around here. *The School Administrator, 54*(11), 24–26.

Cunningham, W. G. (1991). *Empowerment: Vitalizing personal energy.* Atlanta, GA: Humanics.

Cunningham, W. G. (1982). *Systematic planning for educational change.* Palo Alto, CA: Mayfield.

Cunningham, W. G., & Gresso, D. W. (1993). *Cultural leadership: The culture of excellence in education.* Boston: Allyn and Bacon.

Cunningham, W. G., & Sperry, J. (2001a, April). The underpaid educator. *American School Board Journal, 188,* 4:38–44.

Cunningham, W. G., & Sperry, J. (2001b, February). Where's the beef in administrators pay? *The School Administrator, 58,* 2:32–38.

Danzberger, J. P. (1998). School boards—Partners in policy. In R. Spillane & P. Regnier (Eds.), *The superintendent of the future.* Gaithersburg, MD: Aspen.

Daresh, J. C. (1992, May). Teacher evaluation: Are you a drive-by shooter? *Principal, 71*(5).

Darling-Hammond, L. (2003). Enhancing teaching. In W. Owings & L. Kaplan (Eds.), *Best practices. best thinking.* Thousand Oaks, CA: Corwin Press.

Darling-Hammond, L. (February, 1998). Standards for assessing teaching effectiveness are key. *Phi Delta Kappan, 79*(6).

Darling-Hammond, L. (1997). *The right to learn.* San Francisco, CA: Jossey-Bass.

Darling-Hammond L., & Ball, D. (1998). *Teaching for high standards: What policymakers need to know and be able to do.* (Research Rep. No. JRE-04). Philadelphia: Consortium for Policy Research in Education, University of Pennsylvania.

Darling-Hammond, L., & Falk, B. (1997). Using standards and assessments to support student learning. *Phi Delta Kappan, 79*(3), 190–202.

Data Research. (1991). *U.S. Supreme Court education cases.* Rosemount, MN: Data Research.

David, J. L. (1989, May). Synthesis of research on school-based management. *Educational Leadership, 46*(8), 45–53.

Davidman, L., & Davidman, P. T. (1994). *Teaching with a multicultural perspective.* New York: Longman.

Deal, T., & Peterson, K. (1998). *Shaping school culture: The heart of leadership.* San Francisco: Jossey-Bass.

Deal, T. E., & Kennedy, A. A. (1982). *Corporate cultures.* Reading, MA: Addison Wesley.

Deal, T. E., & Peterson, K. E. (1990, September). *The principals' role in shaping school culture.* Washington, DC: Office of Education Research and Improvement.

Delbecq, A. L., Van De Ven, A. H., & Gustafsan, P. H. (1975). *Group techniques for program planning.* Dallas: Scott, Foresman.

Delon, F. (1977). *Legal controls on teacher conduct: Teacher discipline.* Topeka, KS: NOLPE.

Deming, W. E. (1997). Quality leaders. In K. Shelton (Ed.), *A new paradigm of leadership* (pp. 121–126). Provo, UT: Executive Excellence.

Deming, W. E. (1993). *The new economics for industry, government and education.* Cambridge, MA: MIT Center for Advanced Engineering Studies.

Deming, W. E. (1991). Foundations for management of quality in the western world. In *An introduction to total quality for schools.* Arlington, VA: American Association of School Administrators.

Deming, W. E. (1986). *Out of crisis.* Cambridge, MA: MIT Center for Advanced Engineering Studies.

Depree, M. (1989). *Leadership is an art.* New York: Dell.

Detert, J., Kopel, M., Mauriel, J., & Jenni, R. (2000, March). Quality management in U.S. high schools: Evidence from the field. *Journal of School Leadership 10,* 2:158–187.

Detterman, D. (1993). The case for the prosecution: Transfer as an epiphenomenon. In D. Detterman & R. Sternberg (Eds.), *Transfer on trial: Intelligence cognition and instruction.* Norwood, NJ: Ablex.

Deutsch, M. (1963). The disadvantaged child and the learning process. In A. H. Paslow (Ed.), *Education in depressed areas* (pp. 163–180). New York: Teachers College Press.

Dewey, J. (1938). *Logic: The theory of inquiry.* New York: Holt, Rinehart & Winston.

Dewey, J. (1910). *How we think.* Boston: DC Heath.

Diangreco, M. F., Cloninger, C. J., & Iverson, V. S. (1993). *Choosing options and accommodations for children.* Baltimore: Brookes.

Diaz, C. (1992). *Multicultural education for the twenty-first century.* Washington, DC: National Education Association.

Digest of Education Statistics. (1995). Washington, DC: National Center for Education Statistics.

Dillard, C. (1995). Leading with her life: An African American feminist (re) interpretation of leadership for an urban high school principal. *Educational Administration Quarterly, 31*(4), 539–563.

DiPaola, M. F., & Stronge, J. H. (2001, February). Credible evaluation: Not yet state-of-the art. *The School Administrator, 58,* 2:18–21.

DiPaola, M., & Tschannen-Moran, M. (2003, March). The principalship at a crossroads: A study of the conditions and concerns of principals. *NASSP Bulletin, 87* (634), 43–63.

Dolan, L. J. (1992). *Models for integrating human services into the school.* (Report no. 30). Baltimore, MD: Center for Research on Effective Schooling. (ERIC Document Reproduction Service No. ED 347 244).

Doll, R. (1986). *Curriculum improvement, decision making and process.* Boston: Allyn and Bacon.

Donmoyer, R. (1999a). The continuing quest for a knowledge base. In J. Murphy & K. Seashore Louis (Eds.), *Handbook of research in educational administration* (2nd ed.). San Francisco: Jossey-Bass.

Donmoyer, R. (1999b, October). Paradigm talk (and its absence) in the second edition of the handbook on research on educational administration. *Educational Administration Quarterly, 35*(4) 614–641.

Doyle, D., & Finn, C. (1985). Now is the time for year-round schools. *Principal 65,* 29–31.

Doyle, M., & Straus, D. (1993). *How to make meetings work* (3rd ed.). New York: The Berkley Publishing Group.

Drake, T. L., & Roe, W. H. (1999). *The principalship.* Upper Saddle River, NJ: Merrill.

Drake, T., & Roe, W. H. (1994). *School business management: Supporting instructional effectiveness.* Boston: Allyn and Bacon.

Drucker, P. (2002). *The effective executive.* New York: Harper Collins.

Drucker, P. F. (1998). *Managing the nonprofit organization.* New York: Diane Publishing.

Drucker, P. F. (1997). Leaders as doers. In K. Shelton (Ed.), *A new paradigm of leadership.* Provo, UT: Executive Excellence.

Drucker, P. F. (1993). *Managing for the future.* New York: Penguin Books.

Drucker, P. F. (1992). *Managing for the future: The 1990's and beyond.* New York: Truman Tally Books.

Drucker, P. F. (1980). *Managing in turbulent times.* New York: Harper & Row.

Drucker, P. F. (1974). *Management: Tasks, responsibilities, and practices.* New York: Harper & Row.

Drucker, P. F. (1967). *The effective executive.* New York: Harper & Row.

Drucker, P. F. (1954). *The practice of management.* New York: Harper & Row.

Dryfoos, J. (1994). *Full-service schools: A revolution in health and social services for children, youth, and families.* San Francisco: Jossey-Bass.

Duhaney, D., & Zemel, P. (2000). Technology and the education process: Transforming classroom activities. *International Journal of Instructional Media, 27*(3), 27–32.

Duignan, P. A. (1997). *The ideal and the ethics of authenticity in leadership.* Annual Conference of the University Council for Educational Administration. Oct. 31–Nov. 2, Orlando, Florida.

Duke, D. (1998, April). The normative context of organizational leadership. *Educational Administration Quarterly, 34*(2), 165–195.

Duke, D. (1987). *School leadership and instructional improvement.* New York: Random House.

Duke, D., & Grogan, M. (1997). The moral and ethical dimensions of leadership. In L. Beck & J. Murphy (Eds.), *Ethics in educational leadership programs.* Columbia, MO: UCEA.

Duke, D., & Iwanicki, E. (1992). Principal assessment and the notion of fit. *Peabody Journal of Education, 68*(1), 25–36.

Duke, D. et al. (1997, November). *A thousand voices from the firing line: A study of educational leaders, their jobs and the problems they face.* Paper presented at the 1997 Annual Conference of the University Council of Educational Administrations, Orlando, FL.

Eberts, R., & Stone, J. (1988). Student achievement in public schools: Do principals make a difference? *Economics of Education Review, 7*(3), 291–299.

E.C.I.S. (1998). *The directory of the European council of international schools.* Petersfield, England: European Council of International Schools.

Edmonds, R. (1979). Effective schools for the urban poor. *Educational Leadership, 37*(1), 15–24.

Educational Research Services. (2000). *The principal keystone of a high-achieving school: Attracting and keeping the leaders we need.* Arlington, VA: Author.

Educational Research Services. (1998). *Is there a shortage of qualified candidates for openings in the principalship?* An exploratory study. Arlington, VA: Author.

Education Week. (1999, January 11). *Quality counts: Education Week/Pew Charitable Trusts report on education in the 50 states.* Bethesda, MD: Education Week.

Einedar, D., & Bishop, H. (1997). Block scheduling the high school: The effects on achievement behavior, and student-teacher relationships. *NASSP Bulletin, 51*(589), 45–54.

Eisner, E. (1995, Spring). Preparing teachers for schools of the 21st century. *Peabody Journal of Education, 70*(3), 99–111.

Eisner, M. (1997). Creative leadership. In K. Shelton (Ed.), *A new paradigm of leadership* (pp. 105–108). Provo, UT: Executive Excellence.

Ellena, W. G., & Redfern, G. (1972). *Tentative report: Evaluation of personnel.* Richmond, VA: State Department of Education.

Elmore, R. (2000). *Building a new structure for school leadership.* New York: The Albert Shanker Institute.

Elmore, R. F., & Fuhrman, S. H. (1994). The governance of curriculum. *1994 ASCD Yearbook.* Alexandria, VA: Association for Supervision and Curriculum Development.

Elmore, R. F., Peterson, P. L., & McCarthy, S. J. (1996). *Restructuring in the classroom: Teaching, learning, and school organization.* San Francisco: Jossey-Bass.

Elshtain, J. B. (1995). *Democracy on trail.* New York: Basic Books.

English, F. W. (1995). Toward a reconsideration of biography and other forms of life writings as a focus for teaching educational administration. *Educational Administration Quarterly, 31*(2), 203–233.

English, F. W. (1993, Spring). A post-structural view of the grand narratives in educational administration. *Organization theory dialogues.* Bloomington, IN: Organizational Theory SIG (AERA) Indiana University.

English, F. W., & Steffy, B. E. (1997, February). Using films to teach leadership in educational administration. *Educational Administration Quarterly, 33*(1), 107–115.

Epstein, J. (2001). *School, family, and community partnerships: Preparing educators and improving schools.* Boulder, CO: Westview Press.

Epstein, J. (1992). School and family partnerships. In M. Alkin (Ed.), *Encyclopedia of educational research.* New York: Macmillan.

Epstein, J. L. (1995). School/family/community partnerships: Caring for the children we share. *Phi Delta Kappan, 76,* 701–712.

Epstein, J. L., Coates, L., Salinas, K. C., Sanders, M. G., & Simon, B. S. (1997). *School, family, and community partnerships: Your handbook for action.* Thousand Oaks, CA: Corwin Press.

Epstein, J. et al. (2002). *School, family, and community partnerships: Your handbook for action.* Thousand Oaks, CA: Corwin Press.

Epstein, J., & Jansorn, N. (2004, January/February). Developing successful partnership programs. *Principal, 83* (3), 10–15.

Erickson, E. H. (1998). *Identity and the life cycle.* New York: W. W. Norton.

Essex, N. L. (1999). *School law and the public schools.* Boston: Allyn and Bacon.

Etzioni, A. (1993). *The spirit of community.* New York: Crown.

Etzioni, A. (1989). Humble decision making. *Harvard Business Review, 67,* 122–126.

Etzioni, A. (1986). Mixed scanning revisited. *Public Administration Review, 46,* 8–14.

Etzioni, A. (1975). *A comparative analysis of complex organizations.* New York: Free Press.

Etzioni, A. (1967, December). Mixed scanning: Their approach to decision-making. *Public Administration Review, 27:*385–392.

Evers, C. W., & Lakomski, G. (1996). *Exploring educational administration.* New York: Pergamon Press.

Evers, C. W., & Lakomski, G. (1996, August). Science in educational administration: A postpositivist conception. *Educational Administration Quarterly, 32*(3), 379–402.

Evers, C. W., & Lakomski, G. (1991). *Knowing educational administration: Contemporary methodological controversies in educational administration.* New York: Pergamon Press.

Fad, K., Patton, J., & Polloway, E. (2000). *Behavioral Intervention Planning*. Austin, TX: Pro-Ed.

Fairman M., Holmes, M., Hardage, J., & Lucas, C. (1979). *Manual of the organization health instrument*. Fayetteville, AR: Organizational Health: Diagnostic and Development.

Fashola, O. S., and Slavin, R. E. (1998, January). School-wide reform models: What works? *Phi Delta Kappan, 79*, 370–379.

Fayol, H. (1949). Administrator industrielle et generale. In C. Starrs (Ed.), *General and industrial management*. London: Sir Issac Pitman and Sons.

Fiedler, F. (1967). *A theory of leadership effectiveness*. New York: McGraw-Hill.

Fiedler, F. & Cherners, M. (1984). *Improving leadership effectiveness: The leader match concept*. New York: John Wiley & Sons.

Fiedler, F., & Cherners, M. (1974). *Leadership and effective management*. Glenview, IL: Scott Foresman.

Fiedler, F., & Garcia, J. (1987). *New approaches to effective leadership: Cognitive resources and organizational performances*. New York: John Wiley.

Fink, E. (2002). *Interview tape transcript conducted by L. Hubbard*. San Diego: University of San Diego, ELDA archives.

Fisher, C., Duyer, D., & Yocam, K. (Eds.). (1996). *Education and technology*. San Francisco: Jossey-Bass.

Flanery, R. A. (1997). Making your school a safe place for learning. *Schools in the Middle, 7*(20), 43–47.

Fleishman, E., & Hunt, J. (1973). *Current developments in the study of leadership*. Carbondale, IL: Southern Illinois University Press.

Follett, M. P. (1942). *Dynamic administration*. New York: Harper.

Follett, M. P. (1924). *Creative experience*. London: Longmans Green.

Foster, W. (1986). *Paradigms and promises: New approaches to educational administration*. Buffalo, NY: Prometheus Books.

Foster, W. (1998, August). Editor's foreword. *Educational Administration Quarterly, 34*(3), 294–297.

Frank, J. (1970). *Law and the modern man*. Gloucester, MA: Peter Smith. (Original work published in 1930.)

Frankl, V. (1984). *Man's search for meaning*. New York: Simon & Schuster. (Originally published in 1949.)

Franklin, C., & Allen, P. (1997, July). School social workers are a critical part of the link. *Social Work in Education, 19*(2), 131–135.

Franklin, C., & Streeter, C. (1995, November). School reform: Linking public schools with human services. *Social Work, 40*(6), 773–782.

Frase, L., English, F., & Poston, W. (1995). *The curriculum management audit: Improving school quality*. Arlington, VA: AASA.

Freire, P. (1985). *The politics of education*. South Hadley, MA: Bergin and Garvey.

Freire, P. (1973). *Pedagogy of the oppressed*. New York: Seabury Press.

French, D. (1998, November). The state's role in shaping a progressive vision of public education. *Phi Delta Kappan, 80*,(3), 184–195.

Fuhrman, S. H. (1994). Legislature and Education Policy. In R. F. Elmore & S. H. Fuhrman (Eds.), *The governance of curriculum*. Alexandria, VA: Association for Supervision and Curriculum Development.

Fukuyama, F. (1995). *Trust: The social virtues and the creation of prosperity*. New York: Free Press.

Fullan, M. (2003). *Change forces: With a vengeance*. New York: Routledge Falmer.

Fullan, M. (1997). *What's worth fighting for in the principalship*. New York: Teachers College Press.

Fullan, M. (1993). *Change forces*. Bristol, PA: Falmer Press.

Fullan, M. (1993). Innovation, reform, and restructuring strategies. In G. Cawelti (Ed.), *Challenges and achievements of American education*. Alexandria, VA: Association for Supervision and Curriculum Development.

Fullan, M. (1991). *The new meaning of educational change*. New York: Teachers College Press.

Fullan, M. (1990). Staff development, innovation, and institutional development. In B. Joyce (Ed.), *Changing school culture through staff development*. Alexandria, VA: Association for Supervision and Curriculum Development.

Fullan, M., & Hargreaves, A. (1992). *What's worth fighting for in your school*. New York: Teachers College Press.

Fullan, M., with Stiegelbauer, S. (1991). *The new meaning of educational change*. New York: Teachers College Press.

Furman, G., & Gruenewald, D. (2004, February). Expanding the landscape of social justice: A critical ecological analysis. *Educational Administration Quarterly, 40* (1), 49–78.

Gable, R., Baler, G., Wang, M., & Walberg, H. (1995). *Research on school effects in urban schools*. Philadelphia: National Research Center on Education in the Inner City.

Gardner, H. (1993). *Frames of mind: The theory of multiple intelligences*. New York: Basic Books. (Originally published in 1983.)

Gardner, H. (1993). *Multiple intelligences: The theory in practice*. New York: Basic Books.

Gardner, H. (1991). *The unschooled mind: How children think and how schools should teach*. New York: Basic Books.

Gardner, H. (1983). *Frames of mind: The theory of multiple intelligences.* New York: Basic Books.

Gardner, H., & Boix-Mansilla, V. (1994, February 7). Teaching for understanding—within and across the disciplines. *Educational Leadership, 51*(5), 14–18.

Gardner, S. (1993). Key issues in developing school-linked, integrated services. *Education and Urban Society, 25*(2), 141–152.

Gardner, S. L. (1992). Key issues in developing school-linked integrated services. In *The future of children* (2nd ed.) (pp. 85–94). Los Altos, CA: Center for the Future of Children.

Garnos, M. L., & King, R. A. (1994). Non-traditional sources of revenue: South Dakota's experience. *NASSP Bulletin, 78*(566), 27–38.

Garvin, J. R., & Young, A. H. (1993). Resource issues: A case study from New Orleans. *Politics of Education Association Yearbook,* pp. 93–106.

Gee, W. (1997). The Copernican plan and year-round education: Two ideas that work together. *Phi Delta Kappan, 78*(10), 793–796.

Gerber, S. B. (1996, Fall). Extracurricular activities and academic achievements. *Journal of Research and Development in Education, 30*(1), 42–50.

Giangreco, M. F., Cloninger, C. J., & Iverson, V. S. (1993). *Choosing options and accommodations for children.* Baltimore: Brookes.

Gillette, J., & McCollom, M. (1995). *Groups in context. A new perspective on group dynamics.* New York: University Press of America.

Gilligan, C. (1982; 1993). *In a different voice.* Cambridge, MA: Harvard University Press.

Ginsberg, B., Lowi, T., & Weir, M. (1995). *We the people.* New York, NY: Norton and Co.

Giroux, H. (1992). *Border crossings: Cultural workers and the politics of education.* New York: Routledge.

Glass, T. (2001, July). *Superintendent leaders look at the superintendency, school board and reform.* Denver: Education Commission of the States.

Glass, T. (2000, Fall/Winter). The politics of school board education. *The School Community Journal, 10*(2), 83–97.

Glass, T. E. (1992). *The study of the American school superintendency.* Arlington, VA: The American Association of School Administrators.

Glass, T., Bjork L., & Brunner, C. (2000). *The study of the American school superintendency 2000: The superintendency in the new millennium.* Arlington, VA: American Association of School Administrators.

Glatthorn, A. (1997). *The principal as curriculum leader: Shaping what is taught and tested.* Thousand Oaks, CA: Corwin Press.

Glatthorn, A. A. (1994). *Developing a quality curriculum.* Alexandria, VA: ASCD.

Glickman, C. D. (1998). *Revolutionizing American schools.* San Francisco: Jossey-Bass.

Glickman, C. D. (1993). *Renewing America's schools: A guide for school-based action.* San Francisco: Jossey-Bass.

Goerty, M. E., Floden, R. E., & O'Day, J. (October, 1996). *Systematic reform.* Washington, DC: U.S. Office of Educational Research and Improvement.

Goldhammer, R. (1969). *Clinical supervision.* New York: Holt, Rinehart & Winston.

Goldring, E. G. (1990). Elementary school principals as boundary spanners: Their engagement with parents. *Journal of Educational Administration, 28*(1), 53–62.

Good, H. (May, 1998). Then and now: The more boards change, the more they remain the same. *The American School Board Journal, 185,* 5.

Good, T., Biddle, B., & Brophy, J. (1975). *Teachers make a difference.* New York: Holt, Rinehart & Winston.

Goodlad, J. I. (1994). *Educational renewal: Better teachers, better schools.* San Francisco: Jossey-Bass.

Goodlad, J. I. (1991). *Teachers for our nation's schools.* San Francisco: Jossey-Bass.

Goodlad, J. I., & Lovitt, T. C. (Eds.). (1993). *Integrating general and special education.* New York: Macmillan.

Goodwin, R. (2004). The changing principalship: A summary of the finds of the 2003 NCPEA Morphet Award Dissertation. *NCPEA Educational Leadership Review, 5* (1), 16–19.

Goodwin, R. (2002). On the edge of chaos: *Delphi Study of the Changing Role of The Secondary Principal.* Morgantown: West Virginia University.

Goodwin, R., Cunningham, M., & Childress, R. (2003, March). The changing role of the secondary school principal. *NASSP Bulletin, 87,* 26–42

Gordon, B. M. (1985). Toward emanicpation in citizenship education: The case of African-American cultural knowledge. *Theory and Research in Social Education, 12,* 1–23.

Gould, S. J. (1995, November). The geometer of race. *Discover, 109,* 64–69.

Gould, S. J. (1981). *The mismeasure of man.* New York: Norton.

Grant, C. A. (Ed.). (1992). *Research and multicultural education: From the margins to the mainstream.* London: Falmer Press.

Grant Foundation. (1998, January). *The forgotten half: Non-college youth in America.* Washington, DC: William T. Grant Foundation.

Grant Foundation Commission on Work, Family, and Citizenship. (1988). *Citizenship through service.* Washington, DC: Grant Commission.

Graves, B. (1995, February). Putting pay on the line. *The School Administrator, 52*(2), 8–16.

Greenfield, T. B. (1988). The decline and fall of science in educational administration. In D. E. Griffiths, R. T. Stout, & P. B. Forsyth (Eds.), *Leaders for American schools.* Berkeley, CA: McCutchan.

Greenfield, T. B. (1985). Theories of educational organization: A critical perspective. In T. Husen & T. B. Greenfield (Eds.), *International encyclopedia of education.* Oxford: Pergamon Press.

Greenfield, T. B. (1980). The man who comes back through the door in the wall: Discovering truth, discovering self, discovering organizations. *Educational Administration Quarterly, 16* (3), 26–59.

Greenfield, T. B. (1979). Ideas versus data: How can the data speak for themselves? In G. L. Immegart & W. L. Boyd (Eds.), *Problem-finding in educational administration.* New York: Lexington Books.

Greenfield, T. B. (1978, Spring). Reflections on organizational theory and the truth of irreconcile realities. *Educational Administration Quarterly, 14*(2), 1–23.

Greenfield, T. B. (1975). Theory about organizations: A new perspective and its implications for schools. In N. Hughes (Ed.), *Administering education: International challenge.* London: Athlone.

Greenfield, T., & Ribbins, P. (Eds.). (1993). *Greenfield on educational administrations: Towards a humane science.* London: Routledge.

Greenfield, W. D. (1995, February). Toward a theory of school administration: The centrality of leadership. *Educational Administration Quarterly, 31*(1), 61–85.

Greenfield, W. D. (1993). Articulating values and ethics in administrative preparation. In Collen A. Capper (Ed.), *Educational administration in a pluralistic society.* Albany, NY: State University of New York Press.

Greenfield, W. D. (1991). The micropolitics of leadership in an urban elementary school. In J. Blase (Ed.), *The politics of life in schools: Power, conflict, and cooperation* (pp. 161–184). Newbury Park, CA: Sage.

Greenfield, W. D. (1990). Five standards of good practice for the ethical administrator. *NASSP Bulletin, 74*(528), 32–37.

Greenfield, W. D. (1982). *A synopsis of research on school principals.* Washington, DC: National Institute for Education.

Greenleaf, R. K. (1996). *On becoming a servant leader.* San Francisco: Jossey-Bass.

Greenleaf, R. K. (1977). *Servant leadership: A journey into the nature of legitimate power and greatness.* New York: Paulist Press.

Greenleaf, R. K. (1970). *The servant as leader.* Indianapolis, IN: R. K. Greenleaf Center for Servant Leadership.

Griffiths, D. E. (1979). Intellectual turmoil in educational administration. *Educational Administration Quarterly, 13*(3), 43, 65.

Griffiths, D. E. (1969). *Developing taxonomies of organizational behavior in educational administration.* Chicago: Rand McNally.

Griffiths, D. E. (1959). *Administrative theory.* New York: Appleton-Century-Crofts.

Griffiths, D. E., Stout, R. T., & Forsyth, P. E. (Eds). (1988). *Leaders for America's schools: The report and papers on the national commission on excellence in educational administration.* Berkley: McCutchan.

Grogan, M. (2002). Guest editors' introduction: Leadership for social justice. *Journal of School Leadership, 12,* 112–115.

Grogan, M. (2000a, February). Laying the groundwork for a reconception of the superintendency from feminist postmodern perspectives. *Education Administration Quarterly, 36,* 1:117–142.

Grogan, M. (March, 2000b). The short tenure of a woman superintendent: A class of gender and politics. *Journal of School Leadership, 10,* 2:104–130.

Gronn, P. (1984a). On studying administrators at work. *Educational Administration Quarterly, 20*(1), 115–129.

Gronn, P. (1984b). I have a solution. . . .: Administrative power in a school meeting. *Educational Administration Quarterly, 20*(2), 65–92.

Gronn, P., & Ribbins, P. (1996). Leaders in context: Postpositivist approaches to understanding educational leadership. *Educational Administration Quarterly, 32*(3), 452–473.

Gross, J. (March 29, 1992). Collapse of inner-city families creates America's new orphans. *New York Times National, 1,* 616.

Guba, E., & Lincoln, Y. (1994). Competing paradigms in qualitative research. In N. K. Denzin & Y. S. Lincoln (Eds.), *Handbook of qualitative research.* Thousand Oaks, CA: Sage.

Guba, E., & Lincoln, Y. (1989). *Fourth generation evaluation.* Beverly Hills, CA:

Guskey, T. (2003). Analyzing lists of the characteristics of effective professional development to promote visionary leadership. *NASSP Bulletin, 87* (637), 4–20.

Guthrie, J. W., & Reed, R. J. (1991). *Educational administration and policy: Effective leadership for American education.* Boston: Allyn and Bacon.

Hall, G. E., & Hord, S. M. (1987). *Change in schools: Facilitating the process.* Albany, NY: State University of New York Press.

Hallinan, M. (1979). Structural effects of children's friendships and cliques. *Social Psychology Quarterly, 42,* 54–77.

Hallinger, P., Bickman, L., & Davis (1989). *What makes a difference? School context, principal leadership and student achievement.* Paper presented at the annual meeting of the American Educational Research Association, San Francisco.

Hallinger, P., Leithwood, L. E., & Murphy, J. (Eds). (1994). *Cognitive perspectives on educational administration.* New York: Teachers College Press.

Hallinger, P., & Murphy, J. (1987). Instructional leadership in the school context. In W. Greenfield (Ed.), *Instructional leadership: Concepts, issues, and controversies* (pp. 79–207). Boston: Allyn and Bacon.

Halpin, A. W. (1966). *Theory and research in administration.* New York: Macmillan.

Halpin, A. W. (1958). *Administrative theory in education.* Chicago: University of Chicago Press.

Halpin, A. W. (1956). *The leader behavior of school superintendents.* Columbus, OH: Ohio State University College of Education.

Hannaway, J., & Albert, J. (1993). Bringing context into effective schools research: Urban-suburban differences. *Educational Administration Quarterly, 29*(2), 164–186.

Hanson, E. M. (1979; 1991; 1996). *Educational administration and organizational behavior.* Boston: Allyn and Bacon.

Hanushek, E. (1994). *Making schools work: Improving performance and controlling costs.* Washington, DC: Brookings Institution.

Hardage, J. G. (1978). *Development of an instrument to measure the task-centered and the internal state components of organizational health.* Unpublished doctoral dissertation. Fayetteville, AR: University of Arkansas.

Hargreaves, A., & Fullan, M. (1998). *What's worth fighting for out there.* New York: Teachers College Press.

Harris, B., & Monk, B. J. (1992). *Personnel administration in education.* Boston: Allyn and Bacon.

Harris, C. E. (1996). The aesthetic of Thomas B. Greenfield: An exploration of practice that leaves no marks. *Educational Administration Quarterly, 32*(4), 487–511.

Harris, S., Petrie, G., & Willoughby, W. (2002, March). *NASSP Bulletin, 86*(630), 3–14.

Harry, B. (1992). *Cultural diversity, families, and the special education system.* New York: Teachers College Press.

Hart, A. W. (1995, September). Reconceiving school leadership: Emergent views. *The Elementary School Journal. 96,*(1), 9–28.

Hart, A. W. (1994). Creating teacher leadership roles. *Educational Administration Quarterly, 30*(4), 472–497.

Hart, A. W., & Bredeson, P. V. (1996). *The principalship: A theory of professional learning and practice.* New York: McGraw-Hill.

Hartley, H. (1990). Boardroom bottom line. *American School Board Journal, 177*(2), 29–31.

Health Insurance Association of America. (1986). *Wellness at the worksite. A manual.* Washington, DC: Author.

Hechinger, N. (1993). The roles of technology. In S. Rocikman (Ed.), *The future: New visions of schooling.* Electronic School. Alexandria, VA: National School Board.

Heck, R., & Hallinger, P. (1999). Next generation methods for the study of leadership and school improvement. In J. Murphy & K. Seashore Louis (Eds.), *Handbook of research on educational administration.* San Francisco, CA: Jossey-Bass, Inc., p. 141–162.

Heifetz, R. A. (1994). *Leadership without easy answers.* Cambridge, MA: Harvard University Press.

Heller, M. F., & Firestone, W. A. (1995). Who's in charge here? Sources of leadership for change in eight schools. *Elementary School Journal, 96,* 1:65–86.

Hemphill, J. K., & Coons, A. (1950). *Leadership behavior description.* Columbus, OH: Personnel Research Board, Ohio State University.

Henderson, A., & Berla, N. (Eds.). (1994). *A new generation of evidence: The family is critical to student achievement.* Columbia, MD: Center for Law and Education.

Henderson, A., & Mapp, K. (2002). *A new wave of evidence: The impact of school, family and community connections on student achievement.* Austin, TX: Southwest Education Development Laboratory.

Henderson, R. (1985). *Compensation management.* Reston, VA: Reston Publishing.

Henkin, A., & Dee, J. (2001, January). The power of trust: Teams and collective action in self-managed schools. *The Journal of School Leadership, 11,* 1:48–62.

Herman, J., Aschbacher, P., & Winters, L. (1992). *A practical guide to alternative assessment.* Alexandria, VA: Association for Supervision and Curriculum Development.

Herman, J. J., & Herman, J. L. (1993). *School-based management: Current thinking and practice.* Springfield, IL: Charles C Thomas.

Herman, J., & Winters, L. (1992). *Tracking your school's success: A guide to sensible evaluation.* Newbury Park, CA: Corwin Press.

Herman, R., Aladjem, D., McMahon, P., Masem, E., Mulligan, I., O'Malley, A., et al. (1999). *An educa-*

tor's guide to schoolwide reform. Washington, DC: American Institutes for Research.

Hersey, P. (1994, February 12). *AASA/NASSP superintendent leadership development program*. Presented at the American Association of School Administrators, Conference on Education, San Francisco, CA.

Hersey, P., & Blanchard, K. (1993). *Management of organizational behavior: Utilizing human resources*. Upper Saddle River, NJ: Prentice Hall.

Hersey, P., & Blanchard, K. H. (1988). *Management of organizational behavior: Utilizing human resources* (5th ed.). Englewood Cliffs, NJ: Prentice-Hall.

Hersey, P., & Blanchard, K. H. (1977; 1982) *Management of organizational behavior: Utilizing human resources*. Englewood Cliffs, NJ: Prentice-Hall.

Hersey, P., Blanchard, K., & Johnson, D. (1996, 1993). *Management of organizational behavior*. Upper Saddle River, NJ: Prentice Hall.

Heslep, R. D. (1997, February). The practical value of philosophical thought for the ethical dimension of educational leadership. *Educational Administration Quarterly, 33*(1), 67–85.

Hesselbein, F. (1997). Strategic leadership. In K. Shelton (Ed.), *A new paradigm of leadership* (pp. 101–104). Provo, UT: Executive Excellence.

Hewstone, M., & Brown, R. (Eds.). (1986). *Contact and conflict in intergroup encounters*. New York: Basil Blackwell.

Hill, M. S., & Raglan, J. C. (1995). *Women as educational leaders*. Thousand Oaks, CA: Corwin.

Hill, R. B. (1991). *The strengths of black families*. New York: Emerson Hall.

Hirsch, E. D. (1996). *The schools we need: And why we don't have them*. New York: Doubleday.

Hoachlander, G., Alt., M., & Beltranena, R. (2001, March). *Leading school improvement: What research says*. Atlanta, GA: Southern Regional Education Board.

Hodgkinson, C. (1991). *Educational leadership: The moral art*. Albany, NY: State University of New York Press.

Hodgkinson, E. (1982). *Toward a philosophy of administration*. Oxford, MA: Blackwell.

Hodgkinson, H. L. (1995, October). What should we call people? *Phi Delta Kappan 77*(2), 173–179.

Hodgkinson, H. L. (1993). Keynote address by Harold Hodgkinson. In S. Elarn (Ed.), *The state of the nation's public schools*. Bloomington, IN: Phi Delta Kappa.

Hodgkinson, H., & Montenegro, X. (1999). *The U.S. school superintendent: The invisible CEO*. Washington, DC: Institute for Educational Leadership.

Hofstede, G. (1991). *Cultures and organizations: Software of the mind*. London: McGraw-Hill.

Holcomb, E. (1999). *Getting excited about data*. Thousand Oaks, CA: Corwin Press.

Hole, S., & McEntee, G. (1999). Reflection is at the heart of practice. *Educational Leadership Journal, 56*(8), 34–47.

Holland, A., & Andre, T. (1991). Is the extracurriculum an extra curriculum? *American Secondary Education Journal, 19*(2), 1–12.

Holland, S. (1989). (1989, September/October). Fighting the epidemic of failure: A radical strategy for educating inner-city boys. *Teacher Magazine*, 88–89.

Honig, M. (2003, August). Building policy from practice. *Educational Administration Quarterly, 39* (3), 305–338.

Hooper-Brian, K., & Lawson, H. (1994). *Serving children, youth and families through interprofessional collaboration and service integration*. Oxford, OH: Institute for Educational Renewal.

Hooper-Brian, K., & Lawson, H. A. (1994, October). *Serving children, youth, and families through interprofessional collaboration and service integration: A framework for action*. Philadelphia: National Forum for the Danforth Foundation and the Institute for Educational Renewal at Miami University.

Hopfenberg, W. S., & Levin, H. M. (1993). *The accelerated schools resource guide*. San Francisco: Jossey-Bass.

Horner, R., Sugai, G., & Horner, H. (2000, February). A school-wide approach to student discipline. *The School Administrator, 57*, 2:20–23.

Horvat, E., Weininger, E., & Lareau, A. (2003, Summer). From social ties to social capital: Class differences in the relations between schools and parent networks. *American Educational Research Journal, 40* (2), 391–351.

Hottenstein, D., & Malatesta, C. (1993). Putting a schooling year with intensive scheduling. *High School Magazine, 2*, 23–29.

House, R. (1971). A path-goal theory of leadership effectiveness. *Administration Science Quarterly, 16*, 321–339.

House, R., & Boetz M. (1990). Leadership: Some empirical generalizations and new research directions. *In Research in organizational behavior*. Greenwich, CT: JAI Press.

Houston, P. D. (2000, December). A stake through the heart of high-stakes tests. *The School Administrator, 57*, 11:58.

Hoy, W. (Ed.). (1994). *PRIMIS: The University Council of Educational Administration document base*. New York: McGraw-Hill.

Hoy, W. K. (1994, May). Foundations of educational administration: Traditional and emerging perspectives. *Educational Administration Quarterly 30*(2), 178–198.

Hoy, W. K., & Miskel, C. G. (1991; 1995). *Educational administration: Theory, research and practice*. New York: McGraw-Hill.

Hoy, W. K., & Tarter, C. J. (1995). *Administrators solving the problems of practice*. Boston: Allyn and Bacon.

Hoyle, J. R., English, F. W., & Steffy, B. E. (1990). *Skills for successful school leaders* (2nd ed.). Arlington, VA: American Association of School Administrators.

Hughes, L. (1999). *The principal as instructional leader*. Englewood Cliffs, NJ: Prentice-Hall.

Hughes, L. W., & Achilles, C. M. (1971). The supervisor as change agent. *Educational Leadership, 28*(8), 840–848.

Hymes, D. L., Chafin, A. E., & Gonder, P. (1991). *The changing face of testing and assessment*. Arlington, VA: American Association of School Administrators.

Iannoccone, L. (1978). *Public participation in local school districts*. Lexington, MA: Lexington Books.

IBM. (1992, June 22). *EduQuest: The journey begins*. Armonk, NY: IBM Educational Systems.

Industry Report 2000. (2000, October). The tech emergence. *Training, 37*, 10–87–95.

International Society for Technology in Education. (2000). *National education technology standards for students: Connecting curriculum and technology*. Eugene, OR: ISTE.

Janis, I. L., & Mann L. (1977). *Decision making: The psychological analysis of conflict, choice, and commitment*. New York: Free Press.

Jehl, J., & Kirst, M. (1992). Getting ready to provide school-linked services: What schools must do. In *The future of children* (2nd ed.) (pp. 95–106). Los Altos, CA: Center for the Future of Children.

Jerald, C., & Ingersoll, R. (2002). *All talk, no action: Putting an end to out-of-field teaching*. Washington, DC: The Education Trust.

Joint Committee on Standards for Educational Evaluation. (1988). *The personnel evaluation standards: How to assess systems for evaluating educators*. Newbury Park, CA: Sage.

Johns, B. H. (1998). Translating the new discipline requirements of the 1997 Individuals with Disabilities Education Act into practice. In L. M. Bullock & R. A. Gable (Eds.), *Implementing the 1997 IDEA: New challenges*. Reston, VA: Council for Exceptional Children.

Johnson, B., & Galvan, P. (1996). Conceptualizing school partnerships and inter-organizational relationships: A consideration of the public choice and organizational economics frameworks. In P. Cordeiro (Ed.), *Border crossings: Educational partnerships and school leadership*. San Francisco: Jossey-Bass.

Johnson, D. W., & Johnson, R. (1975). *Learning together and alone*. Englewood Cliffs, NJ: Prentice-Hall.

Johnson, S. M. (1996). *Leading to change: The challenge of the new superintendency*. San Francisco: Jossey-Bass.

Johnson, S. M. (1990). *Teachers at work: Achieving success in our schools*. New York: Basic Books.

Johnston, E. W. G. (1988). *Organizational health instrument: Technical manual*. Fayetteville, AR: Organizational Health Diagnostic and Development Corporation.

Joyce, B., Weil, M., & Showers, B. (1992). *Models of teaching*. Boston: Allyn and Bacon.

Kagan, S. L. (1991). *United we stand: Collaboration for children*. New York: Teachers College Press.

Kanter, R. M. (1983). *The change masters*. New York: Simon & Schuster.

Kaplan, D. (1997). Leader as model and mentor. In K. Shelton (Ed.), *A new paradigm of leadership* (pp. 145–148). Provo, UT: Executive Excellence.

Kaplan, D. S., Peck, B. M., & Kaplan, H. B. (1997, August). Decomposing the academic failure—dropout relationship: A longitudinal analysis. *Journal of Educational Research, 90*(6), 331–343.

Kaplan, L., & Owings, W. (2002). *Teaching quality and school improvement*. Bloomington, IN: Phi Delta Kappan.

Kaplan, L., & Owings, W. (1999, November). Assistant principals: The case for shared instructional leadership. *NASSP Bulletin, 83* (610), 80–94.

Kean, T. H. (1986, November). Who will teach? *Phi Delta Kappan, 18*, 205–208.

Kearns, D. (1995, January 9). Are we making progress? *Industry Week,* 12.

Keith, N. (1996). A critical perspective on teacher participation in urban schools. *Educational Administration Quarterly, 32*(1), 45–79.

Keller, B. K. (1995). Accelerated schools: Hands-on learning in a unified community. *Educational Leadership, 52*(5), 10–13.

Kelley, C. (1999, October). Leveraging human and fiscal resources for school improvement. *Educational Administration Quarterly, 35*(4), 642–657.

Kellogg Leadership Studies Project. (1997). *Leadership in the twenty-first century*. College Park, MD: University of Maryland, Center for Political Leadership and Participation.

Khan, B. (Ed.). (2001, 2004). *Web-based training*. Englewood Cliffs, NJ: Education Technology Publications.

Kilmann, R. (1989, October). A completely integrated program for creating and maintaining organizational success. *Organizational Dynamics,* 5–19.

Kimbrough, R. B., & Burket, C. W. (1990). *The principalship: Concepts and practices.* Englewood Cliffs, NJ: Prentice-Hall.

Kimbrough, R. B., & Nunnery, M. Y. (1983). *Educational administration.* New York: Macmillan.

King, A., Clements, J., Enns, J., Lockerbie, J., & Warren, W. (1975). *Semestering the secondary school.* Toronto, Ontario: Ontario Institute for Studies in Education.

Kirby, D., & Lovick, S. (1987). School-based health clinics. *Educational Horizons, 5*(3), 139–143.

Kirst, M. (1994). A changing context means school board reform. *Phi Delta Kappan, 75*(5), 378–381.

Kmetz, J., & Willower, D. (1982). Elementary school principals work behavior. *Educational Administration Quarterly, 18*(4), 62–78.

Knapp, M. S. (1995). How shall we study comprehensive, collaborative services for children and families? *Educational Researcher, 24*(4), 5–16.

Knapp, M., & Shields, P. (1996). *Better schooling for the children of poverty: Alternatives to conventional wisdom.* Berkeley, CA: McCutchan.

Knapp, M., & Associates. (1995). *Teaching in high poverty classrooms.* New York: Teachers College Press.

Knezevich, S. J. (1975). *Administration of public education.* New York: Harper & Row.

Kochan, F. K., Spencer, W., & Matthews, J. Gender-based perceptions of the challenges, changes, and essential skills of principalship. *Journal of School Leadership, 10*(4), 290–310.

Kotlowitz, A. (1991). *There are no children here: The story of two boys growing up in the other America.* New York: Anchor Books.

Kottkamp, R. B. (1982). The administrative platform in administrator preparation. *Planning and Change, 13,* 82–92.

Kouzes, J., & Posner, B. (1993). *Credibility: How leaders gain and lose it, why people demand it.* San Francisco: Jossey-Bass.

Kowalski, T., and Reitzug, U. (1993). *Contemporary school administration: An introduction.* New York: Longman.

Kozol, J. (1991). *Savage inequalities: Children in America's schools.* New York: Crown.

Kramer, S. L. (1997). What we know about block scheduling and its effects on math instruction, part II. *NASSP Bulletin, 81*(587), 69–82.

Krug, S. E. (1992, August). Instructional leadership: A constructivist perspective. *Educational Administration Quarterly, 28*(3), 430–443.

LaMorte, M. W. (1999). *School law.* Boston: Allyn and Bacon.

Land, D. (2002, Summer). Local school boards under review: Their role and effectiveness in relation to students' academic achievement. *Review of Educational Research, 72*(2), 229–278.

Lave, J., & Wenger, E. (1993). *Situated learning: Legitimate peripheral participation.* New York: Cambridge University Press.

Lawler, E. E. (1992). *The ultimate advantage.* San Francisco: Jossey-Bass.

Lawler, E. E. (1986). *High involvement management.* San Francisco: Jossey-Bass.

Lawrence, P. R., & Lorsch, J. W. (1969). *Developing organization: Diagnosis and action.* Reading, MA: Addison Wesley.

Leithwood, K. (1999). *Changing leadership for changing times.* Bristol, PA: Taylor Frances.

Leithwood, K. (Ed.). (1995). *Effective school district leadership.* Albany, NY: State University of New York Press.

Leithwood, K. A. (1994). Leadership for school restructuring. *Educational Administration Quarterly, 30*(4), 498–518.

Leithwood, K. A. (1992, February). The move toward transformational Leadership. *Educational Leadership, 49*(5), 8–12.

Leithwood, K., Aitben, R., & Jantzi, D. (2001). *Making schools smarter: A system of monitoring school and district progress.* Thousand Oaks, CA: Corwin Press.

Leithwood, K., Begley, P., & Cousins, B. (1994). *Developing expert leadership for future schools.* Bristol, PA: Falmer.

Leithwood, K., & Duke, D. (1994). A century's quest to understand school leadership. In J. Murphy & K. Seashore Louis (Eds.), *Handbook for research on educational administration.* San Francisco: Jossey-Bass.

Leithwood, K., Seashore Louis, K., Anderson, S., & Wahlstrom, K. (2004). *How leadership influences student learning.* Bloomington: Center for Applied Research and Educational Improvement. University of Minnesota.

Leithwood, K., & Stager, M. (1989). Expertise in principals problems solving. *Educational Administration Quarterly, 25*(2), 126–161.

Leithwood, K. A., Steinback, R. S., & Raun, T. (1993). Superintendent's group problem-solving process. *Educational Administration Quarterly, 29*(3), 364–391.

Lemann, N. (1991). *The promised land.* New York: Knopf.

Lepering, R., & Moskowitz, M. (1993). *100 Best companies to work for.* New York: Doubleday Currency.

Lepsinger, R., & Yukl, G. (December, 1995). How to get the most out of 360-degree feedback. *Training, 32*(12), 45–50.

Lerner, R. (1995). *America's youth in crisis.* Thousand Oaks, CA: Sage.

Levin, K., Lippitt, R., & White, R. (1939). Patterns of agressive behavior in experimentally created social climates. *Journal of Social Psychology, 10*(3), 43–195.

Levine, A. (2000, May). The private sector's market mentality. *The School Administrator, 57,* 5:6–12.

Levine, D., & Ornstein, A. (1993, November/December). School effectiveness and national reform. *Journal of Teacher Education, 342.*

Levinson, B. (1996). Social difference and schooled identity at a Mexican *secundaria.* In B. Levinson, D. Foley, & D. Holland (Eds.), *The cultural production of the educated person.* New York: State University of New York Press.

Levinson, B., & Holland, D. (1996). The cultural production of the educated person: An introduction. In B. Levinson, D. Foley, & D. Holland (Eds.), *The cultural production of the educated person.* Albany, NY: State University of New York Press.

Levy, E. H. (1948). An introduction to legal reasoning. *University of Chicago Law Review, 15,* 501–574.

Lewin, K. (1951). *Field theory in social science.* New York: Harper & Row.

Lewis, A. (1992). *Urban youth in community service: Becoming part of the solution.* Washington, DC: Office of Educational Research and Improvement (EDO-UD-72–4).

Lezotte, L. (1988). Strategic assumptions of the effective school process. *Monographs on effective schools.* New York: New York State Council of Educational Administration.

Lezotte, L., Edmonds, R., & Ratner, G. (1974). *A final report: Remedy for school failure to equitably deliver basic school skills.* East Lansing, MI: Michigan State University Press.

Lieberman, A. (1991). *Early lessons in restructuring schools.* New York: Teachers College, Columbia University.

Lieberman, A., & McLaughlin, M. (1992). Networks for educational change. *Phi Delta Kappan, 73*(9), 673–677.

Likert, R. (1967). *The human organization: Its management and value.* New York: McGraw-Hill.

Lindblom, C. E. (1995). *The intelligence of democracy.* New York: Free Press.

Lindblom, C. E. (1980). *The policy making process.* Englewood Cliffs, NJ: Prentice-Hall.

Lindblom C. E. (1959, Spring). The science of muddling through. *Public Administration Review, 19,* 79–88.

Lindle, G., & Mawhinney, H. (2003, February). Introduction: School leadership and the politics of education. *Education Administration Quarterly, 39* (1), 3–9

Lippitt, R., Watson, J., & Westley, B. (1958). *The dynamics of planned change.* New York: Harcourt, Brace, and World.

Lipsitz, J. (1984). *Successful schools for young adolescents.* New Brunswick, NJ: Transaction Books.

Lipsky, D., & Gartner, A. (2003). *Inclusion: A service, not a place: A whole school approach.* Port Chester, NY: National Professional Resources.

Lipsky, K. (2003, March). The coexistence of high standards and inclusion. *School Administration.* Web Edition (aasa.org/publications/sa/2003_3/lipsky.htm).

Little, J. W. (1986, September). The effective principal. *American Education, 72,* 3.

Liu, J. Q. (1997). The emotional bond between teachers & students. *Phi Delta Kappan, 79*(2), 156–157.

Lomotey, K. (1989). *African American principals: School leadership and success.* Westport, CT: Greenwood Press.

Louis, K. S., & Miles, M. B. (1990). *Improving the urban high school: What works and why.* New York: Teachers College Press.

Loveless, T., & Jasin, C. (1998). Starting from scratch: Political and organizational challenges facing charter schools. *Educational Administration Quarterly, 34*(1), 9–30.

Lucas, C. J. (1978). *Development of an instrument to measure form dimensions of organizational health: Innovation, autonomy, adaptation, and problem-solving adequacy.* Unpublished doctoral dissertation, Fayetteville, AR: University of Arkansas.

Lum, J. (1997). Student mentality: Intentionalist perspectives about the principal. *Journal of Educational Administration, 35*(3), 210–233.

Lunenburg, F., & Ornstein, A. (1991). *Educational administration: Concepts and practices.* Belmont, CA: Wadsworth.

Luster, R., & McAdoo, H. P. (1994). Factors related to the achievement and adjustment of young African American children. *Child Development, 65,* 1080–1094.

Lynn, R. L. (2003). Accountability: Responsibility and reasonable expectations. *Educational Researcher, 32*(7), 3–13.

Macedo, D. (1994). *Literacies of power: What Americans are not allowed to know.* Boulder, CO: Westview Press.

Machiavelli. (1988). *The prince.* New York: Skinner & Price. (First published in 1515.)

Manatt, R. (1998, Spring), Teacher and administration performance: Benefits of 360-degree feedback. *Journal of Research and Information (ERS Spectrum), 16,* 2:18–23.

Manz, C. (1997). SuperLeadership. In K. Shelton (Ed.), *A new paradigm of leadership* (pp. 45–50). Provo, UT: Executive Excellence.

March, J. G., & Simon, H. A. (1959). *Organizations*. New York: Wiley.

Mark, G. (1996). Superintendency in crisis calls for system thinking: State, national leaders meet at national conference. *Leadership News, 168*, 1.

Marshall, C., & Anderson, G. (1995). Rethinking the public and private spheres: Feminist and cultural studies perspectives on the politics of education. In J. D. Scribner & D. H. Layton (Eds.), *The study of educational politics: The 1994 commemorative yearbook of the politics of education association (1969–1994)* (pp. 169–182). Washington, DC: Falmer.

Marsick, V. J., & Watkins, K. (1999). *Facilitating learning organizations: Making learning count*. Aldershot, England: Grower Publishers.

Martin, J. R. (1993). The school home: Rethinking schools for changing families. *Educational Leadership, 52*(1), 25–31.

Martin, W., & Willower, D. (1982). The managerial behavior of high school principals. *Educational Administration Quarterly, 17*, 69–90.

Martindale, T., Cates, W., & Qian, Y. (2003, November-December). Education web sites: A classification system for educators and learners. *Education Technology, 43*(6), 47–57.

Marzano, R., & Kendall, J. (1997). Curriculum frameworks. *NASSP Bulletin, 81*(590), 26–41.

Matthews, J. (1994, January 19). *Analysis of seven frameworks of educational leadership*. Charlottesville, VA: National Policy Board for Educational Administration, 1–16.

Mayrowetz, P., & Weinstein, C. (1999, August). Sources of leadership for inclusive education: Creating schools for all children. *Educational Administration Quarterly, 35*, 3:423–449.

McCarthy, B. (1997a). *About learning*. Barrington, IL: Excel.

McCarthy, B. (1997b, March). A tale of four learners: 4 MAT's learning styles. *Educational Leadership, 54*(6), 45–51.

McCarthy, M., Bull, B., Quantz, R., & Sorenson G. (1993). *Legal and ethical dimensions of schooling: Taxonomy and overview*. New York: McGraw-Hill.

McCarthy, M., & Cambron-McCabe, N., & Thomas, S. (1987). *Public school law*. Boston: Allyn and Bacon. (1998).

McCarthy, M. M., & Webb, L. D. (2000, March). Legal principles in preventing and responding to school violence. *NASSP Bulletin, 84*, 614: 33–45.

McChesney, J., & Hertling, E. (2000, April). The path to comprehensive school reform. *Educational Leadership, 57*, 7:10–15.

McCollurn, S. (2001, February). How merit pay improved education. *Educational Leadership, 58*, 5:21–24.

McDermott, K. (2000, Spring). Barriers to large-scale success models in urban reform. *Education and Policy Analysis, 22*, 1:85–89.

McFarland, L. J., Senn, L. E., & Childress, J. R. (1993). *Twenty-first century leadership*. New York: Leadership Press.

McGregor, D. (1960). *The human side of enterprise*. New York: McGraw-Hill.

McKenna, B. H. (1965). *Staffing the schools*. New York: Teachers College Press.

McKnight, J. L., & Kretzman, J. P. (1993). Mapping community capacity. *Michigan State University Community and Economic Development Program Community News,* 1–4.

McLaughlin, M. W., Irby, M. A., & Longman, J. (1994). *Urban sanctuaries*. San Francisco: Jossey-Bass.

Meadows, M. E. (1995). *A preliminary program review of the four-period day as implemented in four high schools*. Doctoral dissertation. College Park, MD: University of Maryland.

Meek, J. C. (1972). *Unit cost analysis of the implementary expenditures in an urban system*. Master's thesis. University of Alberta.

Meier, K., & Stewart, J. (1991). *The politics of Hispanic education: Un paso Pa'lante y Dos Pa'tras*. New York: State University of New York Press.

Meno, L. R. (1984). Sources of alternative revenue. In *Fifth annual 1*. L. D. Webb and V. D. Mueller. (Eds.). Cambridge: Ballinger.

Merriam, S. B. (2001). *The new update on adult learning theory*. San Francisco: Jossey-Bass.

Mertz, N. T. (1997). *Voices from the field: Principal perceptions*. Presented at the 1997 Annual Conference of the University Council of Educational Administration, Orlando, FL.

Mertz, N. (1997). Knowing and doing: Exploring the ethical life of educational leaders. In L. Beck & J. Murphy (Eds.), *Ethics in educational leadership programs*. Columbia, MO: UCEA.

Metcalf, H., & Urwick L. (Eds.). (1941). *Dynamic administration and the collected papers of Mary Parker Follett*. New York: Harper.

Metz, M. (1978). *Classrooms and corridors: The crisis of authority in desegregated secondary schools*. Berkeley, CA: University of California Press.

Meyer, H. H., Kay, E. E., & French, R. P. (1965, February). Split roles in performance appraisals. *Harvard Business Review, 48*(2).

Mezirow, J. (1991). *Transformative dimensions of adult learning.* San Francisco: Jossey-Bass.

Miller, E. (1995, November/December). Shared decision making by itself doesn't make for better decisions. *Harvard Education Letter, XI*(6), 1–4.

Millman, J., & Darling-Hammond, L. (Eds.). (1990). *The new handbook of teacher evaluations: Assessing elementary and secondary school teachers.* Newbury Park, CA: Sage.

Milstein, M. (1993). *Changing the way we prepare educational leaders.* Newbury Park, CA: Corwin.

Mintzberg, H. (1989). *Mintzberg on management.* New York: Free Press.

Mintzberg, H. (1987, July-August). Crafting strategy. *Harvard Business Review, 65*(4), 66–75.

Mitchell, B., & Cunningham, L. L. (Eds.). (1990). *Educational leadership and changing contexts of families, communities, and schools.* (Eighty-ninth NSSE Yearbook, Part II.) Chicago: University of Chicago Press.

Moffett, J. (1994). *The universal schoolhouse: Spiritual awakening through education.* San Francisco: Jossey-Bass.

Morris, C. (1992, December). Pressure groups and the politics of education. *Updating School Board Policies, 23*(9) 1–5.

Morse, J. (2000, June 19). Is that your final answer. *Time, 155,* 25: 34–38.

Moursund, D., & Bielefeldt, T. (1999). *Will new teachers be prepared to teach in a digital age?* Research report by International Society for Technology in Education. New York: Milken Exchange on Educational Technology.

Murphy, J. (1999). New consumerism: Evolving market dynamics in the institutional dimension/ schooling. In J. Murphy & K. Seashore Louis. *Handbook of Research on Educational Administration* (pp. 405–420). San Francisco, CA: Jossey-Bass.

Murphy, J. (1995). *School-based management.* Thousand Oaks. CA: Corwin Press.

Murphy, J. (1993). What's in? What's out? American education in the nineties. In S. Elam (Ed.), *The state of the nation's public schools* (pp. 55–56). Bloomington, IN: Phi Delta Kappan.

Murphy, J. (Ed.). (1993). *Preparing tomorrow's school leaders: Alternative designs.* University Park, PA: ULCA, Inc.

Murphy, J. (1991). *Restructuring schools: Capturing and assessing the phenomena.* New York: Teachers College Press.

Murphy, J. (1990). The educational reform movement in the 1980's. In J. Murphy (Ed.), *The reform of American public education in the 1980's: Perspectives and cases.* Berkeley: McCutchan.

Murphy, J., & Beck, L. (1996). *The four imperatives of a successful school.* Thousand Oaks, CA: Corwin.

Murphy, J., & Beck, L. (1995). *School based management as school reform; Taking stock.* Newbury Park, CA: Corwin.

Murphy, J., & Hallinger, P. (Eds.). (1993). *Restructuring schooling: Learning from ongoing efforts.* Newbury Park, CA: Corwin.

Murphy, J., & Louis, K. S. (1999). *Handbook of research in educational administration.* San Francisco: Jossey-Bass.

Myrdal, G. (1944). *An American dilemma: The negro problem and modern democracy.* New York: Harper & Brothers.

Nance, J. (October, 2003). Public school administration and technology policy making. *Education Administration Quarterly, 39* (4), 434–467

Nanus, B. (1992). *Visionary leadership.* San Francisco: Jossey-Bass.

Nathan, J. (1996). *Charter schools.* San Francisco: Jossey-Bass.

National Association of Elementary School Principals. (1991). *Proficiencies for principals: Revised.* Alexandria, VA: NASPP.

National Association of Secondary School Principals. (2003). *Measuring leadership: A guide to assessment for development of school executives.* Reston, VA: NASSP.

National Association of Secondary School Principals. (1998). *Assessment handbook.* Reston, VA: NASSP.

National Association of Secondary School Principals. (1996). *Breaking ranks: Changing an American institution.* Reston, VA: NASSP.

National Association of State Boards of Education. (1992). *Winners all: A call for inclusive schools.* Alexandria, VA: National Association of State Boards of Education.

National Commission on Children. (1991). *Beyond rhetoric: A new American agenda for children and families.* Washington, DC: U.S. Government Printing Office.

National Commission on Child Welfare and Family Preservation. (1990). *A commitment to change.* Washington, DC: American Public Welfare Association.

National Commission on Excellence in Education. (1983). *A nation at risk: The imperative of school reform.* Washington, DC: U.S. Office of Education.

National Commission for Excellence in Teacher Education. (1985). *A call for change in teacher education.* Washington, DC: American Association of Colleges for Teacher Education.

National Commission on the Role of the School and the Community in Improving Adolescent Health. (1990). *Code blue: Uniting for healthier youth.* Alexandria, VA: National Association of State Boards of Education and the American Medical Association.

National Commission on Teaching and America's Future. (1996). *What matters most: Teaching and America's future.* New York: NCTAF.

National Education Goals Panel. (1994). *The National Education goals report: Building a nation of learners.* Washington, DC: U.S. Government Printing Office.

National Education Goals Panel. (1991). *The national education goals report: Building a nation of learners.* Washington, DC: NAEG.

National Governors Association. (1987). *Results in education: 1987.* Washington, DC: National Governors Association.

National Governors Association. (1986). *Time for results.* Washington, DC: National Governors Association.

National Policy Board for Educational Administration. (2002). *Standards for advanced programs in educational leadership for principals, superintendents, curriculum directors, and supervisors.* www.hpbea.org/ELCC.

National School Board Association. (1997). *Urban dynamics: Lessons learned from urban boards and superintendents.* Alexandria, VA: National School Boards Association.

National Science Board. (1983). *Educating Americans for the twenty-first century.* Washington, DC: National Science Foundation.

Negroponte, N. (1995). *Being digital.* New York: Alfred A. Knopf.

Neill, D. M. (1997, September). Transforming student assessment. *Phi Delta Kappan, 79*(1), 34–40.

Neill, M. (2003, February) High stakes, high risk. *American School Board Journal,* 18–21.

Neukrug, E. (2003). *The world of the counselor.* Pacific Grove, CA: Brooks/Cole.

Newmann, F. M., & Wehlage, G. (1993, April). Five standards of authentic instruction. *Educational Leadership, 50*(5), 8–12.

Nieto, S. (2000). *Affirming diversity: The sociopolitical context of multicultural education.* New York: Longman.

Noddings, N. (1992). *The challenge to care in schools: An alternative approach to education.* New York: Teachers College Press.

Norris, C. J. (1994). Cultivating creative cultures. In L. W. Hughes (Ed.), *The principal as leader* (p. 341). New York: Macmillan.

Norris, J. H. (1994, Spring). What leaders need to know about school culture. *Journal of Staff Development, 15*(2).

North Central Regional Educational Laboratory (NCREL). (1994). *Designing learning and technology for educational reform.* Elmhurst, IL: NCREL.

Northhouse, P. G. (1997). *Leadership: Theory and practice.* Thousand Oaks, CA: Sage.

Northwest Regional Educational Laboratory. (2000). *Catalog of school reform models* (2nd ed.). Portland, OR: Author. Retrieved March 17, 2003 from http://www.nwrel.org/scpd/catalog/indes.

Norton, M., Webb, L., Dlugosh, L., & Sybouts, W. (1996). *The school superintendency: New responsibilities, new leadership.* Boston: Allyn & Bacon.

Odden, A. R., & Wohlestetter, P. (1994). Making school-based management work. *Educational Leadership, 51*(6), 32–36.

Ogawa, R. T. (1994). The institutional sources of educational reform: The case of school-based management. *American Educational Research Journal 31,* 519–548.

Ogawa, R. (1991). Enchantment, disenchantment, and accommodating: How a faculty made sense of the succession of its principal. *Educational Administration Quarterly, 27*(1), 30–60.

Ogbu, J. (1992). Understanding cultural diversity and learning. *Educational Researcher, 21*(8), 5–14.

Olson, L. (1997, February 12). Designing for learning. *Education Week, 16*(20), 40–45.

O'Neil, G. (2000, April). Fads and fireflies: The difficulties of sustaining change: An interview with Larry Cubarn. *Educational Leadership, 57,* 7:6–9.

O'Neil, J. (2000, Summer). Integrating curriculum and technology. *Educational Leadership, 9,* 4:14–19.

O'Neil, R. (1995). On lasting school reform: A conversation with Ted Sizer. *Educational Leadership, 52*(5), 4–9.

Oritz, F. (1992). *Women's ways of becoming leaders: Personal stories.* Paper presented at the annual meeting of the American Educational Research Association, San Francisco, April.

Ouchi, W. (1981). *Theory Z.* Reading, MA: Addison-Wesley.

Outtz, J. H. (1993). *The demographics of American families.* Washington, DC: Institute for Educational Leadership.

Ovando, M. (2004). Prospective school leaders' educational platform: A reflection prior to action tool. *NCPEA Educational Leadership Review, 5* (1), 33–40.

Owens, R. G. (2001). *Organizational behavior in education.* Boston: Allyn and Bacon.

Owens, R. G. (1995). *Organizational behavior in education.* Boston: Allyn and Bacon.

Pai, Y. (1990). *Cultural foundations of education.* Columbus, OH: Merrill.

Palmer, P. J. (1998). *The courage to teach: Exploring the inter-landscape of a teacher's life.* San Francisco: Jossey-Bass.

Parker, L., & Shapiro, J. (1993). The context of educational administration and social class. In C. Capper (Ed.), *Educational administration in a pluralistic society.* Albany, NY: State University of New York Press.

Payzant, T. W. (1994). Commentary on the district and school roles in curriculum reform: A superintendent's perspective. In R. F. Elmore & S. H. Fuhrman (Eds.), *The governance of curriculum* (p. 224). Alexandria, VA: ASCP.

Payzant, T. W. (1992). New beginnings in San Diego: Developing a strategy for interagency collaboration. *Phi Delta Kappan 74(2),* 139–146.

Pedersen, P. (1994). *A handbook for developing multicultural awareness.* Alexandria, VA: American Counseling Association.

Peltier, G. (1991). Year-round education: The controversy and research evidence. *NASSP Bulletin, 75* (536), 120–129.

Perkins, D., & Blythe, T. (1994, February). Putting understanding up front. *Educational Leadership, 51*(1), 4–7.

Perman, P., & McLaughlin, M. W. (1978, May). *Federal programs supporting educational change, volume VII: Implementing and sustaining innovation.* R-1589/8-HEW. Washington, DC: Department of Health, Education, and Welfare.

Perot, R. (1997). Caring leaders. In K. Shelton (Ed.), *A new paradigm of leadership* (pp. 237–240). Provo, UT: Executive Excellence.

Peskin, A. (1991). *The color of strangers, the color of friends.* Chicago: University of Chicago Press.

Peters, T. (1997). Brave leadership. In K. Shelton (Ed.), *A new paradigm of leadership* (pp. 73–76). Provo, UT: Executive Excellence.

Peters, T. (1994). *The pursuit of wow!* New York: Vintage Books.

Peters, T. (1987). *Thriving on chaos: Handbook for management revolution.* New York: Knopf.

Peters, T. J., & Austin, N. (1985). *A passion for excellence: The leadership difference.* New York: Random House.

Peters, T. J., & Waterman, R. H. (1982). *In search of excellence: Lessons from America's best-run companies.* New York: Harper & Row.

Peterson, K. (1978). The principal's tasks. *Administrators Notebook, 26,* 1–4

Phinney, J. (1993). A three-stage model of ethnic identity development in adolescence. In M. Bernal & G. Knight (Eds.), *Ethnic identity.* New York: State University of New York Press.

Pollard-Durodola, S. (2003, November,). Wesley Elementary: A beacon of hope for at-risk students. *Education and Urban Society. 36*(1),94–117.

Popham, J. W. (2003, February). Trouble with testing. *American School Board,* 14–17.

Popham, W. J. (1997). The standards movement and the emperor's new clothes. *NASSP Bulletin, 81*(590), 21–25.

Portin, B. S. (1997, November 1). *Complexity and capacity: A survey of principal role change in Washington state.* Paper presented at UCEA annual meeting, Orlando, Florida.

Portin, B., Schneider, P., DeArmond, M., & Gundlah, L. (2003). *Making sense of leading schools.* Center on Reinventing Public Education, University of Washington.

Postman, N. (1995). *The end of education: Redefining the value of school.* New York: Knopf.

Pounder, D. (1995). Theory to practice in administrator preparation. *Journal of School Leadership 5,* 151–162.

Pounder, D, & Merrill, R. (2001). Job desirability of the high school principalship: A job choice theory perspective. *Education Administration Quarterly 37* (1), 27–57.

Pounder, D., Reitzug, V., & Young, M. (2002). Preparing school leaders for school improvement, social justice, and community. In J. Murphy (Ed.), *The educational leadership challenge: Redefining leadership for the 21st century.* One hundred-first yearbook of the National Society for the Study of Education. Chicago: National Society for the Study of Education.

Prawat, R., & Peterson, P. (1999). Social constructivist views of learning. In J. Murphy & K. Seashore Louis (Eds.), *Handbook of research on educational administration* (pp. 203–226). San Francisco, CA: Jossey-Bass.

President's Committee of Advisors on Science and Technology. (1997, March). *Report to the president on the use of technology to strengthen K–2 education in the United States.* Washington, DC: Panel on Educational Technology.

Prestine, N. A. (1995). A constructivist view of the knowledge base in educational administration. In R. Donmoyer, M. Imber, & J. Scheurich (Eds.), *The knowledge base in educational administration.* Albany, NY: State University of New York Press.

Price, W. (2001, February). Policy governance revisited (school boards vs. superintendents. *School Administration, 58*(2), 46–50.

Purkey, S., & Smith, M. S. (1982, December). Too soon to cheer? Synthesis of research on effective schools. *Educational Leadership, 82*(3).

Purkey, W. W., & Novak, J. M. (1984). *Inviting school success* (2nd ed.). Belmont, CA: Wadsworth.

Putman, R. D. (1996, Winter). The strange disappearance of civic America. *The American Prospect, 24,* 34–48.

Quigley, M. (1997). Leader as learner. In K. Shelton (Ed.), *A new paradigm of leadership* (pp. 93–96). Provo, UT: Executive Excellence.

Quinlan, C., George, C., & Emmett, Y. (1987). *Year-round education: Year-round opportunities.* Los Angeles: California State Department of Education. (ERIC Reproduction Service No. ED 285 272.)

Raferty, J. R. (1992). *Land of fair promise.* Palo Alto, CA: Stanford University Press.

Ramirez, A. (February, 2001). How merit pay undermines education. *Educational Leadership, 58*(5), 16–20.

Ramirez, M., & Casteñeda, A. (1974). *Cultural democracy, bicognitive development and education.* New York: Academic Press.

Ravitch, D. (1995). *National standards in American education.* Washington, DC: Brookings Institution Press.

Raywid, M. A. (1994, September). Alternative schools: The state of the art. *Educational Leadership, 52*(1), 25–31.

Razik, T. A., & Swanson, A. D. (1995). *Fundamental concepts of educational leadership and management.* Englewood Cliffs, NJ: Prentice-Hall.

Reagan, B. R. (1981, July). Teacher shortages in Texas. Presentation at the AASA Summer Instructional Leadership Conference. Washington, DC.

Rebore, R. W. (2001). *The ethics of educational leadership.* Upper Saddle River, NJ: Merrill Prentice-Hall.

Rebore, R. W. (1998). *Personnel administration in education: A management approach.* Boston: Allyn and Bacon.

Reeves, D. B. (2000, December). Caught in the middle. *American School Board Journal,* 25–27.

Regan, H. (1990). Not for women only: School administration as a feminist activity. *Teachers College Record, 91*(4), 565, 577.

Regan, R. (1984). Overview of education reform issues. In C. Masshner (Ed.), *A blue print for educational reform.* Washington, DC: Free Congress Research and Education Foundation.

Reich, R. (1997). *Keynote speech: Employment in the twenty-first century conference.* Pittsburgh, PA: University of Pittsburgh and Carnegie Mellon University.

Reid, W. M. (1995). *Restructuring secondary school with extended time blocks and intensive courses: The experiences of school administrators in British Columbia.* Dissertation Abstracts. Spokane, WA: Gonzaga University.

Reith, K. M. (1989, Winter). Minority athletes: Study breaks stereotypes. *National Coach 25*(2), 36.

Reitzug, U. C. (1994). A case study of empowering principal behavior. *American Educational Research Journal, 31*(2), 283–307.

Rhodes, L. A. (1997, January). *Connecting leadership and learning.* A position paper for the American Association of School Administrators. Arlington, VA: American Association of School Administrators.

Rice, J. K., & Malen, B. (2003, December). The human costs of educational reform: The case of school reconstitution. *Education Administration Quarterly, 39*(5), 635–666.

Richards, A. (2000). Panel call for fresh look at duties facing principals. *Educational Week.* www.ed week.org/ew/ewstory.CFM?slug=09iel.hw

Richardson, M. D. (1988, June). The administrative assessment center. Presented at the Kentucky Association of School Superintendent Annual Conference. Louisville, KY. ED 301–930.

Robbins, H., & Finley, M. (1995). *Why teams don't work: What went wrong and how to make it right.* Princeton, NJ: Pacesetter Books.

Robinson, V. (1996). Problem-based methodology and administrative practice. *Educational Administration Quarterly, 32*(3), 427–451.

Robinson, V. M. G. (1994, February). The practical promise of critical research in educational administration. *Educational Administration Quarterly, 30*(1), 56–57.

Roethlisberger, F., & Dixon, W. (1939). *Management and the worker.* Cambridge, MA: Harvard University Press.

Rogers, E. M. (1995). *Diffusion of innovations.* New York: Free Press.

Rosaldo, R. (1989). *Culture and truth: The remaking of social analysis.* Boston: Beacon Press.

Rotherham, A., & Mead, S. (2003, June). "Teacher Quality: Beyond No Child Left Behind. A Response to Kaplan and Owings." *NASSP Bulletin.* 87, 635: 165–76.

Rowan, B. (1990). Commitment and control: Alternative strategies for the organizational design of schools. *Review of Research in Education 16,* 53–389.

Rutter, M., Maughan, B., Mortimore, P., Ouston, J., & Smith, A. (1979). *Fifteen thousand hours: Secondary schools and their effects on children.* Cambridge, MA: Harvard University Press.

Ruskin, K. B., & Achilles, C. M. (1995). *Grantwriting, fundraising and partnerships: Strategies that work!* Thousand Oaks, CA: Corwin.

Ryau, K., & Bohlin, K. E. (1999). *Building character in schools.* San Francisco: Jossey-Bass.

Sagor, R., & Barnett, B. G. (1994). *The TQE principal: A transformational leader.* Thousand Oaks, CA: Corwin.

Salisbury, C. L., Palombaro, M. M., & Hollowood, P. M. (1993). On the nature and change of an inclusive elementary school. *Journal of the Association for Persons with Severe Handicaps,* (8), 2, 75–84.

Sanders, K. P., & Theimann, F. C. (1990). Student costing: An essential tool in site-based budgeting and teacher empowerment. *NASSP Bulletin, 74*(523), 95–102.

San Diego Unified School District. (1997–1998). Statistical report. San Diego, CA: San Diego City School Communications/Public Information Office.

Sarason, S. B. (1996). *Barometers of change: Individual educational social transformation.* San Francisco, CA: Jossey Bass.

Sarason, S. (1994). *The predictable failure of school reforms.* San Francisco: Jossey-Bass.

Sashkin, M., & Walberg, H. (1993). *Educational leadership and school culture.* Berkeley, CA: McCutchan.

Sayers-Kirsch, S. (1985). Understanding behavioral style. *NREL Behavioral Matrix.* Portland, OR: Northwest Regional Education Laboratory.

Schacter, J. (1999). *The impact of educational technology on student achievement: What the most current research has to say.* Santa Monica, CA: Milken Exchange on Educational Technology.

Schacter, J., & Fagnano, C. (1999). Does computer technology improve student learning and achievement? How, when, and under what conditions? *Journal of Educational Computing Research, 20,* 4:329–43.

Schein, E. (1991; 1985). *Organizational culture and leadership.* San Francisco: Jossey-Bass.

Schewick, J., & Skrla, L. (2003). *Leadership for equity and excellence.* Thousand Oaks, CA: Corwin Press.

Schewick, J. J., & Young, M. D. (1997, May). Coloring epistemologies: Are our research epistemologies racially biased. *Educational Researcher, 26*(4), 4–16.

Schlechty, P. C. (1997). *Inventing better schools: An action plan for educational reform.* San Francisco: Jossey-Bass.

Schlechty, P. C. (1990). *Schools for the twenty-first century.* San Francisco: Jossey-Bass.

Schmoker, M. (1996). *Results: The key to continuous school improvement.* Alexandria, VA: ASCD.

Schoenstein, R. (1995). The new school on the block. *Executive Educator, 17*(8), 18–21.

Schmitt, N., Noe, R., Meritt, R., Fitzgerald, M., & Jorgensen, C. (1983). *Criterion-related and content validity of the NASSP assessment center.* Reston, VA: National Association of Secondary School Principals.

Schmuck, R., & Runkel, P. (1994). *The handbook of organizational development in schools.* Prospect Heights, IL: Waveland Press.

Schofield, J. W. (1989). *Black and white in school: Trust, tension, or tolerance?* New York: Teachers College Press.

Schön, D. (1983). *The reflective practitioner: How professionals think in action.* New York: Basic Books.

School Health Resource Services, Office of School Health. (1995). *School-based health centers: Recommended services.* Denver: University of Colorado Health Sciences Center Resource packet Series. [Available by writing: 4200 E. 9th Ave./Box C287, Denver, CO 80262 or calling (303) 270–5990.]

School Health Resource Services, Office of School Health. (1995). *School-based clinics that work.* Denver: University of Colorado Health Sciences Center Resource Packet Series.

School Health Resource Services, Office of School Health. (1995). *State initiative to support school-based health centers.* Denver: University of Colorado Health Sciences Center Resource Packet Series.

Schwartz, W. (1995). *School dropouts: New information about an old problem.* Washington, DC: Office of Educational Research and Development. EDO-OD-96–5.

Scott, C., & Teddlie, C. (1987, April). *Student, teacher, and principal academic expectations and attributed responsibility as predictors of student achievement. A causal modeling approach.* Paper presented at the annual meeting of the American Educational Research Association, Washington, DC.

Scott, W. R. (1992). *Organizations.* Englewood Cliffs, NJ: Prentice-Hall.

Scribner, J. P. (1999, April). Professional development: Untangling the influences of work context on teacher learning. *Educational Administration Quarterly, 35,* 2:238–266.

Scribner, J. P., Aleman, E., & Maxcy, B. (2003, February). Emergence of the politics of education field: Making sense of the messy center. *Education Administration Quarterly, 39*(1), 10–40.

Sears, S. J., & Coy, D. R. (1991). The scope of practice of the secondary school counselor. Washington, DC: *ERIC Clearinghouse on Counseling and Personnel Services.* ED 328830.

Senge, P. M. (1990). *The fifth discipline: The art and practice of the learning organization.* New York: Doubleday Currency.

Senge, P. M. (1990, May). The leader's new world: Building learning retention. *Educational Leadership, 47,* 84–88.

Senge, P., et al. (2000). *Schools that learn.* New York: Doubleday Dell Publishing Group.

Sergiovanni, T. J. (2001). *The principalship: A reflective practice perspective.* Boston: Allyn and Bacon.

Sergiovanni, T. J. (1994, May). Organizations or communities? Changing the metaphor changes the theory. *Educational Administration Quarterly, 30*(2), 214–226.

Sergiovanni, T. J. (February, 1992a). Why we should seek substitutes for leadership. *Educational Leadership, 49*(5), 41–45.

Sergiovanni, T. (1992b). *Moral leadership: Getting to the heart of school reform.* San Francisco, Jossey-Bass.

Sergiovanni, T., & Starratt, R. J. (1998, 2001). *Supervision: Human perspectives.* New York: McGraw-Hill.

Shakeshaft, C. (1995). A cup half full: A gender critique of the knowledge base in educational administration. In R. Donmoyer, M. Imber, & J. Scheurich (Eds.), *The knowledge base in educational administration.* Albany, NY: State University of New York Press.

Shakeshaft, C. (1986). *Women in educational administration.* Newbury Park, CA: Sage.

Shanker, A. L. (1990, April). Restructuring: What is it? *Educational Leadership, 47*(7), 10.

Shapiro, J. P., & Stefkovich, J. (1997). Preparing ethical leaders for equitable schools. In L. Beck & J. Murphy (Eds.), *Ethics in educational leadership programs.* Columbia, MO: UCEA.

Sharp, W. (1994). Seven things a principal should know about school finance. *NASSP Bulletin, 78*(566), 1–5.

Sheldon, S. (2003). Linking school-family-community partnerships in urban elementary schools to student achievement on state tests. *Urban Review, 35*(2), 149–165.

Shelton, K. (Ed.). (1997). *A new paradigm of leadership: Visions of excellence for the twenty-first century.* Provo, UT: Executive Excellence Publishing.

Shen, J. (1997, October). The evolution of violence in schools. *Educational Leadership, 55*(2), 18–22.

Shen, J., & Crawford, C. (2003, March). Introduction to the special issue: Characteristics of the secondary principalship. *NASSP Bulletin, 87* (634), 2–8.

Shoop, R. J., & Dunklee, D. J. (1992). *School law for the principal.* Boston: Allyn and Bacon.

Shoop, R. J., & Sparkman, W. (1983). *Kansas school law.* Dubuque, IA: Bowers.

Short, P. M., & Greer, J. T. (1997). *Leadership in empowered schools.* Upper Saddle River, NJ: Prentice-Hall.

Short, P. M., Green, J. T., & Michael, R. (1991, April). Restructuring schools through empowerment: Facilitating the process. *Journal of School Leadership, 1*(2), 127–139.

Shorten, A. R. (1996). Law and the courts. In K. Leithwood, J. Chapman, D. Corson, P. Hallinger, &

A. Hart. (Eds.), *The international handbook of educational leadership and administration.* Boston: Kluwer Academic.

Shreeve, J. (1994). Terms of estrangement. *Discover 108,* 57–63.

Silins, H. (1994). The relationship between transformational and transactional leadership and school improvement outcomes. *School Effectiveness and School Improvement, 5*(3), 272–298.

Simmons, R. (1994). The horse before the cart: Assessing for understanding. *Educational Leadership 51*(5), 22–23.

Simon, H. A. (1976; 1947). *Administrative behavior* (4th ed.). New York: Macmillan.

Simon, H. (1960). *The new science of management decision.* New York: Harper & Row.

Singh, J. V., Tucker, D. J., & House, R. J. (1986). Organizational legitimacy and the liability of newness. *Administrative Science Quarterly, 31,* 171–193.

Sirotnik, K., & Oakes, J. (Eds.). (1986). *Critical perspectives on the organization and improvement of schooling.* Boston: Kluver-Nighoff.

Sizer, T. R. (1996). *Horace's hope: What works for the American high school.* Boston: Houghton Mifflin.

Slater, R. O. (1995). The sociology of leadership and educational administration. *Educational Administration Quarterly, 31*(3), 449–472.

Slater, R. O. (1994). Symbolic educational leadership and democracy in America. *Educational Administrative Quarterly, 30,* 97–101.

Slavin, R. E., & Fashola, O. S. (1998). *Show me the evidence!* Thousand Oaks, CA: Corwin Press.

Slavin, R. E., Madden, N. A., Dolan L. J., & Waskik, B. A. (1996). *Every child. Every school: Success for all.* Thousand Oaks, CA: Corwin Press.

Slavin, R. E., Madden, N. A., Dolan L. J., & Waskik, B. A. (1994, November). Roots and wings: Inspiring academic excellence. *Educational Leadership, 52*(3), 10–15.

Slavin, R. (1996). Cooperative learning in middle and secondary schools. *Clearinghouse, 69*(4), 200–204.

Slavin, R. (1995). *Cooperative learning and intergroup relations.* Washington, DC: ERIC Document No. ED 382 730.

Slavin, R. (1990). *Cooperative learning: Theory, research, and practice.* Englewood Cliffs, NJ: Prentice-Hall.

Sleeter, C., & Grant, C. (1993). *Making choices for multicultural education: Five approaches to race, class and gender.* New York: Merrill.

Slosson, J. (1999, October). Hiring the right people. *The High School Magazine, 7,* 2:20–32.

Smith, W. F., & Andrews, R. L. (1989). *Instructional leadership: How principals make a difference.* Alexandria, VA: Association for Supervision and Curriculum Development.

Smrekar, C., & Goldring, E. B. (1999). *School choice in urban America: Magnet schools and the pursuit of equity.* New York: Teachers College Press.

Smylie, M., & Hart, A. (1999). School leadership for teacher learning and change: A human and social capital development perspective. In J. Murphy & K. Seashore Louis (Eds.), *Handbook for research on educational administration* (pp. 421–443). San Francisco: Jossey-Bass.

Solomon, R. P. (1992). *Black resistance in high school.* New York: State University of New York Press.

Somech, A., & Drach-Zahavy, A. (2001, January). Influence strategies of principals: Ordinary times compared with times of change. *The Journal of School Leadership, 11*(1), 25–47.

Soto, O.R. (2004, August 22). Officials had feared violence at high school. *San Diego Union Tribune,* p. B3.

Sparks, D. (2000). Results are the reason. *Journal of Staff Development, 21* (3), 1–4.

Sparks, D. (1997, September). A new vision of staff development. *Principal, 77*(1), 20–22.

Spartz, J., Valdes, A., McCormick, W., Meyers, J., & Geppert, W. (1977). *Delaware educational accountability system case studies: Elementary schools grade 1–4.* Dover, DE: Delaware Department of Public Instruction.

Spillane, R. R., & Regnier, P. (1998, Spring). *The superintendent of the future.* Gaitherburg, MD: Aspen.

Spring, J. (1998). *Conflict of interests: The politics of American education.* Boston: McGraw-Hill.

Sredl, H. G., & Rothwell, W. J. (1987). *Professional training roles and competencies—volume I.* New York: Random House.

Stallings, J. (1980). Allocated academic learning time revisited, or beyond time on task. *Educational Researcher, 9,* 11–16.

Starratt, R. J. (1996). *Transforming educational administration: Meaning, community and excellence.* New York: McGraw-Hill.

Starratt, R. J. (1995). *Leaders with vision.* Thousand Oaks, CA: Corwin Press.

Starratt, R. J. (1994). *Building an ethical school: A practical response to the moral crisis in schools.* London: Falmer Press.

Starratt, R. J. (1993). *The drama of leadership.* Bristol, PA: Falmer Press.

Starratt, R. J. (1991). Building an ethical school: A theory for practice in educational leadership. *Educational Administration Quarterly, 27*(2), 185–202.

Stedman, L. (1995, February). The new mythology about the status of U.S. schools. *Educational Leadership, 52*(5), 80–85.

Stedman, L. (1987). It's time we change the effective schools formula. *Phi Delta Kappan, 69*(3), 215–224.

Steinberg, L. (1996). *Beyond the classroom: Why school reform has failed and what parents need to do.* New York: Simon and Schuster.

Steinberg, E. D. (1995, January 6). Margaret Wheatley on leadership for change. *School Administration, 16*–20.

Sternberg, R. (1996). IQ counts, but what really counts is successful intelligence. *NASSP Bulletin, 80*(583), 18–23.

Sternberg, R. (1996). *Successful intelligence.* New York: Simon & Schuster.

Sternberg, R., & Caruso, O. (1985). Practical modes of knowing. In E. Eisner (Ed.), *Learning and teaching the ways of knowing* (*NSSE Yearbook*) (pp. 133–158). Chicago: University of Chicago Press.

Sternberg, R., & Frensch, P. (1993). Mechanism of transfer. In D. Detterman & R. Sternberg (Eds.), *Transfer on trial: Intelligence, cognition, and instruction.* Norwood, NJ: Ablex.

Stevens, R., & Slavin, R. E. (1995). Effects of a cooperative learning approach in reading and writing on academically handicapped and nonhandicapped students. *Elementary School Journal, 95*(3), 241–262.

Stiggins, R. (1994). *Student-centered classroom assessment.* Portland, OR: Assessment Training Institute.

Stodolsky, S., & Lesser, G. (1971). Learning patterns in the disadvantaged. In *Challenging the myths: The schools, the blacks, and the poor.* Reprint Series #5. Cambridge: Harvard Educational Review.

Stogdill, R. (1981). Traits of leadership: A follow-up to 1970. In B. Bass (Ed.), *Handbook of leadership.* New York: Free Press.

Stogdill, R. (1974). *Handbook of leadership.* New York: Free Press.

Strahan, R. D., & Turner, L. C. (1987). *The courts and the schools.* New York: Longman.

Strike, K., Haller, E., & Solitus, J. (1988). *The ethics of school administration.* New York: Teachers College Press.

Strober, M. (1990). Human capital theory: Implications for H. R. managers. *Industrial Relations, 29,* 214–239.

Stronge, J. H. (1997). Improving schools through teacher evaluation. In J. H. Stronge (Ed.), *Evaluating teaching.* Thousand Oaks, CA: Corwin Press.

Stronge, J. H., & Tucker, P. D. (2001). *Student achievement and teacher evaluation.* Manuscript submitted for publication.

Stronge, J. H., & Tucker, P. (2000). *Teacher evaluation and student achievement.* Washington, DC: National Education Association.

Suters, E. (1997). Inspirational leadership. In K. Shelton (Ed.), *A new paradigm of leadership* (pp. 199–202). Provo, UT: Executive Excellence.

Swap, P. (1993). *Developing home-school partnerships: From concepts to practice.* New York: Teachers College Press.

Synder, J., & Ebmeier, H. (1992). Empirical linkages among principal behaviors and intermediate outcomes: Implications for principal evaluation. *Peabody Journal of Education, 68*(1), 75–107.

Takaki, R. (1993). *A different mirror: A history of multicultural America.* Boston: Little, Brown.

Talbert, J., & McLaughlin, M. W. (1994). Teacher professionalism in local school contexts. *American Journal of Education, 102,* 123–153.

Tanner, D. (1993, December). A nation truly at risk. *Phi Delta Kappan, 74,* 288–297.

Tannenbaum, R., & Schmidt, W. H. (1958). How to choose a leadership pattern. *Harvard Educational Review, 57,* 92–106.

Tanner, D., & Tanner, L. N. (1995). *Curriculum development: Theory into practice.* Englewood Cliffs, NJ: Prentice-Hall.

Tanner, L. N. (1997). *Dewey's laboratory school: Lessons for today.* New York: Teachers College Press.

Task Force on Teaching as a Profession. (1986). *A nation prepared: Teachers for the twenty-first century.* New York: Carnegie Forum on Education and the Economy.

Taylor, B. B. (1996). *Education and the law: A dictionary.* Santa Barbara, CA: ABC-CLIO.

Taylor, C. (1991). *The ethics of authenticity.* Cambridge, MA: Harvard University Press.

Taylor, E. W. (2000). Analyzing research on transformative learning theory. In J. Mezirow & Associates (Eds.), *Learning as a transformation: Critical perspectives on a theory in progress.* San Francisco: Jossey-Bass.

Taylor, F. W. (1947). *Scientific management.* New York: Harper.

Thayer, Y., & Short, T. (1994). New sources of funding for the twenty-first-century school. *NASSP Bulletin 78*(566), 6–15.

Thomas, D., & Davis, G. (1998). *Legal and ethical bases for educational leadership.* Bloomington, IN: Phi Delta Kappa International, Inc. Fastback.

Thomas, K., & Kilmann, J. (1975). Conflict and conflict management. In Marvin Dunnett (Ed.), *Handbook of industrial and organizational psychology,* vol. 2. Chicago: Rand McNally.

Thorndike, E. (1910). A scale for merit in English writing by young people. *Journal of Educational Psychology, 2,* 361–368.

Thornton, B., & Perrault, G. (2002, March). Becoming a data-based leader: An introduction. *NASSP Bulletin, 86* (630), 86–96.

Thurston, P., Clift, R., & Schacht, M. (1993, November). Preparing leaders for change oriented schools. *Phi Delta Kappan,* 259–265.

Tice, L. (1997). Limitless leadership. In K. Shelton (Ed.), *A new paradigm of leadership* (pp. 79–82). Provo, UT: Executive Excellence.

Tirozzi, G. (2003). Political education: a conundrum for school leadership. In W. Owings & L. Kaplan (Eds.), *Best practice, best thinking.* Thousand Oaks, CA: Corwin Press.

Traub, J. (1999). *Better by design? A consumer's guide to schoolwide reform.* Washington, DC: Thomas B. Fordham Foundation.

Triandis, H. (1971). *Attitude and attitude change.* New York: Wiley.

Trilling, L. (1974). *Sincerity and authenticity.* London: Oxford University Press.

Trueba, H. T. (1988; 1989). *Raising silent voices: Educating the linguistic minorities for the twenty-first century.* Rowley, MA: Newbury House.

Trump, K. (May, 2002). Be prepared, not scared. *Principal, 81* (5), 10–12

Tucker, M. (1990, April). Restructuring: What is it? *Education Leadership, 47*(7), 9.

Tucker, P. (2001, February). Helping struggling teachers. *Educational Leadership, 58,* 5:52–55.

Turnbull, A. P., Turnbull, H. R., Shank, M., & Leal, D. (1995). *Exceptional lives.* Englewood Cliffs, NJ: Prentice-Hall.

Tyack, D. (1992, Spring). Health and social services in public schools: Historic perspective. *The Future of Children, 2*(1), 19–31.

Tyack, D. (1974). *The one best system.* Cambridge, MA: Harvard University Press.

Tyler, R. W. (1949). *Basic principles of curriculum and instruction.* Chicago: University of Chicago Press.

Ubben, G. C., & Hughes, L. W. (1997). *The principal: Creative leadership for effective schools.* Boston: Allyn and Bacon.

Ubben, G., Hughes, L., & Norris, C. (2001). *The principal: Creative leadership for effective schools.* Boston: Allyn and Bacon.

Underwood, J., & Noffke, J. (1990). Litigation threat has chilling effect. *The Executive Educator, 12*(3), 18–20.

Urwick, L. F. (1937). Organization as a technical problem. In L. Gulick & L. F. Urwick (Eds.), *Papers on the science of administration* (pp. 47–88). New York: Institute of Public Administration, Columbia University.

U.S. Department of Education. (2003). *Twenty-third Annual Report to Congress on the Implementation of the Individual with Disabilities Education Act.* Washington, DC: Author.

U.S. Department of Education. (2002). *Comprehensive School Reform (CSR) program guidance.* Retrieved March 17, 2003 from http://www.ed.gov/offices/OESE/compreform/chifltr.html

Valente, W. D. (1997). *Law in the schools* (4th ed.). New York: Merrill.

Van Horn, G., Burrello, L., & DeClune, L. (1992). An instructional leadership framework: The principal's leadership role in special education. *Special education leadership review.* Albuquerque, NM: Council of Administration of Special Education.

Van Voorhis, F. (2001). Interactive science homework: An experiment in home and school connection. *NASSP Bulletin, 85* (675), 20–32.

Varenne, H. (1983). *American school language.* New York: Irvington.

Varenne, H. (1978). Culture as rhetoric: Patterning in the verbal interpretation of interaction in an American high school. *American Ethnologist, 5*(4), 635–650.

Venezky, R. L., & Winfield, L. F. (1979). Schools that succeed beyond expectations in teaching: Studies in Education Technical Report No. 1. Delaware University (ED1777484).

Villa, R., & Thousand, J. (2003, October). Making inclusive education work. *Educational Leadership,* 19–24.

Vroom, V. H., & Jago, A. G. (1988). *The new leadership: Managing participation in organization.* Englewood Cliffs, NJ: Prentice-Hall.

Vroom, V. H., & Yetton, P. W. (1973). *Leadership and decision-making.* Pittsburgh: University of Pittsburgh Press.

Vygotsky, L. (1978). *Mind in society.* Cambridge, MA: Harvard University Press.

Walberg, H. J., & Lane, J. E. (1989). *Organizing for learning: Toward the twenty-first century.* Reston, VA: National Association of Secondary School Principals.

Walker, A., Bridges, E., & Chan, B. (1996). Wisdom gained, wisdom given: Instituting PBL in a Chinese culture. *Journal of Educational Administration, 34*(5), 12–31.

Walsh, J., & Snyder, D. (1994). Cooperative teaching: An effective model for all students. *Case in Point, 2,* 7–19.

Wang, M. C., Haertel, G. D., & Walberg, H. J. (1993). Toward a knowledge base for school learning. *Review of Educational Research, 63*(3), 249–294.

Wang, M. C., Haertel, G. D., & Walberg, H. (1977). *What do we know? Widely implemented school improvement programs.* Philadelphia: Temple University Center for Research in Human Development and Education.

Wang, M. C., Reynolds, M. C., & Walberg, J. H. (1995). *Handbook of special and remedial education: Research and practice.* Tarrytown, NY: Elsevier Science.

Waters, T., Marzano, R. J., & McNulty, B. (2003). *Balanced leadership: What 30 years of research tells us about the effect of leadership on student achievement.* Aurora, CO: McREL.

Webb, L. D., & Norton, M. S. (1994, 1999). *Human resource administration.* New York: Merrill.

Weber, M. (1947). *The theory of social and economic organization* (trans. by A. M. Henderson; introduction by T. Parsons). New York: Free Press.

Weiss, C. H. (1995, Winter). The four "I's" of school reform: How interests, ideology, information, and institution affect teachers and principals. *Harvard Education Review, 65*(6), 571–592.

Werner, E. E., & Smith, R. S. (1989). *Vulnerable but invincible: A longitudinal study of resilient children and youth.* New York: Adams, Bannister, Cox.

West, C. (1992). The new cultural politics of difference. In S. Seidman (Ed.), *The postmodern turn: New perspectives on social theory.* Cambridge, England: Cambridge University Press.

Wheatley, M. (1992). *Leadership and the new science.* San Francisco: Berrett-Koehler.

White, W. D. (1988, January). Year-round high schools: Benefits to students, parents and teachers. *NASSP Bulletin, 478,* 18–24.

Wiggins, G. (1998). *Educative assessment.* San Francisco: Jossey-Bass.

Wiggins, G. (1990). *The case of authentic assessment.* ERIC ED 328 611.

Wiles, J., & Bondi, J. (1993). *Curriculum development* (4th ed.). New York: Macmillan.

Willoughby, K., & Melkers, J. (1998). *The state of the states: Performance budgeting requirements in 47 out of the 50 states.* Boston: The Pioneer Institute for Public Policy Research.

Willower, D. G. (1979). Some issues in research on school organization. In G. I. Immegart & W. Boyd (Eds.), *Currents in administrative research: Problem finding in education.* Lexington, MA: Heath.

Willower, D. J. (1996). Explaining and improving educational administration. In C. W. Evers & G. Lakomski (Eds.), *Exploring educational administration.* New York: Pergamon.

Willower, D., & Forsyth, P. (1999). A brief history of scholarship on educational administration. In J. Murphy & K. Seashore Louis, *Educational Administration* (pp. 1–23). San Francisco: Jossey-Bass.

Willower, D., & Licata, J. (1996). *Values and valuation in the practice of educational administration.* Thousand Oaks, CA: Corwin.

Wimpelberg, R., Teddlie, C., & Stringfield, S. (1989). Sensitivity to context: The past and future of effective schools research. *Educational Administration Quarterly, 25*(1), 82–107.

Wise, A. E. (2001, January). Differentiated staffing. *The School Administrator, 58*(1), 34–38.

Wolcott, H. (1973). *The man in the principal's office: An ethnography.* New York: Holt, Rinehart & Winston.

Wolf, S. (1997, October). Teach our children well. *Time, 150*(17), 62–71.

Wollons, R. (1992). (Ed.). *Children at risk in America: History, concepts, and public policy.* Albany, NY: State University of New York Press.

Woolfolk, A. (Fall, 2001). *Leading for learning: An educational psychologist's perspective.* UCEA Review, XLIII (3), 1–4.

Yetman, N. R. (1985). *Majority and minority: The dynamics of race and ethnicity in American life.* Boston: Allyn and Bacon.

Yorks, L., & Marsick, V. (1999). Transformative learning in organizations. In J. Mezirow & Associates (Eds.), *Learning as transformation: Critcal perspectives on a theory in process.* San Francisco: Jossey-Bass.

Young, I., & Castetter, W. (2004). *The human resource function in educational administration.* Upper Saddle River, NJ: Merrill.

Young, M., Petersen, G., & Short, P. (2002). The complexity of substantive reform: A call for interdependence among key stakeholders. *Education Administration Quarterly, 38*(2), 137–175.

Yukl, G. A. (1989). *Leadership in organizations.* Englewood Cliffs, NJ: Prentice-Hall.

Zepeda, S., & Logenbock, M. (1999). *Special programs in regular schools.* Boston: Allyn and Bacon.

Zigler, E., Kagan, S., & Klugman, E. (1983). *Children, families, and government.* Cambridge: Cambridge University Press.

Zigmond, N. (2003, September). Where should students with disabilities receive special education services? *The Journal of Special Education, 37* (3), 193–199.

Zirkel, P. (1996). Discipline and the law. *The Executive Educator, 18*(7), 21–23.

Author Index

Aboud, F., 100
Achilles, C. M., 65, 141, 260, 339–340
Airasian, P., 222
Aitben, R., 132
Aladjem, D., 76
Albert, J., 10
Aleman, E., 13
Alexander, L., 42
Allen, M., 80
Allison, G., 64
Allport, G., 105
American Association of School
    Administrators (AASA), 127, 129
American Institutes for Research, 71–74,
    109
Anafara, V., 64
Anderson, G., 10, 17
Anderson, L., 10
Anderson, S., 202, 206
Andre, T., 268
Andrews, R., 10, 141
Anti-Defamation League of B'nai B'rith, 100
Anyon, J., 108
Apple, M., 108
Argyris, C., 23, 24, 158, 160, 162, 356
Armstrong, T., 219, 220
Arons, E. L., 285
Arvey, R., 287
Aschbacher, P., 239
Aspin, D., 17
Atkins, J. M., 234
Austin, N., 178
Avolio, B., 10

Ball, D., 284
Ball, S., 10
Ballinger, C., 10, 237
Bamburg, J., 10
Banks, C., 106
Banks, J., 9, 14, 106

Banks, J. A., 107, 108, 369
Barker, J. A., 8, 11
Barnett, B. G., 8, 23
Bartlett, D., 43
Bartlett, L., 256
Bass, B., 10
Beck, L., 10, 20, 223, 327
Begley, P., 10, 219, 220, 354
Bender, W., 208, 209
Benham, M., 10
Bennett, C. I., 301
Bennis, W. G., 187, 188
Berlew, T., 174
Berman, P., 206
Bernhardt, V., 381
Bickman, L., 10
Biddle, B., 27
Bielefeldt, T., 78
Binkowski, K., 223
Bishop, H., 237
Bjork, L., 17, 124, 128, 129
Black, P., 234
Blake, R. R., 24, 158, 165
Blanchard, K., 167, 169, 175
Blase, J. G., 10, 189
Blau, P. M., 122
Bliss, W., 345
Bloom, B., 66, 218
Bloom, L., 10
Blount, J., 10
Blythe, T., 75
Boardman, G. R., 125
Boetz, M., 162
Boix-Mansilla, V., 75
Bolman, L. G., 8, 16, 62, 186, 187
Borman, G., 68, 69
Bossert, S., 206, 223
Boud, D., 226
Bourdieu, P., 105, 116
Bowles, S., 105

420

Bracey, G., 66
Bracken, D., 291
Bredeson, P. V., 212, 213
Brewer, D., 10
Bridges, E., 10, 13, 226, 354
Brookover, W., 223
Brophy, J., 27
Brown, K., 64
Brown, R., 105
Brown, S., 68, 69
Brown-Ferrigno, T., 137
Brunner, C., 124, 128, 129
Bryk, A., 206, 208, 209
Bull, B., 326, 327
Bullivant, B. M., 95
Bullock, A., 351
Bullock, C. S., 102
Burket, C. W., 262
Burns, J. M., 187, 188
Bynham, W. C., 288

Callahan, R. E., 9
Cambron-McCabe, N., 318
Cameron, T., 237
Campbell, R., 190
Campion, G., 287
Canady. R. L., 237
Candoli, I. C., 344
Capper, C. A., 17
Carella, V., 129
Carlson, R., 132
Carnegie Forum on Education and
    Economy, 42
Carr, N., 130
Carroll, J. M., 237
Carter, G., 46, 63, 64, 65, 126, 301
Caruso, O., 219–220
Cassel, M., 125
Casteñeda, A., 97
Castetter, W., 277
Cates, W., 79
Center for the Future of Children, 249
Cetron, K., 58
Cetron, M., 58
Chafin, A. E., 265
Chan, B., 10
Chapman, J., 17
Chase, S., 10
Checkley, K., 219
Cherners, M., 167
Children's Defense Fund, 56, 249, 362

Childress, R., 138
Chung, K., 10
Church, A., 291
Clark, K. E., 155
Clark, M. B., 155
Clark, M. C., 205
Clarke, G. H., 226
Clements, J., 237
Clemmer, E. F., 278
Clift, R., 189
Cloninger, C. J., 254
Cogen, M., 292
Cohen, D. K., 64
Cohen, J. J., 326
Cole, N., 218
Coleman, J., 7, 116
Collins, G. C., 180
Comer, J. P., 75
Constas, M. A., 15, 16
Coons, A., 163
Cooper, B., 55, 129, 140
Cooper, J., 10
Copper, C., 256
Cordeiro, P., 103, 116, 117, 230, 239
Cortese, P. A., 362
Costa, A. L., 218, 246
Cousins, B., 219, 220, 354
Covey, S. R., 21, 179, 180
Coy, D. R., 252
Craig, R., 20, 21
Cranton, P., 205
Crawford, C., 136, 142
Creighton, T., 381
Cremin, L., 233, 234
Crowson, R., 131
Cuban, L., 128
Cubberly, E., 27
Culbertson, J. A., 190
Cummins, J., 111
Cunningham, L. L., 190
Cunningham, M., 138
Cunningham, W. G., 24, 25, 46, 63, 64, 65,
    67, 126, 155, 185, 187, 206, 223, 294, 301,
    358, 359

Dansberger, J. P., 126
Darling-Hammond, L., 51, 54, 88, 284, 292
Data Research, 318
Davidman, L., 106
Davidman, P. T., 106
Davis, G., 10, 138

Deal, T. E., 8, 16, 62. 187, 186
DeArmond, M., 206
Dee, J., 186
Deming, W. E., 183
DePree, M., 181
Detert, J., 52
Detterman, D., 204, 221
Deutsch, M., 104
Dewey, J., 234, 357
Dickson, W., 156
Dillard, C., 10
DiPaola, M., 130, 148
Dolan, L. J., 74
Donmoyer, R., 7, 9, 12, 27
Doyle, D., 237
Doyle, M., 357
Drake, T. L., 141, 142
Drucker, P., 84, 178
Dryfoos, J., 363
Duhaney, D., 77
Duke, D., 7, 8, 10, 20, 21, 31, 188, 223
Dunklee, D. J., 323, 324
Dwyer, D., 206, 223

Eberts, R., 10
Ebmeier, H., 10
Edmonds, R., 32, 135
Educational Research Services, 3, 301
Education Week, 129, 362
Einedar, D., 237
Eisner, E., 231
Ellena, W. G., 289
Elmore, R., 67, 131, 185
Elshtain, J. B., 43
Emmett, Y., 237
English, F., 11, 236, 305
Epstein, J., 146
Essex, N. L., 319
Etscheidt, S., 256
Etzioni, A., 65, 162, 326
Evers, C. W., 9, 12, 15
Ewns, J., 237

Fad, K., 263, 264
Fairman, M., 153
Falh, B., 51
Fashola, O. S., 52, 75, 76
Fayol, H., 26, 156
Feletti, G., 226
Fiedler, F., 167
Fink, E., 205, 216
Finn, C., 237

Fitzgerald, M., 288
Flannery, R. A., 143
Fleishman, E., 163
Floden, R. E., 67
Follett, M. P., 156
Forsyth, P., 7
Foster, W., 14, 16, 20, 190
Foster-Harrison, E., 351
Frase, L., 236
Frattura, G., 256
Freire, P., 19, 108
French, D., 54
French, R. P., 159
Frensch, P., 219, 221
Fuhrman, S. H., 51, 131
Fullan, M., 63, 65, 84, 149, 190, 208, 209,
   230, 294
Furman, G., 55
Fusarelli, L., 129
Fusarelli, T., 55, 140

Galvan, P., 117, 148
Garcia, J., 167
Gardner, H., 66, 75, 116, 225
Garnos, M. L., 336, 337
Gartner, A., 256
Gee, W., 237
George, C., 237
Geppert, W., 223
Gerber, J. B., 269
Giangreco, M. F., 254
Gillette, J., 359
Gilligan, C., 9, 13, 19
Ginsberg, B., 43
Gintis, H., 105
Giroux, H., 108
Glass, T., 124, 128, 129
Glatthorn, A., 135, 224, 227, 228
Glickman, C. D., 15, 133, 237
Goerty, M. E., 67
Goldhammer, R., 292
Gonder, P., 265
Good, T., 27
Goodlad, J. I., 255
Goodwin, R., 138
Grant, C., 104, 105
Greenfield, T. B., 9, 12
Greenfield, W. D., 8, 9, 10, 12, 15, 20
Gresso, D. W., 25, 67, 185, 187, 206, 223,
   294, 358, 359
Griffiths, D. E., 9, 190
Grogan, M., 20, 21, 55, 128

Gronn, P., 10
Gruenewald, D., 55
Guba, E., 9, 235
Gundlah, L., 206
Guskey, T., 295, 297
Guthrie, J. W., 32

Hack, W. G., 344
Haertel, G. D., 76
Hall, F., 174
Hall, G. E., 65, 214
Hallinger, P., 9, 10, 67, 132, 226, 354
Halpin, A. W., 163, 164, 190, 196
Hannaway, J., 10
Hanson, E. M., 155, 190
Hardage, J., 153
Hargreaves, A., 208, 209
Harris, S., 260
Harry, B., 103
Hart, A. W., 8, 10, 213
Hartley, H., 342
Haynes, N. M., 75
Health Insurance Association of America,
  299
Heck, R., 9, 10
Heifetz, R. A., 214
Hemphill, J. K., 163
Henderson, A., 146
Henderson, R., 281
Henkin, A., 186
Herman, J., 239
Herman, R., 76
Hersey, P., 167, 169, 175, 288
Hertling, E., 71, 74
Heslep, R. D., 12
Hewes, G., 68, 69
Hewstone, M., 105
Hill, M. S., 190
Hodgkinson, C., 9
Hodgkinson, H., 129
Holcomb, E., 381
Hole, S., 157
Holland, A., 268
Holland, D., 94
Hollowood, P. M., 255
Holmes, M., 153
Honig, M., 132
Hooper-Brian, K., 363
Hord, S. M., 65, 214
Horner, H., 263
Horner, R., 263
Horvat, E., 147

Hottenstein, D., 237
House, R., 162
Hoy, W. K., 11, 25, 26, 157, 190, 233
Hoyle, J. R., 305
Hughes, L. W., 65
Hunt, J., 163
Hymes, D. L., 265

Ingersoll, R., 285
International Society for Technology
  in Education, 49
Irby, M. A., 262
Iverson, V. S., 254
Iwanicki, E., 10

Jago, A. G., 174
Jannis, I. L., 65
Jansorn, J., 146
Jantzi, D., 132
Jasin, C., 122
Jehl, J., 116, 362
Jenni, R., 52
Jerald, C., 285
Johns, B. H., 263
Johnson, B., 117, 148
Johnson, D. W., 105, 167, 169, 175
Johnson, R., 105
Johnston, E. W. G., 153
Joint Committee on Standards for
  Educational Evaluation, 290
Jorgensen, C., 288
Joyner, E. T., 75

Kagan, S., 362
Kaplan, D. S., 260
Kaplan, H. B., 260
Kaplan, L., 148, 295, 306
Kay, E. E., 159
Kean, T. H., 239
Keith, N., 10
Kendall, J., 49, 239
Kennedy, A. A., 186
Keyes, M., 256
Khan, B., 79
Kilmann, R., 230
Kimbrough, R. B., 190, 262
King, A., 237
King, R. A., 336, 337
Kirby, D., 362
Kirst, M., 116, 362
Klugman, E., 362
Kmetz, J., 10

Knapp, M. S., 363
Knezevich, S. J., 190
Kochan, F. K., 136
Kopel, M., 52
Kottkamp, R. B., 23
Kramer, S. L., 238
Krathwohl, D. R., 218
Krestzman, J. P., 117
Kuantz, R., 326, 327

Lakomski, G., 9, 12, 15
LaMorte, M. W., 334
Land, D., 126
Lareau, A., 147
Lave, J., 225
Lawson, H. A., 363
Leal, D., 252, 255
Lee, G., 206, 223
Leithwood, K. A., 7, 8, 10, 132, 188, 189,
    202, 206, 219, 220, 354, 356
Lepsinger, R., 291
Lesser, G., 97
Levin, K., 162
Levine, A., 53
Levine, D., 236
Levinson, B., 94, 105
Lewin, K., 300
Lewis, K., 126, 155, 190
Lezotte, L., 32, 135, 223
Lieberman, A., 187
Likert, R., 176, 177
Lincoln, Y., 9, 235
Lindal, J. C., 17
Lindblom, C. E., 65
Lindle, G., 140, 408
Lippitt, R., 162, 300
Lipsitz, J., 223
Lipsky, D., 256
Lipsky, K., 256
Little, J. W., 191
Liu, J. Q., 239
Lockerbie, J., 237
Logenbock, M., 259
Lomotey, K., 10
Loveless, T., 122
Lovick, S., 362
Lovitt, T. C., 255
Lowi, T., 43
Lucas, C., 153
Lum, J., 10
Lunenburg, F., 190
Luster, R., 93

Macedo, D., 109
Macedo, H. P., 93
Madden, N. A., 74
Malatesta, C., 237
Malen, B., 48
Manatt, R., 291
Mann, L., 65
Mapp, K., 146
March, J. D., 65
March, J. G., 164
Marshall, C., 17
Marsick, B. J., 205
Marsick, V., 205
Martin, J. R., 63
Martin, W., 10
Martindale, T., 79
Martinez, L., 103, 116
Marzano, R. J., 49, 202, 206, 214, 239
Masem, E., 76
Mathews, J., 136, 155, 200
Maughan, B., 223
Mauriel, J., 52
Mawhinney, H., 140, 408
Maxcy, B., 13
McCanse, A. A., 24, 158, 165
McCarthy, B., 18
McCarthy, M., 261, 318, 326, 327
McCarthy, S. J., 67
McChesney, J., 71, 72, 73, 74
McCollom, M., 359
McCormick, W., 223
McEntee, G., 157
McGregor, D., 158, 160
McKnight, J. L., 117
McLaughlin, M., 206, 262
McMahon, P., 76
McNulty, B., 202, 206, 214
Mead, S., 285
Meadows, M. E., 237
Meier, K., 102, 103
Melkers, J., 346
Meno, L. R., 336
Meritt, R., 288
Merriam, S. B., 204
Merrill, A. R., 180
Merrill, R. R., 141, 180
Mertz, N., 20
Meyer, H. H., 159
Meyers, J., 223
Mezirow, J., 205
Miles, M., 155
Miller, E., 135

Millman, J., 292
Mintzberg, H., 65, 183
Miskel, C., 10, 157, 190
Moffett, J., 225
Montenegro, X., 129
Morris, C., 33
Mortimore, P., 223
Moursund, D., 78
Mouton, J. S., 165
Mulligan, I., 76
Munro, P., 10
Murphy, J., 10, 51, 57, 67, 126, 132, 189,
    190, 223, 327
Myrdal, G., 104

Nance, J., 50
Nanus, B., 188
National Association of Secondary School
    Principals, 288
National Association of State Boards
    of Education, 255
National Commission for Excellence
    in Teacher Education, 41
National Commission on Children,
    55, 249
National Commission on Child Welfare
    and Family Preservation, 259
National Commission on Excellence
    in Education, 41
National Commission on Teaching and
    America's Future, 294, 384
National Governors Association, 42, 302
Negro Ponte, N., 380
Neill, D. M., 239
Neukrug, E., 252
Newmann, F. M., 208
Nieto, S., 101, 106
Noddings, N., 13, 19, 20, 63
Noe, R., 288
Noffke, J., 316–317
Norris, C., 135
Northhouse, P. G., 155
Northwest Regional Educational
    Laboratory, 71, 74, 76, 160
Novak, J. M., 105
Nunnery, M. Y., 190
Nystrand, R. O., 190

O'Day, J., 67
Odden, A. R., 185
Ogawa, R., 10
Ogbu, J., 104, 108

O'Malley, A., 76
Oritz, F., 10
Ornstein, A., 190, 236
Ouchi, W., 162
Ouston, J., 233
Ovando, M., 204
Overman, T., 68, 69
Owens, R. G., 190
Owings, W., 148, 295, 306

Palmer, P. J., 62
Palombaro, M. M., 255
Parker, L., 93
Passeron, J., 105, 116
Patton, J., 263, 264
Peck, B. M., 260
Peltier, G., 237
Perkins, D., 75
Perrault, G., 381
Peters, T. J., 178, 179
Petersen, G., 4
Peterson, K., 10, 186
Peterson, P. L., 67, 295
Petrie, G., 260
Pollard-Durodola, S., 142
Polloway, E., 263, 264
Popham, W. J., 239
Porras, G. I., 180
Portin, B., 206
Poston, W., 236
Pounder, D., 54, 141
Prawat, R., 295
Prestine, N. A., 16–17
Price, W., 126
Purkey, S., 206
Purkey, W. W., 105

Qian, Y., 79
Quinlan, C., 237

Raferty, J. R., 362
Raglan, J. C., 190
Ramirez, M., 97
Randall, E., 55, 140
Raun, T., 188
Ravitch, D., 229
Ray, J., 344
Razik, T. A., 33, 190
Reagan, T., 103, 116
Rebore, R. W., 277, 305
Redfern, G., 289
Reed, R. J., 32

Regan, H., 10
Reich, R., 331
Reid, W. M., 237
Reith, K. M., 268
Reitzug, V., 54
Rettig, M., 237
Reynolds, M. C., 255
Rhodes, L. A., 28
Ribbins, P., 10
Rice, J. K., 48
Richards, A., 141
Richardson, M. D., 288
Robinson, V., 10
Robinson, V. M. G., 13
Roe, W. H., 141, 142
Roethlisberger, F., 156
Rogers, E. M., 65
Rosaldo, R., 94
Rotherham, A., 285
Rothwell, W. J., 277
Rowan, B., 206, 223
Runkel, P., 301
Ruskin, K. B., 339, 340
Rutter, M., 223

Sackney, L., 17
Salisbury, C. L., 255
Sarason, S. B., 187
Sashkin, M., 187
Sayers-Kirsch, S., 195
Schacht, M., 189
Schacter, J., 77
Schein, E., 185, 187, 213
Schewick, J. J., 14, 55
Schlechty, P. C., 64, 89
Schmidt, W. H., 158
Schmitt, N., 288
Schmuck, R., 301
Schneider, P., 206
Schoenstein, R., 237
Schön, D., 23, 24, 158, 356
Schwartz, W., 260
Scott, C., 10
Scott, W. R., 122
Scribner, J. P., 13, 295
Sears, S. J., 252
Seashore, L. K., 202, 206
Sebring, P., 208, 209
Senge, P. M., 21, 181, 182
Sergiovanni, T., 24, 155
Shakeshaft, C., 9, 13, 14

Shank, M., 252, 255
Shapiro, J. P., 20, 21, 93
Sharp, W., 335
Sheldon, S., 146
Shen, J., 136, 142, 262
Shirley, R., 10
Shoop, R. J., 323, 324
Short, P., 4
Short, T., 337
Shorten, A. R., 327
Silins, H., 10
Simmons, R., 75
Simon, H. A., 65
Skrla, L., 55
Slavin, R. E., 53, 73, 74, 76, 225, 226
Sleeter, C., 104, 105
Slosson, J., 286
Smith, A., 223
Smith, M. S., 206
Smith, P., 141, 260
Smith, W. F., 141
Smylie, M., 8
Snyder, D., 255
Sorenson, G., 326, 327
Soto, O. R., 99
Sparks, D., 66, 381
Spartz, J., 223
Spencer, W., 136
Sperry, J., 301
Spring, J., 58, 246
Sredl, H. G., 277
Stagar, M., 10
Stallings, J., 239
Starratt, R. J., 14, 19, 20, 24, 327
Steele, J., 43
Steffy, B. E., 305
Stefkovich, J., 20, 21
Steinback, R. S., 188
Steinberg, E. D., 182
Sternberg, R., 218, 219, 220, 221
Stevens, R., 225
Stewart, J., 102, 103
Stiggins, R., 243, 245
Stodolsky, S., 97
Stogdill, R., 163
Stollar, D. H., 344
Stone, J., 10
Strahan, R. D., 318
Straus, D., 357
Stringfield, S., 223
Strober, M., 7

Stronge, J. H., 130, 291, 294
Sugai, G., 263
Swanson, A. D., 33, 190
Synder, J., 10

Tannenbaum, R., 158
Tanner, D., 233, 234
Tanner, L. N., 233, 234
Tarter, C. J., 233
Taylor, B. B., 323
Taylor, E. W., 205
Taylor, F. W., 156
Teddlie, C., 10, 223
Thayer, Y., 337
Thomas, D., 138
Thomas, S., 318
Thorndike, E., 27
Thorton, B., 381
Thousand, J., 256
Thurston, P., 189
Tirozzi, G., 58
Traub, J., 76
Triandis, H., 100
Trueba, H. T., 103, 104
Trump, K., 143
Tschannen-Moran, M., 148
Tucker, P., 291, 298
Turnbull, A. P., 252, 255
Turnbull, H. R., 252, 255
Turner, L. C., 318
Tyack, D., 362
Tyler, R. W., 233–234

Ubben, G. C., 174, 175, 344
Underwood, J., 316–317
Urwick, L. F., 156
U.S. Department of Education, 68, 256
Usdan, M. D., 190

Valdes, A., 223
Valente, W. D., 315, 322
VanMeter, E. J., 17
VanVoorhis, F., 146
Vareen, H., 10
Venezky, R. L., 205
Villa, R., 256
Vroom, V. H., 174
Vygotsky, L., 225, 356

Wahlstrom, K., 202, 206
Walberg, H., 76, 187

Walberg, J. H., 255
Walker, A., 10
Walsh, J., 255
Walsh, M., 222
Wang, M. C., 76, 255
Warren, W., 237
Waskik, B. A., 74
Waterman, R. H., 178, 179
Waters, T., 202, 206, 214
Watkins, K., 205
Watson, J., 300
Webb, L. D., 261, 277, 279
Weber, M., 156
Wehlage, G., 208
Weininger, E., 147
Weir, M., 43
Weisenstein, S., 256
Wenger, E., 225
West, C., 15
Westley, B., 300
Wheatley, M., 88, 182
White, R., 162
White, W. D., 237
Wiggins, G., 224, 240, 242, 243, 292
Willoughby, K., 346
Willoughby, W., 260
Willower, D. G., 7, 9, 10, 16
Wimpelberg, R., 223
Winfield, L. F., 205
Winters, L., 239
Wise, A. E., 303
Wohlestetter, P., 185
Wolcott, H., 10
Wollons, R., 362
Woolfolk, A., 222

Yetton, P. W., 174
Yorks, L., 205
Young, I., 277
Young, M. D., 4, 14, 54
Yukl, G. A., 174, 291

Zemal, P., 77
Zepeda, S., 259
Zigler, E., 362
Zigmond, N., 255
Zirkel, P. A., 312, 319

Subject Index

Academic achievement, 218–24
Accounting
 child, 259–65
 fiscal, 348–49
Accumulated knowledge, 7–8
Activities
 extracurricular, 266–70
 funds for, 347
Adaptive change, 214
Administering, school budget, 342–43
Administration
 applications in, 80–82
 case study, 1–3
 central office, 132–33
 effective, 26t
 knowledge base in, 25–28
 process of, 8–17
 of taxes, 331
 theories of, 1–28
Administrative
 platforms, 21–25
 skill dimensions (NASSP), 288
 team (case study), 1–3
Administrator(s)
 school (*See* Principals)
 statement of ethics for, 22
Adult learning, 204–5
AERA. *See* American Educational
 Research Association (AERA)
*Affirming Diversity: The Sociopolitical
 Context of Multicultural Education*
 (Nieto), 106–7
African Americans
 discrimination against, 101–2
 education and, 54
 language programs for, 114
 population demographics, 94
Aggregate costs of provisions for
 education, 341f

Alternative Routes to Teacher Certification
 Act, 37t
Amendments to the U.S. Constitution, 310
American Arbitration Association, 304
American Association of School Adminis-
 trators (AASA), 66, 127, 129
 Commission on Standards for the
 Superintendency, 127, 129
American Educational Research
 Association (AERA), 189, 266
American School Counselors Association
 (ASCA), 252
Americans with Disabilities Act, 36t
Applications, administrative, 80–82
Appraisal, testing and, 265–66
Apprenticeship learning, 225
ASCA. *See* American School Counselors
 Association (ASCA)
Assessing leadership characteristics, 155–56
Assessing student progress, 239–45
 portfolios, 240
 presenting outcomes to the community,
 243–45
 reporting progress, 242–43
Assistant principals, 147–48
Association for School Business Officials
 (ASBO), 347
Audit, 241
 legal, 324
 school budget, 349
 school safety, 143–45
Authentic instruction, 226–27
Autocratic style, 158
Average daily membership (ADM), 333

Behavior
 ethical, 20–21
 immature/mature, continuum of, 160b
 Matrix, NREL, 160

Behavioral intervention plan (BIP), 251, 262, 263
Behaviorist theory of learning, 222
Benefits, 303–4
Benevolent authoritative leadership, 176
Bethel School District v. Eraser, 322
Beyond Rhetoric (NCC), 55–56
Biculturalism, 110
Bilingual education, 110
  promoting, 111–13
Bilingual Education Act, 36t, 110
Black English, 114
Block scheduling, 237–38
  example of, 238
Board of education. *See* School board
Board of Education v. Allen, 312
Bodily-Kinesthetic intelligence, 220t
Borderlands, concept of, 95–96
Brown v. Board of Education, 39, 312, 321
Budget deficit, 57
Budgeting
  incremental, 345–46
  line-item, 343–44
  planning, programming, budgeting
    system (PPBS), 344
  process of, 340–41
  trends in, 346
  zero-based, 344–45
Buildings, maintaining, 351

Caring, ethics of, 19
Case studies
  on building an excellent school, 120–21
  on context/existing conditions, 30–31
  on cultural diversity, 91–92
  on developing an administrative team,
    1–3
  on interview for principalship, 201
  on program improvement, 217
  on pupil personnel services, 248–49
  on resource allocation, 330
  on school board policy, 308
  on school health, 153–54
  on school reform, 60
  on special education, 248–49
  on staffing problems, 273–76
CBAM. *See* Concerns-Based Adoption
    Model (CBAM)
*Cedar Rapids Community School District v.
    Garret F.*, 253

Central office
  departments, 131
  duties and operations of, 130–34
Charter schools, 334
Child accounting, 259–65
Children, 255. *See also* Student(s)
  "at-risk," 109
  in inclusive classrooms, 255
  in poverty, 56, 94t
  in single-parent homes, 56
Children's Defense Fund, 55
Civil Rights Act (1964) (Title VII), 36t, 313
Classrooms
  inclusive, 255–57
  Internet cameras in, 81
Codes of ethics, 21
Coequality of authority and responsibility,
    279b
Cognitive dissonance theory, 104–5
Cognitive theory of learning, 222
Collecting information, 291–92
Collective bargaining, 304–5. *See also*
    Human resource management
    (HRM)
Commission on Standards for the
    Superintendency, AASA, 127, 129
Community(ies)
  connecting schools and organizations
    in, 116–18
  presenting student outcomes to,
    243–45
  relations, diversity and, 91–118
  role in financing schools, 335
Complexity of leadership, 32–33
Compliance, 331
  monitoring with policies and
    procedures, 323–27
  theory, 162
Comprehensive School Reform (CSR), 68
Concerns-Based Adoption Model
    (CBAM), 214
Conferences
  district and/or school, 211–12
  teacher, 211
Confidentiality of student records, 321
Consortium for Policy Research in
    Education (CPRE), 75
Constructivist theory, 12–13
  of learning, 222–23
Consultative leadership, 176

Context
    of leadership, 31–32
    for school reform, 63–67
Contextual knowledge, 31–32
Contingency leadership, 167, 169, 174, 176
Cooperative learning, 104, 105, 225–26
Copernican Plan, 237
Counseling, 251–52. *See also* Pupil
        personnel services
The Courage to Teach (Palmer), 62
Crisis in the Classroom (Silberman), 40
Critical-contextual theory, 13–15
Critical incidents, 138–40
Critical pedagogy, 108
Critical teaching, 108
Critical theory, 12–13
Critique, ethics of, 20
Cultural
    leadership, 185–87
    pluralism, 106
    transitions, 97, 99
Cultural deficiency approach, 103–4
Cultural difference approach, 104
Cultural diversity, 91–118
    case study on, 91–92
    PBL project in, 368–73
    in schools, 93–94
    theories, models, and approaches to,
        102–9
Cultural identity, 94–99
    elements of, 96b
Culture
    of learning, 223–24
    shock, stages of, 98t
Curriculum
    designing and managing, 232–33
    developing, 231–32
    functions of, 227–28
    and instructional change, 230–34
    standards, 229

Data management and analysis (DMA), 81
    PBL project in, 380–84
Davis v. Monroe County Board of Education,
        99
Declarative knowledge, 219–20
Delegation, 279b
Democratic style, 158
Demographics, population, 93–94
Deprived, 103

Desegregation, 109–13
Design, curriculum, 227–30, 232–33
Dictionary of Occupational Titles, 280
Differentiated instruction, 227
Differentiated staffing, 302–3
Disabilities, education for people with,
        252–58
Discipline, 261–63
    and students with disabilities, 319–20
Discrimination, 221
    learning transfer and, 221
    prejudice and, 100–101
    in schools, 101–2
Distance learning, 339
Diversity
    case study, 91–92
    and community relations, 91–118
    language, 110–13
    school boards and, 124
    in schools, 93–94
Due process, 312, 318. *See also*
        School(s) legal issues

Ebonics, 114
Economic competitiveness, 41–43
Economic impact, taxes and, 331
Economic Opportunity Act, 36t
Education
    aggregate costs of provisions for, 341f
    bilingual, 110
    challenges in the twenty-first century,
        55–57
    culture and, 97
    deficit and difference theories in, 103b
    equal opportunity legislation, 39–41
    equity and social justice in, 54–55
    federal government's involvement in,
        33–43, 309–10
    origins, 34
    for people with disabilities, 252–58
    standards and testing in, 50–54
    state's legal role in, 314–15
    technology and, 79
Educational enterprise zones, 338
Educational leadership. *See* Leadership
Education Consolidation Improvement
        Act, 36t
Education Flexibility Partnership Act, 37t
Education for All Handicapped Children
        Act, 36t, 251, 252, 313, 321–22

Education for Economic Security Act, 36t
Education of the Handicapped Act (EHA), 313
Education Professions Development Act, 36t
Education Sciences Reform Act, 37t
Education Testing Service (ETS), 290
Elementary and Secondary Education Act, 36t, 40, 50, 110
ELL. *See* English Language Learners (ELLs)
Emergency School Aid Act, 36t
Employee
  assistance programs (EAP), 298–99
  concerns, 276–77
  development, 294–300
  litigation, 305–6
  planning, 277–79, 282–83
  records, 305–6
Empowerment, 106
Encoding specificity, 221
English as a Second Language (ESL), 111b
English Language Learners (ELLs), 113–14
Epistemological influences, 9–11
Equal educational opportunity legislation, 39–41
Equal Employment Opportunities Commission (EEOC), 314
Equal protection clause, 312
Equipment, managing, 351
Equity, 106, 331
  and social justice, 54–55
ESEA. *See* Elementary and Secondary Education Act
ESL. *See* English as a second language (ESL)
Establishment clause, 312
Ethical behavior, foundations of, 20–21
Ethic(s)
  of caring, 19
  codes of, 21
  of critique, 20
  of justice, 19–20
  statement for administrators, 22
Evaluation
  program improvement and, 235–36
  school budget, 343
Exploitative authoritative leadership, 176
Expulsion, 263
Extracurricular activities, 266–70

Facility management, budgeting, accounting, and, 340–46
Family and Medical Leave Act, 37t
Family Educational Rights and Privacy Act (FERPA), 36t, 259, 321
Fault, 323
Federal courts, 310–14. *See also* U.S. Supreme Court
Federal government
  involvement in education, 33–43, 35t–37t, 309–10
  role in financing schools, 332
Financing schools, 330–36. *See also* Resource allocation
  federal government's role in, 332
  local involvement in, 335–36
  nontraditional revenue sources, 336–37
  revenue sources for independent schools, 338–39
  state government's role in, 332–35
  taxes and, 331
First Amendment, 34, 312, 319
Fiscal accounting, 348–49
Fixed responsibility, 279b
Flat-grant model of finance, 333
Formulating, school budget, 341
Foundation program, 332–33
Fourteenth Amendment, 312, 318
Fourth Generation Evaluation (Guba and Lincoln), 235
Frames of Mind (Gardner), 219
Frames of reference, political, critical, and constructivist, 12–13
Framework for school improvement, 76–77
Franklin v. Gwinett County Public Schools, 321
Free appropriate public education (FAPE), 263, 320
Freedom of speech and expression, 319. *See also* School(s) legal issues
Functional Behavior Assessment (FBA), 262, 263
Function classification, 343
Funds, activity, 347

Gender, 13–15
  roles, 97
Genetic inferiority approach, 104
Goals 2000: Educate America Act, 37t

Good to Great (Collins), 182
Government. *See* Federal government;
    State government
Grant writing, 339–40
Great Depression, 38
Grid, managerial, 165–67, 168t
Grounds, maintaining, 351
Group
    facilitation, 358–62
    process, understanding, 359–62
Guidance, 251–52. *See also* Pupil personnel
    services
Gun-Free Schools Act, 313

7 Habits of Highly Effective People, The
    (Covey), 179–81
Hazelwood School District v. Kuhlmeier, 322
Health services, 258–59
Hispanics, population demographics, 94
Honig v. Doe, 262
Human capital, 7–8
Human relations approach, 104–5
Human resource management (HRM),
    273–306
    case study, 273–76
    collective bargaining and, 304–5
    employee records and reports, 305–6
    functions, 278f
    job analysis, 277–79, 280–81
    job classification, 277–79, 281–82
    organizational development and,
        300–301
    performance appraisal and evaluation,
        289–94
    recruitment, 283–85
    staff concerns, 276–77
    staff development, 294–300
    staff planning, 277–79, 282–83
    wage and salary considerations, 301–4

Identity
    cultural, 94–99
    sexual, 99–100
Immersion, 111b
Improvement(s), 64–66
    leadership challenge, 84–88
    program, 235–36
Improving American Schools Act, 37t
Incentive pay, 303

Inclusion, 255–57
Inclusive schools, 255–57
    characteristics of, 256
Incremental budgeting, 345–46
Independent schools, revenue sources for,
    338–39
Individualized educational plan (IEP), 251
Individuals with Disabilities Education
    Act (IDEA), 37t, 251, 252
Information
    collecting, 291–92
    using, 292–94
Initiating structure, 163
Innovative reform programs, 67–77
Innovative schools, 61–63
In Search of Excellence (Peters and
    Waterman), 178
    lessons from, 179b
Institute for Development of Educational
    Activities, Inc. (I/D/E/A), 358
Institute for Educational Leadership (IEL),
    126
Instruction
    authentic, 226–27
    differentiated, 227
    remedial, 252–58
    thematic, 226
Instructional change, curriculum and,
    230–34
Instrument analyses, leadership, 157–77
Integration, 109–13
Intelligence, theories of, 218–19
Interim alternative education settings
    (IAES), 263
International Society for Technology in
    Education (ISTE), 49, 78–79
Interpersonal attraction theory, 105
Interpersonal intelligence, 220t
Interstate New Teacher Assessment and
    Support Consortium (INTASC), 290
Interstate School Leaders Licensure
    Consortium (ISLLC), 6, 189
    standards, 5, 189
Intervention strategies for improving
    student behavior, 264
Interviewing, process of, 285–89. *See also*
    Human resource management
    (HRM)
Intrapersonal intelligence, 220t

Invitational education, 105
ISLLC. *See* Interstate School Leaders
  Licensure Consortium (ISLLC)

Job analysis, 277–79, 280–81
Job classification, 277–79, 281–82
Job Training Partnership, 36t
Justice, ethic of, 19–20

Kerner Commission on Civil Disorders, 40
Knowledge
  accumulated, 7–8
  administrative process and, 8–18
  contextual, 31–32
  types of, 219–20
Knowledge base
  in administration, 25–28
  growing, 156–57

Land grants, 33, 34, 38
Land Ordinance, 35t
Language diversity, 110–13
Lanham Act, 35t
Latinos
  discrimination against, 101–2
  education and, 54
Lau v. Nichols, 110
Law in the Schools (Valente), 315
Laws and policies, 308–28
  case study, 308
  legal issues and schools, 317–23
  legal responsibility, 309
  monitoring compliance with policies
    and procedures, 323–27
  state legislatures, 315–17
  U.S. legal system, 309–15
Leaders
  challenge of, 33
  context and perspective for, 30–58
  effective, 182
  ISLLC standards for, 5
Leadership, 153–91. *See also* Management;
    Principals; Superintendent
  approaches to studying, 10t
  behavior survey, 164b
  case study, 153–54
  challenge, 84–88
  and the change process, 208–9
  characteristics, assessing, 155–56

complexity of, 32–33
contingency, 167, 169, 174, 176
cultural, 185–87
elements of, 1–28
instrument analyses, 157–77
legal and ethical dimensions of, 324–27
new science of, 182–82
overview, 3–7
paradigms of, 156–57
problem-based learning in, 356–58
recent works on, 178–89
school (*See* School leadership)
school district, 120–49
situational, 167, 169, 174, 176
for special services, 257–58
studies on, 162–64
styles, 165–67, 177t (*See also*
    Management styles)
theories, 157–77
traits and skills, 189
transformational, 187–89
Leading with Soul (Bloman and Deal), 62
Learners, linguistically diverse,
    promoting, 111–13
Learning
  adult, 204–5
  apprenticeship, 225
  approaches, 224–27
  behaviorist theory of, 222
  cognitive theory of, 222
  constructivist theory of, 222–23
  cooperative, 225–26
  culture of, 223–24
  distance, 339
  innovative, 61–63
  online, 79–80
  problem-based, 226–27
  styles, culture and, 97
  transfer, 221
Learning organization concept, 181–82
*Legal and Ethical Bases for Educational
    Leadership* (Thomas and Davis), 139
Legal audit, 324
Legal responsibility, 309
Limited English Proficient (LEP), 111
Line authority, 279b
Line-item budgeting, 343–44
Linguistically diverse learners, promoting
    academic success by, 111–13

Linguistic intelligence, 220t
Litigation
  employee, 305–6
  school districts and, 316–17
Local school division, 122–24
Logical-Mathematical intelligence, 220t
Looping, 238–39

Magnet schools, 109–10
Maintaining school buildings and
    grounds, 351
Maintenance Bilingual Education, 111b
Management. *See also* Leadership
  human resource, 273–306
  managerial grid, 165–67, 168t
  school-based (SBM), 185
  total quality (TQM), 183–84
  trends in budgeting and, 346
Management by walking around
    (MBWA), 178
Management styles
  measuring preferred, 170b—173b
  summary preferred, 169t
Managerial grid, 165–67, 168t
Managing
  the curriculum, 232–33
  school supplies and equipment, 351
Manpower Development and Training
    Act, 35t
Mental set, 221
Merit pay, 302
Meyer v. Nebraska, 312
Minorities, population growth of, 56
Monitoring compliance with policies and
    procedures, 323–27
Morrill Act, 34
Multicultural education approach, 106
Multimedia technology, 80
Multiple intelligence (MI) theory, 218, 219
  summary chart, 220t
Musical intelligence, 220t
Muslims, 97

National Assessment of Educational
    Progress, 36t
National Association of Elementary School
    Principals (NAESP), 135
National Association of Secondary School
    Principals (NASSP), 135, 189, 288
  administrative skill dimensions, 288

National Association of State Boards of
    Education (NASBE), 255
National Board for Professional Teaching
    Standards (NBPTS), 290
National Center for School Leadership
    (NCSL), 136
National Coalition for Parents
    Involvement in Education (NCPIE),
    147
National Commission on Children, 55–56
National Defense Education Act, 35t, 38
National defense legislation, 38–39
National Education Technology Standards
    for Administrators (NETS-A), 50
National goals, establishing, 43–44
National Policy Board for Educational
    Administration (NPBEA), 6
National School Board Association
    (NSBA), 129
National School Lunch Program, 35t
Native Americans
  discrimination against, 101–2
  education and, 54
  population demographics, 94
The Nature of Prejudice (Allport), 105
New Jersey v. TLO, 322
New science of leadership, 182–82
No Child Left Behind Act (NCLB), 37t,
    47–49
Nonstandard English speakers, programs
    for, 113–14
Nontraditional revenue sources, 336–37
  school foundations, 337
Northwest Ordinance, 35t
NSBA. *See* National School Board
    Association (NSBA)

Object budget, 343
Ohio Statehood Enabling, 35t
Ohio State Studies, 163, 164b, 166–67
Older Americans, 56
Online learning, 79–80
Operations
  central office, 130–34
  of superintendent, 127–30
Organization, learning, 181–82
Organizational channels, 279b
Organizational development (OD),
    300–301. *See also* Human resource
    management (HRM)

Organizational structure
    definitions of, 279b
    school district, 120–49

Paradigms
    of leadership, 156–57
    parental involvement, 145–46
    and scientific-rational approach, 11
Parental involvement, 145–47
Parent Teacher Association (PTA), 146
Participative group leadership, 176
Path-Goal theory, 162
PBL. *See* Problem-based learning (PBL)
Peace Corps Act, 35t
Pedagogy, critical, 108
Performance appraisals, 289–94. *See also*
        Human resource management
        (HRM)
    collecting information, 291–92
    and evaluation, 289–94
    planning for, 290–91
    three phases of, 289f
    using information from, 292–94
Performance contracting, 303
Philosophical frames, 9–11
PL 93-380. *See* Family Educational Rights
        and Privacy Act (FERPA)
PL 94-142. *See* Education for All
        Handicapped Children Act
Planning
    performance appraisals, 290–91
    school budget, 341
    staff, 282–83
Planning, programming, budgeting
        system (PPBS), 344
Platforms, administrative, 21–25
Plessy v. Ferguson, 312
Political theory, 12–13
Politics, principals and, 140–42
Portfolios, 240
Postmodernism, 15–18
Poststructuralism, 15–18
Poverty, children living in, 94
Power-equalizing model of finance,
        334
Practical knowledge, 220
Prejudice and discrimination, 100–101
Preschool programs, 338
Presenting, school budget, 341–42
Preventive law, 324

Principals, 135–40
    assistant, 147–48
    changing roles of, 136–38
    critical incidents and, 138–40
    as curriculum leader, 228–29
    as instructional leaders, 212–13
    and the integration of technology, 137
    politics surrounding, 140–42
    as school manager, 141–42
Problem-based learning (PBL), 226–27,
        354–91
    defining the problem, 354–56
    in educational leadership, 356–58
    group facilitation in, 358–62
    main features of PBL projects, 355t
    projects in, 362–91
Procedural knowledge, 220
Process
    administrative, 8–17
    budgeting, 340–41
Program development, 217–46
    case study, 217
    model of, 230f
    technology, 82–83
Program improvement, 217–46
    and evaluation, 235–36
Program within a school (PWS), 109
Property tax, school financing and, 335
Psychological services, 251–52. *See also*
        Pupil personnel services
Pupil personnel services, 248–71
    case study, 248–49
    child accounting, 259–65
    counseling, guidance, and psychological
        services, 251–52
    extracurricular activities, 266–70
    health services, 258–59
    remedial instruction, 252–58
    school safety, 259–65
    special education, 252–58
    student service team, 249–51
    testing and diagnostics, 265–66
Pygmalion effect, 159

Quality improvement. *See* Total quality
        management (TQM)

Race, 13–15
    demographics, 93–94
Rand Institute, 63

Records, 259

Recruitment, 283–85. *See also* Human resource management (HRM)

Reform, 60–88
    case study, 60
    common themes in, 66–67
    context for, 63–67
    innovative programs, 67–77
    leadership challenge, 84–88
    new directions in, 64–66
    PBL project in, 384–91

Rehabilitation Act, 36t

Relief, 38

Remedial instruction, 252–58

Reporting student progress, 242–43

Reports, employee, 305

Reproduction: In Education, Society, and Culture (Bourdieu and Passeron), 105–6

Resource allocation, 330–51
    activity funds, 347
    budgeting, accounting, and facility management, 340–46
    case study, 330
    financing schools, 330–36
    fiscal accounting, 348–49
    grant writing, 339–40
    nontraditional revenue sources and, 336–37
    revenue sources for independent schools, 338–39
    vouchers and, 336

Resource sharing, 339

Revenue sources
    for independent schools, 338–39
    nontraditional, 336–37

Rodriguez v. San Antonio Independent School District, 41

Safe and Drug-Free Schools and Communities Act, 37t

Safe Schools Act, 313

Safety, 259–65
    audit, 143–45

Salary considerations, 301–4

SBM. *See* School-based management (SBM)

Scheduling, block, 237–38

School-based health center (SBHC), PBL project in, 362–68

School-based management (SBM), 185

School board(s), 124–27
    powers of local, 124–25
    responsibilities of, 125–26

School budget development checklist, 342b

School Construction Act, 35t

School district(s)
    case study, 120–21
    central office operations, 130–34
    instructional conferences, 211–12
    and litigation, 316–17
    local, 122–24
    organizational structure, 120–49
    parental involvement, 145–47
    and school safety audits, 143–44
    and the superintendent, 127–30
    teacher selection process, 214–15

Schooling in Capitalist America: Educational Reform and the Contradictions of Economic Life (Bowles and Gintis), 105

School leadership, 120–49, 201–15
    adult/teacher learning, 209–13
    case study, 201
    district organizational structure, 120–49
    effective practices in, 205–9
    importance of, 201204

School(s)
    administrator (*See* Principals)
    budget (*See* Budgeting)
    charter, 334
    connecting with community organizations, 116–18
    discrimination in, 101–2
    diversity in, 93–94
    English Language Learners (ELLs) in, 113–14
    financing (*See* Financing schools)
    improvement in, 64–66, 76–77
    inclusive, 255–57
    innovative, 61–63
    land grants for, 34, 38
    language diversity in, 110–13
    magnet, 109–10
    maintaining buildings and grounds, 351
    managing supplies and equipment, 351
    reform (*See* Reform)
    safety audit, 143–45
    security, 260–61

successful, 223–24
technology and administrative
applications in, 80–82
visitations, 211
School(s) legal issues, 317–23
confidentiality of student records,
321
discipline and students with
disabilities, 319–20
due process, 318
freedom of speech and expression, 319
torts, 322–23
Scientific-rational approach, 11
Security, 260–61
Segregation, 109–13
Selection process, 285–89. *See also* Human
resource management (HRM)
alternate approaches, 287–89
Sexual identity, 99–100
Sheff v. O'Neill, 314
Sheltered English, 111b
Single-group studies approach, 105–6
Situational leadership, 167, 169, 174, 176
model, 175f
Skills, leadership, 189
Smith-Hughes Act, 35t
Smith-Lever Act, 35t
Social class, 93
Social justice
education approach, 106–9
equity and, 54–55
Socioeconomic status (SES), 93
Sociotypes, 100
Span of control, 279b
Spatial intelligence, 220t
Special education
case study, 248–49, 252–58
defined, 252–53
inclusion and, 255–57
and remedial instruction, 252–58
Specially Designed Academic Instruction
in English (SDAIE), 113
Staff
authority, 279b
concerns, 276–77
development, 294–300
employee assistance and wellness
programs, 298–99
planning, 277–79, 282–83
Staffing, differentiated, 302–3

Standards, 5
curriculum, 229
ISLLC, 5
state, 50–54
superintendent, 127, 129
State court systems, 314b
State government
legislatures, 315–17
role in education, 50–54, 314–15
role in financing schools, 332–36
roles and responses, 50–54
Stereotypes, 100
Student-Centered Classroom Assessment
(Stiggens), 243
Student(s)
assessing progress of, 239–45
behavior, intervention strategies for,
264t
records, confidentiality of, 259, 321
rights, 321–22
service team, 249–51 (*See also* Pupil
personnel services)
and technology, 78
testing and appraisal of, 265–66
Study groups, 209–10
Submersion, 111b
Superintendent, 127–30
roles, 128
standards for, 127, 129
Supplies, managing, 351
Supreme Court. *See* U.S. Supreme Court
*Swann v. Charlotte-Mecklenburg Board of
Education,* 39–40

Taxes, financing schools and, 331
Tax Reform Act, 36t
Teacher learning
conferences, 211
district and/or school instructional
conferences, 211–12
instructional walk-throughs, 210
school visitations, 211
study groups, 209–10
Teacher Preparation Act, 37t
Teacher Recruitment and Retention Act,
37t
Teacher(s)
recruiting, 283–85
selection process, 214–15, 285–89
and technology, 78

Teaching approaches, 224–27
Technology, 67
    administrative applications, 80–82
    developing a successful program, 82–83
    harnessing, 77–83
    multimedia, 80
    new opportunities through, 80
    PBL project in, 373–80
Technology Standards for School
        Administrators (TSSA), 49
Telecommunications Act, 37t
Tenth Amendment, 34
Testing
    and diagnostics, 265–66
    state programs, 51–54
Thematic instruction, 226
Theories X and Y, 158–60
Time, 236–39
*Tinker v. Des Moines Independent
        Community School District*, 321
Torts, 322–23. *See also* School(s) legal
        issues
Total quality management (TQM), 183–84
    tools for quality improvement, 184
Traits, leadership, 189
Transfer, 221
Transformational leadership, 187–89
Transitional Bilingual Education (TBE),
        111b
Transitions, cultural, 97, 99
Trends in budgeting and management,
        346
Triarchic theory of intelligence, 218
Two-Way Bilingual Education, 111b

Unity of command, 279b
University Council of Educational
        Administrators (UCEA), 189

University of Iowa studies, 162
University of Michigan studies, 176
U.S. Census categories, 95
U.S. legal system, 309–15
    federal courts, 310–14
    federal role in education, 309–10
    state's legal role in education, 314–15
U.S. population demographics, 93–94
U.S. Supreme Court, 312–13
    on language diversity in schools, 110
    on school voucher systems, 336
    on student discipline, 262
    on student rights, 321–22

Vernonia School District 47 J. v. Acton, 322
Violent Crime Control and Law
        Enforcement Act, 37t
Vocational Education Act, 35t
Vouchers, 336

Wage and salary considerations, 301–4
    benefits, 303–4
Walk-throughs, 210
Washington D.C. School Choice Act, 37t
Weighted-student model of finance, 334
Wellness programs, 298–99
What's Worth Fighting For (Fullan), 208–9
Whites, population demographics, 94
Winners All: A Call For Inclusive Schools
        (NASBE), 255

Yankton School District v. Schramm, 312
Year-round education (YRE), 236–37
Yield, 331

Zelman v. Simmon Harris, 53
Zero-based budgeting, 344–45
Zone of proximal development, 225